Alaska

the Bradt Travel Guide

Traveler Terpening

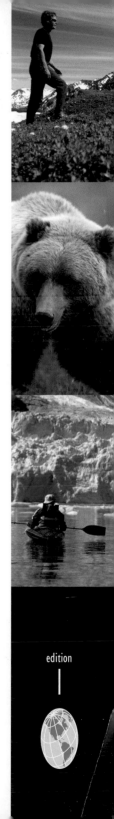

edition
I

www.bradtguides.com

Bradt Travel Guides Ltd, UK
The Globe Pequot Press Inc, USA

Barrow

Chukchi Sea

Deadh
Prudho

Dalton Highway—the State's best scenic road trip
page 414

B   R   O   O   K   S   R

Noatak National Preserve

Cape Krusenstern National Park

Kobuk Valley National Park

Gates of the Arctic National Park

Kotzebue Sound

Kotzebue

Wiseman
Coldfoot

Selawik National Wildlife Refuge

Kanuti National Wildlife Refuge

Diomede Islands

Bering Land Bridge National Preserve

Seward Peninsula

Teller   Taylor

Koyukuk National Wildlife Refuge

Bering Strait

Nome

Council

Manley Hot Springs

St Lawrence Island

Norton Sound

Nowitna National Wildlife Refuge

Yukon

Nenan

Strap on your hiking boots & explore Denali National Park
page 287

Learn about Nome's Gold Rush
page 401

Innoko National Wildlife Refuge

Denali Cant
National Park

Mount McKinley ▲
20320ft/6194m

A
L
A
S
K

Tall

Yukon Delta National Wildlife Refuge

Hike, kayak & cycle to your heart's content in Homer's Kachemak Bay
page 255

Wasilla

ANCHORAGE

Bethel

Kenai National Wildlife Refuge

Kenai   Soldotna

Nunivak Island

Lake Clark National Park

Kuskokwim Bay

Togiak National Wildlife Refuge

Cook Inlet

Homer

**Kenai N
Natio
Pa**

Dillingham

Naknek   King Salmon

See bears dining on salmon in Katmai National Park & Preserve
pages 354–5

Katmai National Park
Becharof National Wildlife Refuge

Fish the rich w of Kodiak Islan the 'Emerald Is
page 351

Bristol Bay

Kodiak

Bering Sea

Kodiak National Wildlife Refuge

Pribilof Islands

Alaska Peninsula National Wildlife Refuge

A
L
E
U
T
I
A
N

R
A
N
G
E

Aniakchak National Park

Chignik

Izembek National Wildlife Refuge

A
e

CONTINUED
ON INSET

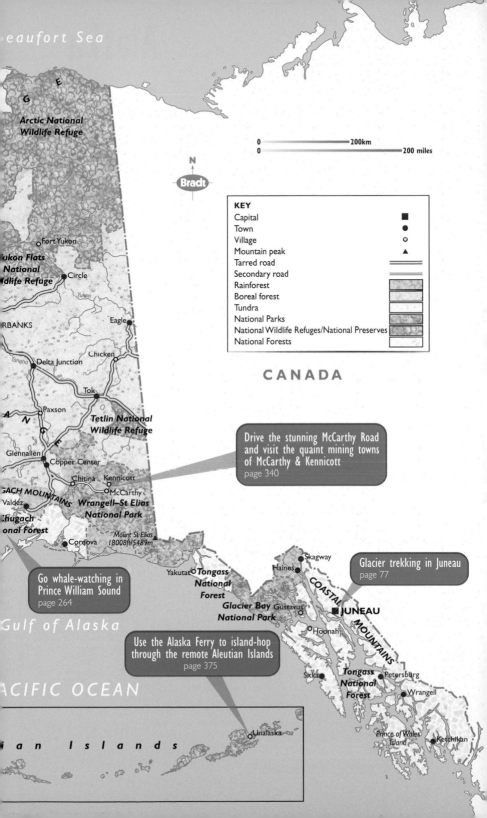

eaufort Sea

G E
G

Arctic National Wildlife Refuge

oFort Yukon

ukon Flats National dlife Refuge • Circle

Yukon

RBANKS   Eagle•

Tanana • Delta Junction   •Chicken

A •Paxson   •Tok
N
G
E •Glennallen   •Copper Center
        •Chitina •Kennicott
GACH MOUNTAINS o McCarthy
•Valdez   **Wrangell–St Elias**
hugach   **National Park**
onal Forest
            •Cordova   *Mount St Elias*
                          18008ft/5489m

Gulf of Alaska

ACIFIC OCEAN

* an   Islands* oUnalaska

N
Bradt

```
0                    200km
0                          200 miles
```

KEY
Capital   ■
Town   ●
Village   ○
Mountain peak   ▲
Tarred road   ═══
Secondary road   ───
Rainforest
Boreal forest
Tundra
National Parks
National Wildlife Refuges/National Preserves
National Forests

CANADA

> Drive the stunning McCarthy Road and visit the quaint mining towns of McCarthy & Kennicott
> page 340

> Go whale-watching in Prince William Sound
> page 264

> Use the Alaska Ferry to island-hop through the remote Aleutian Islands
> page 375

> Glacier trekking in Juneau
> page 77

Yakutat o **Tongass National Forest**

Skagway
Haines

COASTAL

Glacier Bay Gustavus
National Park   ■ **JUNEAU**

oHoonah

MOUNTAINS

Sitka•

Tongass •Petersburg
National
Forest   •Wrangell

Prince of Wales Island   •Ketchikan

Alaska
Don't
miss...

Prince William Sound
Glaciers galore and
superb marine-wildlife
viewing opportunities
(NW/MP/FLPA) page 264

The Alaska Ferry
Reaches towns otherwise
inaccessible by road
(SK/JWL/Alamy) page 48

Northern lights
A once-in-a-lifetime
experience
(I/TIPS) page 414

**Native Alaskan
culture**
Continues to thrive
(KK/TA) page 13

Bears
Grizzlies fishing
for salmon at
Katmai Falls
(B/TIPS) page 25

above **View of downtown Anchorage from the Coastal Trail** (FF/TA) page 194

left **Fur Rondy Festival, Anchorage** (BA/TA) page 68

below **Iditarod Trail Sled Dog Race, Anchorage** (BA/TA) page 69

above **Panning for gold, Fairbanks**
(KK/TA) page 307

right **Native artwork, Sitka**
(BA/TA) page 159

below **Totem park, Ketchikan**
(TT) page 129

above **Ugak Bay, Kodiak Island** (DY/TA)
below **A cycling track just off The Denali Highway** (FF/TA) page 333

AUTHOR

Traveler Terpening was raised in Homer and the Aleutian Islands, Alaska. He is a professional photographer and writer specialising in travel and the outdoors, and his work has appeared in many international periodicals and ad campaigns. He has travelled extensively within Alaska and around the world. He has worked on and off as a commercial fisherman since he was 15, but has also worked as a kayaking, nature, and hiking guide. Nowadays, he divides his time between Homer – where he organises an annual kite-surfing festival – and Arizona, where he's currently studying environmental journalism. He

recently bought a commercial fishing permit on the Ugashik River in Bristol Bay and looks forward to spending his summers working and playing hard on the Alaska Peninsula. This is his first guidebook.

AUTHOR'S STORY

Many people have to search the world to find their home, but – to paraphrase Nancy Lord – I have always taken comfort in the knowledge that I was born into mine. Alaska is a massive, wild place, the likes of which I have rarely seen elsewhere in the world. I feel at home there. Yet despite spending a summer traversing the state while researching this guide, as well as a lifetime of living and travelling there, I always find there is something new to learn about the land. Alaska is perpetually new: massive glaciers recede exposing fresh land to seeds and plant life, volcanoes explode and cover up old life, people leave their mark but then nature erases it within a generation. Researching this guide allowed me to take one more step toward understanding this enigmatic state, and for that reason, if no other, the experience was worth it. My wife and I met hundreds, perhaps thousands, of wonderful people during our travels, each taking the time to show us their secret spots and regale us with their stories. You might need to peer through the cold and wet gloom to see the beauty some days, but that in itself is one of Alaska's clever ploys: it holds its beauty close and shows it only to those most intent on experiencing it. I hope the following pages are infused with enough enthusiasm to encourage you to kick-start your own Alaskan adventure.

PUBLISHER'S FOREWORD   *Adrian Phillips, Publishing Director*

Bradt authors support responsible travel, with advice not only on minimum impact but also on how to give something back through local charities. Thus a true synergy is achieved between the traveller and local communities.

* * *

What's in a name? Well, as a travel publisher, you sit up and take note when a pitch from someone called 'Traveler' crosses your desk. Traveler has certainly engaged wholeheartedly with Alaska's great outdoors, making his living from its land and water – as fisherman and guide – for most of his life. He is at home in this wild place, and there's no-one better equipped to take readers on an adventure in one of the world's great frontiers.

First published March 2010

Bradt Travel Guides Ltd, 23 High Street, Chalfont St Peter, Bucks SL9 9QE, England
www.bradtguides.com
Published in the USA by The Globe Pequot Press Inc, 246 Goose Lane,
PO Box 480, Guilford, Connecticut 06475-0480

Text copyright © 2010 Traveler Taj Terpening
Maps copyright © 2010 Bradt Travel Guides Ltd
Photographs copyright © 2010 Individual photographers
Editorial Project Manager: Emma Thomson

British Library Cataloguing in Publication Data
A catalogue record for this book is available from the British Library
ISBN-13: 978 1 84162 298 9

Photographs Arco Digital Images/ TIPS (ADI/TIPS), Bios/TIPS (B/TIPS), Brian Adams/Travel Alaska (BA/TA), De Young/Travel Alaska (DY/TA), Donald M Jones/Minden Pictures/FLPA (DMJ/MP/FLPA), Frank Flavin/Tourist Alaska (FF/TA), Imagestate/TIPS (I/TIPS), Ingo Arndt/FLPA (IA/FLPA), Kristen Kemmerling/Travel Alaska (KK/TA), Michael Quinton/Minden Pictures/FLPA (MQ/MP/FLPLA), Michale Gore/ Minden Pictures/FLPA (MG/MP/FLPLA), Norbert Wu/Minden Pictures/FLPA (NW/MP/FLPA), Robin Hood/Travel Alaska (RH/TA), Stephen Belcher/Minden Pictures/FLPA (SB/ MP/FLPA), Steve Kaufman/John Warburton-Lee/Alamy (SK/JWL/Alamy), Suzi Eszterhas / FLPA (SE/FLPA), Traveler Terpening (TT), Yva Momatiuk & John Eastcott/Minden Pictures/FLPA (YM&JE/MP/FLPA)
Front cover Grizzly bear crossing river, Katmai National Park (SE/FLPA)
Back cover Totem pole (TT), Bald eagle (TT)
Title page Hiking (TT), Grizzly bear (DMJ/MP/FLPA), Kayaking beside glacier (ADI/TIPS)
Author image Peter Stratton
Maps Dave Priestley

Typeset from the author's disc by Wakewing, High Wycombe
Printed by Ashford Colour Press, arranged by Jellyfish Solutions, UK.

Acknowledgements

This book is dedicated first and foremost to my lovely wife, Nicole Zielger, who should be listed as a second author and given a 'Supportive Wife of the Year' award. I would also like to thank the people of Alaska: their advice, kindness, and smiling faces reminded me daily that Alaska is so much more than mountains, glaciers, and wildlife. I also extend my deepest thanks to all the chambers of commerce and visitor centres.

Contents

FEEDBACK REQUEST

I have made every effort to ensure that the details contained within this book are
as accurate and up to date as possible. Inevitably, however, things move on.
Please feel free to email me with updates, corrections, or to just chat about Alaska
– and if you come to our kite-surfing festival in Homer, please do stop and say
'Hi'. You can contact me directly at feedback@travelerphotography.com, or write
to Bradt Travel Guides Ltd, 23 High Street, Chalfont St Peter, Bucks SL9 9QE,
England; e info@bradtguides.com.

Introduction

Alaska's licence plate slogan 'The Last Frontier' says it all. Where else can you touch the gnarled face of an ancient glacier in the morning, catch a wild king salmon and grill it for lunch, then watch a pod of orcas frolic in the sea as you dine on a gourmet dinner cruise under the midnight sun? What other piece of land boasts arctic sand dunes, lush temperate rainforests rioting with life, and vast ranges of snow-capped mountains enrobed in steely-blue glaciers? Only Alaska.

In addition to its overwhelming natural wonders, America's largest state has a long and fascinating history that is visible everywhere from intricately carved totem poles and onion-domed Russian Orthodox churches, to dilapidated mining claims. It's also one of the few places where native cultures thrive as well today as they have since their ancestors walked across the Bering Land Bridge during the last ice age. Traditional languages, art and subsistence lifestyles – all are visible if you know where to look.

Therein lies Alaska's true accomplishment: unlike the Alaska of old – which was plundered for its gold, timber and oil without concern – modern Alaska, while still learning from the past, is keen to strike a balance between development and preservation, eager to ensure its civilized and art-rich towns do not impinge on its world-class wilderness. So gear up for an unrivalled adventure: bring your camera, a sturdy pair of boots, a sense of adventure, and be prepared for the Frontier State to steal your breath away.

UPDATES WEBSITE

For the latest travel news about Alaska, please visit the new interactive Bradt update website: http://updates.bradtguides.com.

This update website is a free service for readers and for anybody else who cares to drop by and browse, so if you have any comments, queries, grumbles, insights, news or other feedback, you're invited to post them on the website.

Part One

GENERAL INFORMATION

Location Alaska forms the northwest point of North America bordering Canada, the North Pacific Ocean, the Bering Sea and the Arctic Ocean.

Neighbouring countries Alaska shares a 1,538-mile land border with Canada and is 51 miles across the Bering Strait from the Russian mainland. The Diomede Islands (one Russian and one American) are in the middle, just 2.5 miles apart and often joined by ice.

Size 570,373 square miles. One fifth the size of the continental US and more than twice as large as the next largest state, Texas.

Climate Most of Alaska ranges from 15°–27°C during the summer, with some arctic coastal areas as cool as 4°–10°C and some interior areas approaching 38°C.

Political status Alaska is the 49th state of the United States of America.

Population 686,293 (US Census Bureau 2008 estimate)

Capital (and population) Juneau (31,262, US Census Bureau 2008 estimate)

Other main towns Anchorage (261,446), Fairbanks (31,423)

Economy Oil and natural gas, commercial fishing, timber, mining

Languages English is the primary language but Russian and various Native Alaskan languages can also be heard.

Currency US dollar

International telephone code +1

Area code 907

Time zone GMT –9

Electrical voltage 110–120 volts AC

Weights and measures Imperial

Flag Eight gold stars on a dark-blue field forming the Big Dipper pointing at the North Star; designed in 1926 by 13-year-old Benny Benson of Seward.

Background Information

GEOGRAPHY

On maps, Alaska often appears separate from the rest of the US, relegated to the corners of maps with its sibling Hawaii. In so doing, cartographers have convinced many of us that Alaska is almost an island, barely a part of North America, alone in the frozen north with only Canada for company. Pick up a map of the entire continent, however, and you will see that Alaska is in fact firmly joined to the rest of North America with many physical features of the continental US extending through Canada and terminating, often spectacularly, in Alaska.

The Cascade mountain range of the Pacific northwest US flows seamlessly into Canada's Coastal Range with little notice of the international border it crosses. The Coastal Range gains some height as it approaches Alaska, reaching skyward in the Wrangell-St Elias Range and rising to form the continent's highest mountain – Denali (20,320ft) – which forms part of the Alaska Range. While the Chugach and Kenai Mountains head south down the Kenai Peninsula, the Alaska Range continues southwest joining the Aleutian Range and sprouting smoking volcanoes all the way to Russia. Meanwhile the Brooks Range, a much older and more heavily eroded range, cups the North Slope at the top of the state. Of the 20 highest mountains in the United States, 17 are located in Alaska and these are spread through 14 mountain ranges.

In addition to this, there are more than 70 active, or potentially active, volcanoes around the state. A few in the Aleutian Range can even be seen smoking on a clear day from the Kenai Peninsula. Southwest Alaska, in particular, is home to many Mount Fuji-like volcanoes, which rise straight out of the sea and reach heights of 7,000ft or more. In 1912, Novarupta Volcano, at the base of the Alaska Peninsula, erupted violently creating the Valley of Ten Thousand Smokes, where Katmai National Park is today. The eruption was the most violent since Krakatoa in Indonesia. The volcanoes adjacent to the Kenai Peninsula continue to erupt: Mount Spurr erupted in 1992 and Mount Redoubt recently in 2009. Both halted plane traffic with their 55,000–65,000ft plumes of ash and smoke.

The intense tectonic and volcanic activity that has formed Alaska's mountains is also responsible for its regular and occasionally devastating earthquakes. On 27 March, 1964, the Good Friday earthquake shook southcentral Alaska, killing 128 people in the initial quake and later tsunamis. The quake registered 9.2 on the Richter Scale, the largest ever recorded in North America. Every year, Alaska experiences 1,000 earthquakes over 3.5 on the Richter Scale and about 5,000 in total. Three of the ten most significant earthquakes on earth have occurred in Alaska. Spend enough time in southcentral Alaska and you are guaranteed to feel a shake or two.

Alaska's fresh water is contained in some 3,000 rivers, including the 2,000-mile Yukon River (the third longest in the US), more than three million lakes (Lake Iliamna covers more than 1,000 square miles), and most notably in glaciers. As much as three-quarters of the state's fresh water is locked in glaciers. Alaska has more than 100,000 glaciers (just 616 of those are officially named) covering a total area of 29,000 square miles – roughly 3% of the state. While still an icy place today, Alaska has been much icier in its past. Indeed, while the evidence of long-past ice ages can be seen throughout the state – especially in the long fjords carved by glacial movement in the southeast – much of the interior remained a vast grassland and today it is mostly taiga forest.

Glaciers form when snow accumulates, piles on itself, and increases in weight until ice is formed beneath. New snow adds more weight and the mass starts to move with gravity, bulldozing mountains and forests alike as it advances. Interestingly, it's often believed that glacial ice is very old, having formed during the last ice age, but very often that's not the case. In truth, while glaciers, like rivers, are often very old, the water (or ice) in them comes and goes. Just as a river is always receiving new water at its source and dumping it at its mouth, a glacier is perpetually forming and melting. This means most glacial ice in Alaska is no more than 100 years-old.

Of Alaska's 44,000 miles of shoreline (only recently thought to be 33,000 miles), tidewater glaciers are found primarily in the southeast and southcentral regions. The longest glacier in the state is Hubbard Glacier, which starts in Canada and flows 76 miles to the sea near the town of Yakutat. The largest is Bering Glacier at 2,250 square miles.

CLIMATE

Part of what I love about Alaska is the extraordinarily diverse climates found around the state. While some areas receive less than 20 inches of rain per year, others get more than 17 feet. Other areas, such as west and southwest Alaska, get a mixture of rain and sun practically from hour to hour. But generally speaking, May can be cool with snow down to sea level in many areas. Likewise, August and September can be lovely in the southern regions with cool nights, while the western and Arctic regions may be under a few inches of snow. The summer solstice, the longest day of the year, occurs 20–21 June and brings 24 hours of daylight to the Arctic region (for about 84 consecutive days) and more than 18 hours to the southern regions. Alaska is primarily a summer travel destination (May to August) as winters are long and often quite cold, particularly in the western, Arctic and interior regions. In more detail:

SOUTHEAST The southeast is a wet place, particularly in the southern panhandle where Ketchikan holds Alaska's rain record (17ft). Average summer temperatures are 10–15°C with rain possible at any time.

SOUTHCENTRAL This region maintains a mild climate year-round, due largely to the moderating affect of the ocean. While the region doesn't get as much rain as the southeast, it does get its fair share of precipitation, especially in the winter, in the form of snow. Average summer temperatures range from 12 to 18°C with Anchorage and points north averaging 3–6°C warmer.

THE INTERIOR The interior is much warmer with an average temperature of 15–21°C and often pushing 21–26°C or more, but don't stick around for the winter unless you think you can handle −56°C and three hours of daylight.

SOUTHWEST This region includes the Aleutian Islands and the Alaska Peninsula and is generally a cool, wet, and windy place, with summer temperatures ranging from 10 to 15°C.

TEMPERATURE CHART

		Anchorage	Barrow	Bethel	Fairbanks	Juneau	Ketchikan	Kodiak	Nome		
January	Temperature (°C)	8/25	-20/-14	-5/13	-17/-1	22/29	26/38	24/33	-4/13	Temperature	January
	Precipitation (mm)	0.80	0.20	0.81	0.55	3.98	14.01	9.52	0.88	Precipitation	
	Daylight Hours	6.25	0	6.31	5.07	7.07	7.43	7.16	5.16	Daylight Hours	
February	Temperature (°C)	13/27	-24/-20	-2/20	-17/7	25/36	30/40	24/37	-8/10	Temperature	February
	Precipitation (mm)	0.86	0.18	0.71	0.41	3.66	12.36	5.67	0.56	Precipitation	
	Daylight Hours	9.04	6.58	9.07	8.31	9.23	9.41	9.28	8.34	Daylight Hours	
March	Temperature (°C)	12/35	-30/-15	4/26	-5/23	30/40	31/44	27/39	-4/14	Temperature	March
	Precipitation (mm)	0.65	0.15	0.80	0.37	3.24	12.22	5.16	0.63	Precipitation	
	Daylight Hours	11.44	11.32	11.41	11.41	11.46	11.48	11.46	11.41	Daylight Hours	
April	Temperature (°C)	26/45	-8/3	14/36	18/41	37/49	36/49	30/40	7/25	Temperature	April
	Precipitation (mm)	0.63	0.20	0.65	0.28	2.83	11.93	4.47	0.67	Precipitation	
	Daylight Hours	14.42	16.31	14.39	15.10	14.24	14.08	14.21	15.08	Daylight Hours	
May	Temperature (°C)	36/55	14/24	32/51	35/60	38/55	40/59	36/52	26/40	Temperature	May
	Precipitation (mm)	0.63	0.16	0.83	0.57	3.46	9.06	6.65	0.58	Precipitation	
	Daylight Hours	17.27	24.00	17.21	18.39	16.47	16.12	16.39	18.29	Daylight Hours	
June	Temperature (°C)	46/62	28/39	42/61	46/68	43/63	46/63	41/56	38/54	Temperature	June
	Precipitation (mm)	1.02	0.36	1.29	1.29	3.02	7.36	5.72	1.14	Precipitation	
	Daylight Hours	19.18	24.00	19.07	21.39	18.15	17.26	18.04	21.21	Daylight Hours	
July	Temperature (°C)	51/65	34/45	45/66	50/72	48/65	50/64	48/60	45/57	Temperature	July
	Precipitation (mm)	1.96	0.87	2.18	1.84	4.09	7.80	3.80	2.18	Precipitation	
	Daylight Hours	18.27	24.00	18.21	20.11	17.36	16.54	17.26	20.00	Daylight Hours	
August	Temperature (°C)	45/64	34/44	46/61	45/67	48/65	51/66	49/60	45/56	Temperature	August
	Precipitation (mm)	2.31	0.97	3.65	1.82	5.10	10.60	4.03	3.20	Precipitation	
	Daylight Hours	15.51	19.03	15.47	16.35	15.25	15.02	15.20	16.31	Daylight Hours	
September	Temperature (°C)	40/55	28/35	38/53	35/55	44/58	45/59	45/55	35/47	Temperature	September
	Precipitation (mm)	2.51	0.64	2.58	1.02	6.25	13.61	7.18	2.59	Precipitation	
	Daylight Hours	12.57	13.31	12.56	13.06	12.51	12.46	12.50	13.05	Daylight Hours	
October	Temperature (°C)	26/42	9/19	24/38	16/31	38/49	41/51	35/49	23/33	Temperature	October
	Precipitation (mm)	1.86	0.51	1.48	0.81	7.64	22.55	7.85	1.38	Precipitation	
	Daylight Hours	10.07	8.51	10.09	9.47	10.20	10.31	10.22	9.48	Daylight Hours	
November	Temperature (°C)	15/28	-7/4	11/30	-7/11	30/38	35/45	30/43	10/20	Temperature	November
	Precipitation (mm)	1.08	0.27	0.98	0.67	5.13	17.90	6.89	1.02	Precipitation	
	Daylight Hours	7.18	2.37	7.23	6.19	7.52	8.22	7.59	6.25	Daylight Hours	
December	Temperature (°C)	6/21	-19/-12	-2/19	-15/0	25/33	31/39	25/35	-4/11	Temperature	December
	Precipitation (mm)	1.06	0.17	0.95	0.73	4.48	15.82	7.39	0.82	Precipitation	
	Daylight Hours	5.32	0	5.41	3.49	6.25	7.08	6.35	4.00	Daylight Hours	

Background Information CLIMATE

WESTERN This region is cooled by the freezing Bering Sea and experiences extreme variations in rainfall; from ten inches in some places to more than 100 inches in others.

THE ARCTIC As one would expect this region is much cooler, with average summer temperatures hovering around 4.4°C in coastal areas. Inland, the temperatures can warm considerably. The lowest temperature ever recorded in the state was −62.11°C in Prospect Creek on 23 January 1971. The highest temperature in the state was also recorded in this region: Fort Yukon, right on the Arctic Circle, hit 37.8°C on 27 June 1915.

HISTORY

END OF THE ICE AGE As the last Ice Age was ending, about 10,000–12,000 years ago, sea levels were as much as 400ft lower than they are today. Connecting Siberia and Alaska was a land bridge – known as *Beringia*, or the Bering Land Bridge – that early Siberians, as well as countless plants and animals, used to migrate to Alaska. As the planet warmed and glaciers melted, the oceans rose and the Bering and Chukchi Seas covered the land bridge, isolating the newcomers on a strange and new continent. Though it's often called a 'land bridge', the area that went dry may have been 1,000 miles or more wide.

EARLY MIGRATIONS Even before these last waves of people came over to the 'new world', Three-Wave Theory proponents believe there may have been earlier migrations up to 25,000 or more years prior to this. These people continued south and today constitute the majority of the north and south native American groups. Another wave of similar people, the Athabascans, followed and spread through central Alaska and Canada. Though much of the continent was under ice during this time, most of interior Alaska remained vast grassland. Some of these Athabascan tribes followed rivers to the sea and became the Tlingit, Tsimshian, Haida, and Eyak cultures of the Canadian coast and Alaskan panhandle. About 5,000 years ago another wave of immigrants, collectively known as Eskimos, arrived by boat. These hardy people filled the coastal niches of western and Arctic Alaska, using kayaks to hunt marine mammals and catch fish. This community split up and divided along the coast, with the Unangan (Aleut) claiming the Aleutian Islands, the Alutiiq settling around the base of the Alaska Peninsula, the Yup'ik and Cup'ik spreading through the southern and central regions of western Alaska and the Inupiat settling north of the Seward Peninsula and through the arctic region. Eventually, their culture spread across northern Canada all the way to Greenland.

THE RUSSIAN CONQUEST OF SIBERIA Fast forward a few thousand years to the Russian conquest of Siberia and, ultimately, Alaska. Initiated by Tsar Ivan IV, 'The Terrible' (1533–1584), the push east was part of a larger effort to colonise this remote part of the country. Fur, salt, and gold were some of the reasons families struck east. As the country expanded east throughout the 1500s and 1600s, Russian explorers finally reached the north Pacific in 1647. In 1725, Vitus Bering, a Dane in the service of Russia, was sent by Tsar Peter the Great (1672–1725) to explore the unknown waters east of the Kamchatka Peninsula, but failed to see the new world through thick fog. Seven years later, Mikhail Gvozdev, a Russian soldier, explored the Bering Sea with greater success, sighting the mainland and the Diomede Island in the Bering Strait. Sailing south, Gvozdev came across King Island where he was met by native Alaskans in kayaks. This was the first contact between Russians and Alaskans. In June 1741, Vitus Bering and his second-in-command, Aleksi Chirikov, sailed east in two ships, the *St Peter* and *St Paul*. South of the Aleutian Islands the ships were separated in a storm and Chirikov eventually ended up near present day Sitka in southeast Alaska. While he did made contact with native Alaskans there, the experience was far from positive and he left for home with 15 fewer men.

Bering ended up near Prince William Sound, where onboard naturalist, Georg Steller, made notes on wildlife, plants and the uninhabited villages of native people. After just a short time in the new world, both Bering and Chirikov pointed their bows back toward Russia. Bering stopped briefly in the Shumagin Islands (named for a crewmember who died there) in southwest Alaska and traded with the residents. Dying of scurvy, Bering and his crew landed on an island they thought to be mainland Russia, but was actually 115 miles west. After their ship was wrecked on the rocks in November, the original crew of 76 was reduced to 45 from scurvy. Among the dead was Vitus Bering. The island became known as Bering Island. The following spring, the surviving crewmembers built a raft from their wrecked ship and made their way to mainland Russia, arriving safely in August.

Fur trading After those first expeditions, Russian fur traders, or *promyshleniki*, flocked to the newly discovered land, gradually making their way west along the Aleutian chain, depleting the sea otter and fur seal populations as they went – large sums of money could be made by selling the mammals' pelts to Chinese and Russian markets. These fur traders commonly enslaved Unangan hunters and forced them to collect furs by holding their families for ransom. When the work was finished, very often the hunters and their families were killed. In their brutal and relentless search for fur, the traders pushed past the Alaska Peninsula, through southeast Alaska, all the way to California and nearly drove the sea otter to extinction in the process.

In 1784, the fur trader Gregorii Shelikhov established the first permanent Russian settlement in Alaska on Kodiak Island. Others set up shop in Cook Inlet and together they traded with native groups and hunted fur-bearing marine mammals.

European traders While the Russians went about their business in Alaska, other European powers became concerned they might be losing out on Alaska's resources. Between 1774 and 1792, seven Spanish expeditions were dispatched to Alaska but all failed to accurately map or claim the land. In 1776, the English sent Captain James Cook to Alaska where he successfully charted a great deal of the coast from the southeast region to the Bering Sea before sailing off to Hawaii where he was killed in 1779. Shortly afterward, the British navy officer George Vancouver was dispatched to the west coast where he created extremely accurate maps of the coastline from California to southeast Alaska, including Vancouver Island, named in his honour.

Russian expansion In 1790 Alexander Baranov, a Siberian businessman, was hired by Gregorii Shelikhov to run trading operations in Alaska. When Shelikhov died in 1795, Baranov took over and headed the Russian American Company, expanding Russia's sphere of influence more completely to southeast Alaska. After wearing out his welcome in Kodiak and depleting the furred mammal resources, he moved the company headquarters to Sitka (then called New Archangel) in southeast Alaska. The local Tlingit people resisted the strong, new Russian presence and, in 1804, burned the Russian St Michael's Redoubt Fort to the ground. After seeking reinforcements, the Russians retook the area two years later. Running the company between 1799 and 1818, Baranov was responsible for the exploration and development of resources from the Aleutian Islands, through Alaska all the way to San Francisco.

About this same time, the Russian Orthodox religion began to flood into Alaska drastically improving the average, abused native's lot in life. These early missionaries did expect people to convert, but some took the time to learn about native culture. Among them was Ioann Veniaminov – who later became the first Orthodox bishop in Alaska. In 1824 he worked with Unalaska natives to create an alphabet for their language and took detailed notes on their cultural customs. Veniaminov later travelled to Sitka where he studied Tlingit customs before returning to Russia in 1841.

After Baranov, the Russian American Company was run by naval governors who expanded the company's sphere of power through western Alaska and up the Yukon River, where they sought other types of fur. By the 1850s, valuable furred animals were becoming so hard to find, that the company's continued profitability was in question.

Seward's deal with Russia
During the Crimean War between 1854 and 1856, Russia found itself dangerously overextended. With security issues at home and in the southeast with the ever-hostile Tlingit, the Tsar decided the dwindling fur supply in Alaska was not worth the trouble. Right at the end of the American Civil War, the US brokered a deal with Russia to purchase Alaska in 1867 for US$00.02 per acre – a grand total of US$7.2 million. Secretary of State William H Seward spearheaded the deal but after the initial excitement had subsided, he was criticised extensively. For about 15 years Alaska was called 'Seward's Icebox' or 'Seward's Folly.' After the purchase, Russia walked away with a more manageable empire and the US gained what most Americans regarded as a frozen wasteland. However, a few short years later, many Americans changed their tune as they sold their worldly possessions and headed north in search of gold.

THE GOLD RUSH
Some gold had been reported in Alaska as early as 1884 by Russian geologists, but never in commercially viable quantities. The earliest gold prospectors, most of whom still had gold fever from the California Gold Rush of the 1840s, were drawn north by these early reports. Prospectors slowly pushed north finding and claiming gold here and there, but the real prize came in the form of hard rock gold in Juneau in the 1880s. The Treadwell Gold Mining Company extracted US$67 million from the Juneau area before the mines flooded in 1917. Further exploration led to the famous Klondike Gold Rush in 1896. Prospectors with gold fever came to Alaska by the thousands, flooding Skagway and Haines with tents, mules and supplies for the arduous journey through the mountains to the Canadian gold fields. Some quit before they had started, some turned around half-way, others died *en route*. A very select few became rich and most of those were selling goods to prospectors! In addition to the souls lost in the mountains outside Skagway and Haines, some 300 ships were lost on the journey to Alaska. This prompted the government to launch a rigorous mapping and navigational aid programme, installing lighthouses along the panhandle and prying open the doors of Alaska just a little more.

With the increased interest in Alaska, commercial steam ferries began to run a regular Seattle–Juneau service for US$52. After some exploration of the Kenai Peninsula, the majority of gold mining shifted to Nome in northwestern Alaska, after deposits were found inland and on the beaches. During the summer of 1899, 8,000 people travelled to Nome to try their luck. Between 1899 and 1910 more than US$46 million worth of gold was found there. About the same time, one intrepid prospector, Felix Pedro, found gold in the Tanana Hills almost 600 miles to the east of Nome. His discovery led to the city of Fairbanks being established.

Small-scale mining continues today throughout the state, but a very controversial new strike near Lake Iliamna – the Pebble Mine (see box on page 368) – has some seeing dollar signs and others fearing environmental disaster. On the whole though, mining was eventually eclipsed by fishing and by the turn of the 20th century, salmon canneries appeared all over the state, catching millions of fish in giant traps and packing them for the masses.

Road building With more people coming and going than ever before, Alaska needed roads. When Alaska became a territory in 1912, the US government started building roads that mostly followed historic trails. These roads and the Alaska Railroad, built in 1923, opened up vast areas of previously unexplored land. Between 1905 and 1932 alone, more than 1,231 miles of roads were built. Further development came to the territory when the US Military invested heavily in roads, runways and other infrastructure at the onset of World War II.

WORLD WAR I During World War I, a greater percentage of Alaskans joined the armed forces than any other American territory or state. Some were so eager to do their part that before the US entered the war, many volunteered with the Canadian armed forces. Alaska fuelled the war effort by supplying a vast quantity of salmon, which raised prices and the burgeoning industry's profitability. This led to fish piracy and the U.S. Navy eventually intervened. During the build-up to war, Alaska became a focus for the US Military for two reasons: it had immense quantities of the kind of giant, straight-grained spruce trees they needed to build planes, and it was a quick trip from the west coast to many Asian and European destinations.

WORLD WAR II During World War II, military bases were established around the state from Sitka and Unalaska to Fairbanks and many places in between. Despite the incredible build-up of 150,000 troops, the war only briefly directly touched Alaska in the Aleutian Islands (see page 349). The Japanese bombed Unalaska Island on 3 June 1942 and four days later 1,200 Japanese troops landed and entrenched themselves on the Aleutian Islands of Attu and Kiska. This was the first time since the war of 1812 that American soil was held by a foreign power, and was so frightening that martial law was briefly declared in Alaska.

During this time innumerable military resources were poured into Alaska. This included bases, airfields and fortifications in Nome, Sitka, Anchorage, Fairbanks and Kodiak among others. Many of these bases were used as a refuelling point to send more than 7,000 planes to a war ally, the USSR. All this infrastructure, and the people that came with it, helped to catapult Alaska into the modern age. Airplanes buzzed through the sky and vehicles brought goods in via the newly constructed Alaska Highway, completed in 1943. The logging industries of the southeast also saw a short-lived growth with the need for spruce to build war planes. Alaska's gold mines fared poorly from the war's onset. Gold was not considered necessary during a time of war and labour demands forced most Alaska mines to close.

The Japanese were finally routed almost a year after their invasion on 11 May 1943, when 11,000 US troops fought 2,600 Japanese soldiers on Attu Island. When the smoke cleared, 550 Americans and 2,600 Japanese soldiers had lost their lives. On 28 July of the same year, unbeknownst to the nearly 35,000 US troops descending on the island, 5,000 Japanese soldiers fled Kiska in dense fog. The Alaska portion of the war had ended.

During the Aleutian Campaign many Unangan were displaced by both Japanese and American forces. Some were sent to forced labour camps in Japan, while others were interned in southeast Alaska. Many died in horrible conditions, and those lucky enough to return to their villages, often found a destroyed landscape of rotting runways, vehicles, planes and buildings. Their seldom-heard story is one of the war's great tragedies.

AFTER THE WAR Between 1880 and statehood in 1959, the population of Alaska had grown from 33,426 to more than 225,000.

With the increased population, largely due to soldiers choosing to remain in Alaska after the war, the US government was faced with a population of people tired of living in a mere territory. However, Congress was concerned the giant territory of just a quarter of a million people would not be able to support or govern itself. In 1955, Alaskans gathered in Fairbanks to write a state constitution and on 3 January 1959, Alaska was declared the 49th state of the USA. To help Alaska pay for its own government, Congress designated 60% of the state as federal land. By leasing this land for resource extraction, the federal government would reap handsome profits and give 90% to the state.

Oil field discoveries Oil was discovered and drilled successfully off the Copper River in 1900, with more and larger discoveries occurring in various places, including Cook Inlet. However, Alaska did not become an 'oil state' until North America's largest oil field was discovered in Prudhoe Bay in 1967. When the Trans-Alaska oil pipeline was completed in 1974, the state was literally flooded with money. This oil field continues to provide 20% of US domestic production with more than 10 billion barrels pumped to date. With 80% of Alaska's revenue coming directly from oil, the state would be a very different place if the wells were to dry up suddenly. But it looks like that's where the state is headed: oil production has steadily decreased from the late 1980s until today. North Slope oil production alone declined from its 1988 peak of two million barrels per day to just 767,000 barrels per day today.

Native Alaskan land rights During the lead-up to statehood in 1959, there were concerns about the rights of native Alaskans. Large tracts of land were being gobbled up by the federal government. By 1925, the 54-million-acre Tongass National Forest, the Chugach National Forest, Katmai National Monument, Mount McKinley National Park and Glacier Bay National Monument had all been claimed. It became increasingly clear that native Alaskans were going to be landless in no time if they didn't act quickly. An early result of native organisational efforts resulted in a 1947 lawsuit filed by the Tlingit and Haida of the southeast against the federal government. Quite simply, they asked for all of the land they traditionally used – all of southeast Alaska – to be returned to them. Unfortunately, most of the land was already contained within the Tongass National Forest, and though the case was won in 1968, the native groups did not receive their land back, but a belated payment instead.

Land continued to be claimed by the government, so native groups rallied again and their efforts culminated in the Alaska Native Claims Settlement Act (ANCSA) passed by Congress in 1971. The Act granted native Alaskan groups 44 million acres of land and US$962.5 million for native lands already claimed by the government. This made them the largest private land-owners in the state. After the land was divided, 12 groups formed corporations that generated income from their land, then invested it for the benefit of their members. A thirteenth corporation was later formed for natives living outside the state.

While some are more successful than others, total native assets approach US$3 billion state-wide, paying US$40 million or more to their 12,123 members. Further legislature has protected the rights of Alaskans to live off the land and to hunt and fish on federal lands

While native corporations play a significant role in the economy of the state, the continued viability of some is in question. A 1991 amendment and subsequent legislation answered some of the most pressing questions, but raised others. One of the largest hurdles for indigenous corporations is how to make a profit, but at the same time provide leadership, jobs and to protect their culture and their land. Since ANCSA was created, the goal was, and will continue to be, how to balance these diverse needs.

GOVERNMENT AND POLITICS

Due to its small population, Alaska only has two US senators who serve six-year terms in Washington DC, and one US Representative who serves a two-year term. Alaskans elect a governor and lieutenant governor by popular vote, who serve four-year terms. The governor oversees 15 departments including public safety, revenue, natural resources, fish and game and others, and is therefore considered one of the most powerful gubernatorial positions in the country. Current governor, Sean Parnell, assumed office on 26 July 2009. He replaced Sarah Palin – John McCain's surprise candidate for Vice President in the 2008 election – who resigned as governor claiming 'ethics complaints' against her were hindering her ability to govern. It's believed Palin left office early to prepare for the presidency in 2012.

The state legislature consists of 20 senators who serve four-year terms, and 40 representatives who serve two-year terms. The courts are divided into State Supreme Court, Court of Appeals and District Court.

Unlike other states, Alaska is divided into 16 first- and second-class boroughs. These boroughs collect taxes and control education and planning. Within the boroughs are first- and second-class cities, which are governed by a city council and a mayor. Native Alaskans are organised under a federally recognised tribal government.

Though Alaska just about always votes Republican in presidential elections – the last time Alaska was blue (Democratic) was in 1964 when Lyndon Johnson ran against the little known Barry Goldwater – there are four distinct political parties in the state: the Alaska Republican Party, the Libertarian Party, the Alaskan Independence Party, and the Alaska Democratic party. The Alaska Independence Party (www.akip.org) was formed in 1984 and advocates for Alaska to return to territory status, or more radically, to become an independent nation. Todd Palin, husband of Sarah Palin, registered with the party in 1995 and 2000. The information came to light during the 2008 presidential race and was used by democrats to further discredit Sarah Palin.

In a recent, and unfortunately fairly typical, Alaskan political debacle, former Senator Ted Stevens, who served as Alaska's US Senator from 1968 to 2009, was found guilty in federal court on the eve of his re-election of seven counts of failure to report gifts. The charges were eventually nullified.

DID YOU KNOW?

Did you know that Alaskans over the age of 18 are legally allowed to keep and smoke less than one ounce of marijuana if used privately in the seclusion of their own homes?

More than 80% of the state's income is derived from oil revenues, with fishing, timber, mining, agriculture and tourism also playing a role. As a result, the financial prosperity of Alaska is very susceptible to the global whims of oil prices. The rise and fall of these fuel prices also affects tourism and particularly fishing, which generates almost US$2 billion annually.

Interestingly, Alaskan residents also receive an annual Permanent Fund Dividend cheque (see below), just for being a resident. A small reward for toughing out the winters, some might say.

The Alaska Permanent Fund (*www.pfd.state.ak.us*) was created in 1976 with a portion of the income from mineral leases, including oil. In 1980, the fund morphed in the Permanent Fund Dividend (PFD), which pays every resident man, woman and child (as long as they apply) a portion of state investment profits. This can range from US$300 in 1984 to over US$2,000 in 2008. Sadly, though, federal taxes are paid on this income.

TIMBER Alaska's timber resources are significant, but contribute less to the economy than they used to. Many native groups lease their land to timber companies, as does the state and federal government, who own 28 million acres of commercial forest in the Tongass and Chugach National Forests.

MINING Mining continues today, but rarely on the scale of the early 20th-century gold rushes – though the Pebble Mine (see box on page 368) could change things. Alaska is also home to massive coal, zinc and silver reserves.

Alaska has five major mines (Pogo, Red Dog, Usibelli, Greens Creek, and Fort Knox) that employ about 5,000 people and together with smaller claims, total 3.6 million acres of land, about 2% of the state with a total 2007 mineral value of US$3.4 billion. The state of Alaska received US$175 million in mining-related profits in 2007. Most of the state's mineral exports are zinc and lead (from the Red Dog Mine) and account for about 30% of the state's total commodity export. Minerals exported from Alaska go to Canada, Europe and Asia.

FISHING While commercial fishing has been present in Alaska since the state was bought from Russia in 1867, the industry did not gain momentum until around the turn of the 20th century. In 1917, there were 118 canneries in Alaska processing millions of cases of salmon every year. When the fish were first taxed in the 1920's, the revenue was so great that it accounted for nearly 70% of the territories profit. The 1980s saw the boom years of crab fishing with more than 75 million pounds of crab caught in 1980, and 448 boats fishing crab in Kodiak and Bering Sea waters. During the 1980s, Bering Sea pollack fishing took off and combined with the crab fishery make Dutch Harbor one of the top producing ports in the country with 612.7 million pounds of fish and shellfish landed each year.

Today, fishing continues to be a very visible, though relatively small, part of Alaska's economy – just 5%. While some stocks have dwindled, Alaska's fisheries are considered some of the most well-managed in the world. A blow to Alaska salmon fishermen came in the form of farmed fish from South America, Scandinavia and Canada. Raised in pens on artificial diets, these fish grow quickly due to their food and engineered genes. They are also sometimes dyed to look more 'natural'. Farmed fish have been the enemy of environmentalists, health advocates and Alaskans since the idea was first brought to the public. Stickers that read: 'Friends don't let friends eat farmed fish' are a common sight on Alaskan car bumpers. Initial attempts to farm these fish were heavily subsidised in the beginning, but without continued financial support some companies have –

happily, perhaps – folded, unable to pay the mounting costs. Better management of wild stocks seems a healthier, more sensible solution.

OIL As oil production began to fall at the end of the 1980s, the Exxon Valdez oil spill, in 1989, drowned Prince William Sound in oil and shocked the world (see page 272). After a host of new regulations to prevent another spill were put in place, Alaska continued pumping oil just as it had before. With more than 80% of the states revenue coming from oil production even today, the state's economy as we know it, would wither and die without it.

The projected state income from oil for 2010 is US$4.8 billion, US$1 billion less than in 2009. However, in 2008 the income was a record at US$10 billion. Over the last 20 years, oil has accounted for about 89% of the state's total income, but over the next decade is likely to drop to 87%.

TOURISM Though still a small part of the overall economy, tourism has been embraced as a new and major cornerstone of the state's image and economy. The state has spent millions of dollars to promote tourism and current figures show those investments are paying off with 39,420 in-state tourism-related jobs created; $1.15 billion in tourist-related income; $1.6 billion in visitor spending; and 1.7 million visitors in 2007 (60% from cruise ships).

AGRICULTURE Commercial agriculture in Alaska is limited to parts of the interior and the fertile Matanuska Valley near Palmer. The long daylight hours and rich glacial-silt soils regularly produce some of the largest vegetables in the nation. Over the last five years, Alaska's total agriculture production was just over US$3 million with about US$31,000 coming from skins and hides, US$101,000 from livestock, and just under US$100,000 from grains.

PEOPLE

Of the 683,478 Alaskan residents, 70.8% are white, 4.1% are black, 4.6% are Asian, 5.9% are Hispanic or Latino and 15.2% are of native descent. It's commonly thought that Alaska is brimming with men and in possession of only a few precious women, but statistics reveal the split is almost even: males 52%, females 48%. In the larger urban centres this might be true, but the bush is still noticeably the domain of men.

By and large, Alaskans are a fiercely independent breed who like their private property, guns and the freedom to do and say as they please. While this may sound off-putting – and occasionally it is – most Alaskans are very friendly and eager to show off their unique lifestyle and state to visitors. Many people move to Alaska for the same reason visitors come: they want to experience a land ruled by nature and not by man. The more independent folks also like the idea of less governmental control, where they control their own lives and answer to nobody.

This 'frontier' mindset still brings people to Alaska today, just as it has for over 100 years.

NATIVE GROUPS The native cultures of Alaska, while no longer the majority, remain diverse and vibrant, with many groups experiencing a cultural revival amongst younger generations. The Alaska Native Claims Settlement Act of 1971 gave native groups 10% of the state and about US$1 billion, which had the affect of catapulting them into the modern age with internet, TV, westernised diets and snowmobiles. Still, many native groups maintain a traditional lifestyle through subsistence hunting and gathering, and by keeping dance, art and language traditions alive. With a gallon of milk selling for US$11 in remote villages, and food costs on the rise, subsistence living will probably become more popular in the future.

The Tsimshian, Haida, Tlingit and Eyak The lush rainforests of southeast Alaska are home to the Tlingit, Haida, Tshimshian natives. When early Athabascans populated the interior of Alaska and Canada after the last ice age, some tribes split away and made their way to the sea where they established themselves along the coast. With an abundance of food and raw materials, these groups thrived, developing vibrant cultures that are still active today.

The Tsimshian (pronounced 'sim-she-an') live only on Metlakatla on Annette Island near Ketchikan, having migrated there from Canada in the late 1800s (see page 130). The island is the state's only reservation where local government is responsible for every aspect of their society, infrastructure and government.

The Haida also emigrated from Canada and now live mainly on Prince of Wales Island.

The Tlingit are the most numerous group today with 11,000 members living almost exclusively in the southeast. The Tlingit were accomplished boatmen, builders and carvers. They lived in permanent villages of 50 or more people in about ten houses made from cedar planks with low entryways. These villages often faced the ocean or a river and were fronted with totem poles, advertising the resident clan. Marriages were always arranged outside the clan and clan identity was passed from mother to child in a matriarchal system.

The Eyak traditionally lived around the Copper River and along the coast to Icy Bay near Yakutat. The increased presence of salmon fishing and processing in this area quickly led to the decline of the Eyak, with alcohol, drugs and disease being the major culprits. Today, there are no more than 200 Eyak living mostly near the town of Cordova. Though the Eyak are making an attempt to revive their culture – their first potlatch (see opposite) in 80 years was held in 1995 – the last native speaker of Eyak passed away in 2008.

Athabascans Interior Alaska and Canada has traditionally been populated by the Athabascans whose language is closely related to the Navajo of the American southwest. They carved out an existence in a harsh climate of extremely cold winters and blistering hot summers by harvesting salmon from rivers and hunting large game such as moose and caribou. The Athabascans traded extensively with coastal groups and their trails to the coast were later used by gold prospectors. The group consisted of at least 13 distinct tribes, each with its own language and customs.

Inupiat, Yup'ik and Cup'ik Northwestern and Arctic Alaska were settled by the Inupiat (or Inupiaq), sometimes called the Inuit. Their current population is about 16,000 with another 30,000 in Canada and 47,000 in Greenland. The southern part of western Alaska was inhabited by the Yup'ik and Cup'ik who currently number about 25,000 with another 1,400 in Siberia. These groups, while distinct in many ways, all lived off the sea, hunting marine mammals such as whales, walrus, seals and fish from kayaks or umiaks.

Unangan/Alutiiq To the south were the Unangan, or Aleut people of the Aleutian Islands and Alaska Peninsula. They were masters of the rough seas around the Aleutian Islands, paddling seal-skin kayaks, or *baidarkas*, through all kinds of weather to hunt marine mammals. In addition to being master kayak builders and paddlers, they were expert weavers, able to weave beach-grass baskets so tight they could hold water. The Unangan have the dubious honour of being the first people of the new world to have significant contact with Russian explorers. It didn't work out well and of the original 25,000 Unangan, little more than 2,000 remain with less than half being full-blood. Still, their culture is vibrant to this day and is visible throughout the southwest region. The word 'Aleut' is considered derogatory by some and the preferred name is Unangan, which means 'Seasider'.

The Aluttiq people traditionally lived in Kodiak, the base of the Alaska Peninsula and Prince William Sound. Their culture shares many traits with the Unangan, but is distinct in its language and customs. The Aluttiq Museum in Kodiak has spearheaded an ambitious programme to document the language and help teach it to younger generations. The Aluttiq refer to themselves as Sugpiat, which translates as 'real people'.

LANGUAGE

English is the most commonly used language in Alaska, but Russian and various native Alaskan languages are also heard in places. Of the 20 native languages in the state, the Yup'ik and Inupiat languages of western and northern Alaska are the only two commonly heard. A handful are at risk of dying out altogether, and sadly the last speaker of Eyak died in 2008.

Like anywhere, Alaskans have many of their own words and expressions for things that might confuse the visitor. Here are a few:

- **Breakup** Most commonly this refers to the muddy conditions of spring but can also refer to the spring breakup of ice in rivers and lakes.
- **Bush** The remote parts of the state are called 'The Bush', and are often only accessible by boat or bush plane.
- **Cheechako** Someone new to the state that usually hasn't experienced a winter.
- **Combat fishing** Extremely crowded fishing conditions, often when the salmon are running, and fishermen are jockeying (or even fighting) for a spot to cast. The flying hooks and tense mood can put fishermen in a 'combative' mood.
- **Eskimo ice cream** A traditional food made by blending whale or game fat with berries; eaten by some native Alaskans.
- **Fly-out fishing** Flying into a remote area to fish.
- **Freeze-up** A term referring to the freezing of rivers, lakes, bays and harbours in the late fall.
- **Greenhorn** A first-time commercial fisherman.
- **Humpie** The name given to pink salmon by locals on account of their humped backs.
- **Lower 48** Name given the continental US by Alaskans. Many residents also use the term 'outside' to refer to anywhere that's not Alaska.
- **Muskeg** A swamp or bog.
- **Nunatak** A rock peak poking out from a glacier or ice field.
- **Potlatch** A native celebration with food and gifts.
- **Puker** Some Alaskans refer to tourists by this name because when they go whale-watching or charter-fishing, they puke.
- **Socked in** A term used to describe bad weather that has moved in and grounded planes.
- **Sourdough** An old-time Alaskan, or a type of bread.
- **Squaw candy** Dried or smoked salmon.

- **Termination dust** The first snow to grace the tops of the mountains 'terminates' summer and means it's time to harvest potatoes.
- **Williwaw** A sudden, and often violent, gust of wind descending from a mountainous coast to the sea.

RELIGION

Like Pacific northwesterners, Alaskans are some of the least likely Americans to be found in church on Sunday, or any other day for that matter. Only 22% attend any kind of church regularly, though eight out of ten profess to believe in God or some higher being. Those active in religious communities are Protestants, Roman Catholics, Mormons, Quaker, and Baptists, but also Jews, Muslims and Hindus. The Russian Orthodox Church has many Russian and native Alaskan members.

EDUCATION

Alaska has 506 public schools, as well as a number of private schools, both religious and other, organised into 53 school districts. Funding comes from federal, state and local sources and decisions regarding curriculum, budget and teachers are handled by a locally elected school board overseen by the state and federal governments. Students are required to start elementary (primary) school at age six and can leave high (secondary) school at age 16 with or without a diploma. Parents can opt out of public school for private or home school options, which the state supports financially. Between the third and tenth grades, students take standardised tests as part of the 'No Child Left Behind' Act, which actually grades the school's, not the student's, performance. High school exit exams in reading, writing and maths start at tenth grade and continue through to twelfth grade. Students who do not complete high school can take the General Educational Development test (GED), which is roughly equivalent to graduating.

Alaska also has four private colleges, primarily religious schools, and three major state Universities in Juneau, Anchorage, and Fairbanks, each with satellite schools in rural communities around the state.

CULTURE

ARCHITECTURE It could be argued that the climate and terrain of Alaska inform its architecture more than any overwhelming aesthetic sensibility. The rough, hewn log homesteader cabins of old reveal a level of craftsmanship and resourcefulness not often seen outside the state. With a similar sensibility, but different materials, the homebuilders of today still have to fight against the elements (permafrost, low winter light, etc) and the high cost of materials yet manage to produce sturdy, 'funky' looking houses. Numerous add-on extensions are not uncommon since so many people earn their money in spurts and can't afford to build their dream home all at once.

Some of the state's more interesting homes can be found in Palmer, where part of a flight-control tower from Merril Field was combined with an old bar to form a rather modern looking house, and in Fairbanks, a 75-foot space-needle-like home has a panoramic view above the trees. Alaska's most famous example of modern architecture is the University of Alaska's Museum of the North, in Fairbanks. This super-modern structure looks like it might be more at home next to the Guggenheim Museum in Bilbao, Spain, than so near the Arctic Circle.

The Cold Climate Housing Research Center in Fairbanks is a leading researcher in energy efficient buildings for cold climates.

TOTEM POLES

People often assume totem poles are religious objects, worshipped by ancient animalist peoples in place of gods. In reality, totems have more in common with books than they do with religious deities. Totem poles are the largest wooden sculptures in the world and were used to tell stories about family, myths, legends, to make a statement about their owner or tribe, and to commemorate the lives of tribal members. Klingit, Haida, Tsimshian and other northwest native groups all carved totem poles as a tangible record of their lives and to complement their rich oral traditions. While the physical poles tell a story and are fascinating to look at, the full story cannot be known without a verbal explanation from the owner. This was usually done at the pole-raising potlatch (ceremony). If a pole was commemorating a deceased person, their clan animal (often eagle, raven, killer whale and wolf) would be carved at the top of the pole. Their ashes would then be placed in a hollow in the back of the pole.

When Alaska began to modernise in the early 1900s, many native peoples abandoned their traditional lifestyles in favour of city life and jobs, and the art of totem carving was gradually lost. For nearly 30 years, totems and entire villages became overgrown and decomposed back into the earth. In 1938, the Civilian Conservation Corps (CCC), the US Forest Service, and some native leaders began to revive the tradition by salvaging totem poles from their original sites and encouraging young people to learn the art.

CINEMA Alaska's mythical landscape has made it a popular place to set films. One of the earliest films to be shot on location was the silent film *The Chechahcos* (1924), a turn-of-the-century gold rush story complete with revenge, love and the Alaskan landscape. After this, followed *Eskimo* (1932), spoken entirely in the Inupiat language. It was the first big-budget motion picture filmed entirely on location in northwest Alaska. The film earned an Oscar and made the protagonist Ray Mala, a native Alaskan, a movie star. Others include: *The Far Country* (1954), starring James Stewart as a Wyoming cowboy hellbent on driving cattle to the Klondike in the 1890s; and *Never Cry Wolf* (1983).

Production of Alaskan-centred movies picked up during the 1990s and included: *White Fang* (1991), starring a young Ethan Hawke, and filmed in Haines (where the movie set still stands); *North Star* (1996), a typical gold rush film, complete with native Alaskans, guns, knives, sled dogs, snow and some bad acting; *The Edge* (1997), written by David Mamet it tells the tale of a photographer (Alec Baldwin) taking a supermodel and her billionaire husband (Anthony Hopkins) to Alaska for a fashion shoot and the two men's fight for survival when their bush plane crashes; *Mystery, Alaska* (1999), the story of a small Alaskan-town hockey team accepting the challenge to play the New York Rangers, starring Russell Crowe; and *Limbo* (1999).

Some of the better films about Alaska from the last decade include: *Insomnia* (2002) about a policeman who travels to Alaska to investigate a murder, but ends up shooting his partner by 'accident', and making a big show of being driven crazy by the long days, starring Al Pacino, Hillary Swank and Robin Williams; the docu-drama *Grizzly Man* (2005), about Timothy Treadwell, an amateur bear expert from California, who, after travelling to Alaska for 13 years, gets eaten by a bear in Katmai; *30 Days of Night* (2007) about a rural town (Barrow) being eaten alive by vampires; and *Into the Wild* (2007) which, directed by Sean Penn, retells the last days of American teen, Chris McCandless (see box on page 297), who donated his US$24,000 life-savings to Oxfam and travelled into the interior to live out a

Thoreauvian existence. According to a Denali Chamber of Commerce representative, the actual location of Chris's last days weren't scenic enough, so they filmed it elsewhere. The latest offerings are *The Proposal* (2009), which stars Sandra Bullock and Ryan Reynolds and tells the story of two publishing professionals from New York who travel to Sitka, Alaska; and *The Fourth Kind* (2009) an alien abduction film starring Mila Jovovich and supposedly filmed in Nome, but it looks suspiciously like rural Washington.

Most films tend to glorify the rugged northern lifestyle without really digging into the reality of what it means to live in Alaska. A few notable exceptions include the amazing *Alone in the Wilderness* (2005) by Dick Proenneke, who spent 30 years on Lake Clark living alone and off the land, and *Limbo* (1999) a film by by John Sayles about a southeast island community beset by development. This is perhaps the most accurate depiction of southeast available – and it's a fantastic film too!

Alaska has only produced a handful of lesser-known film actors including: Kate Sheldon of *Power Rangers* fame, and Kira Buckland who won the Anime Expo 2007 and Sakura-Con 2007 animated voice acting awards. If you haven't heard of them, perhaps you might have heard of Colleen Shannon who starred on the TV show *Love Island*. No? She was also *Playboy* magazine's Playmate of the Month in January 2004.

LITERATURE As the Last Frontier, Alaska draws creative people of all persuasions looking to be inspired by the endless tracts of wilderness and the hardy people who call it home. Chief among these have always been authors. Although storytelling traditions fed the souls of native Alaskans for thousands of years, Alaska's literature tradition did not start until the Western world began to explore the country in the 1700s. Russian and English expeditions, among others, explored the land and documented what they saw and experienced. Among the first written accounts of Alaska were the expedition reports from these parties.

After Alaska was sold to the US in 1867, the stream of people and US governmental agencies, such as the Army and the Smithsonian Institute, grew and so did the flow of books, articles, and reports about 'the great land'. These accounts of personal adventure, the land, flora, fauna and native cultures inspired the dreams of readers around the world.

One of the best known of these early writers was John Muir, a naturalist and environmental activist, known for rescuing Yosemite Valley in California from development and for his inspirational writing about nature. Muir first visited Alaska in 1879 and made four subsequent trips. His book *Travels in Alaska* recounts many of these stories in vivid and inspiring detail. Another fascinating, but contrasting, look at Alaska came five years later when the letters of Frances Willard were published. Willard carved out a mission in Haines and had a less romantic tale to tell about the reality of living on the frontier.

At the same time, magazine publishers were sending authors to Alaska for stories to feed the public's growing thirst for exotic adventure tales. Fictional novelists also began to set their stories in Alaska, finding that the age-old themes of love, betrayal and redemption could be spiced up and sell a few extra copies if set amongst the jagged peaks of Alaska. Little fictionalising was needed, however, when the Klondike Gold Rush started in 1897 and average citizens sold their possessions to make their fortune in Alaska. During this time more than 100 titles were published to the delights of readers across America fascinated with anything emblazoned with the word 'Alaska'. Among these authors was Jack London, who wrote a number of well-received stories about his adventures in the gold fields in 1897 and 1898, including his most famous works, *The Call of the*

Wild (1903) and *White Fang* (1906). Another notable gold rush-era name was the poet Robert Service. Although he spent his time in the gold fields of Canada, the themes of his poems are as true to the frontier of Alaska and Alaskan historians and authors seem to have accepted him as an honorary Alaskan. Another well-known author of this time was Rex Beach, who wrote about the Klondike and Nome gold strikes in titles such as *The Spoilers* (1906), which tells a true story of corruption and gold fever in Nome around the turn of the century.

As Alaska began to open to the outside world through the first half of the 20th century, new literary themes began to emerge dealing with cultural and political issues such as native rights and what to do with the land and its resources. In the 1920s and 1930s, William Beynon and Frederica de Laguna recorded details of native life and language and author Hudson Stuck began to write and advocate for native rights.

Later still – with the goal of promoting Alaska to developers and travellers alike – magazines like *The Alaskan Sportsman* (which later became *Alaska Magazine*) began to pop up in the 1930s and 1940s. In 1946, the *Anchorage Daily News* started and succeeded where the nearly 200 newspapers published around the state during the first half of the century had failed. Today, the *Alaska Daily News* is Alaska's most widely circulated newspaper.

During the 1960s, 1970s and 1980s another wave of more modern homesteaders moved to Alaska. The authors of this and subsequent generations wrote stories about Alaska's economic, cultural and environmental issues. A well-known example is *Coming into the Country* by John McPhee.

Recent adventure titles include: *Tide, Feather, Snow: A Life in Alaska* by Miranda Weiss and *One Man's Wilderness: An Alaskan Odyssey* by Keith and Richard Proenneke.

Finally, in recent years, a new literary theme has emerged as a result of the public fascination with the dangerous job of commercial fishing. Some of these include *Red Summer: the Danger and Madness of Commercial Salmon Fishing in Alaska* by Bill Carter, *Fishcamp Life on an Alaskan Shore* by Nancy Lord and *Working on the Edge: Surviving In the World's Most Dangerous Profession: King Crab Fishing on Alaska's HighSeas* and *Nights of Ice: True Stories of Disaster and Survival on Alaska's High Seas* by Spike Walker.

Alaska has also been inspirational to poets including John Haines who homesteaded for 20 years in Alaska; Tom Sexton, the former Poet Laureate of Alaska; and Jerah Chadwick who lived in Unalaska in the Aleutian Islands.

For further information on literature, visit **LitSite Alaska** (*www.litsite.org*), an online resource designed to promote the state's literary traditions. The **Alaska Center for the Book** (*http://coolwebak.hypermart.net*) hosts reading conferences in Alaska and promotes literature through its many outreach events and via a newsletter. Finally, some of Alaska's better-known writers' conferences and workshops include the **Kachemak Bay Writers Conference** (*http://writersconference.homer.alaska.edu*) and the **Alaska Writers Guild Workshop** (*http://alaskawritersguild.com*).

MUSIC Just about everyone has heard of the singer-songwriter Jewel, but it's less well known that she spent much of her youth in Homer, Alaska. After performing with her father, Atz Kilcher, in various Alaska venues as a teenager, Jewel left the state to earn her fortune in the Lower 48. After a short time roughing it on the road, she began to receive recognition in the early 1990s. In 1995, she released *Pieces of You*, which catapulted her to the top of the industry, eventually selling more than 12 million copies. She later released *Spirit* in 1998, which was also a great success. A number of other albums followed. In 2008, she married nine-time world champion rodeo star Ty Murray. They now live on a 2,200-acre ranch in Texas. Her father and brother still regularly perform in Homer.

Another reasonably famous group from Alaska is Pumyua, a Yup'ik Alaskan group with a Greenlandic Inuit vocalist. The group has toured internationally and performed at the Grammy Awards. The group has successfully modernised traditional Yup'ik music with world sounds and rhythms but have also remained true to their heritage.

Regularly performing around southcentral Alaska is the old timer Hobo Jim. His catchy country tunes never get old with visitors and only occasionally with locals.

For the classical music lover, the Anchorage Symphony Orchestra, the Fairbanks Symphony Orchestra, the Arctic Chamber Orchestra, and the Juneau Symphony perform in their respective cities and around the state every summer. Anchorage and Juneau also have operas.

NATIVE ART Arts and crafts have played an important role in the lives of native Alaskans for thousands of years, and today those traditions remain strong across the state. They take many shapes and forms, but all embody the ideals and spiritual beliefs of the various native communities. From the intricately carved walrus and petrified mastodon ivory carvings (known as *scrimshaw*) of the Inupiat, and the birch baskets and superbly crafted clothing of the Athabascan, to the beautiful and sometimes frightening masks of the Yup'ik, and the grass baskets, bent-wood hats, and artful tools of the Unangan. And, most famous of all, the totem poles and canoes of the Tlingit.

However, these objects were not always seen as art. In comparison to the functionless objects favoured by Western art, native Alaskan art was designed primarily for utility. As the state became more and more exposed to Western influences, a market was created for mementoes. An ivory carving that once served as a hunter's good luck charm became a souvenir and the nature of native art began to change. Although most native art sold today is decorative rather than traditional, native art is nevertheless thriving in Alaska with a fascinating mix of contemporary and traditional styles, motifs and materials.

New generations of native Alaskan artists have embraced new ways of thinking about art, and are creating pieces that pay homage to their heritage, their culture's place in the modern world, and to the western notion of art. The **Alaska Native Arts Foundation** (*500 West 6th Av;* ☎ *258 2623; www.alaskanativearts.org*) in Anchorage supports the work of native artists with grants, and helps to promote them by selling their work and promoting it further afield too.

Those looking to bring native art home will find the most authentic work by buying directly from the artist, or from a dealer who is intimately connected to the artists and is extremely knowledgeable about their culture and work. Objects that embrace the utilitarian nature of ancient life, such as masks and baskets, will be the most authentic.

NATURAL HISTORY

FLORA Alaskan flora is wonderfully diverse thanks to varying patterns of rain, snowfall, flooding, freezing, and hours of daylight found throughout the different regions. However, all are exposed to an extremely short growing season: during the extended daylight hours of summer there is furious growth and reproduction when conditions are favourable, but this is followed by complete dormancy when winter sets in. In more detail the flora of the various regions is as follows:

Permafrost is a layer of frozen earth – almost entirely devoid of living organisms – that sits just below the active (thawed) soil layer. This frozen soil slows the growth rate of plants and the decomposition of dead matter. However, it also keeps a ready supply of fresh water near the surface for the use of plants, and when it breaks through it forms a pond or lake, used by migratory birds. Currently, over 85% of Alaska is covered by permafrost, but climate change could result in large areas melting. This would drastically alter the ecosystem by increasing soil temperatures and reducing the availability of water. A phenomenon known as 'thermokarst slumping' also promises to change the landscape. This occurs when the insulating layer of tundra is destroyed by human activity – such as driving over the tundra in a vehicle – and the permafrost underneath melts and sinks, killing native plants and creating scars on the landscape.

Southeast Alaska Southeast Alaska is famous for its copious amounts of rain and the resulting riot of life. The Tongass National Forest covers 80% of the panhandle, with 5,000 glaciers and more than 2,000 miles of coastline. Lush forests of immense trees blanket the islands and mainland, while moss and bogs fill in the gaps. Western hemlock accounts for about 70% of the forest cover and can grow to 150ft tall and live for 500 years. Sitka Spruce represents another 20% with trees 225ft tall and 700 years old. Yellow cedars are the old timers of the forest, some are over 1,000 years old. Other trees include red cedar and shore pine. Lichens of all shapes and sizes are found everywhere in the southeast. Lichen are fungi that cultivate tiny algae in a symbiotic relationship. The fungi provide the habitat (the cryptic plant you see hanging from a tree or covering a rock) and the algae inside provide the food (sugars) by transforming the sun's energy via photosynthesis. More than 500 species of lichen thrive in the state and are often the first to colonise an area recently exposed by a receding glacier.

Sundew and butterwort – two of Alaska's insectivorous plants – can be found in the region's bogs and tundra, respectively. The sundew is a small plant that attracts its insect prey with droplets of sweet fluid atop tiny reddish hairs on round, or paddle-shaped, leaves. These droplets shine in the sun and account for the plant's name. Like the purple-flower butterwort, the sundew lures insects by secreting nectar. When prey alights on the plant, it is immediately trapped in the plant's sticky embrace. When the insect thrashes, nearby hairs, each with their own sticky droplet, move toward the insect and help subdue it. Once the insect is dead and the leaf has wrapped around it, it is digested with juices excreted from the leaves. This adaptation allows them to grow in extremely nutrient-poor soils.

Southcentral Alaska Southcentral Alaska is a pleasant mix of the state's floral communities with less rain than the southeast, but just enough to keep the landscape lush. This is where large spruce grow between muskegs, flowers grow in vast fields, and massive mountain ranges a support diverse ecosystem – from forests at their base to hardy alpine plants around their peaks.

Interior Alaska Interior Alaska, on the south side of the Brooks Range, is a vast expanse of spruce known as boreal or *taiga* forest. This landscape has been forged over millennia by short summers of extreme heat (upwards of 100°F/37.8°C in some places), extremely cold and long winters (as cold as –80°F/–62°C), and forests fires sweeping through every 40–200 years. Fires, caused by both lightning and humans, promote health and diversity in the forest by clearing old growth and allowing younger plants and new species to get a foothold and by increasing nutrients in the soil.

Southwest Alaska In southwest Alaska, the volcanic Aleutian Islands – which stretch 1,200 miles from Unimak Island to the Russian mainland – form part of the tundra ecosystem along the coast through western Alaska to the Arctic. The influences of the cold Bering Sea to the north and the slightly less chilly North Pacific to the south create extreme weather of wind and rain, mixed in with days of brilliant sun. Most of the islands are volcanoes, some are perfect cones with spectacular Mount Shishaldin (9,373ft) forming the chain's crown jewel. Summers are cool, but winters are relatively warm and the absence of trees means a verdant green carpet of sedges, grasses, bushes and flowering plants extends from the sea to a few thousand feet.

Western Alaska The western Alaska ecosystem, north of the Alaska Peninsula and south of the Arctic Circle, is a low-lying wet and mostly treeless place with lakes and ponds covering 20% of the land area and wetlands covering 55% of the land in the south and 75% in the north.

The Arctic The Arctic region is a vast treeless plain cloaked in tundra and studded with thousands of lakes extending south from the sea more than 100 miles to the worn peaks of the Brooks Range. The tundra ecosystem consists of willows, sedges and grasses, lichen, mosses, luxurious wildflowers and other plants all growing

These are generally sweeter than the forest variety. High bush berries grow in forest clearings or in areas with limited canopy cover.

CLOUDBERRIES AND NAGOONBERRIES These are somewhat raspberry-like in their shape but grow on tiny plants close to the ground. Both have just a few lobed leaves and are only a few inches tall. The berries are not as sweet as raspberries, but can sometimes be found in great concentrations in open fields.

CROWBERRIES Crowberries are small, black, bland berries found in bogs and on the tundra. When combined with sugar in pies, the subtle flavour comes alive. If not eaten by the birds and bears, crowberries ripen during the winter and can be eaten the following spring. The best way to eat crowberries raw is to collect a handful then pack them into your mouth. Crush them and swallow the juice before spitting out the pulp.

HIGHBUSH CRANBERRIES These are bright-red and can be found in forests on tall, gangly bushes. The berries are sweet and tart, but become sweeter after a frost. Consult a book before gathering highbush cranberries as they look very similar to poisonous baneberries.

LINGONBERRIES Lingonberries are sweet, tart and red and can be found growing close to the ground in forests.

RASPBERRIES These are very thorny and produce small, bright-red berries in the autumn.

SALMONBERRIES These are some of the first to ripen, usually in early August. Salmonberries are closely related to raspberries, but are less thorny, grow much larger and are more tart in flavour. They grow in thickets on mountain slopes. The berries are yellow or orange.

very low to the ground. Most flowering tundra plants are perennials, storing energy for a few years before revealing a delicate flower. While some flowers such as the Arctic poppy track the sun with their bloom to maximise their sun exposure, others such as the woolly lousewort protect themselves from the elements by encasing their foliage in a thick white 'fur'.

Uniquely, the Arctic tundra sits on permafrost (see box on page 21) throughout the year.

FAUNA

The Arctic This habitat supports tens of thousands of caribou, musk ox, arctic fox, brown and polar bears, wolves, many rodents, and millions of migratory birds.

Western Alaska While the entire region is abundant in migratory birds, the Yukon and Kuskokwim River deltas north of Bristol Bay represent one of the most significant concentrations in Alaska. In addition, these rivers support huge populations of all five species of Pacific salmon. The Nushagak and Kvichak Rivers of Bristol Bay are the breeding grounds of the largest red salmon run on earth. This region is home to caribou, moose, brown and black bear (occasionally even polar bears), wolves and millions of migratory birds.

Southwest Alaska Though brown bears live on the first Aleutian Island of Unimak, they are not found elsewhere in the chain. Likewise, other large mammals common to the rest of Alaska are not present here, except feral fox and

The practice of shooting wolves on sight in order to protect game populations has largely been done away with, but occasionally Alaskans still knock heads with wolves over competition for large game. Most summers there are enough moose and caribou to satisfy both parties, but when a hard winter takes its toll on the game, their population becomes extremely fragile and there is only enough to feed the wolves – scuppering poaching opportunities for hunters. In the past, the state solved the problem by killing wolves and allowing a virtual free-for-all on hunting. However, more recently, the state has stopped culling wolves and now allows trophy hunters to shoot them instead (often from planes). This way, predator numbers are still kept in check, but money isn't spent on culling fees and hunting groups are appeased.

The American environmentalist and author, Aldo Leopold, was active in predator control in the 1930s and 1940s. He observed first-hand, the destruction game can wreak on the natural environment when their numbers are not balanced by the natural cycles of predation. In his famous essay *Thinking Like a Mountain*, Leopold had this to say about a wolf encounter:

> In those days we had never heard of passing up a chance to kill a wolf. In a second we were pumping lead into the pack, but with more excitement than accuracy: how to aim a steep downhill shot is always confusing. When our rifles were empty, the old wolf was down, and a pup was dragging a leg into impassable slide-rocks. We reached the old wolf in time to watch a fierce green fire dying in her eyes. I realised then, and have known ever since, that there was something new to me in those eyes – something known only to her and the mountain. I was young then and full of trigger-itch; I thought that because fewer wolves meant more deer, that no wolves would mean a hunter's paradise. But after seeing the green fire die, I sensed that neither the wolf nor the mountain agreed with such a view.

caribou on a few of the islands. The Aleutians are famous, though, for their rich marine ecosystem and abundant sea birds. More than three million sea birds are found in the Pribilof Islands with another seven or more million in the rest of the chain. The most common species include: murrelets, puffins, gulls, stormpetrels, cormorants, terns, kittiwakes, murres, pigeon guillemots and auklets. Non-native rats are found on many of the islands and have harmed ground- and cliff- nesting sea bird populations. While the terrestrial ecosystem is largely intact, the marine ecosystem has faltered recently with declines in sea birds and many marine mammals like Steller sea lions, possibly due to over-fishing in the Bering Sea and North Pacific. Most of the islands are within the Aleutian National Wildlife Reserve.

Interior Alaska The wildlife in the taiga forests of this region are less abundant than in other areas, due to limited food and extreme temperatures. Some species, particularly birds, migrate to warmer climates in the winter, while others simply curl up and go to sleep for the winter. The animals that remain active during the winter are superbly adapted to do so. Wolves, lynx, and other predators grow thick coats, while ptarmigans and snowshoe hares turn white and expand the fur or feathers on their feet to form snowshoes. The physical size of moose and caribou help them cope with the harsh winters, but deep snow means they can't move as quickly and are more susceptible to marauding packs of wolves.

Southeast Alaska The lush rainforests of the Alaska panhandle harbour a huge amount of wildlife, including one of the largest congregations of bald eagles on earth on the Chilkat River outside Haines. Here you'll also find, an astounding 1,600 brown bears on Admiralty Island near Juneau, whales in Fredrick Sound and Glacier Bay National Park, and millions of migratory birds that flood the Stikine River outside Wrangell each spring. The region is also home to other quintessential Alaskan species such as wolves, moose and sea otters.

ALASKAN WILDLIFE
Bears
Black bear (*Ursus americanus*) *Shoulder height: 30 inches; weight: 200lbs.* Black bears (population: 100,000–200,000) are the most common bear in Alaska and are found everywhere except the Seward Peninsula, north of the Brooks Range, the Alaska Peninsula south of Lake Iliamna and on certain islands. They are much smaller than their brown cousins and are opportunistic feeders, eating almost anything. Black bears can be black or brown, and on Kermode Island in Canada they are actually white!

Brown bear (*Ursus arctos*) *Shoulder height: 3–5ft; weight: up to 1,400lbs.* Brown bears (population: 32,000–43,000) are found just about everywhere in the state, except the Aleutian Islands west of Unimak Island. Brown bears are commonly thought to be different from grizzly bears, but the two are actually the same species – grizzly bears are merely a subspecies (*Ursus arctos horribilis*). However, they do occupy different habitats: while grizzlies forage inland and throughout the northern parts of the state and are generally larger (some consider them more aggressive as well), brown bears live along the coast and grow fat on salmon during the summer. Also found is the Kodiak brown bear, sometimes called the Kodiak Grizzly (*Ursus arctos middendorffi*). These are the largest in the world, growing up to 1,500lbs and 10ft tall when standing and are believed to have separated as a subspecies 12,000 years ago.

Ungulates
Caribou (*Rangifer tarandus*) *Shoulder height: 31–59 inches; weight: 300–700lbs.* A widely fluctuating population of about 950,000 caribou – distributed between 32 herds – live in Alaska, with another four million recorded worldwide. Caribou in Europe are called reindeer, but in Alaska are only called reindeer when domesticated. Because caribou exist predominantly in large herds, they must move constantly to find new food. Many herds live in the Arctic during the summer and migrate over the Brooks Range to the taiga forests in the winter. Approximately, 22,000 caribou are killed each year by hunters. Additionally, wolves, bears and eagles kill a large percentage of calves. Their populations vary wildly with the severity of winters, predators and hunting pressure, but overall have not declined significantly.

ANIMAL TRACKS CHART

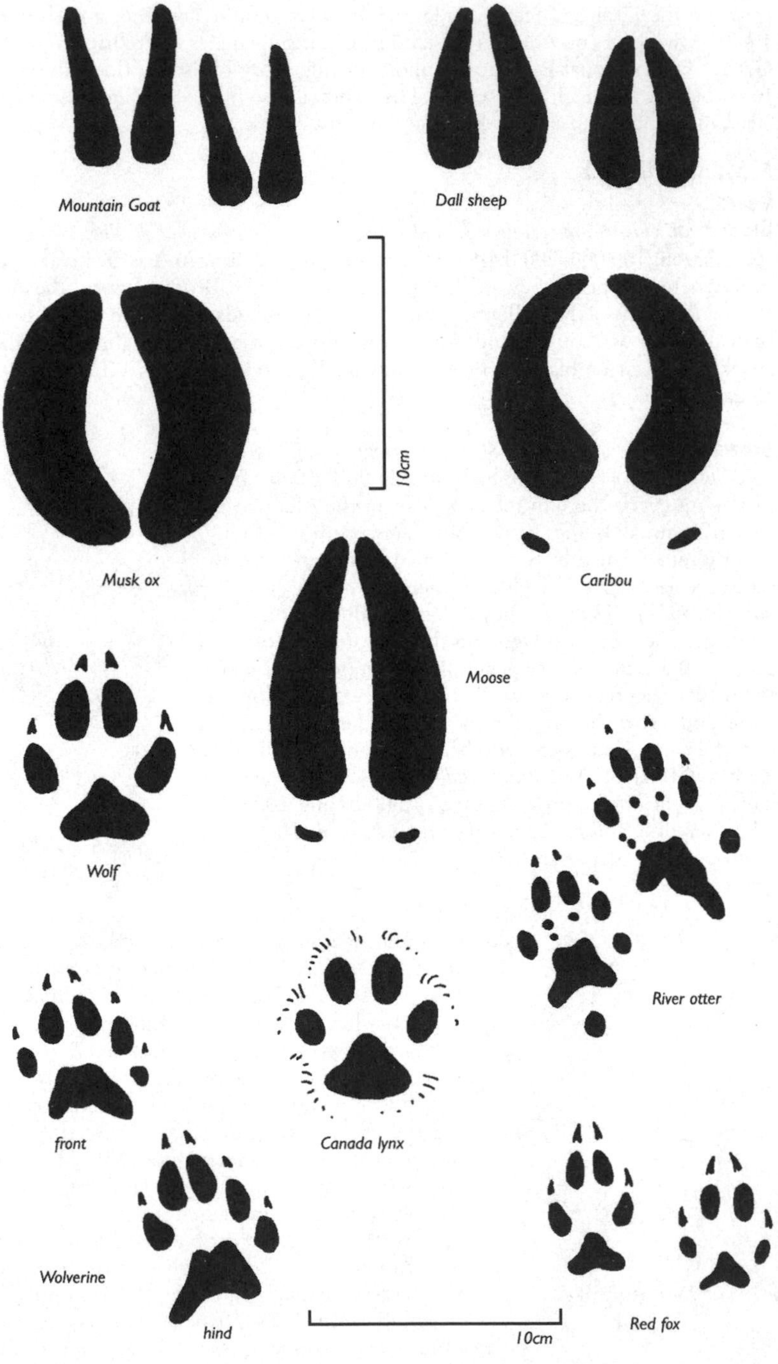

Mountain Goat

Dall sheep

10cm

Musk ox

Caribou

Moose

Wolf

River otter

front

Canada lynx

Wolverine

hind

Red fox

10cm

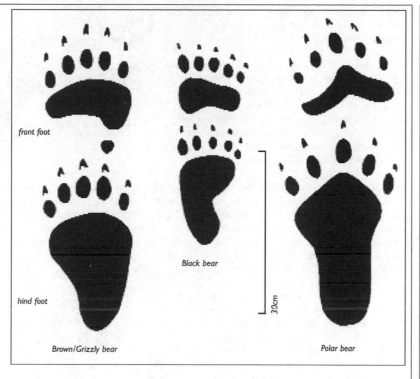

front foot

hind foot

Black bear

30cm

Brown/Grizzly bear

Polar bear

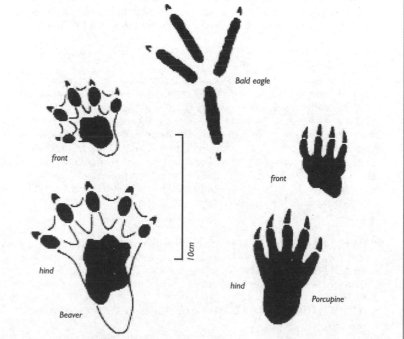

Bald eagle

front

hind

Beaver

10cm

front

hind

Porcupine

Moose (*Alces alces*) *Shoulder height (males): 7ft (50 inch-wide antlers), weight: up to 1,600lbs*. Moose (population: 144,000–166,000) are the largest member of the deer family. They live almost everywhere in Alaska except the Aleutian Island and the southern part of the panhandle. They eat willow and other shrubs, as well as grasses and aquatic plants. They live solitary lives, but in some areas congregate in very high densities. Moose are the state's most important game animal, with 6,000–8,000 killed every year to supply a total of 3.5 million pounds of meat.

Musk ox (*Ovibos moschatus*) *Shoulder height (males): 5ft; weight: up to 800lbs*. Musk ox (population: 3,800) are medium-sized, stocky arctic and sub-arctic animals with long shaggy hair. They've changed little since the last Ice Age and are actually most closely related to sheep and goats. They are best known for their qiviut, or under-hairs, that are some of the softest and rarest fibres on earth. Native Alaskans gather the fibre from bushes after a herd has passed but there are also a number of farms in the state. Musk ox live in herds of up to 75 animals and when they are threatened by predators, which include bear and wolves, they form a circle around their calves, creating a virtually impenetrable ring of snorting muzzles and sharp horns. Unfortunately, this defence did not work against humans who could easily approach these formations. By the 1920s, all the musk ox had disappeared from Alaska, with only small populations still remaining in Greenland and Canada. In the 1930s, 34 musk ox were brought from Greenland and

WILDLIFE VIEWING TIPS

There is always an element of chance when looking for wildlife, but some simple techniques can make things swing a little more in your favour. If you want to see something specific, make sure you visit its favoured habitat when it is most active (most animals are active early and late in the day). If migratory birds only pass through for about a week, find out when and where that is and make sure you're there. Buy really good binoculars and telephoto camera lenses. These will bring the action in, which is often pretty far off, into close view. Use your binoculars or the naked eye to scan the hills (this is particularly rewarding in tundra areas). Doing this slowly and carefully will often produce many animal sightings. Be patient and be prepared to sit still for long periods of time. Animals will often hide if they don't feel safe.

- **THE BEST PLACES TO SEE BEARS** Katmai National Park, McNeil River State Game Sanctuary, Denali National Park, Anan Creek, and Admiralty Island.
- **THE BEST PLACES TO SEE BIRDS** Pribilof Island, Aleutian Islands, Copper River Delta, and the Yukon River Delta. Other locations include Kachemak Bay, and Prince William Sound.
- **THE BEST PLACES TO SEE BALD EAGLES** Homer, Chilkat Bald Eagle Preserve, and Unalaska.

released on Nunivak Island in Western Alaska where they thrived. Their descendants now exist all over Western and Arctic Alaska.

Other Alaskan land mammals Other Alaskan land mammals include: the **American bison** (population: 700), **Dall sheep** (population: 60,000–80,000), **mountain goat** (population: 13,000–15,000), **Roosevelt elk** (population: 475), **Sitka black-tailed deer** (population: 350,000–400,000), beaver, coyote, porcupine, red fox, arctic fox and others.

Wolf (*Canis lupus*) Wolves (population: 5,900–7,200) are common (but rarely seen) throughout the state with a range that covers 85% of the total land area. Wolves are highly social creatures living in packs of around 15 animals and covering a range of about 600 square miles. The wolves of southeast tend to be smaller and darker, while northern wolves can grow to 145lbs and can be any colour, but are usually grey.

Amphibians

Wood frog (*Rana sylvatica*) The wood frog is a small brown frog found throughout Alaska. They may be dull in appearance, but wood frogs have a unique talent: they are one of the few animals on earth that can freeze almost solid during the winter – and survive! Cryogenics researchers are hard at work trying to understand how they do this, but scientists believe that certain minerals and bacteria in the Alaskan environment allow these frogs to freeze more safely without massive cellular damage. In addition, wood frogs can reduce the volume of their cells by drawing the water out of them and promoting ice growth in the extracellular space rather than inside the cell. This stops the cells from being torn apart by sharp ice crystals and allows the frog to thaw out and hop away in the spring.

Birds With 417 species and sea-bird rookeries numbering in their millions, Alaska is a birders' paradise. Millions of birds arrive each spring to take advantage of the long warm days and abundant food. Among the best places to see birds in Alaska are the Copper River Delta, the Yukon Delta National Wildlife Refuge, the Pribilof Islands, and the Aleutian Islands.

Alaska has both the bald eagle and the golden eagle (*Aquila chrysaetos*); the former is the more common species. **Bald eagles** (*Haliaeetus leucocephalus*) gain their white head plumage at about five years old, and are mottled white and brown before that. They are Alaska's largest bird of prey with wingspans that can reach up to 7.5ft (8–14lbs). They are found in greater abundance in Alaska than anywhere else in the US, with an estimated population of 30,000. They nest in large trees in most of their range, but also on cliffs and even sometimes on the ground, particularly in the Aleutian Islands and other treeless places. Bald eagles were protected under the Bald Eagle Protection Act of 1940 and have thrived in the state, unlike their Lower 48 brethren put on the endangered species list because of the pesticide DDT. Today, it remains illegal to kill or harm bald eagles or possess their feathers anywhere in the US.

The playful **arctic tern** (*Sterna paradisaea*) is another fascinating bird, migrating from the arctic to the Antarctic every year – a journey of over 25,000 miles!

Other Alaskan birds Albatross, auklets, cormorants, chickadees, common raven, cranes, eagles, dippers, ducks, eider, geese, grouse, guillemots, gulls, jaegers, kittiwakes, loons, murres, murrelets, osprey, owls, peeps and sandpipers, phalaropes, plovers, ptarmigan, puffins, shearwaters, sparrows, storm-petrels, swans, terns, woodpeckers, yellowlegs and more.

Insects

Mosquitoes The Alaskan mosquito – sometimes referred to as the Alaska state bird on account of its size – is plentiful. These ubiquitous insects breed during the summer in standing water and form buzzing black clouds over the tundra. (Interestingly, females feed on mammalian blood to jumpstart their reproductive system, while males feed only on (phloem) plant juices.) Caribou have been known to run off cliffs, or submerge themselves in pools for hours, to escape the maddening insects. According to the Alaska Almanac, a Canadian study found that a person would be drained of half their blood if standing unprotected on the tundra for two hours. While large and numerous, they are also very slow, making them easy to kill. They are most common at dawn and dusk, near fresh water, and when there is little wind. Their numbers rise in June, peak in July, and quickly descend through August. The best way to protect yourself is to wear tightly-woven clothing that is not tight against the skin and use insect repellent. Headnets can also be nice when they are really bad. At least 25 species of mosquito are found in the state, none of which carry any diseases.

You're also likely to encounter the less well-known but equally voracious 'no-see-um', a tiny biting fly of the Ceratopogonidae family. As the name suggests, they are really small, but their bite packs a punch that makes the mild-mannered mosquito seem positively friendly.

Marine life

Beluga whale (*Delphinapterus leucas*) *Length: up to 15ft; weight: up to 2,000lbs.* Belugas are white, stocky, smallish whales. They have a very small dorsal fin and are the only whales that can move their head on a pivoting neck. This adaptation most likely has to do with feeding on fish, crab and octopus in shallow water. Beluga whales can be found in Cook Inlet and Shelikof Strait near Kodiak and also in the Bering Sea where they regularly travel up large rivers. Other populations live in Greenland, Europe and Asia. Beluga whales are eaten by polar bear and killer whales and occasionally die by fishing net entanglement. Just 400–500 whales remain in Cook Inlet and are on the decline for unknown reasons (see page 218). The Bering Sea population is stable and regularly hunted by native groups.

Bowhead whale (*Balaena mysticetus*) *Length: up to 60ft; weight: up to 120,000lbs.* Bowhead whales have huge, down-turned mouths (the largest in the animal kingdom) for gulping up zooplankton. They are the only Alaskan baleen whale to stay in northern waters year-round. During the summer, they migrate in groups to northern Canadian waters following cracks in the sea ice. When a crack is not present, whales use their heads to break through ice up to two feet thick to breathe.

WHALE IDENTIFICATION

Blue

Bowhead

Fin

Gray

Humpback

Killer

Male Female

Minke

Spout almost invisible

Sei

Sperm

Before commercial whaling, 50,000 bowheads lived in all arctic waters. Today, only 1,000 remain in eastern waters and some 10,000 can be found in Alaska's Bering Sea, down from an original population of 18,000. The Bering Sea variety is the last significant population of their kind on earth. Humans and killer whales are the bowheads' only predators with Native Alaskans allowed to harvest a small number each year for traditional purposes.

Orca (*Orcinus orca*) *Length: up to 27ft; weight: up to 20,000lbs.* The orca, or killer whale, is a white and black whale inhabiting every ocean of the world. They are the largest members of the dolphin family. They live in pods of two varieties: pelagic and resident. Pelagic orcas feed on marine mammals including other whales, sea lions, and seals. Resident orcas feed primarily on fish. Both types work together to subdue their prey, giving rise to their other name, 'wolves of the sea'. Orcas have no predators besides humans who have traditionally used them for meat and oil. In recent years commercial long liners have reported killer whales eating fish off the line as it comes over the side, carefully biting off only the body to avoid the hook. This learned behaviour can be devastating to fishermen.

Polar bear (*Ursus maritimus*) *Length: up to 11ft long; weight: up to 1,400lbs.* Yes, the polar bear is actually considered a marine mammal. They are also carnivores, unlike the brown and black bear that are omnivores. Polar bears – also called *Nanuuq* by Arctic native groups – ranges though the northern polar regions of the world, including northern and northwestern Alaska. Polar bears are the second-largest in the bear family, rivalled only in size by Kodiak brown bears. Though their fur appears white, the hairs are actually clear, designed specifically to channel the suns warmth to their skin. Polar bears eat seals, walrus, and the carcasses of dead marine mammals such as whales. They range over a wide area of both land and sea-ice and are able to swim up to 100 miles. Because these bears use sea-ice so extensively, particularly for hunting the ringed seal, their primary prey, they are especially susceptible to the warming of the Arctic and the associated reduction in sea-ice; the quicker it melts the quicker their potential hunting ground is reduced. As much as 20% of the polar ice cap has already melted, causing polar bears to starve in some of their range. With the reduction in ice, polar bears have been observed recently hundreds of miles from ice or shore, ultimately swimming to exhaustion and death. Recently, two polar bears were recorded swimming from Greenland to Iceland; a distance of 180 miles. There are an estimated 28,000 polar bears worldwide.

Salmon shark (*Lamna ditropis*) *Length: up to 12ft; weight: up to 700lbs.* One of Alaska's top marine predators, salmon sharks can reach swimming speeds of 50 knots. To hunt in the cold waters off Alaska, they have evolved to be some of the warmest-bodied sharks on earth. This allows their muscles to react more quickly with the bursts of speed needed to snatch salmon from a school in 45°F water. They are closely related to both mako and great white sharks and are found throughout the North Pacific region. While they eat all kinds of fish, they feed primarily on salmon in the summer, consuming as many as 146 million salmon (as a species) annually. Salmon sharks were briefly fished commercially, but the fishery was closed because too little was known about them. Today, they are caught by sport fishermen seeking the biggest fish in the state.

Sea otter (*Enhydra lutris*) *Length: up to 5ft; weight: 90lbs.* Sea otters are the largest members of the weasel family and are closely related to river otters and mink. They live in large groups of mostly females. Males are mostly solitary creatures. Unlike other marine mammals that have blubber (a layer of fat beneath the skin) to keep warm in the frigid waters, sea otters have extremely fine and dense fur that they groom constantly; using a rubbing motion that creates insulating air bubbles in their fur. (The Exxon Valdez oil spill (see page 272) was particularly devastating to sea otters because the oil matted their fur and prevented them from staying warm; several thousand died of cold and starvation.) They spend virtually all their time eating (they need to eat one quarter of their body weight every day) shellfish, and can dive to depths of up to 250ft to gather crab, clams and sea urchins. They return to the surface and, while floating on their backs, use their stomachs like a plate. Sea otters occasionally use a rock to smash the mollusc's shell before eating. Sea otters were once present from California all the way through Alaska, to Russia and Japan, but were almost totally annihilated for their rich fur by Russian traders in the 1700s and 1800s. When Alaska was sold to the US in 1867, the Americans continued to hunt the severely depleted creatures until 1911 when their near extinction was acknowledged. Since receiving protection, their numbers have increased dramatically, from a low of less than 2,000, Alaska now has almost 200,000 sea otters. In some areas their numbers are so great that locals complain about there being no more clams or crab.

Steller sea lion (*Eumetopias jubatus*) *Length: 8ft; weight: 1,200lbs.* Steller sea lions differ from other seals because of their external ears and rear flippers, which allow them to walk. Large numbers congregate at established rookeries to breed and give birth. They are found along the Pacific Coast from northern California through Alaska to Japan. Alaska has traditionally had the vast majority of the 281,800 Steller sea lions worldwide but throughout the 1970s and 1980s their numbers declined by 50%. Today, their numbers continue to decline for unknown reasons, but since they are fish eaters, the overfishing of the world's oceans is a likely culprit. Steller sea lions have been hunted for thousands of years by coastal native groups, particularly the Unangan in the Aleutian Islands. Later they were harvested commercially by farmers for fox food and by fur traders for their hides. After the Marine Mammal Protection Act of 1972, Steller sea lions have not been commercially harvested.

Walrus (*Odobenus rosmarus divergens*) *Length: 11ft; weight: 2,000lbs.* Two closely related species of walrus live throughout the polar region and are the world's largest pinnipeds (related to sea lions): the Pacific walrus and the Atlantic walrus. Pacific walrus number over 200,000. Their long tusks are used primarily in fighting for the right to mate and not for feeding. Walrus eat clams and other invertebrates almost exclusively, ploughing the bottom with their muzzles. Clams and other prey are sucked out of the mud, broken and the fleshy bits are sucked out with a powerful piston-like tongue. Bering-Sea native groups have used the many parts of the walrus for thousands of years, making raingear from the intestines, creating art from their tusks and taking food from their flesh.

Other Alaskan marine mammals Other Alaskan marine mammals include: the bearded seal, spotted seal, ringed seal, ribbon seal, northern fur seal, harbour seal, humpback whale, grey whale and blue whale.

Fish Fresh water species include: Brook trout, burbot, arctic char, arctic grayling, dolly varden, cutthroat trout, lake chub, lake trout, northern pike, sheefish, steelhead trout, rainbow trout, lamprey, longnose sucker and whitefish.

SALMON

Salmon is a prized commercial, as well as sport, fish and Alaska has five species. Between 2000 and 2004, Alaskan commercial fishermen harvested (on average) 185.5 million pounds of salmon per year, worth US$40 million.

Salmon hatch from eggs buried in gravel at the bottom of a river or lake, and after spending a period in fresh water (dog and pink salmon skip this), they charge downstream to mature at sea. After spending one to seven years at sea, depending on the species, they return to the same river or lake where they were born to lay their own eggs. After swimming, sometimes thousands of miles upriver, female salmon lay their eggs in a 'redd' (a nest for their eggs in the gravel) and the male fertilises them. At this stage, male salmon develop a hooked nose and often a humped back and are often bright red or striped. Females also 'turn' (see *Glossary*, page 431), but their transformation is less dramatic. Afterward they both die and their corpses provide nutrients for many plants and animals downriver.

CHINOOK SALMON (*Oncorhynchus tshawytscha*) Also called king salmon, this is the state fish and the largest of the Pacific salmon species. Many (myself included), say the king is also the best-tasting salmon. The largest king ever caught weighed 126lbs, but was caught commercially in Petersburg. The largest caught-for-sport king was hooked on the Kenai River on the Kenai Peninsula in 1986 and weighed 97lbs. A more commonly caught size is 15–30lbs. When on the smaller side, king salmon can be hard to differentiate from silver salmon. The best way to identify a king is by its black gums (inside the mouth) and spotted back and tail. After spending three to seven years at sea, kings return to spawn in May and June in most areas. Kings are targeted commercially mainly by trollers, not to be confused with trawlers.

'White' king salmon have been a delicacy in Alaska for a long time, and the word is starting to get out. Some high-end restaurants now serve this pale-fleshed (higher fat) variety and charge a premium for it. Only about one in 100 kings are truly 'white' and whether this has to do with genetics or diet no one really knows. While biologists work on this question, we can go on savouring this tastiest (and rarest) of all salmon.

CHUM SALMON (*Oncorhynchus keta*) Also known as dog salmon, are found around the North Pacific from California to Alaska and on to Japan. Dog salmon are hard to tell apart from both silver and red salmon. They are often larger than reds, weighing 7–15lbs, and do not have silver on their tail like silvers. After three to six years, they return to their home river to complete their life cycle. When they enter fresh water they develop vertical bands on their sides. Less commercially valuable than most other species, 11 million fish were caught in the last few years, worth US$32 million.

Saltwater species include: Eulachon, lingcod, Pacific herring, rockfish, slimy sculpin, Alaska blackfish and black cod plus the five species of Pacific salmon below.

The infamous Pacific halibut (*Hippoglossus stenolepis*) can weigh up to 495lbs and, from evidence of halibut bones found in native midden (see *Glossary*, page 431) sites, possibly much more. Halibut can live for almost 50 years and eat just about anything, including fish and shellfish. Halibut undergo an incredible, almost science-fiction-like transformation as young fish known as 'orbital migration'. After hatching from the egg, the tiny halibut live in the middle water column and swim vertically, rather than resting horizontally on the bottom, like their parents. As they mature, their left eye 'migrates' to the right side of their head and they settle to the bottom. Halibut are commercially fished using 'long-lines'. The commercial harvest of halibut began toward the end of the 1800s when

COHO SALMON (*Oncorhynchus kisutch (Walbaum)*) Are also called silver salmon, generally weighing about 10lbs but can weigh up to 30lbs. Silvers sport a hint of silver on their tails instead of spots like the king. Silver salmon are a prized sport fish and increasingly a commercial one as well. Sport fishermen often catch silvers while trolling for kings. Silver salmon enter streams to spawn mid-summer through the late fall.

PINK SALMON (*Oncorhynchus gorbuscha*) Also known as a 'humpy' (because of its humped back while spawning), the pink salmon is the smallest salmon species. Often weighing just three or four pounds these fish are caught commercially in huge numbers but, because of their small size and mushy flesh, are not very valuable. After just two years, pinks return to their river of birth to spawn, usually June through October. Commercial fishermen catch about 45 million fish per year.

SOCKEYE SALMON (*Oncorhynchus nerka*) Are also called red salmon, and have an immense range from the Pacific Northwest through Alaska to Japan. Their bright red flesh and abundance have made them one of the state's most important commercial fish species. Reds have no spots at all and are often dark blue-black to vivid green along their backs. After feeding at sea on zooplankton, they return to spawn mid–summer weighing five to ten pounds. The largest red salmon fishery on earth is Bristol Bay where 10–30 million fish are caught every year (see *Pebble Mine* box on page 368). Other southcentral and southwest locations bring in another one to six million fish. The Kenai River is home to some of the largest red salmon around, often weighing upwards of 12–15lbs.

COMMERCIAL FISHING METHODS Salmon are commercially caught one of three ways in Alaska: purse sein, gill-net or trolling. Seiners catch salmon by circling them with a large net. As they pull the net back onto the boat, the circle gets smaller, and the fish are concentrated. At a certain point, a line is pulled that closes the bottom of the net and completes the trap. The rest of the net is then hauled onboard, and the fish are dumped into the hold.

Gill-netting comes in two forms: setnetting and drifting. Both involve similar nets of fine monofilament mesh that 'gills' the fish by catching them behind their gills when they swim into the net. Setnetters fish their nets from the beach and pick the fish from the net while it's still in the water from small boats called skiffs. Drifters, on the other hand, fish their nets from boats that are generally 30–58ft long. They let their net out off a drum and tend it closely, pulling it in to pick the fish.

Trolling is done primarily in southeast Alaska for king and silver salmon. Fishermen generally use downriggers to get their bait or lures far below the surface, then tow them waiting for the strike. This can be done with fishing poles or outriggers.

Scandinavian and New England fishermen plied the waters of southeast, packing their catch in glacial ice. Today, halibut are an extremely popular sport fish and are easy to catch, provided there are fish in the area. The problem is that many places formerly teeming with halibut are now practically devoid of them. When my father first came to Homer in the 1970s, he started one of the first charter fishing businesses, Halibut King Charters. He would take his clients out of the small boat harbour, around the tip of the spit then promptly drop anchor. His clients would quickly catch their limit all within a stone's throw from the beach. Though he sold the business long ago, Homer is still one of the state's most popular destinations for halibut fishing and is considered the halibut fishing capital of the world. These days, however, charter fishermen have to travel more than 60 miles to the Barren Islands (practically to Kodiak) to find good fishing for their clients. The moral to the story: keep the small ones (they taste far better) and let the big 'breeders' go free to perpetuate the species.

Other shellfish species Other shellfish species include: Abalone, king crab, Dungeness crab, tanner crab, razor clam, scallop and shrimp.

ENVIRONMENTAL CONCERNS

FISHING Another issue that has come to the attention of the public since the 1990s is destructive fishing methods, such as trawling (not to be confused with trolling (see page 35). These large funnel-shaped nets, deployed by commercial fishing vessels, are dragged either along the bottom (bottom trawling) or through the middle of the water column (mid-water or pelagic trawling) collecting everything in their path. Bottom trawling, in particular, has come under heavy attack because the large nets break up corals, sponges, etc, that are extremely slow growing and provide nurseries for juvenile fish. A UN report found that between 1990 and 2002 in the Aleutian Islands alone, 4.4 million pounds of coral and sponge were killed. Another problem is the indiscriminate nature of trawling, where huge amounts of 'bycatch' are caught and then dumped. (Bycatch is any species caught that was not the intended catch). Bycatch is usually illegal to keep and winds up being dumped over the side, usually dead. While most fisheries have some form of bycatch (often just the occasional flounder that can be tossed back into the sea unharmed), North Pacific bottom trawlers were responsible for 751 million pounds in 1994 (as much as 50% of their total catch). Today, the numbers have improved (332 million pounds in 2005), but bottom trawling remains a poor fishing method in need of serious reform. Some progress has been made, such as large tracts of water made off limits in the Bering Sea and Amendment 79 in 2006, which forced trawlers to retain at least 65% of all bycatch and target species in 2008, and 85% by 2011.

CLIMATE CHANGE The world's Arctic regions are warming at a quicker rate than the rest of the earth, having gained almost 3°C in some areas as opposed to the global average of just 0.6°C since the 1950s. These figures have been confirmed both by scientists and Arctic native peoples. This warming threatens not only human settlements but also virtually all Arctic life, from the tundra itself to the polar bear. Arctic tundra and permafrost hold huge amounts of carbon that could be released with climate change. In addition, the melting of the polar ice-cap (combined with Greenland's ice field) could significantly raise global sea levels and desalinate the ocean, which would alter ocean currents. These currents, to a large extent, drive the planet's weather. As the climate warms, Boreal forestland advances northwards eventually bringing an end to the Arctic ecosystem, with disastrous consequences for its plant and animal life.

MINING/OIL A future environmental concern for Alaska, and the rest of the polar region, is the possibility of oil and natural gas drilling in areas formerly covered by thick sea-ice. A US Geological Survey report speculates that 13–30% of the world's undiscovered oil and natural gas may be under Arctic ice. Leading the charge to develop these fields is ExxonMobil, but others are close behind. Fossil fuel-driven climate change is at least partially responsible for the more than 20% decrease in polar ice, but the irony is clearly lost on these oil giants. While Alaska still relies to a large extent on oil money, it does have an increasing number of forward-looking residents and investors who are starting to realise the potential revenue to be garnered from tourism.

Also looming on the horizon is the Pebble Mine (see box on page 368), which threatens the largest red salmon run on earth in Bristol Bay. In a rare display of brotherhood, environmental groups and commercial fishermen are banding together to combat the proposed gold mine.

CONSERVATION

With the largest tracts of untamed wilderness left in the US, Alaska has become a focal point of the American conservation movement. Unlike so many countries, the US has had the opportunity to preserve a great amount of land. The challenge now is to reconcile the residents' desire and need to use their public lands with the rights of the ecosystem. This can be tricky in a state popular with visiting sport hunters and fishermen, and with so many residents living off the land. While Alaskan fisheries are considered some of the best-managed in the world, the state predator control programmes (see box on page 24) speak to a backwards logic that prioritises the needs of people over those of the ecosystem.

PROTECTED LAND Since Alaska began to see intense development in the early 1900s, conservationists have been increasingly aware that even a place as big as Alaska can be spoiled. In 1925, Congress enacted laws to protect wildlife from over-hunting. Indeed, during the 1930s and 1940s, the Kodiak National Wildlife Refuge was created at the behest of bear hunters, who were also conservationists, and today encompasses 1.9 million acres and is home to some 2,300 of the world's largest brown bears, 600 nesting pairs of bald eagles, 1.5 million sea birds. But the concept didn't gain momentum until the Arctic National Wildlife Refuge was created in 1960. During the 1970s, tens of millions of acres were set aside and, in 1980, Congress passed the Alaska National Interest Lands Conservation Act (ANILCA), which dedicated 104 million acres of land to parks, national forests and wildlife refuges with almost half set aside as wilderness. This was a victory for conservationists, including the long-dead John Muir who explored Alaska in the 1800s and advocated its protection even then.

The ANILCA, with the help of conservation groups like Alaska Conservation Foundation (ACF) and World Wildlife Fund (WWF), designated a further 104 million acres of land, including the 5.4 million acres of the Tongass National Forest, as national parks and preserves and was considered a victory for Alaskan environmental conservation.

But protecting land is never as simple and the well established timber industry of southeast Alaska needed to be compensated for their loss if the land was to be protected. The 1947 Tongass Timber Act promised 4.5 billion board feet of wood to loggers every ten years, but during the 1980s and 1990s an increasingly heated battle raged between forest-use advocates (and most Alaskan residents) and various influential environmental organisations like the Sierra Club. The immense and irreplaceable old-growth forests of the Tongass grabbed the public's attention and eventually pushed the battle in the favour of environmentalists. All subsidies and the 4.5 billion board feet harvest mandate were ended. As compensation for the millions of acres now off limits to loggers, Congress paid US$40 million in subsidies to logging interests. This Act helped to end commercial logging in southeast Alaska with 16.7 million acres protected forever and 300,000 of that designated wilderness. But while environmentalists celebrated, hundreds lost their jobs and part of the Alaskan economy and a way of life began to vanish.

Many effective conservation groups including the Alaska Conservation Society (ACS) founded in 1960, have worked hand in hand with the state of Alaska to protect land. ACS was one of the state's original environmental leaders, helping to block projects like the Rampart Dam on the Yukon River and Project Chariot, a plan to create a harbour on the North Slope with nuclear weapons. In 1980, the ACF took over the ACS and continue their work today.

Today, most conservation groups have a presence in Alaska, including the Nature Conservancy, the Sierra Club, and the World Wildlife Fund.

ENDANGERED SPECIES Alaska, like anywhere, has its fair share of endangered as well as extinct species. While the 1973 Endangered Species Act has done a lot to mitigate the flow of species into memory, there is much more to do. There are currently 13 species on the Endangered Species list, including: the short-tailed albatross, Eskimo curlew, blue whale, humpback whale, right whale, beluga whale, fin whale, sei whale and the sperm whale. There five species on the Threatened Species list, and these are: the spectacled eider, Steller's eider, northern sea otter, Steller sea lion and the polar bear.

Two Alaskan species that did not receive protection in time are the now-extinct spectacled cormorant and the Steller sea cow: the spectacled cormorant was a large, nearly flightless bird of the Aleutian Islands that was large enough to feed several people – the last one died in 1850. The Steller's sea cow also lived in the Aleutians and looked much like today's manatee and the dugong, the major difference being that the sea cow weighed up to 8,800lbs and reached 25ft in length;. they died out in 1768, having been hunted to extinction by Russians and early explorers.

2

Practical Information

WHEN TO VISIT

Alaska is really a summer destination (late-May–mid-August) but ever more visitors are braving the winters to enjoy the northern lights, and the host of winter sports Alaska offers. Still, the winters with their dark and bone-chilling temperatures are not to be taken lightly and the vast majority of the 1.6 million people who visit Alaska annually come in the summer. Many Alaskans themselves flee the state in the autumn, often zipping off to Mexico or Hawaii.

That said, the best time to visit depends on where in the state you plan on going. See *Climate* on page 4.

While the shoulder seasons (May– mid-August/September) can be wonderful, tolerance of a night-time nip and a readiness for almost any weather is required. For those cruising the highways in a recreational vehicle (RV), the shoulder seasons of May and August, with their much-reduced mosquito populations, could be perfect. For campers, cyclists or anyone planning on being outside a lot, June, July and the first week of August are safe almost anywhere. Again, given a tolerance for 'iffy' weather, the shoulder seasons are nearly free of tourists and mosquitoes and are my favourite times to travel, especially the autumn. August brings autumn colours to the tundra and some forests, as well as spawning salmon, complacent bears and wild berries galore.

This guide assumes travel between 1 June and 15 August. At other times businesses, museums and other attractions may be closed.

HIGHLIGHTS

THE MCCARTHY ROAD AND MCCARTHY/KENNICOTT Drive one of the state's most beautiful roads then spend a few days exploring the Wrangell–St Elias Mountains and the charming former mining towns of Kennicott and McCarthy. See pages 340, 343 and 341, respectively.

THE ALEUTIAN RUN Island hop through the Aleutians with the Alaska Ferry then enjoy a week or more in Unalaska, a busy fishing port at the end of the earth. See page 375.

NOME Take in the history and culture of Nome, then road trip through the tundra to see wildlife, catch fish, and soak in hot springs. See page 400.

PRINCE OF WALES ISLAND A little-visited island full of fish, wildlife, old-growth forests and native culture. Road trip around the island or gear up for a canoeing trip or hike. See page 131.

SITKA Where Tlingit, Russian and modern American culture collide. See page 151.

KODIAK ISLAND Take in the fishing ambiance and Russian history of Kodiak town, or hop on a small plane and explore the fish-and-wildlife-rich 'Emerald Isle' from the air. See page 351.

DENALI NATIONAL PARK Push past the glitz of the park entrance and explore this stunning park on foot or by bus. If the mountain is socked in (see *Glossary* on page 431), head south to Cantwell and the stunning Denali Highway. See page 287.

SOUTHEAST BY FERRY The best way to enter Alaska is undoubtedly aboard the Alaska Ferry. Hop on in Bellingham, Washington or Prince Rupert, Canada and island hop all the way to Skagway. Proceed on to the rest of Alaska via the Klondike Highway, once the most beautiful in the state. See page 60.

THE DALTON HIGHWAY Splitting the Arctic in half, the Dalton Highway is the best adventure road trip in the state. See page 414.

HOMER AND KACHEMAK BAY An unrivalled coupling of art, food, and wilderness. See pages 246 and 255.

PRINCE WILLIAM SOUND Take an all-day cruise out of Seward for some of the best marine wildlife viewing in the state or cruise out of Valdez or Whittier for glaciers galore. See page 264.

SUGGESTED ITINERARIES

Trying to decide where to go is hard anywhere, but especially in a place as big and diverse as Alaska. Most travellers long ago realised that trying to cover too much ground means they don't really see anything. Still, every summer I see motorhomes full of Midwesterners racing at top speed towards Denali National Park, where they will presumably stay a night or two, then zip off to Fairbanks, before getting back to Anchorage barely in time to catch their flight home. I am of the mind that experiencing a smaller part of the state – but experiencing it on every level – is a superior way to travel. A tour of the southeast region, or even just Prince of Wales Island, is more than enough for a trip of a few weeks. Those fortunate enough to have the time and money to travel for a month or more can then think about branching out, perhaps riding the ferry to Unalaska, staying a week then touring the interior and Arctic by car and plane. Another enjoyable way to travel is to research an area well, decide on the best location and rent a house for a part of or the entire trip. This means you will effectively become a local, get to know your neighbours and, more importantly, learn about all their secret, favourite places. I can promise you will return home having made new, possibly life-long friends, and with the feeling that you really understand at least a small part of Alaska. That's as much as any of us can hope for.

ART, CULTURE AND FISHING

One week With just a week in the state you can't go wrong exploring Anchorage and Homer and the amazing terrain in between. After flying into Anchorage, spend a day and night recuperating and exploring the city centre. The following day, rent a car and drive south. After Turnagain Arm (see page 218) with its tidal bores, soaring peaks, and dall sheep-studded hills, swing into the Begich, Boggs visitor center to learn all about glaciers. If you're glacier crazy (who isn't?) head through the tunnel to Whittier (see page 265) and board a cruise to see some of the state's most impressive tidewater glaciers in Prince William Sound. Avoid spending the night in Whittier if you can, instead backtrack just a little to Girdwood or press on just a few more hours to Hope (see page 224) or Seward (see page 228). Hope is a fascinating former mining town, but is easily seen in just a few hours. Seward is a must for any Kenai Peninsula Adventure and is *the* place to see marine mammals. Check out the Seward Sealife Center but also be sure to take a full-day cruise into the bird- and marine-mammal-rich waters outside Resurrection Bay. Spend the night in Seward then press on to either Cooper Landing or Soldotna to fish the infamous Kenai River. After a full day of fishing and a night in either place, continue south to Homer (see page 246) where you will want to spend the rest of your time before taking one full day to drive back to Anchorage. While in Homer be sure to explore Kachemak Bay State Park, go halibut fishing, tour the town's fine restaurants, art galleries and museums!

For those who don't want to rent a car, another option is to ride the Alaska Railroad from Anchorage to Seward (a lovely trip), then catch a shuttle to Homer. At the end of the trip, another shuttle can be used to get back to Anchorage.

One week plus With more than a week, your options really open up. You could easily take the above trip and simply stretch it out, but if it's Alaska's heartland you want to see, include a drive or rail trip up to Denali National Park (see page 287). As a conclusion or a start to the one week trip, board the Alaska Railroad in Anchorage and ride it all the way to Denali with an optional stop in the laid-back town of Talkeetna (see page 281), where a day or more can easily be spent. Once in Denali, check into your B&B or hotel and start exploring the park. While bus trips into the park can be wonderful, do yourself a favour and get out into the backcountry. The trip to Denali can also be made by a very scenic car ride. If for some reason you find that you're ready to leave Denali and still have time left in your trip, head south and drive the Denali Highway (see box on page 333), one of Alaska's great road trips.

MOUNTAINS AND GLACIERS GALORE

One week Fly into Anchorage, spend the night and explore the city centre. Then drive north through the Chugach Mountains to Denali National Park (see page 287), home of the continent's highest peak, Denali at 20,320ft. Spend one or two days in Denali then head back toward Anchorage and turn east on the Denali Highway and camp along this amazing gravel roadway. Hit the Richardson Highway and head south to the Wrangell-St Elias National Park visitor centre on the edge of the park at mile 106.8 of the Richardson Highway. There are more glaciers here than anywhere else on the continent. The park is also home to the greatest number of peaks in the continent above 16,000ft including Mount St Elias at 18,008ft. Stay in Glennallen (see page 328) or Copper Center (see page 330) or press on to Valdez (see page 267). The drive to Valdez is truly spectacular with glaciers and mountains pressing in on the road from all directions. Valdez, like Whittier, is not the cosiest place on earth, but it is spectacularly situated. It's also a wonderful place to take a cruise to see tidewater glaciers in Prince William Sound. For the final leg of the journey, drive back to Anchorage on the Glenn Highway, again in the constant company of mountains.

One week plus With a little more time the above trip can simply be extended for a more complete and leisurely trip of two to four weeks. Here are a few amazing extensions to add to the itinerary. After spending some time at the Wrangell-St Elias visitor centre, leave the Richardson Highway and head to the tiny town of Chitina (see page 340). This is where the McCarthy Road starts (see box on page 340), a 60-mile gravel road through the wilderness. At the end of the road are the tiny but lovely towns of McCarthy and Kennicott (see page 340). Mountains and glaciers galore!

Yet another fun way to extend this trip would be to hop on the ferry in Valdez and ride it to Whittier. The scenery is gorgeous and once in Whittier you can head back to Anchorage or on to explore the Kenai Peninsula.

ARCTIC DREAMS

One week Of all the remote places in Alaska, the Arctic is definitely at the top of the list. However, one road does penetrate this region – the Dalton Highway (see page 414). From the modern city of Fairbanks (see page 301), which can be reached by train, car or plane from Anchorage, drive north into the Arctic. This should not be attempted in a standard rental car, instead try GoNorth (see page 62) or Arctic Outfitters (see page 61). This is a rough trip, but folks usually agree that a broken windshield or flat tyre are a small price to pay for the right to drive through such a wild and untouched landscape. While some spend just a few days on the Dalton Highway, others take a week or more, camping, fishing and hiking all the way up.

One week plus A wonderful way to extend this trip is to bed down in a plush Fairbanks B&B and spend a few days eating out and visiting museums, like the hyper-modern Museum of the North at the University of Alaska. When you have eaten at all the good restaurants and are feeling restless, jump in the car and drive out to Chena Hot Springs for a soak in the hot tubs and an 'appletini' in a glass made of ice. Rooms and camping are available. Another day (or overnight) trip is out on the Elliot Highway where the tiny town of Manley and the Manley Hot Springs await. Yet another is the Steese Highway and the town of Circle. Wonderful hiking trails, camping, fishing and historic gold-mining machinery can be found along the road. For more information on these trips see page 311.

RAINFOREST AND TLINGIT CULTURE

One week plus Exploring the southeast by ferry is one of the state's best trips and requires around two to three weeks. While travelling with a car on the ferry is handy, it isn't necessary. But it does allow the exploration of Prince of Wales Island and the many remote logging roads that often branch out from otherwise roadless southeast towns. There are a number of logical ways to start this trip: in Bellingham (Washington), Prince Rupert (Canada) or Ketchikan (Alaska) if going south to north; or from north to south, start in Haines (see page 171) or Skagway (see page 164) both of which are attached to the road system.

For the most complete experience of the southeast, book your passage well ahead and plan for two days or more in places like Ketchikan (see page 116) and Sitka (see page 151), and a handful of days in Juneau (see page 87) and Prince of Wales Island (see page 131). Ketchikan – a 36-hours ferry ride from Bellingham, Washington – is one of the wettest places in the southeast and, as a result, boasts some superb rainforest; nearby Misty Fjords National Monument is a primeval world of sheer granite fjords, ancient forests and water. This is also the staging point for the Prince of Wales Island road trip and the native community of Metlakatla (see page 130) on Annette Island. The next stop is the hard-working fishing community of Wrangell (see page 138), about five hours by ferry from Ketchikan. Here you can tour Chief Shake Island or take a boat cruise to the Stikine River or LeConte Glacier. Bear viewing at Anan Creek is also popular. The next stop on the ferry route, after passing through the famously narrow Wrangell Narrows, is the quaint town of Petersburg (see page 143) with a distinctive Norwegian heritage. Trips to the Stikine River or LeConte Glacier can also be arranged from here.

From Petersburg hop back on the ferry and head to Sitka where fine food meets spectacular scenery and Russian and Tlingit culture. Next is the state capital,

Juneau (see page 87) about four and half hours away by ferry. Juneau is where the wilderness meets civilisation, allowing for a unique adventure of forest and glacier hikes by day, and theatre, art, music and fine dining by night. Other adventures to enjoy while in Juneau include: whale-watching, flightseeing, bear viewing on Admiralty Island, Glacier Bay National Park and Tracy Arm.

From Juneau, hop back on the ferry and enjoy the scenery on your way to Skagway, followed by Haines. Skagway is steeped in gold rush history and Haines has one of the biggest congregations of bald eagles on earth. Both towns are spectacularly situated amidst soaring peaks and are on the road system, making them the perfect place to start a driving tour of the state.

JOURNEY TO THE EDGE OF THE EARTH – EXPLORE THE ALEUTIAN ISLANDS BY FERRY

More than one week Arrive in Anchorage, stay a night or two, then rent a car or hop in a shuttle and get down to Homer. From there board the ferry and start an epic journey to the end of the world, otherwise known as Unalaska. The first leg of the trip takes you to Kodiak (see page 351) on an overnight and sometimes rough trip. This ferry run leaves a few times a week, but the ongoing ferry to Unalaska only goes once a month, so don't miss it! Kodiak is a fascinating island full of Russian and World War II history, bears, and rolling hills of vibrant green – it's sometimes called the Emerald Isle. From there, head out to Chignik, Sand Point, King Cove, Cold Bay, False Pass, Akutan and finally Unalaska/Dutch Harbor over three days. Once you leave Kodiak, the ferry cruises along a wild coast of untouched wilderness. Marine life abounds and an onboard naturalist is there to tell you all about it. The tiny villages between Kodiak and Unalaska are rough places where tourism as the rest of the state experiences it is virtually unknown and subsistence hunting and gathering is a way of life. The fishing town of Unalaska has the same feel but on a larger scale. Here, World War II history is literally strewn everywhere, making it a dream for history buffs. The landscape is also stunning and very accessible to the hiker. Wildflowers carpet the tree-less landscape and a total lack of bears makes it feel that much safer to some hikers. The halibut fishing is out of this world – the state record of 459 pounds was landed here – and there are lots of bald eagles, sea otters and sea birds.

While the trip from Homer to Unalaska takes just five days, choosing to stay in Unalaska for another few days is a good idea for a total trip of seven to ten days. Daily flights back to Anchorage cost an arm and a leg but are the only option short of taking the ferry back. For detailed tips on the Aleutian Run see page 375.

OFF-THE-BEATEN-TRACK

One week For a short trip packed with wildlife, mountains, and wilderness fly into Anchorage and after spending a night and day, head to Seward (see page 228) on the train or by car. Seward is one of the best places in the state to see marine mammals and birds both in the Seward Sealife Center and from a full-day tour outside Resurrection Bay. While a full-day cruise can sometimes be rough, the volume of life is astounding. Sea birds, whales, seals, and sea lions are just some of the creatures you are very likely to see. Seward is also a lovely town. From Seward, drive or take a shuttle to Homer (see page 246) where Kachemak Bay State Park can be explored by small plane, kayak or on foot, but the real prize is the wilderness and unrivalled bear viewing opportunities of Katmai National Park, McNeil State Game Sanctuary and Refuge and Chenik on the Alaska Peninsula. All are accessible from Homer via seaplane and while expensive, are unbeatable trips. Katmai offers a slightly more civilized option where camping and lodge stays are available while Chenik has fewer bears but offers total seclusion and a handful of feeding bears all to yourself. To visit Chenik, hire a Homer guide and they will arrange the trip. The

2

McNeil State Game Sanctuary and Refuge is available only to those who win a lottery, but is undeniably the best place to see bears probably in the entire world. Seventy two bears have been observed at one time at McNeil!

With just a few days left, drive back to Anchorage and on to Denali National Park. While the park entrance is no one's idea of wilderness, the rest of the park is full of wildlife and is totally wild. The beauty of Denali is that leaving the crowds behind is as easy as hiking a half-mile from the road with a tent, some food and a sense of adventure. Those not inclined to hike can ride the park buses through the park for an excellent chance to see all kinds of wildlife.

TOURIST INFORMATION

The state of Alaska maintains a number of visitor services including the **State of Alaska** website (*www.alaska.gov*) with information on government, economy and travel. However, the state's official resource dedicated to the visitor is www.travelalaska.com. They also offer British (*www.travel-alaska.co.uk*), German (*www.alaska-travel.de*), Japanese (*www.alaska-japan.com*) and Korean (*www.alaska-korea.com*) versions.

Once in the Alaska, visitor information is available at the town visitor centre or chamber of commerce. Just about every Alaskan city or town has one; a complete list can be found at the **Alaska Chamber of Commerce** (*www.alaskachamber.com*) website. While smaller towns sometimes do not have a visitor centre office, they usually do have a website and/or a local business owner available by phone.

In addition to a stop at the visitor centre, I always head to a public land information centre. **Alaska's National Parks** (*www.nps.gov/state/ak/index.htm*) all have offices in local communities with knowledgeable staff, displays and printed information about the state's national parks and monuments. Their main office is in Anchorage (*240 West 5th Av, Suite 114;* ☎ *644 3510*), but they also have offices at each park in the state. Some of these include: Wrangell-St Elias National Park and Preserve (*Mile 106.8 Richardson Hwy;* ☎ *822 5234*), Glacier Bay National Park and Preserve (*1 Park Rd;* ☎ *697 2230*), Sitka National Historical Park (*103 Monastery St;* ☎ *747 0110*), Klondike Gold Rush National Historical Park (*Second Av;* ☎ *983 2921*), Kenai Fjords National Park (☎ *422 0500*), Bering Land Bridge National Park (*Nome;* ☎ *443 2522*) and Gates of the Arctic National Park (*Coldfoot;* ☎ *678 5209*).

The **Alaska Department of Natural Resources** (DNR) (*http://dnr.alaska.gov/parks*) also maintain a few offices and, between their staff and their website, offer information about Alaska's state parks and recreations areas. DNR's main offices are in Anchorage (*550 W 7th Av, Suite 1260;* ☎ *269 8400*) and Fairbanks (*3700 Airport Way;* ☎ *451 2705*). They also run offices in: Chugach (*Mile 115 Seward Hwy;* ☎ *345 5014*), Soldotna (*Mile 85, Sterling Hwy;* ☎ *262 5581*), Kodiak (*1400 Abercrombie Dr;* ☎ *486 6339*), Mat-Su Valley (*Mile 0.7 Bogard Rd;* ☎ *745 3975*), and Juneau (*400 Willoughby Av;* ☎ *465 4563*).

The **National Fish and Wildlife Service** (*http://alaska.fws.gov*) has information about all of the Alaska's wildlife refuges. The two national forests in Alaska – the Tongass and Chugach National Forests – are managed by the National Forest Service (*www.fs.fed.us*). They maintain offices in various communities around both national forests. The main office for the Chugach National Forests is in Anchorage (*3301 C St;* ☎ *743 9500*) and the Tongass National Forest office is in Ketchikan (*648 Mission St;* ☎ *225 3101*).

Another fantastic resource for all federal lands in Alaska is www.recreation.gov, where public-use cabins and campsites can be book. See *Further information* on page 66 for a list of useful websites.

TOUR OPERATORS

UK

Audley Travel ✎ 1993 838 700; www.audleytravel.com. Custom trips for any taste including trips for people who just want to see bears, arctic themed trips & even trips that focus on Alaska's rural communities.
Explore ✎ 0845 013 1537; www.explore.co.uk. Offer both hotel- & wilderness-based tours of Alaska with small group sizes. Trips are well organised &, while they may not get far off the beaten-path, they do visit most of the main attractions.
Frontier Canada ✎ 020 8776 8709; www.frontier-canada.co.uk. Offer a host of Alaska travel options from bus tours, to whale-watching, to ferry trips where hotels & activities are organised for you in each port.
North American Highways ✎ 01902 851 138; www.nahighways.co.uk. Organised tours throughout the state from cruise-ship trips in southeast to wildlife excursions in remote western Alaska. They can also set you up with your own vehicle & help you plan a road trip around the state.
Trek America ✎ 870 444 8735; www.trekamerica.co.uk. Specialises in active, flexible trips with no more than 13 participants.

IN ALASKA For most guided trips, it's a good idea to have a reservation a month or more in advance. Some of the more popular tours, or those that only accommodate a limited number of people, should be booked as much as six months ahead. Occasionally, tours such as kayak and hiking trips can be booked only a few days ahead. NB: with rising fuel costs, some tour operators may levy a fuel surcharge in addition to the advertised price.

Alaska Discovery ✎ 888 831 7526; www.mtsobek.com/alaska_Discovery adventures around the state including dog sledding, mountain climbing, river rafting & hiking.
Alaska Mountain Guides and Climbing School ✎ 800 766 3396; www.alaskamountainguides.com. Alaska's premier adventure-guide outfit with wilderness kayaking, high-altitude climbing & remote treks.
Alaska Wildland Adventures ✎ 783 2928, 800 334 8730 (TF); www.alaskawildland.com. Adventures organised by theme, or the amount of time you have. Pick a region, like the Kenai Peninsula or Denali National Park, or an activity, like fishing or photography, & they will find the right trip for you.

AlaskaPass ✎ 463 6550, 800 248 7598 (TF); www.alaskapass.com. Offer package deals for train, car, & ferry travel from US$879 for 15 days.
Explore Tours ✎ 786 0192; www.exploretours.com. Trips in southcentral & southeast Alaska focusing on fishing, wildlife & activities like hiking & kayaking.
Green Tortoise ✎ 800 867 8647; www.greentortoise.com. Offering 14- & 27-day bus trips in Alaska. The funky, but safe, buses are a hostel on wheels catering to young travellers.
St Elias Alpine Guides ✎ 888 933 5427; www.steliasguides.com. Also offer mountaineering trips.

IN AUSTRALIA

Alaska Bound ✎ 1300 650 481; www.alaskabound.com.au. Logistical support for almost any kind of trip in Alaska, from ferry travel to wilderness travel & small cruise ships.
Australian Pacific Touring ✎ 3 9277 8555; www.aptouring.com.au. Offers garden tours, remote wilderness-lodge stays, wildlife excursions & cruises throughout Alaska.

CRUISE SHIPS Not all cruises are created equal, so be sure to shop around and don't just settle for the cheapest. The best cruises are often smaller ships. These have on-board naturalists, offer shore excursions and dock in some interesting places.

Adventures Afloat ✎ 586 3312; http://home.gci.net/~valkyrie. The M/V *Valkyrie*, a 106ft vessel, has been converted to take a small number of passengers on custom wildlife-viewing trips through southeast Alaska. Charter the entire boat, or book a cabin.
Alaska on the Home Shore ✎ 800 287 7063; www.homeshore.com. This 63ft former-fishing-boat

2

turned-adventure-vessel, is an ideal base for kayaking & otherwise exploring some remote & beautiful parts of the southeast.

Alaska Sea Adventures 772 4700, 888 772 8588 (TF); www.yachtalaska.com. High-end adventure planned around your schedule & interest. Fishing, photography, whale-watching, birding etc.

American Safari Cruises 888 862 8881 (TF); www.amsafari.com. Offer a variety of trips in southeast Alaska inc Glacier Bay National Park & a 15-day trip from Seattle to Juneau. These trips focus on wildlife viewing & offer kayaks for further exploring.

Cruise West 888 851 8133; www.cruisewest.com. The smallest of the commercial cruiseship companies, these cruises are high end with an emphasis on culture & natural history.

Lindblad Expeditions 212 765 7740, 800 397 334 8466 (TF); www.expeditions.com. Having teamed up with National Geographic, these guys now offer 1–2 week trips with a natural history & environmental focus.

Pacific Catalyst 360 378 7123, 800 378 1708 (TF); www.pacificcatalyst.com. The 74ft M/V *Catalyst* cruises the waters of southeast Alaska all summer while guests come & go.

Most of the larger cruiseship companies offer cruises all summer in the southeast and in Prince William Sound, with occasional stops in other southcentral ports. Most of the larger companies are slightly different versions of the same thing. All offer shore excursions in all ports of call and arrange other forms of transport to move their passengers to inland locations like Denali. These include:

Celebrity Cruises 888 307 8401; www.celebritycruises.com
Holland America Line 877 932 4259; www.hollandamerica.com

Princess Cruises & Tours 800 774 6237; www.princess.com
Royal Caribbean 888 307 8401; www.royalcaribbean.com

RED TAPE

Everyone entering the US needs a passport valid for at least six months and all foreign nationals need a return ticket and a visa if they are not from a country participating in the Visa Waiver Program. The Visa Waiver Program allows nationals from 35 countries to travel to the US without a visa for up to 90 days if they have an electronic passport (ePassport). These countries are: Andorra, Australia, Austria, Belgium, Brunei, Czech Republic, Denmark, Estonia, Finland, France, Germany, Hungary, Iceland, Ireland, Italy, Japan, Latvia, Liechtenstein, Lithuania, Luxembourg, Malta, Monaco, New Zealand, Norway, Portugal, San Marino, Singapore, Slovakia, Slovenia, South Korea, Spain, Sweden, Switzerland, the Netherlands and the United Kingdom. Citizens of other nations need visas. To find your nearest US embassy, visit www.usembassy.gov.

Other resources include the US Customs website (*www.customs.gov*), state website (*www.travel.state.gov*), and the Canadian Customs website (*www.cbsa-asfc.gc.ca*). Canadians do not need a visa to enter the US.

There are some other things to remember when travelling to Alaska: travellers taking prescription medicine should carry a signed prescription note from their doctor. Single parents travelling with children should have a signed letter from the other parent. Foreign nationals may come and go from the US with US$10,000 without declaring it at the border. Visitors should not buy any native art made from marine mammals as it may not be possible to take the artwork out of the country. Visit www.visahq.com for more information.

EMBASSIES

For a complete listing of foreign embassies in the US and US embassies on foreign soil visit www.usembassy.gov.

OVERSEAS

Austria Boltzmanngasse 16 A-1090, Vienna; ☎ +43 1 31339 0; http://vienna.usembassy.gov
Belgium Regentlaan 27 Bd du Régent, B-1000 Brussels; ☎ +32 2 508 2111; http://belgium.usembassy.gov
Canada 1095 W. Pender St, Vancouver, B.C. V6E 2M6; ☎ 604 685 4311; http://vancouver.usconsulate.gov
Czech Republic Tržiště 15, 118 01 Praha I; ☎ +42 0 257 022 000; http://prague.usembassy.gov
Denmark Dag Hammarskjölds Allé 24, 2100 København Ø; ☎ +45 33 41 71 00; http://denmark.usembassy.gov
Estonia Kentmanni 20, 15099 Tallin; ☎ +37 2 668 8100; http://estonia.usembassy.gov
Finland Itäinen Puistotie 14B, 00140 Helsinki; ☎ +35 8 9 616 250; http://finland.usembassy.gov
France 2, Av Gabriel, 75382 Paris Cedex 08; ☎ +33 1 43 12 22 22; http://france.usembassy.gov
Germany Pariser Platz 2, 10117 Berlin; ☎ +49 030 83050; http://germany.usembassy.gov
Greece 91 Vasilisis Sophias Av, 10160 Athens; ☎ +30 210 721 2951; http://athens.usembassy.gov
Hungary Szabadság tér 12, H-1054 Budapest; ☎ +36 1 475 4400; http://hungary.usembassy.gov
Iceland Laufásvegur 21, 101 Reykjavík; ☎ +35 4 562 9100; http://iceland.usembassy.gov
Ireland http://dublin.usembassy.gov.
Italy Vittorio Veneto 121 – 00187 Roma; ☎ +39 06 46741; http://rome.usembassy.gov
Latvia Raiņa Blvd 7, Riga LV-1510; ☎ +37 1 67036200; http://riga.usembassy.gov

Lithuania Akmenų gatvė 6, Vilnius LT-03106; ☎ +370 5 2665500; http://vilnius.usembassy.gov
Luxembourg 22, Bd Emmanuel Servais, L-2535; ☎ +35 2 46 01 23; http://luxembourg.usembassy.gov
Mexico Paseo de la Reforma 305, Col. Cuauhtemoc, 06500; ☎ +52 55 5080 2000; http://mexico.usembassy.gov
The Netherlands Museumplein 19; 1071 DJ Amsterdam; ☎ +31 0 20 575 5309; http://amsterdam.usconsulate.gov
Norway Henrik Ibsens gate 48, 0244 Oslo; ☎ +47 21 30 85 40; http://norway.usembassy.gov
Poland ul. Stolarska 9, 31-043 Krakow; ☎ +48 12 424 5100; http://krakow.usconsulate.gov
Portugal Avenida das Forças Armadas, 1600-081 Lisboa; ☎ 351 21 727 3300; http://portugal.usembassy.gov
Russian Federation Bolshoy Deviatinsky Pereulok 8, Moscow 121099, -77, APO AE 09721; ☎ +7 495 728 5000; http://moscow.usembassy.gov
Slovakia PO Box 309, 814 99 Bratislava; ☎ +421 2 5443 3338; http://slovakia.usembassy.gov
Slovenia Prešernova 31, 1000 Ljubljana; ☎ +386 1 2005500; http://slovenia.usembassy.gov
Spain Calle Serrano 75, 28006 Madrid; ☎ + 34 91 587 2240; http://madrid.usembassy.gov
Sweden Dag Hammarskjölds Väg 31, SE-115 89 Stockholm; ☎ +46 8 783 5300; http://stockholm.usembassy.gov
Switzerland Sulgeneckstrasse 19, CH-3007 Bern; ☎ +41 31 357 70 11; http://bern.usembassy.gov
UK 24 Grosvenor Sq, London, W1A 2LQ; ☎ +44 0 20 7499 9000; http://london.usembassy.gov

IN ALASKA Some of these consulates do not have offices and are simply contacts for nationals who need help.

Austria K St, Anchorage; ☎ 276 6000.
Canada 310 K St Ste 220, Anchorage; ☎ 264 6734.
Czech Republic 810 N St, Anchorage; ☎ 274 2602.
Denmark 425 G St, Anchorage; ☎ 261 1221.
Finland 1529 P St, Anchorage; ☎ 274 6607.
France 2606 C St, Anchorage; ☎ 222 6232.
Germany 425 G St # 650, Anchorage; ☎ 274 6537.
Italy PO Box 100148, Anchorage; ☎ 762 7664.

Japan 3601 C St, suite 1300, Anchorage; ☎ 562 8424.
Korea 800 E Dimond, Anchorage; ☎ 339 7955.
Mexico 610 C St, Anchorage; ☎ 334 9573.
Norway 203 W 15th Av, Anchorage; ☎ 375 5565.
Poland 7550 Old Seward Hwy, Anchorage; ☎ 344 4722
Sweden 301 W Northern Lights Blvd, Anchorage; ☎ 265 2927.
UK 3211 Providence Dr, Anchorage; ☎ 786 4848

GETTING THERE AND AWAY

Alaska is connected to the rest of America by the Alaska Highway through Canada, the Alaska ferry system, and the Anchorage and Fairbanks international airports.

✈ **BY AIR** Few airlines offer direct flights into Alaska from abroad. Instead, they stop in a continental US city (usually Seattle) before going on to Alaska. The only exceptions are Condor, which flies between Frankfurt and Anchorage, and JAL which flies between Japan and Fairbanks. Since the travel season in Alaska is so short, flights can fill up quickly and the price can rise sharply if not booked well ahead. June and July are usually the most expensive. Prices vary tremendously based on where you're travelling from and from year to year. If booked at least six months ahead, tickets from the UK generally cost £800–1,000. On top of that you'll need to factor in the cost of an internal flight, usually from Seattle to Anchorage, which costs in the region of US$400–500. Flights from Sydney to Seattle cost in the region of AU$2,000–2,500. You could try the following internet operators: **Expedia** (*www.expedia.com*), **Travelocity** (*www.travelocity.com*), **Orbitz** (*www.orbitz.com*), **Travelzoo** (*www.travelzoo.com*) and **Kayak** (*www.kayak.com*). Most offer good savings. Alternatively, contact the various airlines listed below, directly.

From the UK

British Airways ☎ 0844 493 0 787; www.britishairways.com. Daily flights to Seattle from London.

Northwest Airlines ☎ 08705 074074; www.nwa.com. Runs regular services from London to Minneapolis, Detroit & Seattle

KLM/Royal Dutch Airlines ☎ 871 231 0000; www.klm.com. Runs regular services to Anchorage from London.

Continental Airlines ☎ 800 231 0856; www.continental.com. Daily connections from London to Anchorage via Houston & New York.

Delta Airlines ☎ 0845 600 0950; www.delta.com. Connections to Anchorage, from London via Atlanta, Salt Lake City & Seattle.

From the US

Alaska Airlines ☎ 800 252 7522; www.alaskaair.com. Offer the vast majority of flights to Alaska. Hourly departures every day from Seattle to Anchorage & Fairbanks.

British Airways ☎ 800 247 9297; www.britishairways.com.

Condor Airlines ☎ 800 524 6975; www.condor.com.

Continental Airlines ☎ 800 523 3273; www.continental.com. 2 flights per day from Seattle, Washington & Houston, Texas to Anchorage.

Delta Airlines ☎ 800 221 1212; www.delta.com. Flights to Anchorage are twice daily from Salt Lake City, 3 times daily from Minneapolis & once daily from Detroit. 2 flights daily from Minneapolis to Fairbanks

Northwest Airlines ☎ 800 692 6955; www.nwa.com.

US Airways ☎ 800 428 4322; www.usairways.com. One flight daily from Phoenix to Anchorage.

United Airlines ☎ 800 864 8331 (US); www.united.com. 2 flights per day from Seattle to Anchorage.

From elsewhere

Air Canada ☎ 888 247 2262; www.aircanada.com. Daily flights from Vancouver to Anchorage with connecting flights to Europe, Asia & Australia.

Condor Airlines ☎ 180 5 707202; www.condor.com. Daily flights from most of Europe to Fairbanks, Juneau & Anchorage, via Frankfurt.

Delta Airlines ☎ 020 201 3536 (Netherlands); www.delta.com. Connections to Anchorage, from Amsterdam via Atlanta, Salt Lake City & Seattle. Also regular flights from Tokyo & Sydney to Seattle & Los Angeles.

Japan Airlines ☎ 800 525 3663; www.jal.com. Charter flights from Japan throughout the year.

KLM/Royal Dutch Airlines ☎ 130 039 2192; www.klm.au.

Korean Air ☎ 800 438 5000; www.koreanair.com. Regular flights from most of Asia via Seoul to Alaska via Seattle. Flights are also available from Australia.

Northwest Airlines ☎ 1800 144 917; www.nwa.com. Flies from Sydney to Anchorage via Los Angeles.

 BY FERRY

Alaska Marine Highway (☎ *465 3941;* ☎/f *800 642 0066; www.ferryalaska.com*). In 1963 the Alaska Ferry started regular service in the southeast and a year later

expanded to cover southcentral Alaska. The Alaska Ferry serves most of coastal Alaska (except the western and Arctic regions) with a fleet of 11 comfortable, seaworthy ships. The ferry system connects Alaska with two ports outside the state, Bellingham in Washington, and Prince Rupert in Canada. Each ferry can load cars, motorcycles, bikes, kayaks, and other gear. You can book the more expensive rooms with bunks or settle for a chair or bench in the open floor space. The long- haul ferries have a solarium on the top deck and a semi-enclosed space for tents. It's a good idea to book as far ahead as possible so you're sure to get exactly what you want, especially if you are planning on travelling with a car or want to book a cabin. The schedules often don't come out until the late winter or early spring so be in contact with the office regarding the new schedule. As soon as it's released, book. This is of the utmost importance for the once-monthly ferry from Kodiak to Unalaska. Prices for a standard adult ticket (not including meals or a berth) range from US$31 from Skagway to Haines to US$363 from Skagway to Bellingham. Tickets for children aged 6–11 cost half price, while children under 6 travel free.

To book tickets visit the website or call. For arrival in Juneau see page 88.

BY TRAIN There is no train service to Alaska, only within the state. See page 64 for more information. However, Canadian travellers can hop aboard a **VIA Rail Canada** (✆ *888 842 7245; www.viarail.ca*) train to Prince Rupert in British Columbia, board the Alaska Ferry there and connect to the rest of Alaska.

BY BUS Getting to Alaska by bus is far more work than its worth, but if one were so inclined, **Green Tortoise** (see page 45) is the best bet. Another option is to use **Greyhound Canada** (✆ *800 661 8747; www.greyhound.ca*) to get to Whitehorse or another northwestern Canadian city. From there, use **Alaska Direct Bus Line** (✆ *277 6652, 800 770 6652 (TF); www.alaskadirectbusline.com. Buses run all summer on Wed, Fri & Sun to Tok (US$105), Glennallen (US$75) & Palmer (US$10))* to get into the state.

BY CAR The Alaska Highway, also known as the Alcan, is, for some, the road trip of a lifetime. For others it's a long, rough, perpetually under construction nightmare. I personally love the trip, but only in the fall (mid-August) and given enough time (two weeks). The fishing is wonderful and the scenery in northern British Columbia is rivalled only by that of Alaska. The 1,422-mile road was completed in 1942 in one big World War II-push to connect strategically positioned Alaska with the rest of the world. The Alcan proper starts in Dawson Creek, British Columbia and ends in Delta Junction, Alaska, but for most travellers the trip starts somewhere in the US, often Seattle, and continues all the way to Fairbanks or Anchorage. From Seattle to Fairbanks, is just under 2,400 miles and the trip to Anchorage is about 100 miles more. However, petrol is more expensive in Canada than in the US. At the time of going to press, petrol in Whitehorse, Yukon Territory was CAN$4.14 (US$3.90). At that price, a one-way trip would cost US$465.93, about US$00.20 per mile.

While the Alaska Highway is entirely paved, construction delays can slow the trip somewhat. These roadwork areas and the associated gravel patches are also very often the cause of cracked windshields. Another consideration is the two border crossings. Crossing these borders is generally very easy but for those convicted of a DUI (Driving Under the Influence), an intoxicated driving charge, may be prevented from entering Canada. The decision is generally at the border agent's discretion.

✚ HEALTH with Dr Felicity Nicholson

IMMUNISATIONS There are no recommended vaccines for Alaska but it would be wise to be up to date with diphtheria, tetanus and polio as part of routine vaccinations for the UK. This comes as the routine all-in-one vaccine Revaxis, which lasts for ten years. The only other vaccination that may be considered is the rabies vaccine (see page 52).

TRAVEL CLINICS A full list of current travel clinic websites worldwide is available on www.istm.org/. For other journey preparation information, consult www.nathnac.org/ds/map_world.aspx. Information about various medications may be found on www.netdoctor.co.uk/travel.

HEALTHCARE Modern healthcare is available in all Alaskan cities and large towns. Smaller towns do have clinics, but anything more than a broken limb or cut, you will need to be transported to a larger town. Medical help is generally very good, but the immense distances in Alaska can make response times slow. Plan to be self sufficient as much as possible. Purchasing medical insurance before entering the US is always a good idea due to the high cost of medical help. Decent insurance can be purchased through **Endsleigh** (✆ *0800 028 3571; www.endsleigh.co.uk*) for travellers based in the UK or **International Services** (✆ *877 593 5403; www.nriol.net*) for travellers based in the US.

FIRST-AID KIT At certain points during your Alaska trip you'll be away from medical help. Therefore, I'd recommend carrying a first-aid kit everywhere.
A minimal kit contains:

- A good drying antiseptic, eg: iodine or potassium permanganate (don't take antiseptic cream)
- A few small dressings (plasters, bandages)
- Suncream
- Insect repellent; impregnated bed-net or permethrin spray; headnet and tent screen
- Aspirin or paracetamol
- Ciprofloxacin or norfloxacin, for severe diarrhoea
- Tinidazole for giardia or amoebic dysentery
- Antibiotic eye drops, for sore, 'gritty', stuck-together eyes (conjunctivitis)
- A pair of fine pointed tweezers (to remove thorns, splinters, etc)
- Alcohol-based hand rub or bar of soap in plastic box
- Condoms or femidoms
- A digital thermometer
- Space blanket (also known as a first-aid blanket or emergency blanket). These are compact plastic and metallic blankets that can be used to stay warm in an emergency.
- Water sterilisation tablets (in case you need to drink some 'iffy' water)

HYPOTHERMIA A visitor's biggest concern when travelling through Alaska is exposure to the elements. Alaskan weather is extremely variable, especially in coastal and mountainous areas. Wind can cause the temperature to drop considerably. At −9°C, 10mph of wind will reduce the relative temperature to −16°C and 20mph of wind drops it to −19°C. Being wet makes everything worse and can lead to hypothermia very quickly. The general rule when spending any time outdoors is to layer synthetic or wool clothing and plan for the worst-

Dr Felicity Nicholson

Any prolonged immobility, including travel by land or air, can result in deep-vein thrombosis (DVT) with the risk of embolus to the lungs. Certain factors can increase the risk and these include:

- Having a previous clot or a close relative with a history
- People over 40, with increased risk in over 80s
- Recent major operation or varicose-veins surgery
- Cancer
- Stroke
- Heart disease
- Obesity
- Pregnancy
- Hormone therapy
- Heavy smokers
- Severe varicose veins
- People who are tall (over 6ft/1.8m) or short (under 5ft/1.5m)

A deep-vein thrombosis causes painful swelling and redness of the calf or sometimes the thigh. It is only dangerous if a clot travels to the lungs (pulmonary embolus). Symptoms of a pulmonary embolus (PE) – which commonly start three to ten days after a long flight – include chest pain, shortness of breath, and sometimes coughing up small amounts of blood. Anyone who thinks that they might have a DVT needs to see a doctor immediately.

PREVENTION OF DVT
- Keep mobile before and during the flight; move around every couple of hours
- Drink plenty of fluids during the flight
- Avoid taking sleeping pills and excessive tea, coffee and alcohol
- Consider wearing flight socks or support stockings (see www.legshealth.com)

If you think you are at increased risk of a clot, ask your doctor if it is safe to travel.

case scenario. Hypothermia is a life-threatening condition brought on by rapid cooling of the core body temperature that results from ones body temperature falling so significantly that normal bodily functions and metabolism are impaired. The first signs are uncontrollable shivering and confusion. If not treated, this can lead to death very quickly. The best way to prevent hypothermia is to keep dry and plan ahead by bringing extra clothes. This means putting on raingear before it starts raining and staying dry at any cost. If someone with you shows hypothermic symptoms, don't take it lightly. Presumably they are in wet clothes, so remove them and replace them with dry clothes and start to warm the person slowly, using your own body heat if necessary. Avoid warming them too quickly. Hypothermia can set in, even in relatively warm conditions (50°F and higher) and will affect some people more quickly than others. Seek medical help in all but the mildest cases.

MEDICAL PROBLEMS
Giardia (*Giardia lamblia*) is a microscopic parasite found in water across the US including Alaska that causes diarrhoeal illness. The parasite can live in water for months and is transferred through the intestines of animals. Though some water

Practical Information HEALTH

2

is safe to drink in Alaska, most is not. The best bet is to filter all water before drinking. I personally only drink water when it's flowing from a glacier or area of snowpack, but the wise would even filter this. If you are unfortunate enough to become infected, the symptoms are usually obvious. They include eggy burps and greasy bulky diarrhoea. Fortunately the disease is treatable with either tinidazole or metronidazole. Go and see a doctor as soon as possible if you display any symptoms.

Rabies There is rabies in Alaska, which has been observed especially in foxes, and it is not uncommon to spill over into the dog population.

Rabies is passed on to humans through a bite, a scratch or a lick of an open wound. You must always assume that the foxes are rabid and medical help should be sought as soon as is practicably possible. In the interim, scrub the wound thoroughly with soap and bottled or boiled water for five minutes, then pour on a strong iodine or alcohol solution. This can help to prevent the rabies virus from entering the body and will guard against wound infections, including tetanus. The decision whether or not to have the highly effective rabies vaccine will depend on the nature of your trip.

If you do decide to take the vaccine, ideally three pre-exposure doses should be taken over a minimum 21-day period. It is probably only necessary for those (such as veterinarians) who are at unusually high risk of exposure. If you think you have been exposed to rabies, then treatment should be given as soon as possible. At least two post-bite rabies injections are needed, even for immunised people. Those who have not been immunised will need a full course of injections together with rabies immunoglobulin (RIG). Treatment should be given as soon as possible, but it is never too late to seek help, as the incubation period for rabies can be very long. Remember if you contract rabies, mortality is 100%.

SAFETY

Crime in Alaska is relatively high – it's ranked 27 out of 50 in the list of America's safest states – but it certainly won't be obvious to the average visitor. Indeed, half of the state's crime is confined to Anchorage; elsewhere most people feel safe enough to leave their cars and homes unlocked. Nevertheless, to ensure a safe trip, keep valuables hidden and cars and hotel rooms locked. In an emergency call ❧ 911.

SURVIVING IN THE WILDERNESS Those spending a lot of time outdoors should be knowledgeable about treating themselves and others if need be. This means some kind of medical training such as CPR, first-aid awareness and wilderness survival techniques. At the very least, carry a complete first-aid kit (see page 50) and space blanket and know how to use them. While some parks still pay for rescue, don't ever plan on someone coming to get you. Bad weather can also keep rescue away. Travellers embarking on an off-the-beaten-track trip should consider buying or renting a satellite phone or an EPIRB (emergency position-indicating radio beacon). In an emergency call ❧ 911. The emergency radio channel is 16.

WILDLIFE RISKS
Poisonous and harmful plants Picking and eating wild berries is one of life's great pleasures, but eating the wrong berries can be deadly. If you plan on eating wild berries, buy an edible plants guide (see *Further information* on page 435) and follow it religiously until you have them all memorised. In the meantime, just remember, there are no white berries in Alaska that are edible. Another harmful plant is devil's club, a menacing looking plant with bright-red berries whose leaves and stems are

covered in spiky thorns. These grow in great thickets and can be a nightmare for overland hikers. Another less obvious harmful plant is pushki, a flat leafed plant with fleshy hollow stocks and white flowers. The juice that oozes from broken stalks reacts to the sun and can cause blisters.

Wild animals Wild animal attacks are rare in Alaska, but they do happen. For the most part brown and black bears, as well as moose, are the only animals to become knowledgeable about from a safety point of view.

Bear attacks First it's important to stress that bear attacks are very rare – an Alaska US Geological Survey study of the past century shows there have only been 56 fatalities from bear attacks in the last century – and with some basic understanding of bear behaviour, can generally be avoided. Behaving properly around bears and doing the right thing in the event of an attack depends on what you think the bear's motivations might be and what species they are. Alaska is home to black, brown, and polar bear, but the black and brown bears are the most commonly encountered. Both species are drawn by the smell of food and will enter cars or tents in search of it. One of the best ways to avoid negative encounters with bears is to camp cleanly; cook far away from your tent and avoid any food smells (even toothpaste) in your tent and on your person. If you are attacked inside your tent the best response, regardless of species, is to fight back. Punch the nose and try to gouge the eyes.

Attacks also arise as a result of surprise encounters on hiking trails. This situation will sometimes result in an attack, but thankfully can be easily prevented. Make noise while you're walking in bear country. Many travellers dispute the efficacy of jingling bell sounds, whereas singing definitely does work. If you do encounter a bear, don't run. This will only encourage the bear's chasing instinct and, with a top speed of more than 35 miles per hour, there's no chance of outrunning it. Contrary to popular belief, bears generally do not stand up when about to attack. However, they do 'posture', ie: huff and click their jaws, so if the bear starts presenting these signs, yell and clap your hands. Some Alaskans are also starting to bring black plastic bags with them as a bear deterrent. If a bear is acting aggressively or too close for comfort, open the bag to its full size above your head – it makes you look 12ft tall. Bears do 'bluff' charge, ie: run to within 50 feet or less of you, before stopping or veering off. If all else fails, playing dead sometimes works with brown bears (but not black bears – it's always best to fight back if a black bear attacks). To play dead, kneel or lay on the ground to protect your vital organs and stay in this position for as long as possible – bears will sometimes linger nearby and re-attack when they see movement. While brown bears are generally poor tree climbers, black bears are very agile in trees so climbing a tree isn't recommended. Brown bears are also quite tall when standing and are very strong. They may be able to reach you in a tree or even push the tree over.

Moose attacks This tall gangly creature of the north is also responsible for injuries, and even deaths, in the state. Moose are fast and their hooves are sharp. Female moose, or 'cows', are most aggressive in the spring when they often have young calves. Male moose are especially aggressive in the fall during mating season. If charged, run and either climb a tree or get behind something solid. I once climbed a nearby tree when a mother moose charged me, which worked well. However, she seemed to hold a grudge and stood at the bottom of the tree for two hours before sauntering off with her calf.

Other animals not to approach include caribou, bison, and musk ox as well as any injured animals such as bald eagles.

Poisonous shellfish Before digging clams call the local Fish and Game office and ask about paralytic shellfish poisoning, a toxin that accumulates in shellfish from algae and can harm or kill humans.

WOMEN TRAVELLERS Unfortunately, Alaska does have a high rate of rape (529 annually) and assault (3,363 annually). Assaults are often related to domestic problems and do not affect visitors.

While Alaska is a 'tough guy' state, it is also a 'tough girl' state. Alaskan women are known for 'holding their own', so reasonably resourceful female travellers will find they receive respect throughout in the state. Women should not be afraid to travel alone, but should avoid dark or remote, deserted areas and drunk people.

SENIOR TRAVELLERS Alaskan businesses are great about offering senior (65+) discounts. Mention your age every time you take out your wallet and you will be surprised how often you save money. Pick up a Golden Age Pass at any national park office for US$10 for free admission to all national parks and deals on other park services.

GAY AND LESBIAN TRAVELLERS While Alaska can be a bit of a tough-guy state, Anchorage, Fairbanks and Juneau have thriving gay and lesbian scenes. Being

---

NOTES FOR DISABLED TRAVELLERS

Lieke Scheewe (with advice from Gordon Rattray; www.able-travel.com)
Geographically Alaska is one of the most wild and remote of the 50 United States. The rugged nature of Alaska makes many places difficult to visit, so that travelling becomes adventurous for everyone, especially for those with limited mobility. Yet, a remarkable athletic event takes place each July, Sadler's Alaska Challenge, which is the world's longest wheelchair and hand-cycle race covering about 265 miles of mountains and flat terrain from Fairbanks to Anchorage. Alaska has much to offer disabled travellers.

PLANNING AND BOOKING There are several specialised tour operators that may be helpful in planning your itinerary. **Easy Access Travel** (☎ +1 (800) 920 8989 or +1 (951) 549 9325; e debra@easyaccesstravel.com; www.easyaccesstravel.com) and **Accessible Journeys** (☎ +1 (800) 846 4537 or +1 (610) 521 0339; www.disabilitytravel.com) both assist in individual travel planning and offer an Alaska cruise tour (which may be combined with a land tour). Another specialised travel agency is **Alaska Welcomes You! Inc** (☎ +1 (800) 349 6301 or +1 (907) 349 6301; e akwy@customcpu.com; www.accessiblealaska.com).

GETTING THERE AND AROUND
By air Anchorage Ted Stevens International Airport (www.anchorageairport.com) is fully equipped for disabled passengers, including toilets, lifts, parking, etc. To request a wheelchair and/or assistance travellers should contact their airline directly.

By road Accessible van rentals are not easy to find in Alaska due to its remoteness. One company offering nationwide delivery is **America's No 1 Mobility Solution** (☎ +1 (888) 880 8267; www.aavans.com).

By rail Alaska Railroad's passenger trains (☎ +1 (907) 265 2494; www.akrr.com) are wheelchair accessible and comply with the Americans with Disabilities Act. There are wheelchair lifts at all stations and registered service animals are also welcome aboard. It

---

openly gay in many other areas could be met with a sideways glance and possibly worse. While it's not always true that the more remote a place, the less accepting its residents, it would be a safe rule to travel by while in Alaska. See page 199 for listings of gay-friendly bars in Anchorage.

Identity www.identityinc.org. Based in Anchorage, they organise events & offer support to gays & lesbians in Anchorage & around the state.
Gay, Lesbian & Straight Education Network ✆ 441 6140; www.glsen.org. A national organisation with a chapter in Anchorage.

Purple Roofs www.purpleroofs.com. Lists gay- & lesbian- friendly accommodation options around the world.
Southeast Alaska Gay & Lesbian Alliance ✆ 463 4203; www.seagla.org. An Alaskan gay & lesbian group with chapters in Juneau & Anchorage.

TRAVELLING WITH CHILDREN Alaska is a very family friendly location, but because transportation and living costs are expensive, some modifications may have to be made. In addition, road trippers may want to rethink that trip up the Alaska Highway if their kids tend to get fidgety on long trips. Just about every distance in the state is a long one, so travel can take a lot of time. In addition, many of the best things to do in Alaska are outdoors. The trails and mountain ridges that beg to be followed can be taxing for small children. Depending on the age of your children, either slow-paced camping trips or a long-term rental house might be the best option.

is advised to check with an agent for details about varying accessibility on other connecting modes of transport. Inform them in advance if you require boarding assistance.

By boat There are many cruises, which have Alaska as their destination. Besides the tour operators mentioned above, another useful resource is the **Cruise Lines International Association** (www.cruising.org), which provides a 'Special Interest Guide' for wheelchair travellers online. It allows you to search for ships using 13 different levels of accessibility. In cases where you require equipment that is not provided by the cruise ships themselves, you can contact **Cruise Ship Assist** (www.cruiseshipassist.com).

ACCOMMODATION One of the easiest ways to find accessible accommodation is at LocalSearch.com, where you can enter 'Hotels and Motels' for 'AK' (Alaska), resulting in 95 hits once you have specified for wheelchair accessibility.

TRAVEL INSURANCE Most insurance companies will cater for disabled travellers, but it is essential that they are made aware of your disability. Examples of specialised companies that cover pre-existing medical conditions are **Free Spirit** (✆ 0845 230 5000; www.free-spirit.com) and **Age Concern** (✆ 0845 601 2234; www.ageconcern.org.uk), who have no upper age limit.

FURTHER INFORMATION The Alaska Railroad does not only provide transportation, covering over 500 miles from Anchorage to Fairbanks, Anchorage to Seward and Anchorage to Whittier, but also offers tour packages that include many accessible hotels and lodges (which often provide shuttles from the station).
   Challenge Alaska (✆ 344 7399; www. www.challengealaska.org) provides sports and recreation for people with disabilities, including equipment rentals.
   Travellers with disabilities will be able to find suitable services in most moderately-sized towns. Hotels are the only venues that consistently have elevators and wheelchair ramps.

Packing for Alaska's cold climes can seem like a daunting task. In general pack for extremely variable weather, usually 10–15°C.

The first step is to decide on the type of activities you will be undertaking during your trip; you can then tailor your packing list to suit. Anything you forget can usually be found easily in Alaska's larger towns, although goods will be more expensive compared to other American states. Smaller, more remote towns will have less of a choice so plan in advance.

FOR THE CASUAL VISITOR WHO IS ALWAYS SLEEPING UNDER A ROOF, BUT STILL HIKING NOW AND THEN, I RECOMMEND THE FOLLOWING:

- Waterproof, rugged hiking shoes or boots. Those doing a lot of mucking about, may want to wear rubber boots. Many locals wear ExtraTuffs, a flexible and comfortable boot available at fishing supply stores in Alaska.
- Gaiters are a good idea for long hikes through wet grass.
- Insect repellent
- A decent camera (that you know how to use!) (see page 79). Though there are a few camera stores around the state, plan on bringing most of your own gear.
- Sun block
- Waterproof jacket and trousers of high quality Gore-Tex or similar material. The cheap stuff soaks through in no time. Gore-Tex will also eventually soak through, but if new, will generally be waterproof for most of the day. Rubberized raingear (made of thin, flexible rubber instead of Gore-Tex), is indefinitely waterproof but is not breathable. This can be annoying or even dangerous if you're sweating a lot.
- A set of smart clothes for dining out.

FOR THOSE WHO PLAN TO GET OUT AND DO A LOT OF OVERNIGHT HIKING AND CAMPING, I RECOMMEND EVERYTHING ABOVE *PLUS* THE FOLLOWING:

- Bring only wool and synthetic clothing. Cotton kills! Be sure to have many extra changes of clothes and socks.
- Camping stove. Fuel canisters are available in most Alaska's larger towns and cities but rarely in small towns. A multi-fuel stove is the best bet.
- A sturdy tent that can handle high winds and lots of rain. Be sure the screen is very tight, so you are protected from mosquitoes, etc.
- A satellite phone or EPRIB (emergency position-indicating radio beacon).
- Space blankets (see page 50).
- Complete first-aid kit.
- Some form of bear protection. While a gun is best, other items such as a large black bin bag work just as well when trying to scare them off (see page 53). Bear pepper spray can also be effective. Store food in a pile far from camp but still within earshot. Pile silverware, pots and pans and anything that will make noise on your food. This will alert you should an animal get into it.
- Sleeping bag. There is an age-old debate on down versus synthetic sleeping bags, and I don't think I'll solve it here. But, since the weather is so variable in Alaska and synthetic bags will keep you warm even when wet, they are far safer but heavier and more bulky. Down bags on the other hand are warmer and lighter but are useless when wet.
- Sleeping pads are very important for insulation from the ground. Be sure to have a good inflatable pad, such as Thermarest, with a repair kit. Foam pads don't pack down as small but won't pop.

- Headlight. Summer days are long, but a headlight and extra batteries are essential.
- Compass and maps. Alaska's backcountry is bigger than you can imagine and getting lost can easily lead to a very serious situation. National Geographic offers a multi-CD set of Alaska topography maps that is very good for planning adventures. These can be printed and laminated to take with you.
- Dry bags or plastic bags. Wrap your clothes and sleeping bag in bags inside your backpack. While some backpacks claim to be waterproof, they will often seep at the seams, and if you fall into a river your clothes and sleeping bag will be protected.
- Fire starter. Be sure to always have matches in zip-lock bags in various places. If you lose some or they get wet, you should have others. Also bring at least one lighter in case the matches run out or get wet. Another good thing to have is some kind of emergency fire starter; something that will get a fire going fast, even if it's raining. Magnesium works well and can be bought in outdoor stores. Very fine steel wool will also burn. My father recommends emptying a traditional lighter of its fluid, then stuffing it with steel wool. The sparking mechanism can then be used to light the steel wool. Another of his tricks is to melt paraffin wax into toilet paper, then stuff it in a film canister. This will burn slowly but surely in almost any weather.
- Food. For most trips bring light, energy dense foods like pasta and energy bars. As a general rule, bring breakfast and dinner foods that are light and gain their bulk from water. For lunch, I like to have things like energy bars, dried fruit, nuts, bagels, etc. Oatmeal with dried fruit and nuts is a great breakfast food. Try the pre-packaged, single-serving versions. To avoid attracting bears, avoid greasy foods that have very strong smells or might be hard to clean up with cold water.

ELECTRICITY AND GAS Alaska, like the rest of the US and Canada, uses 110–120 volts AC. Bring a converter from home since they can be hard to find in the US.

White gas for camping is not allowed on planes, but is available for sale around the state.

$ MONEY

CASH Alaska uses US dollars except in Hyder on the border of Canada, where they use Canadian dollars, but will accept US dollars as well. Bills commonly come in denominations of one, five, ten, 20, 50 and 100 dollar bills. Coins come in denominations of one (penny), five (nickel), ten (dime), and 25 (quarter). One-dollar coins are also sometimes seen.

Remember that 50 and 100 dollar bills can be hard to break outside larger towns and cities. As of January 2010, the exchange rates were as follows: US$1 = £0.61, €0.70 and AUD$1.09.

CREDIT CARDS Credit and debit cards are widely accepted throughout Alaska, except in some very small towns and in the bush. Mastercard and Visa credit and debit cards are the most commonly accepted.

TRAVELLERS' CHEQUES Travellers' cheques are accepted in many businesses, but credit/debit cards and cash are a much safer bet, especially for smaller towns. Most banks will exchange travellers' cheques.

ATMS ATMs are available in all but the most remote areas and generally charge a withdrawal fee of US$2–3 per transaction. Carry five-, ten- and 20-dollar bills to remote areas to pay for services since ATMs may not be available. ATMs are often found at banks and sometimes in grocery stores. They are also sometimes located right off the main street.

TIPPING Europeans often complain about the American custom of tipping 15% or more for food and drinks when dining out. Although tipping can be annoying, particularly when service is not good, it's important to understand the other socio-economic factors that are at play. Most wait staff earn minimum wage (US$7.75 in Alaska), which is different for every state but generally speaking, forces people to live on, or near, the poverty line. In some states, employers are allowed to pay waiting staff less than the minimum wage because it is assumed that tips are given. Though this is not the case in Alaska, the state does have the sixth highest cost of living in the country. As a rule of thumb, tip 15% unless the service is excellent or poor. My wife and I tip 15–20% for great service and 5%–10% for poor or okay service. Then again, my wife worked as a waitress for years and former or current waiting staff often tip more than the average as a gesture of solidarity. Leaving small change is often considered rude, so only tip with notes or quarters. If taking advantage of a cheap meal offer or two-for-one deal, it's nice to tip on what the full price of the meal would have been.

BUDGETING

Alaska is not a cheap destination. The cost of goods, accommodation and services is high. This is partly because almost everything, short of fresh fish, has to be imported by container ship. Alaska is also a tourism savvy place and many of the more commercial businesses know they can charge a lot for very little.

However, with common sense and a few tips, costs can be cut and a better experience can be had. For example, B&Bs are almost always more comfortable, friendlier and cheaper than hotels and have the added benefit of a free breakfast and advice from your host. Many hotels now also offer free breakfasts, but they are never homemade sourdough pancakes with fresh blueberry syrup! While basic hotels run US$140 for two people per night, a B&B often costs US$75–150 for two with breakfast and sometimes free airport or ferry pick-up and activity booking service. Cheaper yet are hostels, which usually cost less than US$20.

The tremendous expense of meals is another matter to consider. US$75 or more can easily be spent on a nice dinner for two, with wine and a tip raising that to US$100. Fortunately, many B&Bs have half or full kitchens, allowing visitors to prepare much of their own food. Additionally, fresh seafood abounds, meaning you can eat a US$100 meal for the cost of wine and a few veggies every night of the week if you are reasonably resourceful and own a fishing rod (non-resident fishing licence, three-day/four-day costs US$20/50; charter fishing costs US$125–225). This is not to say that eating well for cheap is not possible. Grocery store delicatessens are a classic way to save money at lunchtime and in the larger towns and cities, good and affordable options are always available. Costs, however, vary tremendously from place to place. The cost of goods in Anchorage are some of the cheapest in the state, but those are still about 18% higher than the national average. One half gallon of milk in a remote Alaskan town like Bethel or Barrow will cost US$4–5, while in Anchorage it will only cost about US$2.50. While the average Anchorage resident pays about US$36.90 per week for food (US$3.37 for one pound of ground beef and US$1.19 for bread), someone from Barrow pays US$95.88!

Activities aren't cheap either, but this certainly isn't an area you should skimp on; scenic flights (US$125–250) have to be experienced at least once by everyone. Kayaking is another great Alaskan activity that should be splurged on.

Transport costs quickly mount up too (a rental car can easily cost US$55–75 per day), but the Alaska ferry system doubles up as a cheap cruise ship ideal for exploring the coastline

If these prices seem fair, then have a great time and do as much as you can. If they scare you, then take heart; I have seen many a grinning backpacker touring the state with little more than a thumb and a good attitude. I travel on a budget somewhere in between the two extremes and consistently have a splendid time, never feeling like I'm missing out on anything. Rich or poor, most people come to Alaska for the same reasons: scenery, wildlife, native culture and a profound sense of humility in the face of nature – and all these things are free.

LUXURY Those looking for luxury can certainly find it, even in the most remote locations. A standard/luxury hotel costs US$145–450. Every region of the state has wonderful lodges offering all-inclusive packages (meals, transportation, and activities) from US$2,200 all the way up to extravagant film-star prices. Not all lodges are created equally though, so choose carefully and make sure the feel of the lodge and the nature of the activities suit you. Dining out at a nice restaurant can easily run US$75–100 for two people including wine.

MID-RANGE In general, visitors should expect to spend US$100–150pp/day on food and accommodation. A rental car (US$55–75/day) and any activities should be added on top. Eating out can be kept affordable by choosing local haunts. Lunch will cost US$8–15, while dinner will cost around US$12–25.

BUDGET Campers can slash mid-range expenses by half or more by camping. Hostels are also a good choice, especially when the laundry needs doing. While campgrounds are generally very affordable and offer decent services, some RV parks are surprisingly expensive. Remember that camping is allowed on forest service land for free as long as you're out of sight and well away from roads.

GETTING AROUND

One look at a map will give you an idea of how restricted the road network, and how large and sparsely populated the state. For this reason, small planes and the Alaska Ferry are a common and generally pleasurable way to get around. While small planes or jets can get you almost anywhere, the state's two rail systems are also good options. The road system, while generally in good shape, exists almost exclusively in southcentral and interior Alaska. In these regions, a vehicle of your own is priceless, allowing a flexible schedule and countless side trips. Vehicles can be rented around Alaska but visitors can also drive to Alaska from the Lower 48 US states via the Alaska Highway. Those without vehicles can hitchhike, and though I can't officially recommend it, I consider Alaska among the safest (and best) places on earth to hitch.

BY AIR Flying by small plane, or 'bush plane' as they're known in Alaska, is a lot of fun, and for those wanting to reach remote towns, it's a necessity. Alaska has 14 times as many planes per capita than the rest of the US, and six times more pilots. About one in 50 people are pilots. While these planes do crash, they are not usually the problem, the weather is. Be very cautious about weather, even if your pilot isn't. Conversely, don't be mad if you get picked up from a remote cabin five days late because your pilot refused to fly in a storm.

While some – not all – plane crashes result in injuries or fatalities, other crashes cause death when the pilots and/or passengers are not properly prepared to survive on the ground. When flying in a small plane, wear layered clothes with sturdy boots. If something happens, you may need to hike a long way to the nearest settlement. It's also a good idea to have water, food and a sleeping bag.

Because these planes are grounded or fly according to weather conditions, their schedules vary wildly. Don't plan any tight connections around small planes, even when they advertise a seemingly rigid schedule.

Local bush plane & jet companies

Alaska Airlines ☎ 800 252 7522; www.alaskaair.com. Flies to the Lower 48 states as well as many locations within Alaska.

Arctic Circle Air ☎ 474 0112; www.arcticcircleair.com. Serves much of interior & western Alaska.

Era Aviation ☎ 266 8394, 800 866 8394 (TF); www.flyera.com. Flights around the Kenai Peninsula, Prince William Sound & other locations.

Everts Air ☎ 450 2350; www.evertsair.com. Service to many interior destinations.

Frontier Flying Service ☎ 450 7200; www.frontierflying.com. Flights to most of Alaska except the Alaska Peninsula & the Aleutian Islands.

Grant Aviation ☎ 243 3592; www.flygrant.com. Flights to various Kenai Peninsula locations.

Hageland Aviation Services ☎ 245 0119; www.hageland.com. Flights to many Western & Arctic destinations including Anchorage.

Pen Air ☎ 243 2323, 800 448 4226 (TF); www.penair.com. Regular flights to the Aleutians & Alaska's west coast. An Alaska Airlines partner.

Rusty's Flying Service 4525 Enstrom Cir; ☎ 243 1595, 800 544 2299 (TF); www.flyrusts.com. Flightseeing, fly-out (see *Glossary* on page 431) fishing & charter flights.

Warbelow's Air Ventures ☎ 474 0518, 800 478 0812 (TF); www.warbellos.com. Flights throughout Interior Alaska.

Wright Air Service ☎ 474 0502; www.wrightair.net. Charter flight service in Interior Alaska.

Domestic airlines

Alaska Airlines ☎ 800 426 0333; www.alaskaair.com

American Airlines ☎ 800 433 7300; www.aa.com

Continental Airlines ☎ 800 523 3273; www.continental.com

Frontier Airlines ☎ 800432 1359; www.flyfrontier.com

Northwest Airlines ☎ 800 225 2525; www.nwa.com

United Airlines ☎ 800 241 6522; www.ual.com

US Airways ☎ 800 428 4322; www.usairways.com

🚢 BY FERRY

Alaska Marine Highway (☎ 465 3941, 800 642 0066 (TF); *www.dot.state.ak.us*) This is one of the best ways to get around the state, with many of the benefits of a cruise ship (remote coastlines and a taste of the seagoing life) and none of the drawbacks (tourist-choked ports of call and hordes of people). The ferry system serves 28 Alaskan communities through southeast, southcentral and southwest Alaska with a fleet of ships that carry people, cars, motorcycles, bikes, kayaks, and other gear. Most of the ferries have simple cabins with bunks, but all offer comfortable chairs, floor space and benches for sleeping. The longer haul ferries have a solarium on the top deck, a semi-enclosed space for tents. When planning a trip, be sure to book as far ahead as possible, especially when travelling with a car. Ferry schedules are normally released no later than late spring, but be in touch with the office so you can book as soon as possible. To book tickets visit the website or call.

The water-bound towns of southeast Alaska have benefited enormously from the ferry and today the ferry remains the best (and most affordable) way to explore this part of the state. After leaving Bellingham, Washington, the ferry stops in Prince Rupert, Canada, then in Ketchikan and costs US$239 plus US$515 for a vehicle up to 15ft. From Ketchikan a smaller ferry, the 181ft MV *Lituya*, serves the native community of Metlakatla on Annette Island for US$25.

From there the ferry heads north to Wrangell for US$37 and another US$77 for a car to 15ft. From Wrangell the ferry cruises the Wrangell Narrows and arrives in Petersburg for US$33 and US$54 for a vehicle. From there the ferry goes to Sitka for US$60 and US$115 for a vehicle. After Sitka is Juneau for US$45 and US$79 for a vehicle on the fast ferry, the MV *Fairweather*. The 235ft MV *LeConte* serves the small communities of Hoonah, Tenakee Springs, Angoon, Pelican and Haines. From Juneau to Skagway costs US$50, another US$31 gets you to Haines.

The ferry system connects southeast to southcentral Alaska with two trips a month between Juneau and Whittier via Yakutat on the 382ft MV *Kennicott*. Juneau to Whittier costs US$221 and another US$508 for a vehicle up to 15ft. Daily service within Prince William Sound connects Whittier, Cordova and Valdez on the 235ft MV *Aurora* and MV *Chenega*. Fares are US$50 (plus US$94 vehicle) from Cordova to Valdez and US$89 (plus US$105 vehicle) from Valdez to Whittier.

Once a month the 382ft MV *Kennicott* connects Whittier with Kodiak for US$91 (US$191 vehicle) then on to Homer for US$74 (US$152 vehicle). The 296ft MV *Tustumena* then heads out to Unalaska once per month for US$351, stopping in Chignik, Sand Point, King Cove, Cold Bay, False Pass, Akutan and finally in Unalaska/Dutch Harbor.

Inter-Island Coastal Ferry (✆ *225 4838; www.interislandferry.com*) The Inter-Island ferry serves Prince of Wales Island from Ketchikan for US$37 for an adult and US$5 per foot for vehicles under 20ft. Due to a lack of passengers, the Inter-Island ferry has suspended their Prince of Wales Island to Wrangell and Petersburg trip.

BY CAR Like most places in America, a car is mighty handy for getting around, especially in Alaska where there are often great distances between towns and smaller villages not serviced by local transport. Renting a car gives travellers total freedom and flexibility to go where they please and stop when they want. See box on page 62 for some road-trip suggestions. Be sure to pick up a copy of *The Milepost*, a beefy volume describing every detail of every road in the state.

Rental cars The usual suspects of the car rental business are all represented in the major cities and some of the larger towns. These all offer new cars for US$70–100 per day. Book well ahead to ensure you have a car where and when you want it.

International companies

Avis Fifth & B St; ✆ 277 4567, 800 331 1212 (TF); www.avis.com
Budget 5011 Spenard Rd; ✆ 243 0150, 800 248 0150 (TF); www.budgetalaskaonline.com
Dollar 4940 W International Airport Rd; ✆ 248 5338, 800) 800-4000 (TF); www.dollar.com. Anchorage.

Enterprise ✆ 248 5526, 800 736 8222 (TF); www.enterprise.com
Payless Car Rental 1130 W International Airport Rd; ✆ 243 3616; www.paylesscarrental.com. Anchorage.
Thrifty Car Rental ✆ 279 1326, 800 847 4389 (TF); www.anchorage.thrifty.com

Local companies Local rental companies often have cheaper rates, but the cars are often less than brand new. Still the savings add up (sometimes US$10/day) and some allow their vehicles on roads like the McCarthy Highway, the Denali Highway and the Dalton Highway. The national companies forbid many of these adventure highways. Try Arctic Outfitters for go-anywhere vehicles.

Denali Car Rental 1209 Gambell St; ✆ 276 1230. Near Anchorage city centre.
High Country Car & Truck Rental 3609 Spenard Rd; ✆ 562 8078, 888 685 1155 (TF). Anchorage.
Arctic Rent-A-Car 4500 Dale Road; ✆ 479 8044; www.arcticrentacar.com. Fairbanks.

Arctic Outfitters ✆ 474 3530. Rentals available for Dalton Hwy trips from Fairbanks.
Rent-A-Wreck 615 12th Av; ✆ 452 1606, 800 478 1606 (TF); www.rentawreck.com. Fairbanks.

Recreational vehicles/motorhomes (RVs) RVs or motorhomes are a popular way to explore the state. While they burn up the fuel, they provide accommodation and transportation in one. Plan on US$100–200 or more per day for a small to mid-sized RV, plus fuel. Book well ahead, these book up quickly. Visit www.travelalaska.com for a selection of rental outfits.

ABC Motorhome & Car Rentals 3875 Old International Airport Rd; ☎ 279 2000, 800 421 7456 (TF); www.abcmotorhome.com. A good selection of RVs, & they speak German. Anchorage.

Cheap Motorhomes Alaska ☎ 866 425 0307 (TF), 0808 234 8955 (UK); www.cheapmotorhomesalaska.com. Available in Anchorage, Fairbanks, Haines, Kenai, Seward, Skagway, & Whittier.

Clippership Motorhome Rentals ☎ 800 421 3456; www.clippershiprv.com. Located in Anchorage. RVs for US$100 & up.

Cruise America ☎ 800 671 8042; www.cruiseamerica.com. Not the cheapest, but a well-run national company. Anchorage.

Go North 3500 Davis Rd; ☎ 479 7272; www.gonorthalaska.com. Camper, SUV, & truck rental from Fairbanks.

Great Alaskan Holidays ☎ 888 225 2752 (TF); www.greatalaskanholidays.com. New RVs & decent rates. Anchorage.

AUTHOR'S FAVOURITE ROAD TRIPS

These road trips can be undertaken by car, motorcycle or bike but the remote areas encountered on each necessitate a high degree of self-reliance, especially if traveling by bike or motorcycle. Travelling on two wheels instead of four has its advantages and disadvantages: on the plus side it connects you more closely to the surrounding landscape, but you're also much more exposed to (potentially dangerous) wildlife, insects, sun and the elements. Indeed, while some areas of Alaska are dry, most get their fair share of rain, especially the rainforests in southeast Alaska. Another consideration is the immense amounts of dust that can be kicked up on gravel roads during dry spells. Flying gravel is also a concern, especially on the Dalton Highway, where large trucks travel very fast. Most of these roads are not exactly busy, but dust and rocks can still be an unpleasant variable if traveling by bike or motorcycle.

DENALI HIGHWAY From Fairbanks, head south to Denali National Park and after exploring the park, proceed a little further south to Cantwell and turn east onto the Denali Highway. This 135-mile, mostly gravel road winds through the tundra past rivers, lakes and often herds of caribou and the occasional brown bear. All the while, mountains – including Denali – loom in the distance. When the end finally comes, follow the Richardson Highway north to Fairbanks or proceed south to Wrangell-St Elias National Park, which leads you straight into another of the state's best adventure road trips, the McCarthy Road. See also page 333.

MCCARTHY ROAD The McCarthy Road starts in Chitna, southeast of Fairbanks and continues into the park for 60 miles. This gravel road is a true wilderness road, with mountains on all sides and wildlife a common sight. At the end of the road are the towns of McCarthy and Kennicott, former mining towns sandwiched between mountain and glacier. These remote, almost 'old-west' towns are one of a kind and are perfectly situated in an area blessed with sun for most of the summer. This is also the best place to start a hiking or 'flightseeing' tour of the park. The Alaskan wilderness of dreams comes to life here. See also box on page 340.

DALTON HIGHWAY The 414-mile Dalton Highway, striking north near Fairbanks, all the way to the Arctic Ocean, is the king of all Alaskan adventure highways. This gravel haul road is used to transport supplies to the oil fields of Prudhoe Bay, but the adventurous motorist can make good use of it as well. The camping trip of a lifetime would involve little more

BY BUS/SHUTTLE The southcentral and interior are fairly well connected by bus and shuttle. There are daily departures from Anchorage to the Kenai Peninsula, Denali and Fairbanks.

Alaska Direct Bus Line ✆ 277 6652, 800 770 6652 (TF); www.alaskadirectbusline.com. Buses run all summer on Wed, Fri & Sun to Tok (US$105), Glennallen (US$75) & Palmer (US$10).

Alaska Park Connection ✆ 245 0200, 800 266 8625 (TF); www.alaskacoach.com. Regular service in a large bus between Anchorage & Seward, Whittier, Denali & Talkeetna.

Alaska/Yukon Trails ✆ 479 2277, 800 770 7275 (TF); www.alaskashuttle.com. Daily shuttle service from Anchorage to Denali (US$75) & to Fairbanks (US$99).

Denali Overland ✆ 733 2384, 800 651 5221 (TF); www.denalioverland.com. Shuttle service to Talkeetna & Denali National Park. Since the whole van must be rented, the more people riding, the cheaper it is.

Homer Stage Line ✆ 883 3914; www.homerstageline.com. Serving virtually the entire Kenai Peninsula.

Seward Bus Lines ✆ 563 0800; www.sewardbuslines.net. Daily service between Anchorage & Seward for US$50. Leaves Anchorage at 14.30, arrives Seward 17.30.

than a healthy sense of adventure, a sturdy vehicle and a few spare tyres. The fishing, wildlife viewing, and hiking opportunities are all out of this world. Other, less accessible regions of the Arctic include the Arctic National Wildlife Refuge (ANWR) in the east and the Gates of the Arctic National Park in the west. It's possible to raft or hike in these areas for weeks without seeing a single human being or even a plane or jet trail. Trust me, I've done it. See also page 421.

NOME ROAD TRIP Nome has a small network of three roads leading out to Council, Taylor and Teller , all of which offer spectacular hiking, fishing and wildlife viewing. There's even a hot spring. Taking a week with a rental car in Nome would be time well spent.

DRIVING THE ALASKAN-CANADIAN HIGHWAY ('ALCAN') Driving the Alcan Highway is a monumental road trip allowing a slow build-up to Alaska. The key to this magnificent road trip – which takes in British Columbia and the Yukon territory – is to take your time; two weeks in August is perfect. The road was finished in 1943 and runs from Dawson Creek in British Columbia for 1,422 miles to Delta Junction in Alaska. It is 854 miles from Seattle, Washington, to Dawson Creek. From Delta Junction to Anchorage is another 334 miles, making a total road trip of 2,610 miles! Be sure to stop at Liard River Hot Springs in British Columbia. Take the ferry back to Bellingham, Washington near Seattle, or drive back.

PRINCE WILLIAM SOUND Yet another fantastic trip is an exploration of Prince William Sound by ferry and car. This trip involves a short train or car ride to Whittier from Anchorage, then a fast ferry through the sound to Valdez, passing glaciers dumping tons of ice into the water. If you have your car with you, you can explore the area including Hatcher Pass and Keystone Canyon before jumping back on the ferry to the much smaller and more interesting town of Cordova. From this town (inaccessible by road), the dead-end Copper River Highway traverses some of the wildest land around and ends between two glaciers in the middle of nowhere. For the bold few, this is where the adventure could continue, over hill and dale – and glacier. Anyone visiting Cordova should also consider spending a few nights at the Cape St Elias lighthouse (see page 276), on Kayak Island, 65 miles southeast of Cordova. From Cordova, catch the ferry back to Whittier or stop in Valdez again, then drive the scenic Glen Highway back to Anchorage.

MILEAGE CHART

APPROXIMATE DRIVING DISTANCE IN MILES BETWEEN CITIES	Anchorage	Circle	Dawson City	Eagle	Fairbanks	Haines	Homer	Prudhoe Bay	Seattle	Seward	Skagway	Tok	Valdez
Anchorage		520	494	501	358	775	226	847	2234	126	832	328	304
Circle	520		530	541	162	815	746	1972	2271	646	872	368	526
Dawson City	494	530		131	379	548	713	868	1843	619	430	189	428
Eagle	501	541	131		379	620	727	868	1974	627	579	173	427
Fairbanks	358	162	379	379		653	584	489	2121	484	710	206	364
Haines	775	815	548	620	653		1001	1142	1774	901	359	447	701
Homer	226	746	713	727	584	1001		1073	2455	173	1058	554	530
Prudhoe Bay	847	1972	868	868	489	1142	1073		2610	973	1199	695	853
Seattle	2243	2271	1843	1974	2121	1774	2455	2610		2493	1577	1931	2169
Seward	126	646	619	627	484	901	173	973	2493		958	454	430
Skagway	832	872	430	579	710	359	1058	1199	1577	958		504	758
Tok	328	368	189	173	206	447	554	695	1931	454	504		254
Valdez	304	526	428	427	364	701	530	853	2169	430	758	254	

BY RAIL Started in 1912, the 470-mile **Alaska Railroad** (↘ *265 2494, 800 544 0552 (TF); www.akrr.com*) was finally completed in 1923. The train travels between Seward and Fairbanks, stopping in Whittier, Girdwood, Anchorage, Palmer, Wasilla, Talkeetna, Denali National Park and Nenana. The Alaska Railroad also offers one of the few remaining 'whistle stop' services, where passengers can get on and off the train – even at unscheduled stops – between Anchorage and Fairbanks. Daily services run from mid–May to mid-September. Dinner service is available on the train and the luxury Gold Star service can be had for approximately double the price. Anchorage to Talkeetna costs US$89/45 adult/child, to Denali costs US$146/73 adult/child, and all the way to Fairbanks costsUS$210/105 adult/child. The coastal train travels between Anchorage and Girdwood for US$59/30 adult/child, then on to Seward for US$75/38 adult/child. The Glacier Discovery train serves Whittier for US$65/33 adult/child. Book tickets by calling.

The only other train in the state is the **White Pass and Yukon Route Rail** (*231 2nd Av;* ↘ *983 2217, 800 343 7373 (TF); www.wpyr.com*) in Skagway. This small train connects Skagway with Whitehorse, Canada and offers fantastic views. The train can also be used to start or end the Chilkoot Trail, or hop off *en route* for a glacier hike. For more information see page 170.

If travelling mid-May to mid-August, it is a good idea to book six months ahead. The only way to visit Alaska 'last minute' is if you have a tent and are prepared to use it.

HOTELS Traditional hotels are generic and expensive in Alaska with few exceptions. A standard hotel will often cost in excess of US$150 for a clean, if somewhat soulless, room. For something with the charm of a B&B expect to pay US$250 or more. If you do plan to stay in hotels during your trip, always try to book a room on the top floor, they tend to be quieter. Just ask the receptionist and he/she will help you find the best room. While many hotels offer breakfast nowadays, some still do not. Breakfast fare in hotels usually consists of waffles, yoghurt, canned fruit, cereal, muffins and juice. Nicer places offer hot items such as eggs, sausages and bacon. An advantage of staying in hotels is their consistency. For the most part you know what you're going to get for a given amount of money. Hotels offer Wi-Fi, TV and telephone across the board. Many towns levy a 10% 'bed tax', so budget accordingly. Many hotels offer airport pick-up.

BOUTIQUE HOTELS Alaska has a few boutique hotels that strike a pleasant balance between a B&B and a hotel but are generally much more expensive than B&Bs. When booking a boutique hotel, ask about the beds, views, noise and whether there is a private entrance. Once there, some proprietors will usually allow you to switch to a higher-end room for no additional cost, but only if you ask.

B&BS Bed and breakfasts have sprung up in their thousands in Alaska and cater predominantly to the independent traveller. These almost always include breakfast, Wi-Fi, and free travel advice. B&Bs almost always offer better value (and better service) than hotels. A mid-range B&B will cost around US$150 for two people, but in less popular areas can cost as little as US$75 with no loss in quality. A quality B&B should offer a private, homely room with a delicious breakfast and the company of other travellers. An added benefit is having access to a local; your host. This is how you find out about the best hikes, fishing spots and restaurants. Atmosphere does vary: from madhouses with kids and dogs running around the breakfast table, to lonely fortresses of solitude with no one around at all. The listings in this guide should help you avoid both. Some B&Bs offer cabins or cottages which are independent structures with maximum privacy, usually a full kitchen and all the benefits of a traditional B&B room. I prefer these but always avoid the cookie cutter cottages at more commercial places.

Practical Information ACCOMMODATION

2

ACCOMMODATION PRICE CODES

Accommodation listings are laid out in decreasing price order, under the following categories: Luxury, Upmarket, Mid-range, Budget and Shoestring. The following key (also on the inside front cover) gives an indication of prices. Prices are based on the cost of a double room per night.

$$$$$	£148+	US$275+
$$$$	£108–148	US$200–275
$$$	£67–108	US$125–200
$$	£25–67	US$49–125
$	<£25	<US$49

HOSTELS If a roof is more your style, hostels are available in just about every town for US$20–25, but are generally not much better than camping and with less privacy. A few exceptions do exist and you will find them in this guide.

CAMPING While accommodation is generally expensive in Alaska, camping is almost always available and very cheap. If you headed to the last frontier and haven't camped before and are also on a budget, now is the perfect time to get a tent and sleeping bag. Public campsites are often less than US$12 for the site, while the private variety can be US$20 or more and cater more to RV than campers with tents. Free camping is always available anywhere away from roads on Forest Service land.

PUBLIC-USE CABINS Public-use cabins, managed by federal and state agencies, are found throughout the state. Virtually all of these simple cabins are found in remote areas, with just a few accessible by road. A plane or boat ride and/or a hike is usually required to reach the rest. Most sleep four to eight people on bunks. A gas (bring in your own fuel) or wood stove is usually provided. Those situated by lakes often offer rowing boats free to renters. These cabins are very affordable at US$35–45/night but must be booked far in advance.

For cabins in the Tongass and Chugach National Forests, visit www.fs.fed.us. For National Park cabins visit www.nps.gov.

All can be reserved at www.reserveusa.com or by calling ℡ 877 444 6777.

HOME EXCHANGE Yet another option is home exchange. Travellers around the world have started to use this service whereby two homeowners (or even renters) trade houses simultaneously, or – if either party has a second home – at different times. Home Exchange (*www.homeexchange.com*) is one example and has 44 listings in Alaska. A fee is generally required to join a group.

✕ EATING AND DRINKING

FOOD Different parts of Alaska each have their own speciality. Many are influenced by native Alaskan and also Russian culture; particularly the southeast, where *pelmini* – tasty Russian meat or veggie dumplings – are found. Native foods are harder to come by and are usually only encountered in remote native villages. These villages often dry salmon and other meat on wooden racks to preserve it, so it can be eaten throughout the winter. In the western and Arctic regions caribou is the staple food, and natives occasionally mix the fat with berries to make 'Eskimo ice cream'. Of course, though, Alaska is most famous for its fish and

RESTAURANT PRICE CODES

Restaurant listings are laid out in decreasing price order, under the following categories: Luxury, Upmarket, Mid-range, Budget and Shoestring. The following key (also on the inside front cover) gives an indication of prices. Prices are based on the average price of a main course.

$$$$$	£20+	US$39+
$$$$	£12–20	US$23–39
$$$	£6–12	US$12–23
$$	£3–6	US$6–12
$	<£3	<US$6

seafood. The rivers are teeming with salmon and the oceans consistently yield huge harvests of king crab, shrimp, halibut, rockfish, black cod and other delicacies, which are shipped across the world for rich diners to enjoy.

The main cities and towns like Anchorage, Juneau and Fairbanks also offer a full range of international eateries, so if you're lusting after Thai food you'll be able to satiate your cravings. Outside these areas though, dining options diminish drastically. When visiting the less well-travelled parts of the state, asking after restaurants will likely be returned by a blank stare, a recommendation for a local bar that serves microwaved pizzas, or the reply: 'I just eat at home.' In these instances, you'll need to stock up at local grocery stores or markets. Alternatively, you could attempt to catch your own dinner. Cast your rod into the river, stock up on vegetables from the local farmers' market, and hey presto!

See *Budgeting*, page 58, for information about food prices.

DRINK Given the cold weather, you'd expect spirits to be in high demand in Alaska, but beer is popular too. Several towns – including Anchorage (see page 199), Wasilla (see page 212), Kenai (see page 243), Kodiak (see page 363), Haines (see page 176) and Fairbanks (see page 315) – have their own breweries. Many of these offer tours and tastings. In contrast, you can always fill up your water bottle for free with pure glacial water, which trickles in abundance from the state's glaciers.

PUBLIC HOLIDAYS

1 January	New Year
19 January	Martin Luther King Day
16 February	President's Day
30 March	Seward's Day (The day, in 1867, when US Secretary of State William H Seward signed the treaty that made Alaska part of the US.)
Last Monday of May	Memorial Day. A public holiday occurring on the last Monday of May. Tourism businesses consider this the start of summer.
4 July	Independence Day. Celebrated everywhere with fireworks the night before and usually a parade and party of some kind.
7 September	Labour Day. Considered the end of the summer season.
18 October	Alaska Day. The anniversary of the transfer of Alaska from Russia to the US in Sitka on 18 October 1867.
11 November	Veterans Day
26 November	Thanksgiving Day
25 December	Christmas Day

FESTIVALS AND EVENTS

JANUARY
The Great Alaska Beer and Barley Wine Festival (*auroraproductions.net/beer-barley.html*) Generally held in the middle of January in Anchorage, this is your only chance to taste beer from around the state all in one place.

Polar Bear Jump-Off (*www.sewardak.org/news-events/polarbear.htm*) Show up in Seward on the third week of January to dress up in a costume and jump into the ocean! It's that simple.

The only thing better than tasting regional cuisine is being able to make it for yourself. There are few things I enjoy more than catching a king salmon, picking some fresh lettuce and carrots from my garden and preparing a meal with friends. Visitors can do the same with a fishing rod, a cottage with a fully-equipped kitchen and a trip to the local farmers' market.

BLACKENED ROCK FISH/HALIBUT TACOS
Ingredients

Rock fish or halibut flesh	Coriander
Cajun or Jerk (spicy Jamaican) seasoning	Salt
Vegetable oil	Cumin
Corn or flour tortillas	Jalapeno pepper
Tomatoes	Onion
Olive oil	Mango

Preparation Cube the rockfish/halibut, fillet it, then place in a bowl and coat with a liberal dose of blackening, cajun or Jerk (spicy Jamaican) seasoning.

Heat a cast iron frying pan to smoking point then add butter and fish shortly after. Expect lots of smoke.

Serve in warm corn tortillas with fresh mango salsa.

GRILLED KING SALMON King salmon is the favourite of many Alaskans. Most folk just grill it plain and enjoy its wonderful flavour but the simple sauce in this recipe really makes it sing.

Ingredients

King salmon flesh	Honey
Salt and pepper	Olive oil
Red wine vinegar	Parsley (optional)
Stone ground Dijon mustard	

Preparation Rub one king salmon fillet with salt and pepper and grill under tin foil until the meat lightens in colour and flakes apart. Grill the fillet flesh side down for just a minute on a very clean oiled grill before flipping it to the skin side to finish cooking.

While the salmon is grilling, whisk together one tablespoon of red wine vinegar, one tablespoon of stone ground Dijon mustard, one tablespoon of honey and two tablespoons of olive oil.

Drizzle the sauce over each helping and serve with chopped parsley.

In the absence of a grill, try baking the fillet at 400°F/200°C for about 20 minutes.

Roasted potatoes and mushrooms make great side dishes. Roast the vegetables in a tin foil packet on the grill or with the fish in the oven.

FEBRUARY

Fur Rendezvous (*www.furrondy.net*) Known as 'Rondy' or 'Fur Rondy' to locals, this popular festival has been filling Anchorage for 75 years. Originally organised for trappers to sell their furs, the event now draws people from around the country with shows, food, entertainment and best of all, it now includes the kick off to the Iditarod Sled Dog. The festival takes place at the end of February/early March.

Yukon Quest International Sled Dog Race (*www.yukonquest.com*) Held during the second week of February, this gruelling race runs between Fairbanks and Whitehorse, Canada.

GRILLED TERIYAKI SALMON (from *Chez Alaska* in Juneau, see page 87)

Ingredients

Teriyaki sauce	Tomatoes
Mayonnaise	Spring onions
BBQ sauce	Olive oil
Ginger	Wine vinegar
Red or silver salmon fillets (skin on)	Cucumber
Spinach leaves	Sesame oil
Green bell pepper	Lemon (optional)

Preparation Mix half a cup teriyaki sauce, half a cup BBQ sauce, half a cup mayonnaise and one tablespoon of minced ginger. Marinade up to four fillets for up to one hour with two thirds of this sauce and reserve the rest.

Grill the fillets on a clean, hot and well-oiled grill, basting with the remaining sauce.

Mix ½lb chopped spinach, half a diced green pepper, two diced tomatoes, one diced cucumber and four thinly sliced green spring onions with one tablespoon of olive oil, one tablespoon of sesame oil and three tablespoons of wine vinegar.

Serve grilled salmon with lemon wedges, accompanied by a side salad.

WILLIE CORK MEMORIAL CAESAR SALAD DRESSING AND CROUTONS This is the best Caesar salad recipe in Alaska and is not for the faint-hearted. Willie Cork was a famous ship pilot who worked in the Aleutian Islands.

Ingredients

Garlic	Dry mustard
Extra virgin olive oil	Lemons
Sourdough bread	Tabasco sauce
Red wine vinegar	Worcester sauce
Anchovies packed in olive oil	Parmesan cheese

Preparation Blend three or four large garlic cloves with ⅔ of a cup of high-quality extra virgin olive oil. Mix one tablespoon of the mixture with a few cups diced sourdough bread, then bake on a flat tray until crispy.

To the olive oil and garlic mixture, add two teaspoons red wine vinegar (balsamic is good), a whole tin of anchovies packed in olive oil (half a tin for the squeamish), ½ a teaspoon of dry mustard, the juice of two lemons, a dash of Tabasco, a dash of Worcester sauce, and ¼ a cup of grated Parmesan cheese.

Blend everything together. Toss with fresh, washed and dried, then torn romaine or other local lettuce.

Sitka Jazz Festival (*www.sitkajazzfestival.com*) Jazz performers from around the state play during the first week of the month.

Tok to Dawson International Poker Run (*www.alaskatrailblazers.com*) This event draws almost 1,000 people annually. Participants ride snowmobiles 200 miles from Tok across the border to Dawson where they are wined and dined.

MARCH

Iditarod Sled Dog Race (*www.iditarod.com*) This world-famous 1,000-mile dog-sled race starts in Anchorage in early March and ends in Nome.

Winter King Salmon Tournament (*www.homeralaska.org/winterkingsalmonderby/index.htm*) Held in the third week of March in Homer, the event pays out a cash prize of almost US$18,000 to whomever catches the largest king salmon.

World Ice Art Championships (*www.icealaska.com*) Held in Fairbanks during the first week of March, this event draws ice sculptors from around the globe.

Nenana Ice Classic (*www.nenanaakiceclassic.com*) Guess when the ice is going to break-up in Nenana and win US$283,723 like the 2009 tandem winners, Stephen Gregory and Claudia Russell.

APRIL

Garnet Festival (*www.wrangell.com/visitors/attractions/outdoors/garnet*) The festival welcomes spring and celebrates the return of thousands of migratory birds.

Camai Dance Festival A celebration of native culture held in Bethel during the beginning of April.

Arctic Man Ski and Sno-Go Classic (*www.arcticman.com*) An extreme ski and snow-machine race in Fairbanks. Held during the second week of the month.

Alaska Folk Festival (*www.akfolkfest.org*) A folk music extravaganza held during the second week of the month.

Spring Carneval and Slush Cup (*www.alyeskaresort.com/page.asp?intNodeID=39842*) Head to Girdwood during the last week of the month to see crazy ski stunts and to party.

MAY

Copper River Delta Shorebird Festival (✆ 424 7260; *www.cordovachamber.com*) Gather with Cordova locals and watch as millions of migratory birds pass through the area.

Kachemak Bay Sea Fest (✆ 235 7740; *www.kachemakkayakfestival.com*) Taking place in Homer in the last week of May, this fun event is entirely focused around small boats.

Kachemak Bay Shorebird Festival (✆ 235 7740; *www.homer.alaska.org/shorebird.html*) This multi-day migratory bird festival takes place in Homer during the second week of May.

Kodiak King Crab Festival (✆ 486 5557; *www.kodiak.org/crabfest.html*) Celebrate the bounty of the sea while hunting it during this fun event over Memorial Day weekend (last Monday in May).

Great Alaskan Craftbeer and Homebrew Festival (*seakfair.org/beerfestival.php*) Head to Haines during the last few days of the month for beer galore.

Jazz and Classics Festival (*www.jazzandclassics.org*) Juneau comes alive with music and good food for the last ten days of the month.

Pelican Boardwalk Boogie (*www.pelicanboardwalkboogie.com*) Party in the isolated town of Pelican during the third week of the month to the tune of Alaskan and national bands.

Little Norway Festival (*www.petersburg.org/visitor/littlenorway.html*) Petersburg celebrates its Norwegian heritage during the middle of the month.

JUNE
Midnight Sun Festival (☏ *443 5535*) Nome's big music festival starts in mid June.

Summer Solstice Usually held on 20 or 21 June, this is *the* June event held all over the state. Depending on the town, festivities range from informal bonfire parties on the beach to town-consuming festivals with entertainment, food, music and more. Some of the best include: the Summer Solstice Festival in Anchorage with arts, crafts, food and music; the Seldovia Summer Solstice Music Festival in Seldovia near Homer; the Midnight Sun Festival in Fairbanks with a foot race, music, entertainment, food and city centre shops open through the night; and the Summer Solstice Celebration in Juneau featuring a sailboat race and festivities.

Seldovia Summer Solstice Music Festival (*www.seldoviamusicfestival.wordpress.com*) Takes place in Seldovia across from Homer on Summer solstice, and in Fairbanks.

Nalukataq Whale Festival Assuming a successful hunt, Barrow celebrates with dancing, festivities, and whale meat in mid-June.

Alaska Scottish Highland Games (*www.alaskascottish.org/games.html*) Eagle River hosts these fun games with music and other events in the third week of June.

Gold Rush Days Juneau celebrates its gold mining history with music, food, and events during the third week of June.

JULY
Girdwood Forest Fair (*www.girdwoodforestfair.com*) Takes place on the first weekend of July, and features music and partying like you've never seen before.

Moose Dropping Festival (*www.talkeetnachamber.org*) A small but fun event in Talkeetna during the second week of July, with music, food, softball games, etc.

Mt Marathon Race This race to summit 3,022ft Mt Marathon, near Seward, is something to behold on the first weekend of July. Finalists party in Seldovia afterwards.

World Eskimo-Indian Olympics (*www.weio.org*) Watch native Alaskans compete against one another in traditional sports during the second week of July in Fairbanks.

AUGUST
Alaska State Fair (*www.alaskastatefair.org*) At the end of the month is the state's biggest fair held in Palmer. Parking is a nightmare.

Kenai Peninsula State Fair (*www.kenaipeninsulafair.com*) A smaller fair held in Ninilchik at the end of the month.

Talkeetna Bluegrass Festival (*www.eideticimage.com/bluegrass*) A fun music festival held near Talkeetna during the second week of August.

Tanana Valley State Fair (*www.tananavalleyfair.org*) A funfair in Fairbanks with food, art, livestock, and rides during the second week of August.

SEPTEMBER

Kodiak State Fair and Rodeo (*www.kodiakrodeoandstatefair.com*) Head to Kodiak for music, rodeo, food and more. Held during the first week of September.

Tongass Rainforest Festival (*www.tongassrainforestfestival.org*) Take some time in Ketchikan during the middle of the month to learn all about the rainforest. Art, food and education.

Blueberry Bash Learn to eat and prepare blueberries in every conceivable way at this festival held in the last week of September.

NOVEMBER

Haines Bald Eagle Festival (*www.baldeaglefestival.org*) See art, raptor demonstrations, and lots of eagles in Haines. Held during the middle of November.

Whalefest (*www.sitkawhalefest.org*) Celebrate whales in Sitka during the first week of the month with whale-watching, lectures, art and education.

DECEMBER

New Years Fire and Ice Extravaganza (*http://www.anchorage.net/events.html?eventid =15946*) Downtown Anchorage turns into a giant party on the 31 December.

🧺 SHOPPING

NATIVE ART Visitors often purchase art while in Alaska, particularly native art, which best represents the state. While much of this work is the real deal, some of it is part of a growing counterfeit industry. Common sense will be your best guide in the quest for that perfect mask or doll. Look for quality, hand-worked material and the silver 'hand' logo and 'Alaska-made' stickers. Also talk to the artist, if possible, to learn more about their lives and work and to see if they are really making it. Just because the storeowner is not native or an artist, does not mean the work sold there is any less authentic. Ask a storeowner all the same questions you would ask the artists. The best dealers should take great pride in the work they sell, and the communities of artists they work with. Remember not to buy work made from marine mammals since you may not be able to take it out of the country. For extensive information on buying Alaskan native art visit www.commerce.state.ak.us/oed/nag/nativearts.htm or contact the **Alaska State Council on the Arts** (☏ *269 6610; www.eed.state.ak.us/aksca*) to learn more about the silver hand logo.

ARTS AND CRAFTS Other than native art, Alaska is full of artists making all manner of work in the state's urban as well as far-flung places. Many wonderful galleries can be found around the state, but also look for art in coffee shops.

FOOD AND DRINK Groceries are available in large stores in all the major towns, but be prepared for high prices. As a general rule, the amount it costs to buy four bags of groceries in the Lower 48 states will only buy you two in Alaska. While milk might cost US$4/gallon in Homer, it costs US$10 or more in rural villages. Thankfully, farmers' markets are springing up around the state, offering locally made goods and vegetables for a fraction of the price.

OUTDOOR EQUIPMENT Outdoor equipment can be found at reasonable prices in Anchorage, Fairbanks, Juneau and other large towns (see pages 203, 318 and 106).

⚇ ARTS AND ENTERTAINMENT

In addition to the larger cities of Anchorage, Fairbanks and Juneau, some of the smaller towns such as Homer and Ketchikan place an emphasis on the arts, drawing musicians and artists to their communities from outside the state throughout the year. Alaska Council on the Arts (*www.eed.state.ak.us/Aksca*) is responsible for funding and promoting arts throughout the state.

Most towns of any size have a movie theatre and the smaller communities often play films at their local school.

Where native Alaskan cultures still thrive, traditional performances can usually be seen, even participated in. Southeast Alaska is an especially good place to watch dancers perform. Some of the more spirited performances can be found in rural communities seldom visited by cruise ships, such as Metlakatla near Ketchikan. The World Eskimo Olympics (*www.weio.org*) takes place every year in Fairbanks with competitions, dancing and music. Celebration, a biennial festival of the Tlingit, Haida and Tsimshian tribes, takes place in Juneau every even-numbered year and is something to behold.

ACTIVITIES

Alaska is an adventurer's paradise offering hiking, biking, kayaking, rafting, fishing, mountaineering, and wildlife viewing. Guides can be hired in most towns for any of the activities below.

BEAR VIEWING Both brown and black bears are secretive creatures for the most part and wander across such wide areas, they are seldom seen. However, when salmon are swimming upriver to spawn during the summer, bears congregate to feast. This is the best time to see bears up close. Some of the best places to see bears dining on salmon are Katmai National Park, McNeil River State Game Sanctuary, Anan Creek, and Admiralty Island. Denali National Park is also a good place to see bears roaming the tundra. See page 45 for a list of operators.

BIKING While Alaska may not be laced with bike trails like some states, there are many great bike adventures to be had both on the road and on the trail. Anchorage and the Matanuska Valley have a large collection of paved and dirt bike trails, as does Fairbanks. The book *Mountain Bike Anchorage: A Comprehensive Guide to Dirt, Gravel and Paved Bicycle Trails from Eklutna Lake to Girdwood, Alaska* by Rosemary Austin is a great resource for the Anchorage area, as are the local bike shops where you can find trail maps and glean valuable info from shop employees. Also try the **Arctic Bicycle Club** (*www.arcticbike.org*) in Anchorage. They organise groups tours and races around Anchorage. Elsewhere, local knowledge rules and local shops are the best resource for trails. Also try *Mountain Biking Alaska: 49 Trails in the 49th State* written by Richard Larson.

On the road, the opportunities are nearly endless, from riding the Alaska Highway through Canada (see *You Can't Ride a Bike to Alaska. It's an Island!* by Mickey Thomas) to any of the state's adventure road trips (see page 62) such as the Dalton Highway or the McCarthy Road. In fact, virtually all of Alaska's highways are good for cyclists, with little traffic on most stretches, amazing scenery and nearly unlimited camping all the way. For inspiration pick up a copy of *Alaska Bicycle Touring Guide: Including Parts of the Yukon Territory and Northwest Territories* by Pete Praetorius and Alys Culhane.

However, cyclists touring the state should be resourceful and be able to carry everything they need, including extra parts. The distances can be great between towns with nothing but wilderness in between and with the state's notoriously mountainous terrain, there are some serious hills to climb. If you feel like you need a little support, contact **Sockeye Cycle Co** (✆ 766 2869, 877 292 4154 (TF); *www.cyclealaska.com*) with locations in Haines and Skagway. They rent bikes with everything you need for a seven-day unguided bike tour for US$850 per person. They also offer a guided nine-day bike tour and ferry trip through southeast for US$3,225 per person. Bike rentals are US$35 per day. Another option is **Alaska Backcountry Bike Tours** (✆ 866 354 2453 (TF); *www.mountainbikealaska.com*) in Anchorage with two-eight-day trips by mountain bike from US$445–2,695 per person. Bike rentals are US$28/day.

Another wonderful way to see the state by bike is to ride the Alaska Ferry with your bike, cycling at each stop and branching off when desired. Passage for your bike from Bellingham, Washington to Ketchikan on the Alaska Ferry costs just US$38.

FISHING Alaska is a prime fishing destination – one of the best in the world – and anglers come from all around to try and hook some of the largest, feistiest (and tasty) species of fish. Serious anglers usually bring their own equipment, but rods and tackle can also be purchased and sometimes rented in Alaska. When hiring a guide or going on a charter, gear is usually provided. Alaska has some good roadside fishing, but for the best scenery and fishing, nothing beats a trip to the backcountry. This can be done by booking a stay at a remote fishing lodge, by hiring a guide to walk, fly or boat you to the fishing grounds, or by joining a charter boat heading out for halibut or salmon. All these options are expensive, but if fishing is a priority for you, they will be well worth the money. Alaska's fish are plentiful, but not always easy to find. Local knowledge goes a long way.

Halibut Those looking to catch halibut can head to Homer – known as the halibut fishing capital of the world – where an armada of charters boats will vie for your business and guarantee great fishing. For an adventure trip to the end of the world and the home of the world's largest halibut, head to Unalaska in the Aleutian Islands.

Salmon Salmon are one of the state's most prized fish, making great sport and food. King salmon arrive in rivers in May and June and can be found around the state with the biggest found in the Kenai River. In 1987, a 97 pounder was landed there. Another way to land king salmon at any time of the year is to troll for them at sea.

While charters offer king salmon trolling throughout the state, the southeast ports of Ketchikan, Petersburg and Wrangell are some of the best. To catch the other four species of salmon, the Kenai River is a great bet. Seward is famous for its silver salmon and the river fishing and ocean trolling is excellent there in the early fall.

Trout Those seeking trout should not miss Bristol Bay, where a remote lodge can be booked or a guide can be arranged, usually out of Dillingham. The rivers in the Bristol Bay drainage are considered some of the best in the state. Again, the Kenai River is also an excellent choice for trout and a day-long drift trip starting in Cooper Landing should satisfy any trout angler. For the state sport fish records, visit www.sf.adfg.state.ak.us/Trophy/index.cfm/FA/main.record

HIKING Alaska is a hiker's haven with routes to suite everyone. Most urban centers have a network of well-maintained trails while the parks, national forests and refuges across the state offer everything from single-day hikes on pleasant nature trails to multi-week expeditions crossing streams, ice fields, and rugged peaks both on and off trail. The beauty of hiking in Alaska is the variety. If you would prefer not to see a soul for weeks on end, head to the Wrangell-St Elias Range and set out

The following is an explanation of the various levels of difficulty of hiking trails covered in this guide:

EASY Mostly even walking on reasonably well-maintained trails.

MODERATE Could include rough trails with hills and easily navigable obstacles such as small creeks, tree trunks, rocks, etc. Hikers should be moderately fit and coordinated.

DIFFICULT Trails may contain very steep hills with rocks, mud and significant obstacles. Hikers should be fit and coordinated.

through the tundra; if you'd prefer to hike for a day or two on a pleasant trail following a river between soaring peeks and sleep in public-use cabins every night, then drive just south of Anchorage to the Crow Pass or Resurrections Trails; or, if the comfort of a bed and breakfast is more your style then stay Anchorage, Juneau or Fairbanks city centre and walk groomed trails with the local Audubon Society looking for birds before retiring to a café for lunch.

While just about any trip can be arranged on your own, those who would like some logistical support can go to any of the guides or hiking clubs listed below. A guide service will provide all the gear and expertise, all you need to do is keep up.

There are a great many hiking books about Alaska, here are a few: *Hiking Alaska* by Dean Littlepage, *Denali National Park Guide to Hiking, Photography & Camping* by Ike Waits, *Hiking Alaska's Wrangell-St Elias National Park and Preserve* by Greg Fensterman, *50 Hikes In Alaska's Kenai Peninsula* by Taz Tally, *50 Hikes in Alaska's Chugach State Park* by Shane Shepherd and Owen Wozniak, *Best Hikes near Anchorage* by John Tyson, *Outside in the Interior: An Adventure Guide for Central Alaska* by Kyle Joly, *South Central Alaska: A Comprehensive Guide to the Hiking & Canoeing Trails & Public-Use Cabins* by Alan Jubenville, *Best Easy Day Hikes Fairbanks* by Montana Hodges, and *A Recreational Guide to Kachemak Bay State Park and Wilderness Park* by Joshua Duffus.

Hiking clubs and resources

Alaska Alpine Club www.alaskanalpineclub.org
Fairbanks Area Hiking Club www.fairbankshiking.org
Trail Mix www.juneautrails.org

Southeast Alaska Trails www.seatrails.org
Wrangell-St Elias National Park and Preserve www.wrangellsteliaspark.com

Hiking guides

Trek Alaska ↘ 350 3710; www.trekalaska.com. 2- to 9-day treks in the Wrangell-St Elias Mountains for US$475–2,600.
Denali Trekking Co ↘ 733 2566; www.alaskahiking.com. Offers 3- to 7-day trips for all level for US$1,750–2,250.
The Ascending Path ↘ 783 0505; www.theascendingpath.com. Day hikes out of

Anchorage for US$80–120. They also offer mountaineering, ice & rock climbing & glacier hikes.
Alaska Alpine Adventures ↘ 525 2577; www.alaskaalpineadventures.com. Offers hiking trips around the state including multi-sport trips (include rafting, kayaking, biking etc). 4- to 7-day trips cost US$1,500–3,000.

KAYAKING With 44,000 miles of coastline and a rich marine ecosystem, Alaska is a kayakers paradise. In addition to being a pleasurable way to get around, kayaking is a wonderful, unobtrusive way to view terrestrial and marine wildlife alike because it is so quiet. Understandably kayaking is very popular in Alaska and at least one

Practical Information ACTIVITIES

2

guiding service can be found in each major coastal town. Most are high quality and have high standards of safety. Most offer daily trips for about US$150 for a full day trip, or US$100 for a half day. These include lunch and all the gear you will need. While standards are generally very high, some guides are better than others, so be sure to ask for the most experienced guide available. In addition, most outfitters rent kayaks without a guide to experienced paddlers for US$45–65 per day. While this is a good match for those with experience, be sure to understand local wildlife etiquette, the often dramatic tidal fluctuations, ocean currents, and other environmental factors that may not exist at home.

In addition to the thousands of miles of seashore, Alaska has more than three million lakes. The larger of these make excellent canoe or kayak destinations, while chains of smaller lakes can be linked together by river or portage. These are commonly called 'canoe routes' and some of the best are the Honker Divide and Sarkar canoe routes on Prince of Wales Island, the Admiralty Island canoe route, and those in the Kenai National Wildlife Refuge. Boats and guides can be hired locally.

For further information, try: *Paddling Alaska: A Guide to the State's Classic Paddling Trips* by Dan Maclean and *The Alaska River Guide: Canoeing, Kayaking, and Rafting in the Last Frontier* by Karen Jettmar.

Above and Beyond Alaska ⟍ 364 2333; www.beyondak.com. Offers a multitude of trips from mellow one-day paddles around their base in Juneau, to all-out adventures trips in the most remote corners of southeast. Trips range in price from US$100 for a day-trip to US$1,500 or more for longer trips.
Alaska on the Home Shore ⟍ 360 592 2375, 800 287 7063 (TF); www.homeshore.com. Offers trips through southeast Alaska aboard their 62ft *Home Shore*, a former commercial fishing vessel. Kayak excursions are launched from the boat. 8-day trips are US$3,800–4,200pp & include accommodation on the boat, all meals & gear.
Alaska Sea Kayakers ⟍ 472 2534, 877 472 2534 (TF); www.alaskaseakayakers.com. Based out of Whittier, these guys can offer everything from guided day paddles to multi-day expeditions to boat-assisted trips around Prince William Sound.

They also rent gear & other expedition gear.
Anadyr Adventures ⟍ 835 2814; www.anadyradventures.com. Offering guided single- and multi-day trips as well as boat-assisted & lodge-based kayak trips from their base in Valdez.
Kayak Adventures Worldwide ⟍ 224 3960, 406 980 0762 (winter); www.kayakak.com. A top-notch kayak outfitter based out of Seward offering trips around Seward & Prince William Sound including guided, unguided or boat-assisted trips.
Southeast Exposure ⟍ 225 8829; www.southeastexposure.com. Offers a host of excellent trips around Ketchikan & in Misty Fjords National Monument. S6-day trips in the monument are US$1,150.
Ursa Major ⟍ 206 310 2309; www.myursamajor.com. A similar kayaking experience to *Home Shore*, aboard the 65ft *Ursa Major* for US$2,000–5,000pp.

MOUNTAINEERING AND CLIMBING With 14 distinct mountain ranges in the state, Alaska has so many mountains many have been assigned numbers instead of names. Alaska is home to 19 peaks over 14,000 feet and six peaks over 16,000 feet, including Mount Foraker (17,402 ft), Mount Saint Elias (18,009 ft) and, of course, Denali (20,322 ft), the continent's highest mountain. These majestic summits called to mountaineers in centuries past just as they do today with the promise of pain, cold, and hopefully, glory. But summiting cold, lonely peaks is not the only climbing to be done in Alaska. Recently there has been an influx in the popularity of rock climbing and motivated locals around the state have established new areas. While Anchorage has the most developed scene and some good rock, other areas include Homer (*www.shitflyclimbing.com*) and Juneau. The **Ascending Path** (⟍ 783 0505; *www.theascendingpath.com*) offers rock and ice climbing trips near Anchorage for US$130–220, as well as glacier travel and self-rescue clinics for US$250–275. Another great resource for climbing across the state is www.rockclimbing.com.

Literary resources include *High Alaska: A Historical Guide to Denali Mount Foraker and Mount Hunter* by Jonathan Waterman, *To the Top of Denali: Climbing Adventures on North America's Highest Peak* by Bill Sherwonit, *Alaska: A Climbing Guide* by Michael Wood and Colby Coombs, *The SCAR: Southcentral Alaska Rock Climbing* by Kristian Sieling and a new book called *Alaska Rock Climbing Guide* by Kelsey Gray.

Mountaineering guide services

Alaska Mountain Guides ↘ 800 766 3396 (TF); www.alaskamountainguides.com. Located in Haines & offer trips throughout the state, such as the 12-day Mt Bona (16,421ft) trip for US$3,200. They also offer mountaineering clinics all summer.

Alaska Mountaineering School ↘ 1016; www.climbalaska.org. Located in Talkeetna, they specialise in mountaineering clinics which run all summer. They also offer expeditions to a number of

Alaska Range peaks, including the popular 21-day trip up Denali's West Buttress for US$6,000.

Kennicott Wilderness Guides ↘ 554 4444; www.kennicottguides.com. 8-16-day mountaineering trips in the Wrangell-St Elias Range.

NORTHERN LIGHTS The northern lights, or *Aurora borealis*, are undeniably amazing, and for some, seeing them borders on a religious experience. Unfortunately, the best time to see them is during the long, cold nights of winter. While they can sometimes be visible anywhere in Alaska during the winter, they are best viewed in the northern parts of the state. Fairbanks is one of the best places to see them and has worked to promote themselves as a northern lights destination. There is no trick to seeing them, just book a cosy accommodation away from light pollution and scan the night sky until they appear, which is almost every night Fairbanks residents claim.

RAFTING Rafting is huge in Alaska, and with good reason. The state has thousands of rivers – some contain world-class whitewater rapids, while others are calm waterways allowing access to some of the state's most remote and otherwise inaccessible terrain. Rafting remote rivers is one of the best ways to explore the Alaskan backcountry since there is no other way to cover so much ground so quietly and with so much space for gear, the experience is more akin to car camping than backpacking. While the most common guided raft trips are short jaunts down roadside rivers, other, more spectacular trips can be arranged almost anywhere. Some of these include the incredible Alsek River in southeast Alaska, the Yukon River that crosses the state, the Noatak River following the Arctic Circle, and the incredibly remote and beautiful river flowing north from the Brooks Range such as the Hulahula and Canning rivers.

Guided trips are available on most of Alaska's remote rivers, but to do things on your own time, rent a raft, charter a plane and do it yourself.

ABEC's Alaska Adventures ↘ 877 424 8907 (TF); www.abecalaska.com. Offer excellent 10-day trips to many of the state's best remote river for US$3,000–5,500pp.

Alaska Discovery ↘ 888 831 7526 (TF); http://mtsobek.com. Offers a handful of remote trips as well, but also a number of less remote raft trips near Prince William Sound & Anchorage.

Chilkat Guides ↘ 888 292 7789 (TF); www.raftalaska.com. Specialises in trips in southeast

Alaska, but also offers a few trips in the Arctic.

NOVA ↘ 800 746 5753 (TF); www.novalaska.com. Offers 3–5-day trips in the southern part of the state for US$349–2,950 as well as day trips around Anchorage for US$75–450.

Too-loo-uk River Guides ↘ 683 1542; www.akrivers.com. Offer excellent 10-day trips to many of the state's best remote river for US$3,000–5,500pp.

The following is an explanation of the skills needed to tackle various grades of whitewater rapids covered throughout this guide.

CLASS I Small riffles. No river experience needed.

CLASS II Fast moving water with obstacles that are easily avoided. Basic river skills required.

CLASS III Whitewater with obstacles, drops and conflicting currents. Paddlers should be experienced.

CLASS IV Large waves, strong currents, long rapids, and large rocks and hazards. Extensive whitewater experience required.

CLASS V Like Class IV but whitewater is bigger, longer and more intense. Advanced whitewater paddlers only.

CLASS VI Often described as 'nearly impossible' with huge rapids and drops and frequent dangerous obstacles. Expert paddlers only.

Do-it-yourselfers can rent rafts and other gear at:

Alaska Downstream ☎ 868 3704, 800 608 7238 (TF); www.alaskadownstream.com. In Anchorage
Alaska Raft and Kayak ☎ 800 606 5950 (TF); www.alaskaraftandkayak.com.

Blue Moose Rafting Adventures ☎ 460 7758; www.bluemooserafting.com. In Fairbanks.
GoNorth ☎ 474 1041, 866 236 7272 (TF); www.gonorth-alaska.com. Has offices in Anchorage & Fairbanks. Rafts run US$55–100/ day.

WHALE-WATCHING When whales migrate back to Alaska for the summer, they are best seen in the southeast locations of Frederick Sound and Glacier Bay. While these destinations are consistently productive, most of the protected waters of southeast are good places to see whales and every town has charters that will take you out to look for them. Another wonderful place to see whales and other marine mammals is outside Resurrection Bay near Seward. See page 228 for a list of operators.

WILDLIFE VIEWING

Bald eagles The national bird is fairly common in Alaska, but in certain areas, at certain times of the year, bald eagles congregate in large numbers. The Chilkat Bald Eagle Preserve outside Haines, brings in large numbers of bald eagles from October through to February to feed on a late run of salmon. During August, other rivers rich with salmon, like the Kenai River, see dead fish washing downstream, having completed their lifecycle. This is when eagles make their way to the banks and can be seen feeding on these fish. Homer is another place with a large population of eagles, as is Unalaska.

Other birds Alaska is the summer home of millions of migratory birds that flood into the state in the early spring. Stunning in their volume, these flocks are best seen in May and early June in place like the Copper River Delta, the Yukon River Delta, the Stikine River, Cordova and to a lesser degree in most other coastal or water-rich parts of the state. Millions of sea birds also call th state home and are best seen nesting in the spring on sea cliffs in the Pribilof and Aleutian Islands and to a lesser extent in Kachemak Bay, and Prince William Sound.

PHOTOGRAPHY

Few visitors come to Alaska without a camera, and for good reasons – it's gorgeous! Most visitors come with a simple point-and-shoot digital model, and return home with average shots that preserve the memories, but rarely do them justice. Excellent images can be created with some of the newer high-end point-and-shoot cameras like the Canon G10 or Leica D-Lux cameras. However, the best images come from mid-range digital SLRs combined with a wide and telephoto lens and a tripod. An optional, but highly recommended accessory for shooting in Alaska, is a macro lens. These allow for those stunning close-up shots of Alaska's lovely, but often tiny and overlooked wildflowers. (Inside tip: the perfect light for these tiny beauties? A small piece of frosted plastic food wrap (Glad Press 'n' Seal) held in front of the sun creates a studio light effect every time.)

Unlike wildflower photography, shooting wildlife is usually not cheap or easy. To capture traditional close-up wildlife images, the longer and faster (smaller aperture number such as f2.8) the lens, the better. Good quality 200–600mm lenses can run anywhere from US$1,000–10,000 plus (£625–£6,250). To double the magnification of any lens affordably, purchase a teleconverter, which will remove two stops of speed from the lens but increase the focal length by half or more. I have a relatively affordable 70–200mm f2.8 lens with a 2x teleconverter and I couldn't be happier with the results. Since many of Alaska's most sought-after and photogenic animals are also dangerous to approach, a lens of some length is almost always required. Small point-and-shoot cameras can zoom way in, but the image quality dramatically decreases the more you zoom. If going the SLR route, you can afford to spend less on the camera body, but don't skimp on the lenses; professional quality lenses make all the difference.

In addition to Alaska's natural beauty, its people are often very photogenic. Native peoples, especially when dressed traditionally and performing, make wonderful shots. However, be sure to ask permission first.

MEDIA AND COMMUNICATIONS

Alaska is well plugged into the rest of the world, even in rural areas. Internet is common throughout the state as are telephones, but mobile coverage is patchy and public phones are less common than they used to be. In the medium and large towns and cities, national papers are available at book stores, libraries and sometimes grocery stores, while international papers are available only in the larger towns and cities.

TELEPHONES Landline phones, including public phone booths, are common throughout the state with only very small and remote communities relying on satellite phone or radio. Mobile phone reception can be spotty, even around town – and between towns there is seldom any service at all. Be sure to speak to your mobile service provider about using it in Alaska and any roaming charges involved. To keep costs down, you can buy a local SIM card at an **AT&T** (✆ 888 388 3884; www.attalascom.com) store; there are a number around the state. The SIM card, when inserted into your phone, will give you a new US number and allow you to call within the US. Different rate plans include a flat rate of US$0.25/min or US$0.10/min with a US$1 charge each day you use the phone. Monthly plans are also available. Conversely, a 'GoPhone' can be purchased for US$30–100, which includes a phone and SIM card. One of the above plans would still need to be used. Other mobile service providers include **ACS** (✆ 800 808 8083; www.acsalaska.com) and **GCI** (✆ 800 800 4800; www.gci.com). Some small and remote communities like

Unalaska and the Bristol Bay area require registering with the local and very expensive provider.

Perhaps a cheaper, easier, option is to buy a calling card. These can be bought in just about any grocery store in the state in denominations of US$10 and US$20. A US$20 calling card will charge US$0.12/min to call the UK and has 165 minutes of calling time on it.

For directory services dial ↘ 411 (fee) or look in the phone book. For a free directory (businesses only) call ↘ 1 800 411.

Calling Alaska To call Alaska from abroad dial ↘ 00 1 907 then the number.

Calling abroad To call abroad dial 011 + country code + city code then the number. Some common country codes are:

Australia	61	Germany	49	New Zealand	64	UK	44
France	33	Italy	39	Spain	34		

RADIO Radio is also alive and well in Alaska, with many public and commercial radio stations. The Alaska Public Radio Network (APRN) out of Anchorage is made up of 25 member stations and produces some fantastic programs on Alaska life and politics. Because so much of the state is rural and some people still lack phones, many radio stations air messages from one person to another. They also list 'ride lines' for people looking for a ride somewhere. In Homer, these are called the 'Bushlines', in Barrow 'The Tundra Drum', in Galena 'The Yukon Wireless', and in Nome 'The Ptarmigan Telegraph'. Check out KIAK–FM (102.5 MHz) in Fairbanks, KHNS–FM (102.3MHz) in Haines and Skagway, KBBI (890 MHz) in Homer, KRBD–FM (105.3MHz) in Ketchikan, KVOK (560MHz) in Kodiak, KFSK–FM (100.9MHz) in Petersburg, KCAW–FM (104.7 MHz) in Sitka, KCHU (770 MHz) in Valdez, and KSTK–FM (101.7 MHz) in Wrangell.

PRINT

Newspapers While Alaska's largest and most widely circulated newspaper is the *Anchorage Daily News* (*www.adn.com; US$0.75*), most smaller towns have their own local paper, and many are quite good. These cover local events and are a great way to find out what's going on in the community. Local papers (and the Anchorage Daily News) can be purchased in grocery stores around the state. The *Anchorage Press* (*www.anchoragepress.com*) is a free paper that covers the city's cultural beat.

Magazines Alaska has a number of magazines, most of which are too general or too specific. These are available by subscription or in local bookstores and grocery stores. *Alaska Magazine* (*www.alaskamagazine.com*) tries to cover the whole state, but barely scratches the surface and is more of an appetite wetter for those who are planning to visit the state, than a real source of information. *Fish Alaska Magazine* (*www.fishalaskamagazine.com*) has some great articles on sport fishing in the state while *Alaska Business Monthly* (*www.akbizmag.com*) is self explantory.

POST Every town has a post office that can deliver mail locally or internationally. To send a postcard or normal letter internationally costs US$00.98 and takes one to two weeks. International flat-rate envelopes cost US$12.95 and can be stuffed full for the same price (they have to close properly though). These take six to ten days. International medium flat-rate boxes (11in x 8.5in x 5.5in) cost US$41.95 and again can be packed full of stuff. These also take about six to ten days. A large flat-rate box (12in x 12in x 5.5in) is US$53.95. The weight limit for flat rate-boxes is 20lbs. Most shops that stock postcards will also sell postcard stamps, which are cheaper than stamps for letters.

INTERNET Internet access is available in some form almost everywhere in the state. Coffee shops, libraries and hotel lobbies often have free Wi-Fi as do many B&Bs. Some coffee shops can charge between US$5/day or US$5/hr. Internet cafés are less common these days due to the influx of Wi-Fi hotspots.

BUSINESS

Alaska has a booming economy, but it's still almost entirely dependent on dwindling oil supplies. As a result, there is a lot of energy being put into other business to stimulate growth. Tourism is growing fast, but mining, forestry, transportation, and commercial fishing are also growing. For the most part, Alaskans are pro growth and desperately want their state to be as much of a financial hub as other resource rich states. Local and state politics have generally been favourable to growth, sometimes to the detriment of the environment.

Anchorage is Alaska's financial capital, with many state, national, and international businesses headquartered there.

BUYING PROPERTY

With 2.7 million acres of private land in the state (excluding native land), Alaska isn't short of investment opportunities. The best way to find property is to check with the chambers of commerce in your area of interest. Their websites list real estate businesses, all of which will be happy to show local land and houses for sale. Property in Alaska can be amazingly cheap, but, like anywhere, you get what you pay for. A friend once bought a piece of property in the interior for US$500 from a guy in a bar. As expected, the land turned out to be a mosquito-infested bog hundreds of miles from the nearest road or town.

Sadly, Alaska suffers from a curious property phenomenon: during summer, when the weather is at its best, many tourists buy property with a view to retiring there in later life, or using it as a summer home. But when nature refuses to produce good summer weather the following year, they become disenchanted and sell their property or newly built home, but not before pushing up real estate and property taxes prices. Generally, the market stabilises just in time for another perfect summer and the process starts all over again. Generally speaking, however, desirable land is on par with the national average – just over US$282,000 for a home. A three-acre piece of land in Homer can easily cost US$75,000-100,000 or more, depending on the location, view etc, while a remote five-acre plot 25 miles northeast of Homer, on the other hand, might cost just US$5,000. A comfortable house in Anchorage with three bedrooms will, on average, cost between US$175,000 and US$300,000. Access is a big selling point for most property. If you don't need to drive up to your house, land can be had for a song.

For people who want to 'drop out' of society, Alaska still is a great place to do so. Remote land can be purchased relatively cheaply around the state, and because many places are so rich in fish and game animals, one can live quite independently and cheaply. But there are unexpected expenses associated with this lifestyle, unless you plan to go there and never leave. Coastal properties will require a small boat (US$8,000 – 24,000 with motor), as well as some way of making electricity such as a hydroelectric, solar, wind or a gas-powered system. The cost of getting materials into these locations is also very high. Many inland locations can only be reached by snowmobile in the winter or by plane (lake or landing strip required) in the summer. Many remote tracts are so far from any road that a 'driveway' could cost millions, literally. Still, this can be a rewarding lifestyle, and very unique in this urbanised world. The American environmental author Aldo Leopold, said it best: 'there are two spiritual dangers in not owning a farm. One is the danger of supposing that breakfast comes from the grocery store, and the other is that heat comes from the furnace.'

Those serious about trying out the remote lifestyle would do well to choose an area, move to the nearest town, and spread the word that they are looking to rent or just use a trapper cabin for the summer. I know a number of people who have done this for free. They generally do it for one summer then get burned out and return to civilisation skinnier, but also knowing a little more about themselves.

CULTURAL ETIQUETTE

TERRITORY Visitors should avoid land marked with private property signs and where sled dogs are kept. Alaskans can take their private property very seriously and, according to American gun laws, are perfectly within their rights to shoot you if you stray onto their land. Large groups of sled dogs, while often very nice, can also be extremely aggressive. It's especially important to keep children from running into yards containing sled dogs.

GUNS Because guns are so common, alcohol-related gun violence can occur, so stay away from inebriated people at all times. If you hear gunshots in a remote area, consider the fact that it may be hunters. If that doesn't seem to be the case, leave the area.

VISITING A LOCALS' HOME One of the greatest pleasures when travelling is to be invited to the home of a local.

If you do get invited for dinner at someone's house, ask what you should bring. Often a salad or dessert will be requested. But it's also good to bring something extra, like a nice bottle of wine.

TRAVELLING POSITIVELY

Alaska is a big wild place and we all must work to preserve it. This means responsible living and travelling for visitors and residents alike.

American environmental author Aldo Leopold suggested in the 1940s that we should consider including the natural world in our ethical sphere. Quite simply, this means treating all living things with respect. This doesn't mean you shouldn't hunt or fish – Leopold was active in both – it just means you should do it with respect and thoughtfulness. Catching the largest fish and shooting the biggest game seems a universal human tendency, but a smarter course of action is to keep the smaller ones and let the larger 'breeders' go so they can perpetuate the species. This is especially true for halibut fishermen who may have dreams of landing the biggest fish of their lives.

Try also to treat the landscape with respect. While hiking or camping, take your litter with you– don't scatter it along the trails – and try to recycle it on returning to town.

BEACH CLEAN-UPS In addition to living responsibly and sustainably while in Alaska, visitors can pitch in by participating in organised beach clean-ups. Just about every coastal community organises at least one every summer. Different beaches are assigned to different groups who spend the day walking, talking and collecting rubbish. This is also a great way to see wildlife. Wherever you are, call the local chamber of commerce to find out if a clean-up is taking place nearby. If nothing is happening, clean the beach yourself. In addition to helping the community and the natural world, it usually affords an unforgettable day by the sea. Contact the **Center for Alaskan Coastal Studies** (↘ *235 6667; www.akcoastalstudies.org*) for Kenai Peninsula beach clean-ups.

WILDLIFE VOLUNTEERING Those interested in volunteering to participate in wildlife research in some of the state's most remote and beautiful areas can contact Kristen Gilbert (↘ *786 3391;* e *kristen_gilbert@fws.gov; alaska.fws.gov/volunteers.htm*) at the **Fish and Wildlife Service**. To volunteer and help out with wildlife management issues contact **Defenders of Wildlife** (*333 W 4th Av. #302;* ↘ *276 9453; www.defenders.org*) or **Alaska Center for the Environment** (*807 G Street, Ste 100;* ↘ *274 3621; www.akcenter.org*). The **Alaska Islands and Oceans Center** (see page 262) in Homer also accepts volunteers to help with tours and events like the Shorebird Festival.

Part Two

THE GUIDE

3

Juneau

Population: 31,262

Juneau (⊕ 58°21'5"N, 134°30'42"W) has the dubious honour of being the only state capital (besides the island state of Hawaii) not accessible by road – none lead in or out of the city (see box on page 92). Not hindered by this in the least, Juneau has thrived in its isolation. Quite different from the gold mining frontier town of a century ago, visitors generally find Juneau a welcome island of culture in a vast sea of wilderness. The 1,500 square-mile Juneau Ice Field feeds glaciers up and down the coast and manifests itself most notably in Mendenhall Glacier, which sits literally in Juneau residents' backyard. Juneau is the perfect place to put your feet up and enjoy 'big city' luxuries, or to gear up before heading into the wilderness. Nowhere else in Alaska are wilderness and culture so intimately juxtaposed.

Downtown Juneau is a mix of government buildings and historic homes and, just a few miles north, suburbia unfolds in the Mendenhall Valley. With so little road, motorists can drive just 40 miles north and little more than ten miles south of Juneau. Small communities have sprung up along the Glacier Highway, including the town of Douglas across the Gastineau Channel on Douglas Island.

Juneau's economy once relied heavily on gold, then timber, but today these have been replaced by tourism – the city now receives more than 920,000 visitors annually – and government dollars.

HISTORY

The reason for Juneau's existence is the same as so many other towns in Alaska – gold. Responding to a reward offered for the whereabouts of gold, Tlingit Chief Kowee presented Sitka mining engineer, George Pilz, with some very promising samples from the Juneau area. In August 1880, at the request of Pilz, Richard Harris and Joe Juneau, both veteran prospectors, were brought to the mouth of what is now called Gold Creek where they found large amounts of gold. On their second trip, they discovered the source of the gold in the Silver Bow Basin, near Juneau, and immediately staked a 160-acre claim. After their discovery Harris said: 'it was a beautiful sight to see the large pieces of quartz, spangled over with gold'. Within a month, more than 40 prospectors had set up camp in what had become known as Harrisburg, after original prospector Richard Harris. It was the first town founded in the territory after the purchase of Alaska. In 1881, the town was renamed Juneau, in honour of Joe Juneau. In 1906 the capital of the territory of Alaska was moved from Sitka to Juneau due to Sitka's declining economy.

After the initial nuggets had been gathered, the majority of the mining, which was increasingly industrialised, moved away from what is now Juneau city centre and the Alaska Juneau Mine (AJ) sprung up in the hills behind town. It soon became the state's most profitable mine, making US$80 million dollars in total. Interestingly, Juneau city centre was in fact built on enormous quantities of mine tailings dumped into the sea.

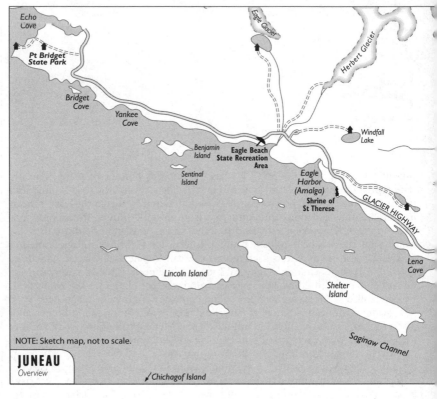

Echo Cove

Pt Bridget
State Park

Eagle Glacier

Herbert Glacier

Bridget
Cove

Yankee
Cove

Windfall
Lake

Benjamin
Island

Eagle Beach
State Recreation
Area

Sentinal
Island

Eagle
Harbor
(Amalga)

Shrine of
St Therese

GLACIER HIGHWAY

Lena
Cove

Lincoln Island

Shelter
Island

NOTE: Sketch map, not to scale.

JUNEAU
Overview

Chichagof Island

Saginaw Channel

Across the Gastineau Channel on Douglas Island, the Treadwell and Ready Bullion Mines went on to produce US$66 million dollars in gold between 1882 and 1917. Though it's hard to believe, the small town of Douglas used to be much larger than Juneau, its two mines employing some 15,000 workers. At the turn of the century the two locales were at odds over which had the honour of being the largest city in Alaska. In 1944, at the onset of World War II, much of Juneau's lucrative mining stopped because gold wasn't considered a valuable addition to the war effort and the mine's many workers were needed as soldiers.

The early 1900s saw a marked increase in timber harvest and the expansion of government. Wood production increased, just as it had during World War I, because the giant straight-grained spruce trees of the southeast were ideal for building war planes. After Alaska became the 49th state in 1959, with Juneau as its new state capital, government work accounted for a great many jobs in the area. To this day, federal, state and local government employ about 50% of the population.

As with just about every city in Alaska, native peoples made full use of the area well before white prospectors began to show up. Juneau was no exception and the Tlingit inhabited the Juneau area for thousands of years. Today, Juneau hosts Celebration (see page 105), a bi-annual gathering of native groups from around Alaska to celebrate their cultural heritage.

GETTING THERE AND AWAY

BY AIR The Juneau International Airport is about nine miles north of the centre; a taxi ride into town costs about US$20. Public buses (see page 92) connect the

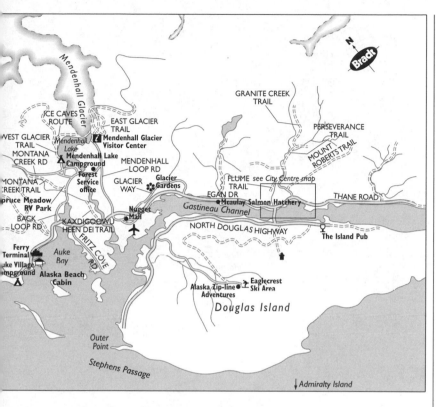

airport to other areas of Juneau, including the centre, for US$1.50, but flights can arrive at odd hours and buses don't run all night. Buses leave the airport Mon–Fri starting at 07.11 and run to the city centre every hour until 17.11. Buses head the opposite direction, toward Auk Bay, starting at 07.46 and depart every hour until 17.45. The airport bus does not operate on weekends. However, the bus does run through the weekend from the nearby Nugget Mall. These start at 09.15 and run every hour through 18.45 to Juneau. To Auk Bay they start at 09.45 and run until 18.15. Many hotels and select B&Bs offer free pick-up, as do some rental-car companies.

✈ **Alaska Airlines** ✆ 800 252 7522;
www.alaskaair.com. Alaska Airlines provides the only jet service to Juneau from Anchorage, 600 miles north, or Seattle, 900 miles south. Flying from many places in the Lower 48 states will generally cost about US$500.
✈ **Air Excursions** 1873 Shell Simmons Dr; ✆ 789 5591; www.airexcursions.com. Charter flights to most of the southeast & flightseeing in the Juneau area.
✈ **Alaska Fly 'n' Fish Charters** (see page 94) Flightseeing, fly-out fishing & charter service.

✈ **Alaska Seaplanes** 1873 Shell Simmons Dr; ✆ 789 3331; www.flyalaskaseaplanes.com. With a fleet of small, sturdy seaplanes, they can drop you & your gear just about anywhere you would like to go.
✈ **Ward Air** 8991 Yandukin Dr; ✆ 789 9150; www.wardair.com. Able to fly you anytime just about anywhere, even Canada.
✈ **Wings of Alaska** 8421 Livingston Way; ✆ 789 0790; www.wingsofalaska.com. Scheduled service to a number of small communities around the northern half of the southeast.

BY FERRY With southeast Alaska's almost countless islands and rugged shoreline, it seems a shame not to arrive in Juneau on a ferry as part of a larger adventure. See

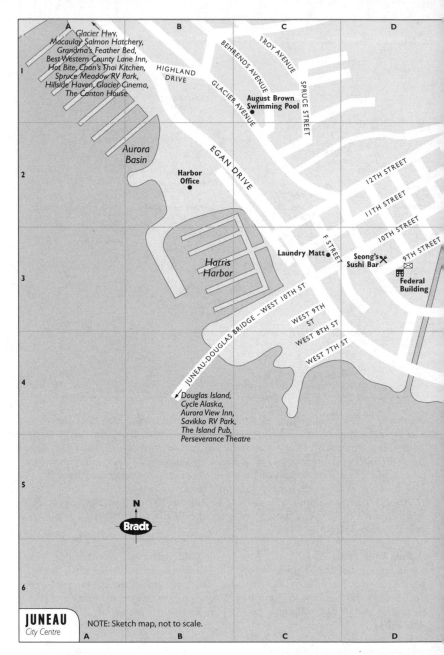

JUNEAU
City Centre

NOTE: Sketch map, not to scale.

Map labels:

Glacier Hwy,
Macaulay Salmon Hatchery,
Grandma's Feather Bed,
Best Western County Lane Inn,
Hot Bite, Chan's Thai Kitchen,
Spruce Meadow RV Park,
Hillside Haven, Glacier Cinema,
The Canton House

HIGHLAND DRIVE

BEHRENDS AVENUE

TROY AVENUE

SPRUCE STREET

GLACIER AVENUE

August Brown
Swimming Pool

EGAN DRIVE

Aurora
Basin

Harbor
Office

12TH STREET

11TH STREET

10TH STREET

9TH STREET

Harris
Harbor

Laundry Matt

F STREET

Seong's
Sushi Bar

Federal
Building

JUNEAU–DOUGLAS BRIDGE – WEST 10TH ST

WEST 9TH ST

WEST 8TH ST

WEST 7TH ST

Douglas Island,
Cycle Alaska,
Aurora View Inn,
Savikko RV Park,
The Island Pub,
Perseverance Theatre

N

Bradt

Getting there, by ferry. Arriving at the **Juneau Ferry Terminal** (℡ *465 3940; http://www.dot.state.ak.us/amhs*), just two miles north of Auke Bay, can be a little bewildering, since it is about 14 miles north of town and has little in the way of services. If it's nice weather, it's an easy enough walk into Auke Bay, where there is a public bus stop. Otherwise, try hitchhiking, or asking around on the ferry for a lift. Once you're there, head for **Dehart's** store (see page 106), where you can hop

E | F | G | H

Flume Trailhead

Silverbow Basin,
Perseverance Trail,
Granite Creek Trail,
Last Chance Mining Museum

Mount Roberts Trailhead

BASIN ROAD

NELSON ST

Rainforest Cottage

Gold Creek

CAPITAL AVENUE

GOLDBELT

CALHOUN

DIXON

7TH STREET

6TH STREET

GOLD STREET

HARRIS STREET

EAST STREET

House of Wickersham

8TH ST

Governor's Mansion

St Nicholas Orthodox Church

Juneau International Hostel

5TH STREET

Theatre in the Rough

Alaska's Capital Inn

Rainbow Foods

State Capitol Building

SEWARD STREET

Juneau-Douglas City Museum

WILLOUGHBY AVENUE

WHITTIER STREET

State Office Building (Juneau Historical Library)

Windfall Fisherman

3RD STREET

2ND STREET

P

Sandpiper Café

Zephyr

Silverbow Inn

Rainy Retreat Books

Foggy Mountain Shop

1ST ST

Valentines Coffee House & Bakery

Alaska State Museum

Centennial Hall

WILLOUGHBY AVENUE

MAIN STREET

Imperial Saloon

FRONT ST

FRANKLIN ST

El Sombrero

EGAN DRIVE

i

Goldbelt (& Zen restaurant)

MARINE WAY

P

City Hall

1, 2
3

Alaskan (& bar)

Juneau Founders

P

The Hanger on the Wharf

4, 5, 6

Paradise Bakery & Café

MARINE WAY

FERRY WAY

Red Dog Saloon

Hard Rock

GASTINEAU AVENUE

Ad Lib

Coast Guard Dock

Seadrome Dock

Miner

i Library

Patsy Ann

P

Raven's Journey

Alaska Steam Ship Dock

USS Juneau Memorial

FRANKLIN STREET

Tracy's King Crab Shack

Archie Van Winkle Memorial

Cruise Ship Terminal

i

Juneau Community Sundial

Mount Roberts Tramway

Twisted Fish

Fisherman's Memorial

Intermediate Vessel Float

THANE ROAD

AJ Dock

South Franklin Street Dock

Gastineau Guiding, Thane Ore House

E | F | G | H

KEY TO NUMBERED SITES
1 20th Century Theatre
2 Hearthside Books
3 Annie Kaill's Fine Art Studio
4 Taku Glacier Lodge
5 Wings Airways
6 Pel'meni restaurant

on the public bus (*departs: every half hour,* ⊕ *06.50–23.22 Mon–Sat &* *09.06–18.20 Sun; tickets: US$1.50*). Route 3 follows the Glacier Highway, route 4 follows Back Loop Road through the suburbs and near the Mendenhall Glacier. Or grab a taxi for US$30 or more to town.

In 2004, Juneau was blessed with the new ultra-fast, luxury catamaran, the 235ft MV *Fairweather*. A trip to Sitka costs about US$50 (US$100 for a car) and takes

Many Alaskans find their isolated, wilderness bound, yet oddly cosmopolitan capital to be the perfect symbol for their state. Others – primarily those not living in Juneau – find the capital and all its political goings-on inaccessible and out of their reach or influence, a decidedly undemocratic idea. Short of flying or taking the ferry to Juneau, many voters are not able to participate in government to the degree they would like. And with the reputations of some Alaskan politicians having been tarnished by corruption, there is a sense among many Alaskans that their politicians need a watchful eye turned their direction at all times.

Alaskans have attempted to move the capital numerous times since statehood. None of the attempts worked, but not for lack of impassioned or downright crazy arguments – or even votes. Capital move opponents cite the city's fantastic website that meticulously chronicles the government's every vote and debate via TV and internet coverage. Alaskans can even testify live at any of the 22 offices around Alaska on events taking place in the capital. But the drawbacks of a roadless capital are too obvious for many to ignore, and a leading solution has been a proposed road connecting Juneau to the outside world. However, several obstacles stand in the way, including the immense cost of negotiating mountains and cleaning up the inevitable avalanches and 16 miles of designated Wilderness Area in Berner's Bay. Governor Frank Murkowski attempted to initiate a 65-mile road and fast ferry combo along this route, but the project was shelved in 2006, when Sarah Palin took the governor's office. Residents – who are largely opposed to the road – breathed a sigh of relief.

Since statehood, Alaskan voters have been presented with no less than ten ballots proposing a move of the capital to the Anchorage area, where most Alaskans live. After defeating propositions in 1960 and 1962, voters finally approved the idea in 1974. In 1976, a site was selected in Willow, near Anchorage but when the obscene price tag of US$966 million was announced, voters scoffed and refused to fund it. In 1982, a proposal for the same move inexplicably carried a price tag of US$2.8 billion and in 1994 voters predictably rejected it. In 2002, voters refused yet another plan, this time to move the capital to Wasilla, also near Anchorage. Whether because of tradition, indecision, or just because it's a great place for a capital, Juneau will very likely remain the political heart of Alaska for years to come.

only four hours. The ferry runs to Sitka five days a week leaving Juneau at 08.00 and arriving at 12.30. The fare is US$45.

GETTING AROUND

Like most places in Alaska, renting a car is the best option to really take advantage of everything the area has to offer. However, thanks to a decent public transport system and a compact downtown, with a little walking one can see quite a bit of Juneau on the cheap. Remember, Juneau is in a rainforest; it rains, and often! If you plan to walk or ride a bike, be prepared to spend some time in the rain.

BY BUS

Capitol Transit (↘ 789 6901; www.Juneau.org/capitoltransit) Buses run from Juneau city centre to Auke Bay via the Mendenhall Valley then back to the city centre. At US$1.50 for a one-way ticket anywhere, the price can't be beaten. A one-month pass can be purchased at the **Treasurer's Office** (155 S Seward St; ↘ 586 5261; ⊕ 08.00–16.30 Mon–Fri), the **Mendenhall Valley Public Library** [90–1 G5] (see page 108), **Fred Meyers Department Store** (see page 106), or **A&P Market** (see page 106) for US$36/12 adult/child and allows unlimited rides anywhere for the month. Schedules can be found at all the tourist information stations around town. Visit http://www.juneau.org/pubworks/captrans/map/index.php for a timetable.

BY CAR For getting around Juneau, renting a car can be handy as there are about 200 miles of roads – more than any other city in the southeast. Be sure to reserve one well ahead as they can go fast mid-summer. Cars generally cost US$70–110 per day.

Car rental companies Inside Juneau International Airport you will find a slew of car rental companies, all of them fairly similar.

🚗 **Avis** ✆ 789 9450; www.avis.com; ⏲ 06.30–22.00 Mon–Sun.

🚗 **Budget** ✆ 790 1086; www.budget.com; ⏲ 06.00–22.00 Mon–Sun. Offers a key drop box at the ferry terminal so you can leave on the ferry & don't have to worry about returning your car.

🚗 **Hertz** ✆ 789 9494; www.hertz.com; ⏲ 06.00–22.00 Mon–Sun.

🚗 **National** ✆ 789 9814; www.nationalcar.com; ⏲ 06.00–22.00 Mon–Sun.

🚗 **Rent-a-Wreck** 2450 Industrial Blvd # C; ✆ 789 4111; www.rent-a-wreck.com; ⏲ 06.00–18.00 Mon–Sun. Located within a few blocks of the airport terminal. Good deals on less-than-new cars. Check cars carefully for damage.

BY TAXI Taxi fares around Juneau rarely exceed US$30. For example, a trip from the ferry to the centre is about US$30–32. If you meet a friendly and knowledgeable driver ask him/her if they're willing to use the car for tours as well. Many of the local taxi companies offer this as a service, but finding a good driver is often pot luck. Tour rates generally run US$50–60 for as many people as can fit in the taxi, sometimes seven or more.

🚗 **Capitol Cab** ✆ 586 2772.

🚗 **EverGreen Taxi** ✆ 586 2121; www.evergreentaxi.com. Tours around Juneau for US$55 for up to 7 people.

🚗 **Juneau Limousine Service** 4269 Marion Dr; ✆ 463 5466; www.juneaulimousine.com. Limo, van tours & transportation.

BY BIKE Renting a bike can be an affordable way to see more of Juneau.

🚲 **Cycle Alaska** 3172 Pioneer Av; ✆ 321 2453; www.cycleak.com. Just across the bridge on Douglas Island, they offer bike tours & rentals. Owned by a friendly Kiwi expat, they offer some fun tours, inc Glacier View Bike & Brew for US$94pp & Mountain

Zip & Bike for US$225pp. Rentals are US$25 for 4hrs, US$35 for 8hrs & US$50 buys you 24hrs.

🚲 **Driftwood Lodge Motel** 435 W Willoughby Av; ✆ 586 2280; www.driftwoodalaska.com. Rent bikes here for US$15 for 6hrs or US$25 for the whole day.

TOURIST INFORMATION

Juneau has a number of small tourist information kiosks around town, but the main office is in Centennial Hall (see below). Others are located at the airport, the Auke Bay ferry terminal, the Marine Park (*downtown on Marine Way across from the Goldbelt Hotel*) and in the cruise-ship terminal on South Franklin Street.

🛈 **Centennial Hall** [90–1 F4] 101 Egan Dr; ✆ 586 2201; www.traveljuneau.com; ⏲ 08.30–17.00 Mon–Fri, 09.00–17.00 Sat–Sun. Main tourist office. Has a public bathroom, a ferry information desk, displays & dioramas & US Forest Service information.

🛈 **City Parks & Recreation** 155 S Seward St Room #218; ✆ 586 5226, hotline 907 586 0428; www.juneau.org/parkrec; ⏲ 08.00–16.30 Mon–Fri. Their office doesn't cater specifically for the public, but they welcome visitors & are knowledgeable about hiking & other outdoor opportunities.

Forest Service 8510 Mendenhall Loop Rd; ☎ 586 8800; www.fs.fed.us/r10/tongass/districts/juneau/ jrd.shtml; ⊕ 08.00–17.00 Mon–Fri. For those wanting to branch out beyond downtown & do some hiking or camping, this place is a must.

LOCAL TOURS AND ACTIVITIES

You will never be without something to do in Juneau. Tours abound, from extreme zip-line courses to the more sedate mine and history tours. Be prepared to spend some money, but also be prepared for the highest quality and best service around. The intense competition for tourist dollars has weeded out most of the low quality businesses. You can book tours directly through the company, at one of the visitor information offices (see page 93), or from aboard your cruise ship.

GENERAL

AJ Mine/Gastineau Tour ☎ 463 5017; adult/child US$49/24.50. A tour for visitors interested in Juneau's historical cornerstone, hard-rock gold mining. Inc a 3hr bus ride & mine tour. Pan for gold on the way home.

Alaskan Brewing Company 5429 Shuane St; ☎ 780 5866; www.alaskanbeer.com; ⊕ 13.00–19.00 daily; free. Few will want to miss the internationally acclaimed brewery tour featuring free beer, history & information on the unique challenges facing beermakers in Alaska. Tours every ½hr.

Chez Alaska Cooking School 2092 Jordan Av #585; ☎ 790 2439 or 957 0327; www.chezalaska.com; adult US$25. A new business aimed at teaching visitors about the finer points of Alaskan cooking. Watch the hilarious head chef Derrick prepare meals in a food TV-channel-like set. Demonstration classes are held 5 times a day. Hands-on classes are held less frequently, cost US$99pp & are fantastic for those who want to really learn to cook the bounty of Alaska's waters.

Glacier Gardens 7600 Glacier Hwy; ☎ 790 3377; www.glaciergardens.com; ⊕ 09.00–18.00; adult/child US$21.95/15.95. Garden & rainforest tours in a motorised cart. This tour is ideal for older visitors who want to get out into the rainforest but are not able to hike. These gardens are famous for upside down trees (with roots in the air) covered in foliage.

Juneau Trolley Car Company 245 Marine Way # 4; ☎ 586 7433; www.juneautrolley.com; adult/child US$19/9. Bus tours downtown & the Mendenhall Glacier with narrated Juneau history.

Macaulay Salmon Hatchery 2697 Channel Dr; ☎ 463 4810; www.dipac.net/Macaulay_hatchery.html; ⊕ 10.00–17.00 daily; adult/child US$3.25/1.75. Compared to some of the southeast's smaller, more casual, salmon hatcheries, the Macaulay Hatchery is quite the tourist trap. During May & June, see immature salmon in outdoor pools before their release into the wild. From July to September, you may see the salmon returning to the hatchery to be 'milked' for their eggs & sperm. Inside is a large aquarium & displays explaining everything anyone would ever want to know about salmon.

Mt Roberts Tramway [90–1 H5] 490 S Franklin St; ☎ 463 3412; www.goldbelttours.com/travel/day_trips/juneau/tram.html; ⊕ 08.00–21.00 Mon–Fri, 09.00–21.00 Sat–Sun; adult/child US$24/13. Head up Mt Roberts (the large mountain behind downtown Juneau) via the tramway for some of the best views in town. Facilities at the top inc an auditorium that shows a decent movie about Tlingit culture, gift shop, nature centre & an expensive restaurant. Fit locals hike the mountain via the Mt Roberts Trail (see page 100) & get the same views others paid US$24 for. Buy a US$5 beer from the restaurant & the receipt will get you a free ride down the mountain in the tram.

SCENIC FLIGHTS Flightseeing can seem expensive at first glance, but seeing Alaska from the air is one of those things that must be experienced at least once. However, these flights can be bumpy, so if you are prone to air sickness take medication beforehand, choose a short flight (half an hour or less) or ask for a trip that may be less bumpy than the rest.

Alaska Fly 'n' Fish Charters 9604 Kelly Court; ☎ 790 2120; www.alaskabyair.com. Flightseeing & fly-out fishing.

Taku Glacier Lodge [90–1 G4] 2 Marine Way; ☎ 907 586 6275, www.takuglacierlodge.com;

adult/child US$225/185. A fantastic trip only slightly diminished by their 'get you in & get you out' mentality. However, few guests complain after a ¹/₂hr scenic flight over Taku Glacier in a small plane, 2hrs at the remote & historic 1923 lodge & a salmon bake featuring local fresh salmon. Many Juneau locals go on this trip despite the price. The

lodge caters only to day-trippers & is not open for overnight stays.

Wings Airways [90–1 G4] 2 Marine Way Ste 175; ↘ 586 6275; www.wingsairways.com. Operated by the Taku Lodge. Glacier flightseeing & Taku Glacier lodge flight & dine trips. A larger company with newer planes & pilots.

WILDLIFE As with just about every town in Alaska, Juneau has a bewildering variety of wildlife-watching options. To see eagles, don't take a tour, just drive to **Auke Bay** and scan the flats as you drive past the **Mendenhall River**; both sites are often teeming with them, especially when the salmon are running. During the early spring (April–May), the 3,800 acre **Mendenhall Wetlands State Game Refuge** near the airport can be a good place to see migratory shore birds. For whales and other marine life, board one of the many tour boats leaving from Auke Bay. For bears, secure a permit or a guide to Pack Creek and fly or boat in for a few days of living with the bears (see page 98).

Dolphin Jet Boat Tours 9571 Meadow Lane; ↘ 463 3422. www.dolphintours.com; adult/child US$109/89. Fast, covered boats zip you out to see humpback whales & other marine life. A 3hr tour.

Harv & Marv's Outback Alaska ↘ 209 7288; www.harvandmarvs.com; adult/child US$149. One of the smaller, more personal wildlife-viewing options.

High Time Charters (see page 98) A smaller whale-watching outfit with tailored itineraries.

National Audubon Society www.juneau–audubon–society.org. Run free bird walks around Juneau.

Orca Enterprises 495 S Franklin St; ↘ 789 6801; www.alaskawhalewatching.com. A 3¹/₂hr trip around Admiralty Island. Captain Larry is active in whale conservation & research & is very knowledgeable.

Bear-viewing trips If bears are more your cup of tea, Pack Creek on Admiralty Island (*www.fs.fed.us/r10/tongass/districts/admiralty/packcreek/gethere.shtml*) is where you want to be. Since it's a remote location full of bears, most visitors choose to go with a guide: you can try the recommended ones listed below or visit the website above for a full list of guides and flight services.

Alaska Fly 'n' Fish Charters Offer a 3hr tour for US$425pp. The price inc the US$50 sanctuary permit.

Discover Alaska ↘ 888 831 7526; www.mtsobek.com. Inc Pack Creek in many of their multi-day trips & offers a 3-day Pack Creek-specific trip for diehard bear watchers. No local office.

It is possible to visit the island without a guide, indeed it works out cheaper and rangers are almost always on hand to answer questions, but I'd only recommend it for bear-savvy self-sufficient travellers. To arrange unguided charter services contact **Alaska Seaplanes** (see page 89) or **Ward Air** (see page 89) or, for a serious adventure, travel from Juneau via water taxi and kayak (see page 98).

Pack Creek is managed jointly by the Alaska Department of Fish and Game and the US Forest Service and requires a permit to visit. If you go with a guide, the permit and most of the gear will be provided, but if you visit independently, you'll need to adhere to the following sanctuary rules and navigate the rather complex permit system:

- Adult/child/senior permits cost US$50/25/25 during peak season (5 July–25 August). Adult/child/senior permits cost US$20/10/10 during the shoulder seasons (1 June–4 July & 26 August–10 September).
- Visitors are only allowed in the sanctuary between 09.00–21.00 daily.

- During peak times one must secure permits months in advance.
- Permits are restricted to just 24 per day during peak season, four of which are held for late arrivals.
- To ensure a permit, visit the Juneau Ranger District (see page 94) or download the application form (*www.fs.fed.us/r10/tongass/districts/admiralty/packcreek/permit.shtml*).
- Apply on or near 20 February; the earliest possible date you can apply for the following summer.
- Camping is not allowed in the sanctuary, but is allowed on nearby Windfall Island and in Windfall Harbour (no fresh water on Windfall Island).

GLACIER VIEWING Great glacier viewing comes in many forms in Juneau: trails lead to the Mendenhall Glacier allowing up-close-and-personal encounters with the ancient ice; flight services will fly you over and sometimes drop you on a glacier; and boat cruises can take you into berg-strewn fjords right up to a calving glacier (ice falling off a glacier's face). The more adventurous and self-sufficient, can rent kayaks and explore the rugged glacier-encrusted stretch of land just south and north of Juneau.

Mendenhall Lake, right in Juneau, is a great and accessible, if not totally secluded, place to see a glacier from the water. Guides are not allowed in the lake to prevent too many boats in the lake, so rent a boat from a local outfitter and go exploring. But be careful of falling ice.

Above & Beyond Alaska Rents kayaks for half-day paddles to Mendenhall Glacier for US$99pp.

Adventure Bound Alaska 215 Ferry Way; ☏ 463 2509; www.adventureboundalaska.com; adult/child US$140/90. More personal tours of Tracy Arm, an amazing fjord south of town.

MENDENHALL GLACIER

Mendenhall Glacier flows from the 1,500-square-mile Juneau Ice Field and spills into Mendenhall Lake. The glacier is amazingly accessible and has an informative visitor centre nearby. A warming climate has caused the glacier to retreat since the 1700s, and today as much as 600ft a year is lost. At its greatest length, the glacier reached more then 2.5 miles down the Mendenhall Valley from where it is today. Most Mendenhall Valley residents now live where a mountain of ice rested just a few hundred years ago.

The **Mendenhall Glacier Visitor Center** (*At the head of Glacier Spur Rd;* ☏ *907 789 6640; www.fs.fed.us/r10/tongass;* ⏰ *08.00–19.30 Mon–Sun; adult US$3*) is usually clogged with visitors. If you can penetrate the writhing throngs, ask an attendant to see the short time-lapse video of the glacier retreating. One viewing is enough to make you want to sell your car and get a bike.

Outside, a new boardwalk system is a great place to see bear, which seem to be surprisingly common. The steep rocky cliffs on either side of the glacier are also excellent places to see mountain goats.

Afterwards, search out the West or East Glacier Trail (see page 99). Another, less time-consuming approach is to walk past the visitor centre towards the glacier and out onto the sand flats. Follow any one of the informal trails to the waterfall. This spot is easy to access and the crowds are limited. The thundering waterfall and the looming glacier really make you feel small. Check out the Mendenhall Glacier 'cam' (*www.fs.fed.us/r10/tongass/districts/mendenhall/webcam.html*).

GETTING THERE You can drive, or take a taxi, to the glacier but should you choose to take the public bus, be warned you will have to cover the last 1.5 miles on foot.

Goldbelt Tours 76 Egan Dr; ☏ 586 8687; www.goldbelttours.com. Glacier-viewing cruises to Tracy Arm for US$139pp, the stunning Ford Terror Wilderness Area for US$139pp, & ferry service to Gustavus where most Glacier Bay adventures begin for US$69pp.

HIKING AND ADVENTURE TOURS

Alaska Canopy Adventures ☏ 523 2920; www.alaskacanopy.com; ⏰ 09.00–17.00 daily; adult US$165. No admission to children under 12. Located near the Treadwell Gold Mine, they incorporate its history into their tour. Cruise across the Gastineau Channel to the camp in a powerboat, then get outfitted before being transported uphill in an off-road vehicle. One of the last zips is over the glory hole, 180ft deep.

Alaska Zip Line Adventures ☏ 321 0947; www.alaskazip.com; ⏰ 08.00–18.00; adult/child US$138/99. Located at **Eaglecrest Ski Resort** (*3000 Fish Creek Rd;* ☏ *790 2000; www.juneau.org/eaglecrest*) this tour is a quieter, less motorised & a more nature-centric zip-line experience in comparison to the competition. Occasionally they offer zip-line tours incorporating wine & food at each stop! The business is run by a young couple who are passionate about nature, adventure & good food.

CRUISE, KAYAK AND CANOE

Above & Beyond Alaska Auke Bay harbour parking lot; ☏ 789 6886; www.beyondak.com; ⏰ 09.00–18.00 daily. Owned & operated by a young local couple who are a lot of fun & very knowledgeable. Hike & ice climb on the Mendenhall Glacier for US$189pp or head out on a day kayak trip for US$100–200pp, depending on the trip theme. Some of these include the Tongass Wildlife Paddle, Coastal Kayak Fishing & the Ocean to Ice Adventure. Overnight trips are also available for US$400pp all the way up to US$1,600pp for trips to Pack Creek on Admiralty Island. Rent kayaks for a self-guided paddle in Mendenhall Lake for US$99pp.

Alaska Discovery (see page 45) Not an Alaskan-owned company, but it's been around for more than 30 years & offers some excellent high-end adventure trips around Alaska.

Juneau Sportfishing & Sightseeing (see page 98) Bus tours of the city & Mendenhall Glacier.

Mighty Great Trips ☏ 789 5460; www.mightygreattrips.com. These folks offer a multitude of trips in southeast Alaska inc rafting trips down the Mendenhall River & glacier tours.

City Parks & Recreation (see page 93) Hosts 2 free hikes a week all year round. Volunteers lead these hikes, which can take place anywhere in the Juneau area & cover any theme the volunteer chooses. Find out about the following day's hike by calling the hotline or checking the website around noon the day before. Hikes take place Wed & Sat at 09.30.

Gastineau Guiding 1330 Eastaugh Way; ☏ 586 8231; www.stepintoalaska.com. Guided hikes to suit anyone, inc glacier hikes, wildlife cruises & photo safaris.

Northstar Trekking ☏ 790 4530; www.northstartrekking.com, ⏰ 09.00–17.00 daily. Offers 1-, 2- & 3-hr glacier treks for US$339/379/479. Fly in via helicopter & learn glacier trekking & ice climbing techniques.

Alaska on the Home Shore ☏ 800 287 7063, www.homeshore.com. Unique & high-end multi-day kayak trips. Trips are centred around the MV *Home Shore*, a 62ft wooden boat built in 1944 for commercial fishing. Travelling by boat allows kayakers to access some of the southeast's most remote & beautiful areas.

Alaska Travel Adventures ☏ 789 0052, 800 323 5757 (TF); www.bestofalaskatravel.com. Kayak & raft trips around Juneau & in Mendenhall Lake & River.

Juneau Steamboat Company 3328 Fritz Cove Rd; ☏ 789 0172; www.juneausteamboat.com; adult/child US$40/35. Under 5s ride free. Juneau's best history tour. If you're looking for scenery & wildlife, go with someone else.

FISHING Though Juneau is not a major fishing destination, there are still fish to be caught. Charter boats are the standard way to go and Juneau has no shortage of them. The Juneau area has all five species of salmon, but also halibut, cutthroat trout, rainbow trout, dolly varden (sea-running trout), and steelhead. Anglers should pick up the Juneau Sportfishing Guide at the Department of Fish and Game.

Admiralty Island is a wild place, filled with lakes, inlets, bays and rivers. In short, a boaters' paradise. For those looking to incorporate the beary location of Pack Creek into a larger Admiralty Island trip, rent a kayak and have a water taxi drop you just a few miles south of Juneau in Oliver Inlet on Admiralty Island. Connecting Oliver Inlet and Seymour Canal (where Pack Creek is located), you will find a strange manual railway called the Oliver Inlet Tram. You can use this one-mile tram to haul your kayak and gear with minimal effort to the head of Seymour Canal, then paddle south 12 miles or so to Pack Creek. Do not arrive in Seymour Cove at low tide or you will be faced with miles of mud rather than water! For more information visit: www.fs.fed.us/r10/tongass/districts/admiralty/canoeroute.shtml.

Once on the island, countless kayaking opportunities exist. A favourite, but not heavily-used route, is to cross the island coast to coast connecting seven mountain lakes with short portages (the moving of a boat across land), often on boardwalks in the heart of Admiralty Island's Kootznoowoo Wilderness. The route connects the small town of Angoon on the east side of the island to Seymour Canal on the west side through 32 miles of old growth rainforest. The normal route has seven portages, the longest is three miles. Four Forest Service cabins are available to rent along the route and reservations are required. Make these far in advance to be on the safe side.

Call the Juneau Ranger District office for more info (see page 94). Be sure to get an Admiralty Island boaters' map and if visiting Pack Creek to see bears, be sure to get a permit. Find more information at: www.fs.fed.us/r10/tongass/districts/admiralty/canoeroute.shtml.

Everyone must have a fishing licence and for those pursuing king salmon, a special stamp is needed. For information on licences and bag limits, visit the **Alaska Department of Fish and Game** (*1255 W 8th St;* ❧ *465 4100; www.adfg.state.ak.us*).

Bear Creek Outfitters ❧ 789 3914; www.juneauflyfishing.com. Offers half-day & full-day fly-out, fishing trips.

High Time Charters ❧ 723 2420; www.hitime.com. A smaller outfit, specialising in both fishing & sightseeing/whale watching. This is one of the few such businesses owned & skippered by a woman. Toni is very friendly & knowledgeable & guarantees to find the fish.

Juneau Flyfishing Goods 175 S Franklin St; ❧ 586 3754; www.juneauflyfishinggoods.com;

⏰ 10.00–17.00 Mon–Fri, 09.00–18.00 Sat–Sun. This is the best fly fishing shop in town & they can book you on just about any fishing trip you may want to take.

Juneau Sportfishing & Sightseeing ❧ 586 1887; www.juneausportfishing.com; ⏰ 07.00–19.00 daily. Sport fishing for halibut & salmon.

Sea Runner Guide Service ❧ 586 3754, www.sea-runner.com. Boat or flight trips to Juneau's back country. Book at Juneau Flyfishing Goods (see page 93).

HIKING AND RECREATION Locals take their hiking seriously. There are 260 miles of hiking trails – in comparison to just 200 miles of road – meandering through 1,352 square miles of wilderness. Juneau does get rain, so if you planned a hike and it turns out to be raining, dress warm and dry and head out anyway. You and the locals will be the only ones on the trails.

Keen hikers should buy the big, thick, waterproof *Juneau Area Trails Guide* map. They can usually be obtained at the visitor centre (see page 75) and at Juneau Park and Recreation Department (see page 93). Other great sources of trail information include the website of the luxury bed and breakfast, Pearson's Pond, the locally published book *90 Short Walks Around Juneau* and the website www.juneautrails.org.

The Juneau-Douglas City Museum (see page 109) has a wonderful walking tour map (free with admission) of Juneau's historic city centre and lists historic sites, totem poles, public art and other points of interest. Also, be sure to join one of the National Audubon Society (see page 95) bird walks. Other great resources for hiking trails include: www.seatrails.org and www.juneautrails.org.

Below is a list of favourite trails. Times listed are for one-way hikes. See box on page 75 for an explanation of hiking grades. See map on pages 88–9 for trailheads.

Flume Trail [90–1 G1] (*Grade: easy; time: 15mins*) The Flume Trail follows an old water flume behind central Juneau. At 3,250ft, it's one of the longest boardwalks in the country. When the trail ends, you will find yourself well up Basin Road, which ends in more trail heads including the Perseverance Trail and the Last Chance Mining Museum. You can walk back to downtown in about 20 minutes by following Basin Road south. The easiest way to find the trail is from the other end, at Basin Road. To find this trailhead from the city centre, head northwest (uphill) on Seward Street, North Franklin Street or Gold Street. Turn northeast (right) on 5th or 6th. Turn left (uphill) again on Harris Street. This flows into Basin Road, which bends around and eventually turns into a long, windy wooden bridge. Just before the Gold Creek Bridge look for the trailhead on the left across the creek. Download an online brochure at: www.aelp.com/Acrobatforms/flume%20trail%20brochure.pdf.

West Glacier Trail (*Grade: moderate; time: 4–6hrs, +6–8hrs inc Mt McGinnis*) On a clear day, this is the trail for Mendenhall Glacier views. From Juneau city centre, take Egan Drive to the intersection with Mendenhall Loop Road. Turn right and follow it for 2.2 miles. Turn left on Back Loop Road for about 1.4 miles, then turn right onto Montana Creek Road. After a third of a mile, turn right onto Skater's Cabin Road. Follow this road to the end and park in the lot. The trail follows the lake and heads off toward the glacier. The first mile is very well worn, but the trail quickly begins to climb. If you have all day, continue along this trail, which will get steeper and progressively less well marked, but gives good glacier views. The trail eventually steers away from the glacier and heads up the steep and gnarly McGinnis Mountain (4,228ft).

Ice Caves Route (*Grade: easy/moderate; time: 1hr*) A better alternative to this exhausting West Glacier Trail is the Ice Caves Route which is unmarked and used mainly by locals. This is the best trail for getting up close and personal with Mendenhall Glacier, apart from splashing out on a helicopter ride. Even though this moderate trail is not formally marked, it's easy to follow and provides the quickest way straight to the ice. For the ice-caves route, branch off the West Glacier Trail at the first viewpoint (covered bench, trail on left). Follow the narrow trail downhill to the lake, then head up and over the large rock dome. There is some steep rock to climb but those with even moderate co-ordination and confidence should be able to get up and down. The glacier reveals itself shortly after mounting the dome. Touch and contemplate the ice before it's gone.

East Glacier Trail (*Grade: moderate; time: 2–3hrs*) Climb the stairs up the hill above the Mendenhall Glacier visitor centre to gain the trailhead. This trail is well maintained and provides great views.

Montana Creek (*Grade: moderate; time: 3–4hrs*) A pleasant trail with plenty of opportunity to see bears during salmon season and/or fish for trout until fall. Find the trail about one mile southwest of the Montana Creek Bridge on Mendenhall Loop Road.

Kaxdigoowu Heen Dei Trail (*Grade: easy; time: variable*) Start at Brotherhood Park where the Brotherhood Bridge crosses the Mendenhall River at mile 10 of the Glacier Highway. There are nice views of the glacier and it's a good spot for fishing in season. Very easy walking on flat ground and decent bird viewing.

Perseverance/Granite Creek Trail (*Grade: moderate; time: 3–4hrs*) A spectacular trail system providing amazing views, lakes, and flowers. Find the trailhead by following the directions to the Flume Trail off Basin Road behind Juneau. From there, simply continue into Silverbow Basin where the Silverbow Basin Gold Mine used to be. The Perseverance Trail used to be used by miners and today provides a moderate and scenic hike. Mount Juneau (3,576ft) is accessible from this trail by taking the marked branch in the road at Ebner Falls. The Mt Juneau Trail is fantastic but difficult, steep and seldom used. The Granite Creek Trail is also accessed here, by taking the marked cutoff about one mile past Ebner Falls.

Mt Roberts Trail [90–1 G1] (*Grade: moderate; time: 2–4hrs*) One of the most popular hikes around is the Mt Roberts Trail from the top of the **Mt Roberts Tram** (see page 94). Ride the tram to its end then intercept the trail and head uphill toward Gastineau Peak (3,666ft), Gold Ridge Peak and Mt Roberts Peak (3,810ft). The tundra provides endless hiking opportunities if you want to explore off-trail. Tough guys can hike the whole thing from Juneau, but bear in mind it's 3,819 vertical feet and 4.5 miles. The tram dock and restaurant are at 1,760ft. If you do hike up, buy a US$5 beer and the receipt will buy you a ride down on the tram. The trail starts on Basin Road just beyond the bridge.

Point Bridget State Park Point Bridget State Park at mile 40 of the Glacier Highway, is a lovely secluded park on a peninsula with a network of trails. Camping and cabins are also available. For more information, visit www.dnr.state.ak.us/parks/units/ptbridg1.htm.

 WHERE TO STAY

Juneau offers a wide variety of places to stay, from luxury B&Bs and hotels to simple hostels or camping. Staying in the city centre doesn't tend to cost any more than staying further out and it's always a bonus to be within walking distance of restaurants, museums and activities. However, if you have a car, parking in the city centre can be a real problem.

Visit www.traveljuneau.com for a full list of Juneau accommodations, sorted by type and location.

HOTELS

Luxury Since no true luxury hotel exists in Juneau look to the Alaska Capitol Inn and Pearson's Pond B&B.

Mid-range

⌂ **Grandma's Feather Bed Best Western** [90–1 A1] (14 rooms) 9300 Glacier Hwy; ✆ 789 5005; www.grandmasfeatherbed.com. A very popular hotel, they are known for their amazing beds & B&B-like décor. Near the airport. Wi-Fi. $$$$

⌂ **Best Western Country Lane Inn** [90–1 A1] (55 rooms) 9300 Glacier Way; ✆ 907 789 5005; www.countrylaneinn.com. Next to Grandma's Feather

Bed, the Country Lane Inn is more affordable, but the rooms are more typical hotel fare. Free airport/ferry shuttle. Wi-Fi. $$$

⌂ **Goldbelt Hotel** [90–1 F4] (105 rooms) 51 Egan Dr; ✆ 586 6900, 888 478 6909 (TF); www.goldbelthotel.com. Great location, but an undeserving reputation for quality, though it is boring & clean. Better than other city centre hotels apart from the Silverbow Inn. Some rooms smell like smoke. Free airport shuttle. Wi-Fi. $$$

🏠 **Silverbow Inn** [90–1 F3] (11 rooms) 120 Second St; ☎ 586 4146, 800 586 4146 (TF); www.silverbowinn.com. While not fancy in any respect, the hotel's rundown charm is quite endearing. The

Budget

🏠 **Alaskan Hotel** [90–1 G4] (44 rooms) 167 S Franklin St; ☎ 586 1000, 800 327 9347 (TF); www.thealaskanhotel.com. The oldest operating hotel in southeast Alaska: they haven't closed since 1913. Rooms are small & simple. Shared bath US$60; private bath US$90; suites US$120. Wi-Fi. $$

B&BS

🏠 **Alaska's Capital Inn** [90–1 F3] (7 rooms) 113 W 5th St; ☎ 586 6507; www.alaskacapitalinn.com. You will be hard pressed to find a more luxurious B&B anywhere in Alaska. The owners have maintained the historic home's traditional style & are friendly & accommodating. The city centre location means it's easy to walk to most major sights. The best value in town for a luxury B&B. Wi-Fi. $$$$$

🏠 **Pearson's Pond** (8 rooms) 4541 Sawa Circle; ☎ 888 658 6328; www.pearsonspond.com. This is one of Juneau's high-end B&Bs. Located in the suburbs of the Mendenhall Valley, guests must have a car to get there. The hosts are very friendly & take the hospitality business very seriously. They are knowledgeable about the city & local activities, particularly hiking. A duck pond, hot tub, & gardens are on the property. Not all B&Bs get the beds right, these folks have! Wi-Fi. $$$$$

🏠 **Rainforest Cottage** [90–1 F1] (2 rooms) 873 Basin Rd; ☎ 586 6898; www.juneaurainforestcottage.com. Private & perched high on the hill behind the city centre, this cute little place has clean, bright rooms & is ideally located for exploring the city centre or hiking in

HOSTELS

🏠 **Juneau International Hostel** [90–1 G2] (7 rooms) 614 Harris St; ☎ 586 9559; www.juneauhostel.org. Often crowded, but decked out with a large kitchen, washer/dryer, computer & within easy walking distance of the city centre. Clean & comfortable.

bakery downstairs is a real bonus too. Though the Silverbow does tend to be expensive for what you get, the free baked goods, juice, organic tea, coffee & other snacks in the lobby make up for it. Those on a budget could eat 3 free meals a day here. Free wine tastings. B/fast inc. Wi-Fi. $$$

🏠 **Shrine of St Therese** (see page 109) Rustic cabins in the grounds of a religious retreat, lovely setting. 23 miles north of the Glacier Hwy. $

the Silverbow Basin. The rooms have full kitchens & access to laundry facilities. Discounts are available for teachers, veterans, non-profit employees, etc. No b/fast. Wi-Fi. $$$$$

🏠 **Hillside Haven** [90–1 A1] (1 room) 4011 Shady Lane; ☎ 523 0845; www.hillsidehavenjuneau.com. This new private suite is very close to the ferry terminal & offers a clean & very comfortable atmosphere with wonderful ocean views. Bikes & kayaks are free to use, as are the laundry facilities & a full kitchen. Wi-Fi. $$$$

🏠 **Alaska Beach Cabin** (2 rooms) 3184 Indian Cove Dr; ☎ 523 1963; www.alaskabeachcabin.com. With a great location right on a sandy beach out of town, you could get picked up by boat in the morning for a kayaking or fishing trip. The friendly owners have kayaks & bikes for rent. A full kitchen is available. No b/fast. Wi-Fi. $$$

🏠 **Aurora View Inn** [90–1 B4] (3 rooms) 2917 Jackson Rd; ☎ 586 3036, 888 580 8439 (TF); www.auroraview.com. Great views, private entrance & friendly hosts with a lovely, quiet position on Douglas Island. This is one of the better value B&Bs in town. $$$

3 night maximum stay & they may ask you to do some simple chores. Make reservations for peak season. If you have children reserve the family room. US$10pp (kids under 5 free, 5–18 US$5). $

CAMPING Camping anywhere in the southeast requires either a love of the rain or really tough gear, preferably both. Having said that, there are a number of great places to camp in Juneau. You will need a car to reach virtually all the sites.

For Juneau camping information, visit: www.fs.fed.us/r10/tongass/recreation/rec_facilities/jnurec.shtml and to reserve a plot www.reserveusa.com

⚐ Auke Village Campground (11 sites) At mile 15 of the Glacier Hwy past the ferry terminal; ⊕ 15 May–30 Sep. Most sites have ocean views. Picnic tables, fireplaces, toilets & water. No reservations. Tent/RV US$10/20.

⚐ Eagle Beach State Recreation Area (16 sites) At mile 28 of the Glacier Hwy; ⊕ 1 May–1 Oct. 5 sites have shelters & are right on the river. Rarely full. Toilet, but no water. Standard/covered site US$10/20.

⚐ Mendenhall Lake Campground (68 sites) For directions see the West Glacier Trail description; ⊕ 15 May–15 Sep. See the glacier from your tent & cool your drinks with 'bergy-bits'. The wonderful West Glacier Trail is very near. Table, toilets & water. Tent/RV US$10/28.

⚐ Point Bridget State Park At the end of the Glacier Hwy mile 40; ☎ 586 2506; www.dnr.state.ak.us/parks/cabins/index.htm. Informal camping down the trail. Public-use cabins near parking area (furthest is a 2hr hike) are for rent for US$35.

RV Camping

⚐ Spruce Meadow RV Park [90–1 A1] (47 sites) 10200 Mendenhall Loop Rd; ☎ 789 1990; www.juneaurv.com. A typical RV park but has some perks: on the public bus route, hot showers, Wi-Fi & microwave. Close to both Mendenhall Glacier & Auke Bay. Limited tent sites. Tent/RV US$20/30.

⚐ Savikko RV Park [90–1 B4] (4 sites, RVs only) ☎ 586 5255; www.fs.fed.us/r10/tongass/recreation/ rec_facilities/jnurec.shtml. Located in Douglas, this small area has no services but has water, sewage, & garbage at the park's maintenance shop. Toilets can be found at the park's recreation area. A permit is required from the Harbour Master's office (*1600 Harbor Way, just north of pedestrian overpass on Egan Dr*). Free for a maximum stay of 3 days.

Cabins The Juneau area and Admiralty Island have almost 30 remote and rustic public-use cabins available for rent. Admiralty Island alone has 16 shelters and cabins. These are managed by the Forest Service and require reservations (☎ 877 444 6777; *www.reserveusa.com*). Rental fees vary from US$25 to US$45 per night. Between 1 May and 30 September, the cabins are only available for a maximum stay of seven days. Each cabin is outfitted slightly differently, so be sure to read the cabin's description online carefully before setting out. Many require you bring all your own gear, as well as No 1 or No 2 heating oil. Most cabins require boat, plane or kayak transportation but some can be reached on foot. Check out the cabin listings and maps at www.fs.fed.us/r10/tongass/cabins/cabinlist.shtml#jnu.

✖ WHERE TO EAT

Just a few towns in Alaska are blessed with fantastic food and Juneau is one of them. In addition to great restaurants and cafés, the Juneau Arts and Humanities Council (see page 104) puts on something called 'Taste the Local Culture'. During the summer months, visitors can arrange to have dinner with a local family (presumably renowned for their culinary skills) for US$35 per person. The host will pick you up, share dinner and conversation, then return you to your hotel.

CITY CENTRE

✖ Twisted Fish [90–1 H6] 550 S Franklin St; ☎ 463 5033; www.twistedfish.hangaronthewharf.com; ⊕ 11.00–22.00 daily. Located inside the Taku Smokeries building, this comfortable eatery has a good selection of local seafood & a bar. **$$$–$$$$**

✖ El Sombrero [90–1 G4] 157 S Franklin St; ☎ 586 6770; www.elsombreroak.com; ⊕ 11.00–21.00 Mon–Fri, 11.00–22.00 Sat. For Mexican food, this is the place. A local hangout. **$$$**

✖ Seong's Sushi Bar [90–1 D3] 740 W 9th St; ☎ 586 4778; ⊕ 11.00–21.30 Mon–Fri, 12.00–21.30 Sat–Sun. Sushi lovers staying in the city centre need to check this place out. The Chinese food offers better value. **$$$**

✖ Thane Ore House 4400 Thane Rd; ☎ 323 3442; www.thaneorehouse.com; ⊕ 11.00–21.00 daily. In business for more than 25 years. Go for great salmon, but skip the rest. **$$$**

✕ Tracy's King Crab Shack [90–1 H5] 356 S Franklin; ✆ 723 1811; www.kingcrabshack.com; ⏰ 11.00–18.30 daily. The Crab Shack serves anything & everything involving crab from an open-air stand near the public library at the cruise-ship dock. **$$$**

✕ Zen [90–1 F4] 51 Egan Dr; ✆ 586 5075; www.zen–restaurant.net; ⏰ 06.00–22.00 Mon–Sat, 08.00–20.00 Sun. Inside the Goldbelt Hotel. A nicer spot to dress up & have a good meal. Asian fusion food in a super chic atmosphere. **$$$**

✕ Zephyr [90–1 G3 Seward St; ✆ 780 2221; www.zephyrrestaurant.com; ⏰ 11.30–14.00 Mon–Fri for lunch & 17.00–21.00 Mon–Sat for dinner. This is where many locals go for dates & special occasions. Next door to the Silverbow Inn. Fantastic food with a Mediterranean flare. The seafood & lamb dishes are always good. **$$$**

✕ Rainbow Foods [90–1 G3] (see page 106) A good lunch spread that you pay for by weight. Lunch is out at 10.30 & is picked over by 13.00, Mon–Fri. Beat the crowd & get there at 11.00. See their web site for the day's menu. Each Thu night

from 17.00–18.00 they serve a different ethnic entrée, often from exotic locals. **$$**

✕ Kenny's Wok & Teriyaki Sushi Bar 124 Front St; ✆ 586 3575; ⏰ 11.00–21.00 Mon–Thu, 11.00–21.30 Fri, 12.00–21.30 Sat, 11.00–21.00 Sun. Affordable lunch specials (you get what you pay for) & decent decór. **$$**

✕ The Hanger on the Wharf [90–1 G4] 2 Marine Way; ✆ 586 5018; www.hangar.hangaronthewharf.com; ⏰ 11.00–01.00 Mon–Fri, 11.00–03.00 Sat, 11.00–01.00 Sun. Great location, ambience & beer but little else. Somehow this place has been elevated to near-shrine status by the local 20-somethings. Normal pub food that is pricey & only average. Sip a beer & watch the seaplanes land at sunset. **$$**

✕ Pel'meni [90–1 G4] In the Wharf; ⏰ 11.30–01.30 Sun–Thu, 11.30–3.30 Fri. This funky little place could scare a squeamish eater but a rural Russian would feel right at home. Serving only veggie or meat pel'menis (a kind of ravioli with hot sauce & coriander) it's pretty easy to decide what to order. The people-watching possibilities are always good & the cooks play Russian LPs from their extensive collection. Good, cheap food. **$**

OUT OF TOWN

✕ Hot Bite [90–1 A1] 11465 Auke Bay Boat Harbor; ✆ 790 2483; ⏰ 11.00–19.00 daily. Good homemade American food served by real, live, surly American teenagers. Burgers, sandwiches & more flavours of milkshake than the law should allow. Food is expensive & slow to arrive, but not bad for what it is. **$$$**

✕ The Canton House [90–1 A1] 8585 Old Dairy Rd; ✆ 789 5075; www.cantonhouse.net; ⏰ 11.30–21.00 Mon–Sat, 11.30–20.30 Sun. This Chinese & sushi place is the best of its kind in town with gleaming new décor after a recent remodel. By the airport. **$$$**

✕ The Island Pub [90–1 B4] 1102 2nd St; ✆ 364 1594; www.theislandpub.com; ⏰ 11.30–22.00 daily. This gem is not on the tourist radar. Great views & amazing thin-crust pizza. The kind of moody/cool décor one normally finds in Seattle or Portland. Great service with a nice selection of beer, wine, local art & historic photos. Ask about the pizza recipe contest. **$$$**

✕ Chan's Thai Kitchen [90–1 A1] 11806 Glacier Hwy; ✆ 789 9777; ⏰ 11.30–14.00 & 16.30–20.30 Tue–Fri. Best Thai food in southeast Alaska. Monstrous portions so share. Across from the Auke Bay harbour on the bottom floor of a hideous strip mall. **$$**

CAFÉS

✕ Paradise Bakery & Café [90–1 G4] 245 Marine Way; ✆ 586 2253; www.paradisecafeyeehaw.com; ⏰ 07.00–15.00 Mon–Fri, 09.00–15.00 Sat–Sun. With the motto: 'eat, drink, live, love' this place is great! The owner recycles everything. Right on the main drag, this is the place to have a quick bite. **$$**

✕ Sandpiper Café [90–1 E3] 429 W Willoughby Av; ✆ 586 3150; ⏰ 06.00–14.00 daily. Another hot spot for grabbing b/fast or lunch. Large portions, everything is homemade & an eclectic assortment of meats inc elk, buffalo & ostrich. If you have 5 friends, order the giant ostrich-egg omelette. **$$**

✕ Silverbow Inn Bakery [90–1 F3] (see page 101) Serves a delightful assortment of baked goods, sandwiches, salads & drinks in a cool funky atmosphere. Wi-Fi. **$$**

✕ Valentines Coffee House & Bakery [90–1 G4] 111 Seward St; ✆ 463 5144; www.valentinescoffeehouse.com; ⏰ 07.00–18.00 Mon–Fri, 09.00–18.00 Sat–Sun. A hip spot to grab lunch; soup, salad, sandwiches, baked goods & drinks. They have the best pizza in town. **$$**

♀ **Alaskan Bar** [90–1 G4] 167 S Franklin St; ✆ 586 1000; www.thealaskanhotel.com; ⊕ 11.00–01.00 Sun–Thu, 11.00–14.45 Fri–Sat. This rustic bar is a great place for great live music. Inside the Alaskan Hotel. **$**

♀ **The Hanger** [90–1 G4] (see page 103) Nearly 30 beers on tap & great views of Gastineau Channel & the harbour. **$**

♀ **Imperial Saloon** [90–1 G4] 241 Front St; ✆ 586 1960; ⊕ 11.00–01.00 Sun–Thu, 11.00–03.00 Fri–Sat. A younger scene with dancing most nights. **$**

♀ **The Island Pub** (see page 103) ⊕ restaurant: closes at 22.00, bar: ⊕ 01.00 Sun–Thu & 02.00 Fri–Sat. Great views, beer, service & food. Escape the downtown crowds. **$**

♀ **Red Dog Saloon** [90–1 G4] 278 S Franklin St; ✆ 463 3777; www.reddogsaloon.com; ⊕ 09.00–22.00 daily. This place is legendary. Like the Salty Dawg Saloon in Homer, the Red Dog is a testament to the longevity of people's desire for seedy environs where they can guzzle alcohol. Unfortunately, the Red Dog Saloon has been somewhat domesticated in recent years. History buffs will want to stop by to see Wyatt Earp's gun mounted on the wall. During the summer of 1900, he checked it IN at the door & couldn't get it back before his boat left for Nome. If you are coming off a cruise ship, be prepared to see all your shipmates. If you're travelling independently, be prepared for legions of tourists who don't take drinking very seriously. **$**

ENTERTAINMENT AND NIGHTLIFE

Being not only a tourist town, but also an active arts community, Juneau has a lot of entertainment to offer. Though nightlife isn't lacking, it can't really be called 'nightlife' since during the summer it barely gets dark! Look for 'what's on' listings in *The Hooligan* (*www.juneauempire.com/entertainment*), a free supplement published every week by Juneau's largest newspaper, *The Juneau Empire*. You'll find them in stands around town.

Alternatively, contact the **Juneau Arts and Humanities Council** (*350 Whittier St;* ✆ *586 2787; www.jahc.org;* ⊕ *09.00–17.00 Mon–Wed, 09.00–18.00 Thu–Fri, 12.00–16.00 Sat*).

CINEMA Juneau has a 'big' commercial theatre as well as some smaller film houses.

20th Century Twin Theatre [90–1 G4] 220 Front St, Mendenhall Valley; ✆ 586 4055. Located in the city centre, this theatre shows new movies every night.
Glacier Cinema [90–1 A1] 9091 Cinema Dr, Mendenhall Valley; ✆ 463 3549; www.grossalaska.com.

A larger theatre in the Mendenhall valley that show most of the newer movies every night.
Silverbow Inn [90–1 F3] (see page 101) Movies are screened in their back room Mon, Tue & Wed. Free.

CONCERTS Two free weekly music concerts, featuring mostly local groups, are worth a visit: **Concerts in the Park** take place in Marine Park in Juneau city centre every Friday between 07.00 and 20.30 June–August; **Concerts on Campus** are held at the Auke Bay campus on Saturdays at the same times. **The Juneau Symphony** (*522 W 10th St;* ✆ *586 4676; www.juneausymphony.org*) play at various venues around town. Call for current performances.

LIVE MUSIC

Alaskan Bar [90–1 G4] A local's haunt located inside the Alaskan Hotel, this is the oldest bar in Alaska. Live music on Fri & Sat with open mic on Thurs. Things generally quite mellow – bring your dancing shoes!
Imperial Saloon [90–1 G4] Popular with young locals. dancing & live bands on the w/ends.

Red Dog Saloon [90–1 F3] Despite the crowds, some fun live acts do pass through the doors. Music starts in the early evening & carries on well into the night.
The Hanger [90–1 F3] Another popular spot to see bands live on the w/ends.

THEATRE Unfortunately most of Juneau's wonderful theatre options go underground during the summer.

Perseverance Theatre [90–1 B4] 914 3rd St; ☎ 364 2421; www.perseverancetheatre.org. Since 1979 the PT has been at the core of the Juneau theatre scene. Month-long performances can be seen throughout the fall, winter & spring.

Theatre in the Rough [90–1 G2] 315 Fifth St; ☎ 209 0867; www.theatreintherough.org. A passionate group dedicated to bringing great music to town & putting on plays. Visit their website for what's current.

Juneau Symphony 522 W 10th St; ☎ 586 4676; www.juneausymphony.org. The orchestra has been performing around Juneau for more than 40 years. See them live between Oct & Jun.

FESTIVALS AND EVENTS

Alaskans work hard and play hard, and take their festivals very seriously. Planning your trip around one of these events is a good idea. The Juneau Arts and Humanities Council website is a good place to look for events. Juneau's vibrant art scene is on display the first Friday of every month when local galleries showcase the new artwork of local artists – usually with wine and nibbles too. Call ☎ 586 2787 for more information. These are free events except where stated.

APRIL
Alaska Folk Festival (☎ 463 3316; www.alaskafolkfestival.org) One of the largest gatherings of Alaskan musicians anywhere. This free event is held during the second week in April.

MAY
Juneau Jazz & Classics Festival (☎ 463 3378; www.jazzandclassics.org) Local musicians and imported talent make for a fun week in Juneau. Some events take place on boats with food and music. Held third week in May. Tickets are US$10–25 depending on the event.

Spring King Derby (☎ 463 7133; www.springkingderby.org) Anglers try for the big one all month. Cash prizes.

JUNE
Celebration (☎ 463 4844; www.sealaskaheritage.org/celebration/index.htm) A bi-annual native cultural conference bringing native Alaskan groups together to dance and participate in cultural events. This event happens only on even-numbered years. If you're interested in Alaskan native cultures, this is an event to plan your trip around.

Festival of Russian Culture (☎ 789 3854) Russian music, dancing and food. Takes place around 21 June at Marine Park and is free to the public.

Gold Rush Days Juneau celebrates its gold mining history with music, food and events during the third week of the month.

JULY
Fourth of July Celebration Festivities begin at midnight on 3 June with fireworks in the city centre. The next day parades and other festivities take over town.

AUGUST
Golden North Salmon Derby (☎ 789 2399) Takes place during the second week of August and attracts those seeking fish and the large cash prizes.

BOOKSHOPS

Friends of the Library Amazing Bookstore 9109 Mendenhall Mall Rd, in airport shopping centre; ☎ 789 4913; www.juneau.org/library/friends/bookstore.php; ⏲ 10.00–19.00 Mon–Fri, 10.00–18.00 Sat, 12.00–17.00 Sun. Very cheap used books. All proceeds go to the Juneau Public Library.

Hearthside Books [90–1 G4] 254 Front St; ☎ 586 1760; www.hearthsidebooks.com: ⏲ 09.00–21.00 Mon & Wed; 09.00–20.00 Fri–Sun & Tue,

09.00–19.00 Thu. A local favourite with a good selection of Alaskan books. Open almost 30 years. Also in the Nugget Mall (*8745 Glacier Hwy;* ☎ *866 789 2750;* ⏲ *10.00–20.00 Mon–Fri, 10.00–18.00 Sat, 12.00–17.00 Sun*) – a shopping centre with several bookshops.

Rainy Retreat Books [90–1 G3] 113 N Seward St; ☎ 463 2665; ⏲ 09.30–18.00 daily. A large & eclectic selection of used & new books.

CLOTHING

Foggy Mountain Shop [90–1 G3] 134 N Franklin St # B; ☎ 586 6780; www.foggymountainshop.com; ⏲ 09.30–18.00 Mon–Fri, 10.00–17.30 Sat, 12.00–17.00 Sun. Find everything you might need for battling the Alaskan elements.

Nugget Alaskan Outfitter 8745 Glacier Hwy # 145; ☎ 789 0956; www.nuggetoutfitter.com; ⏲ 10.00–20.00 Mon–Fri, 10.00–18.00 Sat, 12–17.00 Sun. A full service outdoor shop inside the depressing Nugget Mall.

FOOD

Alaskan & Proud Market 615 W Willoughby Av; ☎ 586 3101; ⏲ 06.00–22.00 daily. Locally called the A&P. The largest selection of food in the city centre. Salad bar & soups are a cheap lunch.

Rainbow Foods [90–1 G3] 224 4th St; ☎ 586 6476; www.rainbow–foods.org; ⏲ 09.00–19.00 Mon–Fri, 10.00–18.00 Sat, 12.00–18.00 Sun. A healthfood store with a great bakery. Fresh bread daily & a lunch spread served by the pound.

For larger quantities of cheaper food drive up to the Nugget Mall area where you will find a number of large grocery stores.

Costco 5225 Commercial Way; ☎ 780 6740: ⏲ 11.00–20.30 Mon–Fri, 09.30–18.00 Sat, 10.00–18.00 Sun. Everything is cheap & in bulk. Membership required.

Dehart's 11735 Glacier Hwy; ☎ 789 7342; ⏲ 06.00–22.00 Mon–Fri, 07.00–23.00 Sat–Sun. A small family-owned grocer in Auke Bay.

Fred Meyers 8181 Old Glacier Hwy; ☎ 789 6500: ⏲ 24hrs. Sells a little of everything, including a large selection of food.

Safeway 3033 Vintage Blvd; ☎ 523 2000; ⏲ 24hrs. A large selection of food.

GALLERIES

Ad Lib [90–1 H4] 231 S Franklin St, in the Decker Bldg; ☎ 463 3031; ⏲ 09.00–18.00 daily. Native crafts & locally made jewellery.

Annie Kaill's Fine Art & Craft Gallery [90–1 G4] 244 Front St; ☎ 586 2880; www.annieandcojuneau.com; ⏲ 09.00–19.00 daily. Quirky selection of local art.

Canvas Community Art Studio & Gallery 223 Seward St; ☎ 586 1750; www.canvasarts.org; ⏲ 09.00–16.00 Mon–Fri, 10.00–17.00 Sat–Sun. This group teaches art classes to the public & work to unify the community through art. Their gallery shows work by artists from around Alaska & they have a nice coffee shop with homemade baked

goods. They also work with an association for handicapped adults.

Juneau Artists Gallery 175 S Franklin St; ☎ 586 9891; www.juneauartistsgallery.com; ⏲ 09.00–22.00 daily. A 27-member artist cooperative who show work from within their ranks.

Rie Muñoz Gallery 2101 N Jordan Av; ☎ 789 7449; www.riemunoz.com; ⏲ 09.00–18.00 daily. One of Alaska's most iconic artists. Her simple, but powerful, work captures the spirit of Alaska & its people. Near the airport.

Silverbow Inn [90–1 F3] (see page 101) Features the work of local artists in their back room. Call ahead to make sure they have pieces on display.

NATIVE ARTS Juneau has a bewildering number of gift shops, many of which sell Alaskan native crafts. Getting the real deal can be harder than you think, even in Alaska (see page 72).

Hummingbird Hollow Gift Shop Located inside the airport; ☎ 789 4672; www.hummingbirdhollow.net; ⏰ 05.00–19.00 daily. One of the better shops in town for native arts. The owner, called Slammer, is a former carpet layer & few are more knowledgeable about native crafts. He buys directly from individual artists & is a wealth of information.
Raven's Journey 435 S Franklin St; ☎ 463 4686; www.ravensjourneygallery.com; ⏰ 09.00–20.00 daily.

Good selection of native arts in the city centre.
Friends of the Alaska State Museum Store 395 Whittier St; ☎ 465 4840; ⏰ 09.00–17.00 daily. At the Alaska State Museum. Most work is bought directly from the artists; they will tell you what is Alaskan & what is a replica. They have another, larger location in the city centre (*124 Seward St; ☎ 523 8431; ⏰ 09.00–18.00 daily*).

OTHER PRACTICALITIES

BANKS A cluster of five banks can be found on the Glacier Highway by the airport. Most have ATMs. In the city centre, it's worth trying:

$ **Key Bank** [90–1 F3] 234 Seward St; ☎ 463 7222; ⏰ 09.00–17.00 Mon–Fri. Branch & 24hr ATM.

$ **Wells Fargo** [90–1 F3] 123 Seward St; ☎ 800 869 3557; ⏰ 09.30–17.00 Mon–Fri. Branch & 24hr ATM.

Those further afield include:

$ **Key Bank** 8800 Glacier Hwy Ste 10, Mendenhall Valley; ☎ 790 5300; ⏰ 10.00–17.30 Mon–Thu, 10.00–18.00 Fri, 11.00–14.00 Sat.
$ **Wells Fargo** 1610 Anka St, Lemon Creek; ☎ 780 5299; ⏰ 10.00–18.00 Mon–Fri. Branch & 24hr ATM.

$ **Wells Fargo** 8181 Old Glacier Hwy; ☎ 800 869 3557 (TF). 24hr ATM only.
$ **Wells Fargo** 9150 Glacier Hwy, Glacier Valley; ☎ 789 9550; ⏰ 10.00–18.00 Mon–Fri, 10.00–17.00 Sat. Branch & 24hr ATM.

HEALTHCARE
Pharmacies
Alaska Infusion Therapy 9109 Mendenhall Mall Rd # 7A; ☎ 789 7570; flexible hrs, call ahead. Inside the Mendenhall Mall.
Ron's Apothecary Shoppe 9101 Mendenhall Mall Rd; ☎ 789 0458; www.ronsapothecary.com; ⏰ 10.00–18.00 daily. Inside the Mendenhall Mall.
Foodland Super Drug 631 W Willoughby Av; 586 2012; ⏰ 09.00–19.00 Mon–Fri, 10.00–18.00 Sat. Located in the city centre.

Juneau Drug Co. 202 Front St; ☎ 586 1233; ⏰ 09.00–19.00 Mon–Fri, 12.00–18.00 Sat. Downtown.
Safeway (see opposite)
Searhc Pharmacy 3245 Hospital Dr; 463 4030, www.searhc.org; ⏰ 08.00–17.00 Mon–Tue & Thu–Fri, 10.30–17.00 Sat. Near the hospital.

Hospitals
✚ **Bartlett Regional Hospital** 3260 Hospital Dr; ☎ 796 8900. Off Egan Dr between downtown & Lemon Creek.

✚ **Juneau Urgent Care** 8505 Old Dairy Rd; ☎ 790 4111. Near the airport.

Dentists You will find at least seven dental surgeries near the airport on Glacier Highway.

Dr Robert White Dentistry Nugget Mall Ste 382; ☎ 789 5880
John Ellenbecker DDS 2211 Jordan Av; ☎ 789 3696

Lonnie Anderson DDS 9211 Lee Smith Dr; ☎ 789 2066

INTERNET Many of the larger hotels, including Juneau's two Best Western hotels (see page 100), have Wi-Fi and don't mind people using it. Ask first. Otherwise the **Juneau Public Library** (*www.juneau.org/library*) has three branches, all of which offer free Wi-Fi and computer terminals with internet access. The city centre branch is a hideous parking garage with a library perched on top; but the views of the channel and town are lovely and free internet make it a worthwhile stop.

🅮 **Douglas Location** 1016 3rd St Douglas; ☎ 364 2378; ⏰ 15.00–22.00 Mon–Wed, 11.00–17.00 Thu, 13.00–17.00 Sat–Sun, closed Fri
🅮 **Downtown Location** [90–1 G4] 292 Marine Way; ☎ 586 5249; ⏰ 11.00–22.00 Mon–Thu, 12.00–17.00 Fri–Sun, closed Tue

🅮 **Seaport Cyber** [90–1 G4] 175 S Franklin St; ☎ 463 9875; 09.00–15.00 daily. Pay internet & calling.
🅮 **Silverbow Inn** [90–1 F3] (see page 100) Free Wi-Fi in the bakery.
🅮 **Valley Location** In the Mendenhall Mall; ☎ 789 0125; ⏰ 10.00–22.00 Mon–Thu, 10.00–17.00 Fri, 10.00–18.00 Sat, 12.00–17.00 Sun

LAUNDRY AND SHOWERS

August Brown Swimming Pool [90–1 C1] 1619 Glacier Av; ☎ 586 5325; www.juneau.org/parkrec/pool; hrs change frequently, call ahead. Ideal for campers, this pool offers free showers with admission. The 32°C pool & sauna aren't bad either.
Auke Bay Harbor Master's Office 11497 Harbor Dr; ☎ 789 0819; ⏰ 06.00–20.00 daily. Showers & bathrooms.

Harbor Washboard 1114 Glacier Av; ☎ 586 1133; ⏰ 08.0–21.00 Mon–Fri, 09.00–21.00 Sat–Sun. Coin laundry & showers.
Mendenhall Laundromat Mendenhall Mall; ☎ 789 9781; ⏰ 06.00–22.00 daily. Laundry only.
The Dungeon 4th & N Franklin St; ⏰ 08.00–18.00 daily. In the basement of the Mendenhall Building. Look for a sign over a dark stairwell leading down. Laundry only.

POST OFFICES

✉ **Auke Bay Location** 11899 Glacier Hwy; ☎ 789 0680: ⏰ 09.30–13.00 & 13:30–17.30 Mon–Fri, 12.00–15.00 Sat
✉ **Douglas Location** 904 3rd St; ☎ 364 2445, ⏰ 09.30–12.30 & 13.00–17.30 Mon–Fri, 12.00–15.00 Sun

✉ **Downtown Location** 145 S Franklin St; ☎ 586 8335; ⏰ 08.30–16.30 Mon–Fri, 09.00–14.00 Sun
✉ **Federal Station** [90–1 D3] 709 W 9th St; ☎ 586 7987; ⏰ 09.00–17.00 Mon–Fri
✉ **Mendenhall Location** 3000 Vintage Blvd; ☎ 586 7984: ⏰ 09.00–18.00 Mon–Fri, 11.00–16.00 Sat

WHAT TO SEE AND DO

GOVERNOR'S MANSION [90–1 E2] (*716 Calhoun Av*) Alaska's first families have lived here since it was built in 1912 for US$40,000, starting with territorial governor Walter Eli Clark. The 14,000-square-foot mansion is not normally open to the public, and beyond its simple but elegant New England design, it's fairly plain. The house is perched high on the hill and affords great views of the channel and city. The 1939 totem pole outside is also worth a look.

STATE CAPITOL BUILDING [90–1 F3] (*On the corner of 4th & Main St;* ☎ *465 3800;* ⏰ *08.00–16.30 Mon–Fri, 09.30–17.00 Sat–Sun; free admission*) A square cement and marble monolith, which tries very hard to look grand. Clearly aware of its negative reputation, the city held a competition in 2004 to redesign the building, but, like a lot of plans for the capital, things were put on hold and haven't progressed since. The public is allowed to walk around much of the building and free tours are held whenever you show up and ask for one.

HOUSE OF WICKERSHAM [90–1 F2] (*213 7th St;* ☎ *586 9001; www.dnr.state.ak.us/parks/units/wickrshm.htm;* ⏰ *10.00–12.00 & 13.00–17.00 daily; adult US$2*) This fine house was built in 1898, at the behest of Frank Hammond, superintendent of the Sheep Creek Mining Co. After being bought and lived in by three more influential men, the house was purchased by Judge Wickersham in 1928. Judge Wickersham, practically singlehandedly, brought the US legal system to much of Alaska, including the semi-lawless gold rush regions like Nome and Fairbanks.

He died in 1939 and the home passed to relatives until 1984 when the State of Alaska purchased the house to preserve it for posterity. The house is a step back in time and some of the former owner's stories can be seen in the objects and photographs around the house.

MUSEUMS
Alaska State Museum [90–1 E4] (*395 Whittier St;* ↘ *465 2901; www.museums.state.ak.us;* ⊕ *08.30–17.30 daily; adult/child US$3/free*) Shows a variety of displays and exhibits, from history and contemporary art to natural history. One of the best museums in the state.

Juneau–Douglas City Museum [90–1 E3] (*114 W 4th St;* ↘ *586 3572; www.juneau.org/parksrec/museum; adult/child US$4/free;* ⊕ *09.00–17.00 Mon–Fri, 10.00–17.00 Sat–Sun*) Has a good collection of exhibits that complement, but do not overlap, with those of the Alaska State Museum (see above). Their relief map of the Juneau area helps you get your bearings. Check out the 30-minute video on Juneau's mining history.

Last Chance Mining Museum [90–1 H1] (*1001 Basin Rd;* ↘ *586 5338; adult/child US$4/free;* ⊕ *09.30–12.30, 03.30–18.30 daily*) Created by the conversion of an old mining building. Only worth a journey for those fascinated by mining history. Drive uphill from downtown to Basin Road and follow it around to the museum.

GALLERIES Juneau's vibrant art scene is on display the first Friday of every month when local galleries showcase new artwork by local artists – usually with wine and nibbles too. It's also worth attending the **Taste the Local Culture** event (see page 104) put on by the Juneau Art and Humanities Council. Not only is it a great way to meet locals and eat homemade food, but to see their private art collections as well. Call the Arts Council (see page 104) and ask to be paired with an art collector for dinner.

Juneau Arts and Humanities Council [90–1 F4] (see page 104) Operates a fine gallery in the Juneau Arts and Culture Building next to Centennial Hall in the city centre.

Juneau Historical Library [90–1 F3] (*8th Flr State Office Bldg;* ↘ *465 2925; www.library.state.ak.us/hist;* ⊕ *10.00–16.30 Mon–Fri; free admission*) Fans of historic photographs and manuscripts should make a beeline for this archive. Call ahead with a wish list and they will set up a private showing. If you don't know what to ask for, look at the Winter and Pond, and the Case and Draper collections.

Sealaska Building (*1 Sealaska Plz # 400;* ↘ *586 1512; www.sealaska.com;* ⊕ *08.00–17.00 Mon–Fri; free admission*) Has a good collection of Alaska native artwork on display throughout the building and in the small gift shop. Visitors are free to wander and look at the art, but must check in with the receptionist first.

AROUND JUNEAU

THE SHRINE OF ST THERESE (*21425 Glacier Hwy;* ↘ *780 6112; www.shrineofsainttherese.org;* ⊕ *08.30–22.00 daily; free*) A nice stop if you're in Auke Bay. There is a lovely stone chapel, a bookshop, gardens and forests interconnected with trails, all of which are dedicated to the patron saint of Alaska, St Therese. To get there drive to Auke Bay and continue through town past the ferry terminal until you see the sign.

MENDENHALL GLACIER One of the more accessible glaciers in Alaska, the Mendenhall Glacier area is often crowded with sightseers, helicopters, planes, kayaks and hikers. Even so, seclusion is often no further than a few miles from any trailhead. See box on page 96.

GLACIER HIGHWAY Also called the Veterans Memorial Highway, this is a pleasant day trip if you have a car. Once past Auke Bay, the road continues another 28 miles before ending at Echo Bay (mile 40). All the way you will be sandwiched between the mountains and the sea. There are many parks and trailheads along the way, including Auke Recreation Area at mile 15, Boy Scout Beach at mile 25, and Eagle Beach at mile 26.

AUKE BAY Auke Bay is a small community at the edge of the Mendenhall Valley with a few basic services, the University of Alaska Southeast campus and Auke Bay Harbor, where wildlife and kayak trips often depart. The Alaska Ferry dock is 1.5 miles west of Auke Bay and the Juneau city centre is 11 miles southeast on the Glacier Highway. Visitors often know Auke Bay as the place to find **Chan's Thai Kitchen** (see page 95), one of the best Thai places in the southeast.

ADMIRALTY ISLAND Accessible only by seaplane or boat, Admiralty Island – located southwest of Douglas Island and 40 miles as the crow flies from Juneau – is known by the Tlingit as *Kootznoowoo* or 'Fortress of the Bear', and with good reason. The island is home to 1,600 brown bears; more than the entire continental US combined! It also claims to support the largest concentration of bald eagles (5,000) in the world.

Most tours land at Pack Creek, but seeing the bears can be hit or miss during the shoulder (low) season or if you're only staying for a few hours. Your chances improve greatly if you visit for a full day or during the peak season when hordes of pink and chum salmon begin their migration upstream to spawn. The bears arrive in droves to profit from the feast and when the bears have had their fill, the eagles swoop in to pick up the scraps.

The trip to Pack Creek takes about 30 minutes by plane and generally costs about US$200 (see page 95 for details of tour operators).

Angoon (*Population: 430*) The lone permanent settlement on Admiralty Island is the Kootznoowoo Tlingit village of Angoon on Kootznahoo Inlet, 45 miles southwest of Juneau and 41 miles northeast of Sitka. In the 18th century, Angoon was developed as a fur-trading hub and later expanded to whaling. In 1882, a whaling accident killed a Tlingit shaman. The village requested the customary 200 blankets from the Northwest Trading Company for the man's family. The company refused and, sensing a conflict, went to the US Navy in Sitka. The village was promptly shelled and destroyed by the USS *Corwin*.

Following the whaling and herring fishing work, villagers moved to nearby Killisnoo, but moved back to Angoon in 1928, when fire destroyed Killisnoo. Today, Angoon is a modern Tlingit village where the smell of smoking salmon lingers in the air along the dirt streets. A number of historic cemeteries are around town and Tlingit art can be seen here and there in the form of totem poles, and carved and painted houses.

The Danger Point Trail follows the peninsula 2.5 miles from town past a cemetery. Admiralty Island has 14 public-use cabins. Some can be reached by plane or boat

A short flight or ferry right from the hustle and bustle of Juneau are the sleepy towns of Pelican and Hoonah.

GETTING THERE The **Alaska Ferry** (✆ 789 7453, 800 642 0066 (TF); www.dot.state.ak.us/amhs) sails the 90 miles between Juneau and Hoonah every Sunday, Monday, Tuesday and Friday for US$33; services to Pelican run just a few times per month, tickets costUS$50.

HOONAH (*Population: 823*) The – mostly Tlingit – town of Hoonah (www.visithoonah.com) sits on Icy Strait at the northern end of Chichagof Island. While the Tlingit culture is very visible around town in the form of totem poles, canoes and carvings, the town is otherwise not very attractive and offers the independent traveller little in the way of services. The town has a pleasant Forest Service office (*430 Airport Way;* ✆ 945 3631), an interesting graveyard across from the ferry terminal, a tackle shop (✆ 945 3463), and a few simple accommodation possibilities including **Icy Strait Lodge** (✆ 945 3636; icystraitnow.com; $$) and the **Wind 'N Sea Inn** (✆ 945 3438; $$). A few gift shops cater to the cruise ships.

PELICAN (*Population: 113*) The miniscule town of Pelican (www.pelican.net) sits on Lisianski Inlet on the western side of Chichagof Island, 80 miles north of Sitka and 70 miles west of Juneau. While many Alaskan towns are located in lovely areas, but are quite ugly themselves, Pelican is both a charming town and splendidly situated between the mountains and the sea. Pelican is known for its scenery, great fishing and, since 1998, the **Boardwalk Boogie** (www.pelicanboardwalkboogie.com), a four-day music and party event at the end of May.

The Takanis Lakes Trail and the Tsunami Trail are both pleasant treks from town. For more information visit www.seatrails.org.

Where to stay and eat Three public-use cabins are available in the Pelican area, including the popular White Sulfur Spring. While some open-ocean canoe paddling is required to reach these cabins, the camping possibilities are endless here. For more information visit www.fs.fed.us/r10/tongass/cabins/cabinlist.shtml. Otherwise try:

Lisianski Inlet Wilderness Lodge ✆ 735 2266, 800 962 8441 TF; www.pelicanalaskafishing.com. $$$$$

Highliner Lodge ✆ 735 2476, 877 386 0397 TF; www.highlinerlodge.com. Offers complete fishing/lodging packages, but also rent kayaks & serve delicious food from their restaurant. The owners also rent 2 apartments along the boardwalk. $$–$$$$

Rose's Bar and Grill ✆ 735 2288. Decent pub food in a bar atmosphere. $$

while others can be used along the cross-island canoe route (see page 98). For more information and booking visit www.fs.fed.us/r10/tongass/cabins/cabinlist.shtml.

TENAKEE SPRINGS (*Population: 99; www.tenakeespringsak.com*) Just 45 miles southwest of Juneau, Tenakee Springs (population: 102) is a popular day trip and second home location for Juneau residents. The town is famous for its **hot spring** (🕐 *daily to men 14.00–18.00 & 22.00–09.00 & women 09.00–14.00 & 18.00–22.00*) near the city dock. Those hopping off the ferry while it's in town sometimes have enough time for a dip, depending on their sex and the time of day. The hot water was originally tapped in 1895 for the increasing number of visitors and has been used constantly every since. According to an Alaska magazine article, the town actually advertised on Craigslist (an internet classifieds page) because they were in danger of losing state school funding due to a lack of kids. They needed ten to maintain their funding. Earlier, in 1997, the town made headlines when they closed up shop and shut themselves indoors when a cruise ship disgorged 120 people in the tiny town. Apparently it's not that they don't like visitors, it's just that they don't like it on an industrial scale.

Getting there The Alaska Ferry (✎ 789 7453, 800 642 0066 (TF); *www.dot.state.ak.us/amhs*) makes the trip twice a week for US$35.

Where to stay and eat

⌂ **Tenakee Spring Lodge** ✎ 364 3640; www.tenakeehotspringslodge.com. Offers 5 dbl rooms for US$150.

✗ **Rosie's Blue Moon Café** This artist's co-op also serves tasty pub-style food & is run by old-timer Rosie. Don't let the rustic décor & low door fool you, the food is good & all made from scratch.

Snyder Mercantile ✎ 736 2205. Established in 1899 by Ed Snyder & still open today.

4

Southeast Alaska

Geographically separated from the rest of the state, the Alaskan 'panhandle' stretches from Yakutat, 420 miles southeast to Ketchikan, and exists mostly within the 17-million-acre Tongass National Forest. Lushly forested islands, soaring glaciated peaks, a rich native heritage and bustling communities rich in culture and steeped in history make the southeast a popular destination for visitors year round. The Tlingit, Haida and Tsimshian native cultures of the region are some of the most active and visible in the state, with totem poles and traditional long houses found throughout the region. The Tlingit language can also sometimes be heard. Other less-expected cultural influences – such as Russian Orthodox churches in Sitka and Scandinavian influences in Petersburg – are also readily visible here. Nearly every part of the region has also been touched by gold mining or logging, often both. Evidence of these two industries, along with commercial fishing, and, more recently, tourism is, for better or worse, everywhere. State and private ferries connect many of the region's communities and small planes are available for accessing the multitude of remote and stunning locations throughout the region. Juneau, the state capital (see

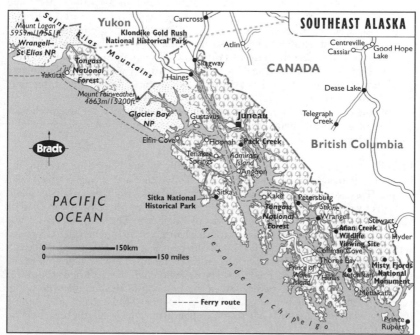

Tongass National Forest – the largest national forest in the United States – is an astonishing 16.8 million acres. That's about the size of the state of Virginia. It is the largest temperate rainforest in the world and forms just a part of a much larger forest that stretches into Canada, and the northwest states of the US. Tongass encompasses virtually all of southeast Alaska from Yakutat Bay to Ketchikan and from the sea to the border of Canada. Red-and-white cedar, Sitka spruce (Alaska's state tree) and western Hemlock cover about half of the park's area in dense, mossy expanses. The only constant in the Tongass is the presence of water. From the 11,000 miles of ocean coastline and 25ft tides, to the glaciers, rivers and lakes, and the 200 inches of rain that can fall annually in some places, the Tongass is a wet place, filled with life and beckoning adventurers.

The Tlingit people thrived on the land for thousands of years before westerners 'discovered' the area. So great was the abundance of food that they never bothered developing a word that conveyed the concept of starvation. Their cultures were also some of the most elaborate and sophisticated of the many Native groups in Alaska.

Chapter 3 on page 87), sits within this region and offers a taste of 'city life', while the wilderness is always just outside the back door.

HYDER (AND STEWART)

With a population of just 72, the quaint town of Hyder (⊕ 55°54'51"N, 130°1'27.7"W) – nicknamed the 'friendliest ghost town in Alaska' – is just three miles across the border from the much larger town of Stewart in British Columbia, Canada. (Stewart can be visited easily despite the international border, due to the road leading in – something most southeast communities lack.) Hyder is found at the head of Portland Canal where the Salmon and Bear Rivers flow into Portland Canal, a 96-mile fjord. As a result of the town's proximity to Stewart, Hyder has assumed the Canadian dollar, time difference, and schooling system.

The town's local culture may not impress you, but Hyder is set in a lovely part of Alaska and the mountain scenery and occasional good bear viewing make it worth the trip.

HISTORY The area was originally used seasonally by the Nass tribe, seeking the protection Portland Canal provided against the weather and the aggressive Haida people. The two towns, Hyder and Stewart, emerged simultaneously when gold and silver were unearthed shortly after the area was originally explored in 1896 by Captain Gaillard of the US Army Corps of Engineers. The town of Hyder was originally known as Portland City, but was changed in 1914 when the US postal service denied a post office application on the basis that too many towns in the US used the name Portland. The town was promptly renamed Hyder in honour of the Canadian mining engineer, Frederick Hyder, who envisioned a bright future for the area. Mining ruled the two towns in the first half of the century with boom years in 1920 and 1930, before going bust in the 1950s. Most major gold mining disappeared in 1956, but the Grand Duc Copper Mine, the last in the area, held on before finally closing in 1984.

GETTING THERE AND AWAY

By car Unlike most of southeast Alaska, Hyder is accessible via a spectacular 38-mile spur road (37A) from British Columbia. The distance from Anchorage is 1,305 miles, 1,231 miles from Valdez, 1,183 miles from Fairbanks, 625 miles from Whitehorse, Canada, and 940 miles from Vancouver, Canada.

By air Taquan Air (↘ *225 8800, 800 770 8800 (TF); www.taquanair.com*) flies to Hyder from Ketchikan a few times a week for US$185. Or **Air Canada** (↘ *888 247 2262 (TF); www.aircanada.com*) flies from Vancouver, Canada to Terrace, Canada, which is 204 miles from Hyder.

By bus Seaport Limousine (↘ *250 636 2622; www.seaportnorthwest.com*) travels between Terrace, Canada and Stewart every weekday, leaving Stewart at 10.00 and returning from Terrace at 17.00. Alternatively, **Greyhound Canada** (↘ *800 661 8747; www.greyhound.ca*) connects Vancouver with Terrace for US$70.

TOURIST INFORMATION For more details on both towns visit the Stewart and Hyder International Chamber of Commerce (*222 5th Av;* ↘ *250 636 9224; www.stewart-hyder.com*) in Stewart.

WHERE TO STAY AND EAT Facilities in Hyder are limited, but if you head over to Stewart there are a handful of accommodation options and restaurants, some of which are of reasonable quality.

⌂ **Ripley Creek Inn** (35 rooms) 306 5th Av; ↘ 250 636 2344; ripleycreekinn.com. These are the best rooms in town & have decent views & Wi-Fi. The rooms are simple, but nice & spread out over a number of buildings in the same part of town. $$–$$$

⌂ **Kathy's Korner B&B** (4 rooms) 505 Main St; ↘ 250 636 2393. Pleasant rooms right in Hyder. ⊕ May–Sep only. $$

✗ **Bitter Creek Café** 313 5th Av; ↘ 250 636 2166; www.bittercreek.homestead.com. A local favourite with a tasty lunch & dinner menu of salads, sandwiches, & seafood & meat entrées. $$$

✗ **Silverado Café** 309 5th Av; ↘ 250 636 2727. Head here for pizza, pub food & breakfast. $$

☕ **Glacier Inn** International St; ↘ 250 636 9248. Is the pick of the bunch from the town's bars.

WHAT TO SEE AND DO
Hyder
Fish Creek Wildlife Observation Site (⊕ *06.00–22.00 daily*) Located three miles north of Hyder, this is a great place to see spawning salmon and, more often than not, brown and black bears. The bears visit from far and wide to dine on pink and dog salmon from mid-July through to late autumn. Rangers are generally on hand to answer questions and ensure safety. For more information, visit www.fs.fed.us/r10/ro/naturewatch/southeast/fish_creek/fishcreek.htm. A quarter mile north of the viewing area is the **Titan Trail**, which heads five miles up the mountain and rewards hikers with great views.

Salmon River Road This spectacular scenic drive continues up the valley then skirts the mountain past the abandoned Grand Duc Mine (closed to the public) to the Salmon Glacier. After passing through Hyder follow the Grand Duc Road for about 25 miles. Ask about the condition of the road before setting out.

Bear Glacier This easily accessible glacier can be found about 20 miles outside Hyder, just off highway 37A. This bright-blue glacier stops in a lake and is flanked by two large mountains.

Stewart

Historical Society Museum (603 Columbia St; ✆ 250 636 2568; US$5 adult/child; ⊕ 13.00–16.00 daily) Located inside the old fire building, it contains details of the the area's mining history.

Toastworks Museum (*Attached to the Ripley Creek Inn, see page 115*) Celebrates the 'seemingly ordinary and mundane' with hundreds of antiquated appliances. For more information contact the Ripley Creek Inn.

KETCHIKAN *(Population: 8,295)*

Ketchikan (✷ 55°21'00"N, 131°40'24"W) is Alaska's fourth largest community behind Fairbanks, Juneau and Anchorage. The town is squeezed into a narrow but spectacular strip of land between the John, Fish and Achilles Mountains and a thin strip of the Pacific sea, known as the Tongass Narrows, on the southwest corner of Revillagigedo Island (Revilla Island for short). The town is so compressed that locals joke it's just three miles long and three blocks wide (a tenth of a mile). Early residents increased the living area by dumping mine tailings into the sea and today,

MISTY FJORDS NATIONAL MONUMENT

The dramatic landscape of the 2.2-million-acre Misty Fjords National Monument is some of the most stunning in all of southeast Alaska. Coastal rainforests of immense trees, 3,000-foot granite walls rising straight out of the ocean, high mountain lakes full of fish, glaciers and a profusion of wildlife make Misty an unforgettable destination for casual sightseers and rugged adventurers alike.

The most striking feature of the park is the mass of granite forming mossy domes and grey, lichen-streaked walls throughout the park. During the last ice age, 12,000 or so years ago, the majority of Misty was covered in as much as a mile of ice. As the climate warmed and the glaciers began to recede, the deep, glacially carved fjords we see today were revealed.

The wet coastal climate created a rich ecosystem fuelled by huge amounts of rain, tides and the ocean. Virtually every species of animal found in the southeast can also be found in Misty including black and brown bears, wolves, deer, mountain goats, river otters, wolverine, beaver, mink and marten. Fjords are sometimes thousands of feet deep and attract marine life with their nutrients. All five species of salmon navigate these waters to spawn in the monument's rivers and lakes and streams are often alive with trout.

There are no roads in the monument so visitors explore by boat, plane, and on foot. Casual visitors will want to hop on one of the many cruises or flightseeing trips that make their way into the park daily. Those seeking a more intimate experience of the park can enter in a number of ways including, fly-in, water taxi or kayak. Kayaking from Ketchikan into the park is possible but dangerous conditions are created by tides funnelled through narrow fjords. A better idea is to be dropped deep in the park by water taxi (see page 122) with kayaks. Adventure seekers can also be dropped by seaplane on a mountain lake for endless hiking and fishing opportunities.

The weather, especially in Misty, is extremely variable and can change in minutes. Be prepared for 24 hours of rain and always take more food than you need in case your ride is postponed due to bad weather.

Forest service cabins are maintained throughout the monument. Make reservations at www.reserveusa.com or by calling the Ketchikan Misty Fjords Ranger District (see page 121).

On the map:

0 — 5km
0 — 5 miles

Betton Island

Revillagigedo Island

Lunch Falls Loop Trail
Lunch Creek
Settlers Cove Campground
Harriet Hunt Lake
Second Waterfall Creek
Lake Emory Tobin
Lake
Harriet Hunt Recreational Area
White River

Clover Pass
Knudson Cove
First Waterfall Creek
Clover Pass Resort
Guard Island Viewpoint
Connell Lake Trail
Whipple Creek
Talbot Lake
Connell Lake
George Inlet

Ward Creek
Totem Bight Historic Park & Potlach Park
Ward Creek Trail
Brown Mountain
Dude Mountain Trail
Mahoney Lake
Mud Bight
Wade Lake Trail
Perseverance Trail
Diana Mountain
Dude Mountain
Upper Mahoney Lake
Last Chance Campground
Ward Lake
Mahoney Mountain
Refuge Cove
Ward Cove
Signal Creek Campground
John Mountain
Lower Silvis Lake
Three Cs Campground
Signal Creek Lake
Perseverance Lake
Upper Ketkchikan Lake
Walsh Creek
Signal Mountain
Fish Mountain
Roy Jones Mountain
Upper Silvis Lake
George Inlet Cannery
Black Bear Inn
Carlanna Creek
Lower Ketchikan Lake
Deer Mountain Trail
Achilles Mountain
Airport Ferry Terminal
Alaska Ferry Terminal
Ketchikan International Airport
Bar Harbor
Casey Moran Float
Gravina Island
Tongass Narrows
KETCHIKAN
Thomas Basin
Deer Mountain
Whitman Lake
Herring Cove
Carroll Inlet
Saxman Totem Park
N
Bradt
Pennock Island
Saxman
Fawn Mountain
Rotary Beach Picnic Area
Hole in the Wall Harbor
Mountain Point

much of the oceanfront is built on these tailings. Unfortunately, though, there still isn't quite enough space and traffic jams on Tongass Avenue mid-summer are common. In addition, some 900,000 visitors (mainly from cruise ships) pour into town every summer to learn about Ketchikan's well-preserved mining, fishing, and native Alaskan history and visit Totem Bight State Park, Saxman Village and the Totem Heritage Center. Indeed, during the high season Ketchikan can receive up to 10,000 visitors per day!

Ketchikan is – above all things – famous for its rain. When it's not raining here, it's snowing. And when it's not snowing or raining, scantily clad locals stumble around staring at the mysterious bright-yellow orb in the sky. Ketchikan has received as much as 202 inches (almost 17ft) of rain in a single year, making it the wettest town in Alaska. The rain doesn't deter visitors, though, because all that moisture has, at least in part, created the majestic maze of towering mist-shrouded peaks, temperate rainforest and chiselled fjord-lands found in the 2.2-million-acre Misty Fjords National Monument. With a little exploration, travellers can experience this timeless landscape in total solitude – a rare treat in today's modern world.

HISTORY Ketchikan was formed in much the same way as Juneau, around a small creek formerly used by the native peoples. In the case of Ketchikan, however, the riches in the stream were not gold, but salmon. Ketchikan was named after

Ketchikan Creek, which was itself called *Kitschk-Hin* by the Tlingit and means 'thundering wings of an eagle.' In 1886, the first salmon cannery opened near the mouth of Ketchikan Creek and, by 1912, four more had been built. Salmon production peaked in 1936 with seven canneries producing more than 1.5 million cases of salmon. Interestingly, during the 1920s, tidal flats that used to exist at the mouth of Ketchikan Creek were used as baseball fields at low tide. Teams from all over southeast Alaska, and even Canada, came to play during the low-tide intervals. Sadly, the flats were dredged in the 1930s to create the Thomas Basin Boat Harbour.

Salmon stocks crashed about the same time World War II started, and Ketchikan's main industry changed from salmon to timber. While timber had been a small industry since the turn of the century, logging did not begin in earnest until the 1940s. The rainforests of the Ketchikan area are some of the richest on earth with immense spruce, cedar and hemlock trees. In the early 1950s, the US Forest Service granted 50-year logging contracts to two mills, promising almost 500 million board-feet of timber. After World War II and during the 1980s, Japan bought much of the large, old-growth spruce from southeast Alaska. But not long after the logging industry had taken off, it began to decline due to increased competition from world markets and tighter environmental laws. In 1997, the government cancelled the Ketchikan Pulp Company's 50-year contract and large-scale commercial logging ceased overnight. A number of small mills have started and failed over the years and today the local economy depends on tourism, federal employment and, to some degree, commercial fishing.

GETTING THERE AND AWAY Ketchikan is accessible only by air and boat with daily jet and ferry service from various Alaskan and Lower-48 destinations.

By air Alaska Airlines fly into Ketchikan from Seattle and other southeast towns daily. Regional small-plane charter services also fly into Ketchikan daily from around the southeast. See list below. While many small-plane companies offer regularly scheduled flights to outer-lying communities, charters are also available. These have the advantage of being private, able to leave whenever you want and hold a handful of people and gear. However, they do have the disadvantage of being quite expensive – about US$650/hour.

✈ **Alaska Airlines** ➘ 800 426 0333; www.alaskaair.com. Daily jet service from Seattle to Ketchikan (90mins) for about US$450 return. They also fly from Juneau (daily flights; US$325), Wrangell (daily flights; US$225), & Sitka (daily flights; US$300).
✈ **Pacific Airways** 1935 Tongass Av Ste B; ➘ 225 3500, 877 360 3500 (TF); www.flypacificairways.com. Offers flights to multiple destinations on Prince of Wales Island (approx

US$100 1-way) & flights to Metlakatla for about US$50 1-way.
✈ **Taquan Air** 4049 Tongass Av; ➘ 225 8800, 800 770 8800 (TF); www.taquanair.com. Flies to 12 locations on Prince of Wales Island & to many locations around Ketchikan. Ketchikan to Coffman Cove (US$145), Hollis (US$105), & Craig (US$125) on Prince of Wales Island. Metlakatla is US$45. For a private charter the price increases by at least 100%.

Getting into town Ketchikan International Airport is located on Gravina Island, one mile across Tongass Narrows from Ketchikan. You can get into town by water taxi, bus, or ferry. The airport is attached to the dock where water taxis and ferries leave for town. **Tongass Water Taxi** (➘ *225 8294; ticket: US$19 adult, US$8 each additional person*) offer 10-minute boat rides from the airport to anywhere along the waterfront; look for the boat driver, or a sign in the baggage-claim section. Alternatively, **Ketchikan Transporter** (➘ *225 9800;www.sitnews.us/frontpage/ ketchikantransporter/ketchikan_transporter.html;* ⊕ *05.46–20.46 Mon–Sat & 09.00–15.46*

The fifth busiest airport in Alaska, Ketchikan International Airport is located not in Ketchikan as one would assume, but on neighbouring Gravina Island. With more than 200,000 airline passengers arriving every summer, some locals decided a bridge to replace the ferry and water taxi service was long overdue. The Ralph M Bartholomew Veterans Memorial Bridge was going to be a stacked bridge 200 feet above the water to allow large ship traffic to pass underneath. Residents of the Ketchikan Gateway Borough approved the project in 1990, despite the US$315 million price tag. Alaska's only congressman, Don Young, quietly inserted an appropriation for US$223 million for the bridge into the federal Transportation Equity Act in 2005, as well as an additional US$229 million for another bridge near Anchorage.

When other 'earmark' spending abuses were uncovered, the overpriced and little-needed Alaskan bridge projects were labelled 'The Bridges to Nowhere' and fierce opposition arose from US senators and the general public. To make matters worse, Don Young and Alaska Senator Ted Stevens refused to allocate any bridge funds to aid reconstruction in New Orleans after the devastation caused by Hurricane Katrina. The project's success seemed to have been based on as few people knowing about it as possible. Once the general public found out they were going to pay for a bridge nearly as long as the Golden Gate Bridge in San Francisco for a small town in Alaska, the democratic process took hold once again and the idea was eventually shelved.

For comparison, the Golden Gate Bridge carries almost 50 million cars a year, while Ketchikan's Bridge to Nowhere would have seen fewer than 200,000 cars a year.

Sun; adult/child US$15/7) run a bus service from the airport, across Tongass Narrows, to anywhere in town. Mid-summer reservations are recommended, otherwise look for their uniformed agents at baggage claim. Finally, the five-minute ferry ride (borough run) to town leaves the airport every half hour and from Ketchikan every 15 minutes. The trip is less than 15 minutes.

Tickets can be purchased at the airport and cost US$5/2 adult/child; cars are US$6 one-way. Taxis are also usually on hand for airport-ferry and state-ferry arrivals.

By sea
Alaska Marine Highway (*7559 North Tongass Hwy;* \ *800 642 0066; www.ferryalaska.com*) Ferries arrive at the ferry terminal from Bellingham, Washington (*departs: 3 times/month; journey time: 36hrs; ticket: US$239*) and Prince Rupert, Canada (*departs: 12 times/month; journey time: 6hrs; ticket: US$54*). Service between the native village of Melakatla on Annette Island is provided by the small passenger-and car-carrying MV *Lituya*. It runs two times a day and tickets cost US$25. Ferries usually leave every day for northern destinations such as Wrangell (US$37), Petersburg (US$60), Sitka (US$83), Juneau (US$107), Haines (US$134), and Skagway (US$147).

Inter-Island Ferry Authority (*3501 Tongass Av;* \ *826 4848, 866 308 4848 (TF); www.interislandferry.com*) Ferries leave Ketchikan for Hollis on Prince of Wales Island daily at 15.30 (US$37), arriving in Hollis at 18.30. Ferries leave Hollis daily at 08.00 and arrive in Ketchikan at 11.00.

The Ketchikan ferry terminal (\ *225 6182, 225 6181;* ⊕ *09.00–16.30 Mon–Fri & when a ship is in port*) is about two miles north of town. Fortunately, the public bus provides transport to and from the terminal.

GETTING AROUND Ketchikan can get congested with traffic midsummer making their public transportation system, **Ketchikan Gateway Borough Transit**

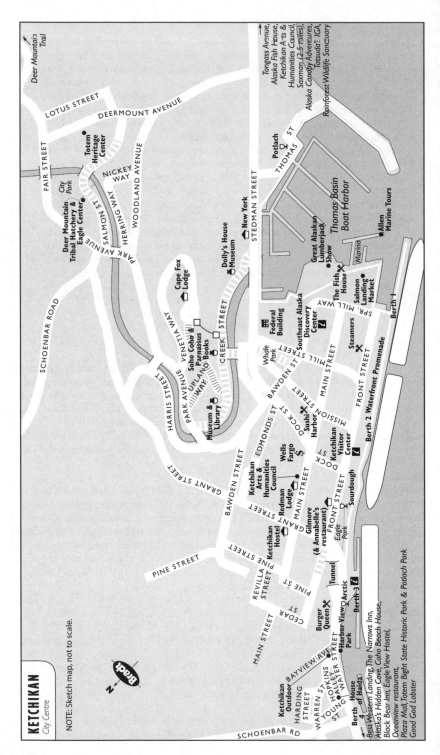

KETCHIKAN
City Centre

NOTE: Sketch map, not to scale.

Bradt

N

Deer Mountain Trail

LOTUS STREET

DEERMOUNT AVENUE

FAIR STREET

SCHOENBAR ROAD

SCHOENBAR RD

City Park

Totem Heritage Center

Deer Mountain Tribal Hatchery & Eagle Center

NICKEY WAY

SALMON ST

HERRING WAY

PARK AVENUE

WOODLAND AVENUE

STEDMAN STREET

THOMAS ST

Potlach

Thomas Basin Boat Harbor

Marina

Allen Marine Tours

New York

Dolly's House Museum

Cape Fox Lodge

VENETIA WAY

Soho Coho & Parnassus Books

MAIN

UPLAND WAY

CREEK STREET

Great Alaskan Lumberjack Show

The Fish House

Salmon Landing Market

Federal Building

Southeast Alaska Discovery Center

Whale Park

SPR MILL WAY

Steamers

Berth 1

PARK AVENUE

HARRIS STREET

Museum & Library

BAWDEN ST

MILL ST

MAIN STREET

EDMONDS ST

DOCK ST

MISSION STREET

FRONT STREET

Berth 2 Waterfront Promenade

GRANT STREET

BAWDEN STREET

Wells Fargo

Sushi! Harbor

Ketchikan Visitor Center

Ketchikan Arts & Humanities Council

Redman Lodge

Gilmore (& Annabelle's restaurant)

MAIN STREET

GRANT STREET

PINE STREET

Sourdough

Eagle Park

FRONT STREET

DOCK ST

Ketchikan Hostel

REVILLA STREET

PINE STREET

PINE STREET

CEDAR ST

PINE STREET

Burger Queen

Harbor View Park

Tunnel

Arctic

Berth-3

MAIN STREET

BAYVIEW AVE

HARDING STREET

WARREN ST

HOPKINS ST

HALLER STREET

YOUNG ST

WATER STREET

Ketchikan Outdoor

Berth House 4 of Haida

Best Western Landing, The Narrows Inn, Alaska's Hidden Cove, Coho Beach House, Black Bear Inn, Eagle View Hostel, Oceanview restaurant, Plaza Mall, Totem Bight State Historic Park & Potlach Park, Good God Lobster

Tongass Avenue, Alaska Fish House, Ketchikan Arts & Humanities Council, Saxon, (2-5 miles), Tatsuda: IGA, Alaska Canopy Adventures, Rainforest Wildlife Sanctuary

(↘ *225 8726; www.borough.Ketchikan.ak.us; adult/child/senior US$1/free/0.5*) a godsend. The blue line travels as far north as Totem Bight State Park and as far south as Saxman Village. Pick up a schedule and route map from a bus driver, or from the visitors' bureau.

By car Rental cars can be arranged and picked up at the airport, as well as in Ketchikan. It's a good idea to remember that public car parks in Ketchikan have time limits. Get a permit at City Hall (*334 Front St;* ↘ *225 3111;* ⊕ *08.00–17.00 Mon–Fri*) for US$5.

🚗 **Alaska Car Rental** 2828 Tongass Av; ↘ 225 5123, 800 662 0007 (TF); www.akcarrental.com

🚗 **Budget Car Rental** 4950 N Tongass Hwy; ↘ 225 8383, 800 478 2438 (TF); www.budget.com

By bike

🚲 **Ketchikan Outdoor** 714 Water St; ↘ 220 9957; www.ketchikanoutdoors.com; ⊕ 07.00–18.00 daily.

New mountain bikes with helmets & locks. US$25 half day; US$50 full day.

By taxi and shuttle

🚗 **Ketchikan Transporter** (see page 118) Shuttle service anywhere in town for US$5pp, as well as airport service.

🚗 **Sourdough Cab** ↘ 225 5544
🚗 **Alaska Cab** ↘ 225 2133
🚗 **Yellow Taxi** ↘ 225 5555

TOURIST INFORMATION

🛈 **Ketchikan Visitors Bureau** 131 Front St; ↘ 225 6166, 800 770 3300 (TF); www.visit-ketchikan.com. A large grey building at the cruise ship dock.
🛈 **Ketchikan-Misty Fiords Ranger District** 3031 Tongass Av; ↘ 225 2148; www.fs.fed.us; ⊕ 08.00–4.30 Mon–Fri.

🛈 **Southeast Alaska Discovery Center** 50 Main St; ↘ 228 6220; ⊕ 08.00–17.00 Mon–Sat, 08.00–16.00 Sun; US$5/free adult/child. This new facility is one of the better sources of information on the Tongass National Forest & other public lands. They also have some handsome, museum-like displays that are well worth the admission fee.

LOCAL TOURS AND ACTIVITIES
City centre

Seahorse Ventures Horse Drawn Tours ↘ 225 3672; www.horsetrolleytours.com. A guide with a husky dog narrates this tour of historic Ketchikan. Fun, warm people & the best way to learn about Ketchikan.
Alaska Amphibious Tours ↘ 225 9899, 866 341 3825 (TF); e info@akduck.com; www.akduck.com.

A fun tour for families with young children, otherwise a little too 'Disneyland'.
Great Alaskan Lumberjack Show ↘ 225 9050, 888 320 9049 (TF); www.lumberjacksports.com/alaska/index.html; adult/child US$34/17. A fun show that's touristy, but perfect for families with young children.

Around Ketchikan

Scenic flights Flights can be bumpy, so be sure to take appropriate measures against air-sickness. With the profusion of flight services in Ketchikan, there's no reason you shouldn't get the best service.

Alaska Seaplane Tours (see page 123) Bear viewing on Prince of Wales Island (US$339) & in Misty Fjords (US$289) as well as flightseeing.
Allen Marine Tours 5 Salmon Landing; ↘ 225 8100, 877 686 8100 (TF); www.allenmarinetours.com. Sightseeing tours of Misty Fjords on high-speed boats with wildlife guaranteed. A larger company with

branches in Sitka & Juneau offering good tours & a streamlined service.
Carlin Air (see page 123) Bear viewing & flightseeing.
Deer Mountain Tribal Hatchery & Eagle Center (see page 128) A good place to see spawning salmon mid to late summer.

Sea Wind Aviation ↘ 225 1206, 877 225 1203 (TF); www.seawindaviation.com. Tours & charter service from Ketchikan. The Misty Fjords Tour is US$229pp & bear viewing is US$349. They also offer fly-in-fishing & public-use cabin drops.

Wildlife The Alaska Department of Fish and Game produces a guide to wildlife viewing in Ketchikan. These can be picked up at the visitor centre. Fly-out trips are a great way to see bears, especially at Anan near Wrangell, Salmon Creek near Hyder or Prince of Wales Island. One of the best places for bear viewing is actually free: Eagle Creek in Herring Cove, eight miles south of town, is unbeatable for seeing bears feeding on salmon in August. Try to get there a few hours before the high tide as the fish start to come in. Margaret Bay is another great spot to try.

Alaska Seaplane Tours 420 Front St; ↘ 225 1974, 866 858 2327 (TF); www.alaskaseaplanetours.com; e ryan@alaskaseaplanetours.com. Misty fjords flightseeing, fly-out fishing & Prince of Wales Island & Hyder bear viewing. Family run, Ryan & Loren are fun outdoor folk.

Carlin Air ↘ 225 3036, 888 594 3036 (TF); www.carlinair.com; e info@carlinair.com. Flightseeing (US$230pp), bear viewing at Anan & Traitor Cove (US$350–450pp), fly-out fishing trips (1/2 day US$425pp, full day US$750pp).

Island Wings Air Service ↘ 225 2444, 888 854 2444 (TF); www.islandwings.com. One of the only commercial female pilots around, Michelle has been flying since 1978 & holds a degree in meteorology! Flightseeing trips into Misty Fjords in a lovely 6-person DeHavilland Beaver seaplane with perfectly clear windows for taking pictures. Michelle will give you the straight answer for any question. Flightseeing & bear viewing.

Pacific Air (see page 130) Flightseeing, fly-out fishing & charter flights.

Promech Air 1515 Tongass; ↘ 225 3845; www.promechair.com. A larger carrier with multiple planes, offering charter flights, flightseeing, bear viewing, etc.

Taquan Air (see page 133) Bear viewing, flightseeing & scheduled flights around Ketchikan.

Hiking/Adventure

Alaska Canopy Adventures 4085 Tongass Av St. 201; ↘ 225 5503; www.alaskacanopy.com. A 4,500ft zip-line course through the trees in Herring Cove, 8 miles south of town. From one line you can actually see Eagle Creek & any bears that may be fishing there in season. A commercial feel & a gaudy gift shop only slightly detract from this facility. The Rainforest Wildlife Sanctuary is also part of this complex. Zip-line tours are US$179 & guided nature/wildlife walks are US$80. Bears are often seen on this walk if fish are in the creek & captive wildlife is on the grounds.

Snorkel Alaska ↘ 247 7783; www.snorkelalaska.com. Encounter wolf eels & even orcas on these guided snorkelling & diving trips. Dry suits provided.

Tongass Rainforest Expeditions ↘ 617 8908; www.kpu.net/~trex. A 3hr hiking tour with company owner Chris on a scenic rainforest trail. Adult US$74.

Wind & Water Charters & Scuba 111 Washington St; ↘ 247 2082; www.wind-water.org. Full service scuba rental outfit & undersea tour operator. US$125+ for a beach dive.

Cruise, kayak and canoe

Bering Sea Crab Fishermen's Tour ↘ 360 642 4935, 888 239 3816 (TF); www.56degreesnorth.com; adult/child US$149/99. Head out on a former Bering Sea crab boat to watch as crewmen bring in crab & shrimp pots & pull long lines. Creatures are kept alive in holding tanks then released. Free snacks & drinks inc.

Experience Alaska Tours 11728 S Tongass Hwy; ↘ 225 6077; www.catchcrabs.com. Guests help pull crab pots before retiring to a historic cannery building where dinner is prepared.

Ketchikan Kayak Fishing Recently started offering kayak trips, as well as kayak fishing.

Ketchikan Outdoors 714 Water St; ↘ 220 9959; www.kethikanoutdoors.com. Boat rentals & sightseeing tours. This new tour allows guests to captain their own 16ft inflatable boat while they follow a guide boat for 30 miles up the coast. Instructions are issued over the radio.

Southeast Exposure 37 Potter Rd; ↘ 225 8829; www.southeastexposure.com. The first kayak outfit in town, these guys are top notch. Short or extended trips by kayak & gear rental. Bike tours & a zip line/ropes course are also available. **Southeast Sea Kayaks** 1621 Tongass Av; ✆ 225 1258, 800 287 1607 (TF); www.kayakketchikan.com. Owner Greg brings his diverse background of music, chemistry, diving & love for the sea to the business. Small groups, rentals & drop offs. Half-day trips cost US$159; all-day Misty Fjords trips cost US$449 & guided overnight trips start at US$1,600 for 4 days.

Fishing Though Ketchikan's title of 'Salmon Capital of the World' is a carry-over from the turn of the century, the area is still rich in fish. Anglers arrive from around the world to fish salmon from the sea and rivers and trout from high-mountain lakes and clear creeks. While there is some fishing around town, most fishermen choose to fly into Misty Fjords or the Tongass National Forest for the best sites.

Alaska Seaplane Tours All-day guided fly-in fishing trips cost US$550.
Baranof Excursions ✆ 225 4055; e info@ exclusivealaska.com; www.exclusivetouring.com. One of the most unique fishing experiences in Alaska. Head out in an open boat with your guide & catch a fish, & then watch or help the chef prepare the evening's meal around a campfire in a remote location for US$295pp.
Carlin Air Fly-out half-day (US$425) & full-day (US$750) fishing trips.
Classic Alaska Charters ✆ 225 0608; e captrob@ classicalaskacharters.com; www.classicalaskacharters.com.

These 5-day trips give guests the full Alaskan subsistence experience. With access to more fishing than anyone can handle, these guys pull their own shrimp & crab pots & their chef prepares the meal. Adult US$2,450.
Experience One Charters 3857 Fairview; ✆ 225 2343; www.latitude56.com. Salmon & halibut charters.
Ketchikan Kayak Fishing ✆ 225 1272; e trips@ yakfishalaska.com; www.yakfishalaska.com. A fishing charter & a kayak trip all in one. Fish for salmon & other species or just sightsee & watch your other half fish.

HIKING AND RECREATION The visitor bureau in the city centre has a fantastic hiking trail guide with detailed information on virtually every hike in the area. Some of the best trails include:

Deer Mountain Trail/Silvis Lake John Mountain Trail (*Grade: difficult; distance:10 miles*) Start at the trailhead just off Ketchikan Lakes Road or 12 miles south of Ketchikan at the end of South Tongass Highway.

Perseverance Trail (*Grade: moderate; distance: 2.3 miles*) This easy walk is lovely and provides excellent berry picking in the fall. Camping is also available. Start at the trailhead (across from the Ward Lake Red Area) eight miles north of town on the Tongass Highway.

Others include the Ward Creek Trail, Connell Lake Trail and the Lunch Creek Trail. For more info on trails visit www.seatrails.org.

WHERE TO STAY Ketchikan has only a few hotels, but competition between B&Bs and vacation rentals is fierce. With the exception of the New York Hotel (see below), Ketchikan's hotels are nothing special, offering mostly clean but bland accommodation. One hotel perk is a free airport- or ferry- pickup. For a more private experience, book a vacation rental or B&B. In fact, it's worth contacting **Alaska Travelers Accommodations** (✆ *247 7117, 800 928 3308 (TF);* e *info@ alaskatravelers.com; www.alaskatravelers.com*). They will make life easier by finding the best accommodation for your needs. They book mid- to upper-end B&Bs and vacation rentals.

Hotels

⌂ **Best Western Landing** (107 rooms) 3434 Tongass Av; ☏ 225 5166; e bwlanding@kpunet.net; www.landinghotel.com. Clean, standard rooms in a good central location with microwaves & refrigerators in all the rooms. The 2 restaurants downstairs are the smoky **Landing Restaurant** *(open 06.00–21.00 Sun–Thu, 06.00–21.30 Fri–Sat)* serving b/fast all day & generic, low quality American food. Upstairs is **Jeremiah's Pub** *(⏱ 11.00–23.00 Mon–Thu, 11.00–midnight Fri, 09.00–midnight Sat, 09.00–23.00 Sun)* with microbrews on tap & an outside deck. $$$$

⌂ **Cape Fox Lodge** (72 rooms) 800 Venetia Way; ☏ 225 8001; www.capefoxlodge.com. Located high on the hill behind Creek St, the hotel is special only for its amazing views & Tlingit artwork. A short tram connects the lodge with the Creek St area & costs US$3. The hotel has a decent restaurant & a bar. Pay Wi-Fi. $$$$

⌂ **Gilmore Hotel** (34 rooms) 326 Front St; ☏ 225 9423; www.gilmorehotel.com. Located in the quaint Creek St district, this hotel offers decent rooms with free b/fast downstairs in Annabell's restaurant. Wi-Fi. $$$

⌂ **New York Hotel** (14 rooms) 207 Stedman St; ☏ 225 0246; www.thenewyorkhotel.com. A lovely, historic, boutique hotel in the best part of town, Creek St. The hotel was originally built in 1924 by a Japanese family who were sent to internment camps at the onset of World War II. 8 standard rooms (US$129) are in the main building & 6 suites (US$189) are off the boardwalk up Ketchikan Creek. Historic furniture & photos can be seen throughout the hotel. Downstairs is the Ketchikan Coffee Company with hot drinks, baked goods, & lunch. Guests can ride the Cape Fox Lodge tram for free. Rates dropped by at least 25% after 1 Oct 2009. One of the best historic hotels in Alaska & great value. Wi-Fi. $$$

⌂ **The Narrows Inn** (46 rooms) 4871 North Tongass Hwy; ☏ 225 2600; www.narrowsinn.com. A large, generic hotel right on the water about 4 miles from the city centre. Ocean view rooms are just US$10 more than a standard. The bar & restaurant downstairs are decent. Free airport/ferry transportation. Wi-Fi, microwave, & fridge. B/fast inc. $$$

B&Bs

⌂ **Alaska's Hidden Cove** (3 rooms) ☏ 225 7934, 800 822 2683 (TF); e reserve@akhiddencove.com; www.akhiddencove.com. Located in a private, secluded cove 9 miles north of town. A lovely large house with every amenity & luxury. Stocked with a wide assortment of foods. Full kitchen. Laundry. BBQ. $$$$$

⌂ **Coho Beach House** (2 rooms) A 2-storey historic home over the water with good views. North of town in Ward Cove. Wi-Fi. BBQ. Laundry. $$$$

⌂ **Black Bear Inn** (6 rooms) 5528 N Tongass Av; ☏ 225 4343; e blackbearalaska@aol.com; www.stayinalaska.com. A lovely home 4 miles north of town & right on the water. One of Ketchikan's best places to stay. Hot tub, BBQ, Wi-Fi, freezer space & fish smoker. $$$

⌂ **Eagle Heights B&B** (4 rooms) 1626 Water St; ☏ 225 1760; e eagleheights@kpunet.net; www.eagleheightsbb.com. A beautiful, historic home near Clover Pass Resort *(www.cloverpassresort.com)*. Simple, but comfortable rooms & great rates. Wi-Fi & fridge. $$$

Hostels

⌂ **Eagle View Hostel** (10 beds) 2303 Fifth Av; ☏ 225 5461; www.eagleviewhostel.com. A nice wood home 1.5 miles from the city centre. No curfew. Laundry is US$3.50. US$25/pp. $

⌂ **Ketchikan Hostel** (19 beds) 400 Main St; ☏ 225 3319; e ktnyh@eagle.ptialaska.net. On the corner of Grant & Main St in the city centre. Closed 10.00–17.00 daily. Located in a church, but guests are not required to attend. Kitchen. ⏱ only Jun, July, Aug. No credit cards. B/fast inc. $

Camping Call ☏ 877 444 6777 to make reservations at any of the federal campgrounds. For more information visit www.fs.fed.us/r10/tongass/recreation/rec_facilities/ktnrec.shtml

⛰ **Last Chance Campground** (19 sites) 10 miles north of town on Revilla Rd. Fire rings, water, toilets, & garbage. No hookups. Fishing nearby. US$10/night.

⚑ Settler's Cove State Recreation Area (14 sites)
⚈ 247 8574; www.dnr.state.ak.us. 18 miles north of Ketchikan at the end of the Tongass Hwy in a majestic forest of ancient trees. The 3.5-mile Lunch Falls Loop Trail is nearby & can be good for seeing & feeding black bears. The recreation site is slated for an overhaul with better facilities, roads & campsites. A total of 13 of the 14 sites can accommodate RVs. No reservations. Toilets.

⚑ Signal Creek Campground (24 sites) Located at the Ward Lake Recreation Area, this campground is near trails & right on the lake. Watch for mid-summer mosquitoes & early-spring flooding. Camped on high ground with an ample supply of anti-bug sprays, you will have a great time at this awesome spot. US$10/night.

⚑ Three Cs Campground (4 sites) Located at the Ward Lake Recreation Area. Closed except for overflow from Signal Creek Campground. US$10/night.

RV Camping

⚑ Clover Pass Resort (36 sites) ⚈ 247 2234. Guided fishing trips & DIY boat rentals (US$250), as well as lodge rooms, RV spaces & a restaurant serving seafood. RV sites US$30 standard & US$35 waterfront.

Cabins The Ketchikan area (⚈ 877 444 6777; *www.recreation.gov*) has 17 cabins and shelters accessible by plane or boat only. Fees range from US$25–45 per night.

✗ WHERE TO EAT There are a number of fine eateries, offering everything from sushi and burgers to fine dining, in and around the city centre. Those closest to the cruise ship docks are usually filled to capacity when ships are in town.

✗ Bar Harbor 2813 Tongass Av; ⚈ 225 2813; www.barharborrestaurantktn.com; ⊕ 16.30–21.00 Tue–Sat. Intimate dining with consistently good food & homely/rustic décor. Famous for prime rib, crab cakes & chunky homemade fries. Small beer selection, but a medley of wines. Reservations are a good idea. $$$$

✗ Cape Fox Lodge, Heen Kahidi Dining Room ⊕ 07.00–21.00 daily. Serves decent seafood, meat & pasta dishes as well as b/fast & lunch. Great view. Restaurant patrons ride the tram up from Creek St for free. Full bar. $$$$

✗ Steamers Restaurant 76 Front St Ste 301; ⚈ 225 1600; ⊕ 10.00–22.00 daily. Right on the cruise-ship dock with a good upper-storey view of the Tongass Narrows. Very popular with cruise-ship passengers. Standard fare with passable seafood & all-you-can-eat crab. A large selection of beers on tap, but small cocktails. Local singers perform on the w/ends. $$$$

✗ Alaska Fish House 3 Salmon Landing; ⚈ 247 4055, 877 732 9453 (TF); www.alaskafishhouse.com; ⊕ 06.00–19.00 daily. Chuck & Debbie are fun people dedicated to bringing great food & experiences to the wilderness. The Alaska Fish House offers good seafood & great salmon chowder. Far more exciting though is their side project called **Chef's Table**: feast on the best seafood, meticulously prepared in their private dining area with boat harbour views. A 5-course meal might inc saffron bouillabaisse, smoked & fresh salmon, halibut & a number of desserts. Reservations required. US$119pp. Ask about **Baranof**, a wilderness dining experience. $$

✗ Annabelle's 326 Front St; ⚈ 225 6009; ⊕ 10.00–22.00 daily. Downstairs from the Gilmore Hotel, this restaurant – named after a prostitute – serves passable food & has a fabulous antique bar. $$$

✗ Sushi Harbor 629 Mission St; 225 1233; ⊕ 10.00–21.00 Mon–Fri, 11.00–21.00 Sat–Sun. Local seafood is used here. Great names for their creative concoctions such as 'monkey brain.' Looks like a brain, tastes great. $$$

✗ The Narrows ⊕ 06.30–14.00 & 17.00–21.00 daily. Located inside the Narrows Inn. Right on the dock with good prices & food. Sunday brunch is very popular, but only served on the 1st Sun of the month. $$$

✗ Burger Queen 518 Water St; ⚈ 225 6060; ⊕ 11.00–19.00 Tue–Sat. This local favourite is north of the tunnel & is run by angsty teens who somehow turn out great burgers. $$

✗ Landing Restaurant On the bottom floor of the Best Western Landing Hotel. A smoky diner with retro décor. The only reason to come here is for the all-day b/fast. $$

✗ **Ocean View Restaurant** 1831 Tongass Av; ☎ 225 7566; ⏱ 11.00–23.00. Mexican & Italian food done well & served in massive quantities. One of town's cheaper & more filling options. **$$**

✗ **Pioneer Café** 619 Mission St; ☎ 225 3337; ⏱ 24hrs. The only restaurant in town that's open 24hrs — handy for those getting off the ferry at 03.00. Though they serve 3 all-American meals a day, b/fast is the best. **$$**

Cafés

✗ **Ketchikan Coffee Company** (see page 124) ☎ 247 2326; ⏱ 07.00–16.00 daily, ⏱ until 22.00 on Fri. Located downstairs of the New York Hotel (see page 124) & sometimes called the New York Café. Hot drinks, baked goods, lunch is served 11.00–15.00. Live music on Fri. A cosy spot to hang out & watch the rain.

✗ **Refiner's Roast Coffees** 2050 Sea Level Dr Ste 105; ☎ 247 6278; ⏱ 06.30–18.00 Mon–Fri, 07.00–17.00 Sat, 08.00–16.00 Sun. A coffee roaster & small coffee house. Free Wi-Fi.

WHERE TO DRINK

☿ **Annabelle's** (see page 125) ⏱ until 23.00 daily. An old-fashioned place with a gorgeous antique bar.
☿ **Arctic Bar** 509 Water St; ☎ 225 4709; www.arcticbar.com. Right on the water with a nice verandah. Drunks & thrill seekers have been known to leap from the deck into the sea.
☿ **Cape Fox Lodge, Heen Kahidi Lounge** (see page 124) ⏱ 11.00–22.00 daily. Frequently full, this bar does offer great views, but the interior lacks character.

☿ **Fat Stan's** Salmon Landing, #108; ☎ 247 9463; www.winesinternational.net. This small haunt is one of the more classy places in town to have a drink. A large selection of martinis, beer & wine with a wine shop attached. Located in Salmon Landing by the cruise-ship dock.
☿ **Potlach Bar** 126 Thomas St; ☎ 225 4855. A fisherman's bar.
☿ **Sourdough bar & liquor store** 301 Front St; ☎ 225 2217. A standard bar with a strange yet fascinating collection of historic sinking-ship photos.

ENTERTAINMENT AND NIGHTLIFE
Live music
First City Players ☎ 225 4792; www.ketchikanarts.org. Founded in 1964, this theatre group puts on 10 or more shows per year. The *Fish Pirate's Daughter* plays twice weekly during Jul & includes a crab feast at the Civic Center for US$40.

First City Saloon 830 Water St; ☎ 225 1494; http://firstcitysaloon.com. A rowdy young scene with dancing, loud music & occasionally policemen throwing people out. Live music Thu & Fri.

Cinema
Coliseum Twine Theatre 405 Mission St; ☎ 225 2294. 2 relatively new movies play at a time.

FESTIVALS AND EVENTS
The **Monthly Grind** (☎ *225 6910; adult/child US$5/1*) is usually held the third Saturday of each month between September and May, and features local talent from kids singing ABCs to great local bands jamming together. Coffee, tea and desserts are included in the admission price, but if you bring your own, it's free. Starts at 19.00 at the Saxman Village Clan House.

April
Alaska Hummingbird Festival A celebration of the return of not only hummingbirds, but many other migratory birds on their way north. Events include guided walks, bird banding, art & bird education for kids and adults. Call the Alaska Discovery Center (see page 129) for details.

July The 4 July celebration takes over Front Street with a parade and mobs of people. A logger's competition takes place at the baseball field on Park Avenue and a pie sale at St John's Church (*423 Mission St*). Fireworks start at 23.00 on 3 July.

August The first weekend of August brings the Blueberry Arts Festival with booths, music, food and some blueberries.

SHOPPING
Bookshops
Parnassus Books 5 Creek St; ☎ 225 7690; www.ketchikanbooks.com; ⏰ 08.30—18.00 Mon—Fri, 09.00—17.00 Sat, 09.00—16.00 Sun. This gem has a great assortment of Alaskan books & others.

Waldenbooks 2417 Tongass Av # 103; ☎ 225 8120; www.borders.com; ⏰ 09.00—20.00 Mon—Sat, 12.00—17.00 Sun. A commercial bookstore in the Plaza Mall.

Galleries
Exploration Gallery 633 Mission St; ☎ 225 4278; www.explorationgallery.com. A wide range of local art from stone sculptures to kelp baskets.
Scanlon 318 Mission St; ☎ 247 4730; www.scanlongallery.com. Native & local art.

Soho Coho 5 Creek St; ☎ 225 9195; www.trollart.com. Downstairs from Parnassus Books, this gallery is owned by the Troll family & features Ray's work & others.

Native arts
Carver on Creek Street 28 Creek St; ☎ 225 3018; www.normanjackson.com. A unique opportunity to watch Nathan Jackson, a Tongass Tlingit, work & speak with him about his art.

Crazy Wolf 607 Mission St; ☎ 225 9653; www.crazywolfstudio.com. A wide variety of native arts, owned by a Tsimshian artist from Ketchikan.
Saxman Arts Co-op (see page 130)

Outdoor
Alaskan Wilderness Outfitting 3857 Fairview Av; ☎ 225 7335; www.latitude56.com/camping. Rent camping gear here.
Murray Pacific Supply 1050 Water; ☎ 225 3135. Raingear, sport & commercial fishing gear.

Tongass Trading Co. 201 Dock St; ☎ 225 5101; e mail@tongasstrading.com, www.tongasstrading.com. Outdoor gear & fishing equipment. Near the city centre.

OTHER PRACTICALITIES
Banks
$ **First Bank** 2530 Tongass Av; ☎ 228 4235; www.firstbankak.com; ⏰ 09.00—17.30 Mon—Fri, 10.00—14.00 Sat. Branch & ATM.
$ **First Bank** 331 Dock St; ☎ 228 4474; ⏰ 09.00—17.30 Mon—Fri. Branch & ATM.
$ **Key Bank** 2501 Tongass Av; ☎ 225 4556; www.key.com; ⏰ 09.30—17.00 Mon—Fri, 09.30—13.30 Sat. Branch & ATM.

$ **Wells Fargo Bank** 306 Main St, city centre; ☎ 225 2184; www.wellsfargo.com; ⏰ 09.00—17.00 Mon—Thu, 09.00—17.30 Fri. Branch & 24hr ATM.
$ **Wells Fargo Bank** 2415 Tongass Av; ☎ 225 4141; ⏰ 10.00—18.00 Mon—Sat. Branch & 24hr ATM.
$ **Wells Fargo Bank** 4966 N Tongass Hwy; ☎ 247 7878; ⏰ 09.30—17.30 Mon—Fri. Branch & 24hr ATM.

Food shopping
A & P 3816 Tongass Av; ☎ 225 1279
Carr's Safeway 2417 Tongass Av; ☎ 225 9880; www.safeway.com; ⏰ 05.00—midnight daily. Delicatessen & good selection of foods.
Good God Lobster 1624 Tongass Av; ☎ 247 8000; www.goodgodlobster.com; ⏰ 10.00—18.00 Mon—Sat. A full selection of fresh seafood.

Tatsuda's IGA 633 Stedman St; ☎ 225 4125; www.tatsudaiga.com; ⏰ 07.00—23.00 daily. Full service grocery store in Ketchikan since 1916. Just south of Creek St.
Wal-Mart 4230 Don King Rd; ☎ 247 2156; www.wal-mart.com. Some food, hardware, sporting goods, clothes, etc.

Healthcare

Pharmacies

Downtown Drug 300 Front St; ☏ 225 3144
Island Pharmacy 3526 Tongass Av; ☏ 225 6186

Wal-Mart 4230 Don King Rd; ☏ 247 2183;
🕐 09.00–19.00 Mon–Fri, 09.00–18.00 Sat

Hospital

✚ **Ketchikan General Hospital** 3100 Tongass Av;
☏ 225 5171; e ketchikan@peacehealth.org

✚ **Ketchikan Medical Clinic** 3612 Tongass Av; ☏ 225 5144. Near the ferry terminal.

Dentists

David A Albertson 130 Carlanna Lake Rd; ☏ 225 9631
J Terry Thompson 306 Main St Ste 211; ☏ 225 3031

Thomas B Nordtvedt Tongass Av Ste 103; ☏ 225 8228

Internet

🄴 **Best Western Landing** (see page 124) Fast Wi-Fi is available in the cosy lobby area for non-guests. An adjoining office is also available.
🄴 **Ketchikan Coffee Company** (see page 124)

🄴 **Ketchikan Public Library** 629 Dock St; ☏ 225 3331; 🕐 10.00–20.00 Mon–Wed, 10.00–18.00 Thu–Sat, 13.00–17.00 Sun. Free internet.
🄴 **Walden Books** (see page 127)

Post offices

✉ **Ketchikan Post Office** 3609 Tongass Av;
🕐 08.30–17.00 Mon–Fri
✉ **Ketchikan Post Office City Centre** 422 Mission St;
🕐 09.00–17.30 Mon–Sat

✉ **Ward Cove Post Office** 7172 N Tongass Hwy;
🕐 07.00–16.00 Mon–Fri, 09.30–12.30 Sat

WHAT TO SEE AND DO

Creek Street A historic part of town a short walk south of the city centre. Shops, restaurants and homes on stilts line the creek connected by boardwalks. High tide from mid-summer onward brings spawning salmon and sometimes hungry seals. Don't stay here in the late autumn when stinky 'spawned out' salmon wash down the creek. See box below.

Museums

Deer Mountain Tribal Hatchery and Eagle Center (*1158 Salmon Rd;* ☏ *228 5530, 800 252 5158 (TF); US$9/free adult/child;* 🕐 *08.00–16.30 daily*) Located near the Totem Heritage Center, the hatchery caters to visitors curious about the salmon lifecycle

---

RED-LIGHT DISTRICT TURNED TOURIST TRAP

These days Creek Street caters to tourists who come to window shop and dine out, but at the turn of the 20th century, it served as Ketchikan's red-light district. Dolly Arthur (1888–1975) was Creek Street's most infamous 'lady of the night' and her former home and brothel at 24 Creek Street is now a museum called Dolly's House.

As local government gained power, they pushed the working girls out of the city centre and into Newtown on Ketchikan Creek. However, Newtown residents were unhappy with the arrangement and, in 1903, petitioned the city to move them back across the creek. The plan stuck, the girls stayed and soon the small houses of what would be Creek Street were built on stilts on the south side of the creek, creating a true red-light district and a one-stop shop for lusty patrons.

For more information visit http://creekstreetketchikan.com.

with information, displays, and demonstrations. They also have a small aviary for a pair of injured bald eagles who have nested in the enclosure. The eagles sometimes hunt for themselves in the creek that passes through their enclosure.

Dolly's House Museum (*24 Creek St;* ✎ *225 2279;* ⊕ *08.00–17.00 daily; US$4/free adult/child*) This historic house – home to Ketchikan's first brothel – is full of great photos and antiques.

Southeast Alaska Discovery Center (see page 121) A huge boon to Ketchikan, the new US$10 million centre is the only one of its kind in southeast Alaska. Native history, the more recent past and natural history, are all carefully assembled into first-class displays.

Tongass Historical Museum (*628 Dock St;* ✎ *225 5600;* ⊕ *08.00–17.00 daily; US$2 adult*) A good collection of native and historic artefacts and photos. Rotating invitational shows are some of the most popular.

Totem Heritage Center (*601 Deermount St;* ✎ *225 5900;* ⊕ *08.00–17.00 daily; US$5/free adult/child, free on days without cruiseships*) A must-see for those interested in the history of totem poles and native traditions. See also box on page 17.

Galleries Ketchikan has a rich arts community and was named one of America's 100 Best Art Towns. Lectures, gallery shows and performances happen here all year and locals often complain of so many things happening, that in a given night they must choose one event over another. One of Alaska's more famous artists, Ray Troll, found most of his original inspiration in the primeval environs around Ketchikan.

Ketchikan Arts and Humanities Council (*716 Totem Way;* ✎ *225 4278*) This outfit is the glue that holds the arts community together. They organise events and bring artists and musicians to town from outside the state.

Mainstay Gallery The gallery of the Ketchikan Art and Humanities Council feature a new show each month.

AROUND KETCHIKAN

RAINFOREST WILDLIFE SANCTUARY (*4085 Tongass Av Ste 201, 8 miles south of town in Herring Cove;* ✎ *225 5503, 877 947 7557 (TF); www.alaskarainforest.com; tours US$80*) This nature reserve hosts an owl, an eagle and a small herd of caribou. When the salmon are in Eagle Creek can attract bears, which can be seen at close range from a boardwalk. Built on the site of an old sawmill, much of the original machinery and wood is still there. A resident totem-pole carver works away while you watch. A worthwhile place to visit when the salmon are in and the bears are around. A zip-line tour is also available.

TOTEM BIGHT STATE PARK (*On main road, 8 miles north of town; www.dnr.state.ak.us/ parks/units/totembgh.htm; free admission*) An amazing collection of totem poles and a traditional long house built to accommodate 50 people. A gift shop is on the grounds. See also box on page 17.

POTLACH PARK (*Adjacent to Totem Bight State Park*) Many visitors miss this amazing collection of buildings and totems.

SAXMAN VILLAGE (*Population: 420*) 2.5 miles south of town, this traditional native village has the largest collection of totem poles on earth. Carvers can sometimes be seen at work on massive cedar logs. Visitors can explore the area on their own for an admission price of US$3, or join a tour led by Cape Fox (*www.capefoxtours.com/saxman.html*). To see the dancers, pay an additional US$35/18 adult/child at the Village Store (↘ *225 4421; open according to cruise ship schedule*). The Saxman Arts Co-op (↘ *225 4166*) sells the work of local native artists. The city bus, Ketchikan Gateway Borough Transit (see page 119), stops at the village.

METLAKATLA (*Population: 1,318*) The Tsimshian native community of Metlakatla (✪ 55°7'37"N, 131°34'35"W), or 'Met' sits on the west side of Annette Island, 15 miles south of Ketchikan. The 86,000-acre island is Alaska's only native reservation, controlled entirely by the Metlakatla Indian Community. The tribe regulates every aspect of its conduct from commercial fishing to the courts, with no state oversight. The land was acquired in 1886 by the Anglican Reverend William Duncan, who petitioned President Grover Cleveland for it. A year later, he set sail from Prince Rupert, Canada, with a group of 826 Tsimshian and landed on Annette Island, Alaska. Duncan ruled the community with a degree of authoritarianism, keeping out state education and overseeing the building and operation of a sawmill and fish cannery. Despite this, he was generally loved by the community and to this day is held in high esteem by many. Duncan died in 1918 and left behind a legacy evident in the Anglican churches that seem to stand on every street corner. During World War II a massive runway (1.5 miles long) was built near the southern end of the island and a base was staffed with some 10,000 men. A well-maintained road connects town with the former base. Commercial fishing and processing dominate the economy today with a few cruise ships docking and providing additional cash flow. A 14.7-mile, US$40-million road is currently under construction from town to Waldon Point where a new ferry terminal will be built, but is currently behind schedule. .

The friendly community has just enough visitor services to make a stay comfortable, but not so many that visitors feel like they are in yet another southeast Alaska tourist trap. Just about everyone in town belongs to one of the traditional Tsimshian clans of the eagle (*Laxsgyiik*), raven (*Ganhada*), wolf (*Laxgyibuu*), and orca (*Gisbutwada*). Clan affiliations are still so important that high school sports teams wear their clan symbol on their shorts. While the town offers a few cultural points of interest, the island itself is rugged, lushly forested, and offers a handful of adventures, such as hiking, fishing, shopping, and cultural performances.

Getting there and away The **Alaska Ferry** (*7559 North Tongass Hwy;* ↘ *800 642 0066; www.ferryalaska.com*) makes the trip from Ketchikan to Metlakatla twice a day with the MV *Lituya*. Alternatively, **Promech Air** (↘ *225 3845; www.promechair.com*) and **Pacific Airways** (↘ *886 3500; www.metlakatla.com*) fly to Met daily for US$50 one-way.

Tourist information City of Metlakatla (↘ *886 4441; www.metlakatla.com*). Culeen at the municipal building is very friendly.

Tours In a non-touristy town like Met, visitors looking for detailed cultural information would do well to arrange a tour with **Laughing Berry Tours** (↘ *886 4133*) or **Metlakatla Tours** (↘ *886 8687; metlakatlatours.com*).

Where to stay and eat

🏠 **Tuck 'Em Inn** (9 rooms) ☎ 886 6611; www.alaskanow.com/tuckem-inn. Small but comfortable rooms & an adjoining restaurant (🕐 11.00–19.00 Mon–Sat; **$$**). The owners also have a 3-bedroom home on Hillcrest that is more comfortable – worth asking about. Roy can arrange fishing or cultural tours. $$

✕ **Pizza Remix** ☎ 886 7779. Call to order. **$$$**
✕ **Mini-Mart** ☎ 886 3000. Basic groceries & a burger & fries joint, perfect for meeting the locals. **$$**

What to see and do

Father Duncan's Cottage (🕐 08.30–12.30 Mon–Fri; US$2) This cottage now houses a small museum. On the west side of town near the harbour is a traditional **long house** and next door is a large building with art shops (open when cruise ships are in town). The exquisite long house is generally open, but don't enter without permission or a guide. Dances are held when cruise ships are in town.

Walking trails Airport Road heads south from town and provides access to the Yellow Hill Trail, Purple Lake Trail, and Sand Dollar Beach but not before passing the city dump (a roadside field of garbage). Yellow Hill is accessible via a short trail leaving the road about 1.5 miles from town. The yellow rock outcrop contrasts wonderfully with the pond on a sunny day. The hike to Purple Lake starts at the end of a narrow road branching off Airport Road 4 miles from town. Turn at the Quonset huts and follow the road to the base of the mountain and hike up to the saddle. A wooden sign off Airport Road marks Sand Dollar Beach. A well-maintained boardwalk traverses a muskeg (marsh) before descending into a spectacular stand of cedars on a lovely sandy beach. Near the end of the road is a 1.5-mile runway built in World War II and used by locals for drag racing. If you brought your own car, this is a fun place to see how fast it can go before you get scared. The road narrows and continues through the trees to the sea at the far south end of the island. The rugged coastline is a good place to see birds and beach comb. The forest in this area is not tall but is extremely lush. A **frog petroglyph** can be found at Tent Point. Ask locally for directions.

Bingo (*8th & Waterfront; 16.00 Thu & Sat, every other week*) To really feel like a member of the community, head over to bingo in the hall across from the Tuck 'Em Inn.

PRINCE OF WALES ISLAND

Those who love adventure, the southeast and a good old-fashioned road trip simply must take the ferry to Prince of Wales Island. The immense island (the third largest in the country) is a veritable wilderness filled to the brim with soaring peaks, remote lakes, ancient moss-draped forests, thousands of rivers and streams, and even one of America's largest cave systems. The land is filled with bear and deer, and wolves still prowl the high country. The rivers and lakes offer some of the best trout and salmon fishing in the state, not to mention long rafting and canoe trips.

Best of all, the island is crisscrossed by more roads than the rest of the southeast combined (1,500 miles), making it both wild and accessible. Alas, no place is a true paradise and Prince of Wales Island, or POW as locals call it, is no exception. Much of the island's vast timber resources were converted to boards and pulp in the last century, leaving fields of stumps and new growth throughout the island. Still, much of the island remains cloaked in lush old growth. In addition to the natural

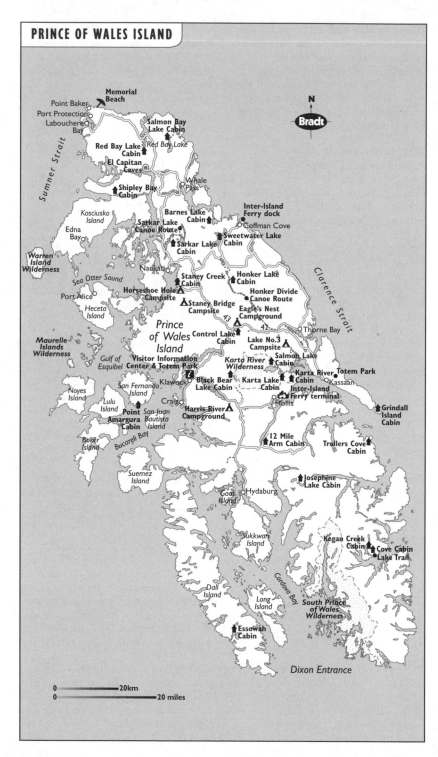

PRINCE OF WALES ISLAND

N

Bradt

Memorial
Beach

Point Baker

Port Protection
Labouchere
Bay

Sumner Strait

Red Bay Lake
Cabin

Salmon Bay
Lake Cabin

Red Bay Lake

El Capitan
Caves

Whale
Pass

Shipley Bay
Cabin

Kosciusko
Island

Edna
Bay

Barnes Lake
Cabin

Inter-Island
Ferry dock

Coffman Cove

Sarkar Lake
Canoe Route

Sweetwater Lake
Cabin

Sarkar Lake
Cabin

Warren
Island
Wilderness

Sea Otter Sound

Naukati

Clarence Strait

Staney Creek
Cabin

Honker Lake
Cabin

Port Alice

Heceta
Island

Horseshoe Hole
Campsite

Honker Divide
Canoe Route

Staney Bridge
Campsite

Eagle's Nest
Campground

Prince
of Wales
Island

Control Lake
Cabin

43

42

Thorne Bay

Maurelle
Islands
Wilderness

Gulf of
Esquibel

Visitor Information
Center & Totem Park

Lake No.3
Campsite

Karta River
Wilderness

Salmon Lake
Cabin

San Fernando
Island

Klawock

Black Bear
Lake Cabin

Karta Lake
Cabin

Karta River
Cabin

Totem Park

Kassaan

Noyes
Island

Lulu
Island

Craig

San Juan
Bautista
Island

Harris River
Campground

Inter-Island
Ferry terminal

Hollis

Grindall
Island
Cabin

Point
Amargura
Cabin

Baker
Island

Bucareli Bay

12 Mile
Arm Cabin

Trollers Cove
Cabin

Suemez
Island

Josephine
Lake Cabin

Goat
Island

Hydaburg

Sukkwan
Island

Kegan Creek
Cabin

Cove Cabin

Lake Trail

Cordova Bay

South Prince
of Wales
Wilderness

Dall
Island

Long
Island

Essowah
Cabin

Dixon Entrance

0   20km

0   20 miles

environment, POW is one of the best places in the southeast to see totem poles, both old and new. Amazing Haida totems can be found around the island, including a particularly amazing village site a short hike from Kasaan.

HISTORY The area was explored in the 1770s by the Spanish and mapped in 1777 by Captain James Cook. The island was named after the then Prince of Wales, who was the oldest son of King George III, by British explorer and cartographer George Vancouver in 1793. In the 19th century, mining took root in many parts of the island, followed closely by logging and commercial fishing. Since the 1970s logging has slowed considerably, with just a few small mills still operating. Today, the island's economy is slowly shifting to tourism, mostly catering to the hunter and fishermen contingent.

GETTING THERE AND AWAY

By sea The **Inter-Island Ferry Authority** (↘ 826 4849; *www.interislandferry.com*) travels from Ketchikan to Hollis (*journey time: 3hrs; ticket: US$37*) on Prince of Wales Island every day. These new ferries are first class and accommodate cars. Be sure to arrange a taxi, or rental car pick-up on POW, since the ferry terminal is isolated.

By air

✈ **Island Air Express** ↘ 888 387 8989; www.islandairx.com. 4 daily flights between Ketchikan & Klowack for US$115 1-way.

✈ **Pacific Airways** ↘ 826 5400, 877 360 3500 (TF); www.flypacificairways.com. Several flights per day from Ketchikan to Craig (US$130), Hollis (US$100), & Thorne Bay (US$100) on POW.

✈ **Promech Air** ↘ 225 3845, 800 860 3845 (TF); www.promechair.com. Daily flights to Ihorne Bay & Hollis for US$105 1-way & Craig for US$130.

✈ **Taquan Air** 4085 Tongass Av; ↘ 225 8800, 800 770 8800 (TF); www.taquanair.com. Daily flights from Ketchikan to just about every POW community. Flights from Ketchikan to Coffman Cove are US$145, to Craig are US$125, to Hollis or Thorne Bay are US$105.

TOURIST INFORMATION The **Prince of Wales Chamber of Commerce** (↘ 755 2626; *www.princeofwales.org*; ⊕ 08.00–16.00 Mon–Fri) is located in the mall in Klawock, and is the only visitor centre on the island. Get a US$12 island map here, or at the southeast Alaska Discovery Center (↘ 228 6220) in Ketchikan, or at the **US Forest Service office** (*900 Main St;* ↘ 826 3271; *www.fs.fed.us*) located in Craig at the end of 9th Street. It's staffed by very knowledgeable rangers. For island trails visit www.seatrails.org.

 WHERE TO STAY AND EAT Accommodation and eating options are listed under the island's various towns below.

HOLLIS (*Population: 172*) Those arriving by ferry will get their first taste of the island in the miniscule settlement of Hollis (⊕ 55°29'4"N, 132°42'57"W). Hollis was a mining site, then a logging camp, and now hosts the ferry port. From here, the road travels east to Hydaburg, Klawock, and 35 miles to Craig.

Practicalities

Hollis Adventure Rentals ↘ 530 7040; www.harentals.com. Rental cars for US$105–125, boats for US$125–145, & kayaks for US$55.

Public Library ↘ 530 7112; www.princeofwalesonline.com/hollis_library.html; ⊕ 13.00–16.00 Tue, 14.00–17.00 Wed, 10.00–14.00 Thu, 10.00–13.00 Sat. An incredibly small library with internet access.

HYDABURG (*Population: 341*) Hydaburg (⊕ 55°12'17"N, 132°49'15"W) is a native Haida community located in the far south of the island off State Road 913. Residents eek out a living through a combination of commercial fishing and subsistence hunting and fishing. This traditional village has some great totem poles and can be fun to walk around, but many islanders recommend against spending the night. While most folks are very friendly, some can be abrasive towards visitors. For more information call **City Hall** (✆ *285 3761*).

🏠 Where to stay and eat

⚑ Harris River Campground Between the turnoff to Hydaburg & Klawock, 11 miles from the ferry; normally US$8/night, but 17 Sep–17 May free. A lovely 14-site campground sat among low mist-enshrouded hills on the rushing Harris River. Fine gravel keeps the mud at bay & a short boardwalk leads through a bog.

Prince of Wales Hatchery Mile 9; ✆ 755 2231; www.powhasalmon.org; ⏰ 08.00–17.00 daily. 8 miles beyond Harris Campground, it produces salmon & trout fry for the island. Visitors can join free daily tours. From Aug–Oct, silver salmon can be bought when available for US$1/lb!

KLAWOCK (*Population: 785*) Next to Hollis, Klawock (⊕ 55°33'18"N, 133°5'7"W; *www.cityofklawock.com*) seems like a booming metropolis. The small town (second largest on the island) isn't very impressive at first sight, but a number of accommodation options, guides, and stores can be found here, as well as the POW visitor centre.

🏠 Where to stay and eat

In town

🏠 Fireweed Lodge PO Box 116; ✆ 755 2930; www.fireweedlodge.com. Offers just rooms or room & meal packages, as well as guided fishing trips. $$$$

✗ B & T Café At the end of the parking lot, ✆ 755 2986. An island institution, locally known as 'Dave's Diner'. Grab a burger & fries in this dark & dingy, yet positively delightful, place. $$

Out of town

🏠 Forget Me Not Big Salt Lake Rd; ✆ 755 2340. The owner, Skip, will set you up with a beach cabin (US$70), apartment (US$95), or suite (US$150). He also runs kayak trips & fishing/whale-watching trips. To get there from Klawock town, follow Route 929 north, & look for Big Salt Lake Rd, which runs next to the water, parallel to Route 929. $$$

⚑ Eagle's Nest Campground (12 sites) Has walk-in-sites & basic facilities for US$8. Free camping between 17 Sep & 17 May. To get there leave

Klawock & head north towards the Control Lake Junction, after about 11 miles the road splits. The east fork leads to Kasaan & Thorne Bay, the west fork heads to Naukati, Coffman Cove, & the rest of the northern portion of the island. A gravel road also connects Thorne Bay with Coffman Cove (can be snowed in during spring), the campground is along this road.

✗ Wildfish Co Off Big Salt Lake Rd. Drop in here to get smoked salmon.

Other practicalities In the mall on the north side of the road is a large grocery store with a sign on the door that prohibits guns inside. Also in the mall is the **post office** (✆ *755 2977*; ⏰ *08.30–13.00 & 14.00–17.00 Mon–Fri, 10.00–14.00 Sat*) and the **Chamber of Commerce**.

The **Black Bear Store** (✆ *755 2292*; ⏰ *04.00–midnight daily*), located next door to the B&T Café is *the* place to get sporting goods on the island. **Misty Mountain Tours** (✆ *755 2885*) rent kayaks (US$50) and offer local kayak tours ranging from a few hours to a few days. **Wesley Rentals** (✆ *617 8837*; *www.wesleyrentals.com*) rent cars in Klawock, but there is a US$70 fee for leaving cars in Hollis.

What to see and do Across the street from the Black Bear Store is **Gaanaxadi Hit**, where John Ronin carves exquisite totem poles and teaches the tradition to others. The yard is full of horizontal poles and an amazing hand-carved boat is at the back of the lot. Feel free to walk around, but be respectful of the poles.

Before leaving town, drive east towards Craig along Route 924 and turn north after the isthmus on Bayview Boulevard. At the top of the hill is one of **POW's best totem parks**. The green paint seen on these and other totems in the area was used on the local cannery's roof; local totem carvers managed to salvage the excess to use on their poles.

CRAIG (*Population: 1,117*) Three miles east of Klawock, Craig (✪ 55°28'35"N, 133°8'54"W) is POW's largest bastion of civilisation. While the town is very well put together, the visitor's first impression is of a houseboat moored in a bay north of the road that has somehow ignored the laws of buoyancy and got away with it. More importantly, it appears that someone lives there. Beyond the houseboat, a pleasant town unfolds.

Tourist information The **US Forest Service** (*900 Main St;* ☎ *826 3271; www.fs.fed.us;* ⊕ *08.00–17.00 Mon–Fri*) has lots of printed information about POW and very helpful staff. Be sure to pick up a US$12 island map. The many public-use cabins on the island cannot be booked here, but their staff can tell you all about them. For additional information and reservations visit www.fs.fed.us/r10/tongass/cabins/cabinlist.shtml.

Where to stay, eat and drink

🏠 **Shelter Cove Lodge** (10 rooms) ☎ 826 2939, 888 826 3474 (TF); www.sheltercovelodge.com. Standard hotel rooms with a pleasant dining area (⊕ 17.00–21.00 daily; $$$$) which serves seafood, meat & pasta. $$$$$

🏠 **Waterfall Resort** ☎ 800 544 5125; www.waterfallresort.com. An exclusive remote lodge a short flight south of Craig. All-inclusive packages start at US$3,400 for 4 days. $$$$$

🏠 **Blue Heron B&B** (4 rooms) ☎ 826 3608; www.littleblueheroninn.com. The owners manage 2 separate B&Bs in Craig: the Blue Heron at Bucareli Bay ($$$) & the Boat Harbor ($$). The Bucareli Bay location is top-notch with a lovely location right on the water & first-rate amenities all around. The Boat Harbor location is quaint & right on the harbour, but the rooms are on the small side.

🏠 **Dreamcatcher B&B** (3 rooms) 1405 East Hamilton Dr; ☎ 826 2238; www.dreamcatcherbedandbreakfast.com. A lovely home right on the water. The owner, Ken Owen, is friendly & knowledgeable about the island & caters to independent travellers rather than hunters. The loft rooms are a little loud in the mornings because one wall is open to the common area. Continental b/fast. US$115 dbl. Wi-Fi, TV. $$

✖ **Ruth Ann's Restaurant** ☎ 826 3377. Decent seafood, meat, & pasta dishes with ocean-view tables. The tasty & affordable b/fast is a local favourite. $$$$

✖ **Papa's Pizza** ☎ 826 2244. Pizza place owned by Ken Owen, proprietor of Dreamcatcher B&B. If you're staying there, don't let him catch you eating anywhere else. $$$

✖ **Zat's Pizza** ☎ 826 2345. Also serves decent pizza. Like, Papa's (see above) it has a loyal following. $$$

✖ **Annie Betty's Bakery & Café** ☎ 826 2299. Occupying a vacant fast food building, this pleasant little eatery offers toasted sandwiches, baked goods & hot drinks. Wi-Fi. $$

✖ **Dockside Café** ☎ 826 5544; ⊕ 05.30–15.00 daily. Across from the city dock, this simple diner serves decent b/fast until 11.00. $$

Other practicalities

Harbour Master's Office ☎ 826 3404. Has showers & toilets – ideal for campers.

Post office 303 Thompson Rd; ☎ 826 3298; 08.30–17.00 Mon–Fri, 12.00–14.00 Sat

Prince of Wales Jeep Rentals ☎ 401 0997

What to see and do A wonderful short and easy **hike** follows the sea, past the graveyard to Cape Suspiro on Cemetery Island just south of town. Follow Hamilton Drive on the south side of town until you reach a dead end. The hike is 1.5-mile round trip.

KASSAAN (*Population: 54*) Kassaan (⊕ 55°32'30"N, 132°24'7"W) is a remote former logging town right on the water. Kasaan's residents include some very interesting recluses, former (and current) loggers, and a small native Haida population. The reason most folks visit Kasaan is to see the totem park a short walk from town. On the east side of town there is also a cute house with buoy decorations.

Tourist information and where to stay
🛈 **Kasaan City Hall** ☎ 542 2212
🛈 **Organised Village of Kasaan** ☎ 542 2230; www.kasaan.org. General information about the native group in Kasaan. Occasionally the tribe rents houses; call for more information.

What to see and do
Totem park Park in town and walk due east to find the totems. This spectacular former village site has a collection of large and small totems in the woods around a central long house. Because it is little visited and set in the woods, this has always been my favourite totem park in Alaska. The school in town also has a lovely new totem. The mayor, Richard, is an interesting guy who lives in the middle of town near the cell towers with a red truck. Stop by to find out more about the area. See also box on page 17.

THORNE BAY (*Population: 440*) The small town of Thorne Bay (⊕ 55°40'38"N, 132°33'22"W) is about 17 miles from the Control Lake Junction and 36 miles north of Klawock. Thorne Bay was once the largest logging camp on the island.

Tourist information Some general history can be found at the **Public Library** (☎ *828 3303*) next to City Hall (internet available here), and at the welcome sign on the way into town. Near the sign on the left side of the road is the **US Forest Service Office** (*1312 Federal Way;* ☎ *828 3304; www.fs.fed.us*) with National Forest information. This is also the place to book El Capitan Cave tours.

🏠 Where to stay and eat
🏠 **Welcome Inn B&B** 4 rooms; ☎ 828 3950; f 828 3940; www.lodginginnalaska.com. Situated on the hill, this is a lovely homely place with rooms & a cabin. Vehicle hire (US$100–110) & skiff rental (US$85–95) also available. $$

🛖 **Thorne Bay RV Park** ☎ 828 3380. Located down the hill near the water. $

Other practicalities
Post office ☎ 828 3490; ⊕ 09.00–17.00 Mon–Fri, 11.00–15.00 Sat
Thorne Bay Market 409 Shoreline Dr; ☎ 828 3306; ⊕ 07.00–19.00 Mon–Sat & 10.00–18.00 Sun

Thorne Bay Business Association www.thornebayalaska.net. A list of local businesses & general information.

What to see and do Sandy Beach Road heads north from town and before connecting to Coffman Cove (40 miles), Sandy Beach presents itself on the east. This lovely beach is where locals go after work and on the weekends. Sandy Beach Road is a narrow gravel road and an unforgettable drive mostly along the sea.

POW has two fantastic canoe/kayak trips through remote and lovely country with unbeatable fishing. Inexperienced boaters will have a lot more fun on the Sarkar Lakes, while those with more experience can tackle the Honker Divide trip.

SARKAR LAKES Just north of the tiny settlement of Naukati is Sarkar Lake and the start of the wonderful Sarkar Lake Canoe Route. Ideal for paddlers of any level, this route meanders through seven lakes, all connected by civilised boardwalks. Tent platforms and public-use cabins can be used along the way. In the autumn, bears can be found at the far end of Sarkar Lake.

For more information visit: www.fs.fed.us/r10/tongass/districts/pow/recreation/rogs/sarkar_canoe_rt.shtml.

HONKER DIVIDE Best for reasonably experienced paddlers in decent shape, this route starts at the Honker Canoe Launch, off Forest Road 30, ten miles south of Coffman Cove. This 30-mile trip covers some remote and rugged ground. Upstream paddling, steep portages (the carrying of a boat overland) and swift downstream paddling are required. The rewards come in the form of remote wilderness, wildlife, amazing fishing, and an extremely small chance of seeing anyone else.

For more information visit: www.fs.fed.us/r10/tongass/districts/pow/recreation/rogs/honker_canoe_trail.shtml.

During the spring the road can be snowed-in at higher elevations, so enquire locally before setting out.

COFFMAN COVE (*Population: 141*) The small, mostly residential town of Coffman Cove (✪ 56°0'44"N, 132°49'44"W; *www.coffmancove.org*) was founded in the 1950s as a logging camp and today hosts the Inter-Island ferry the MV *Stikine*. Along the harbour is a petrol station, general store and a variety of basic accommodation options and charter outfits.

 Where to stay

🏠 **Rock Haven Lodge** ☎ 329 2003; www.rockhavenalaska.com. Sat across the bay, this custom, yet homely, lodge offers a variety of all-inclusive packages starting at US$3,000. Dan & Ellen are gracious hosts that will leave you wanting for nothing. $$$$$

🏠 **Cove Connection Cottage** (2 rooms) ☎ 329 2295. A simple, self-contained place with bunk beds & Wi-Fi. $$$

🏠 **Salmon Shores** (3 rooms) ☎ 329 2311; www.salmonshores.com. Located off the main drag, this small house sleeps 6 for US$220 & the cabin sleeps two for US$180. $$$

🏠 **Coffman Cove Bunkhouse** ☎ 329 2228; www.coffmancovebunkhouse.net. A good place to rent boats (US$95/day) & kayaks (US$45/day), but not rooms. $$

🏠 **Andersonville** Lot 10 Blk 11 Narwhale; ☎ 329 2267; www.coffmancove.org. Run by Dale & Genny Sue, who offer extremely rustic accommodation & are known for their hospitality & fried food. Swing by on Fri, Sat or Sun for cheeseburgers & pizza ($$), or anything that can be deep-fried. $

Other practicalities

Coffman Cove Car Rental ☎ 329 2208

Post office ☎ 329 2317; ◷ 13.00–15.00 Mon–Fri

NORTHERN TIP OF POW A number of sights make the northern portion of the island well worth the extra time it takes to navigate the narrow gravel roads.

El Capitan Caves (*www.usd.edu/esci/alaska/elcap.html*) This immense network of limestone caves (including the largest cave in Alaska) is managed by the US Forest Service and is located just north of the small town of Whale Pass at mile 51. Free tours can be arranged at the US Forest Service office in Thorne Bay (see page 136) or by simply showing up. Palaeontologists have found 9,200-year-old human bones in the caves, the oldest human remains ever found in North America. Much older animal bones have also been found, including black bear skeletons from the late Pleistocene epoch (about 12,000 years old).

Red Bay Lake This 0.8-mile, difficult hike leads to a lovely lake with a cabin on the water at the opposite end. A boat is provided at the lake for fishing and cabin access. Fly in from or drive from Hollis (3.5hrs) or Thorne Bay (2hrs) on road #20. After completing the hike, which may take a few hours, row the 1.5 miles to the cabin.

Memorial Beach This beach on Sumner Strait is an amazing place to see whales feeding and other marine life. Katie, of the Forest Service office in Craig, told me the whales were so close to shore she could hear them exhaling while she slept in her tent! Free camping is available in three sites with a toilet and table but no water. The campsites are located at the end of a 1,000ft trail from the road. To find the beach follow road #20 north toward Point Protection, and turn right onto Forest Service Road 20860; it's three miles from here to Memorial Beach.

Point Protection and Point Baker Off the road system at the far northern tip of the island with 50 residents each, these are remote, heavily logged areas with minimal services.

WRANGELL *(Population 2,062)*

Wrangell (✛ 56°28'15"N, 132°22'36"W) is a rugged little working town, blessed by its proximity to the Stikine River, LaConte Glacier and the Anan Creek bear viewing area. Unlike many of the southeast's well-polished towns, Wrangell's streets are lined with simple, sometimes rundown shops catering mostly to locals while much of the seashore is piled with fishing equipment and other junk. The harbour's perimeter hums with canneries, while fishing boats come and go most of the day. Juxtaposed with Wrangell's working image is the unique Tlingit art found around town. Chief Shakes Island, in the middle of the harbour, is a veritable garden of totem poles with a stunning clan house in the centre. Nearby, the top-notch Nolan Center houses more poles and many other artefacts. North of town is Petroglyph Beach with black stones etched by ancient peoples. Given the time and the money it takes to explore the surrounding area by boat, it's well worth spending a few days in Wrangell. Ferry and cruise-ship passengers with just an hour or two in town can easily see the major sights.

HISTORY In the first half of the 19th century, Russian fur traders began trading with Wrangell area Tlingit natives and eventually built a fort called Redoubt Saint Dionysius. In 1840, the British Hudson Bay Company leased the fort and renamed it Fort Stikine. By the middle of the century the fur-bearing animals had been depleted so the fort was abandoned, but remained in British hands until 1867 when Alaska was purchased from Russia. Within a year the US military had built Fort Wrangell, which continued to grow with military personnel and gold prospectors seeking gold up the Stikine River. At the turn of the 20th century, Wrangell had largely turned to timber and commercial fishing for support. While timber has declined, commercial fishing and tourism continue to do well in Wrangell.

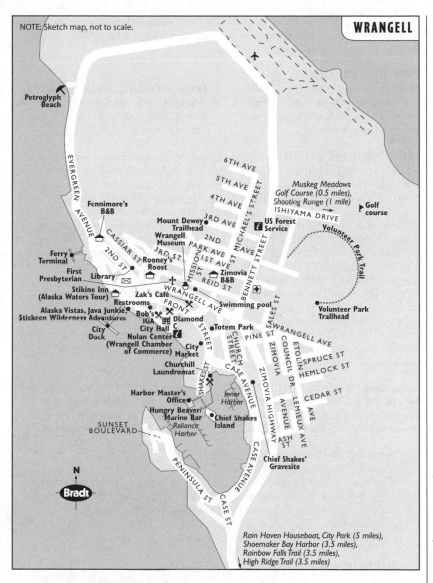

NOTE: Sketch map, not to scale.

Petroglyph Beach

EVERGREEN AVENUE

6TH AVE
5TH AVE
4TH AVE
3RD AVE
2ND

Muskeg Meadows Golf Course (0.5 miles), Shooting Range (1 mile)

ISHIYAMA DRIVE

Golf course

Volunteer Park Trail

Fennimore's B&B

Mount Dewey Trailhead

Wrangell Museum

US Forest Service

CASSIAR ST

3RD ST

PARK AVE

MICHAEL'S STREET

BENNETT STREET

Ferry Terminal

2ND ST

Rooney's Roost

2IST ST

REID ST

Zimovia B&B

First Presbyterian

Library

Stikine Inn (Alaska Waters Tour)

Zak's Café

WRANGELL AVE

FRONT STREET

Swimming pool

Volunteer Park Trailhead

Restrooms

Alaska Vistas, Java Junkie, Stickeen Wilderness Adventures

Bob's IGA

Diamond C

City Dock

City Hall

Nolan Center (Wrangell Chamber of Commerce)

City Market

Totem Park

SALES ST

WRANGELL AVE

PINE ST

CHURCH STREET

CASE AVENUE

ETOLIN AVE

SPRUCE ST

HEMLOCK ST

COUNCIL DR

ZIMOVIA AVENUE

ZIMOVIA HIGHWAY

CEDAR ST

LEMIEUX AVE

Churchill Laundromat

SHAKES ST

Harbor Master's Office

Inner Harbor

Hungry Beaver/ Marine Bar

SUNSET BOULEVARD

Reliance Harbor

Chief Shakes Island

ASH ST

Chief Shakes' Gravesite

N

Bradt

PENINSULA ST

CASE ST

CASE AVENUE

Rain Haven Houseboat, City Park (5 miles), Shoemaker Bay Harbor (3.5 miles), Rainbow Falls Trail (3.5 miles), High Ridge Trail (3.5 miles)

GETTING THERE AND AWAY Wrangell is located at the northern tip of Wrangell Island, 155 miles south of Juneau and 89 miles north of Ketchikan. Wrangell is accessible by air and sea only.

By air Alaska Airlines (❄ *800 252 7522; www.alaskaair.com*) provides daily jet services from Seattle in Washington via Juneau for US$525.

Sunrise Aviation (❄ *874 2319; www.sunriseflights.com*) charter flights to Ketchikan, Petersburg and the Anan Wildlife Observatory (see box on page 140).

By ferry The **Alaska Ferry** (❄ *465 3941, 800 642 0066 (TF); www.dot.state.ak.us/ amhs*) travels five times per week between Wrangell and Ketchikan (US$37),

Petersburg (US$33) and Juneau (US$87). The **Inter-Island Ferry Authority** (↘ 874 4848; *www.interislandferry.com*) stopped their service north of Prince of Wales Island but may start up again in the future.

TOURIST INFORMATION

ℹ US Forest Service 525 Bennett St; ↘ 874 2323; www.fs.fed.us; ⊕ 08.00–16.30 Mon–Fri. Extensive information about the Tongass National Forest & the regional sights & activities.

ℹ Wrangell Chamber of Commerce 224 Front St; ↘ 874 3901; www.wrangell.com. Located inside the wonderful Nolan Center in the city centre along with the museum. Wi-Fi is US$10/hr.

LOCAL TOURS AND ACTIVITIES Wrangell has a number of charter outfits, most of which offer Stikine River, LaConte Glacier, and Anan Creek bear-viewing area trips. All of these are good trips worth doing if you have the money. The **Stikine River** enters the sea about ten miles north of town and enters Canada after 20 miles. Jet boat tours race up the glacial river, passing soaring peaks, glaciers and wildlife on the way. Hot springs, an old garnet mine and the tiny town of Telegraph Creek, 150 miles upstream, are other sights. On a clear day, the scenery is truly stunning. The delta is chock full of migratory birds, such as 10,000 snow geese in the early spring. Seals are also often seen up the river chasing salmon. Public-use cabins are located along the river and can be used by boaters on multi-day downriver trips. The **LaConte Glacier** is 10 miles north of the Stikine River and makes an excellent day trip. This is a spectacular glacier flowing right into the sea at the head of a long steep valley with snow-covered peaks all around; this is North America's southernmost tidewater glacier. To arrange trips to any of these places visit the chamber website or try the following:

Alaskan Waters 107 Stikine Av; ↘ 874 2378, 800 347 4462 (TF); www.alaskawaters.com. Offer guided boat trips, rental kayaks & adventure support in all these areas. Day trips to Anan Creek cost US$212, Stikine River trips US$90–160, while LaConte Glacier & Petersburg trips cost US$190. Kayak rentals & water taxi service are also available. One of the owners, Wilma, is extremely knowledgeable about

ANAN WILDLIFE OBSERVATORY

A wonderful, but expensive, side trip from Wrangell is the Anan Wildlife Observatory, where you can see scores of brown and black bears. The bears gather in late July and August, and are easily seen from a covered viewing area reached after a short hike. Most visitors get to Anan by seaplane, but those with strong arms and a sense of adventure could conceivably take two days and kayak the 30 miles.

GETTING THERE Island Wings (↘ 225 2444; www.islandwings.com) is just one of many air taxis that fly to Anan. For a complete list of guides and air taxis visit www.fs.fed.us/r10/tongass/recreation/wildlife_viewing/ananobservatory.shtml or talk to the rangers at the US Forest Service office in Wrangell. Day trips are generally about US$500.

WHERE TO STAY There is no camping in the area, but there is a public-use cabin a mile away. Book this cabin as early as possible. The Forest Service charges a US$10 fee between 5 July and 25 Aug, which can be paid for at the observatory or in Wrangell at the Forest Service office. Alternatively, the **Rain Haven Houseboat** is moored near Anan during July and August for those who want to live in comfort near the bears.

Wrangell & is eager to help everyone have the best trip possible. Call her to book a trip & she can answer all your questions. Wilma also leads cultural tours for US$65 that include native & non-native historical information about the town.
Summit Charters ☎ 874 2402; www.summitcharters.com. Offer Stikine River jet boat tours, LeConte Glacier tours, as well as water-taxi service to the Anan Wildlife Observatory for US$180.
Rainwalker Expeditions ☎ 874 2549; www.rainwalkerexpeditions.com. Kayaking experts who lead daily kayak (US$75 for ¹/₂ day) & hiking (US$35 2hr ecology) tours. Incidentally, they also run Rain Haven Houseboat (see below).
Breakaway Adventures ☎ 874 2488, 888 385 2488 (TF); www.breakawayadventures.com. Rent canoes or kayaks for US$40–60/day & offer trips to the Stikine River, LaConte Glacier & Anan Creek.
Sunrise Aviation (see page 144) Offers flightseeing trips to many of Wrangell area's best sights. They also fly into Anan Creek.

HIKING AND RECREATION Hikers should stop by the Forest Service office and pick up the free trails map as well as the island map. The miles of Forest Service roads on Wrangell Island provide access to many campgrounds and trails, as well as lakes and creeks. The Sea Trails website (*www.seatrails.org*) is another excellent hiking resource. See box on page 75 for an explanation of hiking grades.

Hiking trails

Mt Dewey Trail (*Grade: easy; distance:* ¹/₄ *mile*) This short trail starts at the end of Reid Road, on the hill behind Wrangell. To find the start, follow Third Street to a set of stairs that lead to Reid Street.

High Country Trail (*Grade: moderate; distance: 2.3 miles*) Starts at the Shoemaker Bay Recreation Area a few miles south of town on the Zimovia Highway. This 2.3-mile trail gets up into the higher country overlooking Zimovia Strait and has some shelters for camping. The trailhead for Rainbow Falls Trail is also here.

Rainbow Falls Trail (*Grade: moderate; distance: 0.8 miles*) This one-mile trail follows Institute Creek through lush forests to the falls. Near the end of the Zimovia Highway, the road turns inland and splits. The right branch (FS 6267) continues along the side of the mountain passing five campgrounds. Locals like to park at the branch and hike this stretch of road for its amazing views.

Nemo Point Trail (*Grade: easy; distance:* ¹/₂ *mile*) The Nemo Point Trail follows boardwalks to the sea and provides amazing views. From Wrangell drive south 13.4 miles then follow Nemo Loop Road (6267) 5.2 miles to the trailhead.

Practicalities The Wrangell area has 22 public-use cabins that allow access to the backcountry. For more information stop by the Forest Service office. Most cabins (the ones worth going to anyway) can only be reached by boat or plane; contact Breakaway Adventures or Sunrise Aviation to arrange transportation. For more information and to book cabins visit www.fs.fed.us/r10/tongass/cabins /cabinlist.shtml.

⌂ WHERE TO STAY

⌂ **Fennimore B&B** (6 rooms) Evergreen Av & Second St; ☎ 874 3012; www.fennimoresbbb.com. Simple rooms in a nice part of town off Second St across from the ferry terminal. Rooms with & without bathrooms & kitchens go for US$85–95 dbl. Bikes are inc. TV. $$
⌂ **Rain Haven Houseboat** (1 room) ☎ 874 2459; www.rainwalkerexpeditions.com. Moored in Shoemaker Bay south of town, this houseboat is Wrangell's most unique accommodation. During Jul & Aug the houseboat is near Anan Creek where it can be rented to live near the bears for US$575. May, Jun & Sep are US$85 dbl. Call 6 months or more ahead to reserve this accommodation. $$

🛏 **Rooney's Roost** (4 rooms) 206 McKinnon St; ☎ 874 2026; www.rooneysroost.com. Lovely & affordable rooms in a custom home, ¼-mile from the ferry terminal & very near town. The owner is very friendly & knowledgeable. Wi-Fi. TV. $$

🛏 **Zimovia B&B** (2 rooms) 319 Weber St; ☎ 874 2626, 866 946 6842 (TF); www.zimoviabnb.com. A lovely custom home on the hill behind town with interesting, comfortable rooms with many artistic

touches. I room has a tiny sauna. The owners are very friendly & offer a free ½hr tour of town & free airport/ferry pick-up. Delicious homemade b/fast. Wi-Fi. TV. $$

🛏 **Wrangell Hostel** 220 Church St; ☎ 874 3534. A simple place on the upper floor of the First Presbyterian Church. Air mattresses on the floor are US$18. TV. $

Camping The island is covered with campgrounds, but many are far out of town to the south, on Forest Service roads. To explore these remote roads, pick up a Wrangell Island map at the US Forest Service office or the visitor centre.

🏕 **City Park Campground** Located I mile south of town, just off the Zimovia Hwy, this free campground has tent sites right beside the ocean. Shelters, fire pits & toilets are provided. Walk back toward town to see the cemetery & hidden gravestones in the trees.

🏕 **Shoemaker Bay Recreation Area Campground** 5 miles south of town off the Zimovia Hwy; ☎ 874 2444. This campground has tent & RV spaces for

US$25. Nearby is Rainbow Fall Trail & Institute Creek with spawning salmon in the autumn.

🏕 **Nemo Point Recreation Area Campground** 14 miles south of town on the Zimovia Hwy, off Forest Service Road 6267. This rough road continues south to five more campgrounds & is a wonderful, little-travelled route with amazing views of the strait, where hikers can also set off for a pleasant day's walk.

✕ **WHERE TO EAT** The dining options in Wrangell are dismal. Locals usually get a sandwich from Bob's IGA and go to the beach. When I visit, I do the same.

✕ **Hungry Beaver** Shakes St; ☎ 874 3005; ⏱ 10.30–22.00 daily. Tasty, but pricey, pizza (US$27 large) served from 16.00–22.00. Burgers & assorted fried items can be had from 10.00. The Marine Bar is also inside. Located on Shakes St near Chief Shake Island & the harbour. $$$

✕ **Stikine Inn Restaurant** 107 Stikine Av; ☎ 874 4388, 888 874 3388 (TF); www.stikineinn.com; ⏱ 11.00–20.00 daily. Water views & Wrangell's best approximation of fine dining. Seafood & steaks. $$$

✕ **Bob's IGA** Brueger St; ☎ 874 2341; ⏱ 08.00–18.00 Mon–Sat. Full-service grocer. $$

✕ **Diamond C Café** 225 Front St; ☎ 874 3677; ⏱ 06.00–15.00. A standard diner with decent, large b/fast. $$

✕ **Zak's Café** 316 Front St; ☎ 874 3355; ⏱ 11.00–20.00 Mon–Sat. Mediocre food served by surly staff with boring décor. Sandwiches, wraps, salads & burgers. $$

FESTIVALS AND EVENTS During the first weekend of May, **Muskeg Meadows** (☎ 874 4653; *www.wrangellalaskagolf.com*), the local golf course, hosts a tournament, and from 10 May to 8 June the **King Salmon Tournament** is held with prizes for the largest fish and tagged fish. Like anywhere, the **4 July** is big in Wrangell with fireworks, food and festivities.

Other practicalities

Bob's IGA Deli & groceries.

City Market ☎ 874 3333. A full service grocery store on Front Street.

Churchill Laundromat ☎ 874 3954; ⏱ 07.00–21.00 daily. Showers & laundry. Near the Hungry Beaver off Shakes Street.

Post office 112 Federal Way; ☎ 874 3714; ⏱ 09.00–17.00 Mon–Fri, 11.00–13.00 Sat

Public library ☎ 874 3535; ⏱ 10.00–12.00 & 13.00–17.00 Mon & Fri, 13.00–17.00 & 19.00–21.00 Tue–Thu, 09.00–17.00 Sat. A cosy library with internet access.

Practical Rent-A-Car ☎ 874 3975

WHAT TO SEE AND DO Most of Wrangell's best sights are only accessible by plane or boat, but for those getting off the ferry with just a few hours to spare, there are still a handful of fascinating sights within walking distance of the ferry:

Chief Shakes' Island (*www.shakesisland.com*) Located in the boat harbour, this is one of Wrangell's most accessible sites. It can be reached via a bridge at the end of Front Street. The tiny island has an amazing variety of totem poles (see box on page 17) all huddled around a replica of Chief Shakes' house. The original was built in the 1800s and the replica was erected in the 1940s by the Civilian Conservation Corp (CCC) and local artists. To arrange a look inside the clan house, call Wilma at Alaska Waters (see page 140).

In town off Front Street, the **Kiksadi Totem Park** has a few poles and nearby off Second Street is the **St Rose of Lima Catholic Church**, the oldest Roman Catholic Parish in Alaska, founded in 1879. Nearby is the **First Presbyterian Church** built in 1879. The neon cross on top is still used as a navigational aid by mariners.

Petroglyph Beach Personally, I can spend hours exploring this beach located half a mile north of the Wrangell ferry terminal off Evergreen Avenue. After reading the interpretive signs, head on down to the beach and look for the fascinating ancient rock carvings. Many of the best ones are to the right. Rock art in non-marine environments are dated by their lichen growth, but these are scoured daily by high tide and salt spray. Best estimates date the carvings to either 3,000 or 5,000 years old. The carvings are thought to delineate property lines and the ownership of natural resources like creeks.

Museums
Wrangell Museum (*296 Outer Dr, inside the Nolan Center;* ✆ *874 3770;* ⊕ *10.00–17.00 Mon–Sat; US$5/2 adult/child*) A splendid collection of native and more recent artefacts, as well as some Alaskan art. The shop has a good selection of books.

PETERSBURG *(Population: 3,072)*
The quaint fishing town of Petersburg (✜ 56°48'15.89"N, 132°56'31.25"W) is picturesque, hard working, but, unfortunately, not on most cruise-ship itineraries. The town is deeply rooted in its Norwegian heritage that can be seen in shutters hand-painted with flowers, tidy houses and yards, and in the complexions of many inhabitants. Even the local grocery store flies a Norwegian flag. All summer the seashore hops with activity as fishing boats and men in yellow raingear come and go from the many canneries and cold-storage facilities. The shrimp, crab, salmon and halibut they process regularly exceed US$40 million in value. In addition to being a lovely little community, Petersburg occupies a stunning location at the northern tip of Mitkof Island on Wrangell Narrows with a backdrop of snow-capped, glacier-enshrouded peaks. Friendly people and top-notch B&Bs complete the town nicely.

HISTORY Early Tlingit natives used the site of present day Petersburg as a summer fish camp until it was settled by Norwegian immigrants, including Peter Buschmann in the 1890s. Buschmann and other homesteaders got right to work and, by the turn of the century, had built a sawmill, cannery and the beginnings of a town. The town was eventually named in his honour. The abundance of ice from the region's glaciers was used to develop one of the state's first fresh fish markets. By 1920 other Scandinavians were travelling to Petersburg, which had grown to a population of some 600 souls. During this time, the shrimp processing plant, Alaska Glacier

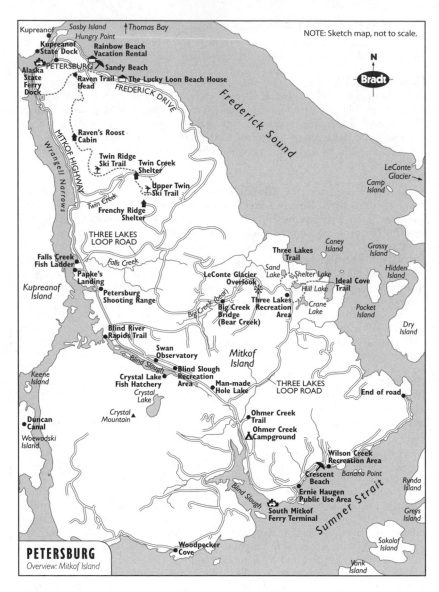

NOTE: Sketch map, not to scale.

N

Bradt

Kupreanof
Sasby Island
Hungry Point
↑Thomas Bay

Kupreanof State Dock
Rainbow Beach Vacation Rental

PETERSBURG
Sandy Beach

Alaska State Ferry Dock
Raven Trail Head
The Lucky Loon Beach House

FREDERICK DRIVE

Frederick Sound

Raven's Roost Cabin

MITKOF HIGHWAY

Wrangell Narrows

Twin Ridge Ski Trail
Twin Creek Shelter

LeConte Glacier

Camp Island

Upper Twin Ski Trail

Twin Creek

Frenchy Ridge Shelter

THREE LAKES LOOP ROAD

Coney Island
Grassy Island

Three Lakes Trail

Hidden Island

Falls Creek Fish Ladder

Falls Creek

Sand Lake
Shelter Lake

Papke's Landing

LeConte Glacier Overlook

Ideal Cove Trail

Kupreanof Island

Petersburg Shooting Range

Hill Lake

Big Creek (bear)

Big Creek Bridge (Bear Creek)

Three Lakes Recreation Area

Crane Lake

Pocket Island

Dry Island

Blind River Rapids Trail

Swan Observatory

Blind Slough

Mitkof Island

Keene Island

Crystal Lake Fish Hatchery

Blind Slough Recreation Area

Man-made Hole Lake

THREE LAKES LOOP ROAD

End of road

Crystal Lake

Duncan Canal

Crystal Mountain

Ohmer Creek Trail

Woewodski Island

Ohmer Creek Campground

Wilson Creek Recreation Area

Crescent Beach
Banana Point

Rynda Island

Blind Slough

Ernie Haugen Public Use Area

South Mitkof Ferry Terminal

Sumner Strait

Greys Island

Woodpecker Cove

Sokolof Island

Vank Island

PETERSBURG
Overview: Mitkof Island

Seafoods, was built and is now called Petersburg Fisheries. Today, Petersburg's thriving fishing industry dominates the economy with tourism filling in the gaps.

GETTING THERE, AWAY AND AROUND Petersburg is accessible by daily jet service, small plane and the ferry.

By air

✈ **Alaska Airlines** ☎ 800 252 7522; www.alaskaair.com. Provides daily jet service from Seattle via Juneau for US$525 & Anchorage via Juneau for US$450.

✈ **Sunrise Aviation** ☎ 874 2319; www.sunriseflights.com. Offer charter flights between Wrangell & Petersburg for US$250 up to 3 people.

✈ **Pacific Wing Air** 1500 Haugen Dr; ✆ 772 4258; www.pacificwing.com. Offer charter flights around Petersburg & the north end of Prince of Wales Island. They use 2 planes: a 3-person Cessna for US$447/hr & a Beaver that carries 6 people for US$747/hr.

By ferry The **Alaska Ferry** (✆ 772 3855, 800 642 0066 TF; *www.dot.state.ak.us/amhs*) connects Petersburg with Ketchikan (US$60), Wrangell (US$37), Sitka (US$60), and Juneau (US$107) five times per week. The ferry terminal is one mile south of town.

The **Inter-Island Ferry Authority** (✆ 874 4848; *www.interislandferry.com*) This ferry has stopped service north of Prince of Wales Island. It could start up again though, so call for more information.

TOURIST INFORMATION

US Forest Service 12 N Nordic Dr, inside the Federal Bldg; ✆ 772 3871; ⊕ 08.00–17.00 Mon–Fri. Knowledgeable staff & a handful of useful brochures inc an island road map.

Visitor Centre [146–7 D3] ✆ 772 4636; www.petersburg.org; ⊕ 09.00–17.00 Mon–Sat, 12.00–16.00 Sun. Located at 1st & Fram St, this adorable office is staffed with friendly locals & has all the normal information.

LOCAL TOURS AND ACTIVITIES In addition to a selection of charter fishing outfits, Petersburg offers some great kayaking options. Visit the Forest Service office for suggestions or try:

Doyles Boat Rentals ✆ 772 4439, 877 442 4010 TF; www.doylesboatrentals.com. Rents skiffs for the self-sufficient traveller who wants to explore, fish or camp in the islands around Petersburg. US$135–300/day.
Tongass Kayak Adventures ✆ 772 4600; www.tongasskayak.com. The owner, Scott, offers a variety of single- & multi-day tours inc a short tour from town for US$85. A much better option is the LaConte Glacier Tour for US$180–225. Those who want to go it alone can rent boats for US$55/day & get pick-up & drop-off service anywhere in the area.

Kaleidoscope Cruises ✆ 772 3736, 800 868 4373 TF; www.petersburglodgingandtours.com. The owner, Berry, is a long-time Petersburg resident & marine biologist. He offers top-notch whale-watching trips & glacier cruises for US$190–275pp, & does not cater to fishermen or hunters.
Whale Song Cruises 212 Harbor Way; ✆ 772 9393. Offers similar trips, but also offers fishing. Jul & Aug are the best times for sightings.
Alaska Sea Adventures ✆ 772 4700, 888 772 8588 TF; www.yachtalaska.com. Offers completely custom high-end trips from their 60ft converted fishing boat, the MV *Alaskan Adventurer*.

Flightseeing can be arranged through **Pacific Wing Air** (see above).

HIKING AND RECREATION Stop by the Forest Service office or visit the Sea Trails website (*www.seatrails.org*) or www.fs.fed.us/r10/tongass/recreation/rec_facilities/ mitkoftrails.html. See box on page 75 for an explanation of hiking grades.

Hungry Point Trail [146–7 F3] (*Grade: easy; distance: 3 miles*) Starts behind town at the baseball field. This pleasant trail crosses a marsh and passes through forests before meeting with Nordic Drive. Walk along the road past Eagle's Roost Park back to town for a wonderful three-mile loop.

Raven's Roost Trail [146–7 G6] (*Grade: moderate/difficult; distance: 4 miles*) Starts behind the airport and ascends the hill to Raven's Roost public-use cabin. The trail is steep and can be muddy, but the views of town, Frederick Sound and Wrangell Narrows are unbeatable. The four-mile trail climbs 1,500ft. Follow Haugen Drive past the airport, then turn left at the T-junction and watch for signs.

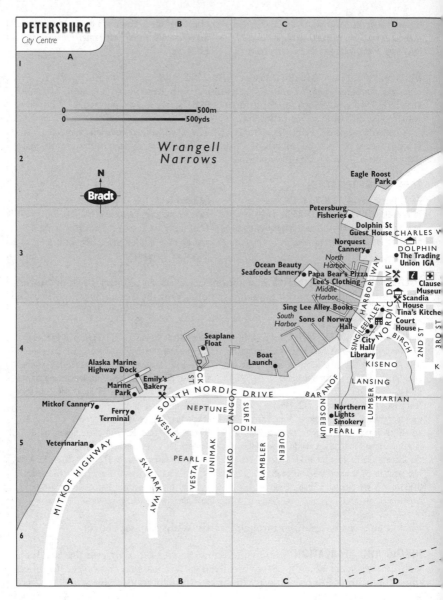

PETERSBURG
City Centre

Wrangell
Narrows

N

Bradt

Eagle Roost
Park

Petersburg
Fisheries

Dolphin St
Guest House CHARLES W

Norquest
Cannery

DOLPHIN
The Trading
Union IGA

North
Harbor

Ocean Beauty
Seafoods Cannery Papa Bear's Pizza
Lee's Clothing

Clause
Museur

Middle
Harbor

Scandia
House

Sing Lee Alley Books

Tina's Kitche

South
Harbor Sons of Norway
Hall

Court
House

City
Hall/
Library

KISENO

Seaplane
Float

Boat
Launch

Alaska Marine
Highway Dock

LANSING

Marine
Park Emily's
Bakery

SOUTH NORDIC DRIVE

MARIAN

Mitkof Cannery

NEPTUNE

Northern
Lights
Smokery

Ferry
Terminal

ODIN

PEARL F

Veterinarian

MITKOF HIGHWAY

SKYLARK WAY

WESLEY

PEARL F

VESTA

UNIMAK

TANGO

RAMBLER

QUEEN

Blind River Rapids Trail (*Grade: easy; distance ¼ mile*) 15 miles south of town on the Mitkof Highway.

Ohmer Creek Trail (*Grade: easy/moderate; distance: 1 mile*) Starts 22 miles south of town at Ohmer Creek Campground (see page 148).

Three Lakes Area Offers boating and hiking in a lovely, forested setting south of town. Drive south on the Mitkof Highway to Lakes Loop Road (6235) that intersects the Highway after ten and 20 miles from town. The roads travel overland to the Frederick Sound side of the island. Three lakes have public-use boats and

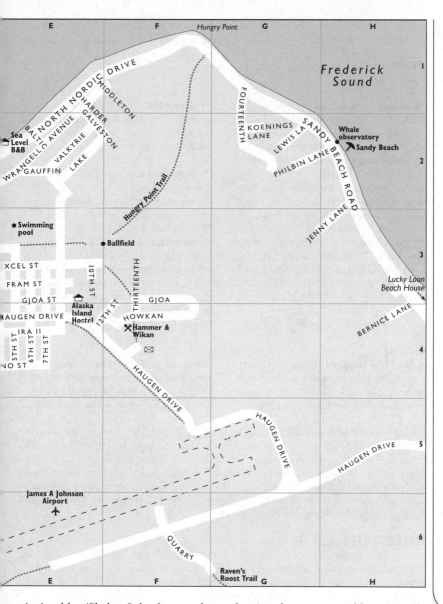

picnic tables (Shelter Lake does not have a boat) and are connected by a 4.5-mile trail system on boardwalks (*grade: easy*). Park at any of the three trailheads.

Ideal Cove Trail (*Grade: difficult; distance:1.5 miles*) Starts at the Hill Creek bridge between the Crain Lake and Hill Lake trailheads on the Three Lakes Trail. The 1.5-mile trail slowly descends through the trees to Ideal Cove.

Crystal Mountain (*Grade: difficult/bushwack/adventure; distance: 4 miles*) Crystal Mountain (3,317ft) is the highest mountain on the island and is occasionally hiked by local 'hard men'. From the south side of the Crystal Lake Fish Hatchery, a water pipe ascends the mountain to Crystal Lake and can be followed. From the lake a mostly alpine environment allows access to the peak. This is an adventure, not a trail.

⌂ WHERE TO STAY
Petersburg levies a 10% bed tax, which must be added to the following prices.

⌂ **The Lucky Loon Beach House** (2 rooms) 181 Frederick Dr; ☎ 772 2345; www.theluckyloon.com. A lovely private cabin 3 miles outside town. US$200 dbl with a 3-night minimum stay. No b/fast. $$$$

⌂ **Rainbow Beach Vacation Rental** (1 room) 913 Sandy Beach Rd; ☎ 772 3457; www.rainbowbeach.us.com. An amazing custom home outside town near Sandy Beach. Owner lives upstairs. Stunning ocean views. US$130 dbl with 3-night minimum stay. No b/fast. $$$

⌂ **Scandia House** [146–7 D3] (33 rooms) 110 N Nordic Dr; ☎ 772 4281; 800 722 5006 (TF); www.scandiahousehotel.com. Standard rooms in a great central location go for US$120–195 dbl. Kitchenette rooms start at US$130. Cars can be rented here for US$58/day. Small boats are guest/non-guest US$125/140/day. Wi-Fi. TV. $$$

⌂ **Sea Level B&B** [146–7 E2] (2 rooms) 913 N Nordic Dr; ☎ 772 3240; www.sealevelbnb.com. A large home, a short walk from town, built on pilings over the water. US$110–140 dbl. B/fast. TV. Wi-Fi. $$$

⌂ **Dolphin Street Guest House** [146–7 D3] (2 rooms) 102 Dolphin St; ☎ 772 4800; www.dolphinstreetguesthouse.com. A small, but adorable, private cabin in town with 2 rooms. US$120. Wi-Fi. TV. B/fast. $$

⌂ **Alaska Island Hostel** [146–7 E3] 805 Gjoa St; ☎ 772 3632, 877 772 3632 (TF); www.alaskaislandhostel.com. A friendly well run & clean hostel a short walk to town. Bunks are adult/child US$25/13. Family rooms are available. The late check-in (17.00–20.00) is the hostel's only drawback. Kitchen, laundry, Wi-Fi. $

Camping
⋏ **Ohmer Creek Campground** (10 sites) Travel south along the Mitkof Hwy for 22 miles to Ohmer Creek. Has toilets, table, grill & water in a lush forested setting. Ohmer Creek Trail travels along a well groomed trail for ¼ mile before continuing along a narrow boardwalk for another mile to Snake Ridge Rd. Follow this back to the campground for a loop. The creek has king salmon & trout fishing. US$6.

Hiking accommodation The Petersburg area has 20 public-use cabins that provide access to many of the area's most remote and secluded land. Ideally cabins need to be booked ahead of time, since they book-up quickly during mid summer. For more information or to book, visit www.fs.fed.us/r10/tongass/cabins/cabinlist.shtml. **Raven's Roost Cabin** is the only one that can be hiked to from town. All others will require a small plane or boat. Try **Tongass Kayak Adventures**, **Doyles Boat Rental** or **Pacific Wing Air** (see page 145).

✗ WHERE TO EAT
Petersburg has just a few decent restaurants, but they will seem positively cosmopolitan if you just came from Prince of Wales Island or Wrangell. When asked where to eat, locals will usually say they eat at home then proudly recite their favourite Norwegian recipes. Check out the locally produced cookbook *Sons of Norway* by local chefs Liv and Heidi.

✗ **Papa Bear's Pizza** [146–7 D3] 306-B N Nordic Dr; ☎ 772 3727; www.papabearspizza.com; ⏲ 11.00–21.00 Mon–Sat, 15.00–20.00 Sun. Located near the ferry terminal, this place serves decent pizza, sandwiches, & ice cream. $$$

✗ **Emily's Bakery** [146–7 B4] 1000 S Nordic; ☎ 772 4555; ⏲ 08.00–16.00 Mon–Fri. Good old fashioned homemade baked goods. A non-descript red building south of town by the shipyard. Look for the massive collection of satellite dishes! $$

✗ **Hammer & Wikan** [146–7 F4] A decent deli for grabbing sandwiches. $$

✗ **La Fonda** ☎ 772 4981; ⏲ 10.00–21.00 Mon–Sat. Decent Mexican food served from a takeaway window. Located inside Kito's Cave on Sing Lee Alley. $$

✗ **Tina's Kitchen** [146–7 D3] 104 N Nordic Dr; ☎ 772 2090; ⏲ 10.00–20.00 Mon–Sat,

11.00–19.00 Sun. Run by an Asian woman & a Mexican woman, the food always has flair. Teriyaki, burritos & sandwiches served from a little stand near the Scandia House in the city centre. $$

FESTIVALS AND EVENTS

Little Norway Festival Four-day event that takes place mid-May and features music, parade, shrimp feed, and dances.

King Salmon Derby Kicks off at the end of May with cash prizes.

4 July Festival Involves a parade and other festivities such as an egg toss, street art, log rolling and more.

Canned Salmon Classic An ongoing summer contest (1 July and 20 August) to guess the total number of cans of salmon produced that year by local processing plants. The 2009 winner won US$2,000 and the total count was 13,291,477 cans!

Octoberfest and the Humpy 500 Go-cart Race Held in October these festivals feature parades, music, and cart races.

SHOPPING
Food

Hammer & Wikan [146–7 F4] 1300 Howkan Dr; ☎ 772 4246; www.hammerandwikan.com
Northern Lights Smokeries [146–7 C5] 501 Noseeum St; ☎ 772 4608; www.nlsmokeries.com; ☺: 08.00–19.00 daily. Belgian transplant, Thomas Cumps, makes the best smoked salmon in town & is a fun guy to talk to besides.

The Trading Union IGA 401 N Nordic; ☎ 772 3881; www.tradingunion.com
Tonka Seafoods 22 South Sing Lee Alley; ☎ 772 3662, 888 560 3662 (TF); www.tonkaseafoods.com. Located near the Nordic Brotherhood Hall, Tonka sells fresh, smoked, & frozen seafood from Petersburg waters.

KAKE

The remote – mostly native – town of Kake (⊕ 56°58'15"N, 133°56'2"W) on the northwestern side of Kupreanof Island is accessible by plane and ferry from Petersburg and Sitka. Its 519 residents live a predominantly subsistence lifestyle, but also fish and log commercially. In 1967, the residents of Kake erected the world's largest totem pole (see box on page 17) on a bluff overlooking town. The 132ft pole details the Tlingit clans of the region.

Kake, Tebenkof Bay nearby and the Kuiu Wilderness areas are popular destinations for experienced kayakers. The two wilderness areas are at the southern end of the island and protect 127,420 acres. The rest of the island has been extensively logged. This is wild country with thousands of islands, mountains, fish-rich rivers and other wildlife. The Petersburg Forest Service (see page 145) office carries a brochure that details a 68-mile paddle from Petersburg to Kake. Those who complete this trip can take the ferry back. Contact Tongass Kayak Adventures (see page 145) for more information on these trips and to arrange boats and transport.

PRACTICALITIES Kake is accessible by charter flight from Sitka or Petersburg, or via the **Alaska Ferry** (see page 145). The ferry travels between Kake and Petersburg twice a week for US$34 and one to two times per week from Juneau for US$66. You can stay at **Keex' Kwaan Lodge** (12 rooms; ☎ 785 3434; www.kakealaska.com; $$), which has simple rooms and a restaurant on location.
Contact the **City of Kake** (☎ 785 3804) for more information.

Miscellaneous

Lee's Clothing [146–7 D3] 212 Nordic Dr; \ 772 4229, 800 478 7702 (TF). Outdoor gear & work clothing.

Sing Lee Alley Books [146–7 D4] 11 Sing Lee Alley; \ 772 4440; ⊕ 09.30–17.30 Mon–Sat. A wonderful bookstore with many Alaska-themed books & gifts.

OTHER PRACTICALITIES

Post office [146–7 F4] 1201 Haugen Dr; \ 772 3121; ⊕ 09.00–17.30 Mon–Fri, 14.00–16.00 Sat
Public library [146–7 D4] 12 Nordic Dr; \ 772 3349; www.psglib.org; ⊕ 12.00–21.00 Mon–Thu, 10.00–17.00 Fri & Sat. Internet access.

High school \ 772 3861. Campers might be pleased to know it has a free gym, saltwater pool, & showers.

WHAT TO SEE Petersburg has some great **public art**, mainly murals. A comprehensive guide is available at the visitor centre. In addition to the public art, the well-groomed homes and yards make Petersburg a fun town to walk around. The north dock is a good place to look for sea lions and a seal affectionately called 'Bob'.

On the ocean side of Nordic Drive, **Sing Lee Alley** was where early Petersburg developed. **The Sons of Norway Hall** [146–7 D4] (\ 772 4575) was built in 1912 and is used today as a fraternity meeting place and centre of Norwegian heritage preservation. Outside, the small, but still spectacular, *Valhalla* is a replica of early Viking vessels. The **Northern Nights Theatre** (*500 N First St, at the Middle School auditorium;* \ 772 7469; *www.northernnightstheater.org*) is a small town movie theatre with shows at 19.00 on Friday and Saturday and 16.00 Sunday. Tickets cost US$8/6 adult/child. Finally, **Clausen Museum** [146–7 D3] (*203 Fram St, city centre;* \ 772 3598; *www.clausenmuseum.net;* ⊕ *10.00–17.00 Mon–Fri; US$3/free adult/child*) showcases Norwegian and Tlingit artefacts, including fish traps, a Tlingit canoe, and a 126.5-pound stuffed king salmon.

AROUND PETERSBURG

Nordic Drive heads north and south, turning into the **Mitkof Highway** on the south end of town. The 32-mile road follows Wrangell Narrows before turning inland and eventually ending at the south end of the island. **Falls Creek** is 11 miles from town and is a good place to see salmon swimming up the fish ladder. A little over 16 miles from town is the **Swan Observatory**, a little shack with peep holes for swan viewing on Blind Slough. From October through December is the best time to see swans but other species can be seen all year. The **Crystal Lake Fish Hatchery** is a mile beyond and allows visitors to explore on their own. During the week of 10 August, king salmon are spawned. The **Blind Slough Recreation Area** is also right there with great salmon fishing in season. A short trail (¼ mile) ends at the river with lovely views of the river and mountains. Further south is **Ohmer Creek Campground** (see page 148) and the **Mitkof Ferry Terminal**.

Nordic Drive leaves the north end of town along the Narrows before turning east and into Sandy Beach Road, then south following Frederick Sound. **Eagle's Roost Park** is a tiny park on the sea where bald eagles are a common sight. The **Whale Observatory** near Philbin Lane has information about whales and scopes for spotting them. Ice from LaConte Glacier is also commonly seen floating out to sea. Adjacent to Haugen Drive is **Sandy Beach**, a lovely picnic spot with a small sandy beach, a playground and covered tables.

The **Devil's Thumb** (9,077ft) is visible behind town on a clear day. The striking peak straddles the US/Canadian border and protrudes from the Stikine Icecap. Because of the temperate maritime climate, conditions change constantly keeping many climbers from the summit. The 6,700ft northwest face has long

been coveted by climbers and to this day remains unclimbed. At le
have perished while trying.

SITKA *(Population 8,788)*

Isolated though it is, Sitka (⊕ 57°3'10"N, 135°19'54"W) has manag
place where visitors of all persuasions and residents of many professions feel at
home. Much of the town's appeal lies in its stunning natural setting on the west
coast of Baranof Island amidst hundreds of tiny islands and facing the Pacific Ocean.
Looming over the entire scene is the extinct volcano Mount Edgecumbe (3,200ft)
on Kruzof Island. Behind town, forested hills climb to a ragged snow-capped range
with a network of hiking trails providing access. It's a popular port of call with cruise
ships and the port receives some 200,000 passengers a year. The local population is
an eclectic mix of fishermen, artists, retirees, and native Alaskans who have kept the
town diverse and welcoming to anyone with the mind to make the journey.

HISTORY Sitka, or *Shee Atika'*, as it was known to the Tlingits, was a thriving native
village in the 18th century, when early Russian explorer Vitus Bering encountered
it in 1799. Five years later, in 1804, Alexander Baranov, the manager of the Russian
American Company (the state sponsored fur trading presence in Alaska), built the
St Michael's Redoubt Fort in their new town of New Archangel, only to see it
burned to the ground by Tlingits. Two years later, Russian forces and their Unangan
(Aleut) captives retook the fort in what was to become the last major stand against
the Russians by the Tlingit. With its abundant resources, New Archangel (present
day Sitka) soon became the capital of Russian-controlled Alaska. The main export
was sea-otter pelts destined for China and Russia, but timber, fish and ice were also
shipped around the North Pacific. Wealthy Russians lived in opulent homes,
enjoying most of the luxuries of big city life, including a library, museum, two
schools and scores of businesses. In 1822, the Tlingits returned and delicately
coexisted with the Russians until Alaska was sold to the US in 1867.

Sitka remained the territory's capital until 1906, when it was moved to the
booming town of Juneau. Sitka's growth slowed in American hands but persisted
through the sale of timber, commercial fishing and gold mining. During World
War II, Sitka's population swelled with the arrival of more than 30,000 servicemen,
who were stationed at Japonski Island across from the harbour. It was fortified and
received a runway. Today, the base belongs to the US Coast Guard. After Sitka's
largest employer, a pulp mill, closed in 1993, locals continued fishing and have
carved out a lucrative niche in tourism.

GETTING THERE AND AWAY Sitka is 95 miles southwest of Juneau, 185 miles
northwest of Ketchikan and 862 miles from Seattle in Washington. Sitka is
accessible by plane and ferry only. The airport [156–7 C7] is on Japonski Island and
about a mile from town over the O'Connell Bridge.

By air

✈ **Alaska Airlines** ☎ 966 2926, 800 426 0333 (TF); www.alaskaair.com. Daily jet service directly into Sitka from Seattle for US$525. Also offers 3 flights a day from Juneau for US$225.

By ferry

Alaska Ferry *(5307 Halibut Point Rd;* ☎ *747 8737, 800 642 0066 (TF);
www.dot.state.ak.us/amhs)* runs between Sitka and Juneau four to five times per week
for US$45. The MV *Fairweather* makes the trip in about six hours at a dizzying 32
knots. The ferry terminal is seven miles north of town. **Sitka Tours** (☎ 747 8443)
operates a shuttle into town from the ferry terminal for US$8.

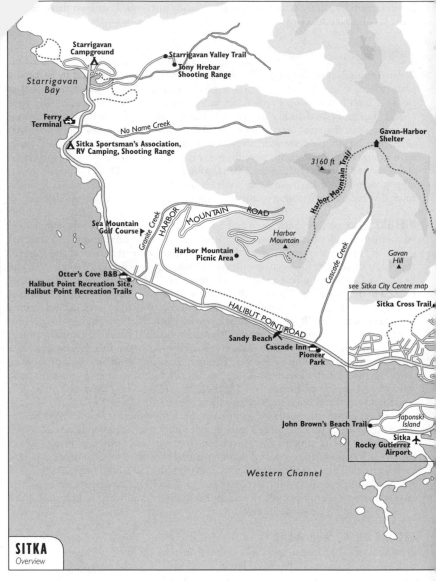

SITKA
Overview

GETTING AROUND
By car
🚗 **North Star Rent-A-Car** ☏ 966 2552, 800 722 6927 (TF); www.northstarrentacar.com. Office in the airport.

🚗 **Avis Rent-A-Car** ☏ 966 2404; www.avis.com. Office in the airport.

By taxi
🚗 **Esther G Sea Taxi** ☏ 747 6481; www.puffinsandwhales.com. Offers water taxi pick-up & drop-off service for hikers & kayakers. 🚗 **Hank's Taxi & Tour Service** ☏ 747 8888

🚗 **More Taxi & Tours** ☏ 738 3210; www.moorebusi.com
🚗 **Nina's Taxi and Tour Service** ☏ 738 1931. Offer taxi & tour services around town.

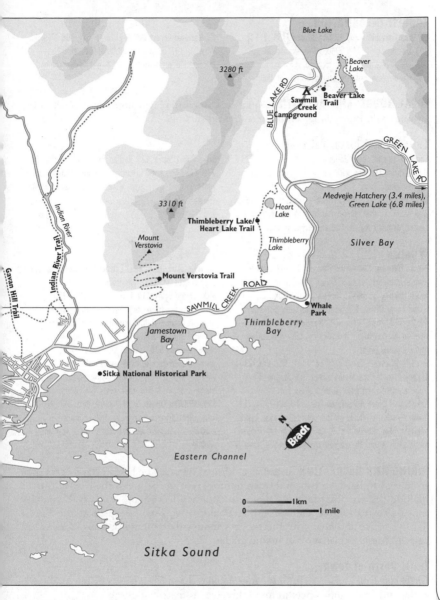

By bus

🚌 **Sitka Community Ride Bus** ☎ 747 7103;
www.publictransit.sitkatribe.org; runs w/days
06.30–18.30. Connects the city centre with Halibut
Point Road & Sawmill Creek Boulevard. Tickets cost
US$2/trip or US$5/day.

By bike

🚲 **Yellow Jersey Cycles** [156–7 F4] 329 Harbor Dr;
☎ 747 6317; www.yellowjerseycycles.com; ⊕
Mon–Fri 09.00–18.00, Sat 09.00–17.30. Bike rentals
cost US$30 for 24hrs.

TOURIST INFORMATION

Z Sitka Convention and Visitors Bureau [156–7 C4] 303 Lincoln St; ☎ 747 5940; www.sitka.org. In addition to the city centre location, there is a summer information desk inside Harrigan Centennial Hall.

Z National Forest Office [156–7 C4] 204 Siginaka Way; ☎ 747 6671; ⊕ 08.00–16.30 Mon–Fri. Information on hiking trails & public-use cabins.

LOCAL TOURS AND ACTIVITIES Sitka is an ocean playground with world-class fishing, wildlife viewing, kayaking, and even surfing.

Cultural and historical tours
Shore to Summit 801 Halibut Point Rd; ☎ 747 7244. Half & full-day hikes with proceeds going to trail improvement.
Sitka Tours ☎ 747 8443. History walks around town with stops at the salmon hatchery & the Raptor Center; detailed Russian era history. 3hr tour.

Sitka Tribal Tours 429 Katlian St; ☎ 747 7290, 888 270 8687 TF; www.sitkatribe.org. 2hr guided history walks around town with a special emphasis on the Tlingit history.

Wildlife
Alaska Outdoor Tours 409 Mills St; ☎ 747 7266; www.akoutdoortours.com. Offers half-day & full-day tours starting at US$75 on up to US$300.
Island Fever Diving & Adventures 805 Halibut Point Rd; ☎ 747 7871; www.islandfeverdiving.com. A dive shop in Alaska? Here it is. Diving, hiking, & biking tours around Sitka.
Sea Life Discovery Tours ☎ 966 2301, 877 966 2301 TF; www.sealifediscoverytours.com. See marine life from a customised boat with a glass bottom.
Sitka Sound Ocean Adventures Crescent Harbor; ☎ 752 0660; www.kayaksitka.com. The only full service kayak outfit in town. Kayak rentals for US$60 & day trips for US$200 & up. The ragged coastline around Sitka is

a magic place to paddle. Extended guided & unguided trips can be started right from town.
Sitka Sound Tours 312 Cascade; ☎ 738 1190; www.sitkasoundtours.com. Some of the best wildlife tours in town led by long time Sitka resident & biologist Jim Seeland.
Sitka's Secrets 500 Lincoln St; ☎ 747 5089; www.sitkasecret.com. Head out to sea for wildlife viewing with a very knowledgeable husband-&-wife-biologist team. A 3hr tour costs US$120pp.
Sitka Wildlife Quest ☎ 747 8100, 888 747 8101 TF; www.allenmarinetours.com. A slightly more commercial experience, but still a good way to see wildlife.

HIKING AND RECREATION Sitka has a number of fantastic hiking trails that range from easy to hard, and around town to more remote. Some of the best resources include the www.seatrails.org, www.sitkatrailworks.org and www.fs.fed.us/r10/tongass/recreation/rec_facilities/sitkatrails.html websites. Stop in at the Forest Service office and chat with the rangers about other hiking options. See box on page 75 for an explanation of hiking grades.

Trails north of town
Gavin Hill Trail [156–7 E3] (*Grade: easy; distance: 3.5 miles*) This accessible trail starts at the end of Baranof Street in town. Involves a steep stair climb.

Harbor Mountain Trail (*Grade: moderate; distance: 6 miles*) Starts at the end of Harbor Mountain Road, a few miles out Halibut Point Road. This moderately steep trail provides excellent views of town and connects to the Gavin Hill Trail. Can be muddy.

Indian River Trail [156–7 F1] (*Grade: easy; distance: 5.5 miles*) This trail is a mellow walk along Indian River just outside town, at the end of Indian River Road. At the end of Halibut Point Road, just past the ferry terminal is Starrigavan Bay with walk-in camping and three short trails.

Mount Verstovia Trail (*Grade: difficult; distance: 2.5 miles*) This steep 2.5-mile trail starts from a point about two miles down Sawmill Creek Road. Total elevation gain is 2,550ft and spectacular views can be had toward the top.

Beaver Lake Trail (*Grade: moderate; distance: 1 mile*) This trail circumnavigates Beaver Lake, providing excellent views of the surrounding peaks. Just past Whale Park on Sawmill Creek Road turn north on Blue Lake Road and follow it to the Sawmill Creek Campground. The trail starts at a bridge over the creek. Public-use rowboats are generally available at the lake.

Mount Edgecumbe (*Grade: difficult; distance: 6.5 miles*) Hikers can also ascend Mount Edgecumbe via a 6.5-mile trail for a total elevation gain of 3,000ft. Fred's Creek public-use cabin can be rented near the trail for US$35. Reserve this cabin early at www.fs.fed.us/r10/tongass/cabins/cabinlist.shtml. Catch a ride to the island with Esther G Sea Taxi (see page 152).

Stop in at the **Yellow Jersey Cycle Shop** (*329 Harbor Dr;* ⟍ *747 6317; www.yellowjerseycycles.com*) to hire a bike for the day (US$25) or pick their brains for information on local trails.

WHERE TO STAY

Public-use cabins The Sitka area has 28 public-use cabins, managed by the Forest Service. For more info and to reserve visit the Forest Service office or their website www.fs.fed.us/r10/tongass/cabins/cabinlist.shtml. All are accessible by small plane and boat.

Hotels

With a few notable exceptions, Sitka's accommodation possibilities are nothing special. For a full list visit the chamber website (*www.sitka.org*).

Cascade Inn [156–7 A5] (10 rooms) 2035 Halibut Point Road; ⟍ 747 6804, 800 532 0908 TF; www.cascadeinnsitka.com. Generic waterfront hotel. $$$

Fly-In Fish Inn [156–7 D5] (10 rooms) 485 Katlian St; ⟍ 747 7910; www.flyinfishinn.com. Standard rooms with nice views of the water from half of the rooms on the upper floor. $$$

Westmark Hotel [156–7 E4] (105 rooms) 330 Seward St; ⟍ 747 6241, 800 544 0970 (TF); www.westmarkhotels.com. A ubiquitous Alaska hotel chain with standard rooms with TV, laundry & free airport shuttle. $$$

Sitka Hotel [156–7 E5] (57 rooms) 118 Lincoln St; ⟍ 747 3288; www.sitkahotel.com. Another waterfront location, but with reasonable rates. $$

B&Bs

Alaska Ocean View B&B Inn [156–7 B4] (3 rooms) 1101 Edgecumbe Dr; ⟍ 747 8310, 888 811 6870 (TF); www.sitka-alaska-lodging.com. An efficiently run & extravagantly decorated B&B off a quiet street behind town. Rooms are very comfortable but the best reason to stay here is the owner Carole, whose infectious energy & local knowledge are something to behold. Hot tub. TV & Wi-Fi. $$$

Otter's Cove B&B [156–7 A5] (3 rooms) 3211 Halibut Point Rd; ⟍ 747 4529; www.ottercovebandb.com. Lovely simple rooms with access to laundry & a kitchen. Wi–Fi. $$$

Raven's Peek B& [156–7 B4] (2 rooms) 4260 Halibut Point Rd; ⟍ 738 0140; www.ravenspeekbandb.com. A fancy new home across the street from the water. Pleasant & private with full amenities. The owner roasts his own coffee. $$$

Hostel

Sitka Youth Hostel [156–7 F3] 109 Jeff Davis St; ⟍ 747 8661. Located at the Sheldon Jackson College, the hostel offers simple, but clean accommodation. If arriving late by ferry call ahead. $

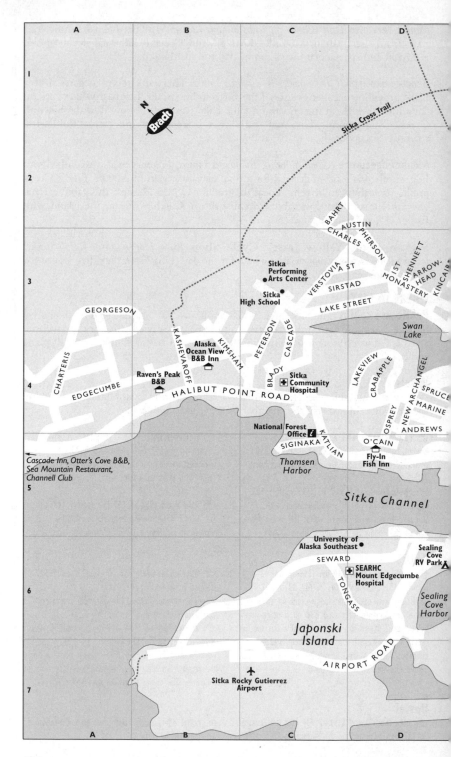

N
Bradt

Sitka Cross Trail

BAHRT
CHARLES
AUSTIN
PHERSON
IST
SHENNETT
MONASTERY
ARROW-
HEAD
KINCAP

A ST
VERSTOVIA
SIRSTAD

Sitka
Performing
Arts Center

Sitka
High School

LAKE STREET

GEORGESON

Swan
Lake

KASHEVAROFF

KIMSHAM

PETERSON

CASCADE

Alaska
Ocean View
B&B Inn

LAKEVIEW
CRABAPPLE
NEW ARCHANGEL
SPRUCE

CHARTERIS

Raven's Peak
B&B

BRADY

Sitka
Community
Hospital

OSPREY
MARINE

EDGECUMBE

HALIBUT POINT ROAD

ANDREWS

National Forest
Office

O'CAIN

*Cascade Inn, Otter's Cove B&B,
Sea Mountain Restaurant,
Channell Club*

SIGINAKA

KATLIAN

Fly-In
Fish Inn

Thomsen
Harbor

Sitka Channel

University of
Alaska Southeast

Sealing
Cove
RV Park

SEWARD

SEARHC
Mount Edgecumbe
Hospital

Sealing
Cove
Harbor

TONGASS

Japonski
Island

AIRPORT ROAD

Sitka Rocky Gutierrez
Airport

E
F
G
H

Indian River Trail

Indian River

2

Gavan Hill Trail

Alaska Raptor Center

JARVIS ST

INDIAN RIVER ROAD

SAWMILL CREEK ROAD

SAWMILL CREEK ROAD

Sheldon Jackson College

Sheldon Jackson Museum

JOHN BRADY DR

JEFF DAVIS

METLAKATLA

KELLY

Sitka National Historic Park

3

FIRST

MERRILL

BARANOF

DEGROFF

PARK

BJORKA

OJA

SAWMILL CREEK ROAD

BARANOF

Sitka Youth Hostel

ETOLIN

BARLOW

STREET

FINN ALCE

Sitka Sound Science Center

SJC Aquarium & Salmon Hatchery

Crescent Harbor

Russian Bishop's House

LINCOLN

St Peter's by the Sea Episcopal Church

Highliner Coffee

LAKE ST

Westmark

Yellow Jersey Cycles

ERLER

Russian Cemetery

HARBOR DR

Harrigan Centennial Hall (Sitka Visitor's Bureau)

4

OBSERVATORY

Sitka Historical Museum

Little Tokyo

Library

MARINE

Lutheran Cemetery

LINCOLN

St Michael's Cathedral

Russian Block House

Sitka Lutheran Church

KOGWANTON

Totem Square

Castle Hill

Victoria's Café

KATLIAN

LINCOLN

Pioneer

Ludwigs Bistro

Sitka Pioneer's Home

Sitka

O'Connell Bridge Visitor's Dock

5

ANB Harbor

ANB Hall

O'Connell Bridge

Sitka Sound

Aleutski Island

6

0 —————— 1,000m
0 —————— 1,000yds

7

E
F
G
H

ping

Sawmill Creek Campground (11 sites) Free primitive sites with toilets & tables 8 miles down Sawmill Creek Road, then 1.8 miles up Blue Lake Road. The Beaver Lake Trail (see page 155) starts here.

Starrigavan Campground (35 sites) 7 miles out on Halibut Point Rd, less than a mile past the ferry terminal; www.recreation.gov. Drive-up & walk-in tent sites & RV spaces US$12–30. Toilets, water, & tables available. Reservations are a good idea mid-summer.

RV parks

Sitka Sportsman's Association RV Park (18 sites) 5211 Halibut Point Rd; 747 6033. This RV park, located near the ferry terminal, has sites for US$20. Be aware that there's also a shooting range on the grounds.

Sealing Cove RV Park [156–7 D6] This parking lot on Japonski Island, near the Sealing Cove Harbour at the base of the O'Connell Bridge, accommodates RVs for US$21/night. It's run by the city, so call the Harbour Master (747 3439) for more information.

✕ WHERE TO EAT Sitka is arguably the best place to eat in all of southeast Alaska. That claim may not seem much in a region with culinary black holes like Prince of Wales Island and Wrangell, but don't forget the region is also home to Juneau and Skagway, both well known for their fine eateries. Sitka beats them both, however, in variety, quality and sheer dedication to food.

✕ Ludwig's Bistro [156–7 E5] 256 Katlian St; 966 3663; ⊕ 16.00–21.00 Mon–Sat. An intimate womb-like bistro serving excellent handmade & often local food. Their head chef travels to Europe every winter to learn more about wine & cuisine. Groups of 4 or more should make reservations weeks – or even months – ahead. $$$$

✕ Bayview Restaurant 407 Lincoln St; 747 3900; ⊕ 04.30–21.00 Mon–Sat, 04.30–19.00 Sun. Good handmade burgers, ribs on Fri, & a simple but filling b/fast buffet every day from 04.30–10.00. $$$

✕ Little Tokyo [156–7 E4] 315 Lincoln St; 747 5699; ⊕ 11.00–21.00 Mon–Fri, 12.00–21.00 Sat & Sun. Decent sushi & bento at a great price. $$$

✕ Roma's 327 Seward St; 966 4600; ⊕ 11.00–21.00 daily. This fine little Italian eatery is owned & run entirely by... Koreans. Everything is handmade, served with a smile & tastes great. $$$

✕ Larkspur Café 2 Lincoln St; 966 2326; ⊕ 11.00–22.00 Wed–Sat, 10.00–15.00 Sun. A hip, casual place with beer, wine & simple meals. $$

✕ Ludwigs at Lincoln Lincoln St, near the bridge; ⊕ 11.30–14.30 Mon–Sat. This soup cart serves the best clam chowder on earth. $$

✕ Victoria's Café [156–7 E5] 118 Lincoln St; 747 9301; ⊕ 06.00–21.00 daily. A Victorian diner? Here it is. The food is OK, with sandwiches, burgers & the like filling the menu. $$

✕ The Back Door Café 104 Barracks St; 747 8856; ⊕ 06.30–17.00 Mon–Fri, 06.30–14.00 Sat. Located in the back of Old Harbor Books, this cute little locals' café serves quiche, baked goods, & hot drinks. Local art hangs on the walls. $

✕ Highliner Coffee [156–7 E4] 327 Seward St; 747 4924; ⊕ 05.30–18.00 Mon–Fri, 07.00–17.00 Sat & Sun. Fresh roasted coffee, baked goods, & internet. $

WHERE TO DRINK

♀ Pioneer Bar [156–7 E5] 212 Katlian St; 747 3456. This maritime-themed joint is known locally as a 5-star dive because of its delightfully seedy

atmosphere. Located near Ludwig's Bistro on the waterfront, this is where folks start drinking during a night out. Lots of boat pictures.

ENTERTAINMENT AND NIGHTLIFE The **New Archangel Dancers** (see page 160) and the **Sheet'ka Kwaan Naa Kahidi Native Dancers** (see page 160) both perform in town, primarily for cruise-ship members, but anyone can buy tickets and attend. Otherwise, try **Kelly's Sports Pub** (*1617 Sawmill Creek Rd;* 623 3910*)*; has live music and dancing on the weekends. The brand-new (2009) **Sitka Performing Arts Center** is located immediately next to the high school (*http://shs.ssd.k12.ak.us*) on Lake Street. Readers can visit Old Harbor Books (see opposite) for shows and tickets.

Cinema Sitka has two movie theatres, one is in the **city centre** (*335 Lincoln St;* ℄ *747 0646*) and the other is out on **Sawmill Creek Road** (*1321 Sawmill Creek Rd;* ℄ *747 0646*). Both are similar and play newish movies all year. For show times, call or visit www.sitkamovies.com.

SHOPPING Sitka's main shopping district is along Lincoln Street in the city centre, but sadly many of the shops are quite generic. A few exceptions are:

Sitka Rose Gallery 419 Lincoln St. ℄ 747 3030; www.sitkarosegallery.com. A good assortment of Russian & native Alaskan arts & crafts.

Fishermen's Eye 239 Lincoln St; ℄ 747 6080; www.fishermenseye.com. Showcases painting & art from local & state-wide artists.
Robertson's Gallery 128 Lincoln St; ℄ 747 6764. A good selection of local 2-D artwork.

For native arts head over the **Sitka Historical Museum gift shop** (see page 161). Also check out the **Sheet'ka Kwaan Naa Kahidi** (see page 160) building, where native dances are held along the waterfront. Another great stop is the **Baranof Arts and Crafts Guild** (℄ 747 6536) in Centennial Hall.

FESTIVALS AND EVENTS
May
Sitka Salmon Derby (℄ 747 6790) Takes place during the last week of May with cash prizes.

June
Home Skillet Music Festival (*www.homeskilletfest.com*) Held during mid-June this festival features an eclectic assortment of music from local and out-of-town bands.

Sitka Music Festival (℄ 277 4852; *www.sitkamusicfestival.org*) Brings classical music to town with a crab feed and ice cream through June.

July
4 July The celebrations start 2 July with parades, parties and fireworks and continue through 4 July.

November
Sitka WhaleFest (*www.sitkawhalefest.org*) Kicks off in the first week of November with speakers, programs, and whale watching.

OTHER PRACTICALITIES
Baranof Laundromat 1211 Sawmill Creek Rd
Evergreen Health Foods 1321 Sawmill Creek Rd; ℄ 747 6944; ⏰ 10.00–06.00 Mon-Fri & 10.00–05.30 Sat. A complete selection of health foods in a new & much larger location.
Lakeside Grocery 705 Halibut Point Rd; ℄ 747 3317; ⏰ 06.00–midnight daily. A decent grocery store with lots of Asian foods.
Old Harbor Books 201 Lincoln St; ℄ 747 8808; ⏰ 08.00–19.00 Mon-Fri, 08–18.00 Sat & 10.00–16.00 Sun. A good selection of Alaska & travel books.

Post Office (Lincoln) [156–7 E4] 338 Lincoln St; ℄ 747 8491; ⏰ 08.30–17.45 Mon–Sat
Post office (Sawmill) [156–7 G2] 1207 Sawmill Creek Rd; ℄ 747 3381; ⏰ 09.30–17.00 Mon–Fri
Public Library [156–7 F4] 320 Harbor Dr; ℄ 747 8708; www.cityofsitka.com/dept/library/library.html; ⏰ 10.00–21.00 Mon–Fri, 13.00–21.00 Sat & Sun. A cozy little seaside library with Wi–Fi with the Back Door Café in the back. Open times vary with cruise-ship schedule.

Sea Mart 1867 Halibut Point Rd; ☏ 747 6266; www.seamart.com. Deli, bakery, & full assortment of foods.

Sitka Laundry Center 906 Halibut Point Rd
Super O Laundromat 404 Sawmill Creek Rd

WHAT TO SEE AND DO Sitka is packed with history and full of amazing scenery. On a clear day head to:

Harbor Drive [156–7 E4] where your attention will be divided between views of town with a backdrop of rugged peaks to the northeast and hundreds of islands dominated by Mount Edgecumbe to the southwest. Nearby is **Castle Hill** [156–7 E5], the site of Baranof's original castle, built in 1837. Before that it was central to the Tlingit people. This is where the official transfer of power took place in 1867 between Russia and the US.

On the sea off Katlian Avenue is **Totem Square** [156–7 E5] with a Russian cannon, some anchors and a totem pole with a double-headed eagle. On the same street is the **Sheet'ka Kwaan Naa Kahidi tribal house** (☏ 747 7290; US$8/5 adult/child) where Tlingit dancers perform, primarily for cruise-ship passengers, in full traditional regalia.

Up the hill on Kaagwaantaan Street is the **Russian Block House** [156–7 E5], a replica of the original structure that separated Tlingits and Russians after the Tlingit returned to Sitka in the 1820s. Nearby is the **Sitka Pioneer's Home** [156–7 E5], an original structure built in 1934 for elderly Alaskan residents. A gift shop can be found on the second floor. North of the city centre is the **Lutheran Cemetery** [156–7 E4] with the grave of Princess Maksoutoff, the wife of Russian-Alaska's last governor, Dimitrii Maksoutoff.

In the centre of town is one of Sitka's most striking buildings, the **St Michael's Cathedral** [156–7 E4] (⊕ 09.00–16.00 Mon–Fri & when a cruise ship is in town; US$2). The onion-domed church, built in 1844, was the first of its kind in America. The building burned in 1966 and was rebuilt. Inside are all manner of icons, paintings, and other religious artefacts. The church holds regular services. On the west side of Crescent Harbor is **Harrigan Centennial Hall** [156–7 F4] where the **New Archangel Dancers** (☏ 747 5516; US$8/4 adult/child), a group of local women, perform traditional dances. Also inside this building is a spectacular hand-carved Tlingit canoe and the **Sitka Historical Museum** [156–7 F4]. Near Baranof Street and Lincoln Street, north of Crescent Harbor, is the **Russian Bishop's House** [156–7 E4] (☏ 747 6281; ⊕ 09.00–15.00 daily; US$4). Built in 1842, it is the oldest Russian building in Sitka. On the east side of Crescent Harbor, off Lincoln Street, is the **Sitka Sound Science Center** [156–7 F3] (☏ 747 8874; ⊕ 08.00–17.00 daily; US$2), fish hatchery, and aquarium. Stop by to learn all about the undersea life of southeast Alaska. Nearby is **Sheldon Jackson Museum** [156–7 F3].

At the east end of Lincoln Street is the 107-acre **Sitka National Historic Park** [156–7 G3] (☏ 747 8061; ⊕ 08.00–17.00 daily; US$4). The centre features information on the Tlingit and Russian cultures and the famous Russian–Tlingit battle that took place on the grounds. Local artists including weavers and totem carvers occasionally demonstrate traditional techniques. Call ahead for talk and demonstration times. A network of forest trails covers the grounds, including a scenic walk along the sea with totem poles and interpretive signs all the way.

Off Sawmill Creek Road east of town is the **Alaska Raptor Center** [156–7 G2] (☏ 747 8662; www.alaskaraptor.org; ⊕ 08.00–16.00 daily; US$12/6 adult/child) where injured bald eagles and over 100 other birds of prey are rehabilitated every year. The birds that cannot be released back into the wild are kept at the facility to educate the public. This is a top-notch facility that's fun to explore alone or with a tour. If going on the tour route, ask for someone who has been at the centre for a year or more. A walking trail from the Sitka National Historic Park also leads to the centre. A taxi from town costs US$6.50. Six miles out on Sawmill Creek Road is **Whale Park**, a roadside pullout where whales can sometimes be seen.

The **Sea Mountain Golf Course** (*301 Granite Creek Rd;* ✆ *747 5663; seamountaingolf.com*) is special, mainly because it's a favourite haunt of local black bears. According to locals, bears do 'number twos' every morning at hole number two! Located four miles north of town off Halibut Point Road.

Museums

Sheldon Jackson Museum [156–7 F3] (*104 College Dr;* ✆ *747 8981;* ⊕ *10.00–16.00 Tue–Sat; US$4 adult/child*) Sheldon Jackson founded Sheldon Jackson College, the first in the state, and amassed an impressive collection of native artwork from around the state between 1880 and 1900. The first concrete building in the state was erected in 1895 to store this priceless collection.

Sitka Historical Museum [156–7 F4] (*330 Harbor Dr;* ✆ *747 6455; www.sitkahistory.org;* ⊕ *09.00–17.00 Sun–Fri, 11.00–15.00 Sat; US$2 adult/child*) Located inside Harrigan Centennial Hall, this small museum features artefacts from Sitka's Russian, American and native history.

GLACIER BAY NATIONAL PARK AND PRESERVE AND GUSTAVUS

As far as primeval, glacier-encrusted landscapes go, Glacier Bay cannot be beaten. More than a dozen major glaciers split towering peaks to crash into the bay and what is more the Bay is also renowned for its abundant marine life. Most of the landscape, only newly uncovered from ice, supports a hardy collection of verdant green plants that contrasts sharply with the predominantly white and grey landscape. Wildlife to be seen here includes porpoises, sea lions, humpback whales seabirds, bear, moose, mountain goats and bald eagles. Though reasonably remote (25 miles from Haines and 45 miles from Juneau), the 3.3-million-acre park has seen an ever-increasing number of visitors since John Muir first explored the bay in 1879. The Scottish-born American naturalist first visited Glacier Bay in 1879 and later made a number of other trips to the state. Since that time, the ice has receded substantially and records show that since 1750 the bay's glaciers have retreated some 65 miles! Today, the park is visited by more than 350,000 people annually, almost all of whom arrive and depart on cruise ships. While not a cheap destination, the independent traveller can explore the park in a variety of ways. Others can board a boat for a day tour of the park from Gustavus near the park entrance, or Juneau 45 miles to the south.

HISTORY In 1794 George Vancouver sailed by Glacier Bay, but instead of seeing the majestic valley of ice and rock of today, he saw only a wall of ice, and sailed on without a second thought. But the bay had not always been like that. Before the ice surged forward to completely fill the valley a few hundred years before Vancouver sailed by, the Huna Tlingit lived there for centuries. When the ice moved forward, they were forced from their home. Later, in the time of John Muir , the ice receded, revealing several miles of new land. We know today that before glaciers start to recede, they often advance, just as the glaciers of Glacier Bay did. Muir studied the landscape intently, recognising that California's Yosemite Valley must have been formed by a similar process of glaciation. Ever since then, the bay has been a source of fascination for scientists, artists, writers and the general public. It was designated a monument in 1925, but didn't receive national park status until 1980. Since then, the number of boats in the park has skyrocketed and sadly affected the whale population, prompting park management to limit boat traffic during the summer.

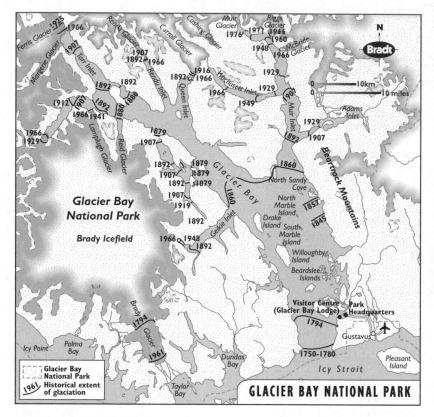

Labels on map: Ferris Glacier 1925, 1766, Renu Glacier, Carroll Glacier, Cushing Glacier, Muir Glacier 1976, 1977, Riggs Glacier 1966, 1960, McBride Glacier 1948, 1966, N, Bradt, Margerie Glacier 1907, Tarr Inlet, 1907, 1892 1966, 1892, 1916 1966, Rendu Inlet, 1892 1966, Hugh Miller Inlet, 1929, 1929, 1966, 1949, Adams Inlet, 10km, 10 miles, 1912 1901, 1892, 1880, 1966 1941, 1880, Queen Inlet, Muir Inlet, 1907, 1929, 1892, 1907, 1966 1929, Reid Glacier, 1879, 1907, Lamplugh Glacier, 1860, North Sandy Cove, Beartrack Mountains, 1892, 1879, 1879, Glacier Bay, North Marble Island, 1907, 1892 1879, 1860, 1857, Drake Island, 1845, Glacier Bay National Park, 1907 1919, Geikie Inlet, 1892, South Marble Island, Brady Icefield, 1966 1948, 1892, Willoughby Island, Beardslee Islands, Brady Glacier, 1794, Visitor Centre (Glacier Bay Lodge), Park Headquarters, Icy Point, Palma Bay, 1961, 1794, Gustavus, Dundas Bay, 1750–1780, Pleasant Island, Taylor Bay, Icy Strait

Legend:
Glacier Bay National Park
1961 Historical extent of glaciation

GLACIER BAY NATIONAL PARK

GETTING THERE AND AWAY

By air Apart from cruise ships, the best way to get to Glacier Bay is to fly. Alaska Airlines (see below) offers a quick jet service, indeed the 15-minute flight is over before it begins. Flying with one of the smaller outfits (see list below) doubles as a flightseeing trip.

✈ **Air Excursions** ☎ 789 5591. Flies out of Juneau.
✈ **Alaska Airlines** ☎ 800 252 7522; www.alaskaair.com. Flies daily from Juneau to Gustavus for US$300 round-trip.
✈ **Fjord Flying Service** ☎ 697 2377, 877 460 2377 (TF) Flies from Juneau.

✈ **Haines Airways** ☎ 877 359 2467. Flies from Haines.
✈ **Wings of Alaska** ☎ 789 0790; www.wingsofalaska.com. Flies from Juneau.

By ferry The privately owned **Glacier Bay Ferry** (☎ *888 229 8687 (TF); www.visitglacierbay.com*) operates between Bartlett Cove (inside the park) and Auke Bay near Juneau Friday and Sunday (24 May–2 Sep); tickets cost US$75.22/37.61 adult/child each way. The ferry departs Glacier Bay at 16.00 (arrives Juneau 19.00) and leaves Juneau at 19.30 (arrives Glacier Bay 22.30).

GETTING AROUND Once in Gustavus a shuttle is always on hand at the airport to take passengers to Bartlett Cove (on the edge of the park) for US$10. Those staying at local lodges generally get a free pick-up. **TLC Taxi** (☎ *697 2239*) runs anywhere there's a road and will happily haul kayaks and bikes. **Bud's Rent-A-**

Car (℡ *697 2403*) rents cars, but the limited road system hardly makes it worth it. Hitching and biking (bikes can be rented at the Glacier Bay Lodge and are available at some accommodations) are good ways to get around town.

TOURIST INFORMATION

ℹ Park Service Visitor Centre ℡ 697 2230; ⏱ 11.00–21.00 daily. Located in Bartlett Cove, it has a number of educational displays & a bookstore. Catch a ranger presentation in the auditorium at 20.00, or one of 3 films at 14.00, 17.00 & 19.00. Daily ranger walks depart from the visitor centre at 14.00 for a 1.5-mile stroll through the woods.

ℹ Visitor Information Station Bartlett Cove; ⏱ 08.00–19.00 daily. Good source of information for campers, boaters, & other independents.
ℹ Gustavus Visitor Association ℡ 697 2454; www.gustavusak.com. Have a helpful website.

🏠 WHERE TO STAY

Options within the park are restricted to camping. You can either head for Glacier Bay Lodge – a free campground located ᶜ mile south of the Bartlett Cove dock and ten miles from Gustavus – or camp wild, as long as you stop by the visitor information centre for an orientation. If, however, you'd prefer to have a roof over your head you'll need to stay in Gustavus.

🏠 Bear Track Inn (14 rooms) ℡ 697 3017, 888 697 2284 (TF); www.beartrackinn.com. A monumental log inn with luxurious rooms, fine food, & all the amenities one expects when paying US$500 plus (with meals) per night. The lodge is located in a secluded area east of town, past the airport. Fine overland hiking can be had right out the back door. $$$$$

🏠 Glacier Bay Country Inn (10 rooms) ℡ 697 2288, 800 628 0912 (TF); www.glacierbayalaska.com. Located on 160 acres with a large central lodge & rooms for US$408 & cabins for US$506, both including 3 meals. $$$$$

🏠 Glacier Bay Lodge (56 rooms) ℡ 264 4600, 888 229 8687 (TF); www.visitglacierbay.com. Located 10 miles from Gustavus at Bartlett Cove inside the park, the Glacier Bay Lodge offers simple rooms for US$170–225. The visitor centre & hiking trails are nearby. There is little reason to stay here unless you want to be near the visitor centre or don't have a car. Wi-Fi. $$$$

🏠 A Bear's Nest B&B (3 rooms) ℡ 697 2440; www.gustavus.com/bearsnest. 2 well-appointed cabins (1 is round) & a private room go for US$120–225 dbl. $$$

🏠 Aimee's Guesthouse (2 rooms) ℡ 697 2330; www.gustavus.com/guesthouse. A lovely home right in town divided into 2 apartments with full kitchens & all the conveniences of home. US$100–150 dbl. $$$

🏠 Annie Mae Lodge (11 rooms) ℡ 697 2346, 800 478 2346 (TF); www.anniemae.com. A comfortable, but simple, B&B in town. $$$

🏠 Blue Heron B&B (4 rooms) ℡ 697 2293; www.blueheronbnb.net. Pleasant rooms with kitchenettes. The owners maintain a large garden on the property. $$$

🏠 Good River B&B (5 rooms) ℡ 697 2241; www.glacier-bay.us. A lovely wood home in the woods with artful touches. 4 private rooms (shared bath) & a rustic cabin for US$130–140 dbl. $$$

🏠 Gustavus Inn (14 rooms) ℡ 697 2254, 800 649 5220 (TF); www.gustavusinn.com. A lovely home surrounded by forests & gardens, this 1928 homestead was converted to an inn in the 1960s & has gained a reputation as one of the area's best accommodations. Rooms start at US$209 dbl. Wi-Fi. $$$

🏠 Homestead B&B (2 rooms) ℡ 697 2777; www.homesteadbedbreakfast.com. Long-time Alaskans, Tom & Sally McLaughlin, have a lovely custom-made home with a large veggie garden outside. $$$

✘ WHERE TO EAT

The **Bear Track Inn** and the **Gustavus Inn** both serve top-notch, fresh seafood dinners for US$35–40. Also worth a try are:

✘ Bears Nest Café ℡ 697 2440; www.gustavus.com/bearsnest; ⏱ 11.00–20.00 daily. Amazing local seafood & local organic greens. $$$
✘ Homeshore Café ℡ 697 2822; ⏱ 11.30–19.00 Tue–Fri. Pizza & sandwiches. $$$

✘ Bear Track Mercantile ℡ 697 2358; ⏱ 09.00–19.00 daily. A 'sell-everything' store with a decent delicatessen. $$

OTHER PRACTICALITIES

Public library ☏ 697 2350; www.cms.gustavus-ak.gov/ services/library; ⊕ 13.30–16.30 & 19.00–21.00 Mon | & Wed, 13.30–16.30 Tue & Fri, 10.00 12.00 & 13.30–16.30 Thu, 11.00–15.00 Sat. Internet access.

EXPLORING THE PARK Kayaks are a popular way to explore the park, and arguably the best. Those who don't want a workout can board the *Baranof Wind*, a tour boat run by **Glacier Bay Lodge** (☏ *264 4600, 888 229 8687 TF; www.visitglacierbay.com*). The vessel makes a 130-mile, seven-hour loop through the bay past many tidewater glaciers for adult/child US$170/85. An onboard naturalist gives presentations on various aspects of the park's wildlife, glaciers, and geology. Reservations are required well in advance.

Kayakers can rent boats from **Glacier Bay Sea Kayaks** (☏ *697 2257; www.glacierbayseakayaks.com*) for US$45 or head out with a guide for US$95/150 half day/full day. Those camping in the park must swing by the visitor information station (see page 163) for an orientation.

Since most people come to Glacier Bay to see glaciers, they will probably want to get beyond the nearby Beardslee Islands. While kayakers can get to tidewater glaciers under their own power, it's a good 45 miles from Bartlett Cove to the first glacier with rough water a distinct possibility. A better option is to book a drop-off on the *Baranof Wind* for US$190 return. Alternatively, the eastern portion of the bay is less crowded and generally preferable to kayakers. Areas that do not allow motorised boats and are perfect for kayakers include: Adams Inlet, Muir Inlet and Wachusett Inlet. The Rigg's, Muir and McBride glaciers all touch the sea and are spectacular to approach in a kayak.

Several companies offer extended kayak trips in Glacier Bay for US$2,000 plus. These companies include **Alaska Discovery** (☏ *800 780 6505; www.akdiscovery.com*), **Alaska Mountain Guides** (☏ *800 766 3396; www.alaskamountainguides.com*), **Packer Expeditions** (☏ *983 2544; www.packerexpeditions.com*), and **Spirit Walker Expeditions** (☏ *800 529 2537; www.seakayakalaska.com*).

Hiking The **Bartlett Lake Trail** (*Grade: moderate; distance: 4 miles*) starts near the Glacier Bay Lodge and continues for four miles through the forest to Bartlett Lake. The **Bartlett River Trail** (*Grade: moderate; distance: 2 miles*) branches off the lake trail, meandering in and out of the trees along an intertidal area for four miles before ending at the Bartlett River. Two short walks start from the lodge, one follows the sea, the other loops through the forest. See box on page 75 for an explanation of hiking grades.

SKAGWAY *(Population: 846)*

The town of Skagway (⊕ 59°28'7"N, 135°18'21"W) occupies a narrow strip of flat land – some of the only flat ground for miles – along the Skagway River at the head of Taiya Inlet. Few towns, except nearby Haines, are so spectacularly situated. Soaring peaks sprout from the water along the inlet and continue right along the valley through White Pass to Canada. In addition to a great location, Skagway is significantly drier than the rest of the southeast, receiving just over 26 inches of rain annually. Compare that to Ketchikan's excess of 12 feet! Moreover, the town's past is steeped in the fascinating history of the world famous Klondike Gold Rush. Yet Skagway is not quite a heaven on earth. Legions of tourists (more than one million a year) descend on the tiny town between May and August. When a cruise ship is in town it's positively overwhelmed by thousands of tourists looking to stretch their legs. The upshot is that nearly everyone keeps to the main drag and the edges of town, hiking trails, and nearby Dyea Valley remain tranquil, serene places in which to escape. Despite the town's unappealing desire to accommodate tourists in every way, Skagway remains a lovely place to hike (the Chilkoot Trail jumps to mind), absorb history and take advantage of the excellent dining options.

For further information, it's also worth consulting *Yukon: The Bradt Travel Guide* written by Polly Evans.

HISTORY Skagway's heyday, in the 1890s, was short but furious. In 1896, gold was discovered on the Klondike River in Canada's Yukon Territory. As word leaked across the border, then across the ocean, would-be prospectors arrived in Skagway by the thousands. One of the original settlers in Skagway, William Moore, was inundated by more than 10,000 prospectors attempting to gather the year's worth of supplies the Canadian government required to enter. From Skagway, the White Pass Trail headed inland and, though pack animals could be used, thousands died *en route* and the Chilkoot Trail, located in the neighbouring Dyea Valley, was so steep that pack animals could not be used at all. Both routes consisted of 35-mile journeys by foot (with a year's worth of supplies that could consist of 400lbs of flour, 200lbs of bacon, and 100lbs of beans) then a further 560 miles by boat to the gold fields. For a few years, tens of thousands made the trip and most returned home broke. By the end of the century, the Klondike Gold Rush had ended as quickly as it had begun and those who had struck it rich, or had not learned their lesson, immediately moved on to the newly discovered strike in Nome.

GETTING THERE AND AWAY Skagway is accessible via road, rail, ferry and charter flight from Juneau. The Klondike Highway ends in Skagway after branching off the Alaska Highway 108 miles northeast in Whitehorse, Yukon Territory, Canada.

By air Skagway is most commonly accessed by charter flight from Juneau, 100 miles (45 minutes) to the south. The following offer a daily service.

✈ **Air Excursions** ↘ 789 5591; www.airexcursions.com. Charter service in the upper-panhandle. US$120 from Juneau to Skagway with a generous 70lb baggage allowance, US$00.40/lb after that. Free shuttle service to & from the airport.
✈ **Wings of Alaska** 301 S Terminal Way; ↘ 983 2442; www.wingsofalaska.com. Daily service from

Juneau to Skagway for adult/child US$119/89 1-way, US$238/178 round trip, as well as scheduled flights to neighbouring villages from Juneau. 50lb baggage allowance, US$00.50/lb after that.
✈ **Alaska Mountain Flying Service** (see page 172) Charter flights to Haines for US$60.

By ferry
⛴ **Alaska Ferry** ↘ 983 2941, 800 642 0066 (TF); www.dot.state.ak.us/amhs. Ferries connect Skagway with Juneau 4–5 times a week through the summer for US$50, then head for neighbouring Haines for US$31.
⛴ **Alaska Fjordlines** ↘ 766 3395, 800 320 0146 (TF); www.alaskafjordlines.com. Hop on the catamaran *Fjord Express,* for a quick & scenic day trip to Juneau. The ferry leaves Skagway daily at 08.00,

Haines at 08.45 & arrives in Juneau at 11.00 for adult/child US$155/125. The ferry returns to Haines at 07.30 & Skagway at 08.15.
⛴ **Haines-Skagway Fast Ferry** 142 Beach Rd; ↘ 766 2100, 888 766 2103 (TF); www.hainesskagwayfastferry.com. Daily ferry service between Skagway & Haines. As many as 6 trips per day for adult/child US$35/18 one way.

By rail
🚂 **White Pass & Yukon Route Rail** 231 2nd Av; ↘ 983 2217, 800 343 7373 (TF); www.wpyr.com. Connects Whitehorse, Canada with Skagway on an all day bus/train trip Sun–Fri for adult/child US$195/97.50. Scenic train trips through White Pass

are their speciality, they also offer pickup for those finishing the Chilkoot Trail at Lake Bennett railway stop for US$95. They also offer a trip to Carcross, Canada with a stay in the Foxhollow B&B (*www.yukonalaska.com/foxhollow*) for US$170pp.

Skagway is connected with the Alaska Highway via a 98-mile road called the Klondike Highway. This stretch of road is considered by some to be the most scenic in the state – even though much of it is in Canada. Many visitors travelling the Alaska Highway make this detour for the scenery and to get a good bite to eat in one of Skagway's top-notch eateries. The highway crosses into British Columbia 14 miles north of Skagway and into the Yukon Territory 38 miles later. Those crossing the border at an odd hour (⊕ *midnight–08.00*) be sure to call Canadian customs ☏ 867 821 4111 or US customs ☏ 983 2325.

By bus

🚌 **White Pass & Yukon Route Rail** One bus a day (except Sun) connects Whitehorse, Canada & Skagway for US$60pp. The bus leaves Skagway at 14.00. They would rather sell a train ticket for US$116, so the bus fares are not shown on their website.

GETTING AROUND

By bike
Skagway is a reasonably flat place, making bikes an ideal way to get around.

🚲 **Sockeye Cycles** 381 Fifth Av; ☏ 983 2851; www.cyclealaska.com. Bike rentals (US$35/day) & tours, including a train & bike tour that involves a train ride up the mountain & a fast bike ride back down. US$179.

By shuttle and bus

🚐 **Dyea Dave's Shuttle** ☏ 209 5031; www.dyeadavetours.com. Dave offers fun tours around town, general transportation as well as Chilkoot Trail hiker drop-off & pick-up.

By rental car and RV

🚗 **Alaska Motorhome Rentals** 246 12th Av; ☏ 983 3333, 800 254 9929 (TF); www.alaskarv.com.
🚗 **Avis** 3rd Av; ☏ 983 2247; www.avis.com. Cars for US$113/day. Located inside the Westmark Hotel.

🚗 **Sourdough Vehicle Rentals** 351 6th Av; ☏ 983 2523; www.geocities.com/sourdoughcarrentals. Cars & trucks are US$80–140/day.

TOURIST INFORMATION

🈳 **National Park Visitor Centre** ☏ 983 2921; www.nps.gov/klgo; ⊕ 08.00–18.00 daily. Located across the street from the visitor centre, the park office has lots of information about the gold rush days & offer free daily tours of Skagway (⊕ 09.00, 10.00, 11.00, 14.00 & 15.00) & the Dyea town site (⊕ 14.00 Mon–Thu, 10.00 & 14.00 Fri–Sun). Be sure to watch the gold rush movie screened a few times a day.
🈳 **Skagway Visitor Center** ☏ 983 2854; www.skagway.com; ⊕ 08.00–18.00 daily. Located between Second & Third Av & Broadway inside the Arctic Brotherhood Hall. The facade is entirely encased in driftwood sticks, you can't miss it.

LOCAL TOURS AND ACTIVITIES

Alaska Mountain Guides 370 4th Av; ☏ 766 3366, 800 766 3396 (TF); www.alaskamountainguides.com. Guided trips of all kinds, from climbing to the summits of the highest Alaskan peaks to mellow half-day rock climbing trips just outside of town.

Frontier Excursions 1602 State St; ☏ 983 2512, 877 983 2512 (TF); www.frontierexcursions.com. Bus tours around town & White Pass for US$45.
Mt Flying Service ☏ 766 3007; www.flyglacierbay.com. Flightseeing trips to Glacier Bay National Park from Skagway & Haines. This is a decent way to see the park & infinitely cheaper than a traditional lodge stay trip.

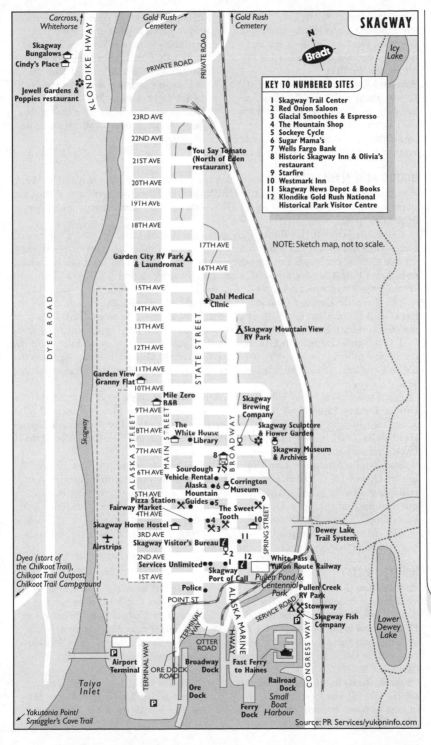

SKAGWAY

KEY TO NUMBERED SITES

1 Skagway Trail Center
2 Red Onion Saloon
3 Glacial Smoothies & Espresso
4 The Mountain Shop
5 Sockeye Cycle
6 Sugar Mama's
7 Wells Fargo Bank
8 Historic Skagway Inn & Olivia's restaurant
9 Starfire
10 Westmark Inn
11 Skagway News Depot & Books
12 Klondike Gold Rush National Historical Park Visitor Centre

NOTE: Sketch map, not to scale.

Carcross, Whitehorse

Gold Rush Cemetery

Gold Rush Cemetery

Icy Lake

Skagway Bungalows
Cindy's Place

KLONDIKE HWY

PRIVATE ROAD

PRIVATE ROAD

Jewell Gardens & Poppies restaurant

23RD AVE
22ND AVE
21ST AVE

You Say Tomato (North of Eden restaurant)

20TH AVE
19TH AVE
18TH AVE
17TH AVE
16TH AVE

Garden City RV Park & Laundromat

15TH AVE
14TH AVE

Dahl Medical Clinic

13TH AVE

STATE STREET

12TH AVE

Skagway Mountain View RV Park

11TH AVE

DYEA ROAD

Garden View Granny Flat

10TH AVE

Mile Zero B&B

9TH AVE

Skagway Brewing Company

ALASKA STREET

MAIN STREET

8TH AVE

The White House
Library

BROADWAY

Skagway Sculpture & Flower Garden

Skagway Museum & Archives

7TH AVE

6TH AVE

8
Sourdough 7
Vehicle Rental

Corrington Museum

Alaska Mountain Guides

5TH AVE

6

Pizza Station

5

Fairway Market

4TH AVE

The Sweet Tooth

9

SPRING STREET

10

Skagway Home Hostel

3RD AVE

4
3

11

Airstrips

Skagway Visitor's Bureau

Dewey Lake Trail System

2ND AVE

1

12

Dyea (start of the Chilkoot Trail), Chilkoot Trail Outpost, Chilkoot Trail Campground

Services Unlimited

2

White Pass & Yukon Route Railway

1ST AVE

Skagway Port of Call

Pullen Pond & Centennial Park

Pullen Creek RV Park

Police

POINT ST

ALASKA MARINE HWY

SERVICE ROAD

Stowaway

Skagway Fish Company

CONGRESS WAY

Lower Dewey Lake

TERMINAL WAY

OTTER ROAD

Airport Terminal

ORE DOCK ROAD

Broadway Dock

Fast Ferry to Haines

Railroad Dock

Taiya Inlet

Ore Dock

Ferry Dock

Small Boat Harbour

Yakutania Point/ Smuggler's Cove Trail

Source: PR Services/yukoninfo.com

Skagway

Southeast Alaska SKAGWAY

4

Skagway Float Tours ✆ 983 3688; www.skagwayfloat.com. Spend a day on the Taiya River in the Dyea Valley. The hike & float trip including a short hike up the Chilkoot Trail then a raft trip down for US$85.

White Pass & Yukon Route Railroad (see page 165) The most popular tour in town. The railroad was built during the Klondike Gold Rush in 1898 & is now a Historic Civil Engineering Landmark. The popular White Pass Summit Tour takes 3½ hrs & ascends almost 3,000ft into the mountains & costs US$103/51.50 adult/child. Hikers can hop on the train in Skagway & get off at the Denver Glacier stop (US$30) for a 6-mile hike to the ice. Further up the valley is the Laughton Glacier stop (US$60) where a 3-mile hike leads to the ice. Hikers can catch the train on its way back to town later in the day. Call the Forest Service Office in Juneau (✆ 586 8800) to book either of the cabins found at these glaciers. Be sure to enquire about schedules at the rail office.

HIKING AND RECREATION
Skagway has some great hiking near town and in White Pass toward Canada. Of course the **Chilkoot Trail** (see box on page 170) is the quintessential Skagway trek, but is only for those with some energy and a couple of days to spare.

Outside town, off the White Pass and Yukon Rail Line, are the Denver and Laughton Glacier trails at miles 5.8 and 14 of the line. The train offers flagstop service to these trailheads through the summer (May–September). Both trails have public-use Forest Service cabins that can be rented by calling ✆ 877 444 6777 or by visiting www.reserveusa.com.

The 4.6-mile **Denver Glacier Trail** (*Grade: moderate*) starts at mile 5.8 of the tracks and follows the east fork of the Skagway River to Lower Elway Falls then into the tundra for wonderful views of Denver Glacier and Upper Elway Falls.

The 3.5-mile **Laughton Glacier Trail** (*Grade: difficult*) starts at mile 14 of the tracks and follows the Skagway River to the glacier. This trail allows access to the ice and endless off-trail hiking, but is more challenging than the Denver Glacier Trail.

From town, the Dewey Lake Trail System provides some nice, short hikes. The **Lower Dewey Lake Trail** (*Grade: moderate*) circles Lower Dewey Lake and takes about two hours. The trail is just under four miles. The **Icy Lake and Upper Reid Falls Trail** (*Grade: moderate*) heads six miles north from the Lower Dewey Lake Trail and offers great views.

The 7-mile **Sturgill's Landing Trail** (*Grade: moderate*) also branches off the Lower Dewey Lake Trail and ends at a beach with an old sawmill. A tough 6-mile trail heads straight uphill to the lovely Upper Dewey Lake where there is a public-use cabin. From Upper Dewey Lake, it's another 2.5 miles to the Devil's Punchbowl, a small but dramatic mountain lake.

The **Mountain Shop** (*355 4th St;* ✆ *983 2544; www.packerexpeditions.com;* ⊕ *09.00–20.00 daily*) rents basic equipment.

⌂ WHERE TO STAY
⌂ **Cindy's Place** (2 rooms) ✆ 800 831 8095; www.alaska.net/~croland/skagway/index.html. Nice cabins on Dyea Rd stocked with b/fast foods. $$$

⌂ **Chilkoot Trail Outpost** (11 rooms) ✆ 983 3799; www.chilkoottrailoutpost.com. A collection of nice new cabins near the Chilkoot Trailhead in the Dyea Valley. B/fast. TV. $$$

⌂ **Historic Skagway Inn** (10 rooms) ✆ 983 2289, 888 752 4929 (TF); www.skagwayinn.com. Lovely old fashioned rooms with or without private bathrooms, right in the city centre. When choosing a room, check the beds for softness, as some are better than others. The Alice room is one of the best. Ferry pick-up service & drop-off at the Chilkoot trail for those staying 2 nights. Olivia's Restaurant is also here where dinner is served & garden & cooking tours & demonstrations take place. B/fast. Wi–Fi. $$$

⌂ **Mile Zero B&B** (7 rooms) ✆ 983 3045; www.mile-zero.com. A well-designed & newer B&B near the city centre (9th & Main St) with simple, but pleasant, rooms. B/fast. $$$

🏠 **The White House** (10 Rooms) 475 8th Av; ✎ 983 9000; www.atthewhitehouse.com. Simple rooms in a historic 1902 house near the city centre. Homemade baked goods every morning. Wi–Fi, TV. $$–$$$

🏠 **Skagway Bungalows** (2 rooms) ✎ 877 983 2986; www.aptalaska.net/~saldi. 2 simple but nice cabins in the woods near where the Dyea Rd.

connects with the Klondike Highway about 2 miles from the city centre. $$–$$$

🏠 **Skagway Home Hostel** (12 beds) 3rd & Main; ✎ 983 2131; www.skagwayhostel.com. A friendly, clean hostel with mixed gender bunks for US$15 & single sex bunks for US$20. Located in the city centre in a historic building with a kitchen & laundry facilities. 23.00 curfew. $

Camping Skagway's RV parks offer camping and RV spaces for about US$15–28 on average. They include:

🏕 **Garden City RV Park** 1575 State St; ✎ 983 2378, 866 983 2378 (TF); www.gardencityrv.com.

🏕 **Pullen Creek RV Park** 501 Congress Way; ✎ 983 2768, 800 936 3731 (TF); www.pullencreekrv.com.

🏕 **Skagway Mountain View RV Park** 246 12th Av; ✎ 983 3333, 888 778 7700 (TF); www.bestofalaskatravel.com.

🏕 **Chilkoot Trail Campground** 22 sites; US$10. Located at the Chilkoot Ranger Station in the Dyea Valley near the Chilkoot Trailhead.

✗ **WHERE TO EAT AND DRINK** I can say with confidence that Skagway's restaurants will impress almost everyone.

✗ **Olivia's Restaurant** Located at the Historic Skagway Inn, this quant dining room features local seafood & veggies grown on the property. $$$

✗ **Poppies** ✎ 983 2111; www.jewellgardens.com; ⏱ 11.00–14.00 daily. Enjoy a tasty meal of local, organic foods in a greenhouse overlooking their luxurious gardens, free for restaurant patrons. $$$

✗ **Red Onion Saloon** 271 Broadway Av; ✎ 983 2222; www.redonion1898.com; ⏱ 10.00–close daily. Skagway's most famous eating & drinking establishment — & former brothel. The food & service are mediocre, but the dining room art & upstairs bedpan collection are worth a look (US$5 for a tour). $$$

✗ **Skagway Brewing Company** 7th & Broadway; ✎ 983 2739; www.skagwaybrewing.com; ⏱ 10.00–closing. Great pub food & locally made beers. Try the Spruce Tip beer. $$$

✗ **Skagway Fish Company** 201 Congress Way; ✎ 983 3474; ⏱ 11.00–22.00 daily. Also near the cruise ship dock is this family run seafood joint that's decidedly more casual. Local seafood & red meat are their specialties. $$$

✗ **Starfire Restaurant** 4th Av & Spring St; ✎ 983 3663; ⏱ 11.00–22.00 Mon–Fri, 16.00–22.00 Sat & Sun. Tasty Thai food & outdoor seating. A local favourite. $$$

✗ **Stowaway** 205 Congress Way; ✎ 983 3463; http://stowaway.eskagway.com; ⏱ 10.00–22.00 daily. Great food in a quirky mermaid-themed building with harbour views out by the cruise ship dock. Caesar salad connoisseurs will fall in love with the spicy dressing. Excellent ribs. $$$

✗ **Glacial Smoothies** 336B 3rd Av; ✎ 983 3223; ⏱ 06.00–18.00 daily. Skagway's best place to cosy up with a hot drink & a book. The monster baked potatoes should not be missed. $$

✗ **North of Eden** (see page 170) Located inside You Say Tomato, this cute little place serves organic food to go. $$

✗ **Sugar Mama's** 5th Av, between Broadway St & State St; ✎ 983 2288; ⏱ 10.00–19.00 Sun–Thu, 12.00–17.00 Fri–Sat. The cupcake fad has hit Alaska! The unholy combination of flour, sugar, butter & food colouring never tasted so good. $

✗ **The Sweet Tooth** 315 Broadway; ✎ 983 2405; ⏱ 06.00–14.00 daily. Hikers looking for lunches in a sack should drop in here for sandwiches for the trail, or a burger & fries after a long hike. $

FESTIVALS AND EVENTS
The Elks Solstice Party Takes place 13 June at the ball field near town. Beer, games and food are always on hand.

4 July Parade and Street Fair Has been an event in town since the 1890s. Fireworks and festivities, including a pie-eating contest, a horseshoe toss, and an egg toss.

The Fish Derby Kicks off on 16 July and runs through to 19 July. Fish for a few days for cash prizes and pride and glory.

SHOPPING Like many cruise-ship towns, Skagway has many gift shops that do little for the community and generally don't sell anything made in the state. Look for 'Made in Alaska' and 'Locally Owned' tags.

Skagway News Depot 260 Broadway; ✆ 983 3354; www.skagwaybooks.com: ⊕ 09.00–18.00 daily. Books, magazines & newspapers.
You Say Tomato On corner of State St & 21st St; ✆ 983 2784. Sells organic, fairtrade & locally grown goods. Their small café, North of Eden, is also very good.
Fairway Market 4th & State St; ✆ 983 2220. A good selection of foods.

OTHER PRACTICALITIES
Public library 769 State St; 983 2665; www.skagway.org; ⊕ 13.00–20.00 Mon–Fri, 13.00–17.00 Sat & Sun. No Wi-Fi, but computer terminals with internet access.
Post office 641 Broadway; ✆ 983 2330; ⊕ 08.30–17.00 Mon–Fri

Services Unlimited 170 State St; ✆ 983 2595. The only gas station in town & it does laundry.
Skagway Ports of Call 375 2nd Av; ✆ 983 9503; ⊕ 10.00–20.00 daily. International snacks, internet for US$6/hr & phones for international calls.

WHAT TO SEE AND DO Skagway is an excellent walking town with history around every corner. Start by walking along **Broadway**, Skagway's main drag (if a cruise ship is in town, it might be worth going for a hike instead). Along Broadway you will find a great many restored historic buildings, many of which are owned by the Klondike Goldrush National Historic Park. At the southern end of Broadway is the White Pass and Yukon Route Rail depot. Trains come and go daily and on a sunny day are extremely photogenic against the mountain backdrop. A train ride up through White Pass is definitely worth the price. On the other side of the track are **Pullen Creek**

CHILKOOT TRAIL

The historic, 33-mile Chilkoot Trail is not only a tremendously scenic, three-five day wilderness hike, it's also steeped in history with artefacts from the 1890s found along the trail's length. The Chilkoot Trail was one of two routes used by prospectors to reach the Klondike gold fields in the 1890s. Before the gold rush, Tlingit natives used these same routes to trade inland. The most authentic (and challenging) way to hike the Chilkoot Trail is from the Dyea Valley north (uphill) to Lake Bennett. Those without the time for an overnighter can hike the first part of the trail and still see many historic artefacts on the way.

The first thing to do is head over to the **Chilkoot Trail Centre** (✆ 983 9234; ⊕ 08.00–17.00 daily) in the city centre where permits and current trail conditions can be obtained. To talk to their counterparts in Canada (✆ 667 3910, 800 661 0486 (TF); www.pc.gc.ca/chilkoot). To get to the trailhead, call Dyea Dave (see page 166). To get back into town, hop on the train at Bennett Lake at 13.00 Sunday to Friday for US$95. This ticket needs to be booked as early as possible.

For a list of national and international guides licensed to operate inside the park visit: www.nps.gov/klgo/planyourvisit/outfitters.htm.

Park and **Centennial Park**, which are nice for lounging on sunny days or for watching pink salmon in Pullen Creek. Near Spring and 8th Avenue is the **Skagway Sculpture and Flower Garden** (✆ *983 3311,* ⊕ *09.00–17.00; US$7.50 adult/child*) with 29 bronze sculptures scattered among wildflowers. Follow State Street for two miles north to the **Gold Rush Cemetery**. Located before the river turns north onto a road that follows the train tracks, the funky and fascinating cemetery is tucked in the woods. Beyond is a trail to **Lower Reid Falls**; a spectacular canyon full of white water. The falls were named after Frank Reid who killed the infamous swindler, Soapy Smith on 8 July, 1898. Reid was also shot in the incident, and died himself 12 days later. Both are buried in the cemetery.

The **Dyea Valley** parallels Skagway 2.5 miles west as the crow flies but is a world apart. When the Chilkoot Trail was active in the 1890s, the valley was filled with tens of thousands of prospectors. The Chilkoot Ranger Station and campground are at mile 6.5. Just beyond where the road crosses the river is the start of the historic Chilkoot Trail. The Dyea town site is near the end of the road with a series of collapsed buildings and information signs. **Slide Cemetery** is where those killed in the 3 April, 1898 avalanche are buried. A series of small slides, followed by a very large avalanche in the morning of 3 April, killed dozens of prospectors. To the dismay of those profiting from prospectors in the Dyea Valley, many left for the White Pass trail in Skagway, presuming it was safer. The fact that all the graves bear the same date of death is a little eerie.

For a pleasant day trip drive up the Klondike Highway to Carcross (66 miles from Skagway) in the Yukon Territory. The drive through White Pass is stunning and Carcross offers rental canoes, horseback riding trips and some delicious ice cream at **Matthew Watson Store** (✆ *867 821 3501*), which is the oldest continuously running store in the Yukon.

Skagway Museum (*700 Spring St;* ✆ *983 2420;* ⊕ *09.00–17.00 Mon–Fri, 10.00–17.00 Sat, 10.00–16.00 Sun; US$2/1 adult/child*) Wonderful historic displays and some odd ones, such as a feather quilt and gold-nugget watch. Can get very busy when cruise ships are docked.

Corrington Gift Shop (*525 Broadway;* ✆ *983 2579;* ⊕ *09.00–17.00 daily*) A gift shop with crafts for sale.

HAINES (Population: 1,474)

The quaint, mountain ringed town of Haines (⊕ 59°14'1.68"N, 135°26'49.23"W) is just 17 miles south of Skagway, but is more than a world apart. The first thing visitors notice about Haines is the truly monumental range of mountains rising behind town. Between the peaks are a handful of glaciers making their way toward the sea from Glacier Bay National Park just beyond. The peaks continue in an unbroken line along the Haines Highway and the Chilkat River, making the drive into or out of Haines one of the best stretches of road in the state.

The community consists of two semi-distinct groups: those who work in timber or commercial fishing, and the smaller group of guides and creative types. With generally dry weather and amazing surroundings, Haines is a great place to explore the outdoors. Hiking, rafting, biking, kayaking, and just about any other outdoor activity is available here in abundance. During the winter, pro-extreme skiers come from all over the world to hurl themselves down the surrounding mountains.

For more coverage of Haines, I'd like to recommend *Yukon: The Bradt Travel Guide* written by Polly Evans.

HISTORY Like Skagway, Haines was used by early Chilkat Tlingit native peoples to trade with native groups inland. They called it *Dei Shu* or 'end of the trail'. The first white folks to thoroughly explore the area were American naturalist, John Muir, and his friend, the Presbyterian minister, Samuel Young, in 1878. While Muir was content to revel in the natural beauty, Young was there to convert the natives. Young built a school and mission with the permission of the Tlingit.

The mission was renamed Haines in 1884 in honour of Mrs FE Haines, a church member. When the Klondike Gold Rush started in the late 1890s, Haines grew to accommodate prospectors. After the short gold rush abated, the town turned to commercial fishing and a few canneries were built. At the same time the US Military invested in the town with the construction of Fort Seward in 1898. The fort remained the only military presence in Alaska until World War II. In 1946, the fort was deactivated and sold for a song to former servicemen. They renamed it Fort Chilkoot and in 1970 the town of Haines and the former fort merged, forming what we know today as Haines.

GETTING THERE AND AWAY Haines is accessible via the Haines Highway 155 miles from the Alaska Highway in Canada, by ferry from Juneau or Skagway or by small plane from Juneau or Skagway. Haines is 80 air miles north of Juneau and 775 miles by road from Anchorage.

By ferry

Alaska Ferry ✆ 983 2941, 800 642 0066 (TF); www.dot.state.ak.us/amhs. Ferries connect Haines with Juneau via Skagway 4–5 times a week throughout the summer. Tickets cost US$37. Trips to Skagway cost US$31 & leave 5 times a week.

Alaska Fjordlines ✆ 766 3395, 800 320 0146 (TF); www.alaskafjordlines.com. Hop on the catamaran *Fjord Express,* for a quick & scenic day trip to Juneau. The ferry leaves Haines daily at 08.45 &

arrives in Juneau at 11.00 for US$155/125 adult/child. The ferry returns to Haines at 07.30 & Skagway at 08.15.

Haines-Skagway Fast Ferry 142 Beach Rd; ✆ 766 2100, 888-766-2103 (TF); www.hainesskagwayfastferry.com. Daily ferry service between Skagway & Haines. As many as 6 trips per day for US$35/18 adult/child 1-way.

By air

Air Excursions ✆ 789 5591; www.airexcursions.com. US$105 from Juneau to Haines with a generous 70lb baggage allowance, US$00.40/lb after that. Free shuttle service to & from the airport.

Alaska Mountain Flying Service 132 2nd Av. Charter flights to Skagway for US$60.

Wings of Alaska (see page 174) Haines to Juneau is US$109 & Haines to Skagway is US$60. 50lb baggage allowance, US$00.50/lb after that.

DRIVING THE HAINES HIGHWAY

The Haines Highway connects the town of Haines with the Alaska Highway in Haines Junction, Yukon Territory, Canada 145 miles away. This scenic drive takes about four hours and passes countless rivers and mountains. North of Klukwan and Mosquito Lake, the road crosses the border into British Columbia, in Canada, 41 miles from Haines and 106 miles from Haines Junction. The US border station is open 24 hours a day but Canadian customs is only open 08.00–midnight. If you plan to drive into Canada from Haines at an odd time, be sure to call to confirm their hours (✆ 767 5511, US; ✆ 767 5540, Canada; www.cbp.gov/xp/cgov/toolbox/contacts/ports/ak/3106.xml). Rumour has it the Canadian border may be open 24/7 in the future. There is no gas between Haines and Haines Junction.

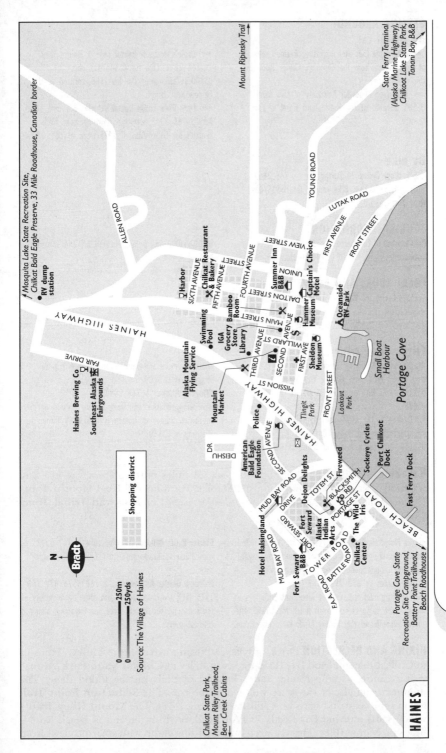

HAINES

N

Bradt

0   250m
0   250yds

Source: The Village of Haines

Shopping district

*Chilkat State Park,
Mount Riley Trailhead,
Bear Creek Cabins*

*Mosquita Lake State Recreation Site,
Chilkat Bald Eagle Preserve, 33 Mile Roadhouse, Canadian border*

RV dump
station

HAINES HIGHWAY

FAIR DRIVE

Haines Brewing Co

Southeast Alaska
Fairgrounds

ALLEN ROAD

Mount Ripinsky Trail

SIXTH AVENUE

Harbor

Chilkat Restaurant
& Bakery

FIFTH AVENUE

Swimming
Pool

FOURTH AVENUE

Summer Inn
B&B

VIEW STREET

UNION STREET

DALTON STREET

Hammer
Museum

Captain's Choice
Motel

Oceanside
RV Park

FIRST AVENUE

FRONT STREET

YOUNG ROAD

LUTAK ROAD

*State Ferry Terminal
(Alaska Marine Highway),
Chilkoot Lake State Park,
Tanani Bay B&B*

IGA
Grocery
Store

Library

Bamboo
Room

MAIN STREET

WILLARD ST

SECOND AVENUE

FIRST AVE

Sheldon
Museum

Alaska Mountain
Flying Service

THIRD AVENUE

Mountain
Market

MISSION ST

HAINES HIGHWAY

FRONT STREET

Tlingit
Park

Lookout
Park

Small Boat
Harbour

Portage Cove

Police

American
Bald Eagle
Foundation

DEISHU DR

SECOND AVENUE

MUD BAY ROAD

DRIVE

Dejon Delights

Fort
Seward

Fireweed

TOTEM ST

BLACKSMITH

PORTAGE ST

RD

Sockeye Cycles

Port Chilkoot
Dock

Fast Ferry Dock

BEACH ROAD

Hotel Halsingland

MUD BAY ROAD

Fort Seward
B&B

TOWER ROAD

FORT SEWARD ROAD

F-A-A ROAD

BATTLE ROAD

Alaska
Indian
Arts

The Wild
Iris

Chilkat
Center

*Portage Cove State
Recreation Site Campground,
Battery Point Trailhead,
Beach Roadhouse*

GETTING AROUND
By rental car

🚗 **Affordable Cars** (see opposite) A small selection of cars rented from the Captain's Choice Hotel in the city centre.

🚗 **Avis** (see opposite) A variety of cars from US$80. Located at the Halsingland Hotel at Fort Seward.

🚗 **Eagle's Nest Car Rental** mile 1 Haines Hwy; ✆ 766 2891. Cars for US$45/day plus US$00.35/mile after the first 100. Located at the Eagle's Nest Motel.

🚗 **Lynn View Lodge Rental Vehicles** 3.5 mile Lutak Rd; ✆ 766 3713; www.lynnviewlodge.com. AWD vehicles for US$69/day, US$425/week or US$20/hr.

By bike

🚲 **Sockeye Cycles** 24 Portage St; ✆ 766 2851; www.cyclealaska.com. Bike rentals for US$35/day. Near Fort Seward.

TOURIST INFORMATION

ℹ️ **Chamber of Commerce** ✆ 766 2234; www.haines.ak.us; 🕐 08.00–18.00 Mon–Fri,

09.00–18.00 Sat & Sun. Located off 2nd St near Willard Street.

LOCAL TOURS AND ACTIVITIES

Sockeye Cycles 24 Portage St; ✆ 766 2851; www.cyclealaska.com. Offer a host of single & multi-day tours for US$80 plus. Near Fort Seward.

Flightseeing trips

Alaska Mountain Flying Service ✆ 766 3007; www.flyglacierbay.com. Glacier Bay flights from US$160–300 with an optional glacier landing for US$75.
Fly Drake ✆ 314 0675; www.flydrake.com. Flightseeing around Haines & Glacier Bay for US$160–300 for a 1 or 2hr flight, as well as

charter service anywhere in the area. A trip to Skagway is US$180 for 1–3 people.
Wings of Alaska ✆ 766 2030; www.wingsofalaska.com. Daily service around northern southeast. Haines to Juneau is US$109 & Haines to Skagway is US$60.

Kayaking The Tlingit village of Klukwan, 22 miles north of Skagway is a tiny, traditional Native community of just 100 folks. For tours call **Keet Gooshi Tours** (✆ *766 2168, 877 776 2168 (TF); www.keetgooshi.com*) or **Klukwan Tribal Tours** (✆ *767 5505*).

Alaska Mountain Guides 35 Portage St; ✆ 766 3366; alaskamountainguides.com. Single & multi-day kayak, hiking, & mountaineering trips. Kayak rentals.
Chilkat Guides ✆ 888 292 7789 (TF); www.chilkatguides.com. Chilkat River raft trips through the eagle reserve with lunch for US$90. The guides recommend the 13-day Alsek River expedition.

Glacier Valley Wilderness Adventure ✆ 767 5522; www.glaciervalleyadventures.net. Chilkat River raft trips.
Rainbow Glacier Adventures ✆ 766 3576, 877 766 3516 (TF); www.joeordonez.com. Offering a variety of tours around the Haines area, inc kayaking, biking & cultural tours.

HIKING AND RECREATION Drive, or bike, east from town over the Chilkat Peninsula to Chilkat Inlet on Mud Bay Road for seven miles to **Chilkat State Park**. A small visitor centre, a campground, and a handful of trails can be found there. The mountain and glacier views are well worth the trip. The **Seduction Point Trail** follows the coast and starts on Chilkat State Park Road. The **Mount Riley Trail** – which starts on Mud Bay Road, off FAA Road, or from the end of Beach Road – heads up Mount Riley. This is a steep but rewarding climb with amazing views from the top. The **Battery Point Trail** also starts at the end of Beach Road and follows the coast for just over a mile to Kelgaya Point. From there, the trail proceeds over Mount Riley then back to the FAA Road or Mud Bay Road Trailheads.

North of town, past the ferry terminal, is the **Mount Ripinski Trail**, a 3,500ft climb through the forest that eventually breaks out into fields of flowers and berries (in autumn) and offers amazing views. Three trailheads all converge on the mountain. One way to get there is: follow 2nd Avenue to Young Blood Road where the trailhead starts on the left before a gate. Those in shape can get up and back in one day.

At the other end of the peninsula, **Chilkoot Lake State Recreation Site** is accessible via the Lutak and Chilkoot River roads for five miles past the ferry terminal. Hiking and camping are available here amidst towering spruce trees.

For other hikes consult www.seatrails.org.

WHERE TO STAY
Hotels

Fort Seward B&B (7 rooms) #1, Fort Seward Dr; 766 2856; www.fortsewardalaska.com. Pleasant rooms in a historic 3-storey house at Fort Seward. Rooms 3 & 4a are the best. Guests can use the kitchen, bikes & the BBQ. The quirky owner, Norm, has run the B&B for 26 years! $$$

Beach Roadhouse (6 rooms) 1 Mile Beach Rd; 766 3060; www.beachroadhouse.com. Nice cabins spread out around Phil's compound about 1 mile out on Beach Road. Private chalet cabins with kitchens for US$150 dbl are the best. Duplex rooms are US$105–115, with or without a kitchen. $$

Captain's Choice Motel (39 rooms) 108 2nd Av; 766 3111, 800 478 2345 (TF); www.capchoice.com. A generic hotel in the city centre with rooms with a view & suites. Car rentals also available $$

Hotel Halsingland (42 rooms) 13 Fort Seward Dr; 766 2000, 800 542 6363 (TF); hotelhalsingland.com. This historic hotel at Fort Seward once served as officer's quarters. Simple rooms for US$109–119 dbl & shared bathrooms for US$69. Be sure to get a room with a sea view. TV, Wi-Fi. $$

Summer Inn B&B (5 rooms) 117 Second Av; 766 2970; www.summerinnbnb.com. Located right in the heart of the city centre, this lovely house has 5 rooms, all with shared bathrooms. Friendly & knowledgeable innkeepers & a delicious hot b/fast. Nice, but not romantic. $$

Tanani Bay B&B (1 room) 46 Dolphin St; 766 3750; www.tananibaybnb.com. A large private suite with a full kitchen & good view. Sleeps 4. $$

Hostels

Bear Creek Cabins & Hostel (7 rooms, 8 bunks) 766 2259; www.bearcreekcabinsalaska.com. 5 rustic cabins for US$20, 2 bunk cabins for US$68 & bunks for US$18. Tents are US$12. Full kitchen & laundry. South of town a few miles along Small Tract Rd. $$

Camping

Chilkat State Park Campground (15 sites) Pleasant well-equipped sites with hiking trails & the State park visitor centre nearby. Located 7 miles south of town on Mud Bay Rd. US$10.

Chilkoot Lake State Recreation Area (80 sites) Camp among the spruce trees on Chilkoot Lake north of town past the ferry dock. US$10.

Mosquito Lake State Recreation Area (5 sites) A small, quiet & forested campground on Mosquito Lake 27 miles north of town off the Haines Highway. US$10.

Portage Cove State Recreation Site Campground An open lawn beautifully positioned by the sea just southeast of town on Beach Road. The campground is for hikers & cyclists as there is not overnight parking. Walk to Fort Seward. US$5.

RV Camping

Oceanside RV Park 766 2437; www.oceansiderv.com. A boring RV park in an amazing location right on the water within walking distance to most of town. US$30.

✕ WHERE TO EAT AND DRINK

✕ **Commanders Room** ⊕ 05.30–21.00 daily. Good meals & a fine-dining atmosphere. Located in the Hotel Halsingland (see page 175) at Fort Seward. **$$$$**

✕ **Bamboo Room** Main & Second St; ☎ 766 2800; www.bamboopioneer.net; ⊕ 06.00–21.00 daily. A classic diner with good burgers, & fish & chips. Christy, the owner, grew up in Haines & has covered the walls with images of her family & other local characters. Check the mural outside. If you would like to know anything about the history of Haines, ask Christy when she works 06.00–10.00 Thu–Sun. Live music most w/ends. Pioneer bar is attached. **$$$**

✕ **Chilkat Restaurant & Bakery** 5th Av & Dalton St; ☎ 7663653; ⊕ 07.00–15.30 daily plus 17.00–21.00 Fri & Sat. Bare bones décor, but decent baked goods & lunches. Thai special on Thu. **$$$**

✕ **Fireweed Restaurant** ☎ 766 3838; ⊕ 16.30–21.00 Tue–Sat. Known for their excellent pizza & desserts. Located near the sea & Fort Seward, this is a great place to grab lunch on a sunny day. **$$$**

✕ **Mountain Market** ☎ 766 3340; ⊕ 07.00–19.00 Mon–Sat, 08.00–18.00 Sun. A lovely café with hot drinks & baked tasty goods. Attached is a health food store with a limited selection of food, but lots of booze! **$$**

✕ **33 Mile Roadhouse** 33 Mile Haines Hwy; ☎ 767 5510; www.33mileroadhouse.com; ⊕ 07.00–18.00 Mon, 07.00–18.00 Wed–Sat, 08.00–18.00 Sun. A helicopter/skiing-themed roadside diner known for their burgers & pies. It's 33 miles from Haines, so stop on the way out of town. **$$**

♀ **Haines Brewing Company** 108 White Fang Way; ☎ 766 3823; ⊕ 13.00–18.00 Mon–Sat. Located at the fairground in old Dalton City, this walk in closet micro-brewery is the place any beer lover must visit. 5oz samples cost US$1.25. Grab a jug to go.

♀ **Harbor Bar** 101 Front St; ☎ 766 2444. The quintessential working man's bar.

FESTIVALS AND EVENTS

King Salmon Derby (☎ *766 3885*) Two weekends of king fishing right at the end of May.

Kluane to Chilkat Bike Relay (☎ *766 2455*) A 160-mile bike race from Haines to Haines Junction. Starts on 19 June.

4 July Is a hoot in Haines, with a parade, contests and fireworks. Contact the visitor centre for more information.

Southeast Alaska State Fair (☎ *766 2476*) Takes place in Haines at the fairground at the end of August every year. Five days of music, events and performances.

OTHER PRACTICALITIES

IGA 209 Main St; ☎ 766 2040. A dismal grocery store with a large selection of foods. Fresh food comes in on Tue & is picked over after a day or so. **Post office** 55 Haines Hwy; ☎ 766 2930; ⊕ 08.30–17.00 Mon–Fri, 13.00–15.00 Sat.

Public library 111 3rd Av; ☎ 766 2545; www.haineslibrary.org; ⊕ 10.00–21.00 Mon & Tue, 12.00–21.00 Wed & Thu, 10.00–18.30 Fri, 12.30–16.30 Sat & Sun. A lovely new library with cosy reading chairs & pay Wi–Fi or 60 mins free at terminals.

WHAT TO SEE Haines has two good walking districts: the proper city centre on Second Street behind the harbour, and in the south side at Fort Seward. Tlingit totem poles (see box on page 17), representing the many clans of the area, are scattered throughout town. A 16ft example representing the eagle clan can be found in **Lookout Park** overlooking the harbour, off Front Street. In the woods due west are some fascinating old gravestones. The 1991 film *White Fang* (see page 17) was filmed in Haines. The turn-of-the-century town that was built as a set can still be explored at the southeast Alaska State Fairgrounds south of the Haines Highway just after the 'Y' as you come into town.

Over in Fort Seward, the central **Tribal House** is an intricately-carved Tlingit building surrounded by totem poles representing the house's clans. Around the clan house are the buildings that used to comprise the fort, but are now privately owned. Near the southeast corner of the fort is the **Alaska Indian Arts** (✆ 766 2160; www.alaskaindianarts.com; ☉ 09.00–17.00 Mon–Fri) building where a group of artists are keeping the rich Tlingit artistic traditions alive. Their small gallery shows off some of their best work and the backroom is where they transform giant trees into beautiful totem poles. Feel free to poke around whenever they are open.

A handful of locally owned businesses are a block toward the sea from the fort including **Sockeye Cycles** (see page 174) with bike rentals and tours, **The Wild Iris** (✆ 766 2300) with gifts, art and a lovely garden (the owner is the mayor), **Alaska Mountain Guides** (see page 174) with kayaking trips and mountaineering and **Dejon Delights** (✆ 766 2505; www.dejondelights.com) with smoked salmon and other treats.

The **Chilkat Bald Eagle Preserve** is found 18 miles north of town on the Haines Highway along the Chilkat River. Created in 1982, this preserve protects an unusual winter population of bald eagles that congregate to feed on a winter salmon run. As many as 3,000 eagles can be seen between October and January, but mid-November is often best. Informational signs can be found at many of the roadside pullouts.

Museums
American Bald Eagle Foundation Interpretive Center (113 Haines Highway; ✆ 766 3094; www.baldeagles.org; ☉ 09.00–18.00 Mon–Fri, 10.00–16.00 Sat & Sun; US$3 adult/child). Everything anyone ever wanted to know about bald eagles. Stuffed and live specimens and daily informative talks. Located at the Haines Highway and 2nd Avenue.

Hammer Museum (108 Main St; ✆ 766 2374; www.hammermuseum.org; ☉ 10.00–17.00 Mon–Fri; US$3/free adult/child) Haines has the dubious honour of being the only place on earth with a museum dedicated exclusively to that ancient and gloriously simple device, the hammer. Swing through this odd little museum so you can say, 'I once saw 1,400 hammers…'

Sheldon Museum (11 Main St; ✆ 766 2366; www.sheldonmuseum.org; ☉ 10.00–17.00 Mon–Fri, 13.00–16.00 Sat & Sun; US$3/free adult/child). A charming museum with Tlingit and pioneer history. Located across from the small boat harbour.

YAKUTAT (Population: 621)

Like any traveller, I love to look at maps, and extremely remote places like Yakutat (✪ 59°32'4"N, 139°42'1"W) always draw my eye. However, to truly appreciate this tiny settlement on the edge of nowhere, you have to take the time to travel there. Located a little over 200 miles from both Cordova and Sitka at the far northern tip of Southeast, Yakutat enjoys the protected waters of Yakutat Bay, while the ocean pounds the shoreline just outside. Intimidating peaks such as Mt Elias (18,114ft) and Mt Fairweather (15,388ft) form the town's backdrop and are only broken by still larger glaciers, many of which tumble into the sea. The 1,500 square mile Malspina Glacier oozes out of the mountains west of town, while the Hubbard Glacier travels 76 miles from Canada to dump ice into Yakutat Bay.

Yakutat itself is a small fishing town with a population comprised of almost 50% Tlingit natives. The town is attempting to expand its image to include tourism, but the difficulty of getting there is slowing efforts. Despite its isolation, Yakutat does have a small number of visitor services, including B&Bs, restaurants and guides for fishing and sightseeing. Currently fishing and hunting are the main reasons people visit, but the natural beauty of the place and total isolation should make it more popular with nature lovers and outdoor enthusiasts in the future.

Yakutat is now known as a surfing destination and even has its own surf shop (see page 180)!

HISTORY Yakutat was originally a cultural crossroads with influences from the Athabascans inland, the Eyak from the Copper River, and Tlingit from Canada and north southeast Alaska. When the bay was first explored by the Russians in the mid 1700s, the people supposedly had mixed heritage of inland and coastal people and called their village *Yakutat* meaning 'the place where the canoes rest', presumably referring to the protection the bay afforded ancient mariners. In 1805, the Russian-American Company built a fort in Yakutat Bay to harvest and process sea otter pelts. During the latter part of the 1800s, Yakutat grew with gold mining (on the beach), followed by a cannery and a sawmill.

During World War II, a runway was built to accommodate war planes and the population boomed with the influx of people and goods. Today, Yakutat subsists on commercial fishing, subsistence hunting and fishing and, increasingly, on tourism.

GETTING THERE AND AWAY
By air Charter flights are a great way to explore the backcountry, whether it be flightseeing, fly-in fishing, or a drop-off at a remote public-use cabin. To hire a plane that seats three people plus gear is usually US$450–500/hr.

✈ **Alaska Airlines** ☏ 800 426 0333; www.alaskaair.com. A daily flight from Anchorage via Juneau (US$300–400), from Juneau (US$300) & from Seattle via Juneau (US$400–650).
✈ **Alsek Air Service** ☏ 784 3231; www.alsekair.com. Offer charter flights, flightseeing, & fly-in fishing as well as drop-off for adventurers. Their 2 small planes seat 3–4 people with gear, 4–5 without. Both planes charter at US$400/hr for the whole plane. Flightseeing

to Russel Fjord is US$425 for the plane & their general glacier tour is US$550 for the plane.
✈ **Yakutat Air** ☏ 784 3831; www.flyyca.com. Serving the entire Yakutat area as well as the northern part of the panhandle with charter service to remote locations, fishing trips & flightseeing. Tour the sights around Yakutat for US$100pp (4 person minimum) or charter one of their planes for US$425–1,300/hr, depending on the plane.

GETTING AROUND
By rental car
🚗 **Leo's Vehicles** ☏ 784 3909. Not the only car rental in town, but the most affordable.

TOURIST INFORMATION The best place to get information is on www.yakutatalaska.com or www.yakutat.net. Again, the **Forest Service Office** (*712 Ocean Cape Rd;* ☏ *784 3359*) provides the most information about Wrangell-St Elias Nation Park and the Tongass National Forest. Call them a few months ahead to book any of the public-use cabins in the area, including one that can be driven to at Harlequin Lake. It's also worth stopping by the **Park Service Office** (☏ *784 3295*), which has some Tlingit art, a film and some amusing historic photos.

LOCAL TOURS AND ACTIVITIES
Glacier tours and fishing The **Yakutat Charter Boat Company** (☏ *784 3433, 888 317 4987 (TF); www.alaska-charter.com*), **Pacific Pleasures** (☏ *784 3976; www.yakutatcharter.com*) and **Ross Marine Tours** (☏ *784 3698*) all offer glacier tours and charter fishing trips on safe boats with knowledgeable captains. Also good for

fishing is Bob who is extremely knowledgeable about local fishing and runs **Situk River Fly Shop** (*101 The Hangar;* ↘ *784 3087; www.situk.net*). He is a purist who treats the resource with respect and runs a lovely shop in town. If it's not open just honk!

Flightseeing The natural environs around Yakutat are some of the most dramatic in the state, making flightseeing a must-do here. The Malaspina and Hubbard Glaciers, not to mention Mount St Elias are views you will never forget. Either of the two air taxis in town can arrange this.

HIKING AND RECREATION For a good full-day adventure, rent a car and drive 30 miles northeast to **Harlequin Lake**. Yakutat Glacier pours in and fills it with ice. Camping is allowed anywhere along the road or at the lake, and the overland hiking is excellent. Call the Forest Service about the public-use cabin here.

Halfway between Harlequin Lake and town, a trail heads north to **Russell Fjord**. When the trail ends, countless overland hiking opportunities exist. Both Harlequin Lake and Russell Fjord can be reached by taking the only road that heads northeast, Dangerous River Road.

For a pleasant stroll along the sea, head to **Cannon Beach**, located near the airport, where the beach goes on for 150 miles.

For a chance to see bears, head northeast of town to the trail leading to Situk and Mountain Lakes in the autumn. A public-use cabin can be found on the east side of Situk Lake. Call or visit the Forest Service office to book it.

For an all-day or even multi-day adventure, charter a boat to **Esker Stream** and hike up into the hills. This is where some of the biggest trees and loveliest mountain lakes in the area can be found. This is rough, off-trail hiking with stream crossings, but well worth the effort.

WHERE TO STAY
Hotels

🏠 **Ryman's On The Beach** (2 cabins) ↘ 866 784 3396 (TF); www.rymansitalio.com. Simple, self-contained cabins on the beach with a kitchen, TV, etc. US$300 for up to 8 people. $$$$$

🏠 **Blue Heron Inn** (4 rooms) ↘ 784 3287; www.johnlatham.com. Yakutat's higher end establishment, lovely rooms on the water. $$$

Camping Camping can be found along Cannon Beach on 16x16 platforms with a toilet nearby. All the driftwood you could ever want can be gathered in minutes along the beach. Camping is also allowed on Tongass National Forest Land as long as you're away from the road.

✘ WHERE TO EAT
Savvy visitors bring their own food in and with local seafood, prepare their own meals. Milk is US$11/gallon! But otherwise you can try:

✘ **AC** ↘ 784 3386. Another good deli. $$
✘ **Glacier Bear Lodge** ↘ 784 3202; www.glacierbearlodge.com. Has a decent restaurant & the prices are not too exorbitant. $$

✘ **Mallott's General Store** ↘ 784 3355. Has a good deli. $$
✘ **Yakutat Lodge** ↘ 784 3232, 800 925 8828 (TF). Near the airport & does a good burger. $$

FESTIVALS AND EVENTS Be sure to check out **Fairweather Day** on 1 August for live music, dancing, and free seafood!

OTHER PRACTICALITIES
Post office 447 Mallotts Av; ↘ 784 3201; ⏰ 09.00–17.00 Mon–Fri, 10.00–13.00 Sat.

WHAT TO SEE AND DO

Hubbard Glacier Interestingly, in 1986, Hubbard Glacier advanced across Russell Fjord creating a dam and trapping seals and other marine mammals behind a wall of ice. The ice eventually receded and is now 1,000 feet from where it had touched Gilbert Point. During tide swings, the strong currents sheer ice off the glacier. Once again the glacier is advancing and scientists are tracking its progression. In the near future the glacier may once again block off Russell Fjord. For a tour of Hubbard and other area glaciers, call any of the charter boat companies listed above.

Surfing Head over to **Icy Waves Surf Shop** (❦ 784 3226; *www.icywaves.com*) and say 'hi' to the owner, Jack Endicott, who will tell you all about town and set you up with a surfboard and wetsuit. Though Yakutat has become known for its surf, the waters are cold and the environment wild, so beginners should learn to surf before showing up here.

5

Southcentral Alaska

If you can only visit one area in the state, make it southcentral Alaska. The region's natural beauty is complemented by a number of interesting communities and is easily and cheaply reached by trains, planes, ferries and an extensive network of roads. In the north, the cosmopolitan city of Anchorage offers every urban convenience plus spectacular mountain views. To the south, the Kenai Peninsula is a playground that offers fishing in the world-famous Kenai River, kayaking in Seward and art and fine food at the end of the road in Homer. Finally, nobody should miss the chance to see Prince William Sound. 'The Sound' is the heart of southcentral Alaska and even though it's accessible by ferry, plane, and car, it remains an immense marine wilderness rimmed by mountains and tidewater glaciers, and filled with islands, marine life and fish. Everyone will find something to enjoy in southcentral Alaska; it is the most accessible, unique, and diverse region in the state.

HISTORY Southcentral Alaska has been occupied by native groups for almost 8,000 years. The earliest inhabitants were Athabascans, who travelled from the interior, via river valleys, to the rich coastal areas of the Kenai Peninsula and Prince William Sound. As they made their way south along the Kenai Peninsula and into Prince William Sound, they were influenced by both southeastern and Aleutian cultures, developing various kayak shapes to navigate coastal areas. In June 1778, Captain James Cook was searching for the Northwest Passage and sailed into Cook Inlet where the shallow water forced him to turn his ship several times in order to get out – hence the name of the arm at the end of the inlet, Turnagain Arm. Not long after, in 1783, Russian explorer, Potap Zaikov, led an expedition past the Aleutian Islands to southcentral Alaska in search of fur bearing animals. He discovered what is now known as the Copper River on the east side of Prince William Sound. During the 1780s, Russian fur trading companies competed aggressively with one another for the rights to much of southcentral Alaska. In 1787, the first Russian settlement on mainland Alaska was established at St George Redoubt by the Lebedev-Lastochkin Company. A shipbuilding site was developed at the mouth of the Kasilof River and, in 1791, Fort St Nicholas on the Kenai River was also settled. As resources dwindled and native groups became increasingly hostile, Russian fur traders moved to southeast Alaska and, by 1819, only a handful of Russian fur traders remained in the southcentral region.

Fur had been the main reason for Russian interest in Alaska, but the Californian gold rush in 1849 created a new market; coal. The gold rush brought thousands of people to California and coal was a key component in the excavation and processing of the metal. Russian companies, already entrenched in Alaska, seized the opportunity to ship coal to the Lower 48 states. More than 800 tons of coal were shipped to California from the Kenai Peninsula prior to 1860. But not long after the industry had started, the high cost of coal production forced the mines to close.

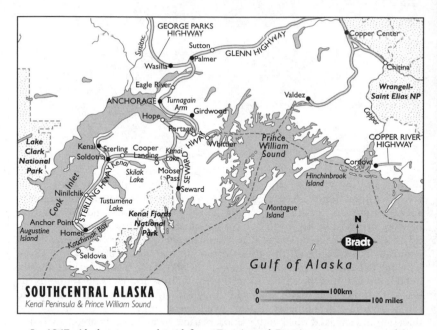

SOUTHCENTRAL ALASKA
Kenai Peninsula & Prince William Sound

George Parks Highway — Sutston — Sutton — Copper Center — Glenn Highway — Palmer — Wasilla — Chitina — Eagle River — Valdez — Wrangell-Saint Elias NP — Anchorage — Turnagain Arm — Girdwood — Hope — Portage — Copper River Highway — Lake Clark National Park — Kenai — Sterling — Cooper Landing — Kenai Lake — Whittier — Prince William Sound — Cordova — Soldotna — Kenai — Skilak Lake — Moose Pass — Hinchinbrook Island — Ninilchik — Tustumena Lake — Seward — Kenai Fjords National Park — Montague Island — Anchor Point — Augustine Island — Homer — Seldovia — Kachemak Bay — Gulf of Alaska

N

Bradt

0 — 100km
0 — 100 miles

In 1867, Alaska was purchased from Russia and Russian interests were driven out. The first few years of the 1880s saw the foundation of the southcentral region's first salmon canneries located at the mouth of the Kasilof River. Salmon canneries sprang up all over the region, particularly on Prince William Sound, where countless rivers supported huge numbers of salmon. As many as 25,000 fish could be trapped in a single day. However, many were wasted with inefficient processing and storage while native villages upstream, who relied on salmon swimming upriver to spawn, starved. In 1907, the Chugach National Forest was created by the government of the forward-thinking Theodore Roosevelt in an effort to conserve the state's rapidly disappearing natural resources.

In 1913, Anchorage had just a few settlers camping along Ship Creek. Congress approved a plan to push the Alaska Railroad through Anchorage to connect Seward with Fairbanks. The tracks passed through Ship Creek where the station is today. A job rush ensued and soon thousands of people were camping by the river. Land was sold and people began to settle in the area. In 1917, Anchorage's population had swelled to 7,000 people.

The state saw more growth as midwest farming families, who had been bankrupted during the depression, were relocated to the fertile Matanuska Valley north of Anchorage in the 1920s and 1930s. Helping to civilise other hard-to-reach parts of the state at this time was the new railroad allowing access to the interior as well as the Kenai Peninsula.

During World War II, huge amounts of military spending and large numbers of military personnel and their families were funnelled into the Anchorage area as a result of its strategic location and easy access. Fort Richardson and Elmendorf Air Force Base were built at that time just outside the city. In the autumn of 1950, the Sterling Highway was constructed to connect Homer with Seward and Hope. A year later, the highway linked up with Anchorage, opening up the Kenai Peninsula for further development. Shortly after World War II, the Richardson Highway from Valdez to Fairbanks was completed allowing access to the east side of Prince William Sound. Until the George Parks Highway was completed in 1971, the

Richardson Highway provided the only access to Interior Alaska from the southcentral region.

By the end of World War II, Anchorage was home to almost 50,000 people and was fast becoming the state's financial centre with oil discoveries on the Kenai Peninsula. During the latter part of the 1950s, the Kenai Peninsula saw extensive oil exploration and drilling. Kachemak Bay fishermen successfully blocked development in their bay fearing the harm an oil spill would do their small but successful fishery. To this day, oil drilling has been kept out of Kachemak Bay.

On 27 March 1964, the Good Friday earthquake rocked southcentral Alaska for nearly five minutes. The quake registered 9.2 on the Richter Scale and destroyed much of the Kenai Peninsula and many towns across the southcentral region. Tsunamis followed the quake and were responsible for the majority of the 114 people killed in the disaster. Valdez and other Prince William Sound communities suffered the most significant loss of life while Anchorage suffered the most financially. Roads buckled and buildings collapsed at an estimated cost of over US$300 million. The quake shifted the majority of shipping traffic from Seward to Anchorage. The dock in Anchorage was only minimally damaged while Seward's was almost completely destroyed. Elsewhere in the state, populations and financial centres shifted after the quake. At the bottom of the Kenai Peninsula, people and canneries moved from the ruined town of Seldovia to Homer, helping to make it the population centre it is today.

In 1977 the Trans-Alaska Pipeline from the North Slope to Valdez was completed, turning Valdez into one of Alaska's most important ports. The pipeline turned Alaska into an 'oil state' and changed the economy to one driven by oil overnight. As if forseeing the eventual decline of oil production, the region invested heavily in tourism around the same time and the fruits of their labours are only now paying off. With oil production and tourism on the rise, Anchorage quickly became the state's financial capital and has become one of the most common places for visitors to start their Alaskan adventure.

ANCHORAGE (Population: 277,498)

Despite its reputation as a staging point rather than a destination, Anchorage (⊕ 61°13'6"N, 149°53'57"W) has much to offer the visitor. Beneath the city's grim façade of strip malls, sky scrapers and suburbs, visitors will find a vibrant cultural scene, an extensive network of city trails and parks, world-class dining and, best of all, it's sandwiched between the soaring peaks of the Chugach Mountains and the turbulent waters of Cook Inlet. Some 60 glaciers and hundreds of mountains can be found within 50 miles of Anchorage, giving rise to the Alaskan expression: 'you can see Alaska from Anchorage'. Within a day's drive are many of the state's most notable attractions, including Denali National Park and the Kenai Peninsula, as well as the cultural and adventure destinations of Homer and Talkeetna. As the largest city in the state, the city can be a destination in itself or a jumping-off point for the rest of the state.

The city centre is located in north Anchorage and is where many visitors spend their time. The area is famous for its brilliant flowers that erupt from every pot and patch of earth. While not cheap, north Anchorage represents the most condensed and diverse part of the city with eateries, galleries, shops and accommodation options all within walking distance. For those who have more than a day or two in town, a rental car is a must. Excellent hiking and views are found in Hatcher Pass north of town, along Turnagain Arm and at Portage Glacier to the south. In addition, the city has many wonderful restaurants and shops outside the city centre that are easily reached by car. The natural and cultural attractions of the Anchorage area will keep any visitor busy for a few days or even a week.

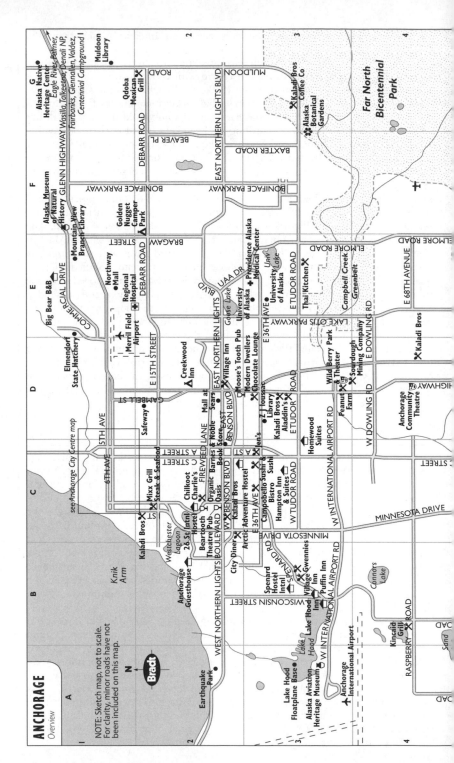

ANCHORAGE
Overview

NOTE: Sketch map, not to scale. For clarity, minor roads have not been included on this map.

Bradt

Knik Arm

Earthquake Park

Lake Hood Floatplane Base

Alaska Aviation Heritage Museum

Anchorage International Airport

W INTERNATIONAL AIRPORT RD

Connors Lake

Sand Lake

Kincaid Grill

RASPBERRY ROAD

MINNESOTA DRIVE

WISCONSIN STREET

Spenard Hostel Intnl

Gwennies

Puffin Inn

Village Inn

City Diner

Arctic Adventure Hostel

Spenard Hostel

Bearttooth Theatre Pub

Anchorage Guesthouse

Westchester Lagoon

Kaladi Bros

26 St Intnl Hostel

Mixx Grill Steak & Seafood

Chilkoot Charlie's

Organic Oasis

Kaladi Bros

Campobello Sushi & Bistro

Hampton Inn & Suites

Aladdin's

MINNESOTA DRIVE

SPENARD RD

W TUDOR ROAD

Glen's

Homewood Suites

Z Tousaa

Library

Kaladi Bros

Aladdin's

ETUDOR RD

Peanut Farm

FIREWEED LANE

Barnes & Noble Book Store

Mall at Sears

Safeway

E 15TH STREET

5TH AVE

6TH AVE

GAMBELL ST

A STREET

C STREET

L ST

BENSON BLVD

Elmendorf State Hatchery

Merril Field Airport

Big Bear B&B

COMMERCIAL DRIVE

Mountain View Branch Library

Northway Mall

Regional Hospital

Alaska Museum of Natural History

Creekwood Inn

EAST NORTHERN LIGHTS

Village Inn

Moose's Tooth Pub

Modern Dwellers Chocolate Lounge

DEBARR ROAD

EAST NORTHERN LIGHTS BLVD

Goose Lake

Golden Nugget Camper Park

BONIFACE PARKWAY

BRAGAW STREET

Alaska Native Heritage Center

Qdoba Mexican Grill

Muldoon Library

MULDOON ROAD

Kaladi Bros Coffee Co

Alaska Botanical Gardens

Far North Bicentennial Park

GLENN HIGHWAY Wasilla, Talkeetna, Denali NP, Fairbanks, Glennallen, Valdez, Centennial Campground

Eagle River, Palmer

BEAVER PL

BAXTER ROAD

EAST NORTHERN LIGHTS BLVD

DEBARR ROAD

University Lake

UAA DR

University of Alaska

Providence Alaska Medical Center

UAA DRIVE

Thai Kitchen

Wild Berry Park & Theater

Sourdough Mining Company

Campbell Creek Greenbelt

ELMORE ROAD

E 36TH AVE

LAKE OTIS PARKWAY

ETUDOR ROAD

E DOWLING RD

W DOWLING RD

Kaladi Bros

Anchorage Community Theatre

E 68TH AVENUE

HIGHWAY

C STREET

AIRPORT RD

W INTERNATIONAL AIRPORT RD

see Anchorage City Centre map

N

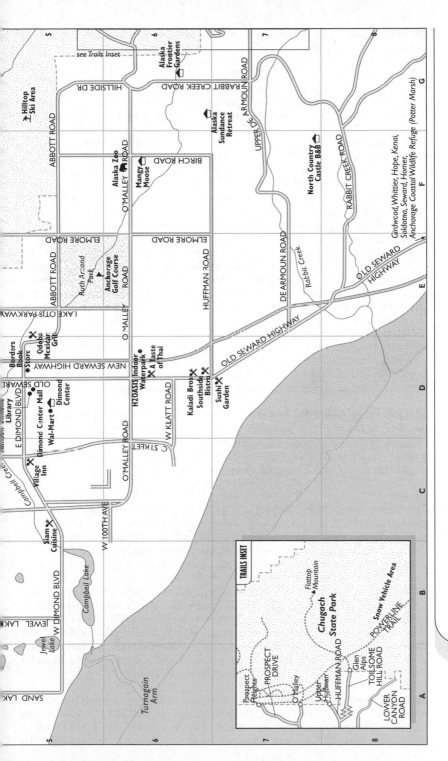

TRAILS INSET

Chugach State Park

Flattop
▲ Mountain

Snow Vehicle Area

POWERLINE TRAIL

Prospect
Heights

PROSPECT
DRIVE

O'Malley

Upper
'Huffman'

Glen
Alps

HUFFMAN ROAD

TOILSOME
HILL ROAD

LOWER
CANYON
ROAD

Hilltop
Ski Area

see Trails Inset

Alaska
Frontier
Gardens

HILLSIDE DR

RABBIT CREEK ROAD

ABBOTT ROAD

Alaska Zoo

O'MALLEY ROAD

Mangy
Moose

BIRCH ROAD

Alaska
Sundance
Retreat

UPPER DE ARMOUN ROAD

North Country
Castle B&B

RABBIT CREEK ROAD

Girdwood, Whittier, Hope, Kenai,
Soldotna, Seward, Homer,
Anchorage Coastal Wildlife Refuge (Potter Marsh)

ELMORE ROAD

ABBOTT ROAD

Ruth Arcand
Park

Anchorage
Golf Course

O'MALLEY ROAD

ELMORE ROAD

HUFFMAN ROAD

LAKE OTIS PARKWAY

DE ARMOUN ROAD

Rabbit Creek

OLD SEWARD
HIGHWAY

Borders
Book
Store

Qdoba
Mexican
Grill

NEW SEWARD HIGHWAY

H2OASIS
Indoor
Waterpark

A Taste
of Thai

Kaladi Bros
Southside
Bistro

Sushi
Garden

OLD SEWARD HIGHWAY

O'MALLEY ROAD

W KLATT ROAD

C ST REET

Library

E DIMOND BLVD

Dimond Center Mall

Wal-Mart

OLD SEWARD

Dimond
Center

Campbell Creek

Village
Inn

O'MALLEY ROAD

W 100TH AVE

Siam
Cuisine

W DIMOND BLVD

JEWEL LAKE

Jewel
Lake

Campbell Lake

Turnagain
Arm

SAND LAKE

Southcentral Alaska ANCHORAGE

185

HISTORY A permanent population of Athabascan natives, called the Upper Cook Inlet Tanaina, established themselves in the Anchorage area around 1650. Following the Russian 'discovery' of Alaska in 1741, Russians began to trade with native groups around the state, building trading posts and Russian Orthodox Churches in western and southcentral Alaska. In 1778, Captain James Cook passed the present site of Anchorage while searching for the Northwest Passage. By 1913, Anchorage consisted of a handful of settlers camping along Ship Creek near the location of today's city centre. After Congress approved the Alaska Railroad project (which connected the coastal port of Seward with Fairbanks and allowed goods to be delivered all year round) and the tracks were planned to pass right through the Ship Creek area, job seekers flooded into the area. The name 'Anchorage' was formalised by the post office in 1915, but was hotly contested by residents who wanted to call it Alaska City. Land was bought and sold and, by 1917, a town had sprung up with a population of 7,000 and a school. The population dropped again as the railroad project slowed and World War I demanded soldiers. During the drought and depression of the 1920s and 1930s, Midwest farming families were moved to the Matanuska Valley north of Anchorage to develop agriculture in the state. The strategic location of Anchorage brought huge amounts of military spending, as well as personnel and their families. Fort Richardson and Elmendorf Air Force Base were built at that time just outside the city. The city was also fast becoming the state's financial centre with the discovery of oil on the Kenai Peninsula. The Good Friday earthquake shook southcentral Alaska on 27 March 1964, killing 114 people and causing millions of dollars in damage. In 1968, oil was discovered in Prudhoe Bay, securing the state's financial future. By the 1980s, the state was filling its coffers with oil revenue and Anchorage started to invest in beautification and tourism. Today, Anchorage continues to be the state's financial centre and invests heavily in the growth of the tourism industry.

GETTING THERE AND AWAY If you are flying to Alaska, you will probably arrive at Ted Stevens International Airport in Anchorage. If you are driving in you will pass through Anchorage on your way to the Kenai Peninsula. If you're arriving aboard a cruise ship, you will likely be bussed into Anchorage from Whittier or Seward. Anchorage is very well connected and on nearly every visitor's itinerary.

By air
Ted Stevens International Airport [184–5 A3] (*www.anchorageairport.com*) With corruption rampant in Alaskan politics, it's fitting that the state's largest airport was named after US Senator Ted Stevens, who was convicted in 2009 of seven counts of receiving and hiding monetary gifts. Still, the former senator brought millions of dollars into the state and was involved in state politics from the state's birth, doing far more good than harm along the way. The airport is one of the world's busiest cargo terminals and approximately five million people pass through the terminal every year. Most of the 20 or so passenger flights leaving every day are operated by Alaska Airlines from Seattle. A few others serve Asia, Europe and even Russia. The airport offers free Wi-Fi and a number of small information desks. The **South Terminal information desk** (✎ 266 2437; ☉ 09.00–16.00 *every day*) and **North Terminal information desk** (✎ 266 2657; ☉ 09.00–16.00 *daily*) are both located in the arrivals hall. Head for the mezzanine in the south terminal to sleep or to look at native art.

Shuttle service Free transportation between the terminals is provided by a shuttle running every 15 minutes. The **People Mover** (✎ 343 6543; *www.muni.org*) provides transportation from the airport into Anchorage for US$1.75/1/0.50 adult/child/senior. The bus stops every 30 minutes at various locations around the airport from 06.00–23.00, delivering passengers to either the Transit Centre near the city centre or the Diamond Centre mall.

Airlines Many of the larger commercial airlines fly domestically between Alaska and the Lower 48 including:

✈ **Alaska Airlines** ☏ 800 426 0333;
www.alaskaair.com
✈ **American Airlines** ☏ 800 433 7300; www.aa.com
✈ **Continental Airlines** ☏ 800 523 3273;
www.continental.com

✈ **Frontier Airlines** ☏ 800432 1359;
www.flyfrontier.com
✈ **Northwest Airlines** ☏ 800 225 2525;
www.nwa.com
✈ **United Airlines** ☏ 800 241 6522; www.ual.com
✈ **US Airways** ☏ 800 428 4322; www.usairways.com

Alaska regional air services include:

✈ **Alaska Airlines** Flies to the Lower 48 states, as well as many locations within Alaska such as the Aleutians or within the Arctic Circle.
✈ **Era Aviation** ☏ 266 8394, 800 866 8394 (TF); www.flyera.com. Flies around the Kenai Peninsula, Prince William Sound & other locations
✈ **Frontier/ERA Flying Service** ☏ 450 7200; www.frontierflying.com

✈ **Grant Aviation** ☏ 243 3592; www.flygrant.com. With flights to various Kenai Peninsula locations.
✈ **Hageland Aviation Services** ☏ 245 0119; www/hagland.com
✈ **Pen Air** ☏ 243 2323, 800 448 4226 (TF); www.penair.com. Flies to the Aleutians & Alaska's west coast.

By rail

Alaska Railroad [190–1 E2] (*411 W 1st Av;* ☏ *265 2494, 800 544 0552 (TF); www.akrr.com;* ⊕ *05.00–16.00 daily*) Even for those with a car, the trip from Anchorage to Seward on the *Coastal Classic* (US$160/80 adult/child) is well worth the money. The views are some of the best on the Peninsula, with mountains and wild rivers everywhere. Wildlife is fairly common, and is seen especially easily in May before the trees are covered in leaves. Another fantastic trip, particularly during the last two weeks in August when the autumn colours are ablaze, is the *Hurricane Turn* train from Talkeetna or Anchorage. This is one of America's last 'flag stop' trains, meaning passengers can get on and off almost anywhere. Even if you're not getting off and hiking into the wilderness, seeing those who do is always interesting. Depending on the season, you may see backpackers, trappers or dog mushers. The 5.5hr trip runs in a loop from Talkeetna, or from Anchorage, via the Denali Star route. The *Denali Star* train leaves Anchorage at 08.15 and arrives in Denali at 16.00 (US$146/73 adult/child) and later at Fairbanks at 20.00 (US$210/105 adult/child). Upgrading to the Goldstar service means the train cars are double-decker and the views are far superior to the standard cars. However, the price is almost double the standard fare.

The train depot near the city centre has pay parking. Once on the train – assuming you aren't in the Goldstar cars – passengers are called to the dining car row by row, starting at the front of the train. On the trip to Seward, head to the dome car after Girdwood for some great views.

By ferry The Alaska Ferry does not go to Anchorage at all; the closest port is Whittier.

By bus and shuttle

🚌 **Alaska Direct Bus Line** ☏ 277 6652, 800 770 6652 (TF); www.alaskadirectbusline.com. Buses run all summer on Wed, Fri & Sun to Tok (US$105), Glennallen (US$75) & Palmer (US$10).

🚌 **Alaska Park Connection** ☏ 245 0200, 800 266 8625 (TF); www.alaskacoach.com. Regular service in a large bus between Anchorage & Seward, Whittier, Denali & Talkeetna.

Alaska/Yukon Trails ✆ 479 2277, 800 770 7275 (TF); www.alaskashuttle.com. Daily shuttle service from Anchorage to Denali (US$75) & Fairbanks (US$99).
Denali Overland ✆ 733 2384, 800 651 5221 (TF); www.denalioverland.com. Shuttle service to Talkeetna & Denali National Park. Since the whole van must be rented, the more people riding, the cheaper it is. Custom trips are available, for a price.

Homer Stage Line ✆ 883 3914; www.homerstageline.com. Serving virtually the entire Kenai Peninsula.
Seward Bus Lines ✆ 563 0800; www.sewardbuslines.net. Daily service between Anchorage & Seward for US$50 1-way. Leaves Anchorage at 14.30, arrives Seward 17.30.

GETTING AROUND
By public transport
People Mover (see page 186) A modern bus system, the People Mover will get you almost anywhere in the city for US$1.75/1 adult/child. Timetables are available at the Transit Centre on 6th Av, at city centre visitor centre & elsewhere around town.

MASCOT ✆ 376 5000; www.matsutransit.com. The Mat-Su transit system runs between Anchorage & Wasilla & Palmer for US$2.50.

By rental car Rental cars are generally US$50–100 per day with unlimited mileage. Larger 4x4 vehicles cost double. Renting two to six months ahead with one of the discount travel websites such as www.travelocity.com, www.orbitz.com or www.expedia.com can save you money. Conversely, the locally owned rental companies are often cheaper and, if not located at the airport, will charge less in taxes. Try Denali or Payless.

Avis Fifth & B St; ✆ 277 4567, 800 331 1212 (TF), 243 4300 (airport); www.avis.com. Has offices in the city centre & at the airport. Free pick-up from downtown hotels.
Budget 5011 Spenard Rd; ✆ 243 0150, 800 248 0150 (TF); www.budgetalaskaonline.com. Situated near the airport.
Denali Car Rental 1209 Gambell St; ✆ 276 1230. Located near the city centre.
Dollar 4940 W International Airport Rd; ✆ 248 5338, 800, 8004000 (TF); www.dollar.com. Dollar cars, mini vans, SUVs, 12 passenger vans available from 2 locations: inside Homewood Suites & at the airport. Vehicles can be rented by the day, week or month. Local corporate accounts available.

Enterprise ✆ 248 5526, 800 736 8222 (TF); www.enterprise.com. Available at Ted Stevens International Airport.
High Country Car & Truck Rental 3609 Spenard Rd; ✆ 562 8078, 888 685 1155 (TF); www.highcountryanchorage.com. Shuttle service, quality new-model vehicles. Not located at the airport; closer to the city centre.
Payless Car Rental 1130 W International Airport Rd; ✆ 243 3616; www.paylesscarrental.com. Situated near the airport.
Thrifty Car Rental ✆ 279 1326, 800 847 4389 (TF); www.anchorage.thrifty.com. Anchorage now has two locations: one inside Anchorage airport & another situated on Spenard Road & Minnesota Drive.

RV hire
ABC Motorhome Rentals 3875 W International Airport Rd; ✆ 279 2000, 800 421 7456 (TF); www.abcmotorhome.com.

Alaska Dream RV Rental ✆ 278 7368, 888) 357 7368 (TF); www.home.gci.net/~akdream. Available near the city centre.

PARKING IN THE CITY CENTRE

Parking in the Anchorage city centre can be difficult and expensive. New parking meters around the city accept credit cards, bills and coins and dispense a receipt. Public car parks can be found around the city and most charge US$1–3/hr. For longer durations it's much cheaper. A convenient lot near the city centre can be found next to the post office at C Street and 3rd Avenue, where parking is US$1/hr.

Alaska Motorhome Rentals 9085 Glacier Hwy, Ste 301; ☏ 800 323 5757; www.bestofalaskatravel.com.
Clippership Motorhome Rentals 5401 Old Seward Hwy; ☏ 562 7051, 800 421 3456 (TF); www.clippershiprv.com. Can arrange airport pick-ups.

Great Alaskan Holidays 9800 Old Seward Hwy; ☏ 248 7878, 888 225 2752 (TF); www.greatalaskanholidays.com.
Lulay Rentals 4010 Romanzof Cir; ☏ 243 5120; www.lulayrentalsllc.net. Can arrange airport pick-ups.

By taxi The size of Anchorage and the exorbitant taxi rates mean you will pay an arm and a leg to get almost anywhere. Taxis are available at any time from the airport, but the bus is certainly cheaper (see opposite).

Alaska Cab Company ☏ 562 5353
Alaska Shuttle ☏ 338 8888. Door-to-door van service.
Alaska Yellow Cab ☏ 222 2222
Anchorage Checker Cab ☏ 276 1234

Rickshaws Taxi & Tours ☏ 250 6076. Try the eco-friendly alternative to a taxi. A charge of US$5 will get you anywhere in the city centre.
Taylor Taxi ☏ 248 0993

By bike Anchorage has more than 200 miles of cycling trails. The Tony Knowles Trail along the coast is unbeatable on a sunny day.

Alaska Backcountry Bike ☏ 866 354 2453; www.mountainbikealaska.com. Mountain bike tours around the Anchorage area. Bike rentals cost US$28/day.
Coastal Trail Rentals & Tours 4800 Spenard Rd; ☏ 301 2165; www.coastaltrailrentals.com; ⊕ 09.00–19.00 daily. Bicycle rentals & tours. City bikes are US$30/day. Mountain bikes are US$4/day & electric bikes are US$60/day.
Downtown Bicycle Rental 333 W 4th Av; ☏ 279 5293; www.alaska-bike-rentals.com. Rental bikes cost US$32/day. The company also runs the Flattop Mountain Shuttle (☏ 279 3334; www.alaska-bike-

rentals.com), which will shuttle you with or without a bike to Flattop Mountain. Located near Buttress Park in the city centre.
Pablo's Bicycle Rentals ☏ 250 2871; www.pablobicyclerentals.com, ⊕ 08.00–19.00 daily. Pablo's staff are some of the most friendly people in Anchorage. Plus, he has 52 great rental bikes in tip-top shape. Bikes cost US$30/day or US$5/hr. His shop is located near the city centre in front of the Copper Whale Inn on L St.
Sunshine Sports 1231 W Northern Lights Blvd; ☏ 272 6444. Mountain bikes for rent at US$40/day.

TOURIST INFORMATION The best place to start learning about Anchorage and Alaska in general is right in the city centre. Here you will find the quaint log cabin visitor centre as well as the Department of Natural Resources Public Information Centre and the Alaska Public Lands Information Centre.

Anchorage Convention & Visitors Bureau Visitor Center [190–1 D4] 524 W 4th Av; ☏ 276 4118; www.anchorage.net; ⊕ 07.30–19.00 daily. The quaint visitor centre is the best place to start any exploration of Anchorage. The building in the back is where most of the printed information can be found.
Alaska Public Lands Information Center [190–1 D3] 605 W 4th Av; ☏ 644 3661, 866 869 6887 (TF); www.nps.gov/aplic; ⊕ 09.00–17.00 daily. Located in the federal building across the street from the visitor centre, this is the place to start

learning about the state as a whole &/or to research adventures. A bookstore & various displays will keep you entertained for hours.
Alaska Department of Natural Resources [190–1 D5] 550 W 7th Av; ☏ 269 8400; www.alaskastateparks.org; ⊕ 10.00–17.00 Mon–Fri. Located on the 12th floor, the DNR office has a great view of the city & helpful staff, but limited printed resources. Public-use cabins anywhere in the state can be booked here & staff can help with general information about trails, campsites & state land.

LOCAL TOURS AND ACTIVITIES Anchorage is chock full of tours and guides ready to take you out and show you the sights. City tours are popular as are the many

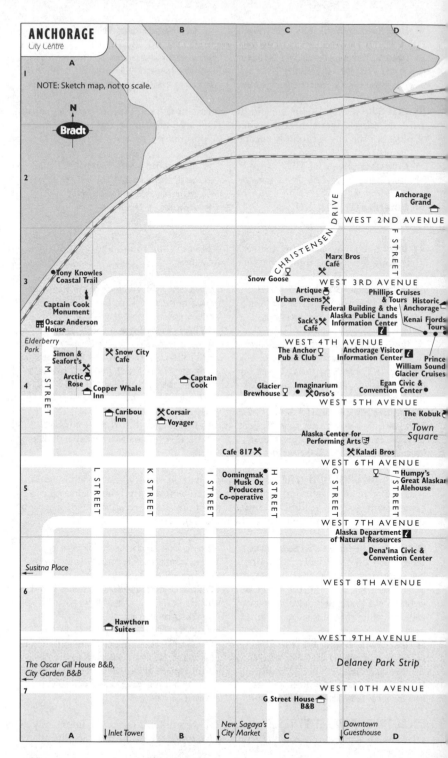

ANCHORAGE
City Centre

NOTE: Sketch map, not to scale.

N

Bradt

A

B

C

D

I

2

CHRISTENSEN DRIVE

F STREET

Anchorage Grand

WEST 2ND AVENUE

Marx Bros Café

Snow Goose

WEST 3RD AVENUE

3

● Tony Knowles Coastal Trail

Captain Cook Monument

Oscar Anderson House

Elderberry Park

Artique
Urban Greens

Phillips Cruises & Tours Historic Anchorage

Federal Building & the Alaska Public Lands Information Center

Sack's Café

Kenai Fjords Tours

WEST 4TH AVENUE

Simon & Seafort's

Snow City Cafe

Arctic Rose

Copper Whale Inn

Captain Cook

M STREET

The Anchor Pub & Club

Anchorage Visitor Information Center

Prince William Sound Glacier Cruises

Glacier Brewhouse

Imaginarium
Orso's

Egan Civic & Convention Center ●

4

WEST 5TH AVENUE

The Kobuk

Caribou Inn

Corsair
Voyager

Town Square

Alaska Center for Performing Arts

Cafe 817

Kaladi Bros

WEST 6TH AVENUE

5

L STREET

K STREET

I STREET

Oomingmak ● Musk Ox Producers Co-operative

H STREET

G STREET

F STREET

Humpy's Great Alaskan Alehouse

WEST 7TH AVENUE

Alaska Department of Natural Resources

● Dena'ina Civic & Convention Center

Susitna Place

WEST 8TH AVENUE

6

WEST 9TH AVENUE

Hawthorn Suites

The Oscar Gill House B&B, City Garden B&B

Delaney Park Strip

7

WEST 10TH AVENUE

G Street House B&B

A

↓ Inlet Tower

B

New Sagaya's ↓ City Market

C

Downtown ↓ Guesthouse

D

190

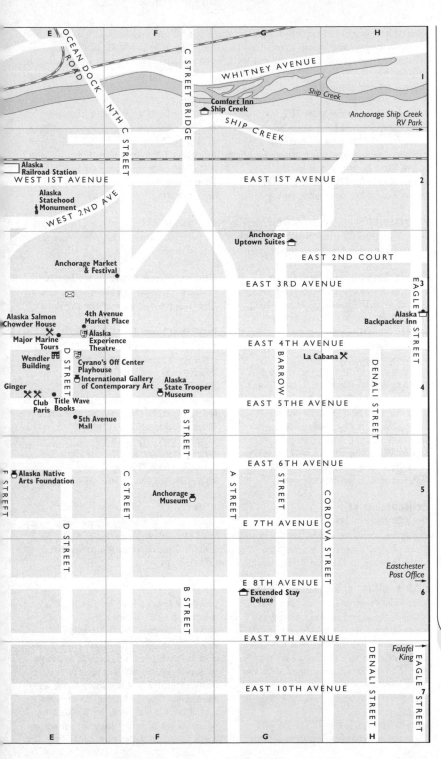

E   F   G   H

OCEAN DOCK ROAD

C STREET BRIDGE

WHITNEY AVENUE

I

NTH C STREET

Ship Creek

Comfort Inn
Ship Creek

Anchorage Ship Creek
RV Park

SHIP CREEK

Alaska
Railroad Station

WEST 1ST AVENUE

EAST 1ST AVENUE

2

Alaska
Statehood
Monument

WEST 2ND AVE

Anchorage
Uptown Suites

EAST 2ND COURT

Anchorage Market
& Festival

EAST 3RD AVENUE

EAGLE STREET

3

Alaska Salmon
Chowder House

4th Avenue
Market Place

Alaska
Experience
Theatre

Alaska
Backpacker Inn

Major Marine
Tours

Cyrano's Off Center
Playhouse

D STREET

EAST 4TH AVENUE

BARROW

La Cabana

DENALI STREET

Wendler
Building

International Gallery
of Contemporary Art

Alaska
State Trooper
Museum

4

Ginger

EAST 5THE AVENUE

Club
Paris

Title Wave
Books

5th Avenue
Mall

B STREET

EAST 6TH AVENUE

Alaska Native
Arts Foundation

F STREET

C STREET

Anchorage
Museum

A STREET

C STREET

CORDOVA STREET

5

D STREET

E 7TH AVENUE

Eastchester
Post Office

E 8TH AVENUE

B STREET

Extended Stay
Deluxe

6

EAST 9TH AVENUE

DENALI STREET

Falafel
King

EAGLE STREET

5

EAST 10TH AVENUE

DENALI STREET H

EAGLE STREET

7

E   F   G   H

Southcentral Alaska ANCHORAGE

191

guided and unguided trips to be had in the Chugach Mountains. If you can't find the activity you are looking for in Anchorage, just drive an hour north or south. Girdwood (see page 219) is loaded with outdoor adventures from paragliding to rafting. North of town, Eagle River, Wasilla, and Palmer offer fishing, rafting and hiking, among other things.

Anchorage Audubon Society ✆ 338 2473; www.anchorageaudubon.org. The society has a variety of free events for bird lovers all summer, but especially when birds are migrating through the area in April, May & the early part of June.
Segtours of Anchorage 325 E. St; ✆ 441 1124; www.segtours.net. Alan shows visitors the city he has

called home for 20 years. A fun & informative 90–120min tour costs US$65 & leaves at 09.00, 13.00 & 17.00 daily.
Trolley Tours Tickets are available from a vendor in front of the visitor centre every day for US$15. The 1hr tour covers much of the city's history from inside a covered & heated bus.

Flightseeing
Seeing the city from the sky is a great way to be reminded of the city's size as well as its utter isolation. Flights can be booked over the city or as far as Denali, Homer or even to see bears in Katmai National Park.

Aero Tech Flight Service 1100 Merrill Field Dr; ✆ 279 6558; www.aerotechalaska.com. Flightseeing to Denali for US$300pp, Knik Glacier for US$180pp, Prince William Sound for US$216pp & around Anchorage for US$96pp.
Alpine Air Alaska ✆ 783 2360; www.alpineairalaska.com. 6 flights/day to area glaciers. A short 30-min flight gets you up & around Anchorage for US$215pp. A 1hr trip with a glacier landing is US$320pp & their Prince William Sound tour costs US$425pp. A 3hr trip to Columbia Glacier in Prince William Sound costs US$640pp.
Regal Air A flightseeing (Chugach Mountains US$95pp, Denali US$365pp, & Prince William Sound for US$239pp), fly-in fishing (US$430pp guided,

US$230pp unguided) & charter service from Lake Hood. Everyone should have the experience of taking off & landing in a seaplane at least once in their life.
Rusty's Flying Service 4525 Enstrom Cir; ✆ 243 1595, 800 544 2299 (TF); www.flyrusts.com. Flightseeing trips to Denali, over area glaciers & around the city for US$100–400.
Sound Aviation 2400 E Fifth Av; ✆ 229 2462; www.soundaviation.com. A short flight around Anchorage costs US$49pp, while trips to Prince William Sound cost US$169–199pp.
Spernak Airways 1707 Merrill Field Dr; ✆ 272 9475; www.spernakair.com. Fly-out fishing & flightseeing (Denali US$325pp & Prince William Sound US$160pp) with 50 years' experience.

Helicopter trips
Alpine Air Alaska ✆ 783 2360; www.alpineairalaska.com. 6 flights per day to area glaciers. A short 30min flight gets you up & around Anchorage for US$215pp. A 1hr trip with a

glacier landing is US$320pp & their Prince William Sound tour costs US$425pp. A 3hr trip to Columbia Glacier in Prince William Sound costs US$640pp.

Hiking, biking and horseback rides
Alaska Alpine Adventures 2133 Dahl Lane; ✆ 222 6147; www.alaskaalpineadventures.com. Widely recognised as one of the best backcountry guiding outfits in Alaska. They offer trips of all sorts just about anywhere in the state. They are not cheap but they are also serious & professional about what they do. Multi-day kayaking, rafting, hiking & mountaineering trips start at US$2,000 & go up to US$4,000 or more.
Alaska Backcountry Bike Tours ✆ 866 354 2453 (TF); www.mountainbikealaska.com. Offers bike tours.

Coastal Trail Rentals & Tours (see page 189) Offers bike tours & rentals in Anchorage.
Alaska Kite Adventures ✆ 888 716 9463; www.alaskakiteadventures.com. Owner, Tom Fredericks offers kiteboarding lessons in Turnagain Arm during the summer & 'snowkiting' (a combination of skis or snowboard attached to a kite) lessons & trips around Alaska in the winter. Kiteboarding is a new sport & a lot of fun. Tom is a friendly guy & offers a fun day out as well as the best instruction this side of Hawaii. Introductory lessons start at US$150 for 3hrs.

Ascending Path Climbing Guide Service ✆ 783 0505, 877 783 0505 (TF); www.theascendingpath.com. Winter & summer adventures on the glaciers & mountains around Anchorage. Half-day hikes around Anchorage start at US$79pp. A 3hr glacier hike is US$139pp.
Horse Trekkin Alaska ✆ 868 3728; www.horsetrekkinalaska.com. Single day & extended

horse trips outside Anchorage. For a shorter trip try the 1hr trip for US$60pp, or the 2hr trip for US$85pp.
Matanuska Ice Climbing Adventures Mile 102.5 Glenn Highway; ✆ 746 4026, 800 956 6422 (TF); www.micaguides.com. Glacier trekking, ice climbing, rafting & kayaking, all outside Anchorage.

Cruise, kayak, canoe and raft trips

Though it's on the ocean, Anchorage doesn't offer many ocean-going excursions, for the simple reason that much of Upper Cook Inlet is a turbid, shallow and muddy place. For those who want to kayak or cruise up to glaciers and wildlife, many Prince William Sound tours can be booked in Anchorage. Most offer transportation to Whittier or Seward where boats wait to take visitors to the foot of a glacier where they will – hopefully – see some wildlife on the way. To book such a tour, walk along 4th Av between C and F Street. Their gaudy signs are hard to miss. See Whittier and Seward for more information.

Alaska Kayak Academy 2201 Palmer Wasilla Hwy; ✆ 746 6600, 877 215 6600 (TF); www.kayakcenterak.com. Guided sea-kayaking trips in Prince William Sound for US$190pp, as well as multi-day trips starting at US$3,100pp. Glacier treks US$190pp. Located in Wasilla.
Chugach Outdoor Center Mile 7.5 Hope Hwy; ✆ 277 7238, 866 277 2738; www.chugachoutdoorcenter.com. 1-day raft trips near Anchorage for US$80–149pp.

Extended trips on the Talkeetna & Tana Rivers cost US$1,450–2,400pp. Visit their other location in Seward, off Exit Glacier Road.
NOVA River Runners ✆ 800 746 5753; www.novalaska.com. Day trips down some of the Anchorage area's most vicious streams. Calmer river trips are also available. Their helicopter/raft trip costs US$450pp & short river raft trips around Anchorage cost US$75–110pp.

Fishing

Fishing trips can be booked out of Anchorage or from Wasilla to the north. Those looking to guide themselves to hook a big one can try Ship Creek in town and Bird Creek south of town on the Seward Highway. The Kenai Peninsula is a fisherman's paradise where both 'combat fishing' (see *Glossary* on page 431) and secluded mountain streams can be found. Call the **Alaska Department of Fish and Game** (✆ 465 4180; *www.sf.adfg.state.ak.us*) for fishing reports and tips. In addition, virtually every newspaper in the state prints fishing reports and tides.

Acord Guide Service ✆ 376 0692; www.acordguideservice.com
Fisherman's Choice Charters ✆ 892 8707, 800 989 8707 (TF); www.akfishermanschoice.com.
Fishtale River Guides ✆ 746 2199; www.fish4salmon.com.
Mat-Su Salmon Charters ✆ 841 0499; www.mat-sucharters.com. Hunt various salmon species from a boat in Anchorage area rivers for US$135 for a half day & US$215 for a full day.

Regal Air 4506 Lake Shore Dr; ✆ 243 8535; www.regal-air.com. Guided & unguided fly-in fishing trips from US$250–450.
Rusty's Flying Service All-day fly-in fishing for US$535 with a pick-up from the airport.
Women's Flyfishing ✆ 274 7113; www.womensflyfishing.net. Guided fly-fishing trips & classes run by women for women.

HIKING AND RECREATION

Anchorage and the Chugach Mountains are a hiker's paradise. For those interested in hiking, be sure to pick up a copy of the Chugach State Park map for US$7 from the Public Lands Information Centre in Anchorage (see page 189). The website www.trailsofanchorage.com is also a great resource. Southeast Anchorage borders the Chugach State Park and provides excellent access to park trails. Follow the Seward Highway south through Anchorage and turn east on any of the main east to west thoroughfares, including Huffman, Abbott, or O'Malley Road. Huffman eventually turns into Toilsom Hill Drive and ends at the

Glen Alps trailhead where a number of wonderful trails head into the park. O'Malley Road leads to Upper Prospect Drive and the Prospect Heights trailhead. See box on page 75 for an explanation of hiking grades.

Flattop Mountain (*Grade: moderate; distance: 1.5 miles*) Located behind town off the Glen Alps trailhead, this extremely popular trail has views that are worth braving the crowds. The hike is all uphill but moderated by switchbacks. At the top there is a little scrambling required, but the views of Anchorage, Turnagain Arm and the Chugach Mountains are stunning. The Flattop Mountain Shuttle (see page 192) will pick up in Anchorage and drop you off at the trailhead for US$22 per person.

Bird Ridge Trail (*Grade: difficult; distance: 2.5 miles*) This starts at mile 102 of the Seward Highway between Anchorage and Girdwood. This is a steep trail (entirely uphill in fact) that rewards hikers with amazing views of Turnagain Arm and the Chugach Mountains.

Crow Pass Trail (*Grade: moderate; distance: 24 miles*) One of the best and longest hikes in the area, Crow Pass follows the historic Iditarod trail from Crow Creek Road in Girdwood all the way to the Eagle River Nature Centre (see page 206) north of Anchorage. The trail passes through the heart of the Chugach Mountains with wildlife, glaciers, mountains and mining ruins along the way. The hike is a serious undertaking mainly due to the length and remoteness. Hikers should pack for all weather conditions, be self-sufficient and be bear-savvy.

Tony Knowles Coastal Trail (*Grade: easy; distance: 11 miles*) Located near the city centre, the Knowles Trail follows the coastline from 2nd Avenue to Kincaid Park. There is nothing like riding or walking this paved trail on a sunny day.

Ship Creek Trail (*Grade: easy; distance: 3 miles*) Follows Ship Creek from C Street north for three miles. This is a fun walk when the salmon are running and fishermen line the banks. The trailhead is near the Alaska Railroad building.

⌂ WHERE TO STAY Those arriving in Anchorage after visiting more remote parts of the state are generally thrilled to have so many choices. Of the thousands of hotel rooms and hundreds of bed and breakfasts, few are worth staying at and even fewer are affordable or even fairly priced. Here are some notable exceptions. The Anchorage visitor centre has a complete list of local accommodation. The **Anchorage Bed & Breakfast Association** (☏ *272 5909, 888 584 5147 TF; www.anchorage-bnb.com*) and the **Bed & Breakfast Association of Alaska** (*www.alaskabba.com*) can also help you find the right B&B. Bear in mind that Anchorage is large and spread out. Many B&Bs are located in midtown or on the outskirts of town where a taxi ride costs US$15–30 from the city centre. Book all Anchorage accommodation as far in advance as possible. Four to eight months ahead is not an exaggeration. Anchorage has a variety of corporate hotels and 'all-suite' hotels that are generally clean, nice but decidedly un-Alaskan and generic. All offer some kind of breakfast and have Wi-Fi.

Hotels
Luxury

⌂ **Homewood Suites** [184–5 C3] (122 rooms) 140 West Tudor Rd; ☏ 762 7000; www.homewoodsuites.com. Pleasant large rooms; b/fast & dinner incl. Wi-Fi. $$$$$

⌂ **Dimond Center Hotel** [184–5 D5] (109 rooms) 700 E Dimond Blvd; ☏ 770 5000, 866 770 5002; www.dimondcenterhotel.com. A lovely hotel in an ugly part of town. The hotel is owned by the

Seldovia Native Association & caters to rural Alaskans visiting the big city. The hotel is situated near many large box stores for this reason. Common areas & rooms are very well designed & organised with top quality furnishings & amenities. A car is essential for getting to & from the hotel. Wi-Fi, restaurant, TV, b/fast, airport shuttle. $$$$

🏠 **Hawthorn Suites** [190–1 A6] (112 rooms) 1110 West 8th Av; ☎ 222 5005; www.hawthorn.com. Nice rooms, free airport shuttle & b/fast. Wi-Fi. $$$$

Mid-range

🏠 **Inlet Tower** (180 rooms) 1200 L St; ☎ 276 0110; www.inlettower.com. Decent rooms with great views. Try to get a corner room on one of the upper floors. Restaurant on the premises. Near the airport with a shuttle. Wi-Fi, TV. $$$$

🏠 **Voyager Hotel** [190–1 B4] (40 rooms) 501 K St; ☎ 277 9501; www.voyagerhotel.com. Clean, simple rooms with a good city centre location. $$$–$$$$

🏠 **Anchorage Grand Hotel** [190–1 D2] (31 rooms) 505 W. 2nd Av; ☎ 929 8888, 888 800 0640 (TF); www.anchoragegrand.com. Right in the city centre, this pleasant hotel offers suite style rooms with full kitchens. Wi-Fi, free b/fast & decent rates for the location. $$$

🏠 **Anchorage Uptown Suites** [190–1 G3] (19 rooms) 235 E 2nd Ct; ☎ 279 423; www.anchorageuptownsuites.com. Simple rooms, some with kitchenettes. $$$

🏠 **Comfort Inn Ship Creek** [190–1 F1] (100 rooms) 111 Ship Creek Av; ☎ 277 6887; www.comfortinn.com. Basic rooms near Ship Creek, the rail station & the city centre. Wi-Fi, shuttle. $$$

Budget

🏠 **Anchorage Guest House** [184–5 B2] (3 rooms) 2001 Hillcrest Dr; ☎ 274 0408; www.akhouse.com. Not quite a hostel, not quite a B&B. The bunks are the best value (US$29). There are 2 private rooms

B&B

🏠 **Copper Whale Inn** [190–1 A4] (14 rooms) 440 L St; ☎ 866 258 7999; www.copperwhale.com. The rooms are simple & clean but the city centre location is what makes this place special. Weekend parking is free, week day parking is a nightmare. Near the ocean & the Tony Knowles trail. TV, Wi-Fi. $$$

🏠 **City Garden B&B** [190–1 A7] (3 rooms) 1352 W 10th Av; ☎ 276 8686; www.citygarden.biz. Offers 3

🏠 **Hotel Captain Cook** [190–1 B4] (547 rooms) 939 W 5th Av; ☎ 276 6000, 800/843 1950 (TF); www.captaincook.com. Offers the standard hotel experience except for the top floor rooms which have great views. The hotel was built by former governor Wally Hickel & is one of the largest & least tastefully coloured buildings in town. A full spa & workout area are on the premises as well as 3 bars & 4 restaurants including the **Crow's Nest** (see page 197), an excellent dress-up place on the top floor. Wi-Fi, TV. $$$$

🏠 **Extended Stay Deluxe** [190–1 G6] (89 rooms) 108 E 8th Av; ☎ 868 1605; www.extendedstayamerica.com. One building in midtown & another a few blocks away in the city centre. Skip the midtown location, unless you have pets. $$$

🏠 **Hampton Inn & Suites** [184–5 C3] (101) 4301 Credit Union Dr; ☎ 550 7000; www.hamptoninn.com. Simple rooms near the airport, with a free shuttle service. Wi-Fi. $$$

🏠 **Historic Anchorage Hotel** [190–1 D3] (26 rooms) 330 E St; ☎ 272 4553; www.historicanchoragehotel.com. Located right in the city centre, the small hotel has a restaurant, bar & small, but comfortable, suites on the 3rd floor for US$250 & standard rooms on the 2nd floor for US$190. The hotel was originally built in 1916 & is listed on the National Register of Historic Places. The hotel was formerly the home of famed Alaskan artist Sydney Laurence. $$$

🏠 **Puffin Inn** [184–5 B3] (85 rooms) 4400 Spenard Rd; ☎ 243 4044, 866 494 4841 (TF); www.puffininn.net. Only worth a stay if you can secure a corner room in the new wing on an upper floor. Wi-Fi, shuttle, b/fast. $$$

(US$92) & 1 shared room with bunks. Everyone shares 3 bathrooms, a large kitchen & a common area. Bikes are US$8/hr. A good hr's hike to the city centre. Laundry, Wi-Fi. $$

modern rooms with/without shared bathroom. $$$

🏠 **Downtown Guesthouse** [190–1 D7] (2 rooms) 1236 G St; 279 2359; www.downtownguesthouse.com. An excellent option for anyone like myself who wants some privacy & quiet to balance their hectic travel schedule. This 2-bedroom apartment has everything one needs to be entirely self-sufficient & is just a short walk from the city centre. US$150 for the entire place with a 3-night minimum & up to 4 people. $$$

🏠 **Susitna Place** [190–1 A6] (9 rooms) 727 N St; ☎ 274 3344; www.susitnaplace.com. Pleasant rooms with shared & private bathrooms. Wi-Fi. $$$

🏠 **The Oscar Gill House** [190–1 A7] (3 rooms) 1344 W. 10th Av; ☎ 279 1344; www.oscargill.com. Former Anchorage Mayor Oscar Gill built this historic home across Cook Inlet in 1913. The current owners moved the house to its present location in 1993. The owners are friendly, the rooms are nice & the central location is ideal. 1 room has its own bathroom & the other 2 share. TV, Wi-Fi. $$–$$$

🏠 **Caribou Inn** [190–1 A4] (14 rooms) 501 L St; ☎ 272 0444, 800 272 5878 (TF); www.cariboubnb.com. Spectacular only for its location. Shared & private bathrooms; internet access & free airport shuttle. $$

🏠 **G Street House B&B** [190–1 C7] (3 rooms) 1032 G St; ☎ 276 3284; www.gstreethouse.com. Simple, pleasant & affordable rooms. Wi-Fi, b/fast. $$

Around Anchorage

🏠 **Mangy Moose** [184–5 F6] (3 rooms) 5560 E 112th Av; ☎ 346 8052, 877 346 8052 (TF); www.alaskamangymoose.com. A huge house in a forested neighbourhood on the outskirts of town. Hiking trails nearby. The 2 rooms downstairs have a private entrance & sleep 7. Honeymoon couples should take the Royal Alaskan suite. TV, Wi-Fi. $$$$

🏠 **North Country Castle B&B** [184–5 F7] (2 rooms) 14600 Joanne Ct; ☎ 345 7296; www.castlealaska.com. A large & lovely home south of Anchorage along Turnagain Arm. Secluded, quiet & always romantic & relaxing. Wonderful views. Bathrobes, TV, Wi-Fi. $$$$

🏠 **Alaska Frontier Gardens** [184–5 G6] (4 rooms) ☎ 345 6556; www.alaskafrontiergardens.com. Lovely, extremely well-appointed rooms with all the amenities. Rita is very friendly & has cultivated an amazing array of flowering plants outside. $$$

🏠 **Alaska Sundance Retreat** [184–5 G6] (4 rooms) 12351 Audubon Dr; ☎ 344 7714; www.aksundanceretreat.com. One of the best B&Bs in town. This new luxury B&B will not remain affordable for long. Grand views overlook the bay & horses are kept on the property. Trails nearby. $$$

🏠 **Lake Hood Inn** [184–5 B3] (4 rooms) 4702 Lake Spenard Dr; ☎ 258 9321; www.lakehoodinn.com. A great, if noisy location right on Lake Hood where float planes take off & land continuously. B/fast, freezer, Wi-Fi. $$$

🏠 **Big Bear B&B** [184–5 E1] (4 rooms) 3401 Richmond Av; ☎ 277 8189; www.alaskabigbearbb.com. Pleasant & affordable rooms & an extremely friendly hostess. The area is not the most attractive, but the B&B is like an oasis. $$

Hostels There are a surprising number of hostels in Anchorage, but due to bad neighbourhoods and poor management, just a few are worth staying at. If they are not listed here, then skip them.

🏠 **Alaska Backpacker Inn** [190–1 H3] (80 beds) 327 Eagle St. Football, TV & some artistic touches. Near the city centre. Beds are US$25. B/fast incl. $

🏠 **Arctic Adventure Hostel** [184–5 C2] (42 beds) 337 W 33rd Av; ☎ 562 5700, 888 886 9332 (TF); www.arcticadventurehostel.com. Clean, simple rooms & bunks. Discounts for climbers. US$22 for a bunk & US$44 for a room. Ingredients to cook your own b/fast. Midtown. Wi-Fi. $

🏠 **Spenard Hostel International** [184–5 B3] (47 beds) 2845 W 42nd Av; ☎ 248 5036; www.alaskahostel.org. A pleasant hostel that's got it right with no curfew. 3 kitchens & a laundry. Buses stop regularly at the front door heading to various parts of the state incl Denali & Homer. Beds are US$25 or US$27 if you use a credit card. Located near the airport. Laundry, bikes, Wi-Fi. $

🏠 **26 Street International Hostel** [184–5 C2] (20 beds) 1037 W 26th Av; ☎ 274 1252; www.26streethostel.com. A simple but adequate hostel with b/fast incl. Bunks are US$25 & private rooms are US$67. Laundry, Wi-Fi. $

Camping In addition to the in city camping options listed below, three campgrounds can be found outside the city. North of town is the **Eklutna Lake Campground** (see page 206) and the **Eagle River Campground** (see page 206). South of town is the **Bird Creek Campground** (see page 206).

🏕 **Anchorage Ship Creek RV Park** [190–1 H1] (150 sites) 150 Ingra St; ☎ 277 3808; www.bestofalaskatravel.com. Located at Ship Creek, but also next to the railroad tracks. Situated a short walk from the city centre. Tents cost US$26, RVs US$46. Wi-Fi available.

Ⓐ **Centennial Campground** [184–5 G1] (108 sites) 8300 Glenn Hwy; ☎ 343 6986; www.muni.org/parks/camping.cfm. A pleasant campground 15mins from the city centre. Tents & RVs cost US$20. Showers US$5.

Ⓐ **Creekwood Inn** [184–5 D2] (68 sites) 2150 Seward Hwy; ☎ 243 0432; www.creekwoodinn-alaska.com. RV sites for US$30 as well as rooms & cabins. No tent camping.

Ⓐ **Golden Nugget Camper Park** [184–5 F2] (215 sites) 4100 Debarr Rd; www.goldennuggetcamperpark.com. Located near the malls & large stores. Tents cost US$22, RVs are US$37.

✗ **WHERE TO EAT** Anchorage is a foodie's paradise with gourmet restaurants and hole-in-the-wall places serving some of the state's best food, much of which is grown in the Mat-Su Valley or caught in Alaskan waters. The city centre is the obvious place to dine, but be sure to explore the many gems hidden away around town in shabby buildings and grey strip malls. For cheap eats while walking around the centre check out the kilt-clad hot dog vendor in front of the Federal Building near the visitor centre. After you get a sausage, head over to the visitor centre to get a copy of *Local Flavour*, a guide to Anchorage dining. Be sure to make reservations for all dining venues in the city centre.

The farmers' market can also be a good place to grab lunch. **Anchorage Market and Festival** [190–1 F3] (☎ *272 5634; www.anchoragemarkets.com*) is held every Saturday and Sunday near the city centre at 3rd Avenue & C Street from 10.00–18.00. Live music, arts and crafts, local produce and ready-to-eat food. Though some breakfast options can be found, the lunch scene is much better. Park across the street in front of the post office for US$1/hr. Another much smaller market is held on Saturday 09.00–14.00 in the car park of the Central Lutheran Church at 15th Avenue and Cordova Street.

City centre

✗ **The Crow's Nest** [190–1 B4] (see page 195) ⏲ 17.00–23.00 Tue & Wed, 17.00–midnight Thu–Sat. Located on the top floor of the Captain Cook Hotel. Romantic atmosphere with great views & inspired food. Entrées cost US$25–50. **$$$$$**

✗ **Marx Brothers Café** [190–1 C3] 627 W 3rd Av; ☎ 278 2133; www.marxcafe.com; ⏲ 17.30–22.00 Tue–Sat. Wonderful seafood & meat dishes served in a historic building with only 14 tables. The menu changes daily. The Caesar salad is divine. Dinner costs US$30–45. **$$$$$**

✗ **Club Paris** [190–1 E4] 417 W 5th Av; ☎ 277 6332; www.clubparisrestaurant.com; ⏲ 11.30–14.30 Mon–Sat (lunch), 17.00–22.00 Sun–Thu & 17.00–23.00 Fri–Sat (dinner). A variety of lunch & dinner options, but famous for their amazing steaks. The strange & dark atmosphere turns some people off. **$$$$**

✗ **Corsair Restaurant** [190–1 B4] 944 W 5th Av; ☎ 278 4502; www.corsairrestaurant.com; ⏲ 17.00–22.00 Mon–Thu, 17.00–23.00 Fri & Sat. A romantic fine-dining establishment known for theatrically preparing your meal at your table. Located in the bottom of the Voyager Hotel. **$$$$**

✗ **Ginger** [190–1 E4] 425 West 5th Av; ☎ 929 3680; www.gingeralaska.com; ⏲ 11.30–14.00 Mon–Fri (lunch); 17.30–late daily (dinner). This hip Asian fusion restaurant is right in the city centre. **$$$$**

✗ **Orso's** [190–1 C4] 737 W 5th Av; ☎ 222 3232; www.orsoalaska.com; ⏲ 11.30–16.00 (lunch); 17.00–22.00 Sun–Thu & 17.00–23.00 Fri & Sat (dinner). Steaks, seafood & pasta all done extremely well. There is a large wine list. **$$$$**

✗ **Sacks Café & Restaurant** [190–1 C3] 328 G St; ☎ 276 3546; www.sackscafe.com; ⏲ 11.00–14.30 Mon–Fri (lunch); 17.00–21.00 Sun–Thu & 17.00–22.30 Fri & Sat (dinner); 11.00–14.30 Sat & 10.00–14.00 Sun (brunch). A modern fine dining place with a small, but good, menu. A pleasant place to sit quietly & sip one of their fine wines. **$$$$**

✗ **Simon & Seafort's** [190–1 A4] 420 L St; ☎ 274 3502; www.r-u-i.com/sim; ⏲ 11.00–14.30 Mon–Fri (lunch); 17.00–21.30 Mon–Thu, 17.00–22.00 Fri, 16.30–22.00 Sat & 16.30–21.00 Sun (dinner); 11.00–23.00 Mon–Fri, 16.00–23.00 Sat & 16.00–22.00 Sun (bar). An excellent fine dining establishment with good views. **$$$$**

✗ **Urban Greens** [190–1 C3] 304 G St; ☎ 276 0333; ⏲ 09.00–17.00 Mon–Fri. A hip city centre eatery ideal for a quick & tasty bite. The fresh sandwiches are great & the Thai chicken salad rocks! Owners participate in the First Friday Art Walk (see page 203). **$$**

Around town

✗ **Jen's** [184–5 C3] 701 W 36th Av; ☎ 561 5367; www.jensrestaurant.com; ⊕ 11.30–14.00 Mon–Fri (lunch);18.00–22.00 Tue–Sat (dinner); 16.00–midnight Tues–Sat (appetisers). A cosy little place in an unassuming strip mall in midtown. Wonderful steak, pasta & seafood. More than 150 wines. Make a reservation & bring a date. $$$$

✗ **Kincaid Grill** [184–5 B4] 6700 Jewel Lake Rd; ☎ 243 0507; www.kincaidgrill.com; ⊕ Tue–Sat 17.00–22.00. Chef Al is a local character & host of the local TV show 'What's Cookin'?' Al is constantly updating his menu with new & exciting dishes & desserts. The wild salmon & scallops are always great. $$$$

✗ **Southside Bistro** [184–5 D6] 1320 Huffman Park Dr; ☎ 348 0088; www.southsidebistro.com; ⊕ 11.30–22.00 Tue–Thu, 11.30–23.00 Fri & Sat. An upbeat & chic atmosphere with good, well-presented food. Price ranges from US$12 for a pizza to more than US$25 for a beef, seafood or pasta dish. Famous rack of lamb. Extensive wine list. $$$$

✗ **Aladdin's** [184–5 D3] 4240 Old Seward Hwy; ☎ 561 2373; ⊕ 17.00–22.00 Wed–Sat. Great Mediterranean food. $$$

✗ **A Taste of Thai** [184–5 D6] 11109 Old Seward Hwy; ☎ 349 8424; ⊕ 11.00–21.00 Mon–Thu, 11.00–22.00 Fri & Sat. Great food, service & ambiance. $$$

✗ **Campobello Bistro** [184–5 C3] 601 W 36th Av; ☎ 562 2040; ⊕ 11.00–14.30 Mon–Fri (lunch);17.00–21.00 Tue–Sat (dinner). Creative fare in a comfortable atmosphere. Located in the same mall as the wonderful bakery Europa. $$$

✗ **Chiang Mai Ultimate Thai** 3637 Old Seward Hwy; ☎ 563 8900; ⊕ 11.00–20.30 Mon–Fri, 16–21.00 Sat. Not much to look at from the outside, but the food & service are both great. $$$

✗ **Organic Oasis** [184–5 C2] 2610 Spenard Rd, ☎ 277 7882; www.organicoasis.com; ⊕ 11.00–20.00 Mon, 11.00–21.00 Tue–Fri, 11.00–20.00 Sat, 13.00–18.00 Sun. Located in mall at Spenard & 26th. Fresh juices & smoothies plus coffee & tea. Simple but excellent pizza, wraps, & sandwiches. Free Wi-Fi. $$$

✗ **Siam Cuisine** [184–5 C5] 1911 W Dimond Blvd; ☎ 344 3663; ⊕ 11.00–21.00 Mon–Fri, 12.00–20.00 Sun. Great food in a boring atmosphere. $$$

✗ **Snow City Café** [190–1 A4] 1034 W. 4th Av; ☎ 272 2489; www.snowcitycafe.com; ⊕ 07.00–15.00 Mon–Fri, 07.00–16.00 Sat & Sun. A light, modern atmosphere combined with creative & tasty food has kept this café a local favourite for years. B/fast served all day. Expect to wait for a table. Lunch served after 11.00. $$$

✗ **Sushi Garden** [184–5 D7] 1120 Huffman Rd; ☎ 345 4686; ⊕ 11.00–23.00 daily. Boring ambience but good sushi. $$$

✗ **Sushi & Sushi** [184–5 C3] 3337 Fairbanks St; ☎ 764 7544. A local's favourite, this is located behind the Moose's Tooth. Great ambiance & food. $$$

✗ **Thai Kitchen** [184–5 E3] 3405 E Tudor; ☎ 561 0082; www.thaikitchenalaska.com; ⊕ 11.00–15.00 & 17.00–21.00 Mon–Fri, 17.00–21.00 Sat, 17.00–20.30 Sun. A huge menu & tasty food, but not the most exciting décor. In Anchorage since 1986! $$$

✗ **The Moose's Tooth Pub & Pizzeria** [184–5 D2] 3300 Old Seward Hwy; ☎ 258 2537; www.moosestooth.net; ⊕ 10.30–23.30 Mon–Thu, 10.30–24.30 Fri, 11.00–24.30 Sat, 11.00–23.30 Sun. Other Anchorage pizza establishments have been folding in the face of the awesome Moose's Tooth for years. If you love good pizza & crave beer, look no farther. Half of the restaurant is lacking character due to a recent expansion, but the old section is still grungy & cool. You'll probably have to wait for a table. Cheap slices from 10.30–14.00 daily. Free Wi-Fi. $$$

✗ **Yak & Yeti** 3301 Spenard Rd; ☎ 743 8078; www.yakandyetialaska.com; ⊕ 11.00–14.30 Mon–Fri, 17.00–20.30 Thu–Sat. Friendly & small with cheerful staff. Excellent food from India, Nepal & Tibet. $$$

✗ **Yamato Ya** 3700S Old Seward Hwy; ☎ 561 2128; www.yamatoyasushi.com; ⊕ 11.00–15.00 & 16.00–22.00 Mon–Fri, 16.00–22.00 Sat. Tasty sushi served in an authentic atmosphere. $$$

✗ **Gwennies Old Alaska Restaurant** [184–5 B3] 4333 Spenard Rd; ☎ 243 2090; www.gwenniesrestaurant.com; ⊕ 06.00–22.00 Mon–Sat, 08.00–21.00 Sun. The only thing separating this from a typical dinner experience is the cave-like atmosphere & the stuffed animals on the walls. Always crowded, Gwennies serves b/fast all day & is famous for its sourdough pancakes. You may have to wait for a table. Unless you have an abnormally large appetite, one meal will feed 2 people. $$

✗ **New Sagaya's Midtown Market** (see page 203) A wonderfully complete Asian market with a deli & the tasty L'Aroma Bakery inside. The seating area is a little dismal, so take your food to go. They also offer fish filleting & freezing. The other location is called **City Market** (900 W 13th Av; ☎ 274 6173). $$

✗ **Taco King** 113 W Northern Lights Blvd; ☎ 276 7387; www.tacokingak.com. Corner of Northern Lights & A St. A US$6.75-burrito deluxe feeds 2! One of the best-value places in Anchorage. Also at 1330 Huffman Rd, 3561 E Tudor Rd & the Burrito King at 111 E 38th Av. $$

Cafés L'Aroma Bakeries, serving wonderful baked goods and pastries, can be found in both New Sagaya's (see page 203) locations.

✕ **Europa Bakery** 601 W 36th; ✆ 563 5704; ☺ 06.00–18.00 Mon–Sat, 08.00–17.00 Sun. The high prices for these pastries & loaves of European style bread deter few people. $$$

✕ **Middle Way Café** 1200 W Northern Lights Blvd; ✆ 272 6433; www.middlewaycafe.com; ☺ 07.00–18.30 Mon–Fri, 08.00–18.30 Sat, 09.00–17.00 Sun. Located in the same mall as REI (see page 204), this café serves the usual hot drinks, but also great healthy & organic food & fresh juices at affordable prices. Delicious brunch Sat & Sun 08.00–13.00. The kitchen is open 10.30–16.30 Mon–Sat. Free Wi-Fi. $$$

✕ **Modern Dwellers Chocolate Lounge** [184–5 D3] 751 E 36th Av, Ste 105; ✆ 677 9985; www.moderndwellers.com; ☺ 11.00–18.00 Mon, 10.00–20.00 Tue–Thu, 10.00–22.00 Fri & Sat . Amazing handmade chocolates in a chic atmosphere. Try at least 1 of their stranger concoctions such as the smoked salmon or anchovy chocolate. $$$

✕ **Café Del Mundo** 341 East Benson Blvd; ✆ 562 2326, 800 770 2326 (TF); www.cafedelmundo.com; ☺ 08.00–17.00 Mon–Thu, 08.00–16.00 Fri. Free Wi-Fi & cheap drinks but not particularly cosy. Located inside the Dimond Mall. $$

✕ **Kaladi Brothers** [184–5 D3] www.kaladi.com. The famous Alaskan coffee place has 9 locations around Anchorage, including in New Sagaya's (see page 203), downtown at the Performing Arts Centre & next to REI (see page 204). $$

WHERE TO DRINK

♀ **The Anchor Pub & Club** [190–1 C4] 712 W Fourth Av; ✆ 677 7979; www.anchorak.com; ☺ 11.30–late Mon–Sat. A dark retro club in the city centre with dancing Thu–Sat after 22.00. Full bar. $$$

♀ **Glacier Brewhouse** [190–1 C4] 737 W 5th Av; ✆ 274 2739; www.glacierbrewhouse.com; ☺ 11.00–16.00 Mon–Sat, 12.00–16.00 Sun (lunch); 16.00–21.30 Sun & Mon, 16.00–22.00 Tue–Thu, 16.00–23.00 Sat (dinner). A huge selection of wine, sake & beer, incl a number of varieties they make on site. Also serves wood-fired pizzas (US$10–12) & other meals for around (US$15–20). $$$

♀ **Humpy's Great Alaskan Alehouse** [190–1 D5] 610 W 6th Av; ✆ 276 2337; www.humpys.com. Live music, a wide selection of beers on tap, decent pub food & right in the heart of Anchorage. A better place for drinking than eating. $$$

♀ **Midnight Sun Brewing Co** 7329 Arctic Blvd; ✆ 344 1179; www.midnightsunbrewing.com. Offers tasting sessions.

♀ **Snow Goose Restaurant & Brewery** [190–1 C3] 717 W 3rd Av; ✆ 277 7727; www.alaskabeers.com; ☺ 11.30–22.00 Mon–Thu, 11.30–23.30 Fri & Sat. Good beer, bad food. The beers made on tap are popular & their deck can't be beaten on a sunny Anchorage afternoon. Occasionally closed on Sun. $$$

♀ **The Moose's Tooth Pub & Pizzeria** [184–5 D2] 3300 Old Seward Hwy; ✆ 258 ALES; www.moosestooth.net. A great selection of beers & wonderful pizza. Fantastic homemade root beer.

ENTERTAINMENT AND NIGHTLIFE In addition to the city's many bars and clubs, Anchorage also has a vibrant music and performing arts scene. The city centre has some good options for the kids and a number of movie theatres show films every day.

The *Anchorage Daily News* and the *Anchorage Press* both print the latest shows to hit town. The Anchorage Zoo (see page 208) hosts live music on Friday at 19.00. The visitor centre puts on live music shows on Wednesday and Friday from 12.00–13.00. **Alaska Center for The Performing Arts** [190–1 D5] (*621 W 6th Av*; ✆ *263 2900*; *ww.alaskapac.org*) offers performances and music shows through the summer. The Anchorage Symphony Orchestra and the Anchorage Opera both play here. The

---

GAY BARS IN ANCHORAGE

Some gay hangouts in Anchorage include: **Kodiak Café** (*225 E 5th Av*; ✆ *258 5233*) which is next to **Mad Myrna's** (*530 E 5th Av*; ✆ *276 9762*) and **The Raven** (*708 E 4th Av*; ✆ *276 9672*).

lobby has a great collection of native masks and inside a film about the northern lights plays hourly every day. The **Egan Center** [190–1 D4] (*555 West 5th Av; www.anchorageconventiondistrict.com*) hosts conferences and also puts on shows. The **Anchorage Concert Association** (*430 West 7th Av;* ☏ *272 1471; www.anchorageconcerts.org*) brings music, dance and theatre to town all year. **Cyrano's Off-Center Playhouse** (*413 D St;* ☏ *274 2599; www.cyranos.org*), **Out North Contemporary Art House** (*3800 DeBarr Rd;* ☏ *279 3800; www.outnorth.org*) and the **Anchorage Community Theatre** [184–5 D4] (*1133 E 70th Av;* ☏ *344 4713; www.actalaska.org*) put on plays all year.

Alaska Experience Theatre [190–1 E3] 333 West 4th Av; ☏ 276 3730. 2 films — *Alaska the Greatland* (length: 45mins; ticket: US$11) & *Earthquake* (length: 20mins; ticket: US$6) — are shown several times an hour all summer. The earthquake film is shown in a theatre with shaking seats.

Beartooth Theatre Pub [184–5 C2] A theatre as well as a restaurant & a concert venue. Eat pizza & sip beer while you watch a movie or a performance.

Chef's Inn 825 W Northern Lights Blvd; ☏ 272 1341. Food, booze & blues.

Chilkoot Charlie's [184–5 C2] 2435 Spenard Rd; ☏ 272 1010; www.koots.com; ⊕ 11.00–03.00

Mon–Fri, 11.30–03.00 Sat & Sun. There are 8 bars on 3 floors with different music & scenes everywhere you turn. Live music every night of the week & crowded on the w/ends. Cover charges are US$2 Thu & US$5 Fri & Sat. Free the rest of the week.

Humpy's Great Alaskan Alehouse [190–1 D5] (see page 199) A large selection of beers as well as food & a regular supply of decent music from Alaska & beyond.

The Snow Goose [190–1 C3] (see page 199) Live music throughout the week with local music & no cover charge on Sat. The in-house theatre plays an Alaskan spoof show called *Hullabaloo* every evening.

Cinema The largest cinemas in town are the **Century 16** (*301 East 36th Av;* ☏ *770 2602*), **Regal Fireweed 7** (*661 East Fireweed Ln;* ☏ *566 3328*) and the **Dimond Center 9** (*Dimond Mall*). All three play movies all day, every day; tickets cost US$9–10.

Up the road in Wasilla and Eagle River are the **Valley River 6 Cinemas** (*11701 Business Blvd;* ☏ *694 5858*) and the **Mat-Su Cinema** (*2430 E Parks Hwy;* ☏ *373 7003*). Finally, also worth a visit is **Beartooth Theatre Pub** [184–5 C2] (*1230 W 27th Av;* ☏ *276 4200; www.beartooththeatre.net;* ⊕ *11.00–22.30 Mon–Sat, 12.00–11.30 Sun*). Established by the owners of the Moose's Tooth, the Beartooth has beer, pizza (**$$$**), and movies (US$3). Was a better idea ever conceived?

FESTIVALS AND EVENTS The **Visitors' Bureau** (*www.anchorage.net*) has a complete listing of the many events that take place each summer. The Iditarod and Fur Rendezvous are popular events that happen in March and February, respectively. The Anchorage International Film Fest in December is also a lot of fun.

January
Great Alaskan Beer and Barleywine Festival (*www.auroraproductions.net/beer-barley.html*) A beer-centric festival at the Egan Center taking place in mid-January..

Anchorage Folk Festival (*www.anchoragefolkfestival.org*) A free music event held during the last ten days of the month often with more than 100 bands from Alaska and around the world.

February
Duct Tape Ball (*http://octanecreative.com/ducttape/ducttapeball/index.html*) Held in the first few days of the month, this fun event features art and clothing made entirely from duct tape.

Fur Rendezvous (see page 68)

March
Iditarod Sled Dog Race (see page 69)

Miners and Trappers Ball (*www.minersandtrappersball.org*) Held during the first week of the month, this event features a 'Mr Fur Face competition', a beard competition, music, food and dancing.

April
Arctic Man Classic (✎ *456 2626; www.arcticman.com*) This crazy event involves the combination of snowboarders, snowmobiles and a lot of speed. As many as 15,000 people head out to Summit Lake at mile 195 of the Richardson Hwy 8–12 April to watch the mayhem.

Alyeska Spring Carnival & Slush Cup (✎ *754 1111; www.alyeskaresort.com*) Skiing, snowboarding and crazy costumed events at Alyeska Mountain in Girdwood 23–26 April.

Heart Run (✎ *263 2014; www.heartrun.com*) The largest foot race in the state starts at 09.00 25 April at the UAA arts building.

May
Anchorage Market & Festival (see page 197) The market starts up on 16 May and runs throughout the summer.

June
Alaska Oceans Festival (✎ *274 3647; www.alaskaoceansfestival.org*) Music and events oriented around the state's connection to the ocean. Takes place 12.00–22.00 6 June at West Delaney Park.

Arctic Thunder (✎ *552 7469; www.elmendorf.af.mil*) The Elmendorf Air Force Base puts on a fantastic air show every June to show its appreciation to the people of Alaska.

Salmon in the City Festival (*www.muni.org/salmoninthecity*) Held 5–14 June, this is a celebration of the city's healthy salmon runs. Events include the 'Slam'n Salm'n' Salmon Derby, ecological talks and other salmon oriented events.

Three Barons Renaissance Fair (✎ *868 8012; www.3barons.org*) Held 7–15 June, this is a bizarre and hilarious medieval event for all ages.

July
4 July Celebration (✎ *279 7500*) Parades, fireworks and other patriotic events at Delaney Park.

Bear Paw Festival (✎ *694 4702; www.cer.org*) Held 8–12 July, the Bear Paw Festival features a salmon cook-off, foot race, live music and food at Eagle River.

Sadler's Ultra Challenge (✎ *344 7399; www.challenge.ak.org*) Held 19–27 July, this is a 267-mile race across southcentral Alaska by wheelchair! The strongest and toughest handicapped contestants in the world take part in this challenge.

Girdwood Forest Fair (see page 71) Held in the first week of the month in Girdwood south of Anchorage.

August
Alaska State Fair (✆ 745 4827; *www.alaskastatefair.org*) Held 27 August–7 September in Palmer, north of Anchorage, Alaska State Fair is the largest of its kind. Music, crafts, food... and veggies so freakishly large on display, they give children nightmares.

Talkeetna Bluegrass Festival (see page 284) Dirty, rowdy and completely awesome music festival held in Talkeetna in the first week of the month.

October
Make it Alaska Festival (*www.miafestival.com/festival_gen_info.html*) A large fair of Alaskan-made products. US$6 admission.

December
New Years Fire and Ice Extravaganza (see page 72)

SHOPPING Shopping options in Anchorage are definitely more exciting for rural Alaskans than for visiting tourists. Rural Alaskans will travel for days to have the opportunity to shop in one of the city's large stores such as Costco or Sam's Club. The city centre, with its galleries and souvenirs shops, is where most visitors will do their shopping. The 3rd and 4th Avenues are lined with gift shops selling every manner of trinket and craft, from embarrassing bald eagles made in China to truly extraordinary garments, jewellery and other crafts made by Alaskan artists. The Anchorage Market and Festival (see page 197) is a good place to grab lunch and buy locally made gifts and crafts.

Anchorage has a number of malls, selling all the usual stuff. The **5th Avenue Mall** (*320 W 5th Av*) has more than 100 stores including Nordstrom and JCPenney and is located in the city centre. The **Dimond Center Mall** (*800 E Dimond Blvd; www.dimondcenter.com*) houses more than 200 shops, including the electronics giant Best Buy as well as the Dimond 9 Cinema. Others include the **Mall at Sears** (*600 E Northern Lights Blvd*) in the centre of town and the **Northway Mall** (*3101 Penland Pkwy*) near Merrill Field Airport. **Nordstrom** (*603 D St;* ✆ *279 7622; www.nordstrom.com;* ⏰ *10.00–21.00 Mon–Sat, 11.00–18.00 Sun*) and **JCPenny** (*406 W 5th Av;* ✆ *279 5656; www.jcpenney.com;* ⏰ *10.00–21.00 Mon–Fri, 10.00–20.00 Sat, 11.00–18.00 Sun*) both sell just about everything except food and are located in the city centre.

Bookshops In addition to the commercial bookshops of **Barnes and Noble** (*200 E Northern Lights Blvd;* ✆ *279 7323*) and **Borders** (*1100 E Dimond Blvd;* ✆ *344 4099*), Anchorage has some great independent booksellers.

Title Wave Books Downtown [190–1 E4] 415 W 5th Av; ✆ 258 9283; www.wavebooks.com; ⏰ 10.00–18.00 daily. Lots of new & used books, as well as coffee.

Title Wave Books Midtown 1360 W Northern Lights Blvd; ✆ 278 9283; ⏰ 10.00–20.00 Mon–Thu, 10.00–21.00 Fri & Sat, 11.00–19.00 Sun. The other location, in midtown near REI.

Food shopping
Costco 330 W Dimond Blvd; ✆ 349 2335; www.costco.com. If you haven't been to a Costco grocery before, head on over & witness the scale of American consumerism. Memberships are required, so tell the doorman you are considering joining.
Fred Meyers 1000 E Northern Lights Blvd; ✆ 264 9600; www.fredmeyer.com. A complete selection of

foods incl a deli, bulk & organic foods. Other locations can be found at 7701 Debarr Rd, 2300 Abbott Rd & 2000 W Dimond Blvd. **Natural Pantry** 3801 Old Seward Hwy; ✎ 770 1444; www.natural-pantry.com. Lunch foods & natural foods. **New Sagaya's Midtown Market** 3700 Old Seward Hwy; ✎ 561 5173, 800 764 1001 (TF);

www.newsagaya.com. A fantastic Asian market in the middle of town. The other branch is called New Sagaya's City Market (*900 W 13th Av;* ✎ *274 6173*). **Safeway/Carrs** 7731 E Northern Lights Blvd; ✎ 331 1700; www.safeway.com. Groceries & a pharmacy. Other branches can also be found at 3101 Penland Parkway & 5600 Debarr Rd.

Galleries
Anchorage participates in the 'first Friday' tradition whereby galleries open their doors and serve wine and appetisers on the first Friday of each month. An Art Walk map is printed in the Thursday edition of the *Anchorage Press*. Though they are not for sale, the Alaska Center for Performing Arts (see page 199) has a wonderful collection of 23 native Alaskan masks on display in their lobby. The Snow City Café (see page 198) hangs a new collection of local art every month. To buy photographs and other local art, check out the Anchorage Market and Festival (see page 197).

Arctic Rose Gallery [190–1 A4] 420 L St; ✎ 279 3911; www.articrosegallery.com; ☉ 12.00–21.00 Mon–Fri, 17.00–21.00 Sat & Sun. Paintings, sculpture, ceramics & glass by local artists.
Artique [190–1 C3] 314 G St; ✎ 277 1663; www.artiqueltd.com; ☉ 11.00–17.00 Tue–Sat. A wide variety of styles & media are represented in this 'Alaskana' gallery.

International Gallery of Contemporary Art [190–1 E4] 427 D St; ✎ 279 1116; www.igcaalaska.org; ☉ 12.00–16.00 Tue–Sun. A very modern gallery showcasing Alaska's most cutting edge artists.
Mts Gallery 3142 Mountain View Dr; www.mtsgallery.wordpress.com; ☉ 16.00–20.00 Wed & Fri, 12.00–16.00 Sat & Sun. A non-profit gallery dedicated to pushing the visual & performing arts in Alaska.

Gift shops
To find gifts, one need look no further than 4th Avenue in the city centre.

Anchorage Museum Shop [190–1 F5] (see page 209) A good selection of native crafts, souvenirs & Alaska themed books.
The Kobuk [190–1 D4] 504 W. 5th Av; ✎ 272 3626; www.kobukcoffee.com; ☉ 11.00–18.00

Mon–Sat. Right next to Town Square Park, this gift/coffee shop has a somewhat uninspired selection of gifts, but a lovely little coffee house in the back. Baked goods, teas & coffee are served.

Native arts
Alaska Native Arts Foundation [190–1 E5] 500 W 6th Av; ✎ 258 2623, 800 979 2623 (TF); www.alaskanativearts.org; ☉ 10.00–17.30 Mon–Sat. A large selection of work from around the state.
Alaska Native Heritage Center Gift Shop 8800 Heritage Center Dr; ✎ 330 8000, 800 315 6608 (TF); www.alaskanative.net; ☉ 09.00–18.00 daily. Artwork from the Tlingit, Haida, Aleut, Yup'ik, Athabascan & Inupiat people.
Alaska Native Medical Center Craft Shop 4315 Diplomacy Dr; ✎ 729 1122; www.anmc.org; ☉ 10.00–14.00 Mon–Fri & the 1st & 3rd Sat of

each month from 11.00–14.00. One of the best places in town to buy Alaskan native crafts. Masks, baskets, dolls, ivory & beadwork are all sold on commission for the artists.
Oomingmak Musk Ox Producers Co-operative [190–1 C5] 604 H St; ✎ 272 9225, 888 360 9665 (TF); www.qiviut.com; ☉ 09.00–21.00 daily. Forget high tech fabrics, *qiviut* (the belly hair of a musk ox) is eight times warmer than wool & much more lightweight. The Co-op is owned by 250 native Alaskan women from around Alaska.

Outdoor
Alaska Mountaineering & Hiking 2633 Spenard Rd; ✎ 272 1811; www.alaskamountaineering.com; ☉ 09.00–17.00 Mon–Fri, 09.00–18.00 Sat,

12.00–18.00 Sun. AMH, as the locals call it, is the small independent outdoor shop in town. Located near REI, but with more knowledgeable staff.

Alaska Raft & Kayak 401 W Tudor Rd; ☎ 561 7238, 800 606 5950 (TF); www.alaskaraftandkayak.com; ⏰ 10.00–18.00 Tue–Sat. Specialises in river & running gear, but also has general camping & outdoor gear.

Mountainview Sports Center 3838 Old Seward Hwy; ☎ 563 8600; www.mtviewsports.com; ⏰ 10.00–19.00 Mon–Sat, 10.00–18.00 Sun. A great place to get fishing equipment & general camping supplies.

REI 1200 W Northern Lights Blvd; ☎ 272 4565; www.rei.com; ⏰ 10.00–20.00 Mon–Fri, 10.00–19.00 Sat, 11.00–18.00 Sun. Despite their national expansion, this outdoor chain is still one of the better places to buy outdoor gear. Check the 'used gear' section for good deals.

OTHER PRACTICALITIES
Banks
$ Key Bank ☎ 888 539 4249; www.key.com. Branches can be found at: 601 W Fifth Av (☎ 257 5502, ⏰ 10.00–18.00 Mon–Fri); 101 West Benson Blvd(☎ 562 6100, ⏰ 10.00–18.00 Mon–Fri, 10.00–15.00 Sat); 9041 Old Seward Hwy,(☎ 267 3865, ⏰ 09.00–18.00 Mon–Fri, 11.00–14.00 Sat); 10928 Eagle River Rd (*located in Eagle River;* ☎ 694 4464, ⏰ 10.00–19.00 Mon–Fri, 11.00–15.00 Sat)

$ Wells Fargo 320 W 5th Av, ☎ 297 2557, ⏰ 10.00–18.00 Mon–Fri; www.wellsfargo.com. ATMs can be found at 1500 E 5th Av, 320 W 5th Av, & 500 Hollywood Dr

$ Northrim Bank 550 W 7th Av; ☎ 263 3226; www.northrim.com. Other branches can be found at:

811 E 36th Av (☎ 261 6241, ⏰ 09.00–18.00 Mon–Fri); 1501 E Huffman Rd (*inside Carrs;* ☎ 348 5334, ⏰ 10.00–19.00 Mon–Fri, 10.00–16.00 Sat); 9170 Jewel Lake Rd (☎ 266 7448, ⏰ 09.00–18.00 Mon–Fri, 10.00–15.00 Sat); 3111 C St (☎ 562 0062, ⏰ 09.00–18.00 Mon–Fri, 10.00–15.00 Sat); 517 W 7th Av (☎ 263 3226, ⏰ 10.00–18.00 Mon–Fri); 8730 Old Seward Hwy (☎ 522 8886, ⏰ 09.00–18.00 Mon–Fri, 10.00–15.00 Sat); 2709 Spenard Rd (☎ 263 3389, ⏰ 09.00–18.00 Mon–Fri, 10.00–15.00 Sat). ATMs open 24hrs can be found at all the listed branches & at the Sulivan Arena (*1600 Gambell*), & Bear Tooth Theatre & Pub (*1230 W 27th Av*).

Healthcare
Pharmacies
Fred Meyers 1000 E Northern Lights Blvd; ☎ 264 9600; www.fredmeyer.com; ⏰ 09.00–21.00 Mon–Fri, 09.00–19.00 Sat, 10.00–18.00 Sun. Other branches can be found at: 7701 Debarr Rd (☎ 269 1700; ⏰ 09.00–21.00 Mon–Fri, 09.00–18.00 Sat, 10.00–18.00 Sun), 2300 Abbott Rd (☎ 365 2000; ⏰ 09.00–21.00 Mon–Fri, 09.00–19.00 Sat, 10.00–18.00 Sun) & 2000 W Dimond Blvd (☎ 267 6700; ⏰ 09.00–21.00 Mon–Fri, 09.00–18.00 Sat, 10.00–18.00 Sun)

Geneva Woods Pharmacy 501 W Intl Airport Rd; ☎ 565 6100; www.genevawoods.com;

⏰ 09.00–18.00 Mon–Fri, 08.00–17.00 Sat.

Safeway/Carrs 1340 Gambell St; ☎ 339 0200; www.safeway.com; ⏰ 09.00–19.00 Mon–Sat (grocery store ⏰ 24hrs). Other locations can be found at: 600 E Northern Lights Blvd (☎ 297 0600; ⏰ 09.00–19.00 Mon–Sat, 10.00–19.00 Sun) & at 1650 W Northern Lights Blvd (☎ 297 0500; ⏰ 09.00–21.00 Mon–Fri, 09.00–19.00 Sat & Sun)

Wal-Mmart 8900 Old Seward Hwy; ☎ 344 7300; www.walmart.com; ⏰ 09.00–21.00 Mon–Fri, 09.00–19.00 Sat

Hospitals
✚ **Alaska Regional Hospital** [184–5 E1] 2801 Debarr Rd; ☎ 276 1131; www.alaskaregional.com

✚ **Providence Alaska Medical Center** 3200 Providence Dr; ☎ 565 6400; www.providence.org

Dentists
Burton Miller 2600 Denali St; ☎ 277 2600
Jerry Zemlicka 1330 Annapolis Dr; ☎ 789 0131

Nathan Lukes 3340 Arctic Blvd; ☎ 561 5154
Stephen Maloney 1020 W Fireweed Ln; ☎ 277 7667

Internet The internet – increasingly wireless – can be accessed all over Anchorage. Most cafés, hotels and public libraries in town offer the service for free. Try www.wififreespot.com.

Libraries All Anchorage's libraries offer internet and a cosy place to spend the day with a book.

Muldoon Library [184–5 G1] 5530 E Northern Lights Blvd; ✎ 338 4590; http://lexicon.ci.anchorage.ak.us; ⊕ 10.00–20.00 Tue–Thu, 10.00–18.00 Fri & Sat.
Samson-Dimond Library [184–5 D5] 800 E Dimond Blvd; ✎ 343 4051; ⊕ 10.00–20.00 Tue–Thu, 10.00–18.00 Fri & Sat. Located inside the Diamond Centre.
Z J Loussac Library 3600 Denali St; ✎ 343 2983;

⊕ 10.00–21.00 Mon–Thu, 10.00–18.00 Fri & Sat, 13.00–17.00 Sun.
Chugiak-Eagle River Library 12001 Business Blvd; ✎ 343 1531; ⊕ 10.00–20.00 Tue–Thu, 10.00–18.00 Fri & Sat.
Mountain View Branch Library [184–5 E1] 120 S Bragaw; ✎ 343 2983; http://lexicon.ci.anchorage.ak.us. This brand new library should be open in 2010.

Post offices Anchorage has many post offices but only a few are convenient for the city centre. Others can be searched for on www.usps.com.

✉ **Downtown Post Office** [190–1 E3] 344 W 3rd Av; ✎ 279 9188; ⊕ 10.00–17.30 Mon–Fri
✉ **Eastchester Post Office** 800 Ingra St; ✎ 272 8266; ⊕ 10.00–17.30 Mon–Fri

✉ **5th Avenue Post Office** 320 W 5th Av; ✎ 276 6790; ⊕ 10.00–18.00 Mon–Fri

WHAT TO SEE

Most visitors spend the majority of their time in the city centre, and rightly so, as nearly everything is within walking distance and there is a lot to do. The midtown area is also a lively place filled with shopping malls, large stores and wide, grey streets that conceal countless eateries, shops, bars, clubs and parks.

City Centre When the city of Anchorage decides to spend money on city beautification, they usually dump the whole lot into the city centre. While some hidden gems exist around the whole town, the centre is where most visitors want to be. The first and most obvious sight is the **Visitor Centre** [190–1 D4] (see page 189). Log cabins were never the norm in Anchorage, but the city decided that a sod-roofed log-cabin visitor centre would be emblematic of the state's frontier spirit. Built in 1955 for US$8,000, it didn't incur any damage until recently when the original builder, John R King, was brought in to sort out some stray grass roots on the roof that were pushing through and creating leaks. Behind the visitor centre, is the two-storey, historic **City Hall**. While the structure may not look special to most visitors, it was quite unique and the only building of its kind in 1930s Anchorage. During its heyday, the building housed every branch of the city government, from the mayor's office to the fire department and it even had three jail cells. The lobby has a free exhibition about early Anchorage and city tours leave at 13.00 Monday–Friday all summer. One block north at the corner of 3rd Avenue and C Street is the **Anchorage Market and Festival** [190–1 F3] (see page 197) held every weekend all summer. Grab lunch, listen to music or shop for arts and crafts.

At 4th Avenue and G Street, the historic **4th Avenue Theatre** was built in 1947 entirely in Art Deco style. The building is currently closed, but there is talk of it re-opening to the public. The **Alaska Statehood Monument** [190–1 E2] (*2nd Av & E St*) commemorates 3 January 1959, when President Eisenhower made Alaska the 49th state.

Where 3rd Avenue bends to the south and joins L Street, the **Resolution Park** and **Captain Cook Monument** [190–1 A3] look out over Cook Inlet. In 1778, Captain Cook anchored off the coast looking for the fabled Northwest Passage.

Anchorage is blessed with almost 11,000 acres of parkland, 223 parks and 250 miles of trails, not to mention the half-million-acre Chugach State Park, right in the city's backyard.

CHUGACH STATE PARK Many Anchorage residents consider the half-million-acre Chugach State Park to be both their backyard and their playground. Fishing, hiking, mountain biking, skiing, rafting and many other activities can be enjoyed here. Despite its proximity to the urban centre of Anchorage, the park is still very wild and wildlife is common once off the beaten track.

Getting there The Chugach State Park is accessible by vehicle from either the Seward Highway, between Anchorage and Girdwood or from the Glenn Highway, between Anchorage and Palmer.

Tourist information
☑ DNR Public Information Center 550 W 7th Av, Ste 1260; ☎ 269 8400; www.dnr.alaska.gov/parks/units/chugach/index.htm. Located in Anchorage.
☑ Eagle River Nature Center 32750 Eagle River Rd; ☎ 694 2108; www.ernc.org. Located 45mins north of Anchorage at the end of Eagle River Rd. Daily guided walks & interpretive programs available. Those not renting a cabin or yurt from the Nature Center must pay US$5 to park.

Where to stay Three campsites can be found in the park: the Eagle River and Eklutna Lake campgrounds are north of Anchorage, while the Bird Creek Campground is south of the city. These are all developed campgrounds with water, toilets and tables.

⅄ Bird Creek Campground (28 sites) South of Anchorage, in the woods off the Seward Hwy at mile 101. Pitches cost US$15/night. The park has one public-use cabin at Yuditna Creek, a shelter at Serenity Falls, plus cabins & yurts for rent at the Eagle River Nature Center.
⅄ Eklutna Lake Campground (57 sites) Found 45 mins north of Anchorage, off the Eklutna Exit at mile 26. The campground is 10 miles from the highway. It costs US$10/night.
⅄ Eagle River Campground (57 sites) ☎ 694 7982; 12 miles north of Anchorage, 1 mile before the city of Eagle River. US$15/night. Half the sites are available for reservation.
⅄ The Yuditna Creek Cabin Sleeps 6 & is located 3 miles from the parking area at the end of Eklutna Lake Rd, north of Anchorage. It costs US$50/night.
⅄ Serenity Falls public-use hut Sleeps 13 in sgl or dbl bunks for US$10–15/night. The hut is located 12 miles down the Lakeside Trail at Eklutna Lake. Guests can walk or bike in. ATVs (all-terrain vehicles) are allowed Sun–Wed. Reservations can be made at the DNR Public Information Center (550 W 7th Av, Ste 1260; ☎ 269 8400) or at www.dnr.alaska.gov/parks/cabins/anch.htm.
⅄ Eagle River Nature Center Rent a cabin & a yurt for US$65/night. The cabin sleeps 8 & is in a secluded & quiet setting. The yurt sleeps 4. Call to reserve.

What to see and do A huge collection of trails can be found in the park. Near Eagle River, the Eklutna Lakeside Trail starts at the end of Eklutna Lake Road and follows the lake for seven miles before meeting the Eklutna Glacier. Also in Eagle River, the Eagle River Nature Center has a network of trails. Hillside Drive divides the suburbs from the wilderness and this is where many trailheads are located. For others see the Anchorage Hiking and Recreation section.

Eagle River offers rafting for all difficulty levels. Access is from the Eagle River Road off the Glenn Highway north of Anchorage. Lifetime Adventures (☎ 746 4644; www.lifetimeadventures.net) offers rafting trips from 1–3hrs for US$30–75, depending on how much white-water you would like.

INDEPENDENCE MINE STATE HISTORICAL PARK AND SUMMIT LAKE STATE RECREATION SITE North of Palmer in the Talkeetna Mountains, Hatcher Pass is a magnet for outdoor enthusiasts as well as history buffs. The Independence Mine and the Summit Lake State Recreation Site in Hatcher Pass are accessible from the George Parks Highway in Willow or from Palmer off the Glenn Highway. A winding gravel road makes its way through the mountains with clear mountain lakes, creeks and tundra everywhere. Excellent hiking can be found off the road and even paragliders and rock climbers regularly visit. The area was developed by Robert Lee Hatcher after gold was discovered in 1886. A collection of 22 families lived in Boomtown nearby and in 1941 the mine employed 204 men and made US$1,204,560. In 1943, the government closed the mine because of World War II. After another brief period of activity, the mine closed for good in 1951. In the late 1970s, the mine and some 270 acres of land were donated to the state. Today, mining equipment and buildings are scattered around the landscape of towering mountains, rolling tundra and clear water creeks.

Practicalities
▣ The Independence Mine State Historical Park Visitor Center ☏ 745 2827; ⏱ 11.00–18.00 daily. Can be found north of the road & west of the pass. Displays about the mine's history & guided walks are available. The centre offers guided tours starting 4 June at 13.00 & 15.00.
Summit Lake State Recreation Site Located at mile 19 on Hatcher Pass Road, just west of the Independence Mine State Historic Park at an elevation of 3,886ft. Summit Lake perches on the edge of a spectacular drop where paragliders regularly take flight. The lake is ringed by a very short trail but more paths follow the ridges on both sides of the road. For excellent views & another gorgeous & less crowded lake, hike east & uphill to April Bowl. For more information visit the Mat-Su Park Office at mile 0.7 (*Bogard Rd;* ☏ 745 3975).

NANCY LAKE STATE RECREATION AREA Located near the town of Willow, 90 minutes by car north of Anchorage, the Nancy Lake State Recreation Area is a 22,685-acre canoeist's paradise. Interconnecting lakes form 'canoe trails' ideal for fishing and spotting moose, migratory birds and beavers, all of which are relatively common in the area. The Lynx Lake Loop canoe trail is a well-marked route traversing eight miles of linked lakes. The trip can be easily done in a single day. Canoeists can also paddle down the Susitna River from mile 57 of the George Parks Highway and portage into the Nancy lakes. The Susitna is an easy river to paddle and provides an adventurous approach to the lakes. Canoes can be rented in Willow from Tippecanoe Rentals (☏ 495 6688; *www.paddlealaska.com*) in Willow. Those in non-motorised boats may want to stick to the lakes where motorised boats are banned, at least at weekends. Motorised boats are allowed on Nancy, Lynx, Butterfly and Red Shirt lakes. All others are motor-free.

The park is not ideal for hiking but the Red Shirt Lake Trail provides decent views. The three-mile trail starts across from the entrance to South Rolly Lake Campground at the end of Nancy Lake Parkway.

Where to stay The park has two campgrounds with the usual amenities for US$10 per night. The first has 30 sites and is located just off the George Parks Highway at mile 66.5. The second, South Rolly Lake Campground, has 96 sites and is located 6.5 miles off the George Parks Highway at the end of Nancy Lake Parkway.

Public-use cabins can be found on the Red Shirt (US$45), Lynx (US$35), Nancy (US$45), James (US$45) and Bald (US$60) lakes. Reserve cabins by calling the Mat-Su Park office (*Mile 0.7, Bogard Rd;* ☏ 745 3975) or by visiting dnr.alaska.gov/parks/cabins/matsu.

For more information, visit the Nancy Lake Ranger Station (☏ 495 6273) on Nancy Lake Parkway or the Mat-Su Park Office (see above).

Between the Captain Cook Monument and the beach is the 11-mile **Tony Knowles Coastal Trail** [190–1 A3]. Walk or bike the paved path from 2nd Avenue to Kincaid Park, enjoying mountains and ocean views all the way. The **Oscar Anderson House** is located just southwest of the Captain Cook Monument at the end of M Street on the ocean. Running parallel to the city centre is **Ship Creek**, a historic landmark in its own right but also a popular place to fish and watch salmon spawn.

Around town Off W Northern Lights Boulevard, just past Satellite Drive, **Earthquake Park** [184–5 A2] commemorates the 1964 Good Friday earthquake (see page 219). Displays detail the event. Just to the south, **Hood Lake** is the busiest seaplane base on Earth with as many as 600 planes coming and going per day. On the southwest side of the lake, the **Alaska Aviation Heritage Museum** is a must-see. South of town off the Seward Highway is the **Anchorage Coastal Wildlife Refuge** at Potters Marsh. Following part of the 16-mile wetlands is a raised boardwalk with informational placards. A total of 130 species of birds have been seen here.

Alaska Botanical Gardens [184–5 G3] (*4601 Campbell Airstrip Rd;* ✆ *770 3692; www.alaskabg.org;* ⊕ *24hrs; US$5/free adult/child*) A few miles of trails wind through 110 acres of forests and native plants. Guided tours leave every day at 13.00. The People Mover bus #75 stops nearby. There is also a gift shop (⊕ *10.00–17.00 Tue–Sun*).

Alaska Zoo [184–5 F6] (*4731 O'Malley Rd;* ✆ *346 3242; www.alaskazoo.org;* ⊕ *09.00–18.00 daily; US$12/6 adult/child*). A great collection of Alaskan wildlife. See it here in case you miss it elsewhere. Be sure to visit at 19.00 on Tuesday for a lecture, or Friday at the same time for live music on the lawn. The Zoo Shuttle stops at most of the centre's major hotels.

Elmendorf State Hatchery [184–5 E1] (*Reeve Blvd & Post Rd;* ✆ *274 0065;* ⊕ *08.00–22.00 daily; free admission*). See the inner workings of a Fish and Game salmon hatchery. See king salmon late May–July and silver salmon August–September. The viewing deck will be closed until 2011 or 2012. Tour the hatchery from 08.00–16.00 Monday–Friday.

Museums

Alaska Aviation Heritage Museum [184–5 A3] (*4721 Aircraft Dr;* ✆ *248 5325; www.alaskaairmuseum.org;* ⊕ *09.00–17.00 daily US$10/6 adult/child*) Right on Lake Hood – the busiest seaplane base on Earth – the museum houses a number of planes in hangars as well as bits and pieces from World War II Japanese and US planes collected in the Aleutian Islands. This is a wonderfully detailed account of the aviation history of Alaska.

Alaska Heritage Museum (*301 W Northern Lights Blvd;* ✆ *265 2834; www.wellsfargohistory.com/museums;* ⊕ *12.00–16.00 Mon–Fri; free admission*) Located in the lobby of the Wells Fargo Bank, this private museum has a great collection of books, documents and Alaskan native artefacts.

Alaska Museum of Natural History [184–5 F1] (*201 N Bragaw;* ✆ *274 2400; www.alaskamuseum.org;* ⊕ *09.00–17.00 Mon–Sat, 12.00–17.00 Sun; US$5/3 adult/child*) This museum has a decent collection of mineral and fossil samples from around the state, as well as other natural history information.

Alaska Native Heritage Center *(8800 Heritage Center Dr;* ✆ *330 8000;*
www.alaskanative.net; ◷ *09.00–17.00 daily; US$25/17 adult/child).* The museum
provides an excellent, if somewhat expensive, introduction to the state's native
cultures and traditions. A joint ticket can be purchased for US$26 for both the
Anchorage Museum and the Alaska Native Heritage Center. A free bus travels
between the two.

Alaska State Trooper Museum [190–1 F4] *(245 W 5th Av;* ✆ *279 5050;*
www.alaskatroopermuseum.com; ◷ *10.00–16.00 Mon–Fri, 12.00–16.00 Sat; free
admission)* This museum commemorates Alaska's State Troopers – the brave souls
in uniform who attempted to bring law and order to this great land.

Anchorage Museum [190–1 F5] *(121 W 7th Av;* ✆ *343 4326;*
www.anchoragemuseum.org; ◷ *09.00–18.00 daily; US$8/2 adult/child)* Alaska has just
a few things worth doing indoors; this is one of them. The Anchorage Museum
has displays, films and art which chronicle 10,000 years of Alaskan history.
Travelling shows spice up the permanent collection. The Marx Brothers Café
(see page 197) runs a kitchen here serving simple, but elegant, and scrumptious
food. You'll also find The Imaginarium *(625 C St;* ✆ *929 9201;*
www.imaginarium.org; ◷ *09.00–18.00 daily; US$10/7 adult/child),* a science
discovery centre for kids, here.

Oscar Anderson House *(420 M St,* ✆ *274 2336,* ◷ *13.30–17.30 Mon–Fri, US$3/1
adult/child)* An interesting 'museum' house built by a Swedish immigrant in 1915.
Many of the family's original possessions are still on show inside the house.

NORTH OF ANCHORAGE

The Susitna and Matanuska River Valleys form the area 35 miles north of
Anchorage known as the Mat-Su. Famous for its monstrous vegetables and
productive salmon rivers, the area is increasingly known for its unchecked urban
spread, particularly in Wasilla.

Palmer has lost little of its charm since impoverished Midwest farming families
were relocated there in the 1930s. Musk ox farms and the famous Alaska State Fair
can also be found in Palmer.

The Glenn Highway leads 35 miles north from Anchorage, past Eagle River,
dividing into the Glenn Highway and the George Parks Highway at the
Glenn/Parks Interchange. The George Parks Highway travels seven miles west
through Wasilla, then onto Willow for 27 miles after. The highway eventually
passes the Denali National Park and ends in Fairbanks. Follow the Glenn
Highway northeast at the Glenn/Parks Interchange and enter a land where
American pastoral meets rugged mountains. The scenic Glenn Highway
continues to Glennallen and Valdez. The Palmer-Wasilla Highway and the
Hatcher Pass Road connect Wasilla and Palmer.

EAGLE RIVER *(Population: 30,000)* Eagle River (✜ 61°19'12"N, 149°34'19"W) is 13
miles north of Anchorage off the Glenn Highway. The area was filled with
homesteads in the 1940s and 1950s and, because of its proximity to Anchorage, has
grown significantly. Today, the city consists mostly of residential neighbourhoods,
chain restaurants and large stores. The main reason to visit this part of Alaska is the
Eagle River that flows through a lovely valley from deep within Chugach State
Park. Eagle River Road follows the river for almost 13 miles and allows boating
visitors access to the class II–IV river. At the end of the road is the **Eagle River**

Nature Center (see page 206) with natural history displays, hiking trails, accommodations and general information about the park. The Iditarod–Crow Pass Trail (see page 221) starts here.

Be sure to check out the **Bear Paw Festival** taking place in mid-July. Camping is available at the **Eagle River Campground** (see page 206) and north of town at **Eklutna State Campground** (see page 206). The Danaina Athabascan village of **Eklutna** (population: 350) is just off the highway 27 miles north of Anchorage. The Eklutna Lake Road provides access to Thunderbird Falls and the Eklutna Lake recreation area (see page 206) which has camping and hiking trails.

Tourist information
🛈 Chugiak–Eagle River Chamber of Commerce 11401 Old Glenn Hwy; ✆ 694 4702; www.cer.org

WASILLA (*Population 5,568*) An hour north of Anchorage, Wasilla (⊕ 61°34'54"N, 149°27'53"W) is quintessential 'Anytown, USA'. Malls, large stores and chain restaurants crowd the busy streets, while typical suburbs occupy the remaining spaces. The city is surrounded by the Chugach and Talkeetna mountains and a host of pleasant museums make a short stop here worthwhile. Wasilla was carved from the wilderness when the Alaska Railroad pushed through in 1917. Further growth in the region was fuelled by regional gold mining. Nearby, Palmer stole the spotlight in the 1930s and 1940s, when the Matanuska Valley started becoming the agricultural centre it is today. In the 1970s, the George Parks Highway was completed and Wasilla was directly connected to Anchorage. The immense growth of Anchorage has driven Wasilla's growth since then. Today, more than 30% of Wasilla's residents commute to Anchorage to work. Wasilla achieved international notoriety when local resident, former mayor, – and now former governor – Sarah Palin was named as John McCain's running mate in the 2008 US presidential election.

Getting there and away
By bus
Mat–Su Transit (✆ 376 5000; *www.matsutransit.com*) Also called MASCOT, the public buses serve the entire Mat-Su Valley and connect it with Anchorage. A journey anywhere in the valley costs US$2.50, a ride to Anchorage costs US$3.

By train
Alaska Railroad (*415 E Railroad Av; www.akrr.com*) From Anchorage, the fare is US$51/26 adult/child and, from Wasilla onto Denali costs US$117/59 adult/child and to Fairbanks costs US$167/84 adult/child.

By taxi
🚗 **Diamond Cab** ✆ 376 5592
🚗 **Mat-Su Independent Taxi** ✆ 373 5861
🚗 **Valley Cab Alaska** ✆ 357 8294

Tourist information
🛈 Wasilla Visitor Center 415 E Railroad Av; ✆ 376 1299; www.visitwasilla.org. Located near the Dorothy Page Museum (see page 212).

 Where to stay In addition to a number of pleasant B&Bs around town, generic hotels line the highway in Wasilla. For more help finding accommodation, contact the **Mat-Su Bed & Breakfast Association** (*www.alaskabnbhosts.com*), the **Mat-Su Convention & Visitors Bureau** (see page 213) or the **Wasilla Chamber of Commerce**. Three public campsites are situated near Wasilla, but be prepared for crowds at the weekends and during holidays.

⌂ **Agate Inn** (11 rooms) 4725 Begich Circle; ✆ 373 2290, 800 770 2290 (TF); www.agateinn.com. In addition to pleasant but simple rooms in a lovely wooded setting, this B&B has its own herd of reindeer! $$$

⌂ **Alaska Garden Gate B&B** (5 rooms) 950 South Trunk Rd; ✆ 746 2333; www.gardengatebnb.com. A lovely & secluded B&B in the woods with good views. A slight drawback is that guests are not allowed at the B&B at midday during cleaning. $$$

⌂ **Lake Lucille B&B** (4 rooms) 235 West Lakeview Av; ✆ 357 0352, 888 353 0352 (TF); www.alaskaslakelucillebnb.com. A lovely home & garden right on the lake. $$$

⌂ **Pioneer Ridge B&B** (7 rooms) 2221 Yukon Circle; ✆ 376 7472, 800 478 7472 (TF); www.pioneerridge.com. Quiet & off the beaten path, this B&B has great views, a friendly hostess & unique affordable rooms. Wi-Fi. $$$

⌂ **Wild Iris B&B** (3 rooms) 550 W Selina Ln; ✆ 357 4184; www.akwildirisbandb.com. Simple but pleasant rooms & an amazing location on Lake Lucille. Wi-Fi. $$$

⌂ **Shady Acres B&B** (2 rooms) 1000 Easy St; ✆ 376 3113, 800 360 3113 (TF); www.shadyacresbnb.com. Affordable, comfortable rooms in a cosy house. $$

⌂ **Gatehouse B&B** (3 rooms) 2500 Bogard Rd; ✆ 376 5960, 888 866 9326 (TF); www.gatehousealaska.com. Quaint cabins on Wasilla Lake. $$

Camping

▲ **Big Bear RV Park** (43 sites) MP 37 Parks Hwy; ✆ 745 7445. US$22. Wi-Fi.

▲ **Finger Lake Campground** (39 sites) Located near the end of Bogard Rd. Toilets, tables, water & lake access. Sites are US$10.

▲ **Lake Lucille Campground** (59 sites) ✆ 745 9690. Located off Knik-Goose Bay Rd, south of Wasilla. A pleasant wooded area on the lake with toilets, fire rings, tables, water & trails. Sites are US$10. Call for more information.

▲ **Little Susitna River Campground** (86 sites) Located near the town of Houston north of Wasilla at mile 57.4 of the Parks Hwy. Toilets, tables, water & access to the river. Sites are US$10. Call the city of Houston (✆ 892 6869) for more information.

✕ Where to eat

✕ **Alpine Garden Grille** Mile 45.2 Parks Hwy; ✆ 357 6313; www.alpinegardengrille.com; ⊕ 16.00–8.30 Wed–Sun. Fresh & often organic local foods are combined into breathtaking dishes. Make a reservation. $$$$

✕ **Settlers Bay Lodge** Mile 8, Knik-Goose Bay Rd; ✆ 357 5678; www.settlersbaylodge.com; ⊕ 17.00–closing. Good food & even better views. The dining area is decorated with a bar & large windows looking towards the Chugach Mountains. Dress up & bring a date. Seafood, steak & pasta. US$25 for entrées. $$$$

✕ **Bombay Valley** 991 S Hermon Rd; ✆ 376 9565; ⊕ 11.00–14.00 & 17.00–21.00 daily. Skilfully prepared Indian food. $$$

✕ **Chepo's Fiesta Restaurant** 731 W Parks Hwy; ✆ 373 5656; ⊕ 11.00–22.00 Mon–Fri, 11.00–23.00 Sat & Sun. Decent food & good prices. $$

✕ **Rib Shack** 3801 S Foothills Blvd; ✆ 376 7461. Mike grills the best meat in the Mat-Su. Highlights include corn fritters, pork & ribs. $$$

✕ **Windbreak Café** 2201 East Parks Hwy; ✆ 376 4484; www.windbreakalaska.com; ⊕ 06.00–23.00 Mon–Sat, 07.00–21.00 Sun. Locally known as the 'Trout House', the Windbreak is a fishy-themed joint with good dinner & b/fast menus served all day. $$$

✕ **Mekong Thai Cuisine** 473 W Parks Hwy; ✆ 373 7690; ⊕ 11.00–21.00 Mon–Fri, 12.00–21.00 Sat. Great Thai food in Wasilla. Located in the Wasilla Mall, off the Parks Hwy. $$

✕ **North Star Bakery** 4931 E Mayflower Ln; ✆ 357 2579; ⊕ 08.00–17.00 Mon–Tue. Tasty pastries, sandwiches, soup & hot drinks, all made from scratch. $

✕ **Tailgaters Sports Bar & Grill** 161 W Parks Hwy; ✆ 376 1314. Grab a pint & relax on the restaurant side, or get sloshed in the dive bar around back. $

Other practicalities

Carrs 595 E Parks Hwy; ☏ 352 1100; www.safeway.com; ⊕ 24hrs. A good selection of groceries & a pharmacy (⊕ 09.00–21.00 Mon–Fri, 09.00–19.00 Sat, 10.00–18.00 Sun).

Pandemonium Books 1325 E Palmer-Wasilla Hwy; ☏ 376 3939; www.akbookstore.com; ⊕ 06.30–22.00 Mon–Thu, 06.30–23.00 Fri & Sat, 08.00–20.00 Sun. The place to sip a hot drink & read a book on a rainy day. Music at the w/ends. Wi-Fi.

3 Rivers Fly & Tackle 390 Railroad Av; ☏ 373 5434; www.3riversflyandtackle.com. If you would like to hear the locals talk about the big one that got away, this is the place. There is no one more knowledgeable about local fishing than the owner, Mike Hudson.

Public library 391 N Main St; ☏ 376 5913; ⊕ 14.00–18.00 Mon, 10.00–20.00 Tue & Thu, 10.00–18.00 Wed & Fri, 13.00–17.00 Sat. Wi-Fi.

Post office 5050 E Dunbar Dr; ☏ 376 5008; www.usps.com; ⊕ 10.00–17.00 Mon–Fri, 10.00–15.00 Sat.

Fred Meyers 1601 E Parks Hwy; ☏ 352 5017; www.fredmeyer.com. A good selection of groceries & goods.

What to see and do

Dog Race Headquarters (*Mile 2.2, Knik-Goose Bay Rd;* ☏ *376 5155;* ⊕ *08.00–19.00 daily*) Everything anyone ever wanted to know about sled dogs and the Iditarod race can be found here. Sled dog rides are available for a fee on a wheeled cart.

Dorothy Page Museum (*323 N Main St; 373 9071; www.cityofwasilla.com;* ⊕ *09.00–17.00 Mon–Fri; US$3/free adult/child*) Located at the Wasilla historic town site, the museum houses artefacts from the area's agricultural and mining history. A number of historic buildings can be explored, including Wasilla's first sauna, which opened in 1942.

Farmers' Market (*Behind the Public Library;* ☏ *376 5679;* ⊕ *every Wed 11.00–18.00*) Find local veggies, jams and other goods. Call for more information.

Goose Bay State Game Refuge (*www.wc.adfg.state.ak.us/index.cfm?adfg= refuge.goosebay.htm*) A coastal wetland full of migratory birds, moose, beaver and a host of other wildlife. During certain seasons there can also be a lot of hunters. A small but worthwhile collection of trails can be found here. Follow Knik-Goose Bay Road from the Parks Hwy in Wasilla to the end, then follow Point MacKenzie Road.

Knik Museum (*Mile 13.9 Knik Rd;* ☏ *376 2005;* ⊕ *14.00–18.00 Fri–Sun; free admission*) Sled Dog Musher's Hall of Fame. Sled dog rides can be arranged from Iditarod racers from their homes off the George Parks Highway north of Wasilla.

Museum of Alaska Transportation and Industry (*3800 Museum Dr;* ☏ *376 1211; museumofalaska.org;* ⊕ *10.00–17.00 Tue–Sun; US$8/5 adult/child*) Relics from local industry, including fishing boats, farming equipment, cars, train paraphernalia and airplanes.

Great Bear Brewing Co (*238 N Boundary St;* ☏ *373 4782; www.greatbearbrewing.com*) Offers tours and tastings.

PALMER (*Population: 5,500*) The quaint farming town of Palmer (⊕ 61°36'6"N, 149°7'2"W) occupies the Matanuska Valley just east of Wasilla and 42 miles north of Anchorage on the Glenn Highway. Palmer is comprised of suburbs and farms, interwoven with forests, rivers and lakes, while towering mountains ring the entire area. The town itself offers every amenity including some interesting visitor sites such as musk ox and reindeer farms as well as outdoor activities and events such as the Alaska State Fair.

History The Dena'ina Athabascans were the first people to settle the area, existing mainly around the Matanuska and Kinik Rivers, but also living from trade with the surrounding tribes. Russian fur traders established trading posts in the Cook Inlet in the 1740s and 1750s but most of them left when Alaska was sold to the US in 1867. Shortly after the sale, George Palmer arrived and built a trading post on the Matanuska River. As the fur trade declined, prospectors started finding gold in local streams. By 1916, the Alaska Railroad had pushed through Palmer, fuelling its slow but steady growth with an influx of prospectors and settlers.

Small-scale farming was a way of life for most settlers, but, on seeing the rich soil and impressive yields, the US Department of Agriculture established an experimental station in Palmer in 1917. While the population declined during World War I, it rebounded somewhat in 1935 during the Great Depression when President Franklin Roosevelt sent 203 farming families from the Midwest to Palmer as part of the 'New Deal' relief program. Many of the families failed in the harsh climate, but many of the descendants of those who persevered still live there today and grow some of the country's largest vegetables in the rich soil during the long summer days.

Getting there and around
By bus
Mat–Su Transit (☏ 376 5000; www.matsutransit.com) Public buses serve the Palmer area and connect it with Wasilla and Anchorage. A ride to Anchorage is US$3 and US$2.50 will get you anywhere in the Mat-Su Valley.

By taxi
🚖 **R&B Taxi** ☏ 775 7475.

Tourist information
🛈 **Matanuska-Susitna Visitor Center** 7744 E Visitors View Ct; ☏ 746 5000; www.alaskavisit.com; ⏰ 08.30–18.30 daily. Be sure to stop at this lovely log cabin visitor centre with a flower garden outside & heaps of information inside. A small museum showcases the area's unique history. Free Wi-Fi & coffee.

Local tours and activities
Dream A Dream Dog Farm Mile 64.7, Parks Hwy; ☏ 495 1197, 866 425 6874 (TF); www.vernhalter.com. Dog kennel tours & dog sled rides 11.00–15.00 every day for US$74pp.

Happy Trails Kennels Mile 4.5, West Lakes Blvd; ☏ 892 7899; www.buserdog.com. Dog kennel tours for US$35pp.

Huskytown Kennels ☏ 733 4759; www.huskytown.com. Dog kennel tours 10.00–19.00 daily for US$35pp.

Lifetime Adventures ☏ 800 952 8624; www.lifetimeadventures.net. Canoe, kayak & bike rentals, camping & tours from their Eklutna Lake location.

Meekin's Air Service ☏ 745 1626; www.meekinsairservice.com. The eco-minded father & daughter team offer charter flying, flightseeing & custom backcountry trips.

MICA Guides ☏ 351 7587, 800 956 6422 (TF); www.micaguides.com. Ice-climbing & glacier trekking on the Matanuska Glacier.

NOVA River Runners ☏ 800 746 5753; www.novalaska.com. Glacier trekking & river floats in the Mat-Su Valley.

Hiking and recreation Hatcher Pass is one of the best day trips around, with hiking and vistas galore. The Independence Mine State Historical Park documents

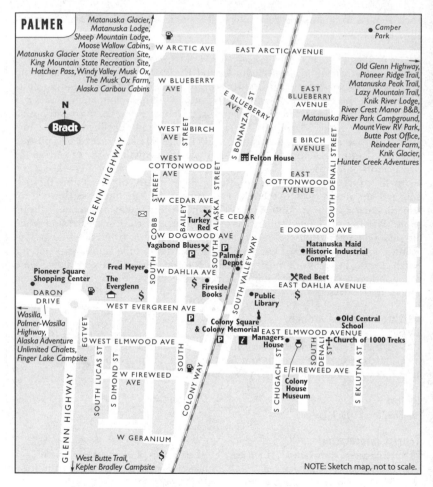

PALMER

Matanuska Glacier, ↑
Matanuska Lodge,
Sheep Mountain Lodge,
Moose Wallow Cabins,
Matanuska Glacier State Recreation Site,
King Mountain State Recreation Site,
Hatcher Pass, Windy Valley Musk Ox,
The Musk Ox Farm,
Alaska Caribou Cabins

W ARCTIC AVE   EAST ARCTIC AVENUE

W BLUEBERRY
AVE

• *Camper*
   Park

Old Glenn Highway, →
Pioneer Ridge Trail,
Matanuska Peak Trail,
Lazy Mountain Trail,
Knik River Lodge,
River Crest Manor B&B,
Matanuska River Park Campground,
Mount View RV Park,
Butte Post Office,
Reindeer Farm,
Knik Glacier,
Hunter Creek Adventures

N

Bradt

GLENN HIGHWAY

W ARCTIC AVE

E BLUEBERRY AVE

E BONANZA ST

EAST
BLUEBERRY
AVENUE

WEST
AVE BIRCH
STREET

WEST
COTTONWOOD
AVE

S BONANZA ST

Felton House

E BIRCH
AVENUE

SOUTH DENALI STREET

W CEDAR AVE

COBB STREET
BAILEY STREET
SOUTH ALASKA STREET

Turkey
Red
E CEDAR

EAST
COTTONWOOD
AVENUE

W DOGWOOD AVE

E DOGWOOD AVE

Vagabond Blues

SOUTH ALASKA ST

Matanuska Maid
• Historic Industrial
Complex

Palmer
Depot

SOUTH VALLEY WAY

Fred Meyer

Pioneer Square
Shopping Center

The
Everglenn

W DAHLIA AVE

Red Beet
EAST DAHLIA AVENUE

DARON
DRIVE

Fireside
Books

WEST EVERGREEN AVE

• Public
Library

Wasilla,
Palmer-Wasilla
Highway,
Alaska Adventure
Unlimited Chalets,
Finger Lake Campsite

Colony Square
& Colony Memorial

EAST ELMWOOD AVENUE

• Old Central
School

EGTVET
SOUTH LUCAS ST

WEST ELMWOOD AVE

SOUTH DIMOND ST

SOUTH ST

COLONY WAY

Managers
House

CHUGACH ST

SOUTH DENALI ST

Church of 1000 Treks

S EKLUTNA ST

GLENN HIGHWAY

W FIREWEED
AVE

E FIREWEED AVE

Colony
House
Museum

W GERANIUM

West Butte Trail,
↓ *Kepler Bradley Campsite*

NOTE: Sketch map, not to scale.

the area's rich mining history. The **Matanuska Glacier** is an hour northwest on the Glenn Highway and is one of the few 'drive up' glaciers in the state. There are lots of hiking and exploring opportunities in the vicinity.

The book *50 Hikes in Alaska's Chugach State Park* by Shane Shepherd and Owen Wozniak (see page 435) is a great resource for anyone planning to do a lot of hiking. For a free option, the Mat-Su Borough website (*www.matsugov.us*) has a complete hiking guide.

While Knik Glacier can be seen from the river aboard a motorboat, a more spectacular but distant view is from the top of the **Pioneer Ridge Trail**. The trail is steep and often muddy; only experienced hikers should try this 12-mile roundtrip. The trailhead is on the south side of Knik River Road. On the north side of the Knik River is one of Palmers most popular hikes, **Lazy Mountain**. The five-mile roundtrip is steep but ends in an alpine setting with great views of the farmland below. Nearby is the **Matanuska Peak Trail**, a lovely but steep eight-mile roundtrip with great views at the top. To get to the trail, travel for 3.5 miles southeast on the Old Glenn Hwy, then turn left onto Smith Road. **West Butte Trail** is a three-mile roundtrip and moderate in difficulty level. Once high on the ridge, hikers are rewarded with lovely views of the farms below. To reach the trail from Palmer travel southwest on the Glenn Hwy. Five miles from Palmer head right on Bodenburg Loop Road, after ½ mile turn left on Mothershead Circle.

Where to stay The **Mat-Su Bed & Breakfast Association** (*www.alaskabnbhosts.com*) lists many valley B&Bs, including some in Palmer.

Chalets and B&Bs

Matanuska Lodge (4 rooms) 34301 West Glenn Hwy; 746 0378; www.matanuskalodge.com. A lovely log home B&B with fabulous rooms & every amenity. Wonderful b/fast & dinner upon request. $$$$$

Alaska Adventure Unlimited Chalets (3 rooms) 373 3494, 800 580 3494 (TF); www.alaskaadventureunlimited.com. Offers 3 lovely chalets & valley van tours. $$$

Knik River Lodge (15 rooms) 29979 E Knik River Rd; 745 5002 www.knikriverlodge.com. Simple but cute cabins perched on a hill above the Knik River at the end of Knik River Rd. The glacier is just around the corner & tours can be booked from the lodge. A decent restaurant serves 3 meals a day, but is also a good spot to sip a beer & relax. Wi-Fi. $$$

Moose Wallow Cabins (3 rooms) 13388 E Moosewallow Av; 745 7777; www.moosewallow.com. Great little cabins with good rates. $$$

Sheep Mountain Lodge (11 rooms) 17701 W Glenn Hwy; 745 5121, 877 645 5121(TF); www.sheepmountain.com. A pleasant collection of cabins on the Glenn Hwy northeast of Palmer. Classic cabins are simple with limited amenities. The deluxe cabins have a kitchenette & other refinements. $$$

Alaska Caribou Cabins (2 rooms) 746 6881, 888 408 2246; www.akcariboucabins.com. Simple but cosy cabins with kitchens. $$

River Crest Manor B&B (3 rooms) 2655 S Old Glenn Hwy; 746 6214; www.rivercrestmanor.com. Plush rooms in a modern house. $$

Remote lodges

Riversong Lodge 350 2392; www.riversonglodge.com. A simple lodge for the die-hard fisherman. All-inclusive lodge stays start at US$1,000. $$$$$

Tordrillo Mountain Lodge 783 4354; www.chugachpowderguides.com. Fishing & skiing

adventures from a remote lodge southwest of Palmer. 2–7 nights cost US$1,300–4,300. $$$$$

Winterlake Lodge 274 2710; www.withinthewild.com. A remote luxury retreat with every comfort. All-inclusive package trips from 1 to 4 days for US$1,330–3,860. $$$$$

Camping

Matanuska River Park Campground (86 sites) Off Arctic Blvd east of town; 745 9690; www.matsugov.us. The park features flush toilets, hot showers, grills, tables, shelter & a lovely setting for tent/RV US$10/15.

Matanuska Glacier State Recreation Site (6 sites) Located at mile 101 of the Glenn Hwy, northeast of Palmer. Toilets, tables, water & trails. US$15.

Mount View RV Park (96 sites) 1405 N Smith Rd; 745 5747, 800 264 4582 (TF); www.mtviewrvpark.com. RV campsite with hot showers & laundry. Knik River boat trips can be booked here. Wi-Fi.

The following campgrounds are operated by **Lifetime Adventures Alaska** (*800 952 8624; www.lifetimeadventures.net*) and in addition to camping and basic services, offer canoe rental for US$10 for the first hour, and a dollar for each hour after.

King Mountain State Recreation Site (32 sites) Located northeast of Palmer at mile 76 of the Glenn Hwy, on the Matanuska River. Camping is US$15.

Kepler Bradley Campsite (6 sites) Located south of Palmer at mile 36 of the Glenn Hwy, this

campground in tucked into a collection of 11 lakes. Camping is US$10/night.

Finger Lake Campsite (36 sites) Located northeast of Palmer, this well run campground costs US$15/night & is right on Finger Lake with fishing & swimming.

Public-use cabins

⚠ Matanuska Glacier public-use cabin Near the Matanuska Glacier State Recreation Area; ☏ 745 5151; www.longriflelodge.com. Accessible by road; has electricity & great views. The cabins sleeps 4. US$50. $$

✗ Where to eat
In addition to the restaurants listed here, a good lunch can be eaten at the Farmers' Market every Friday.

✗ Red Beet 320 E Dahlia Av; ☏ 745 4050; ⏰ 11.30–15.00, 18.30–21.30 Tue–Sat. Fresh food that almost always incorporates local veggies, & yes, beets. Hot drinks, baked goods & desserts too. $$$

✗ Turkey Red 550 South Alaska St; ☏ 746 5544; www.turkeyredak.com; ⏰ 07.00–21.00 Mon–Sat. A socially & environmentally conscious eatery with a great mission & even better food. Serves 3 meals, all prepared with love & local ingredients. An amazing selection of homemade breads. $$$

✗ Vagabond Blues 642 S Alaska St; ☏ 745 2233; www.whistlingswan.net/vagabond.htm; ⏰ 18.00–20.00 Mon–Sat & 08.00–18.00 Sun. Tasty food & a pleasant atmosphere. Hot drinks, baked goods, soups & bread with occasional live music. $$

Other practicalities

Fireside Books 720 S Alaska St; ☏ 745 2665; www.goodbooksbadcoffee.com; ⏰ 10.00–19.00 Mon–Sat, 12.00–17.00 Sun. New & used books with a good selection of Alaskan books. Their official motto is 'Good books, bad coffee'.

Post office 550 S Cobb St; ☏ 745 5051; www.usps.com; ⏰ 10.00–17.30 Mon–Fri, 09.00–12.00 Sat.

Butte Post Office 16500 E Marilyn Dr; ☏ 746 6510; www.usps.com; ⏰ 12.00–18.00 Mon–Fri.

Public library 655 South Valley Way; ☏ 745 4690; www.matsulibraries.org; ⏰ 10.00–20.00 Mon & Wed, 10.00–18.00 Tue, Thu & Fri, 10.00–14.00 Sat. A cosy place to hang out with internet access.

Fred Meyers 650 N Cobb St; ☏ 761 4233; www.fredmeyer.com; ⏰ 07.00–21.00 daily. A good selection of groceries & goods, including a delicatessen, bulk & organic foods.

What to see Palmer is a good deal more picturesque than both Wasilla and Anchorage and offers visitors a pleasant one-day stop-over on their way north. For those with a more relaxed schedule, Palmer is well worth a few days of hiking, dining and exploring.

Alaska State Fair (*2075 Glenn Hwy;* ☏ *745 4827; www.alaskastatefair.org; US$10/6 adult/child*) Palmer's biggest attraction is held in the last week of August. The event draws people from all over the state and the rest of the world and is an event to behold despite the age it takes to find parking. Food, music, rodeo, events and giant vegetables make up the attractions.

Colony Village (⏰ *10.00–16.00 Mon–Fri*) Where some of the area's original farmers were relocated in the 1930s. It is situated at the fairground and is the best place to see how Palmer looked more than 70 years ago.

Farmers' Market Palmer hosts a Farmers' Market every Friday from 11.00–18.00 across from the visitor centre. Bread, jellies and jams, fresh veggies, lunch food vendors and other goods are usually for sale. The market is open from mid-May through to mid-August.

To see some of Palmer's best **farmhouses and bucolic landscapes** follow the Old Glenn Highway north to Farm Loop Road or Bodenberg Loop Road north of town, and then Inner Springer Loop south of town. The striking mountains set the landscape apart from any other farming community in America.

Palmer is home to two musk ox farms. The ice age beasts are kept primarily for their *qiviut* – the animal's silky and warm underhairs. Just about all baby animals are cute, but musk ox calves are in another league of cuteness. See them in May just after they are born.

Windy Valley Musk Ox 9523 N Wolverine Rd; ☏ 745 1005; www.windyvalleymuskox.net. The Nash family have a large herd of musk ox from which they gather *qiviut* to make yarn & a variety of wearable products. Tours of the farm are available, but the Nash family's focus is on making & selling musk ox products, rather than tours, so be sure to call before visiting.

The Musk Ox Farm Mile 50 Glenn Hwy; ☏ 745 4151; www.muskoxfarm.org; ⊕ Jun & Jul 09.00–19.00 daily, May & Aug 10.00–18.00daily; US$8/6 adult/child. A much more formal & commercial experience. Frequent tours led by bored youths take visitors through the musk ox enclosures. The farms works with native Alaskan weavers to produce goods sold there & around Alaska (for more information visit www.qiviut.com).

Reindeer Farm 5561 S Bodenburg Loop Rd; ☏ 745 4000; www.reindeerfarm.com; ⊕ 10.00–18.00 daily; US$6/4 adult/child. Admire, photograph & even feed & pet this quintessential Alaskan tundra animal. A moose, an elk & a deer also live here.

Hatcher Pass A wonderful day trip from Palmer (see page 207).

Havemeister Dairy Farm (☏ 745 2040) Is Alaska's oldest dairy farm. Tours of the milking parlour and gardens are offered daily. Call ahead to arrange a tour.

Matanuska Glacier The Matanuska Glacier, north of Palmer at mile 102 of the Glenn Highway, is 24 miles long and 4 miles wide. The ice flow is cradled by the Chugach Mountains and offers easy access onto the ice on an easy 15-minute hike.

Practicalities Tours are also available through **Glacier Park** (*mile 102 Glenn Hwy;* ☏ *745 2534, 888 253 4480 (TF); www.matanuskaglacier.com*). **MICA Guides** (*200 W 34th Av;* ☏ *351 7587, 956 6422 (TF); www.micaguides.com*) in Anchorage, also offer glacier walks and ice climbing on Matanuska.

Knik Glacier The Knik Glacier sits at the headwaters of the Knik River southeast of Palmer. Knik River Road branches off the Old Glenn Highway and travels 11 miles before ending about 10 miles short of the glacier. Because of its proximity to Palmer and Anchorage and easy access, the glacier is well travelled and motorboats zoom up the river at regular intervals. Hiking or biking from the end of the road is possible but the trails are rutted and frequented by ATVs (All Terrain Vehicles) .

Practicalities A better option for seeing the glacier in all its glory, but from afar, is the **Pioneer Ridge Trail** (see page 214). To meet the glacier face to face, get on a jet boat tour up the river. **Hunter Creek Adventures** (☏ *745 1577; www.knikglacier.com*) offers transportation to the glacier as well as wall tents and meals for US$250 in their glacier-side camp. Day tours are US$80–100. **Mt View Knik-Glacier Boat Tours** (*1405 N Smith Rd;* ☏ *745 5747, 800 264 4582 (TF); www.mtviewrvpark.com*) has an RV park near the Old Glenn Hwy and runs visitors up the river to see the glacier. At the end of the Knik River Road is the **Knik River Lodge** (*29979 E Knik River Rd:* ☏ *745 5002; www.knikriverlodge.com*).

Colony House Museum (*316 E Elmwood Av;* ↘ *745 1935;* *www.palmerhistoricalsociety.org;* ⊕ *10.00–16.00 Tue–Sat; US$2/1 adult/child*) Located near the visitor centre, the Colony House Museum was once owned by Irene and Oscar Beylund who came to Palmer in the 1930s as members of the Matanuska Colony project. The museum gives visitors an idea of what 1930s frontier living was like.

SOUTH OF ANCHORAGE

The Seward Highway strikes southeast from Anchorage and follows the Turnagain Arm for 52 miles before reaching the Kenai Peninsula. In those short miles there are many camping and hiking possibilities and also the well-known attractions of the Portage Glacier and the town of Girdwood. The highway also leads to the small town of Whittier via the Portage Glacier Road.

Leaving Anchorage on the Seward Highway, the grey urban sprawl soon fades into the background and the popular wildlife-viewing area of Potter Marsh appears on the left. Just as the landscape opens up, the highway dives into the wide but steep-sided valley of Turnagain Arm. Arm views are mud at low tide and brown, turbid water at high tide. Beluga whales frequent the Arm and can sometimes be seen from the many rest stops between Potter Marsh and the turnoff to Girdwood. The beluga population in Cook Inlet and Turnagain Arm number fewer than 375 and are currently protected by the Endangered Species Act. Since 1994, the Cook Inlet population has declined by 50%. This was originally attributed to overhunting. However, when all hunting was stopped in 1999, the population did not recover. No-one knows why the Cook Inlet beluga whales are declining. Some biologists point to the increased oil exploration and drilling at Cook Inlet, while others think it may be due to a greater number of killer whales in the Inlet. See page 30 for more beluga information.

On both sides of the Arm the soaring Chugach Mountains rise up for 4,000ft. On the north side of the highway, Dall sheep can usually been seen feeding high on the mountains. Some of the rest stops have telescopes to make the white spots in the distance look more like what they are: live sheep.

About 14 miles southeast of Anchorage, a popular rock climbing area can be seen right off the highway. Less than three miles beyond that, the Beluga Point rest stop has information about Captain Cook's brief visit to the area as well as information on mountain goats, Dall sheep, beluga whales and bore tides. Bore tides, or tidal bores, are walls of water that form with an incoming tide. The Turnagain Arm and the Knik Arm are the only places in the US where tidal bores regularly form. Tidal bores consist of a two- to four-foot wave that moves with the incoming tide at about 12mph. Beluga Point is a good place to see bore tides about 45 minutes after low tide.

Just southeast of Bird Creek and the day use area, the Bird Creek Campground (see page 206) is a pleasant place to spend the night. The campground is about 26 miles east of Anchorage. A paved bike trail follows the old highway northwest and southwest from the campground. Bird Creek is extremely popular with fishermen when the salmon are in. A nice but steep five–mile round trip trail heads into the mountains from the day use area. Here parking costs US$5 per day. Girdwood Junction, 37 miles from Anchorage, consists of a strip mall with gas, food, gifts and little more. Get petrol here, particularly if you plan to visit Hope.

Trails south of here include:

FALLS CREEK TRAIL Located at mile 105 of the Seward Hwy, this steep 1.5-mile trail follows a creek and provides access to a lovely alpine area that can be further explored off-trail.

INDIAN VALLEY TRAIL Located at mile 102 of the Seward Hwy, at the end of a 1.4-mile road. This 6-mile trail climbs 2,100ft on steep terrain to an alpine pass.

BIRD RIDGE TRAIL Located at mile 100 of the Seward Hwy. A steep, 1.5-mile trail through the trees to the tundra. One of the first trails to be free of snow in spring.

GIRDWOOD (*Population: 1,794*) Girdwood (⊕ 60°56'33"N, 149°9'59"W) is 37 miles southeast of Anchorage and occupies a low valley surrounded on three sides by the Chugach Mountains. The Alyeska Resort sits at the base of Mount Alyeska right in town and is a popular winter destination for locals. Not quite as 'happening' during the summer as the winter, Girdwood is still worth visiting for the wonderful mountain views, hiking trails and even paragliding adventures from the top of Mount Alyeska!

History The town began to take shape around the turn of the century when James Girdwood and others staked mining claims on Crow Creek. The Alaska Railroad passed through in 1915 further inspiring growth. During World War II, the town was all but abandoned and only began to flourish again in 1951 when the Seward Highway was completed. A few locals with a dream founded the Alyeska Ski Corporation in 1954. Chairlifts were gradually built including one built then disassembled in France and then shipped all the way to Girdwood! In 1964, the Good Friday earthquake shook the town causing the land to sink 10ft. The dead trees visible at the Girdwood Junction are still standing since 1964, when the land sunk and their roots went below sea level. The town's growth became increasingly based around the ski area, which changed hands a few times before being bought by the Seibu Corporation, who installed high-speed chairs and a tram. They also built the massive Westin Alyeska Prince Hotel and a dining room near the top of the mountain.

Getting there and away
By bus Buses providing transportation to Girdwood generally stop at the junction, which is three miles from town. Public buses run every hour or so between the junction and town; tickets cost US$1.

🚌 **Girdwood Tours and Transportation** ↘ 783 1900; www.girdwoodshuttle.com. Bus service between Anchorage, Girdwood, Whittier & Seward. Anchorage to Girdwood US$40/35 adult/child, Girdwood to Whittier US$40/35 adult/child, Seward to Girdwood US$65/55 adult/child.
🚌 **Glacier Valley Transit** ↘ 754 2547; www.glaciervalleytransit.com. Buses run on a fixed route around town; tickets cost US$1.
🚌 **Home Stage Line** ↘ 235 2252; www.thestageline.net. Bus service from Anchorage to

Girdwood for US$36 & from Girdwood to Homer for US$73. A more economical option is to ask for a ticket from Anchorage to Homer with a stopover in Girdwood. This stopover can be as long as you like. Tickets cost US$88.
🚌 **Seward Bus Lines** ↘ 563 0800; www.sewardbuslines.net. Bus service from Anchorage to Girdwood & onto Seward. Anchorage to Girdwood costs US$35 & Girdwood to Seward costs US$30.

By train
Alaska Railroad (*415 E Railroad Av; www.akrr.com*) From Anchorage to Girdwood the fare is US$59/30 adult/child one-way and from Girdwood to Seward is US$75/38 adult/child one-way.

Tourist information
🎫 **Girdwood Chamber of Commerce** www.girdwoodchamber.com. Girdwood does not have

a visitor centre, but the chamber's website is excellent.

Ⓘ Glacier Ranger Office Mile 0.3 Alyeska Hwy, ☏ 783 3242. Drop in here to ask about hikes & learn about the Chugach Mountains. A ranger is on duty 08.00–17.00 daily.

⌂ **Where to stay** The booking agency, **Alyeska Accommodations** (☏ *783 2000, 888 783 2001 (TF); www.alyeskaaccommodations.com*) specialises in matching visitors with accommodation options, including the many B&Bs in Girdwood. **Girdwood Bed & Breakfast Association** (☏ *222 4858, www.gbba.org*) is also good.

⌂ **Alyeska Prince Hotel** (304 rooms) 1000 Arlberg Av; ☏ 754 1111, 800 880 3880; www.alyeskaresort.com. The luxurious hotel features 3 restaurants, pool, sauna, & a spa. The rooms are surprisingly pleasant & start at US$299 dbl & get about US$20 more expensive with each ascending floor. Prices soar at the top, where the suites are US$750–2,200 dbl. The mountain tram leaves from the back of the hotel. Internet & TV. 💲💲💲💲💲

⌂ **Hidden Creek B&B** (3 rooms) 739 Vail Dr; ☏ 783 5557; www.hiddencreekbb.com. A high end B&B in a lovely, but sparsely decorated new home. The hosts are gracious & their dog is sweet. Great b/fast & treats. Wi-Fi. 💲💲💲💲

⌂ **Timberline Drive B&B** (2 rooms) 923 Timberline Dr; ☏ 783 2404; www.timberlinedrivebnb.com. Set in a quiet neighbourhood, the B&B has 2 comfortable & private rooms with full kitchens. Virgin Creek Falls can be easily reached on foot via a short trail. 💲💲💲

⌂ **Alyeska Hostel** 227 Alta Dr; ☏ 783 2222; www.alyeskahostel.com. A cosy & atypical hostel, this place is more like a simple B&B. Bunks for US$20, rooms for US$50 dbl, & cabins for US$65 dbl. Full kitchen, showers, sauna & a comfy common area. With just a few beds & rooms, the hostel fills up quickly, so call ahead. 💲

Camping
⛺ Forest Fair Campground (18 sites) A brand-new campground is located in the fairground. For more information contact the **Glacier Ranger Office**.

✖ **Where to eat**

✖ **Seven Glaciers Restaurant** ☏ 754 2237; www.alyeskaresort.com; ⏲ 17.00–22.00 daily. Perched near the top of Mount Alyeska, this romantic mountain dining room is a great place for a date. Delicious food with an awe-inspiring view, but also very expensive. Dinner will cost US$40–60. Take the tram to & from the hotel. 💲💲💲💲💲

✖ **Double Musky Inn** Mile 0.3 Crow Creek Rd; ☏ 783 2822; www.doublemuskyinn.com; ⏲ 17.00–22.00 Tue–Thu, 16.00–22.00 Fri–Sun. Decent food but long waits, iffy service & odd décor. Steaks, pasta & Cajun fare. Avoiding the crowds at off-meal times will greatly improve the experience. A local favourite. 💲💲💲💲

✖ **Jack Sprat Restaurant** 165 Olympic Mtn Loop; ☏ 783 5225; www.jacksprat.net; ⏲ 17.00–22.00 daily, 09.00–15.00 Sat & Sun (brunch). An intimate restaurant with tasty food & friendly staff. Great soups & salads & a number of dishes with an Asian theme. Dinner will run US$20–30. Salads & sandwiches are US$10–15. 💲💲💲💲

✖ **Maxine's Glacier City Bistro** Mile 0.3 Crow Creek Rd; ☏ 783 1234; wwwmaxinesbistro.com; ⏲ 17.00–midnight Wed–Mon. One of town's hidden gems with great food in a funky atmosphere. Music on w/ends & open mic on Wed. Delicious Sun brunch. Expect to spend US$20–30 for dinner. 💲💲💲💲

✖ **Chair 5 Restaurant** Hightower Rd; ☏ 783 2500; www.chairfive.com; ⏲ 11.00–01.00 daily. While not the classiest place in town, the restaurant does decent pub food with a twist. Pizza, wings, burgers as well as salads, steaks & some seafood. US$10–20 for dinner. 💲💲💲

✖ **Coast Pizza** 36511 Seward Hwy; ☏ 783 0122; ⏲ 11.00–22.00 Mon–Fri, 11.00–23.00 Sat & Sun. Nice décor & good pizza. 💲💲💲

✖ **The Bake Shop** Olympic Circle Dr; ☏ 783 2831; www.thebakeshop.com; ⏲ 07.00–19.00 daily. Baked goods, pizza, sandwiches, salads & amazing sourdough pancakes. A great lunch spot. 💲💲

✖ **Casa Del Sol** 158 Holmgren Place; ☏ 783 0088; ⏲ 11.00–22.00 daily. Good & cheap Mexican fare. The cheapest place to fill up in town. 💲💲

Local tours and activities

Alaska Backcountry Access ☎ 783 3600; www.akback.com. Based out of Girdwood, ABA offers adventure of all kinds & lengths in the area & around southcentral Alaska.

Alaska Paragliding ☎ 301 1215 www.alaskaparagliding.com. Head up Mount Alyeska with a fun, knowledgeable & extremely safe instructor & leap off the edge with a tandem flight.

The Ascending Path ☎ 783 0505; www.theascendingpath.com. The best in Girdwood for glacier trekking, forest day walks &, for the more extreme sport-loving visitor, ice & rock climbing.

Drift Away ☎ 877 999 8677; www.guidekenairiver.com. Drift-boat fishing trips on the Kenai & Kasilof Rivers. Tell them what you want to catch &, assuming the season is right, they will take you to the fish!

Girdwood Ski & Cyclery ☎ 783 2453; www.girdwood-ski-and-cyclery.com. Mountain bike rentals & sales.

Hiking and recreation The **Iditarod Trail** can be picked up at a number of points throughout the valley, including the fairgrounds and the Glacier Ranger Office. It is 2.2 miles from the fairgrounds to the ranger station. The public bus stops at the ranger station and at the turn-off to Crow Creek Road. Winter Creek Trail, also known as the Hand Tram Trail, traverses some lovely terrain between the Alyeska Resort and the end of Crow Creek Road. The four-mile trail has a hand tram, or cable car, in the middle that crosses a creek. If starting from the hotel, walk along the trail, then follow Crow Creek Road to the junction with the Alyeska Hwy and catch the public bus back to town for an all-day excursion.

Other practicalities

Public library 250 Egloff Dr; ☎ 343 4024; ⏰ 13.00–18.00 Tue & Thu, 13.00–20.00 Wed, 10.00–18.00 Fri & Sat. A cosy library with Wi-Fi.

Post office 118 Lindblad Av; ☎ 783 2922; www.usps.com; ⏰ 09.00–17.00 Mon–Fri, 09.00–12.00 Sat.

Festivals

Forest Fair (*www.girdwoodforestfair.com*) Held every year in early July, the Forest Fair puts on a rocking good show, with live music and food for three solid days. The event is now in its 34th year.

Alyeska Blueberry and Mountain Arts Festival Held at the end of July, this festival features art, music, BBQ and a blueberry-concoction competition.

What to see

Crow Creek Mine (*Crow Creek Rd;* ☎ *278 8060; www.crowcreekgoldmine.com;* ⏰ *09.00–18.00 daily; US$ 3/free adult/child*) This was once one of the most productive mines in southcentral Alaska, gathering as much as 700oz of gold per month! The old mining camp is interesting to explore and the wildflowers are lovely. The owners rent all kinds of gold-finding tools from pans to metal detectors. Both casual gold panners and serious prospectors still find gold in the creek to this day. Crow Creek Mine is located at mile 0.3 of Crow Creek Road, which turns off the Alyeska Highway at mile 0.3.

Crow Pass Trail Four miles beyond the mine on Crow Creek Road is the Crow Pass Trail. The trail cuts through the Chugach Mountains for some 26 miles, ending near Eagle River. The first few miles provide lovely views and pleasant but steep hiking.

Alaska Wildlife Conservation Center (*79 Seward Hwy;* ☎ *783 2025; www.alaskawildlife.org;* ⏰ *08.00–20.00 daily; US$7.50/5 adult/child*) This non-profit animal care and rehabilitation centre is set in 160 acres. Get up close and personal with much of Alaska's wildlife, including musk ox, brown and black bears, elk, moose, coyotes, eagles and others. Drive or walk through the park. The centre is located 11 miles southeast of Girdwood Junction, on the Seward Hwy.

Mount Alyeska Mount Alyeska is best explored on foot after riding the aerial tramway to the top; die-hards can hike up the mountain. The 60-person tram costs US$16 pp and takes just a few minutes to reach the restaurant. Hiking trails branch out from the viewing area, allowing access to a lovely alpine environment. The Seven Glaciers Restaurant and the Glacier Express Café are the two dining options at the top, the former much better (and more expensive) than the latter. For more information call the tram office at ↘ 754 2275.

20 Mile About ten miles past the Girdwood Junction is an area known as 20-Mile. This is a popular place for **kitesurfers** to tear up and down the Arm. Most are friendly and would be happy to talk about their sport. If you would like to try it, take a lesson from Tom Fredericks at Alaska Kite Adventure (see page 192). A mile or so beyond is the **Alaska Wildlife Conservation Center** (see page 221). Immediately following is the turnoff to **Portage Glacier** and the town of **Whittier** (see page 265). From the turnoff, Portage Glacier is 5.4 miles and Whittier is 11.5 via the creepy Anton Anderson Tunnel.

SOUTH OF GIRDWOOD

Moose Flats Day-Use Area About one mile down Portage Glacier Road, Moose Flats Day-use Area has a short trail on a boardwalk. The much longer **Trail of Blue Ice** can be intercepted here and followed to the Begich, Boggs Visitor Center on Portage Lake. At mile 3.7, the **Black Bear Campground** (*12 sites; US$11*) is located in a wooded area near the creek. Just beyond is a fish-viewing platform where spawning fish can be seen in season. Immediately after is the **Williwaw Campground** (*60 sites; camping places for tents US$13 & US$20 for RVs*) with the usual facilities and a number of trails. After a mile, the road splits and to the left is the tunnel to Whittier, to the right is the **Begich, Boggs Visitor Center** (↘ *783 2326; www.fs.fed.us; ☼ 09.00–18.00 daily*) on Portage Lake. This wonderful visitor centre has a wealth of information on the Chugach National Forest and, of course, glaciers. When the centre was built in 1986, the glacier was a stone's throw away. Today, it has receded around the corner and a boat tour is the only way to see it. To see the glacier, hop on the 80ft, 200-passenger **MV Ptarmigan**. Tours leave at 10.30, 12.00, 13.30, 15.00 and 16.30 and cost US$29/14.50 adult/child. The vessel is operated by **Gray Line of Alaska** (↘ *888 452 1737; www.graylinealaska.com*). Right across from the visitor centre, you will also find the **Portage Glacier Lodge** (*Portage Glacier Hwy;* ↘ *783 3117; www.portageglacierlodge.com*), which has a small gift shop and a cafeteria with burgers and sandwiches at reasonable prices.

Byron Glacier Trail Ranger-led interpretive hikes follow the Byron Glacier Trail every Tuesday and Saturday from 15.30–17.30. Some of these involve looking for ice worms on the glacier. To find the trailhead, follow Portage Glacier Road southeast from Boggs Visitor Center toward the glacier and leave your car in the car park on the right.

Portage Pass Trail A guided hike on the Portage Pass Trail leaves at 13.00 every Sunday from the Whittier side of the tunnel at the trailhead. This is also a wonderful hike to do independently.

Anyone with an adventurous bone in their body will want to spend at least one day at Spencer Glacier just south of Portage Glacier. While most visitors zip past the glacier on the train to Seward, those who take advantage of the whistle-stop train service can get off near the glacier and spend any number of days camping and hiking and exploring the glacier on foot. The train leaves the Portage Station (off the Seward Hwy near the turnoff to Portage Glacier) daily at 13.15 and arrives at Spencer Glacier about 30 minutes later. The train stops again on its way north at 16.30 daily. Two group campsites (free) are less than a mile from the tracks, while nine individual sites are scattered along the trail. A new trail that climbs the mountain is being built now, but for those who can't wait, the bush-wacking is worth it. Once above treeline, the views go on forever and the bulk of the glacier is clearly visible. To book tickets visit the Alaska Railroad website (265 2494; www.akrr.com), or call their office at the Begich, Boggs Visitor Center. Tickets are US$64 from Portage one-way, and US$103 from Anchorage or Girdwood one-way. Rafting trips from Spencer Glacier down the Placer River can also be arranged through the Alaska Railroad.

THE KENAI PENINSULA

NORTH KENAI PENINSULA (PORTAGE TO SEWARD) Shortly after the junction with Portage Glacier Road, the Seward Highway unceremoniously crosses onto the Kenai Peninsula. Though the Chugach and Kenai Mountains prevent views of Prince William Sound, 15 miles to the east, the narrow isthmus of land is all that connects the Kenai Peninsula to the rest of the state.

The Kenai Peninsula is one of the state's most visited geographic areas, and for good reason. From the wonderful restaurants and art in Homer, to the amazing fishing of the Kenai area and all the adventures in between, the peninsula has it all. The Kenai Peninsula is 150 miles long and 115 miles wide and has a total area of 25,600 square miles. That's larger than the states of Massachusetts, New Jersey and Connecticut combined, and with just 1/360th the number of people, it's a big piece of land, and still quite wild once you leave the highway.

PORTAGE TO THE HOPE HIGHWAY JUNCTION Heading southeast onto the Kenai Peninsula, a large sign welcomes visitors to the peninsula at mile 75. Over the next seven miles, the road climbs almost 1,000 feet into **Turnagain Pass**, at 988ft above sea level. This is a great place to use the toilets, stretch your legs and take a stroll across the tundra. At mile 65, the road crosses Bertha Creek and a turnoff to **Bertha Creek Campground** immediately follows. The campground has 12 good sites, each costing US$11 in the woods and near a creek. A mile later, at mile 64, the **Johnson Pass Trail** traverses some beautiful alpine terrain and passes a number of lakes where fishing is possible. The 23-mile trail is smooth and easy to hike. For some it's a day's hike, for others it takes two or three days. At mile 63, the **Granit Creek Campground** has ten sites, each costing US$11. The paved **Sixmile Trail** follows the road from here, eight miles to the Hope Highway cut-off. The Sixmile River, a turbid Class V river, is at the bottom of the gorge to the northeast. The river is one of the most popular white-water kayaking and rafting rivers on the peninsula. **Nova Riverrunners** (745 5753, 800 746 5753 (TF); www.novalaska.com) and **Chugach Outdoor Center** (277 7238, 866 277 7238 (TF); www.chugachoutdoorcentre.com) offer daily trips on the Sixmile River.

At mile 56, the Hope Highway branches off the Seward Highway and heads 18 miles north to the small town of Hope. Between miles 7 and 8.1 are the **Chugach**

Covering two million acres, the Kenai National Wildlife Refuge protects the majority of the Kenai Peninsula's land area. The land is diverse from mountains to lowland forests to marsh. The refuge has a thriving moose population and also bears, caribou, Dall sheep, mountain goats and others. Despite the refuge's remote location, it is also very accessible via road, air and water. The refuge is famous for its salmon runs, namely in the Kenai River. Most of the lakes and streams also offer fishing, as well as some unique canoe trips. Scattered around the refuge are 13 public-use cabins and numerous campsites.

GETTING THERE The refuge is crossed by the Sterling Highway at mile 55, southwest of the Seward turn-off. The refuge is also accessible from many points along the road between Cooper Landing and Kasilof. Skilak Lake Road, Funny Lake Road, Swanson River Road and Tustumena Lake Road all provide access. Small planes are an ideal way to get deep into the refuge and there are many small lakes where they can land.

WHERE TO STAY

Campsites Most of the organised camping in the refuge can be found off the Swanson River Road and the Skilak Lake Road. In addition to the 14 campsites, back-country camping is allowed anywhere in the refuge as long as it is a quarter of a mile from any road. The Skilak Lake and Kenai River areas have ten campgrounds in total. Of these, all are free except the Kenai-Russian River Campground, the Upper Skilak Lake Campground and the Hidden Lake Campground, all of which cost US$10 per night. Three more campgrounds can be found along the Swanson River Road, all of which are free.

Public-use cabins The refuge has 13 public-use cabins at Skilak Lake, Tustumena Lake and in the Swanson Lakes area. Cabins range in price from US$35–45 per night and generally sleep about six people. In the Swanson Lakes area are the Big Indian Creek Cabin, the Dolly Varden Cabin, the McLain Lake Cabin, the Snag Lake Cabin and the Vogel Lake Cabin, all available by reservation only. The Trapper Joe Lake Cabin is also in this region but it is rented on a first-come-first-serve basis. On Tusumena Lake hikers can stay in the Caribou Island Cabin, the Nurses Cabin and the Pipe Creek Cabin by reservation only. The Emma Lake Cabin is another first-come-first-serve hire. Skilak Lake offers the Doroshin Bay Cabin and the Engineer Lake Cabin by reservation only. The Upper Ohmer Lake Cabin can be rented on a first-come-first-serve basis. To reserve cabins, call or visit the Kenai National Wildlife Refuge Visitor Centre (*Ski Hill Rd;* ↘ *262 7021; http://kenai.fws.gov;* ⊕ *08.00–16.30 Mon–Fri, 09.00–17.00 Sat & Sun*) in Soldotna.

Outdoor Center (see page 193) and **Angle 45 Adventures** (↘ *782 3165; www.angle45.com*). Angle 45 Adventures has two pleasant cabins and offer guided hiking and drift-fishing trips around Hope and elsewhere on the Kenai Peninsula.

HOPE (*Population: 148*) The tiny town of Hope (⊕ 60°55'10"N, 149°38'31"W) is one of the best-preserved turn-of-the-century mining towns in the southcentral region. A museum, post office and library, as well as restaurants and accommodation opportunities can all be found here. Old mining cabins litter the area in various states of ruin, but some have been lovingly maintained or restored and are used today.

History Hope City, as it was called in 1896, was a booming gold town with some 3,000 residents named after a 17-year-old prospector, Percy Hope. Nearby, Sunrise, on Sixmile Creek, also had a period of success but was abandoned along with many

Another office can be found at mile 58 on the Sterling Highway at the eastern edge of the refuge. The location is staffed during the summer 10.00–16.00 daily, although cabin reservations cannot be made here.

ACTIVITIES The refuge offers something for everyone, from multi-day hikes to canoe trips and even combat fishing for salmon on the Kenai River. A hiking guide called *Kenai Pathways* is available at all peninsula public-land offices.

The Skilak Lake has a network of pleasant, day-hiking trails. For those who want to get out and explore, the soaring ridge lines and tundra landscape on the south side of Skilak Lake are a paradise. Few trails exist here but hiking the high country can be excellent and camping is permitted everywhere. Just outside the refuge in the Chugach Nation Forest is the **Resurrection Pass Trail**, an excellent two-mile trek through a lovely high country environment. Lakes, rivers and some public-use cabins can be found along the way. If the weather forecast is good, plan for extra time to lounge by the pristine mountain lakes. The trail can be started in Hope at mile 15 of the Hope Highway or from the Sterling Highway at mile 52. The trail can also be reached by taking Trail 48 just south of Summit Lake on the Seward Highway or from the Devil's Creek Trail just north of the turn-off to Seward.

Since the 1960s, the refuge has maintained two wonderful canoe trails, the Swanson River and Swan Lake Routes. The routes make their way through lowland forests where wildlife is common and various species of fish can be caught. Lakes are connected by rivers and overland portages. The more popular of the two routes is the **Swan Lake Route,** located at the northern end of the refuge. The route covers more than 60 miles in total, 30 lakes and 17 miles along the Moose River. Follow the Swanson River Road from Sterling to Swan Lake Road. Most parties start at Canoe Lake located at mile 3.5 of Swan Lake Road and allow three days for this trip. The **Swanson River Route** is longer and has more difficult portages. Because of the length, this route is seldom completed. The route covers 80 miles in total and 40 lakes, including 46 miles along the Swanson River. Allow for as long as a week to complete this trip.

OPERATORS
Weigner's Backcountry Guiding ➲ 262 7840; www.alaska.net/~weigner. Single or multi day guided canoe trips in the refuge for US$230 per day for extended trips & US$185 for a single day. Canoe rentals are also available.
Alaska Canoe & Campground 35292 Sterling Hwy; ➲ 262 2331; www.alaskacanoetrips.com. Camping (US$13), cabins (US$150), as well as guided trips of all kinds. They also rent all manner of outdoor equipment, including canoes (US$42/day) & fishing gear.

of Hope's miners when word of larger strikes, such as the Klondike, reached Turnagain Arm. The 1964 Good Friday earthquake destroyed much of Hope.

Tourist information
🖅 **Hope Chamber of Commerce**
http://hopealaska.info. Hope does not have a visitor centre, but their website lists most of the businesses & services in town.

🏠 **Where to stay** Around mile 16 of the Hope Highway, as you enter town, there are a number of accommodation options including:

🏠 **Alaskan Byways B&B** (3 rooms) Mile 16 Hope Hwy; ➲ 301 2499; www.alaskanbyways.com. A private home with all the amenities. Wi–Fi. $$$

🏠 **Alaska Dacha** 19742 Hope Hwy; ➲ 782 3223; www.alaskadacha.com. In addition to cabins, there is also RV camping, laundry, showers, Wi-Fi & a general store (🕐 10.00–17.00 daily). $$$

🛏 **Bowman's Bear Creek Lodge** (5 rooms) Mile 15.9 Hope Hwy; ☎ 782 3141; www.bowmansbearcreeklodge.com. Rustic cabins with wood stoves, a sauna & boats for guests to use. $$$

🛏 **Discovery Cabins** (5 rooms) Discovery Dr; ☎ 782 3730; www.advenalaska.com/cabins.htm. Nice cabins on the creek with laundry available. $$
🛏 **Seaview Café** Maine St; ☎ 782 3300; www.home.gci.net/~hopeak; ⊕ 12.00–midnight daily. Meals, campsites (US$10–15) & cabins (US$40) at the end of Main Street in the city centre. $

Camping

⚑ **Porcupine Campground** (24 sites) Located at the end of the Hope Highway, past the town of Hope. The campground overlooks the sea & offers tables, water & fire pits & costs US$11. The Gull Rock Trail starts here.

⚑ **Coeur d'Alene Campground** (4 sites) Located 7 miles up Palmer Creek Rd which heads southeast at mile 16.2 of the Hope Highway.

In addition to these two campgrounds, remote camping is allowed anywhere on Chugach National Forest land, as long as you are not in sight of a road or any homes. At the end of the five-mile Gull Rock Trail is a lovely place to camp with no facilities.

✖ Where to eat

✖ **Seaview Café** Decent lunch & dinner with a bar attached. $$$

✖ **Tito's Discovery Café** Mile 16.5 Hope Hwy; ☎ 782 3274; ⊕ 07.00–21.00 daily. 3 tasty home cooked meals a day for US$10–20. $$$

Hiking and recreation For Sixmile Creek float trips, see page 223.

Resurrection Pass Trail The 38-mile trail traverses the Chugach National Forest and ends on the Sterling Highway at mile 53. This amazing trail is a must for anyone who loves backpacking. The trail was used at the turn of the century by gold prospectors, coming from Resurrection Bay to Hope. Eight public-use cabins can be found along the trail. These must be reserved beforehand by calling ☎ 877 444 6777 or visiting www.recreation.gov. Cabins cost US$25–45 per night and some have free rowing boats to use in the lake. The trail starts at the end of Resurrection Road off Palmer Creek Road.

Gull Rock Trail This trail starts at the Porcupine Campground at the end of the Hope Highway, past the town. The five-mile trail follows Turnagain Arm through forests and past old saw-mill equipment.

Hope Point Trail This trail starts at the Porcupine Campground at the end of the Hope Highway and climbs 3,900ft up Mt Hope. The trail is steep and poorly maintained, but for those in shape and with a healthy sense of adventure, the views are worth it.

Twin Lakes Trail To reach this trail, follow the Palmer Creek Road to the end, park your car and continue on foot. Follow the road up switchbacks to a lovely alpine environment with a number of lakes.

Other practicalities

Post office 19059 Logman Lane; ☎ 782 3352; www.usps.com; ⊕ 08.00–13.00 & 14.00–16.30 Mon–Fri, 10.00–13.30 Sat.
Hope Library 2nd & A St; ☎ 782 3121; ⊕ 13.00–16.00 Mon, 10.00–13.00 Wed &

12.00–16.00 Sat. This historic building is a cosy place to relax & read a book. Internet is available at computer terminals. A gift shop can be found next door.

What to see The best way to see Hope is to park your car and continue exploring on foot. The city centre has many historic buildings including the **Social Hall** off Main Street

Hope Museum *(Maine St;* ↘ *782 3740;* ⊕ *daily; free admission).* The museum houses a great collection of historic photographs and artefacts, and has a number of historic structures in the grounds.

HOPE HIGHWAY JUNCTION TO SEWARD From the Hope Highway junction, the Seward Highway continues south toward Seward and the rest of the Kenai Peninsula. At mile 46, the **Tenderfoot Creek Campground** *(27 sites; US$11)* is just off the highway on the shores of Summit Lake. The alpine mountains surrounding the area are ideal for hiking (although there are no trails) and the lake has trout. **Summit Lake Lodge** (↘ *244 2031; www.summitlakelodge.com; US$100*) is between the lake and highway and offers rooms and decent meals. **Devil's Creek Trail** starts on the west side of the highway at mile 39.5. This wonderful, but difficult ten-mile trail follows Devil's Creek to Devil's Pass, where it intersects the Resurrection Trail. A public-use cabin is located near the top of the trail. Call 877 444 6777 or visit www.recreation.gov to book.

At mile 37, the Seward Highway continues southeast to Seward and the Sterling Highway branches off west to the southern stretch of the Kenai Peninsula where towns worth visiting include Soldotna, Kenai and Homer. Heading toward Seward, **Turn Lake** is to the south and can be a good place to see migratory birds. At mile 33 the **Carter Lake Trail** climbs two miles to Carter Lake, where trout are stocked. One mile further on, the **Trail Lake Fish Hatchery** (↘ *288 3688; www.ciaanet.org;* ⊕ *daily 08.00–17.00*) offers some basic information for the public. The hatchery raises 19 million red salmon and almost one million silver salmon every year.

MOOSE PASS *(Population: 186)* If you blink, you will miss the town of Moose Pass located near mile 30 on the Seward Highway. In fact, the large sign that reads 'Moose Pass Gas' is often the only reason visitors notice the town at all.

Local tours
Scenic Mountain Air ↘ 288 3647; www.scenicmountainair.com. Offers charter & flightseeing trips around the peninsula.

Where to stay and eat Visit the chamber of commerce website (*www.moosepassalaska.com*) for more options.

⌂ **Spruce Moose B&B** Mile 29.9 Seward Hwy; ↘ 288 3667; www.sprucemoosealaska.com. Lovely chalets, each with a hot tub & kitchen. $$$$
⌂ **Trail Lake View Luxury Cottage** 29 Seward Hwy; ↘ 288 3646; www.traillakeview.com. A large cottage with views & all the amenities. $$$$
⌂ **Tern Lake Inn** Mile 36 Seward Hwy; ↘ 288 3667; www.ternlakeinn.com. Standard rooms in a large, lovely home. $$$
⌂ **Trail Lake Lodge** ↘ 288 3103, 800 865 0201 (TF); www.traillakelodge.com. Provides standard rooms & has a restaurant on location. $$

⋀ **Primrose Campground** At mile 17, 1 mile down Primrose Spur Road, Primrose has 8 sites for US$11.
⋀ **Ptarmigan Creek Campground** A mile down the road from Trail River Campground, at mile 23, Ptarmigan has 16 sites for US$11. Don't miss the 3.5-mile trail to Ptarmigan Lake, a long skinny lake squished between 2 4,000ft mountains. Salmon travel up the creek & trout can be found in the lake.
⋀ **Trail River Campground** Located at mile 24 & has 91 sites, each costing US$11.
✗ **Estes Brothers Grocery** ↘ 288 3151. Serves hot drinks, delicatessen fare & sells basic groceries.

What to see and do The **Primrose Creek Trail** follows the edge of the mountains for seven miles to Lost Lake and connects to the **Lost Lake and Lost Creek Trails**, which connect back to the highway near Bear Lake just before Seward.

SEWARD Population: 2,619

Few towns in the state are as quintessentially 'Alaskan' as picturesque Seward. The town (⊕ 60°07'03"N, 149°26'25"W) sits at the head of Resurrection Bay on the eastern side of the Kenai Peninsula in the heart of the Kenai Mountains. Besides the quaint feel of Seward with its countless great eateries, accommodation possibilities and the world class Sealife Center, the town is a major access point for Kenai Fjords National Park. The park encompasses the Harding Ice Field and its many icy fingers as well as hundreds of miles of ragged, wildlife-rich coastline and soaring coastal peaks. Exit Glacier, one of the state's best-known glaciers, protrudes from the ice field's northeastern side, cascading nearly as far as the road just behind the town.

Far from undiscovered, Seward is often packed full of people, making its small, compact size a little cramped. Visiting Seward in the spring or autumn is a much more pleasurable experience than mid-summer.. Just 127 miles from Anchorage, Seward is accessible by vehicle, plane, train and cruise ship. Like Homer, but a little cosier, Seward has something for everyone including art, fine food, fishing and just about every imaginable outdoor adventure.

HISTORY In 1792, Russian fur trader and explorer, Alexander Baranov escaped a nasty storm in a protected bay on the eastern side of the Kenai Peninsula. Since the day happened to be a Russian holiday – the Sunday of Resurrection – Baranof decided on the name Resurrection Bay. Almost 100 years later, in 1867, Alaska was purchased from Russia. The town of Seward in Resurrection Bay was named around that time after US Secretary of State, William Seward, who was largely responsible for the purchase of Alaska. Around the turn of the century, Seward attracted a number of businessmen and settlers eager to build a railroad to Anchorage and the rest of Alaska. In 1903, the railroad was started but it didn't reach Girdwood until 1911. Years later, the government picked up the reins and, in 1923, finished laying the tracks to Anchorage and later to Fairbanks. Seward's destiny as an important, ice-free port town was solidified with the completion of the tracks. In 1960, Seward was the largest town on the Kenai Peninsula and along with Valdez, played an important role in the transport of the goods heading for interior Alaska. The 1964 Good Friday earthquake and the ensuing tsunamis and fires destroyed much of the town and killed a number of residents. Seward was slowly rebuilt after the quake including a US$10 million 'earthquake-proof' dock. Today, the town is focused around tourism, with the Alaska Sealife Center featuring as one of the biggest draws. Across the bay is the Spring Creek Correctional Center, a maximum-security prison built in 1988 employing 200 Seward residents. The prison houses 500 'hard-core' criminals, but don't worry; in more than 20 years, only one felon has ever escaped.

GETTING THERE AND AWAY
By road
Seward Bus Lines ` 563 0800; www.sewardbuslines.net. Bus service from Anchorage to Girdwood & onto Seward. Anchorage to Seward costs US$50 for a 1-way trip.
Girdwood Tours and Transportation ` 783 1900; www.girdwoodshuttle.com. Bus service between Anchorage, Girdwood, Whittier & Seward. Anchorage to Seward costs US$75 1-way.
Stage Line ` 235 2252; www.thestageline.net. Bus service from Anchorage to Girdwood, Kenai/Soldotna, Homer & Seward. Anchorage to Seward costs US$60 1-way.

☎ Park Connection ✆ 245 0200, 800 208 0200 (TF); www.alaskacoach.com. A large bus connects Seward with Anchorage & north to Talkeetna &

Denali. Seward to Anchorage costs US$65, to Talkeetna costs US$120 & onto Denali costs US$145.

By rail
〰 Alaska Railroad 410 Port Av; www.akrr.com; ⏱ 10.00–19.00 daily. From Anchorage to Seward,

this rail journey is considered the most scenic in the state. Tickets cost adult/child US$75/38 1-way.

By air
✈ Scenic Mountain Air ✆ 288 3646, 800 478 1449 (TF); www.scenicmountainair.com. A charter service to

Seward's back country as well as the Prince William Sound & Kenai Peninsula communities, plus Anchorage.

GETTING AROUND Those heading to Exit Glacier can take the hourly shuttle offered by Exit Glacier Guides (see page 238) for US$10. Even those with a car might want to use this service because their van is powered by vegetable oil!

🚗 Hertz of Seward ✆ 224 4378, 800 654 3131 (TF); www.rentacaralaska.com
🚲 Seward Bike Shop 411 Port Av; ✆ 224 2448; www.sewardbikeshop.com. Bikes for sale & rent at the Train Wreck across from the train depot.

🚗 Seward Cab ✆ 224 2000
🚗 Handlebar Taxi Company ✆ 362 2221; www.handlebartaxi.com
🚗 PJ's Taxi & Tours ✆ 224 5555; www.pjstaxi.com

TOURIST INFORMATION
☑ Seward Visitor Center 2001 Seward Hwy; ✆ 224 8051; www.seward.com; ⏱ 08.30–18.00 daily. Knowledgeable staff & lots of printed information; on the west side of the highway 2 miles out of town.
☑ Park Visitor Center ✆ 224 2125; www.nps.gov/kefj; ⏱ 09.00–18.00 daily. Located near the harbour, the

staff are very knowledgeable about the recreational opportunities in Kenai Fjords National Park.
☑ Chugach National Forest Ranger District 334 4th Av; ✆ 224 3374; www.fs.fed.us/r10/chugach; ⏱ 08.00–17.00 Mon–Fri. Head here with questions about activities in the Chugach National Forest.

LOCAL TOURS AND ACTIVITIES
Sea kayaking Sea kayaking is a popular pastime in Seward. For those wanting to head out, a number of outfits offer rental kayaks or tours of the bay as well as multi-day trips in Kenai Fjords National Park. Half-day trips generally cost around US$70 while full-day trips cost US$120. Multi-day trips can run upwards of US$1,000 or more. Day and half-day trips start at Lowell Point, while overnight trips generally involve a water taxi ride to Aialik Bay.

Adventure Sixty North 11421 Seward Hwy; ✆ 224 2600, 888 334 8237 (TF); www.adventure60.com. Outdoor gear rental & a multitude of kayak trips.
Liquid Adventures 13990 Beach Dr; ✆ 224 9225, 888 325 2925 (TF); www.liquid-adventures.com

Kayak Adventures Worldwide 328 3rd Av; ✆ 224 3960; www.kayakak.com
Sunny Cove Sea Kayaking ✆ 224 4426, 800 770 9119 (TF); www.sunnycove.com

Sailing
Sailing Inc ✆ 224 3160; www.sailinginc.com. Day tours of the bay with an emphasis on those who want to learn to sail.

Alaska Sailing Tours ✆ 224 4363; www.alaskasailingtours.com. Day & overnight trips with all the details arranged for you.

Dogsledding
Seavey's Ididaride Sled Dog Tours Mile 1.1 Old Exit Glacier Rd; ✆ 224 8607, 800 478 3139 (TF); www.ididaride.com. Like most sled dog kennels, this

one relies on its adorable puppies to bring in the crowds. The ride is short & expensive, but the puppies are cute.

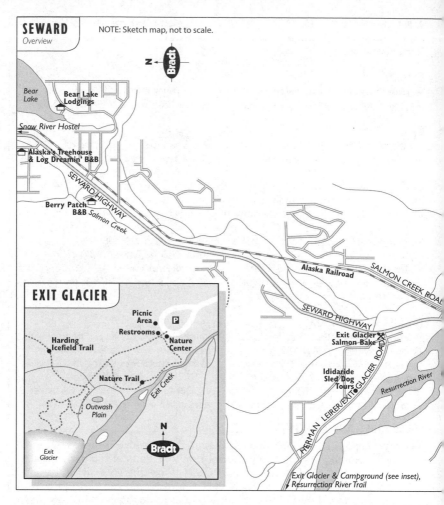

Godwin Glacier Dogsled Tours ✎ 224 8239, 888 989 8239 (TF); www.alaskadogsled.com. Those who can easily part with US$450 will enjoy the helicopter ride & dogsled ride on top of a glacier. Helicopter flightseeing is also available for US$300.

Hiking Exit Glacier hiking can be arranged through **Exit Glacier Guides** (see box on page 238).

Boat tours of fjords Though I personally avoid the large tour companies, there really is no better way to see Kenai Fjords National Park than on one of the larger tour boats. Most of these companies offer both half- and full-day tours. While the half-day tour is enticing in its cost and length, it does not explore the rich waters east and west of Resurrection Bay. It's common to see whales, sea lions, sea otters and legions of seabirds on the full-day trip. So is seasickness, as the outside waters are open to the full force of the north Pacific.

Kenai Fjords Tours ✎ 224 8068, 888 478 3346 (TF); www.KenaiFjords.com. The best tours of the bay. Full-day tours cost US$140, half-day tours are half that.

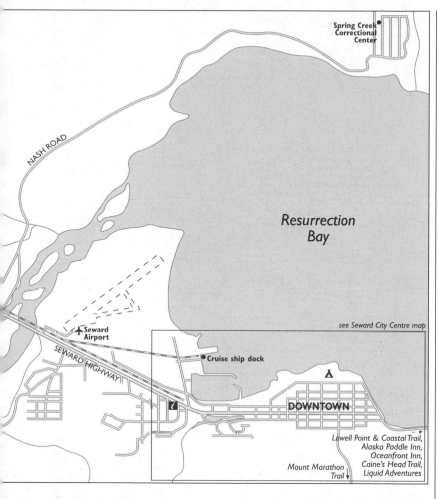

see Seward City Centre map

Major Marine ✆ 224 8030, 800 764 7300 (TF); www.majormarine.com

Kenai Fjords Sea Treks ✆ 224 6595, 877 907 3677 (TF); www.kenaifjordsdaytrips.com

HIKING AND RECREATION Seward is blessed with a large network of hiking trails offering everything from coastal strolls to glacier treks. A number of trails are found along the Seward Highway north of town. The Forest Service Office (see page 229) has detailed information on each and **Miller's Landing** (✆ *224 5739; www.millerslandingak.com*) offers guided hikes on several trails around town.

A local favourite that starts right in town is the **Mount Marathon Jeep Trail**. This steep one-mile hike is clearly marked and starts at the end of Monroe Street just out of the city centre. The trail climbs through many types of vegetation before emerging into a lovely alpine setting with amazing views.

Another wonderful hike is the **Lost Lake Trail**, which offers fishing and wilderness camping opportunities. This hike takes the better part of a day and starts at mile 5 of the Seward Hwy in the Lost Lake subdivision.

The **Primrose Trail** starts at mile 17 and goes to Lost Lake as well.

5

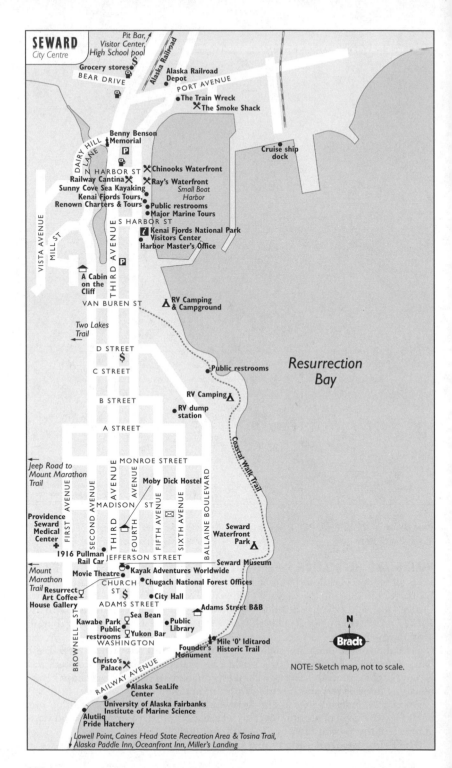

SEWARD
City Centre

Pit Bar,
Visitor Center,
High School pool

Grocery stores
BEAR DRIVE

Alaska Railroad

Alaska Railroad
Depot
PORT AVENUE

The Train Wreck
✕ The Smoke Shack

Cruise ship
dock

Benny Benson
Memorial
DAIRY HILL LANE

N HARBOR ST ✕ Chinooks Waterfront
Railway Cantina ✕ ✕ Ray's Waterfront
Sunny Cove Sea Kayaking   Small Boat
Kenai Fjords Tours,   Harbor
Renown Charters & Tours ● Public restrooms
                         ● Major Marine Tours
S HARBOR ST
             Kenai Fjords National Park
             Visitors Center
             Harbor Master's Office

A Cabin
on the
Cliff
VAN BUREN ST   ⛺ RV Camping
                       & Campground

Two Lakes
Trail

VISTA AVENUE
MILL ST
THIRD AVENUE

D STREET
$
C STREET

B STREET   RV Camping ⛺

A STREET   ● RV dump
                      station

Jeep Road to
Mount Marathon
Trail

FIRST AVENUE
SECOND AVENUE
THIRD AVENUE
FOURTH ST
FIFTH AVENUE
SIXTH AVENUE
BALLAINE BOULEVARD

MONROE STREET

Moby Dick Hostel

MADISON

Providence
Seward
Medical
Center ✚

1916 Pullman
Rail Car
JEFFERSON STREET

Mount
Marathon
Trail
Resurrect
Art Coffee
House Gallery

Movie Theatre ●
● Kayak Adventures Worldwide
CHURCH ST ● Chugach National Forest Offices
$
● City Hall

ADAMS STREET

● Public restrooms

● Public restrooms

Coastal Walk Trail

*Resurrection
Bay*

Seward
Waterfront
Park ⛺

Seward Museum

Adams Street B&B

BROWNELL ST

Sea Bean
Kawabe Park
Public
restrooms Yukon Bar
WASHINGTON

RAILWAY AVENUE

Christo's
Palace ✕

● Public
Library

Founder's
Monument

Mile '0' Iditarod
Historic Trail

N

Bradt

NOTE: Sketch map, not to scale.

Alaska SeaLife
Center
University of Alaska Fairbanks
Institute of Marine Science
Alutiiq
Pride Hatchery

Lowell Point, Caines Head State Recreation Area & Tosina Trail,
↓ Alaska Paddle Inn, Oceanfront Inn, Miller's Landing

Seward has five marine parks all within easy reach of town. The breathtaking scenery throughout Resurrection Bay and beyond draws legions of tourists. However, most venture out on boat tours and miss the opportunity the intrepid traveller enjoys of camping on a remote beach with glaciers and mountains in all directions. Guided or unguided kayak trips, as well as a water taxi service, can be arranged in Seward.

TOURS

Aquetec Water Taxi 362 1291; www.sewardwatertaxi.com
Kayak Adventures 224 3960; www.kayakak.com
Liquid Adventures 224 9225, 888 325 2925 (TF); www.liquid-adventures.com
Miller's Landing 224 5739, 866 541 5739 (TF)
Sunny Cove Sea Kayaking 224 4426, 800 770 9119 (TF); www.sunnycove.com

For more information, contact the **Kenai Parks Office** (*Morgan's Landing, Soldotna;* 262 5581).

CAINES HEAD STATE RECREATION AREA Fort McGilvray at Caines Head defended the port of Seward and its valuable railroad connection during World War II. Today, the abandoned site is well worth the 4.5-mile hike via the Coastal Trail. The park can be reached by boat or on foot from the Lowell Point parking area. Part of the trail is on the beach and a low tide of less than four feet is necessary before hikers can pass. Near the end of the trail at North Beach, there are campsites and toilets as well as a seasonally-staffed ranger station. Two public-use cabins are located on either side of Caines Head. Derby Cove Cabin can be found a $^1/_4$ mile past Caines Head and Callisto Canyon Cabin is situated just before that. The cabins cost US$65 per night and can be reserved by visiting the **Kenai Parks Office** (*Morgan's Landing;* 262 5581) in Soldotna or by visiting www.dnr.alaska.gov/parks/cabins/kenai.htm.

THUMB COVE STATE MARINE PARK Thumb Cove is a small, protected body of water with dramatic mountains and hanging glaciers all around. The park is located a little over seven miles from Seward and right across from Caines Head. The park is popular with campers all summer, but is particularly busy at the weekends. Primitive camping is available along all the beaches. Two public-use cabins are located in the bay and can be rented for US$65 per night. Both cabins sleep eight people. Reserve the cabins by visiting the **Kenai Parks Office**.

Also check out the remote marine parks of the Sandspit Point State Marine Park, the Sunny Cove State Marine Park, the Driftwood Bay State Marine Park and the Safety Cove State Marine Park. These are best explored by kayak.

From Lowell Point, south of town, is the **Caine's Head Trail**, a 5-mile coastal hike with stunning scenery, salmon creeks, and World War II relics at Fort McGilvary. Since the hike follows the sea, only travel the three-mile section between Tonsina Point and North Beach on a very low tide (no higher than 2.5ft). The Callisto Derby Cove public-use cabins are along this route and can be rented for US$50. Visit http://dnr.alaska.gov/parks/cabins/kenai.htm#tcsmp.

WHERE TO STAY Like Homer, Seward seems to have few houses that are not B&Bs. To help make the choice simpler, call the **Alaska Point of View Reservations** (224 2323; *www.go2seward.com*) or call in at the visitor centre and tell them what

Southcentral Alaska **SEWARD**

5

you are looking for. However, finding an accommodation at the last minute can be tricky if not downright impossible mid-summer. To reserve at the best places, call months ahead.

🏠 **A Cabin on the Cliff** (1 room) ☏ 224 2411; www.acabinonthecliff.com. A renovated trapper's cabin high on a cliff overlooking Resurrection Bay. The cabin can sleep up to 6 people with a downstairs suite. The cabin has a huge hot tub with sea views. $$$$$

🏠 **Orca Island Cabins** (4 rooms) ☏ 491 1988, 888 494 5846; www.orcaislandcabins.com. 3 comfortable yurts & 1 houseboat in a secluded part of Resurrection Bay off the road system. Water taxi fees of US$60 are added on top of the normal rates. Kayaks are available for US$40. Hard to reach. $$$$

🏠 **Adams Street B&B** (3 rooms) 611 Adams St; ☏ 224 8879; www.adamsstreetseward.com. 3 nice rooms are made even better by a great central location. $$$

🏠 **Alaska's Treehouse** (2 rooms) 14593 Rainforest Circle; ☏ 224 3867; www.virtualcities.com/ak/treehouse.htm. A unique home in the trees with a 2-room suite & a smaller room. $$$

🏠 **Alaska Paddle Inn** (2 rooms) 13745 Beach Dr; ☏ 362 2628; www.alaskapaddleinn.com. Lovely little rooms on the Lowell Point area, right next to the beach. Half-kitchens & Wi-Fi. $$$

🏠 **Bear Lake Lodgings** (5 rooms) 33820 Bear Lake Rd; ☏ 224 2288; www.bearlakelodgings.com. Friendly folk & comfortable rooms in a B&B located 6 miles out of town. $$$

🏠 **Bell in the Woods** (7 rooms) ☏ 224 7271; www.bellinthewoods.net. Multi-room suites & smaller

rooms all with Wi-Fi & a wonderful b/fast. $$$

🏠 **Berry Patch B&B** (3 rooms) 14247 Victor Dr; ☏ 491 0164; www.berrypatchbnb.net. Out of town in a wooded neighbourhood. The rooms upstairs are pleasant. $$$

🏠 **Sourdough Sunrise** (3 rooms) ☏ 224 3600; www.sourdoughsunrise.com. Outside town, in a secluded wooded area, this lovely custom house is divided into 3 rooms for guests. The owners live out the back in a cabin & prepare sourdough pancakes for b/fast. TV. $$$

🏠 **Oceanfront Inn** 14150 Beach Dr; ☏ 224 5699; www.seward.net/~ocean. The room is nondescript, but the location is amazing, right on the beach at Lowell Point. $$$

🏠 **Whistle Stop** (2 rooms) 411 Port Av; ☏ 224 5252. A converted sleeper-train car that has been converted to 2 rooms at the Train Wreck Plaza. US$125–135. $$$

🏠 **Log Dreamin' B&B** (2 rooms) 14694 Willow Dr; ☏ 224 5410; www.logdreaminbb.com. Just out of town, this small & cosy house offers a less than private loft & a nice, small, private room with a shared bathroom. TV, Wi-Fi. $$

🏠 **Kayakers Cove** ☏ 224 8662; www.kayakerscove.com. A remote, rustic lodge 12 miles from Seward by water. Simple hostel-style beds are available for US$20 or cabins can be rented for US$60. Bedding is available for an extra US$5. Kayaks cost US$20 per day. $

Hostels

🏠 **Moby Dick Hostel** 432 3rd Av; ☏ 224 7072; www.mobydickhostel.com. Simple cabins & bunks. $–$$

🏠 **Snow River Hostel** 22634 Seward Hwy; ☏ 440 1907; www.snowriverhostel.org. Located out of town with bunks & cabins. $–$$

Camping

🏕 **Miller's Landing** 13880 Beach Dr; ☏ 224 5739, 866 541 5739 (TF); www.millerslandingak.com. Expensive camping (US$26/tent) but found in a great location on the beach at Lowell Point. Hot showers, laundry, Wi-Fi & kayaks are also available.

🏕 **Seward Waterfront Park** (450 sites) Ballaine Blvd; ☏ 224 4055; www.cityofseward.net/sprd. This city-run campground is right on the water, but is often

crowded & noisy. Located within walking distance of the city centre. Camping places are booked on a first-come-first-serve basis. US$10.

🏕 **Exit Glacier Campground** (12 sites) Free walk-in tent sites at mile 8.1 on Exit Glacier Road. Food storage, shelter, toilets & water are available. Arrive in the morning to get a site.

✕ **WHERE TO EAT** Seward has many great eateries, however many of them are very poor quality. A general rule is that the more obvious a restaurant is, the worse it is.

The tour bus pales into
insignificance against the
backdrop of Mt McKinley,
Denali National Park
(FF/TA) page 287

Explore Prince William Sound on a
day cruise (FF/TA) page 265

top	**Try your hand at dog-sledding** (RH/TA)
above	**Join a guided glacier climb** (BA/TA) page 76
right	**Camp wild** (IA/FLPA)

above left   **Raft glacial-river rapids**
(FF/TA) page 77

above right   **Catch supper!** (DY/TA) page 74

below   **Splash out on a scenic flight**
(FF/TA) page 94

opposite

top   **Fly above the trees on a zip-line**
(BA/TA) page 97

centre   **Hiking: choose from hundreds of trails**
(TT) page 74

bottom   **Kayaking: get up close and personal with
glaciers and icebergs** (BA/TA) page 75

above left **Bull moose**
(MQ/MP/FLPLA)
page 28

above right **Arctic ground squirrel**
(MQ/MP/FLPLA)

left **Cow moose**
(YM&JE/MP/FLPA)
page 28

above left   Caribou bull in 'velvet'. During this period, the males' new antlers grow underneath a protective layer of fur (DMJ/MP/FLPA) page 25

above right   Grizzly bear; these are a subspecies of brown bear, but grow much larger (DMJ/MP/FLPA) page 25

below   Brown bear with salmon (SB/ MP/FLPA) page 25

above left   **Sea otter** (MG/MP/FLPLA) page 33

above right   **Crested auklet, Pribilof Islands** (ADI/TIPS)

below   **Steller sea lions, Aleutian Islands** (ADI/TIPS) page 33

✕ Ray's Waterfront 1316 4th Av; ☏ 224 5606; www.rayswaterfrontak.com; ⊕ 11.00–16.30 & 17.00–close daily. Very similar to $$$$
✕ Chinooks Waterfront Restaurant 1404 4th Av; ☏ 224 2207; www.chinookswaterfront.com; ⊕ 12.00–22.00 daily. Sat right on the harbour, it serves fair but expensive seafood. Popular with the cruise-ship crowd & the waiting time can be an hour or more. Great harbour views. $$$
✕ Christo's Palace 133 Fourth Av; ☏ 224 5255; www.christospalace.com; ⊕ 11.00–23.00 daily. The service can be iffy, but the food is consistently good. The historic bar at the back is worth a look. Meat dishes, pasta, seafood, as well as some Mexican fare. $$$
✕ Exit Glacier Salmon Bake Exit Glacier Rd; ☏ 224 2204; www.sewardglacierlodge.com; ⊕ 17.00–22.00 daily. Their motto is 'cheap beer & lousy food', but most visitors find the food to be good & the beer not so cheap. A 'frontier'

atmosphere & a mob of locals make this place a must for anyone who loves burgers, beer & seafood. Located out of town where the Exit Glacier Rd turns off the highway. $$$
✕ Railway Cantina 1401 4th Av; ☏ 224 8226; ⊕ 10.00–23.00 daily. Located near the small boat harbour, this gem serves up wonderful Mexican seafood concoctions like blackened halibut burritos & fish tacos. Anyone can fill up for US$10. The Cantina has an impressive hot sauce collection. $$
✕ The Smoke Shack 411 Port Av; ☏ 224 7427; ⊕ 07.00–20.00 daily. A motley group of waiters & cooks serve smoked meat dishes that cannot be beaten. Everything is made (& smoked) in-house &, unless you're a vegetarian, you will love everything. The prices are also some of the best in town. Located in the Train Wreck by the train depot at the northern end of town. $$

Where to drink

♀ Pit Bar Mile 3.5 Seward Hwy; ☏ 224 3006; www.pitbarak.com. Located north of town, this bar's clientele tends to be a little rough around the edges – full of fishermen & very few tourists.
♀ Resurrect Art Coffee House Gallery 320 Third Av; ☏ 224 7161; www.resurrectart.com; ⊕ 07.00–19.00 daily. A hip art & coffee house located in a historic 1916 building. The outdoor seating area can't be beaten on a sunny day. Open till 22.00 on Tue with live music. Free Wi-Fi.

♀ Sea Bean 225 4th Av; ☏ 224 6623; ⊕ 07.00–21.00 daily. Cosy chairs, baked goods & free Wi-Fi. Located in the city centre just a few blocks north of the Sealife Center.
♀ Yukon Bar 4th & Washington St; ☏ 224 3065. A local's bar with music on the weekends & often during the week too. Located in the city centre.

FESTIVALS AND EVENTS The only reason to be in Seward during the extremely crowded 4 July weekend is to witness the **Mount Marathon Race** at 09.00. The brutal race ascends the 3,022ft Mt Marathon. Competitors are often so beaten up from the gruelling ascent and brutal descent that they can hardly move when done, much less stop bleeding from all the cuts and grazes they get from the rocks. This race is an amazing sight for spectators.

In August, the **Silver Salmon Derby** takes over town. The ten-day event brings fishermen from all over the country and at the end, more than US$100,000 in cash prizes are awarded.

OTHER PRACTICALITIES

Public library 238 5th Av; ☏ 224 4082; www.cityofseward.net/library; ⊕ 10.00–20.00 Mon–Thu, 10.00–18.00 Fri & Sat, 13.00–18.00 Sun. Free Wi-Fi & visitors can see the original Alaska flag designed by local boy, Benny Benson.

Post office 507 Madison Av; ☏ 224 3001; ⊕ 09.30–16.30 Mon–Fri, 10.00–14.00 Sat.
High school pool 600 Cottonwood St; ☏ 224 3900. You can grab a free shower or a swim here. Pool hours change so call ahead.

WHAT TO SEE The visitor centre has a walking tour map detailing most of Seward's sights and points of interest.

City centre

Alaska Sealife Center (*301 Railway Av;* ☎ *224 6300; www.alaskasealife.org;* ⊕ *09.00–18.30 Mon–Thu, 08.00–16.30 Fri–Sun; US$20/10 adult/child*) One of Seward's biggest tourist draws. Woody the 1,500lb sea lion is a sight to behold. The seabird aviary, tide-pool touch tank (where visitors can touch inter-tidal creatures in an enclosure), educational displays and many tanks filled with all manner of marine creatures aren't bad either. In addition to catering to the public, the facility rehabilitates marine mammals, many of which can be seen in outdoor enclosures. Anyone interested in seeing the real Sealife Center should go on a behind-the-scenes tour. The only problem with the centre is that they don't allow adults to attend their Nocturn program, where children are invited to spend the night at the centre and find out what the animals do in the dark. Puffin and octopus 'encounters' can be arranged for US$75.

Public library (see page 235) Located in the city centre, it shows an interesting video about the 1964 Good Friday earthquake that destroyed 90% of Seward. The library also has the original Alaska flag designed by local boy, Benny Benson. It was adopted by the Alaska Territorial Legislature on May 1927 and later became the state flag.

KENAI FJORDS NATIONAL PARK

Encompassing just under 700,000 acres of ice, rock and ecologically-rich coastal fjords, this park is one of the most rugged in the state. The park is located just south of Seward on the Kenai Peninsula, following the coastline from Bear Glacier to the border of Kachemak Bay State Park at the Petrof Glacier. The park was established in 1980 to protect the unique rainforest habitat in the park's many fjords as well as the 700-square-mile Harding Ice Field. The park is famous for the Exit Glacier (see box on page 238), which cascades off the Harding Ice Field nearly to Exit Glacier Road. The park's numerous fjords are also a draw with tour boats taking visitors into the park to see glaciers and wildlife all summer.

GETTING THERE Seward is the main access point for the park. Visitors can drive to the park via the Exit Glacier Road off the Seward Highway north of Seward or take a boat for approximately 20 miles around Callisto Head to the park.

TOURIST INFORMATION
🛈 **Exit Glacier Nature Center** ☎ 224 7600; www.nps.gov/kefj; ⊕ 09.00–20.00 daily. Located at the end of Exit Glacier Road off the Seward Highway just north of Seward.
🛈 **Kenai Fjords Information Center** 1212 4th Av; ☎ 224 3374; ⊕ 08.30–19.00 daily. Near the Seward small boat harbour.

WHERE TO STAY Camping is allowed anywhere in the park for free except near a public-use cabin or Exit Glacier or the road. The only organised campground is the 12-site walk-in Exit Glacier Campground. It is not possible to reserve at this free campground. To get a spot, arrive early as the sites fill up by early evening.
    Within the park are three public-use cabins available by reservation for US$50 per night. To reserve call the **Alaska Public Lands Information Center** (☎ *644 3661, 866 869 6887 (TF)*). Holgate Cabin in Aialik Bay is a two- to four-hour boat ride or 35-minute flight from Seward. The Holgate Glacier is located nearby. The North Arm Cabin is in Nuka Bay and situated three to six hours by boat or one hour by plane from Seward. The spectacular 900ft Kvasnikoff Falls, bears, an old growth forest and an occasional pink salmon run are the area's main attractions. The **Aialik Bay Cabin** is located on a piece

St Peter's Episcopal Church Three blocks west of the public library, the church was built in 1906 and is famous for its 1925 mural by Dutch artist Jan van Emple.

Boat harbour The small boat harbour on the north end of town is a great venue for a pleasant evening stroll, especially when fishermen return with their catch. The deep-water dock to the east is where coal is transferred from train cars to ships bound for various Pacific ports.

Coastal Walk Trail Another lovely place to wander is along the Coastal Walk Trail connecting the north end of town to the south end via the seashore.

Around town
Seward Museum *(336 3rd Av; ☎ 224 3902; www.museumsusa.org; ⏰ 10.00–17.00 daily; US$3/0.50 adult/child)* A cross section of local history including native art work, Russian history and the Good Friday earthquake that nearly destroyed Seward. The gift shop has some good books on the Seward area. Evening programmes on Monday, Wednesday and Friday at 19.00.

of park land within Port Graham Native Corporation Land, two to four hours by boat from Seward. The Port Graham Corporation (☎ 284 2212) can issue permits to use their land. Bears and berries arrive in the early autumn.

ACTIVITIES Kenai Fjords National Park is a rugged piece of land where nearly any outdoor activity is an adventure. Kayakers often use the park but must be reasonably experienced since the coastline can be rough. However, the hikes around Exit Glacier are generally easy and short. Beyond Exit Glacier few developed hiking trails exist.

From the Exit Glacier visitor centre at the end of the road, a network of easy, short trails branch out toward the foot of the glacier. Short, ranger-led walks leave the Exit Glacier Nature Center at 10.00, 14.00 and 16.00 daily. Guided hikes on the Harding Ice Field Trail take place on Sat at 09.00. Those interested in local native cultures should head to the **Alaska Sealife Center** at 11.00 for a presentation or at 15.00 for a talk on glaciers.

For a more serious but also more rewarding hike, follow the four-mile **Harding Ice Field Trail**. The trail rises for 1,000 vertical feet over rocky terrain before ending at a point overlooking the Harding Ice Field. The views are amazing with snow, ice and lonely peaks as far as the eye can see. Allow all day for this eight-mile round trip hike. Camping is permitted along the trail but tents must be pitched at least ⅛ mile from the trail and on bare rock or snow. Another fantastic trail is the Resurrection River and Russian Lakes Trail. From mile 8 of the Exit Glacier Road, the Resurrection River Trail follows the Resurrection River through the mountains for 16 miles before intersecting the Russian Lakes Trail. Following the trail to the northeast will take you to the Snug Harbor Road on Kenai Lake after eight miles. Following the trail northwest you will reach the Sterling Highway near Cooper Landing after 15 more miles. Those wishing to complete the 72-mile trek from Seward all the way to Hope can continue across the Sterling Highway onto the Resurrection Pass Trail (see page 226). Brown bears are very common in the Resurrection River valley.

Guided or unguided kayak rentals can be obtained from **Liquid Adventures**, **Kayak Adventures** or **Sunny Cove Sea Kayaking**. Water taxi companies include **Aquetec Water Taxi** and **Miller's Landing**.

Lowell Point Has lovely beaches and hiking trails, and can be found at the southern end of town. The scenic drive hugs the mountains for 1.5 miles before entering a small community. Head to the southern end of the community to a beach access point. Bring a picnic or go for a hike on the **Coastal Trail** to Caines Head (see page 233).

WESTERN KENAI PENINSULA

The Sterling Highway traverses the western part of the Kenai Peninsula from its junction with the Seward Highway for 143 miles to the end of the road in Homer. Not long after Cooper Landing, the road leaves the mountains and heads across a vast flat plain dotted with lakes and stunted black spruce before meeting the Cook Inlet near Soldotna. From the Kenai/Soldotna area, that road travels south along Cook Inlet through Ninilchik and Anchor Point to Homer where the Kenai Mountains are once again visible.

Between the Seward Highway junction and Cooper Landing at mile 48, the **Crescent Creek** (*9 sites; basic facilities for US$11*) and **Quartz Creek** (*44 sites*) campgrounds (*both at mile 60.5 Sterling Hwy*) can be found off the Quartz Creek Road. To reserve, visit www.recreation.gov.

COOPER LANDING (*Population: 357*) After skirting Kenai Lake, the road bends and crosses the Kenai River where it flows out of the lake. This spot marks the beginning of Cooper Landing (⊕ 60°29'25"N, 149°47'40"W), a tiny town surrounded by mountains and blessed with some of the best fishing and rafting in the region. The town hugs the highway for a few miles and consists of a petrol station, a few accommodation options and a handful of rafting and fishing outfits. The town was named after Joseph Cooper who mined the area in the 1880s. The post office and surrounding structures are historic buildings dating from that period.

Tourist information
🛈 Cooper Landing Chamber of Commerce ➲ 595 8888; www.cooperlandingchamber.com. The website is a good source of information. The visitor centre can be found east of town at mile 47.5 on the Sterling Highway.

Local tours and activities
Fishing Most of the drift-fishing companies in Cooper Landing offer a version of the same thing: amazing fishing for salmon, rainbow trout and dolly varden on half-day & full-day trips costing US$175–265. Many can also arrange fly-out trips

EXIT GLACIER

Exit Glacier is one of the state's most accessible glaciers, and is easily explored on foot. The glacier flows from the Harding Ice Field high above and feeds the Resurrection River, which supports an annual flood of spawning salmon. From Seward, drive north on the Seward Highway to mile 3.7 then turn west onto Herman Leirer/Exit Glacier Road. Follow the road along the Resurrection River for 8.4 miles to a carpark and the Exit Glacier Nature Center. Along the road just before the centre are small signs indicating the year that the glacier had reached that point.

Exit Glacier Guides (➲ 224 5081; *www.exitglacierguides.com*) the local experts on Exit Glacier can take you for a simple hike near the glacier or on a full-scale trek over the ice.

for truly spectacular fishing in a remote setting. These trips start at US$475. Half-day scenic raft trips can be booked for prices starting at US$45.

Alaska Drifters 598 2000; www.alaskadrifters.com. Fish for salmon or trout from a rigid drift boat outfitted with comfy chairs.
Alaska River Adventures 595 2000, 888 836 9027 (TF); www.alaskariveradventures.com. Raft trips, fishing floats & custom trips of all kinds.
Alaska Rivers Company Mile 51 Sterling Hwy; 595 1226, 888 595 1226 (TF); www.alaskariverscompany.com. Rafting & fishing trips plus nice cabins right on the water.

Alaska Streamers 595 2200; www.alaskastreamers.com. These guys are the experts on a handful of local rivers & offer salmon & trout fishing for US$150/half day & US$250/full day.
Kenai Cache Outfitters 595 1401; www.kenaicache.com. The main tackle shop in the 'city centre' selling all kinds of fishing gear as well as Alaskana books & gifts. Book a fishing guide here.
Kenai River Fly Fishing 595 5733; www.kenaicache.com

Tour operators
Kenai Lake Sea Kayak Adventures 595 3441; www.kenailake.com. All-day bike rentals for US$45. Kayak trips in Kenai Lake cost US$65.

Where to stay
⌂ **Kenai River B&B** (4 rooms) Mile 49.1 Sterling Hwy; 888 688 9002 (TF); www.kenairiverbandb.com. A lovely private home on the river that can accommodate a large group; well worth the money for groups of up to 10 people. B/fast. $$$$$
⌂ **Kenai Princess Lodge** (86 rooms) 17245 Frontier Circle; 595 1425, 800 426 0500 (TF); www.princesslodges.com/kenai_lodge.cfm. Comfortable, self-contained rooms with all the amenities, including a restaurant, lounge (⊕ 07.00–22.00 daily; $$$$) & gift shop on the premises. Popular with the cruise-ship crowd. $$$$

⌂ **Alaska Rivers Company** (4 rooms) Has private cabins on or near the river. $$$
⌂ **Upper Kenai River Inn** (5 rooms) Mile 48.6 Sterling Hwy; 595 3333; www.upperkenairiverinn.com. Clean standard rooms right on the river. B/fast incl. $$$
⌂ **Stevenson Retreat** (4 rooms) 48.1 Sterling Hwy; 595 348; www.stevensonretreat.com. A lovely 2-storey home on Kenai Lake outside town. B/fast incl. $$

Where to eat
✗ **Kenai Princess Lodge** ⊕ 07.00–22.00 daily. One of town's more reliable, but expensive venues. $$$$
✗ **Sunrise Inn** Mile 45 Sterling Hwy; 595 1222; www.alaskasunriseinn.com; ⊕ 07.00–22.00 daily. Simple diner food. Nothing special, but the meals fill the stomach. $$

✗ **Wildman's** Mile 47.5 Sterling Hwy; 595 1456; www.wildmans.org; ⊕ 07.00–23.00 daily. Delicatessen, groceries, showers, laundry & auto repairs. There is really very little one *can't* get here. $$

What to see
Cooper Landing Museum (*Mile 48.7 Sterling Hwy;* 595 3500; *www.cooperlandingmuseum.com;* ⊕ 13.00–18.00 Wed–Mon; free admission) A small but pleasant museum with local and natural history displays.

AROUND COOPER LANDING Heading west out of Cooper Landing, the **Cooper Creek Campground** (30 sites) is at mile 50.5 with campsites costing US$11. One mile beyond is **Gwin's Lodge** (595 1265; *www.gwinslodge.com*) with decent homemade food in their restaurant. They hold fish bakes with live music on almost every evening of the week. Just beyond is a two-mile road leading to the ever-popular

Russian River Campground (*84 sites*; ☎ *877 444 6777; www.recreation.gov*) at the confluence of the Russian and Kenai Rivers. To reserve, call. Sites cost US$14–22 and dayparking will set you back US$5. The salmon fishing mid-summer is very good but it can get very crowded. If you haven't seen 'combat fishing' – when large numbers of people jostle and sometimes fight along an over-crowded body of water for the best spot to cast their line – this is one place to do it. A lovely trail follows the Russian River from the campground to the Russian River Falls and the Russian Lakes and provides great opportunities to see spawning salmon in season.

The highway follows the Kenai River until mile 58, where the mountains start to give way to lowland black spruce forests. Here, the Skilak Lake Loop Road leaves the highway and provides access to Skilak Lake. The fishing along this stretch of the Kenai River can be very good, even by the side of the road. The best trout fishing is generally in the late summer and autumn, when the gruesome sounding 'flesh flies' can be used as bait to imitate pieces of salmon flesh. At mile 58, the Skilak Lake Loop Road leaves the highway and heads southwest toward Skilak Lake for 16 miles.

Around mile 80, the Highway passes through the community of Sterling (population: 5,134). The town has little to offer the visitor except basic groceries, simple lodging and petrol. The Swanson River Road is one of two access points leading to the **Moose River** and **Swanson Lakes area** (see box on page 224).

Where to stay The area has a handful of campsite grounds. To reserve, visit www.recreation.gov.

⛺ **Hidden Lake Campground** (14 sites) 3.2 miles down Skilak Lake Road with good trout fishing.
⛺ **Lower Skilak Lake Campground** (14 sites) At mile 13.6 of Skilak Lake Road with good lake access near the outflow of the Kenai River.
⛺ **Lower Ohmer Lake Campground** (5 sites) At mile 8.4 of Skilak Lake Road on Skilak Lake.
⛺ **Upper Skilak Lake Campground** (26 sites) Next door to Lower Ohmer Lake Campground (see above).

⛺ **Izaak Walton Campground** (31 sites) Offers camping at the confluence of the Moose & Kenai Rivers with pitches costing US$10. An archaeological site was excavated at the campsite, revealing prehistoric house pits belonging to the Kenaitze Indians, who inhabited the area for hundreds of years.

For those who choose to stay on the highway, the **Jean Lake Campground** (3 sites) sits by a pretty lake. More basic camping can be found at the Kelly and Peterson Lakes near mile 70 and also at Watson Lake a mile further.

SOLDOTNA (*Population: 4,016*) The sprawling roadside town of Soldotna (⊕ 60°29'12"N, 151°4'31"W) consists of strip malls, commercial hotels and restaurants all contrasting sharply with the lovely turquoise Kenai River flowing right through town. The Kenai River is one of the state's most accessible and productive salmon rivers with millions of fish making their way upstream every summer, running the gauntlet of sport fishermen, that can line the banks so densely (and occasionally violently) they are locally called 'combat fishermen'. Supporting the industry are many guides and tackle shops. In addition to sport fishing, Soldotna is a shopping destination for people from less urban Peninsula towns and is also home to many of Cook Inlet's oil and natural gas workers. Visitors not obsessed with fishing can get a good taste of the town by simply passing through after a bite to eat and a stroll along the river.

History The Soldotna area was originally inhabited by Kenaitze Indians, but was developed immediately after World War II because of its rich resources of timber, water, fish and oil. Shortly after, the northern part of the Sterling Highway was completed, connecting the Upper Peninsula with both Soldotna and Kenai. The oil and natural gas exploration continued through the 1950s and 1960s and, combined with the popularity of fishing on the Kenai River, turned Soldotna into one of the Peninsula's fastest growing towns.

Tourist information

🛈 **Kenai National Wildlife Refuge Visitor Center** (see page 224) A great overview of the area's natural environment & the available recreation opportunities. The centre shows wildlife dioramas, films & has other information available. The rangers are generally on hand to answer questions.

🛈 **Visitor Information Centre** 44790 Sterling Hwy; ☎ 262 1337; www.soldotnachamber.com; ⊕ 09.00–19.00 daily. This centre has heaps of information, most of which relates to fishing. Located near the Kenai River bridge.

Hiking and recreation
Soldotna is one of the main access points for the **Kenai National Wildlife Refuge** (see page 224), where an extensive network of lakes and rivers makes ideal canoe routes.

Where to stay
Soldotna is full of accommodation options, most of which are ordinary or worse. Some lovely B&Bs and lodges can be found nestling in the wood or along the river. Try the **Kenai Peninsula Bed and Breakfast Association** (☎ 866 436 2266; www.kenaipeninsulabba.com) or the **Alaska Bed and Breakfast Association** (www.alaskabba.com).

🏠 **Longmere Lake Lodge Bed & Breakfast** (6 rooms) 35955 Ryan Ln; ☎ 262 9799; www.longmerelakelodge.com. Lovely rooms in a hunting-themed house. $$$$

🏠 **Sprucewood Lodge** (8 rooms) ☎ 260 5420, 888 844 9737 (TF). www.kenairiver.com. Mainly catering to fishermen, this lovely lodge has simple but elegant rooms & is located right on the river. $$$$

🏠 **Kenai River Raven B&B** (8 rooms) ☎ 262 5818; www.kenairiverraven.com A large log home right on the river with simple, but pleasant rooms. $$$–$$$$

🏠 **Alaskan Serenity B&B** (3 rooms) 41598 Alaska Ln; ☎ 800 764 6648; www.alaskanserenitybb.com. Simple accommodation in hunting-style cabins. $$$

🏠 **Best Western King Salmon Motel** (48 rooms) 35546A Kenai Spur Hwy; ☎ 262 5857; www.bestwesternalaska.com. Basic rooms with kitchenettes, Wi-Fi, & TV. An OK restaurant is in the main building (⊕ 06.00–21.00 daily; $$). $$$

🏠 **Escape for Two** (1 room) www.escapefortwo.com. A cosy private cabin designed for a couple, located 7 miles outside town. $$$

🏠 **Soldotna Inn** (30 rooms) 35041 Kenai Spur Hwy; ☎ 262 9169; www.mykels.com. A simple place with no frills. $$$

🏠 **Call of the River B&B** (3 rooms) 34199 Keystone Dr; ☎ 260 6533; www.kenairiversalmon.com. Lodge-style rooms share an entrance & adjoin a kitchenette & sitting area. $$

Camping

⛺ **Centennial Park** (176 sites) Located along the river & within walking distance of the museum. To get there, turn west south of the bridge onto Kalifornsky Beach Rd, the campground is on the north side of the road. The park costs US$15 for camping & US$6.50 for day use.

⛺ **Swiftwater Park** (40 sites) A civilised & popular campsite right on the river. To find the park, turn east south of the bridge onto Funny River Road. The campground is on the north side. The park costs US$15 for camping & US$6.50 for day-use.

Where to eat
Soldotna is not known for its cuisine. However, a few decent meals can be found if you know where to look.

✗ **Charlotte's Café at River City Books** 43977 Sterling Hwy; ☎ 260 7722; ⊕ 09.00–19.00 Mon–Sat & 11.00–17.00 Sun. Good salads, soups & sandwiches. Enjoy lunch surrounded by used books. $$

✕ **Jersey Subs** 44224 Sterling Hwy; ☎ 260 3343; ⏱ 00.00–19.00 daily. Great, authentic east coast submarine sandwiches. Try the Philly cheese steak. $$

Other practicalities

Post office 174 N Binkley St; ☎ 262 4760; www.usps.com; ⏱ 10.00–17.00 Mon–Fri, 10.00–14.00 Sat

Public library 235 N Binkley St; ☎ 262 4227; ⏱ 09.00–20.00 Mon–Thu, 12.00–18.00 Fri, 09.00–18.00 Sat. Computer terminals with internet & free Wi-Fi.

What to see

Soldotna Homestead Museum (*44790 Sterling Hwy;* ⏱ *10.00–16.00 Tue–Sat, 12.00–16.00 Sun; free admission*) Historic homestead cabins are located in the grounds, while native artefacts and wildlife displays can be found inside.

Kenai National Wildlife Refuge Visitor Center (see pages 224–5) A good place to learn about the area's natural resources, as well as the refuge.

Kenai River Brewing Co (*241 N Aspen St;* ☎ *262 2337; www.kenairiverbrewing.com*) Offers tours and tastings.

KENAI (*Population: 7,134*) From Soldotna, the Kenai Spur Highway branches off the Sterling Highway and heads 10 miles northwest to the town of Kenai, at the mouth of the Kenai River. Kenai (✛ 60°33'31"N, 151°13'47"W) is financially supported by Cook Inlet oil drilling and commercial fishing and has traditionally given the traveller little reason to visit beyond sport fishing.

Recently Kenai has become better equipped to accommodate visitors with B&Bs, restaurants and some well-preserved sites of Russian history.

History When the Russians arrived in the Kenai area in 1741, Dena'ina Athabascans had already been living there for hundreds of years. Then, 50 years later, Fort St Nicholas – the second permanent Russian settlement – was built to control the fur and fish trade. In 1849, the Holy Assumption Russian Orthodox Church was established by one Egumen Nicholai and, 20 years later, Fort Kenay was built by the US Military. Homestead owners and commercial fishermen developed the town during the first half of the 20th century, but it did not grow further until the 1950s, when oil was discovered in Cook Inlet. Commercial fishing, oil and natural gas continue to drive the economy.

Tourist information

🛈 Kenai Visitors Center 402 Overland Av; ☎ 283 7183; www.visitkenai.com; 09.00–19.00 Mon–Fri, 10.00–18.00 Sat & Sun. The centre has information & a small museum with native artefacts, wildlife displays, films & presentations with a US$3 admission. This is a good place to park & start a walking tour of old town.

🏠 Where to stay

🏠 **Daniels Lake Lodge B&B** (6 rooms) ☎ 776 5578; www.danielslakelodge.com. Located north of Kenai near Nikiski. There are 3 rooms in the main house & 3 pleasant cabins. $$$–$$$$

🏠 **Harborside Cottages** (5 Rooms) ☎ 283 6162; www.harborsidecottages.com. Delightful little cottages right in old town & near the beach. Wi-Fi but no b/fast. $$$

🏠 **Tanglewood B&B** (8 rooms) 2528 Beaverloop Rd; ☎ 283 6771; www.tanglewooedbandb.homestead.com. This B&B has amazing views & tasty home cooked meals. $$$

🏠 **Uptown Motel** (50 rooms) 47 Spur View Dr; ☎ 283 3660; www.uptownmotel.com. This motel has a healthy dose of Alaskana. $$–$$$

The world's largest king salmon was pulled from the Kenai River on 17 May 1985, weighing 97lbs 4oz. A photo of the fish hangs inside the visitor centre. King salmon suspected of being larger have been hooked but never landed – they sometimes struggled on the hook for days – and thus never had their weight confirmed. The Kenai River also holds the state's red salmon record which stands at 16lbs. Other state (although not from the Kenai Peninsula) records include rainbow/steelhead trout weighing 42lbs 3oz, pink salmon weighing in at 12 lbs 9oz, silver salmon weighing 26lbs and dolly varden at 27lbs 6oz.

Camping

Ă Captain Cook State Recreation Area (see page 244) A number of camping options can be found north of Kenai.

Ă Beluga Lookout RV Park (65 sites) 929 Mission Av; ✎ 283 5999; www.belugalookout.com. Well-equipped but expensive sites with a great view & location. Sites cost US$35–60.

✗ Where to eat and drink

✗ Louie's Restaurant 47 Spur View Dr; ✎ 283 3660; www.uptownmotel.com; ⊕ 17.00–22.00 daily. A great place to see locals & stuffed local wildlife. Provides good hearty meals too. The lounge out at the back is a classic Kenai watering hole. **$$$**

✗ Kassik's Kenai Brew Stop 47160 Spruce Haven St; ✎ 776 4055; www.kassikskenaibrewstop.com; ⊕ 12.00–19.00 Mon–Thu, 12.00–20.00 Fri & Sat, 12.00–17.00 Sun. Excellent beers, all made on location. Have a free taste & take home a jug. **$$**

✗ Veronica's Café 604 Petersen Way; ✎ 283 2725; ⊕ 09.00–21.00 daily. This café has a laid-back, cosy atmosphere & serves good food, hot drinks with live music. Open mike is on Fri at 18.30, bands play at 18.30 on Sat. **$$**

♀ Kassiks Kenai Brew Stop 47160 Spruce Haven St; ✎ 776 4055; www.kassikskenaibrewstop.com. Offers tours & tastings.

Other practicalities

Nikiski Pool Mile 23.4 Kenai Spur Hwy; ✎ 776 8472; www.northpenrec.com. This amazing leisure centre has water slides & multiple interconnected pools. The waterslide costs US$7 for the day & general swimming is US$4. Swim times change frequently so call ahead.

Post office 140 Bidarka St; ✎ 283 7771; ⊕ 08.45–17.00 Mon–Fri, 09.30–13.00 Sat. **Public library** 163 Main Street Loop; ✎ 283 4378; www.kenailibrary.org; ⊕ 10.00–20 Mon–Thu, 10.00–17.00 Fri & Sat, 12.00–17.00 Sun. The library has free internet.

What to see Near the visitor centre is a replica of **Fort Kenay** (the way the military chose to spell Kenai), a former US military fort originally built in 1869, two years after Alaska was purchased from Russia. When troops were needed to fight Indians in the American southwest, the fort was abandoned in 1870 after just 17 months. Also here is the **Holy Assumption Russian Orthodox Church** (✎ 283 4122), one of the oldest Russian Orthodox churches in the state and also one of the most visited. The original church was built in 1845, but fell into disrepair and was rebuilt at its present site in 1895. The architecture, with its three onion-shaped domes, is lovely and the relics and paintings inside are really something to see. Regular church services are held on the weekends and tours Monday through Sunday. Nearby, the **St Nicholas Chapel**, built in 1906, was constructed on the site of the original Holy Assumption Russian Orthodox Church built to honour the parish's founder, Fr Nikolai, and Makary Ivanov, the church reader, for saving the lives of hundreds of Dena'ina after a smallpox outbreak. Both structures are inside what used to be Fort St Nicholas, which was built in 1791 and was only the second permanent Russian settlement in Alaska. The nearby bluff provides great views of the Aleutian Range.

The beach in front of old town is a wonderful place to walk or have a picnic on a wind-free day. During incoming tides, dip-net fishermen can be seen at the mouth of the river trying to scoop fish with giant nets.

On Saturdays from 10.00–17.00, head over to the **Farmers' Market** at the visitor centre (*402 Overland Av*) for veggies and crafts.

For a short day trip, head north, passing through Nikiski to **Captain Cook State Recreation Area**. Off the beaten path and little-visited, this recreation area is a wonderful place to hike along the beach, go boating on the lake or just relax and enjoy nature. The fishing is good at Stormy Lake and Swanson River and the long beach is lovely. The recreation area is located 25 miles north of Kenai on the North Kenai Road at mile 36.

The tiny community of **Kasilof** (*population: 56*) follows the highway around mile 109 where the highway crosses the Kasilof River and into the surrounding area. The town of Kasilof has three recreation areas popular with those who want to go camping and fishing (see box on page 246).

The Kasilof River supports a commercial fishing fleet and several fish processing plants.

NINILCHIK (*Population: 853*) Ninilchik village is beautifully situated on a bluff where the Ninilchik River empties into Cook Inlet. Originally inhabited by the Dena'ina, in the 1820s the area became something of a retirement community for Russian fur traders who had taken native wives or were too elderly to make the long voyage back to Russia. In 1847, Grigorii and Mavra Kvasnikoff moved from Kodiak to Ninilchik and, with others, constructed the Transfiguration of Our Lord Church in 1846. The town slowly grew from the descendants of the Kvasnikoff and native residents. In the 1940s homesteaders came to the area and in the 1950s, the Sterling Highway passed through town. Commercial fishing and increasingly sport fishing and tourism are the town's major sources of income. In the bight of the river, on the north side, are many historic buildings and a lovely Russian Orthodox Church.

 Where to stay The **Ninilchik Beach Campground** (35 sites) is on the south side of the river on the beach. Pitches cost US$10. **Ninilchik Chamber of Commerce** (✆ *567 3571; www.ninilchikchamber.com*) has information about the handful of local sport fishing guides and accommodations.

What to see and do
Ninilchik State Recreation Area Camping and razor-clam digging is available on Ninilchik Beach in Ninilchik State Recreation Area, located at mile 135 of the Sterling Highway. Camping is also available along the river. Another campsite on a bluff overlooking the beach is accessed at mile 135.7 of the Sterling Highway, where a stairway leads to the beach.

Deep Creek Located at mile 136, Deep Creek is popular for fishing and partying with southern peninsula residents. During late May and June, king salmon are pursued relentlessly here. Sport fishing charter boats launch from the beach here via tractor. **Deep Creek Custom Packing** (✆ *567 3395; www.deepcreekcustompacking.com*) packs and sells fish. Private and state camping (US$10) can be found off the highway and on the beach.

Stariski State Recreation Area At mile 151, the Stariski State Recreation Area (13 sites) has simple sites for US$10 on a bluff overlooking the Cook Inlet.

Clam Gulch is situated – at mile 117 on the Sterling Highway – on a bluff overlooking the Cook Inlet. The beaches below are full of razor clams, at least where people haven't over-harvested them. The elusive bivalves can dig through the hard sand as quickly or more quickly than a human, making them surprisingly hard to catch. Get a fishing licence and head out on an ebbing tide. The best clamming is far from any road outlet. In my opinion, eating razor clams is rather like eating rubber bands, but some people rave about them. The preferred ways of preparing them are to fry the clams or put them in a seafood chowder. To catch them, a clam shovel is essential. When you spot a dimple in the sand, quickly push the shovel into the sand just to the side of the dimple and pry open. If you have done everything right, the clam will be near the bottom of the hole. You then drop to your hands and knees and begin digging furiously. Be careful not to slice your fingers on their shells. They aren't called razor clams for nothing! Camping available for US$10 per pitch.

ANCHOR POINT (*Population: 1,829*) Five miles south of Stariski State Recreation Area is the town of Anchor Point on the Anchor River. When Captain James Cook explored the Cook Inlet in 1778, he named Anchor Point after losing an anchor offshore. The funky fishing town has the distinction of being the westernmost town on the road system in North America. Silver and king salmon as well as dolly varden and steelhead, draw anglers from around the southern peninsula throughout the summer. The Anchor River Road heads west along the river immediately after the Old Seward Highway bridge. A handful of campgrounds can be found along the road and there is also one at the end of the beach. Sites cost US$10 and can fill up on weekends and holidays.

Where to stay and eat On the western side of the highway, north of the river is the infamous **Blue Bus Diner** (✆ 235 6285). Here, the burgers are mouth-wateringly huge and greasy. They keep your tummy full for days! Don't miss it! The **Anchor River Inn** (✆ 235 8531; *www.anchorriverinn.com*) at the junction with the Old Seward Highway has standard rooms and a restaurant serving dinner. The **Anchor Point Chamber of Commerce** (✆ 235 2600; *www.anchorpointchamber.org*) has information on the handful of services in town.

What to see and do
Anchor River State Recreation Area The park is a favourite spot to fish and camp with wonderful views of Mount Augustine, Mount Iliamna and Mount Redoubt to the west. The river has king, silver and pink salmon runs, as well as runs of steelhead and dolly vaden. Organised camping can be found in a number of campsites between the Anchor Point Spur Road and the Anchor River for US$10 per night. The weekends are crowded and not very quiet.

Stariski State Recreation Site Just north of Anchor Point, this site perches on a high bluff and offers amazing views of the Augustine, Iliamna and Redoubt mountains. The campground has nine sites with pitches costing US$10 per night.

NIKOLAEVSK (*Population: 296*) Nine miles inland from Anchor Point off the North Fork Road is the Russian Old Believer (see *Glossary* on page 431) town of Nikolaevsk. This town is one of a few on the peninsula where Russian Old Believers maintain a traditional way of life, largely separated from the prevailing

KASILOF STATE PARKS

The town of Kasilof has three recreation areas popular with those who want to go camping and fishing. Campsites cost US$10 per night and many of the day use carparks cost US$5 per day.

CROOKED CREEK STATE RECREATION SITE This 79-place site is located at the confluence of Crooked Creek and the Kasilof River, off the North Coho Loop Road. The Kasilof River turns into a zoo in the spring as people try to land a king salmon. Steelhead trout run in the spring and autumn and good silver salmon and dolly varden fishing can be enjoyed in the autumn. Pitch sites here cost US$10.

JOHNSON LAKE STATE RECREATION AREA Located shortly after the turn-off from the Sterling Highway on to Tustumena Lake Road, at the giant red 'T', this area has a lovely 50-site campground by Johnson Lake where visitors can fish and canoe. Pitches cost US$10. Tustumena Lake is 115 square miles and is the source of the Kasilof River.

KASILOF RIVER STATE RECREATION SITE The site is also popular for fishing and camping. The recreation area can be found where the Sterling Highway crosses the Kasilof River. This area can be very crowded when the salmon are running. Camping is available right next to the river.

culture. Residents speak Russian and English and wear traditional handmade clothes. Residents originally purchased land here in 1967 with a grant from the Tolstoy Foundation. The community is interesting but not set up for tourists and some folk are wary of outsiders so be sensitive. However, don't miss the church and the only visitor-oriented business in town, the **Samovar Café** (❀ *235 6867; www.russiangiftsnina.com*) offering homemade Russian food and gifts. Camping is available for US$10.

From Anchor Point, the Sterling Highway continues south for 16 miles to Homer and the end of the road.

HOMER *Population 5,390*

At the end of the Alaskan road system lies the small, arty, fishing town of Homer (⊕ 59°38'35"N, 151°31'33"W). Some know it as the end of the road, or the 'cosmic hamlet by the sea', while still others know it as the halibut fishing capital of the world. The beauty of Homer is that it's all these things and so much more. The tight-knit and creative community is dedicated to the idea that a town in the Alaskan wilderness can be both an outdoor, working town, but also a cultural Mecca. In creating a town where world-class eateries, galleries, and museums meet the tremendous expanse of wilderness known as the Kenai Mountains and Kachemak Bay, they have succeeded admirably.

For those arriving in Homer on the Sterling Highway, the Kenai Mountains and Kachemak Bay form the welcoming committee. The mountains are split by glaciers and beyond, the immense Harding Ice field flows into the distance. Protruding from mainland Homer like an odd proboscis is the Homer Spit, a five-mile sandbar. This natural formation is the terminal moraine (a formation of glacial debris) of a great glacier that once crept down the bay, pushing millions of tons of sand and gravel in front of it. When the glacier stopped and began to recede about 10,000 years ago, the Homer Spit was left. For the majority of the town's

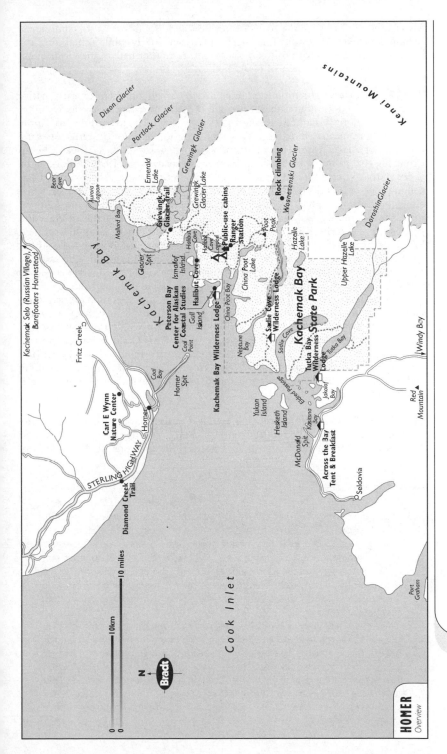

HOMER
Overview

Cook Inlet

Southcentral Alaska HOMER

5

247

Kenai Mountains

Dixon Glacier

Portlock Glacier

Grewingk Glacier

Emerald Lake

Grewingk Glacier Lake

Aurora Lagoon

Bear Cove

Mallard Bay

Glacier Spit

Grewingk Glacier Trail

Public-use cabins

Ranger station

Rock climbing

Wosnesenski Glacier

Doroshin Glacier

Kachemak Bay

Kechemak Selo (Russian Village), Barefooters Homestead

Fritz Creek

Coal Bay

Homer Spit

Homer

Coal Point

Peterson Bay Center for Alaskan Coastal Studies

Gull Island

Coal Island

Halibut Cove

Ismailof Island

Halibut Cove Lagoon

Kachemak Bay Wilderness Lodge

China Poot Bay

China Poot Lake

Poot Peak

Hazelle Lake

Upper Hazelle Lake

Kachemak Bay State Park

Sadie Cove Wilderness Lodge

Sadie Cove

Neptune Bay

Tutka Bay Wilderness Lodge

Tutka Bay

Carl E Wynn Nature Center

STERLING HIGHWAY

Diamond Creek Trail

Yukon Island

Hesketh Island

Eldred Passage

McDonald Spit

Kasitsna Bay

Jakolof Bay

Across the Bay Tent & Breakfast

Seldovia

Red Mountain

Windy Bay

Port Graham

10km

10 miles

N

Bradt

0

0

history, the spit has been the focus of business and life, from coal to commercial fishing and today for tourism. Some find the Spit lovely while others find the tourist-saturated sand bar positively abhorrent. Love it or hate it, the Homer Spit is the starting point for many of Homer's best adventures.

HISTORY Homer was traditionally inhabited by small numbers of early native people who lived mostly on the south side of Kachemak Bay. In the early 1800s, Russian explorers named Kachemak Bay – which according to some interpretations means 'smoking cliffs' – after the smouldering coal seams. After the purchase of Alaska from Russia, the Cook Inlet Coal Fields Company began extracting coal from the bluffs along Homer's beaches in the 1890s. A dock and a short railroad were built and miners were brought in to extract the estimated 400 million tons of coal deposits. The railroad was the first in the state and stretched along the spit for 7.3 miles to a dock where coal could be loaded onto ships. At that time, the community was located at the end of the spit where fields of grass and groups of trees thrived. In 1964, the Good Friday earthquake sunk the spit and killed off most of the flora. In 1869, Homer Pennock arrived looking for gold but soon departed when all he found was coal, leaving only his name. The town of Homer grew around the coal industry until 1902 when the coal market collapsed and the community at the end of the spit was abandoned. The few who remained, settled on the reasonably fertile land in the hills behind the spit, subsisting on farming and fishing. As the population of Homer hovered just above zero, the town of Seldovia, across the bay from Homer, was thriving with a new salmon cannery. Homer didn't see much growth until the 1964 Good Friday earthquake destroyed most of Seldovia. The people and industry relocated to Homer and started the rapid growth of Homer. Today, Homer thrives on commercial fishing and tourism. Coal is still used but only by a few locals who gather it from the beach and use it in their homes.

GETTING THERE AND AWAY Homer is attached to the Alaska road system by the Sterling Highway and is 223 miles from Anchorage, or a five hour drive. Regular shuttles connect Homer with other Peninsula destinations such as Seward,

---

BAREFOOTERS

It says a lot about Homer that one of its most beloved, colourful and deeply influential residents was a Californian mystic who, with a group of followers in 1955, came to Homer and refused to wear shoes until world peace was achieved. Coming from anyone else, this mission would have seemed crazy. However, coming from Brother Asaiah it made sense, and before he died in 2000, there was no-one in town who didn't adore and respect him. Shortly after their arrival, the Barefooters built a homestead near the head of the bay, calling their community the Wisdom, Knowledge, Faith and Love Homestead. They wore no shoes during both summer and winter.

Years later, after moving into town, Brother Asaiah worked as a janitor and gave freely of his money, time and love. Although world peace remains elusive, Brother Asaiah's legacy brought a little peace to the hearts of everyone he met in his long life, and will also hopefully affect those who hear his story. The Barefooters' homestead near the head of the bay has been preserved by the Homer Land Trust and is open to the public. For those looking to meditate on world peace or the meaning of courage and resolve, or for those with a picnic, there is no better place to spend a sunny day.

Girdwood, and Anchorage to the north. Daily small-plane flights arrive in Homer from Anchorage and Kenai. The Alaska Ferry also docks in Homer and connects to Seldovia, Kodiak and Prince William Sound locations.

By air

✈ **Frontier/Era Aviation** ☏ 235 5205; www.frontierak.com. ERA flies between Homer & Anchorage as much as 5 times/day for just under US$300 return.

✈ **Grant Aviation** ☏ 235 2757; www.flygrant.com. Flies between Homer & Anchorage 4 times/week on w/days & 3 times on w/ends. A round-trip costs US$229 with discounts for seniors, students & children.

✈ **Homer Air** [252–3 F4] 2190 Kachemak Dr; ☏ 235 8591; www.homerair.com. Offers flightseeing & a daily service to Seldovia for US$96 return.

✈ **Smokey Bay Air** [252–3 F4] 2100 Kachemak Dr; ☏ 235 1511; www.smokeybayair.com. Provides charter flights & a service to Seldovia.

By bus

🚌 **Homer Stage Line** ☏ 235 2252; www.thestageline.net. A daily bus service between Homer & Anchorage with many stops in between for US$144 return.

By ferry

⛴ **State Ferry** ☏ 235 8449, 800 642 0066 (TF); www.ferryalaska.com. Homer is well connected to the rest of the state via the Alaska Marine Highway. Ferries leave for Seldovia (US$33) & Kodiak (US$74) 3 to 4 times a week & connect to the Aleutian Islands (see page 392) & Whittier (US$159) in Prince William Sound once a month. The ferry office & dock are located at the end of the Spit.

GETTING AROUND Homer is a hard place to get around if you don't have a car. Many visitors rent cars or RVs in Anchorage then make the journey south. Furthermore, water taxis are big business in Homer and with good reason. Virtually all the best places to explore, kayak, hike and camp are on the other side of the bay and require a water taxi. For a list of water taxis, see page 250.

Car rental Homer's airport is tiny with just a few rental car companies represented.

🚗 **Polar Car Rentals** ☏ 235 5998, 800 876 6417 TF. At the airport.

🚗 **Hertz** ☏ 235 0735, 800 654 3131, TF. At the airport.

🚗 **Adventure Alaska Car Rentals** ☏ 235 4022, 800 882 2808 TF). Just down the street from the airport on Ocean Drive. The owner, Trace, is fun guy & offers used cars for lower rates as well as a pick-up service.

By taxi

🚕 **Chux Cab** ☏ 235 2489

🚕 **Kachecab** ☏ 235 1950. Zip around town, often in Subarus.

TOURIST INFORMATION

ℹ **Homer Chamber of Commerce** [252–3 C4] ☏ 235 7740; www.homeralaska.org. Located in a blue building where the Sterling Highway enters town, the chamber has heaps of printed information.

LOCALS TOURS AND ACTIVITIES The **Homer Wilderness Leadership School** (☏ 399 0504; *www.howlschool.net*) offers a variety of outdoor classes and trips for children and adults alike. The young owners grew up in Homer and are extremely knowledgeable about the outdoors, survival in the wilderness and the area in general.

Kayaking Across the bay from Homer is a convoluted and lovely coastline, ideal for kayaking. These kayaking outfits lead tours and many rent boats to experienced paddlers. Rentals usually cost US$50 per day and half- & full-day tours on average cost US$100–150. Most tours include lunch and all gear.

Across the Bay Tent & Breakfast Kasitsna Bay; ↘ 235 3633; www.tentandbreakfastalaska.com. A semi-remote camp set up to give visitors a taste of living simply & off the beaten path. Bikes, kayaks, tents & meals can all be had for a modest sum.
Seaside Adventures ↘ 235 6672; www.seasideadventures.com. Based out of Tutka Bay, this remote lodge offers kayaking excursions for US$110/half day & US$150/full day (inc water taxi from Homer), as well as fishing trips & accommodation.
St Augustine's Charters ↘ 235 6126; www.homerkayaking.com. Another well-established kayak guiding service. Based out of Peterson Bay &

offering cabins, kayak rentals & tours. Central Charters (*4241 Homer Spit Rd;* ↘ *235 7847*) books for them on the spit.
Three Moose Glacier Kayaking 4416 Mariner Dr; ↘ 235 0755 or 888 777 0930 (TF); www.threemoose.com. Glacier kayaking & trekking adventures are US$175pp while a half-day kayak trip in Halibut Cove is US$95.
True North Kayak Adventures 4308 Homer Spit Rd; ↘ 235 0708; www.truenorthkayak.com. A reputable & established company with top-notch boats & a water taxi service. Their office is located on the spit behind **Mako's water taxi** (↘ *235 9055; www.makoswatertaxi.com*).

Fishing

Homer calls itself the halibut capital of the world and with good reason. The commercial fleet bring in more flatfish than anywhere else and, since the late 1970s, halibut charter fishing has become incredibly popular. The spit is lined with charter fishing offices and most offer slightly different versions of the same thing. One difference worth noting is that the more conscientious businesses have seen the halibut populations decline and now advocate catch and release for larger fish. Fish weighing more than 100lbs are almost always females and are capable of laying millions of eggs every year. These large female fish are responsible for perpetuating the species but are also what many fishermen are after. However, listen to a word from the wise; the small fish taste much better. Keep ones that weigh under 50lbs, your palate and the species will thank you. The **Coal Point Trading Co** (*4306 Homer Spit Rd;* ↘ *235 3877; www.welovefish.com*) on the spit is the best place to get your fish flash frozen & shipped. Most charters head to the Barren Islands. If the trip doesn't make you feel a little sick, bobbing around in the swell almost certainly will. The upshot is that getting 'skunked' (not catching any fish) is virtually unheard of and the non-drowsy version of the anti-motion sickness drug Dramamine is quite good. For those who tend to win things, be sure to get a ticket at the **Homer Jackpot Halibut Derby** (*www.homerhalibutderby.com*). One of the largest halibut to win weighed in at 376lbs and the most prize money paid out was US$51,298 in 2004. The derby is now offering prizes for those who release fish weighing more than 60lbs. Tickets cost US$10 per day.

Boat charters

Central Charters 4241 Homer Spit Rd; ↘ 235 7847; www.centralcharter.com. Books halibut fishing trips, kayaking adventures through St Augustine's Charters, bear viewing trips to Katmai National Park for US$525, day trips to Seldovia for US$45 & can arrange lodging besides. Halibut or salmon trips are US$225–250pp.
Homer Ocean Charters [252–3 G6] 4287 Homer Spit Rd; ↘ 235 6212; www.homerocean.com. Offer many of the same services as Central Charters. Kayaking rentals are US$40/day, guided trips are US$135pp, guided hikes across the bay with transportation are

US$125pp, & cabin rentals across the bay are US$80.
Inlet Charters [252–3 G6] 4287 Homer Spit Rd; ↘ 235 6126; www.acrossalaska.com. Books halibut fishing trips, kayak trips, lodging & handle a variety of other visitor services.
North Country Charters [252–3 G6] 4287 Homer Spit Rd; ↘ 235 7620; www.northcountrycharters.com. This family-run business is one of the oldest in Homer. These friendly folk advocate releasing the big ones & run a great business. Halibut fishing trips are US$220–240pp.

Flightseeing The sky above Homer and the Kenai Mountains is a spectacular place to be. The Harding Ice Field and the ragged outside coast of the Kenai Peninsula are well worth seeing from the air, and are in fact, nearly impossible to see any other way. Homer is also where many flights take off for the brown bear-rich Katmai National Park (see page 354).

Smokey Bay Air [252–3 F4] 2100 Kachemak Dr; ⟍ 235 1511; www.smokeybayair.com
Bald Mountain Air Homer Spit Rd; ⟍ 235 7969; www.baldmountainair.com

Emerald Air [252–3 E4] 1320 Lake Shore Dr; ⟍ 235 6993; www.emeraldairservice.com

All are reputable and safe flying services, which offer bear viewing in the Katmai National Park as well as a charter service. Full-day bear viewing trips start at US$600 per person and quickly climb to the thousands of dollars if you stay overnight. **Hallo Bay Bear Camp** (⟍ *235 2237; www.hallobay.com*) offers simple accommodation and guide services in the heart of bear country. For more information on Katmai see page 354.

Walks and trips
Trails End Horse Adventures 53435 East End Rd; ⟍ 235 6393. Guided horseback trips at the head of the bay.

Historic Harbour Walks Hosted by the Pratt Museum (see page 262) all summer costing US$5pp. The walks start in front of the Salty Dawg Saloon on the spit at 15.00 on every Fri & Sat.

HIKING AND RECREATION Homer and the surrounding areas offer a huge range of activities.

Cycling Cyclists with a sense of adventure will love the ride from Jakolof Bay to **Red Mountain** across the bay from Homer. Catch a water taxi from the small boat harbour on the spit to Jakolof Bay. A gravel road heads south for ten miles to Red Mountain and northwest to the town of Seldovia (see page 262). Follow the gravel road up the valley then climb some steep hills. At the fork in the road stay right and climb into a lovely alpine valley coloured red by minerals. Wildflowers are abundant and a crystal clear stream flows through the valley. Those with a tent can camp anywhere but there are no services and generally no other people. An old mine high on the hill can be explored but proceed with caution, it's icy all summer and less than stable. To go on to **Windy Bay** on the outside coast head back to the fork in the road and bushwack for mile after mile (unless someone has cleared the trail) to the remote and wild outside coast. This 15- to 20-mile trip requires river crossings and a healthy sense of adventure. Ask about trail conditions at Mako's Water Taxi. To rent mountain bikes, head over to **Homer Saw and Cycle** [252–3 E1] (*1532 Ocean Dr;* ⟍ *235 8406; homersawcycle.com*) near the airport. For a gym workout or to do some rock climbing, check out the **Bay Club** (*2395 Kachemak Dr;* ⟍ *235 2582*).

Kayaking Kayakers can rent sea kayaks from most of the tour companies as well as many of the water taxi outfits such as Mako's Water Taxi. Because of the extreme tides (35 vertical feet and more) in Kachemak Bay, kayakers, even experienced ones, lose their boats every summer. Be sure to pull boats as high up the beach as possible when stopping for the night. Some parts of the bay are better for kayaking than others and the company you rent from will have the best advice on where to go. One of my favourite spots is the Herring Islands near the mouth of Tutka Bay. There are lots of campsites but watch for private land. The Grace Ridge Trail

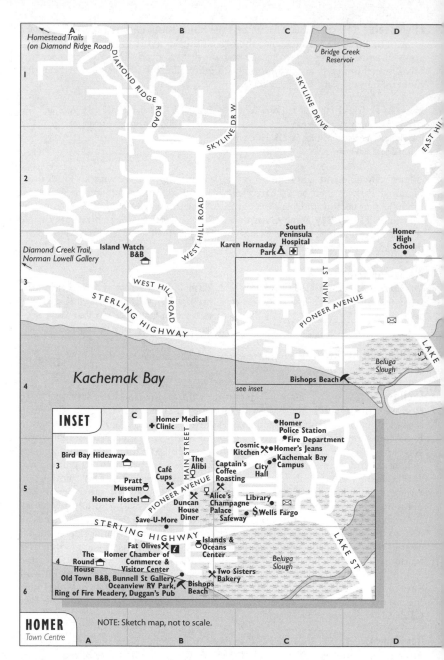

Homestead Trails
(on Diamond Ridge Road)

DIAMOND RIDGE ROAD

SKYLINE DR W

SKYLINE DRIVE

Bridge Creek
Reservoir

EAST HI

WEST HILL ROAD

Homer
High
School

South
Peninsula
Hospital

Karen Hornaday
Park

PIONEER AVENUE

N MAIN ST

Diamond Creek Trail,
Norman Lowell Gallery

Island Watch
B&B

WEST HILL ROAD

STERLING HIGHWAY

Kachemak Bay

LAKE ST

Beluga
Slough

Bishops Beach

see inset

INSET

C

Homer Medical
Clinic

Bird Bay Hideaway

MAIN STREET

The
Alibi

Cosmic
Kitchen

D

Homer
Police Station

Fire Department

Homer's Jeans

Kachemak Bay
Campus

Café
Cups

Captain's
Coffee
Roasting

City
Hall

Pratt
Museum

PIONEER AVENUE

Alice's
Champagne
Palace

Library

Homer Hostel

Duncan
House
Diner

Safeway

Wells Fargo

Save-U-More

STERLING HIGHWAY

Fat Olives

The
Round
House

Homer Chamber of
Commerce &
Visitor Center

Islands &
Oceans
Center

Beluga
Slough

LAKE ST

Old Town B&B, Bunnell St Gallery,
Oceanview RV Park,
Ring of Fire Meadery, Duggan's Pub

Bishops
Beach

Two Sisters
Bakery

HOMER
Town Centre

NOTE: Sketch map, not to scale.

A   B   C   D

---

follows the north side of Sadi Cove and is worth every gruelling step on a sunny day. In the autumn there can be lots of black bears. **True North Kayaks** (see page 250) is based here so contact them for boats and information.

Another wonderful, but less secluded place to kayak is around **Peterson and China Poot Bays**. If paddling in this area, contact St Augustine's Charters (see page 250) who are based out of Peterson Bay. They rent boats as well. While Peterson Bay

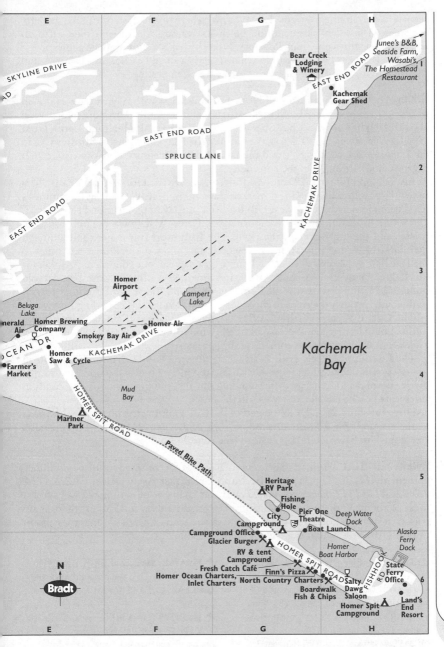

itself has quite a few houses these days, the surrounding areas are lovely. A fine beach on the northeast side of the bay has decent clam digging and lots of blueberries in the late summer. Behind the beach is a lagoon that warms a little at low tide. Hard-core swimmers may want to have a dip here. The Center for Alaskan Coastal Studies (see page 254) has a facility near St Augustine's where hikes are led. A boardwalk winds through a bog near the centre where the tiny carnivorous plant, the sundew, can be seen. Deeper in the bay are oyster farms where fresh oysters can be bought. Experienced paddlers can continue northwest toward Gull Island then catch an incoming tide through China Poot Bay. Near the head, a short portage allows access back into Peterson Bay. Just inside China Poot is a small beach with a cabin. A trail heads up to the point where a pair of eagles are often nesting.

Hiking The hiking in and around Homer is world class with rugged trails galore on the opposite side of the bay and mellow trails behind Homer. For more information about hiking in Kachemak Bay State Park. The **Kachemak Heritage Land Trust** (*395 East Pioneer Av;* ✆ *235 5263*), the **Center for Alaskan Coastal Studies** (✆ *235 6667; www.akcoastalstudies.org*), and the **Islands and Oceans Center** (see page 262) organise hikes throughout the summer.

Just behind Homer, off Diamond Ridge Road, are the **Homestead Trails**. This network of well-maintained and marked trails are unbeatable on a warm summer's day. From Homer, drive up West Hill Road and turn west on Diamond Ridge Road. Leave your wheels in the carpark at Rucksack Drive. Walk down the hill past some houses and the trail starts on the right. The **Ridgetop Inn** is here and although their large black dog is scary, he is very friendly. Follow the trail for a few miles to the Ruben Call Memorial Bench where you can spread out your picnic blanket for lunch and enjoy the view. From there, the trail continues west past an old homestead cabin, then past some homes to Diamond Ridge Road. Another branch leads south through the trees to the Rogers Loop Road and the Sterling Highway.

The **Carl E Wynn Nature Center** occupies 135 acres off Skyline Drive in the hills behind Homer. A boardwalk and trails wind through the woods where moose, eagles, and wildflowers can sometimes be spotted.

The **Diamond Creek Trail** starts where the west end of Diamond Ridge Road intersects with the Sterling Highway west of town. The trail and road head towards the sea beyond a locked gate. After winding through the trees, the road descends to a deserted beach. Hike east or west on the beach.

Drive for about 20 miles to the end of the East End Road. A dirt track plummets to the sea and the Russian Orthodox town of Kachemak Selo is situated here. Beyond is the Barefooters' homestead (see page 248).

WHERE TO STAY Homer has a vast array of accommodation possibilities, particularly B&Bs. The **Homer Bed and Breakfast Association** (✆ *226 1114, 877 296 1114 (TF); homerbedbreakfast.com*) and chamber of commerce website list most of them. With such a profusion of excellent B&Bs and cabins, there is no reason to stay in a hotel. For those who seek the kind of privacy sometimes absent in B&Bs, the best option is to rent a house or cabin.

🏠 **Bear Creek Lodging** [252–3 G1] (3 rooms) Bear Creek Dr; ✆ 235 8484; www.bearcreekwinery.com. Lovely cabins in a wooded setting with a pond, fire pit, BBQ & hot tub. Bear Creek Winery is on the grounds. Private & oriented toward couples. $$$
🏠 **Bird Bay Hideaway** [252–3 C3] (4 rooms) 394 No View Av; ✆ 299 2430; www.birdbayhideaway.com. Ideal for larger groups, this simple & artsy house in town has lots of space at a great price. A new eagle's nest is visible from the house! No b/fast. $$$

🏠 **Island Watch B&B** [252–3 B3] (5 rooms) 4241 Claudia St; ✆ 235 2265; www.islandwatch.net. A lovely custom home & cabin off West Hill. Spectacular views. $$$
🏠 **Junee's B&B** [252–3 H1] (4 rooms) Glacier View St; ✆ 235 4779, 888 265 4779 (TF); www.juneebb.com. Stay with Junee, one of Alaska's true old timers, in her lovely & rustic home out on East End Road. Junee is a fascinating woman with a story for every hour of the day. Rooms are simple but nice. Great homemade b/fast. $$$
🏠 **Mermaid B&B** (1 room) 3487 Main St; 235 7649; www.mermaidcafe.net. A very well-appointed

Homer residents like to refer to 120,000-acre Kachemak Bay State Park as their back yard. Located in the Kenai Mountains across Kachemak Bay from the town of Homer, the park is ringed by a further 280,000 acres of wilderness area. Numerous glaciers, the Harding Ice Field and countless miles of rugged coastline typify the park.

The rich marine ecosystem of the park's waters support a large number of sea otters as well as sea birds, whales, seals, intertidal life and sport fish including salmon and halibut. The park's forests and high tundra areas are home to bears, moose, mountain goats and others animals.

GETTING THERE The remote park enjoys relatively easy and affordable access by boat or small plane from Homer, making it particularly popular with hikers and sea kayakers. Homer has numerous water taxis (see page 250) and flight services (see page 251).

TOURIST INFORMATION
☑ **The Pratt Museum** (see page 262) & the **Islands and Oceans Center** (see page 262) also have information on the park.
☑ **Alaska State Parks** ☎ 262 5581; www.dnr.alaska.gov/parks/units/kbay/kbay.htm. Located in Soldotna.
☑ **Halibut Cove Ranger Station** ☎ 235 6999. This summer-only location is in Halibut Cove Lagoon across the bay from Homer. Found on the VHF radio channel 16.

WHERE TO STAY Camping is allowed just about anywhere in the park and some sites are developed. For those who like a roof, the park has six public-use cabins that can be rented for US$65 per night with a seven-night maximum stay. Three cabins can be found in Halibut Cove Lagoon as well as camping, hiking and good fishing for king salmon in early June. The China Poot Lake Cabin can be found at the end of a 2.4-mile hike. A plane also drops guests at the lake. These cabins sleep six to eight people. Moose Valley Cabin sleeps two and is 2.4 miles from Halibut Cove Lagoon. In Tutka Bay, the Sea Star Cove Cabin sleeps six. A short trail connects the cabin, some campsites and the Tutka Lagoon where pink salmon fishing can be first rate during mid-summer. Reserve by visiting www.dnr.alaska.gov/parks/cabins/kenai.htm or calling the **Kenai Parks Office** (☎ 262 5581).

Alaskan Yurt Rentals (☎ 299 1680; www.alaskanyurtrentals.com) Has nine simple but charming yurts located in wilderness settings around the park that can be rented for US$65 per night. The Humpy Creek location is a good one to stay in if you want to see black bears during the pink salmon season. The park has a number of remote lodges ranging from the very upper end to simple but nice.

WHAT TO SEE AND DO Hiking, camping, kayaking and even skiing are popular in the park. While trails are somewhat limited, a number of trails penetrate the park's interior and are maintained by the community and the park. A fantastic guide to local hiking *A Recreational Guide to Kachemak Bay State Park and Wilderness Park* by Joshua Duffus can be ordered from the author by sending US$17.95 plus US$3 postage to the author (*PO Box 84, Girdwood, AK 99587*).

Some of my favourite trails include the China Poot Peak Trail, the Emerald Lake Trail and the Alpine Ridge Trail. One of the best ways to see the park is by kayak. Many outfitters offer guided trips and rent kayaks for those who want to do it by themselves. For local outfitters and guides, see page 250.

Southcentral Alaska HOMER

5

apartment above the Old Inlet Book Shop/Mermaid Café near the city centre. The apartment has a full kitchen, hot tub & b/fast is provided by the café. $$$

⌂ **The Round House** [252–3 C4] (1 room) 534 Hidden Way; ☎ 235 5249; www.homerroundhouse.com. A unique venue on a bluff overlooking the beach, this yurt is spacious, cosy, & within walking distance of a number of restaurants & other businesses. Miles of beach hiking right out the back. $$$

⌂ **Old Town B&B** [252–3 C4] (2 rooms) 106 W Bunnell St; ☎ 235 7558; www.oldtownbedandbreakfast.com. 2 pleasant rooms in the creaky old 1936 Inlet Trading Post building. Upstairs from Bunnell St Gallery & near Bishops Beach. $$

⌂ **Spit Sisters B&B** (1 room) A small but cute apartment with a great location on the spit. Includes a full b/fast downstairs. $$

Hostels

⌂ **Homer Hostel** [252–3 C3] (5 rooms) 304 Pioneer Av; ☎ 235 1463; www.homerhostel.com. The hostel has a central location & all the amenities budget travellers expect from a good hostel, like internet, kitchen, laundry, etc. $$

⌂ **Seaside Farm** [252–3 H1] 40904 Seaside Farm Rd; ☎ 235 7850; www.xyz.net/~seaside. This is a

great place to meet other travellers & lay your head down cheaply. The setting is lovely with horse pastures, mountain & water views, & beach access. The only drawback is that it's 5 miles out of town on East End Road. Cabins are US$55, camping is US$10 & bunks are US$20. $$

Wilderness lodges

⌂ **Kachemak Bay Wilderness Lodge** ☎ 235 8910; www.alaskawildernesslodge.com. Located in China Poot Bay across from Homer, the Wilderness Lodge is one of original remote lodges in the Homer area. Guests are flown or boated in from Homer & put up in private cabins for 3- to 6-night stays. Hiking, kayaking, fishing & gourmet meals are all available & included in the price. US$2,100–2,800pp. $$$$$

⌂ **Sadie Cove Wilderness Lodge** ☎ 888 283 7234; www.sadiecove.com. Located deep in Sadie Cove across from Homer, this lodge is rustic yet charming & much less expensive than others. Private cabins line the beach, including the unique sailboat cabin. US$350–400pp. $$$$$

⌂ **Tutka Bay Wilderness Lodge** ☎ 907 235 3905; www.tutkabaylodge.com. A lovely collection of cabins in Tutka Bay with all activities & meals included for US$770–2,640pp. $$$$$

Camping City-maintained camping is available on the **Spit** for US$8, but the conditions are bleak and noisy due to the road and weekend partiers. **Karen Hornaday Park** [252–3 C3] (33 sites) offers camping in the woods for the same price. Turn onto Bartlett St from Pioneer Av and head uphill to Fairview Av. Turn right at the park sign. A number of RV parks can be found on the Spit but the prices are steep: US$25 and upward for tents at the **Homer Spit Campground** [252–3 H6] (☎ 235 8206). The **Seaside Farm** offers budget accommodation with cabins, bunks and camping for US$10.

RV parks include the plush new **Heritage RV Park** [252–3 G5] (☎ 235 8019; www.alaskaheritagervpark.com) near the fishing hole and the **Oceanview RV Park** [252–3 C4] (☎ 235 3951; www.oceanview-rv.com) in town. **The Washboard** (1204 Ocean Dr; ☎ 235 6781) at the base of the Spit across from the farmers' market is where you go to get showers, laundry service and hot drinks.

✖ WHERE TO EAT

✖ **Fresh Catch Café** [252–3 G6] 4025 Homer Spit Rd; ☎ 235 2289; ⏱ 11.30–21.00 daily. The ambience is nothing special & the prices are high, but the seafood is always fresh & amazing. Don't miss the fresh Prince William Sound shrimps. $$$$

✖ **The Homestead Restaurant** [252–3 H1] Mile 8.2 East End Rd; ☎ 235 8723; www.homesteadrestaurant.net; ⏱ 17.00–22.00 daily. Homer's original fine dining restaurant & still one of the best. Everything is divine & the service is always impeccable. Be sure to make a reservation & be ready to spend quite a few bucks. Dinner generally costs US$22–38 or more. $$$$

✗ **Wasabi's** [252–3 H1] 52917 East End Rd; ☎ 226 3663; ⏰ 17.00–closing time Wed–Sat. A newer addition to Homer's restaurant line-up, Wasabi's serves amazing sushi at outrageous prices & at a glacial pace. Still, if sushi & mountain views are what you crave, this is the only place to go. $$$$

✗ **Boardwalk Fish & Chips** [252–3 H6] 4287 Homer Spit Rd; ☎ 235 7749; www.vtown.org; ⏰ 11.00–22.00 daily. Don't get excited about the food, the service or the ambience; eat here because it's a classic Homer establishment & you have to be able to say that you did. The halibut is local, fresh & deep-fried into oblivion. $$$

✗ **Café Cups** [252–3 C3] 162 W Pioneer Av; ☎ 235 8330; www.cafecupsofhomer.com; ⏰ 11.00–22.00 Mon–Sat. You can't miss it, it's in the middle of town & there is a giant teacup on the roof. The food is good & the décor is crazy & fun with lots of local art. Lunches are US$10–12 while dinners cost US$16–22. $$$

✗ **Fat Olives** [252–3 C4] 276 Ohlson Ln; ☎ 235 8488; www.fatolives.net; ⏰ 11.00–22.00 daily. Homer's hippest place to sit down for a fine meal or grab a slice of gourmet pizza (largest slices in town). Cool northwest décor & good food. Dinner will cost you US$16–25. $$$

✗ **Finn's Pizza** [252–3 G6] ☎ 235 2878; ⏰ 12.00–21.00 daily. In a town with so many good pizza places, dare I say this is Homer's best pizza? Finn's & a few other places are invalidating the derogatory term 'Spit food'. Gourmet pizzas made by hand in front of you, then cooked in a wood-fired oven & served with local beer. The upstairs dining area is funky & has great views. $$$

Cafés

✗ **Captain's Coffee Roasting** [252–3 D3] 295 E Pioneer Av; ☎ 235 4970; www.captainscoffee.com; ⏰ 06.30–18.00 Mon–Fri, 07.30–17.00 Sat & Sun. Grab a hot drink & a bag of their coffee roasted in-house. $$

✗ **Mermaid Café** 3487 Main St; ☎ 235 7649; www.mermaidcafe.net; ⏰ 09.00–14.00 Tue–Sun. Pour over the used books in the adjoining book shop, then grab lunch in the café. $$

✗ **Spit Sisters** Harbor View Boardwalk, Homer Spit Rd; ☎ 235 4921; www.spitsisterscafe.com;

WHERE TO DRINK

🍷 **Bear Creek Winery** [252–3 G1] Bear Creek Dr; ☎ 235 8484; www.bearcreekwinery.com;

✗ **Sourdough Express Bakery** 1316 Ocean Dr; ☎ 235 7571; www.freshsourdoughexpress.com; ⏰ 07.00–21.00 daily. One of Homer's oldest restaurants, the Sourdough Express is half tourist trap & half local hangout. Good simple meals & over the top baked goods. Look for me as a kid in one of the photo albums on the tables. $$$

✗ **Starvin' Marvin's Pizza** 1663 Homer Spit Rd; ☎ 235 0544; ⏰ 11.00–22.00 Mon–Thu, 11.00–midnight Fri & Sat, 11.00–21.00 Sun. Decent sweet crust pizza, but take it to go, the ambience is nothing special. $$$

✗ **Cosmic Kitchen** [252–3 D3] 510 E Pioneer Av; ☎ 235 6355; www.cosmickitchenalaska.com; ⏰ 09.00–18.00 Mon–Fri, 09.00–15.00 Sat. High-quality food & cheap prices make this a local favourite. Burgers, burritos & a host of Mexican fusion meals. $$

✗ **Duncan House Diner** 125 E Pioneer Av; ☎ 235 5344; www.duncanhousediner.com; ⏰ 06.00–14.00 daily. Food doesn't get much more American than this! This is diner food served by the pound 3 times a day. $$

✗ **Glacier Burger** [252–3 G6] 3789 Homer Spit Rd; ☎ 235 7148; ⏰ 11.00–18.00 Tue–Sun. The Glacier Burger is a long-time Homer establishment with a long & venerable tradition of making big, greasy & amazing burgers. Locals order a Glacier Burger Deluxe (GBD) & a shake, thendon't eat again until the following year. $$

✗ **Spit-Fire Grille** 4246 Homer Spit Rd; ☎ 235 9379; ⏰ 05.00–17.00 Mon–Sat. Amazing food made by hand from local & often organic ingredients. The owner's wife, Marjorie Scholl, is one of Homer's finest artists. Her amazing work adorns the walls. Located in the Harbor View Boardwalk on the Spit. $$

⏰ 05.00–17.00 daily. Pleasantly removed from the hustle & bustle of the Spit, Spit Sisters, run by a couple of cool local girls, is the place to grab a coffee & pastry in the morning. They also have lunch food & a cute B&B upstairs. $$

✗ **Two Sisters Bakery** [252–3 D4] 233 E Bunnell Av; ☎ 235 2280; www.twosistersbakery.net; ⏰ 07.00–18.00 Mon–Sat, 09.00–16.00 Sun. Tasty baked goods, filling lunches & a great location near Bishops Beach. $$

⏰ 10.00–18.00 daily. Fine wines made from local berries & imported grapes. Samples are available.

♀ **Chart Room at Land's End** 4786 Homer Spit Rd; ☌ 800 478 0400 (TF); www.lands-end-resort.com; ☉ 11.00–15.00 & 17.00–22.00 daily. There is little reason to eat or stay here, but it's a fine place to sip a drink & gaze across the bay to the mountains.
♀ **Duggan's Pub** [252–3 C4] 120 W Bunnell Av; ☌ 235 9949. A decent dive with music AT w/ends.
♀ **Homer Brewing Company** [252–3 E4] 1411 Lake Shore Dr; ☌ 235 3626; www.homerbrew.com; ☉ 12.00–19.00 Mon–Sat, 12.00–18.00 Sun. Fine locally made beers since 1996. Get a 64oz jug or 20oz bottle to go. Next door is a serve-yourself beer garden. Bratwurst are often for sale from a cart.

♀ **Ring of Fire Meadery** [252–3 C4] 178 E Bunnell Av; ☌ 235 2656; www.ringoffiremeadery.com. Yes, Homer has its own meadery (mead is a fermented honey drink). Buy it by the glass at Douggan's, Finn's & Café Cups or by the bottle from the meadery.
♀ **Salty Dawg Saloon** [252–3 H6] 4380 Homer Spit Rd; ☌ 235 6718; www.saltydawgsaloon.com. The Dawg used to be Homer's roughest, toughest fisherman's bar but today is mostly a tourist attraction. Still, its original character has not been changed & it's worth diving in for a drink & to tack your ID onto the wall.
♀ **The Alibi** [252–3 C3] 453 E Pioneer Av; ☌ 235 9199. A decent dive with music on the w/ends.

ENTERTAINMENT AND NIGHTLIFE For music at the weekends head to almost any of Homer's bars.

Alice's Champagne Palace [252–3 D3] 195 E Pioneer Av; ☌ 235 6909. Recently reopened under the management of Tiny Nolan, who also owns Fat Olives. This classic Homer bar is now open on & off with creative drinks, live music & performing arts shows throughout the week. Call for hours & shows.
Pier One Theatre [252–3 G5] ☌ 235 7333; www.pieronetheatre.org. On the Spit near the fishing hole is a first-rate, locally run theatre with fabulous & usually very funny shows all summer.
Downward Dog Productions ☌ 235 1921; www.downwarddogalaska.com. Responsible for many of Homer's best musical shows. Check out

their website for a calendar of upcoming performances.
Homer Council on the Arts ☌ 235 4288. Organises workshops & performances of all kinds. Their website calendar lists everything.
Homer Family Theatre Pioneer Av; ☌ 235 6728. The only movie theatre in town. They show all the Hollywood movies & sometimes feature independent films. The back right corner of the theatre has some couches, but the rest of the seats are also reasonably comfortable.
Cinema 127 Bunnell St. Shows local art films now & then. Enquire at Bunnell Street Gallery (see page 260).

FESTIVALS AND EVENTS For more information on any event, contact the Homer Chamber of Commerce.

March
Winter King Salmon Tournament (*www.homeralaska.org/winterkingsalmonderby/index.htm*) A few hundred anglers gather every 21 March to catch kings in Kachemak Bay. A recent winner caught a 28.5 pound king and won US$16,863.

April
Ski-to-Sea Triathlon Held the first week of the month, this event involves a gruelling 5km run down the Homer Spit, 7km bike up West Hill and a 5km ski on the Homestead Trails. The record time is 57.20 minutes, set by local hard-man Ricky Hankins in 2002.

May
Kachemak Bay Shorebird Festival (☌ *235 7740; www.homeralaska.org/shorebird.htm*) Welcomes more than 130 species of migratory birds back to Homer with speakers, bird walks and more.

Kachemak Bay SeaFest (☌ *235 7740; www.kbayseafest.com*) Generally held during the third week of the month and features kayaking demos, seminars, food and interesting boats on display.

KiteFest Alaska (↘ *299 1119; www.kitesurfalaska.com*) An annual gathering of Alaskan and visiting kitesurfers. Cold waters are tempered by warm wetsuits and lots of fun. Lessons, competitions, demo gear and a movie night are all available for a donation. The event generally takes place at the end of May or early June.

June

Kachemak Bay Writers Conference (↘ *235 7743; writersconference.homer.alaska.edu*) Held each summer and draws Alaskan poets and writers out of the woodwork. The conference features world-class writers such as Amy Tan who teach and give talks.

Seldovia Summer Solstice Music Festival (↘ *234 7612*) Takes place in Seldovia 19–21 June. Call the Seldovia Chamber of Commerce for more information.

Strut Your Mutt (↘ *234 3779*) A small, fun event where Homer's finest dogs are walked and run through agility courses.

Land's End Regatta (*www.homeryachtclub.org*) Put on in the last few days of the month by the Homer Yacht Club. Watch the race from the end of the Spit.

July

4 July Calls for a big party everywhere on the peninsula and Homer is no exception. Celebrations generally involve a parade and fireworks off the end of the Spit, though their colours are not very vibrant because it's not very dark!

Concert on the Lawn (↘ *235 7721; www.kbbi.org*) Has been filling Homer with two days of music for more than 30 years. The event is put on by local radio station KBBI and features food, crafts and some amazing music come rain or shine.

August

Homer PhotoFest (↘ *235 1895*) Celebrates the art of photography during the first week of the month with workshops, visiting professionals and photography shown around town in local galleries.

Kenai Peninsula State Fair (↘ *567 3670*) Held in the middle of the month at the fairgrounds in Ninilchik, just north of Homer.

SHOPPING In addition to many galleries and gift shops, the Spit now has a shop entirely dedicated to the *Time Bandit* boat, Homer's own star of the Discovery Channel TV show, the *Deadliest Catch* about king-crab fishing in the Bering Sea. The show is so popular visitors will stand in line for an hour to shake hands with the crew (who are rarely there). Locals enjoy watching the mayhem unfold from afar. If you're a fan, stop on by for a beer holder or T-shirt, but don't expect to meet anyone from the boat since they are usually out tendering salmon (buying salmon from fishermen on behalf of fish processors), an activity too mundane for TV. Check out the store on the Spit next to Finn's Pizza.

Bookshops

The Book Shop 332 E Pioneer Av; ↘ 235 7496; www.homerbookstore.com; ⏰ 10.00–19.00 Mon–Sat, 12.00–17.00 Sun. A lovely bookshop with a huge selection of Alaska & Homer specific titles.

Old Inlet Book Shop 3487 Main St; ↘ 235 7984; www.oldinletbookshop.com; ⏰ 10.00–18.00 daily. Mountains of new & used books with an attached café & B&B.

Galleries The **first Friday of the month** is not to be missed. Just about every gallery in town takes down last month's artwork and hangs a new batch to the accompaniment of artists' talks, food and wine.

Bunnell Street Gallery [252–3 C4] 106 W Bunnell Av; ☎ 235 2662; www.bunnellstreetgallery.org; ⏰ 10.00–18.00 Mon–Sat, 12.00–16.00 Sun. Asia Freeman owns the gallery & with her board, is responsible for some of the most amazing art Homer has seen. The gallery shows local & out-of-town artists & has a wonderful gift shop in the back.

Fireweed Gallery 475 E Pioneer Av; ☎ 235 3411; www.fireweedgallery.com; ⏰ 10.00–19.00 Mon–Sat, 11.00–18.00 Sun. Local arts & crafts with a new show every month. Right next door to Ptarmigan Arts.

Ptarmigan Arts Gallery 471 E Pioneer Av; ☎ 235 5345; www.ptarmiganarts.com; ⏰ 10.00–18.00 daily. A wide variety of Alaskan made arts & craft as well as a small room reserved for new work.

Norman Lowell Gallery [252–3 A3] ☎ 235 7344; www.normanlowellgallery.net; ⏰ 09.00–17.00 Mon–Sat, 13.00–17.00 Sun. An interesting gallery located 4 miles south of Anchor Point at mile 160.9 of the Sterling Highway. Lowell's moody & atmospheric paintings bring something new to 'Alaskana'.

Sea Lion Gallery 4241 Homer Spit Rd; ☎ 235 3400; www.sealiongallery.com. Owned by local artist, Gary Lyon.

Groceries

Kachemak Wholesale 601 E Pioneer Av; ☎ 235 1862; ⏰ 08.00–21.00 daily. A decent selection of foods & goods at the corner of Pioneer Av & Lake St.

Safeway [252–3 D3] ☎ 235 2408; www.safeway.com; ⏰ 05.00–midnight daily. A good selection of food with a deli & bakery. Located on the Bypass near the post office. Though it's expensive, the fruits & veggies are the best here.

Save-U-More [252–3 C3] 3611 Greatland St; ☎ 235 8661; ⏰ 08.00–21.00 Mon–Sat, 09.00–20.00 Sun. A warehouse of bulk foods. This is where most locals, & all commercial fishermen shop.

Outdoor

Homer's Jeans [252–3 D3] 564 E Pioneer Av; ☎ 235 6234; ⏰ 10.00–18.00 daily. Outdoor clothing & related gear.

NOMAR 104 E Pioneer Av; ☎ 235 8363; www.nomaralaska.com; ⏰ 09.00–18.00 Mon–Sat, 22.00–17.00 Sun. Top-quality, handmade clothing & gear.

Kachemak Gear Shed [252–3 H1] 3625 East End Rd; ☎ 235 8612; www.kachemakgearshed.com; ⏰ 08.00–21.00 daily. Homer's local fishing supply super-store. Marine hardware & all manner of serious weather gear & clothing.

Main Street Mercantile 104 E Pioneer Av; ☎ 235 9102; ⏰ 09.00–17.00 Mon–Sat. A lovely building next to NOMAR with basic groceries & outdoor gear, everything from stoves to clothing.

OTHER PRACTICALITIES

Post office [252–3 D3] 3658 Heath St; ☎ 235 6120; ⏰ 08.30–17.00 Mon–Fri,12.00–14.00 Sat.

Public library [252–3 D3] 500 Hazel Av; ☎ 235 3180; www.library.ci.homer.ak.us; ⏰ 10.00–18.00 Mon–Sat. A spacious new library off the Homer Bypass with Wi-Fi & cosy reading spots.

Banks

$ **Wells Fargo Bank** [252–3 D3] 88 Sterling Hwy; ☎ 800 869 3557; www.wellsfargo.com; ⏰ 10.00–17.00 Mon–Fri, 10.00–14.00 Sat

$ **First National Bank Alaska** 3655 Heath St; ☎ 235 5800; www.fnbalaska.com; ⏰ 10.00–17.00 Mon–Thu, 10.00–18.00 Fri, 10.00–14.00 Sat

Hospitals

✚ **South Peninsula Hospital** [252–3 C3] 4300 Bartlett St; ☎ 235 8101; www.sphosp.com. Located at the end of Bartlett St behind town. Large hospital with ER.

✚ **Homer Medical Clinic** [252–3 C3] 4136 Bartlett St; ☎ 235 8586. For non-emergencies.

WHAT TO SEE The **Homer Spit** is not only where the original settlement was located, it is also where the majority of today's visitor development has occurred. Driving along the spit is the best place to see **bald eagles** in Homer. The **small boat harbour** and surrounding businesses can occupy hours or days depending on how interested you are in boats, bars and gift shops. In addition to a huge number of boats on the southwest side of the harbour, a large vessel dock on the northeast side is worth a visit for those interested in boats. On the southeastern side, a commercial dock is where commercial fishermen offload their catch. Halibut and salmon are delivered here by crane and vacuum pump to small processors – Homer has no cannery – and the fresh market.

Also near the end of the spit is the **Salty Dawg Saloon** (see page 258), one of Homer's first buildings. The structure housed many local businesses before it became a bar and has been added to many times. Once the fisherman's bar, it has now become a tourist destination. Sweatshirts are for sale, but the bar's original charm has been maintained. It's still the filthy, dank, dark and decidedly wonderful place it has always been. The **beaches** around the end of the spit and Land's End Resort are wonderful for walking and fishing. Flounders can be caught by the bucketful here, and salmon can be had in season. Walk along the boardwalks in front of the charter fishing businesses in the afternoon to see the day's catch of **halibut**.

About three miles down the Homer Spit, the **fishing hole** [252–3 G5] has become famous as *the* place to catch a king or silver salmon. Though it can be very crowded, the lagoon is stocked with enough fish for everyone to catch one, and often many more. The best place to fish is near the inflow, during the incoming tide. The tackle shop across the Homer Spit Road has all the gear and information. A **bike path** follows the road from the fishing hole to the base of the spit and can be a lovely walk when the wind isn't blowing. At low tide, skip the pavement and walk along the beach on the other side of the road. If you see **kiteboarders** tearing it up and want to have a go, contact local instructor George Overpeck (*www.kitesurfalaska.com*). The **Farmers' Market** [252–3 E4] is open on Wednesdays and Saturdays. Local arts and crafts are on display as well as baked goods and fresh vegetables and there is also music on Saturdays. The market is located on Ocean Drive at the base of the Spit. Call ☎ 299 7540 or visit www.homerfarmersmarket.org for more information.

THE EAGLE LADY

Jean Keene – known as the 'Eagle Lady' – was one of Homer's most interesting and controversial characters. Keene started feeding local bald eagles with fish scraps from the cannery where she worked shortly after she arrived in 1977. Before long she had attracted most of Homer's eagles, and soon after bald eagles from around southcentral Alaska started coming to Homer for handouts during the winter. Though the feeding of bald eagles was prohibited in 2006, Keene was given special permission by the city to continue. In the past decade, Homer has become known throughout the world as one of the best places to see bald eagles. With essentially no winter tourism, Homer suddenly saw photographers flying in from around the world to shoot the birds at close range. Many of the eagles remained in Homer during the summer and brought more visitors. Environmentalists were concerned the huge number of eagles would create conflict with people, reduce the numbers of other birds and increase the likelihood of a disease outbreak among the eagles. After Keene died aged 85 in January 2009, the eagles were fed for the remainder of that winter but a new city resolution then prohibited the act for the future. With the natural order restored, Homer will be home to a more independent, healthier but smaller bald eagle population.

At the end of Maine Street, **Bishops Beach** [252–3 C4] is where locals go for an evening or morning stroll. There is often a breeze, so put on a coat and head east. Before long the cliffs are 100 or more foot tall and coal seams can be seen splitting their expanse. The black lumps on the beach are not rocks, but fuel, ready-made by nature. You may see locals in beaten-up trucks on the beach, collecting the coal.

East End Road starts where Pioneer Avenue ends, and travels northeast from Homer to the head of Kachemak Bay and the Russian Old Believer village of Kachemak Selo and the Barefooters' homestead (see page 248). The drive is lovely in parts and provides an ever-changing view of the Kenai Mountains and the many glaciers that bisect them. From the very end of East End Road (about 20 miles from Homer), park and walk down the steep dirt road to the beach and continue northeast for three quarters of a mile to the Russian village. Don't be surprised if people don't welcome you with open arms. They live traditional lives and thrive on seclusion. Follow the dirt road for five miles to the Barefooters' homestead. Because of the distance, a bike is the best way to make this trip.

For an unbeatable view of Homer, drive up the East Hill Road (east of town on East End Road) and turn left onto **Skyline Drive**. At the top of the hill, look left and be prepared to have your breath taken away.

Across the bay from Homer, **Kachemak Bay State Park** (see box on page 255) offers hundreds of adventures, including hiking, camping, biking, kayaking and fishing. The many water taxis (see page 250) in Homer can whisk you across the bay and pick you up hours or days later. One of my favourite spots is **Glacier Spit** near Halibut Cove Lagoon where there is rock climbing, camping and hiking. Another is **Halibut Cove Lagoon** where king salmon swarm the banks in the spring and early summer and hiking trails lead inland to a number of peaks including China Poot Peak. Organised camping is available there. The **Wosnesenski Glacier** area is accessed by plane and has an increasing number of **rock climbing venues** as well as wilderness hiking, camping and glacier access. For climbing information visit www.shitflyclimbing.com. For cyclists with a sense of adventure, catch a water taxi to **Jakolof Bay** and ride along the gravel road inland to the **Red Mountain** or **Windy Bay** (see page 251) on the other side of the Kenai Mountains.

Museums

Islands and Oceans Center [252–3 D4] (*95 Sterling Hwy;* ☏ *235 6961; www.islandsandocean.org;* ⊕ *09.00–18.00 daily; free admission*) Extensive and top-notch displays and information about the Alaska Maritime National Wildlife Refuge. Beach walks leave the centre daily and a host of other summer programmes are offered. Don't miss *Journey of the Tiglax*, shown daily in their comfortable theatre.

Pratt Museum [252–3 C3] (*3779 Bartlett St;* ☏ *235 8635; www.prattmuseum.org;* ⊕ *10.00–18.00; US$6/3 adult/child*) The Pratt Museum has long been an important part of the local art scene. The museum has high-quality displays on local human and natural history as well as a marine pet tank and a controllable live camera located in the McNeil Bear Sanctuary. Their display about the Exxon Valdez oil spill is unrivalled in the state and their gallery shows some of Homer's best contemporary art.

SELDOVIA Population: 284

Located 16 miles across Kachemak Bay from Homer, Seldovia is a quiet fishing town nestling in the Kenai Mountains. The area was originally settled by the Alutiiq people and later by the Russians. Between 1869 and 1882, a Russian trading post occupied the Seldovia Bay. Seldovia grew into a major commercial fishing port and booming town while Homer saw little growth. In 1964, the Good Friday earthquake all but destroyed the town and all of its commercial fishing and processing infrastructure. The earthquake and the newly completed Sterling Highway shifted the growth from Seldovia to Homer.

Today, the town exists on limited tourism and commercial fishing and is a wonderful place to escape the hustle and bustle of Homer. The tiny town is ideal for a day or more of exploring on foot.

GETTING THERE AND AWAY The Alaska State Ferry (↘ 786 3800, 800 526 6731 (TF); www.dot.state.ak.us/amhs) makes the trip from Homer every few days through the middle of the summer for US$33. The MV Discovery (↘ 235 7847) makes the trip from Homer every day at 11.30 for US$50 round trip. Virtually every Homer water taxi will make the trip as well (see page 250). The air taxis in Homer will also make a round trip for about US$100. Homer Air (↘ 235 8591; www.homerair.com) and Smokey Bay Air (↘ 235 1511; www.smokeybayair.com) fly from Homer to Seldovia daily for about US$100 round trip.

TOURIST INFORMATION Visit the **Visitor Center/Museum** (Main St; ↘ 234 7898; www.seldovia.com; ⊕ 10.30–16.30 daily).

WHERE TO STAY AND EAT

🏠 **Alaska Treetops Lodge** (7 rooms) ↘ 234 6200; www.alaskatreetops.com. A lovely building with well-appointed rooms. The lodge is set up for stays of 3 or more nights with all activities & meals incl. $$$$$

🏠 **Dancing Eagles B&B** (2 rooms) ↘ 234 7627; www.dancingeagles.com. This B&B has 2 cabins in a great location on the water. $$$$

🏠 **Boardwalk Hotel** (12 rooms) ↘ 234 7816; www.seldoviaboardwalkhotel.com. Boring rooms but in a great location by the water & in the city centre. $$$

🏠 **The Bridgekeeper's Inn** (2 rooms) ↘ 234 7535; www.thebridgekepersinn.com. Located near the bridge over the bay. $$$

✖ **Madfish Restaurant** ↘ 234 7676; www.seldovia.com/madfishrestaurant; ⊕ 11.30–16.00 & 17.30–21.00 daily. A selection of fresh seafood as well as some diner favourites like French dip sandwiches and chicken strips. $$–$$$

✖ **Tide Pool Café** ↘ 234 7502; ⊕ 07.00–20.00 Wed–Sun, 07.00–16.00 Mon & Tue. A tasty lunch spot with local art on the walls. $$–$$$

Camping Camping is available at Outside Beach, about 1 mile from town, for US$5. Register and pay at City Hall near the ferry dock.

FESTIVALS Don't miss the **Seldovia Summer Solstice Music Festival** on 19–21 June. And the **4 July Celebration** is not to be missed either. The party takes over town with greased pole climbing, canoe jousting, food and more. Call the visitor centre for more information.

OTHER PRACTICALITIES

Crabpot Grocery 266 Main St; ↘ 234 7435; ⊕ 09.00–20.00 daily. There are other grocery stores in town, but this one has the most character.

Post office 251 Main St; ↘ 234 7831; ⊕ 08.30–18.30 Mon–Fri & 12.00–17.00 Sat.

Public library 260 Seldovia St; ↘ 234 7662; ⊕ 14.00–16.00 & 19.00–21.00 Tue, 12.00–14.00

Wed, 14.00–16.30 Thu & 12.30–16.30 Sat. A good place to relax & read a book or check your email.

Fenske's Shoreline Dr; ↘ 234 7850; ⊕ variable, call ahead. Located on Seldovia Slough near the bridge, this funky waterside building sells books, baked goods & hot drinks. This is my favourite spot in town to sit quietly & watch the water go by.

WHAT TO SEE AND DO Looking down on town from a hill near Main Street is the St Nicholas Russian Orthodox Church; at the end of Main Street, a series of boardwalks follow the lagoon and are lined with interesting houses and boats; and on the other side of town, at the end of Main Street, is the Otterbahn Trail leading to Outside Beach. Bikes are a great way to get around and can be rented from the Boardwalk Hotel.

Visitors can also bring their own bike from Homer on the ferry or water taxi. Bikers can ride along the 15-mile gravel road to Jakolof Bay, then cycle on to Red Mountain (see page 251). Kayak tours (US$120) & rentals (US$150) can be had from Kayak 'Atak (🕿 234 7425; www.alaska.net/~kayaks).

HALIBUT COVE Population: 23

Across the bay from Homer, the quaint art and fishing community of Halibut Cove is well worth a day's visit. Ismailof Island hugs the coastline between Peterson Bay and Halibut Cove Lagoon, forming a protected stretch of water ringed by homes, boardwalks and trails. The island has a few galleries and one restaurant.

GETTING THERE AND AWAY Most visitors arrive on the ferry, the *Danny J*, which can be booked through Central Charters (see page 250). The ferry runs twice a day, once at 12.00 for US$52 and again at 17.00 for US$32. Most people take the earlier ferry so they can return on the later.

 WHERE TO STAY AND EAT Other lodges and accommodation options are listed at www.halibutcove.com.

🏠 **A Stillpoint in Halibut Cove** 🕿 296 2283; www.centreforcreativerenewal.com. Cabins & a lodge on the mainland for US$500 dbl. $$$$$
🏠 **Quiet Place Lodge** 🕿 235 1800; www.quietplace.com. All-inclusive trips from US$1,680 upward. $$$$$
🏠 **Cove Country Cabins** 🕿 235 6374; halibutcovealaska.com. Has cabins for US$150. $$$
🏠 **Hideaway Cove Lodge** 🕿 235 0755, 888 777 0930(TF); www.hideawaycovelodge.com. Has simple cabins for US$155–195. $$$

✕ **The Saltry** 🕿 235 7847; ⊕ 13.00–16.00 & 16.00–21.00 daily. Fresh seafood, local art & a waterside location make the Saltry a truly unique dining experience. Everything is made by hand & served in an outdoor area with a fireplace & a ceramic pool full of marine life. Bread is baked on location & salad greens are grown on the island. Reservations are required. Entrées start at US$25. $$$$

WHAT TO SEE AND DO From the ferry dock, follow the boardwalk past the Saltry to the Halibut Cove Experience Gallery (🕿 296 2215) where local artists show their work. Beyond that, local artist Diana Tillion shows her unique octopus ink work from The Cove Gallery. Past the sand spit is the home of the nationally renowned but now deceased artist, Alex Combs. His painting and pottery are still on display.

PRINCE WILLIAM SOUND

Prince William Sound is a remote and vast body of island-studded water in the heart of southcentral Alaska. The 10,000-square-mile sound is hemmed in by the towering Chugach and Kenai Mountains to the north, east and west, and by a series of wild islands to the south. The towns of Whittier, Cordova and Valdez are the only centres with significant populations, and Valdez is the terminus of the Alaska Pipeline. The Sound is famous for its rugged coastlines, deep fjords, tidewater glaciers and abundant wildlife. Boat tours from Whittier and Valdez explore the glaciers at the northern end of the sound, but the rest remains in a true state of wilderness and is little visited. Because of the intricate coastline and many islands, the area is ideal for kayakers and other small boats.

WHITTIER (*Population: 161*) Tucked between the mountains and the sea, the small town of Whittier (⊕ 60°46'27"N, 148°40'40"W) is grey and ugly but is at least partially redeemed by its spectacular surroundings and access to the many adventures in Prince William Sound. Whittier is located on the west side of a 2.5-mile one-way tunnel (the longest in the US) that accommodates trains as well as cars. The town was created during World War II because its deep-water and ice-free access allowed troops and supplies to be moved to the state's interior military bases. The railroad was completed in 1943 and, in 1948, the town's massive buildings were erected. The Begich Towers were built at this time to house military families. More than half the population still live there. The rest live in Whittier Manor, built in the 1950s. When the military left, Whittier took up commercial fishing and tourism. Because of its proximity to Anchorage, Whittier is a popular place from which to explore Prince William Sound.

Getting there and away
By car In 2000, the Anton Anderson Memorial Tunnel, previously reserved for trains, began accepting cars. The dripping, dark tunnel is only one lane wide, so every half hour the tunnel is opened for cars going one direction. After those cars are let through, the cars waiting to go through the other direction are admitted. The tunnel is open every day from 17.30–23.15 with cars being let into Whittier every hour on the half hour. Every hour, on the hour they are let out. The toll costs US$12 each way. Interestingly, on the Whittier side of the tunnel, the **Portage Pass Trail** heads up the mountain and provides the spectacular views of Portage Glacier you may have missed when visiting the Begich, Boggs Visitor Center.

By ferry The **Alaska State Ferry** (↘ *786 3800, 800 526 6731 (TF); www.dot.state.ak.us/amhs*) also serves Whittier, connecting it to Cordova, Valdez as well as the southeast and the rest of southcentral Alaska.

By train The **Alaska Railroad** (↘ *265 2494, 800 544 0552 (TF); www.akrr.com*) travels between Anchorage and Whittier once a day for US$65/33 adult/child one-way.

Tourist information
The **Whittier Chamber of Commerce** (*www.whittieralaskachamber.org*) is the best source of information.

Local tours and activities
Kayaking
Prince William Sound Kayak Center Billings St; ↘ 472 2452; www.pwskayakcenter.com. These are the guys to go to for expedition & extended trip planning & outfitting. They rent every conceivable bit of kayaking gear from their huge warehouse south of the tracks. They also lead single- & multi-day guide trips.

Alaska Sea Kayakers ↘ 472 2534; www.alaskaseakayakers.com. Similar trips as well as basic rentals. Day trips are US$79–175.

Fishing
Whittier Boat & Tackle Rental ↘ 632 1188; www.alaska-boat-rentals.com. Motor boat & fishing gear rentals for US$425–725/day.

Boat cruises All of the operators listed below offer glacier and wildlife viewing from large boats in Prince William Sound for around US$140/80 adult/child, including lunch.

Phillips Tours and Cruises ☏ 276 8023, 800 544 0529 (TF); www.26glaciers.com
Prince William Sound Tours and Cruises ☏ 835 4731, 800 992 7300 (TF); www.princewilliamsound.com

Major Marine Tours ☏ 274 7300, 800 764 7300 (TF); www.majormarine.com

A handful of smaller and more private operators can take you fishing, sightseeing or provide drop-off and pick-up services. These include:

Honey Charters ☏ 472 2493; www.honeycharters.com
Lazy Otter Charters Harbor View Dr: ☏ 694 6887, 800 587 6887 (TF); www.lazyotter.com

Prince William Sound Eco-Charters ☏ 472 2581; www.pwseco.com
Sound Eco Adventures ☏ 472 2312, 888 471 2312 (TF); www.soundecoadventure.com

⌂ Where to stay
The accommodation options in Whittier are nothing special and sometimes downright depressing. A better option is to spend the day in Whittier and sleep in Girdwood, a short drive away (see page 219). However, if you would like to stay the night, here are your best options:

⌂ **Inn at Whittier** (25 rooms) Harbor Loop Rd; ☏ 472 7000; www.innatwhittier.com. A new & lovely building surrounded by a construction site. The overpriced rooms & restaurant are not consistent enough in their quality to really be recommended. $$$–$$$$
⌂ **June's B&B** Kenai St; ☏ 472 2503; www.whittiersuitesonline.com. Has 11 rooms in the Begich Towers. $$$

⌂ **Soundview Gateway B&B** Blackstone St; ☏ 472 2358; 800 515 2358 (TF); www.soundviewalaska.com. Has a decent apartment. $$$)
⌂ **Anchor Inn** Whittier St; ☏ 472 2354, 877 870 8787 (TF); www.anchorinnwhittier.com. Offers drab rooms upstairs from a bar. Also houses a restaurant ($$), laundry, store & the local museum (⊕ 09.00–19.00 daily; US$3 donation), which has a small but interesting collection of historic documents & artefacts. $$

✕ Where to eat
Whittier's few dining options are at the east end of the harbour in a small visitor-centric area that locals call 'the triangle'.

✕ **Café Orca** Harbor Triangle; ☏ 472 2549; www.cafeorca.com; ⊕ 09.30–19.30 daily. Tasty & reasonably priced sandwiches, salads & seafood. Outdoor seating. $$
✕ **China Sea Restaurant** Harbor Triangle; ☏ 472 3663. US$10 buffet. $$

✕ **Swiftwater Seafood Café** Harbor Rd; ☏ 472 2550; www.swiftwaterseafoodcafe.com; ⊕ 11.30–21.00 Sun–Thu, 11.30–22.00 Fri & Sat. Fish & chips, burgers, & smoked prime ribs on Fri night. Open mic on Sat at 20.00. $$
✕ **Lazy Otter Café** Baked goods & hot drinks. Books kayaking trips & provides a water taxi service. $

Shopping
The Harbor Store Harbor View Dr: ☏ 244 1996. Sells a little of everything & rents Avis cars.

Log Cabin Gifts Harbor Rd; ☏ 472 2501. Aside from the mountains & glaciers, this building is the most photogenic thing in Whittier.

What to see and do
Crowded around the harbour are a series of disparate structures catering to visitors. This is where virtually all of Whittier's visitor services are located. The cruise ship and ferry docks are on either side of the harbour. For a taste of the real Whittier, cross the tracks and head towards the towers. At the far east end of town is a lovely bay where campers can generally stay. Salmon swim up the creek mid-summer and bears frequent the area.

Whittier Area Parks Whittier is one of just a few major access points to the amazing and largely pristine Prince William Sound. Boaters may use any of the eight marine parks near Whittier for camping, hiking and general exploring. These state marine parks include:

Decision Point On Passage Canal and totals 460 acres. The park has basic camping facilities and is an 8-mile boat ride from Whittier. A public-use cabin on Squirrel Cove can be rented for US$65 at www.recreation.gov.

South Esther Island Accessible only by boat and comprises 3,360 acres on the south end of Esther Island. Platforms are provided for camping and toilets are nearby.

Lake Bay There is a salmon hatchery that swarms with fish and commercial fishermen in the late summer. Some of the nearby bays are secluded and quiet even during fishing season.

Surprise Cove (2,260 acres) Also has toilets, campsites and trails, but is much quieter than Esther Island.

Others include: **Bettles Bay** with 680 acres and primitive camping only, and the undeveloped parks of **Entry Cove** (370 acres), **Ziegler Cove** (720 acres) and **Granite Bay** (2,105 acres). Most of these parks are popular places for motor boaters and kayakers to camp, fish, hike and relax.

A handful of public-use cabins are available here as well. Book cabins at the **DNR Public Information Center** (*550 W 7th Av, Ste 1260;* ✆ *269 8400*) in Anchorage or by visiting www.dnr.alaska.gov/parks/cabins/pws.htm.

VALDEZ *Population: 4,353*

At the head of the Valdez Arm on the far eastern side of Prince William Sound, the town of Valdez (⊕ 61°7'51"N, 146°20'54"W) occupies a truly stunning natural location. The Chugach Mountains rise 5,000ft straight out of the ocean and glaciers cascade from between the peaks like icy fingers reaching for the sea. The area's natural beauty and plentiful wildlife draw visitors who board tour boats to see glaciers spilling into the sea and explore the waters of Prince William Sound. Summers can be a little wet, but the winters, with nearly 30ft of snowfall, are truly spectacular. Helicopter skiing (which involves catching a ride to the top of a mountain to then ski down) and shovelling roofs are popular winter activities. In contrast to its many natural wonders, Valdez is the terminus for the Trans-Alaskan Pipeline, which accounts for the town's prosperity. Oil is pumped from Prudhoe Bay on the North Slope for almost 800 miles to Valdez, then loaded onto ships bound for the Lower 48 states. To avoid drawing exasperated sighs from locals, remember to say Val-DEEZ, not Val-DEZ.

HISTORY Valdez was named after the Spanish naval officer Antonio Valdes in 1790. As Alaska's northernmost ice-free port, Valdez was settled in 1898 as a staging point by gold prospectors seeking riches in the Klondike and elsewhere. In the 1920s, Valdez was connected to Fairbanks via the Richardson Highway. The Good Friday earthquake of 1964 destroyed much of the waterfront, forcing residents to rebuild inland and to the west. The town's economic security was sealed in the 1970s when the Trans-Alaska pipeline was built. The date 24 March 1989 is a day all Alaskans know. At 24.04, the 987ft oil tanker *Exxon Valdez* (see box on pages 272–3) ran aground on Bligh Reef, spilling 11 million gallons (125 Olympic-sized swimming pools) of crude oil into Prince William Sound.

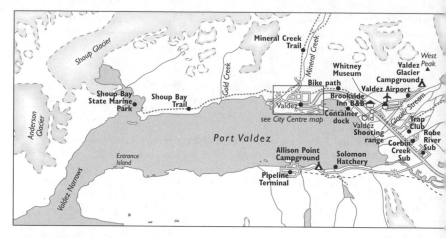

GETTING THERE AND AWAY

By road and air Valdez is 366 road miles from Fairbanks and 300 miles from Anchorage. **Era Aviation** (✎ *248 4422, 800 866 8394 (TF); www.flyera.com*) makes the trip from Anchorage two to three times per day for US$320 round-trip. **Valdez U-Drive** (✎ *835 4402, 800 478 4402 (TF); www.valdezudrive.com*) rents cars, truck, and vans from the airport. Call **Yellow Cab** (✎ *835 2500*) for a ride anywhere in town, or from the airport, which is out of town.

By ferry The **Alaska State Ferry** (✎ *465 6643, 800 526 6731 (TF); www.dot.state.ak.us/amhs*) connects Valdez with Whittier, Cordova, Kodiak, Seward and Homer all summer. The new and very fast MV *Chanega* serves Prince William Sound communities.

TOURIST INFORMATION

☑ **Valdez Visitor Center** [270–1 F3] 200 Fairbanks St; ✎ 835 4636; www.valdezalaska.org.

Knowledgeable staff & lots of printed information, all housed in a tremendously ugly brown building.

LOCAL TOURS AND ACTIVITIES
Kayaking

Anadyr Adventures [270–1 F4] 225 N Harbor Dr; ✎ 835 2814, 800 865 2925 (TF); www.anadyradventures.com. The ever-friendly & knowledgeable Hedy, owner of Anadyr, offers a wide range of tours from short half-day paddles (US$79+) to single (US$189) & multi-day (US$1,000 or more) trips to the Shoup, Columbia & Sawmill Glaciers. She also rents kayaks for US$45/day & offers a water taxi

service for do-it-yourselfers. Their office rents bikes, has computers with internet access & sells native art.
Pangaea Adventures [270–1 F4] 101 N Harbor Dr; ✎ 835 8442; 800 660 9637; www.alaskasummer.com. Pangaea offers a similar line-up of tours as Anadyr Adventures but does not enjoy the same reputation. They also offer a number of trekking & ice climbing trips. Prices are generally a little lower than at Anadyr.

Boat tours Though these are 'get you in, get you out' commercial tours, they are an excellent way to see glaciers dumping ice into the sea and local wildlife.

Lu-Lu Belle Glacier & Wildlife Tours [270–1 F4] 244 Kobuk Dr; ✎ 835 5141, 800 411 0090 (TF); www.lulubelletours.com. Offers 5–7hr tour for US$100.
Stan Stephens Glacier & Wildlife Cruises [270–1 F4] 112 N Harbor Dr; ✎ 835 4731, 866 867 1297 (TF);

www.stanstephenscruises.com. Offers the 9hr Columbia & Meares Glacier Excursion for US$147/73 adult/child & the 6hr Columbia Glacier Cruise for US$112/56 adult/child. Stan is one of a few captains doing tours; he has strong political views. Recommended.

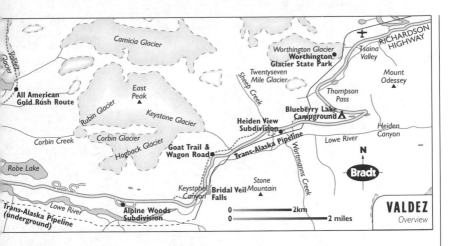

Map labels:
Camicia Glacier; Worthington Glacier; Worthington Glacier State Park; Tsaina Valley; RICHARDSON HIGHWAY; Twentyseven Mile Glacier; Sheep Creek; Mount Odessey; Thompson Pass; East Peak; Keystone Glacier; Rubin Glacier; All American Gold Rush Route; Corbin Glacier; Heiden View Subdivision; Blueberry Lake Campground; Heiden Canyon; Corbin Creek; Hogback Glacier; Goat Trail & Wagon Road; Trans-Alaska Pipeline; Lowe River; Wortmanns Creek; N; Robe Lake; Bradt; Keystone Canyon; Bridal Veil Falls; Stone Mountain; Trans-Alaska Pipeline (underground); Lowe River; Alpine Woods Subdivision; 0 — 2km; 0 — 2 miles; **VALDEZ** Overview

Other tours

Keystone Outfitters 835 2606; www.alaskawhitewater.com. For a wild (& cold) ride on a local river, head out of town to their office at mile 16.5 of the Richardson Hwy. Single & multi-day raft trips on many of the area's rivers, incl the Class III Lowe River in Keystone Canyon.

Fish Central 217 N Harbor, 835 5002, 888 835 5002 (TF); www.fishcentral.net. They book a variety of services incl fishing trips.

HIKING AND RECREATION From the east end of the harbour follow the **Dock Point Trail** [270–1 H3] less than a mile out onto the point via boardwalks and a path. At the far north end of town, Mineral Creek Road follows a lovely valley for 5.5 miles before ending at a locked gate. Hikers can continue for about one mile after the gate to the 1913 WL Smith Stamp Mill. In Keystone Canyon just east of Valdez, the **Goat Trail** follows the 1899 pack trail used by gold prospectors travelling inland from Valdez. The four-mile trail starts at mile 14 at Bridal Veil Falls and ends at mile 18 of the Richardson Highway. For a longer hike follow the **Shoup Bay Trail** from the end of Egan Drive on the west side of town. Camp at Gold Creek six miles in. A further six miles leads to Shoup Glacier and a seabird rookery.

WHERE TO STAY

Best Western Valdez Harbor Inn [270–1 F4] (88 rooms) 100 Harbor Dr; 835 3434, 888 222 3440 (TF); www.valdezharborinn.com. Hotel with standard rooms on the water. $$$

Brookside Inn B&B (5 rooms) 1465 Richardson Hwy; 835 9130, 866 316 9130 (TF); www.brooksideinnbb.com. Lovely rooms, friendly hosts, & b/fast served in a sunroom. Wi-Fi, TV. $$$

Totem Inn [270–1 F3] (46 rooms) 144 E Egan Dr; 835 4443; www.toteminn.com. Hotel with cabins, kitchen suites & standard rooms. $$$

Wild Roses by the Sea [270–1 A4] (3 rooms) 629 Fiddlehead Lane; 835 2930; www.alaskabytheseabnb.com. A lovely home with great views & a full b/fast. $$$

Cedar House B&B [270–1 D2] (2 rooms) 719 Copper Dr; 835 5515; www.cedarhousebedandbreakfast.com. Located in a quiet neighbourhood & owned by a friendly & quiet couple. Free bikes, kayaks, & a fridge stocked with food. Those seeking total privacy may want to look elsewhere as this is their home. Wi-Fi, laundry, TV. $$

L&L's B&B [270–1 D1] (5 rooms) 533 W Hanagita St; 835 4447; www.lnlalaska.com. A new all-wood home located in north Valdez with good rates & simple but clean rooms. $$

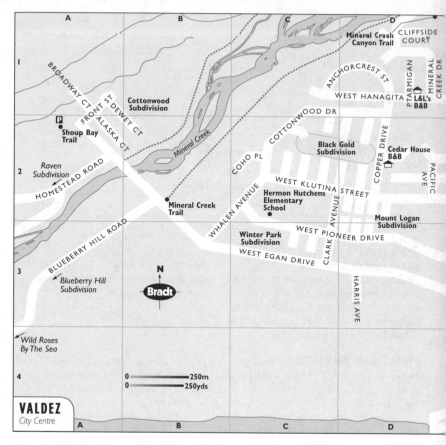

Camping and RV parks

Ⓐ Valdez Glacier Campground (104 sites) Located on Valdez Airport Rd east of town, this campground is pleasantly located near the mountains & rent a variety of camping equipment incl bikes for US$8 & tents for US$7.

Ⓐ Allison Point Campground (61 sites) Located near the end of Dayville Rd about 15 miles from Valdez.

There are 10 tent sites & 51 RV sites available in this popular fishing area for US$12.

Ⓐ Bayside RV Park [270–1 G3] ☎ 835 4425; www.baysiderv.com

Ⓐ Bear Creek Cabins & RV Park 3181 Richardson Hwy; ☎ 835 4723; www.bearcreekcabinsrvpark.com

Ⓐ Sea Otter RV Park [270–1 G4] ☎ 835 2787

✖ WHERE TO EAT AND DRINK

✖ Alaska Bistro [270–1 F4] Located inside the Best Western Hotel (see page 269); ⊕ 07.00–10.00, 11.00–14.00 & 17.00–22.00 daily. The home of a locally famous paella. Place your order 45mins ahead. $$$

✖ Ernesto's Tequeria [270–1 E3] 328 Egan Dr; ☎ 835 2519; ⊕ 05.30–22.30 Mon–Sat. Decent Mexican food served in a boring restaurant. $$

✖ Fu Kung Chinese Restaurant [270–1 F3] 207 Kobuk St; ☎ 835 5255; ⊕ 11.00–23.00 daily. For all kinds of Asian foods, including decent seafood,

check out the Quonset hut (a round-roofed military-style structure) on Kobuk St. $$

✖ The Harbor Café [270–1 G4] 255 N Harbor Dr; ☎ 835 4776; ⊕ 11.00–21.00 Mon–Sat, 11.00–15.00 Sun. Outdoor seating right on the harbour & good burgers make this place a favourite. $$

✖ Magpies Bakery [270–1 E4] 224 Galena St; ☎ 461 3092; www.magpiesbakery.com; ⊕ 07.00–17.00 Tue–Fri, 09.00–17.00 Sat. Homemade breads & soups, & baked goods. $$

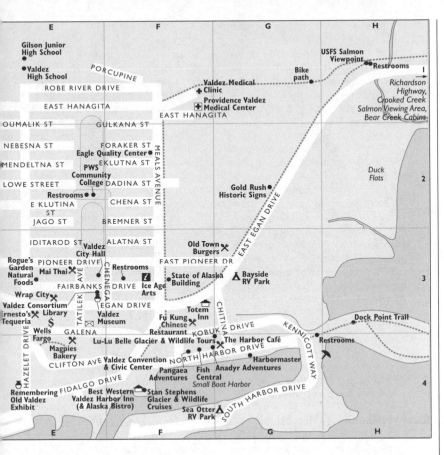

The map shows various locations in Valdez, including:

Gilson Junior High School, Valdez High School, PORCUPINE, ROBE RIVER DRIVE, EAST HANAGITA, OUMALIK ST, GULKANA ST, NEBESNA ST, FORAKER ST, Eagle Quality Center, EKLUTNA ST, MENDELTNA ST, PWS Community College, DADINA ST, LOWE STREET, Restrooms, E KLUTNA ST, CHENA ST, JAGO ST, BREMNER ST, IDITAROD ST, ALATNA ST, Valdez City Hall, Old Town Burgers, Rogue's Garden Natural Foods, PIONEER DRIVE, Mai Thai, Restrooms, EAST PIONEER DR, FAIRBANKS DRIVE, Ice Age Arts, State of Alaska Building, Bayside RV Park, Wrap City, EGAN DRIVE, Valdez Consortium Library, Ernesto's Tequeria, Valdez Museum, Totem Inn, Fu Kung Chinese Restaurant, Wells Fargo, GALENA, KOBUK DRIVE, Lu-Lu Belle Glacier & Wildlife Tours, The Harbor Café, Restrooms, Magpies Bakery, CLIFTON AVE, Valdez Convention & Civic Center, NORTH HARBOR DRIVE, Harbormaster, Pangaea Adventures, Fish Central, Anadyr Adventures, Small Boat Harbor, Remembering Old Valdez Exhibit, FIDALGO DRIVE, Best Western Valdez Harbor Inn (& Alaska Bistro), Stan Stephens Glacier & Wildlife Cruises, Sea Otter RV Park, SOUTH HARBOR DRIVE, HAZELET DRIVE, CHENEGA AVE, TATITLEK AVE, CHITINA, KENNICOTT WAY, EAST EGAN DRIVE, MEALS AVENUE, Valdez Medical Clinic, Providence Valdez Medical Center, EAST HANAGITA, Gold Rush Historic Signs, Duck Flats, USFS Salmon Viewpoint, Bike path, Restrooms, Richardson Highway, Crooked Creek Salmon Viewing Area, Bear Creek Cabins, Dock Point Trail

✕ **Mai Thai** [270–1 E3] 310 Pioneer; ☎ 835 5606; ⏰ 11.00–22.00 daily. Tasty Thai food made with local seafood & served in a cosy atmosphere. Try a smoothy. **$$**

✕ **Old Town Burgers** [270–1 G3] E Pioneer Dr; ☎ 831 1434; ⏰ 11.00–22.00 daily. Wi-Fi.

OTHER PRACTICALITIES

Eagle Quality Center [270–1 F2] 1313 Meals; ☎ 835 2100; ⏰ 04.30–midnight daily. A well stocked grocery store.

Post office [270–1 E3] 221 Tatitlek St; ☎ 835 4449; ⏰ 09.00–17.00 Mon–Fri, 10.00–12.00 Sat.

Prospector Outfitters 141 Galena St; ☎ 835 3858; www.prospectoroutfitters.com; ⏰ 08.00–21.00 Mon–Fri, 08.00–20.00 Sat, 10.00–18.00 Sun. Summer & winter outdoor equipment.

Freshly made fish & chips & handmade burgers. **$$**

✕ **Wrap City** [270–1 E3] 321 Egan Dr; ☎ 835 8383; www.rosecache.com; ⏰ 11.00–13.00 Tue–Fri. Wraps & sandwiches of all kinds. Great for a picnic. **$$**

Providence Valdez Medical Center [270–1 F1] 911 Meals Av; ☎ 834 1659; www.providence.org/alaska/valdez.

Public library [270–1 E3] Fairbanks St; ☎ 835 4632; www.ci.valdez.ak.us/library; ⏰ 10.00–18.00 Mon & Fri, 10.00–20.00 Tue–Thu, 12.00–17.00 Sat. Wi-Fi.

Rogue's Garden Natural Foods [270–1 E3] 354 Fairbanks St; ☎ 835 5880; ⏰ 07.30–18.00 Mon–Fri, 09.00–17.00 Sat. A lovely little natural foods store with a small book section.

WHAT TO SEE

Harbour The harbour is well set up for visitors and fishermen alike. North Harbor Drive is lined with businesses catering to the visitor, including restaurants, kayak

The 987ft *Exxon Valdez* oil tanker left the Alyeska Pipeline Terminal in Valdez at 21.12 on 23 March 1989 with 53 million gallons (1,264,155 barrels) of crude oil, bound for Long Beach, California. After leaving their shipping lane to avoid icebergs from the Columbia Glacier, the *Exxon Valdez* made its way across the oncoming shipping lane, and neglecting to straighten its course, ran aground on Bligh Reef at four minutes past midnight on 24 March 1989.

What would later become known as the worst environmental disaster in America since Three Mile Island, was later described by helmsman Robert Kagan as 'a bumpy ride'. Snow and rain fell and a steady wind blew from the north at ten knots. The temperature was 1°C/33°F. Within the first three hours, 5.8 million gallons of crude oil had poured out of the tanker's eight ruptured tanks. The *Exxon Valdez* oil spill had begun.

During the ensuing hours, days and months, the Exxon Corporation and the US Coast Guard proved utterly incapable of controlling the spread of oil along more than 1,300 miles of Alaska's coastline. Exxon spent hundreds of millions of dollars hiring more than 10,000 workers, including fishermen and their boats, to collect oil from the sea and beaches. High-pressure water jets, chemical agents and shovels were among the techniques used to clean the beaches. Some would later criticise Exxon for attempting to buy off the public by grossly overpaying for just about every service. While some Alaskans were paid by Exxon, others donned their raingear and took to the beaches on their own, attempting to save their local beaches and wildlife. My mother, Kim Terpening, once told me about her part of the clean-up:

outfitters and gift shops. On the other side of the street, the harbour bustles with activity all summer and is fun to explore. Sea lions and seals can sometimes be seen in the water or hauled out on the docks.

Remembering Old Valdez Exhibit [270–1 E4] (*436 S Hazelet Av;* ⟍ *835 5407;* ⊕ *09.00–18.00 daily; US$5/4 adult/child*) North Harbor intersects Fidalgo Drive, then ends at Hazelet Av and a warehouse containing this exhibit, which includes a scale model of Valdez before the devastating 1964 earthquake and a film showing real footage from the quake.

Park A block north, a small wooded park has a trail that provides good views of town and the pipeline terminal across the bay.

Valdez Museum [270–1 E3] (*217 Eagan Dr;* ⟍ *835 2764; www.valdezmuseum.org; 09.00–18.00 daily*) North a few blocks off Eagan Drive is this museum which features a complete cross section of Valdez history, from the gold rush days to the pipeline and the *Exxon Valdez* oil spill and cleanup, including a section of the original ship.

Prince William Sound Community College and the Whitney Museum [270–1 E2] (*303 Lowe St;* ⟍ *834 1600; www.pwscc.edu/museum.shtml;* ⊕ *09.00–19.00 daily; US$5/3 adult/child*). Six blocks north along Hazelet Av off Lowe Street, the museum houses an incredible collection of native art as well as some mounted Alaskan wildlife.

Crooked Creek Salmon Viewing Area [270–1 H1] East of town on the Richardson Highway after about one mile is the Crooked Creek Salmon Viewing Area. From the middle of July through to autumn, salmon can be seen spawning in the river. Across the highway is a wetland rich in bird life, particularly during the early spring migration.

I remember sitting in a truck, driving down the beach. We were picking up dead wildlife. I looked in the back seat and saw a pile of dead bald eagles so covered in oil I could hardly tell what they were. I remember thinking that's our national bird.

While no one knows the true number of dead animals, estimates place the number of dead birds alone at 250,000. Dead sea otters may have numbered 2,800, as well as 300 seals, 250 bald eagles, 22 killer whales as well as entire future generations of salmon, herring and other fish.

In court, evidence suggested that Captain Hazelwood was quite possibly drunk when the grounding took place, and Cousins, the first mate, was almost certainly fatigued from lack of sleep. Exxon paid US$900 million in damages and was ordered to pay US$150 million for their crime against the environment. US$125 million of that amount was disregarded because Exxon had spent US$2.1 billion on the clean-up. More than 20 years after the spill, punitive damages were finally awarded late in 2008 to 33,000 fishermen affected by the spill. The original amount awarded to fishermen in 1994 was US$5 billion but multiple appeals by Exxon reduced that amount to US$507 million. This settlement represents the final stage of the litigation between the State of Alaska, the Federal Government and the Exxon Corporation. The Exxon fleet of ships were later renamed the *Sea River* fleet, and the ship formerly known as the *Exxon Valdez* was transferred to the Atlantic and was recently protested against by environmentalists in Scotland. Captain Joseph Hazelwood was convicted of negligent discharge of oil and sentenced to 1,000 hours of community service and a US$50,000 fine.

Solomon Hatchery (✆ 835 4874) Dayville Road leaves the Richardson Highway at the head of the bay and heads out to the pipeline terminal. At mile 3 is the Solomon Hatchery. They rear huge numbers of salmon and allow visitors to walk through the facility and ask questions. Camping can be found near the end of the road. The road is closed at mile 5.4 and there is no access to the pipeline terminal.

Ice Age Arts [270–1 F3] (*104 Chenega Av, near the Visitor Centre;* ✆ *373 6166;* ⊕ *9.00–20.00 Mon–Fri, 9.00–18.00 Sat–Sun*) Located in the same building as the visitor centre, this locally owned native arts and crafts shop sells work from around the state including St Lawrence Island, King Island and from southeast. The owner is a friendly fellow who knows all about the artwork he sells and the artists who made it.

Valdez Area Parks Shoup Bay, Sawmill Bay and Jack Bay State Marine Parks are all within an hour of Valdez and each offer something very different. Glaciers, icebergs, seabird rookeries and other wildlife as well as great kayaking are a few of the area's draws. Sawmill Bay and Jack Bay, in particular, both offer great kayaking and tent platforms. See page 268 for more information on kayak outfitters.

Shoup Bay State Marine Park Closest to Valdez, Shoup Bay is accessible by kayak, water taxi or on foot via the 11-mile trail [270–1 A2] from Valdez. The major draw here is Shoup Glacier, which fills the bay. The steep rocky cliffs around the lagoon are a good place to look for mountain goats and bear. Icebergs float in the protected lagoon where a seabird rookery is located and the glacier looms in the background.

Practicalities Two public-use cabins can be found around the lagoon and another is on the bay beyond the sand spit. The cabins are US$65 per night and can be reserved by visiting the **DNR Public Information Center** (*550 W 7th Av, Suite 1260;* ✆ *269 8400*) in Anchorage or by visiting www.dnr.alaska.gov/parks/cabins/pws.htm.

The remote fishing town of Cordova (⊕ 60°32'21"N, 145°42'8"W) is one of Alaska's last frontiers. While the town does have a few tourist services, the lack of a road in from the outside world and its remote and wild location have kept the flow of tourists to a mere trickle. While some find the town isolated and boring, many independent visitors thrive on its natural beauty, interesting and quirky people, and working town atmosphere. Located on Orca Inlet 52 airmiles southeast of Valdez, Cordova is nestled in the Chugach Mountains and just a short drive or boat ride from the 700,000-acre Copper River Delta, one of the largest wetlands in North America. In May, as many as 20 million birds descend on the prime habitat, including swans, geese, sandpipers, terns and bald eagles. The Copper River also fuels Cordova's commercial fishing industry with more than two million salmon travelling up the river annually to spawn.

HISTORY The Eyak natives traditionally occupied the Cordova area. In 1790, Don Salvador Fidalgo named the area Puerto Cordova and in 1906 the growing town was named Cordova. Michael Heney poured money into the area with the ambition of laying railroad tracks from the sea to the rich Bonanza-Kennicott copper mines inland. In 1911, the first load of copper reached the coast and was loaded onto the steamship *Northwestern*, then transported to a smelter in Tacoma, Washington. The mines ceased operation in the 1930s and the town made a shift to commercial fishing. Despite the 1964 earthquake that pushed the land up six feet and destroyed much of the town, Cordova continued to catch and process what are known today as some of the world's best salmon. Copper River red salmon are among the first of the year and are known for their size and vibrant red colour.

GETTING THERE AND AWAY There are no roads into Cordova, which is probably the reason it's such an interesting an unspoiled place. However, the town is served by daily flights and a ferry service.

By air
✈ **Alaska Airlines** ℡ 426 0333, 800 225 2752 (TF); www.alaskaair.com. Daily service from Seattle via Juneau & another from Anchorage.

✈ **ERA Aviation** ℡ 424 327, 8800 426 0333 (TF); www.flyera.com. 2 flights per day from Anchorage. **Fishing and Flying** ℡ 424 3324. Charter flights anywhere in the area.

By ferry
Alaska Marine Highway ℡ 465 3941, 800 642 0066; www.dot.state.ak.us/amhs. Daily service from Whittier (US$89) & Valdez (US$50) on the MV *Chenega*, the new fast ferry. The ferry terminal is north of town, catch a taxi or plan for a ½hr walk.

GETTING AROUND
By taxi
🚕 **Wild Hare Taxi** ℡ 424 3939. Less than US$5 anywhere in town.

By rental car
🚗 **Cordova Auto Rentals** ℡ 424 5982; www.ptialaska.net/~cars. New & older cars for US$75–85/day.

🚗 **Chinook Auto Rental** ℡ 424 5277, 877 424 5279 (TF); www.chinookautorentals.com. Cars for US$65/day. Located at the airport.

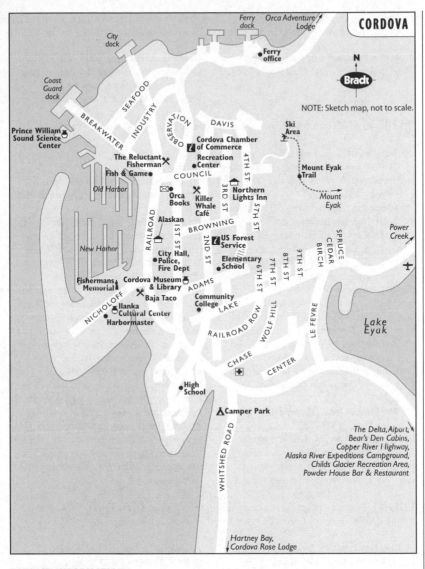

Cordova

NOTE: Sketch map, not to scale.

Southcentral Alaska CORDOVA

5

TOURIST INFORMATION

US Forest Service Office 612 2nd St; 424 7661; www.fs.fed.us/r10/chugach/cordova/index.html; 08.00–17.00 Mon–Fri. Stop by here to get help planning your outdoor adventure. They also have historic & wildlife displays & information. Cordova's

original post office & courthouse are on location & open to the public.

Cordova Chamber of Commerce 404 First St; 424 7260; www.cordovachamber.com.

HIKING AND RECREATION Cordova is an outdoor paradise with hiking, kayaking, fishing and remote trips galore. A total of 14 US Forest Service cabins can be found on islands and in coves for miles around (enquire at the USFS office in Cordova and make great fly-in destinations.

Much of Cordova's hiking trails are found off the Copper River Road east of town (see opposite). The USFS and chamber of commerce offices offer hiking maps. Behind town, a steep but lovely trail heads up the mountain from the ski lift.

Alaska River Expeditions River rafting, hiking, & glacier trekking trips around Prince William Sound.

Cordova Coastal Outfitters ↘ 424 7424; www.cordovacoastal.com. Half- & full-day kayaking trips into lovely protected waters for US$75–115 as well as overnight trips & a water taxi service.

🏠 WHERE TO STAY Cordova levies a 12% tax on all accommodation.

🏠 **Bear's Den Cabins** (5 rooms) Copper River Hwy; ↘ 424 7168; www.bearsdencabins.com. Simple cabins in the woods outside town. Owners offer fishing guide service. $$$

🏠 **Cordova Rose Lodge** (11 rooms) 1315 Whitshed Rd; ↘ 424 7673; www.cordovarose.com. This is a strange & wonderful place. The grounds are decorated with nautical paraphernalia & a working lighthouse sits in the front yard. The rooms in the main building are small, dark & musty but decorated in a unique & interesting way. The building is actually a barge towed from Kodiak, then beached at its present location. The cabins are a better option with more space & privacy. $$$

🏠 **Northern Nights Inn** (4 rooms) 3rd St; ↘ 424 5356; www.northernnightsinn.com. Pleasant clean rooms in a great location on the hill behind town. Hosts also own Chinook Auto Rentals. Wi–Fi. No b/fast. $$$

🏠 **Orca Adventure Lodge** (35 rooms) 1.2 miles NE of the ferry dock; ↘ 424 7249; www.orcaadventurelodge.com. North of town, past the ferry terminal is a historic cannery that's been renovated into a lodge. Sterile modern rooms & suites with kitchens. They offer kayaking, biking &

fly-out fishing trips. Their chefs will prepare any fish you catch. $$$

🏠 **The Reluctant Fisherman Inn** (40 rooms) New rooms in a great location on the harbour in town. $$$

🏠 **Alaskan Hotel** (9 rooms) Railroad Av; ↘ 424 3299. Shared & private bathrooms that are small, rustic & haven't changed for 100 years. The bar can be loud at the w/ends. Wi–Fi, TV. $$

🏠 **Cape St Elias Lighthouse** ↘ 424 5182; www.kayakIsland.org. An amazing remote adventure location. Fly from Cordova with **Fishing and Flying** (↘ 424 3324) for US$650 (3 people & gear) roundtrip to this lighthouse on remote Kayak Island 62 miles to the southeast. Pinnacle Rock towers in front of the lighthouse where sea lions gather & miles of rocky beaches provide world-class beachcombing. The lighthouse sleeps up to 10 on bunks (bring your own sleeping bags) & provides a stove, oven, pots & pans etc. $$

🏠 **Lupine Inn** (1 room) Davis Court; ↘ 529 1796; www.cordovalupineinn.com. Located in the lower level of the owner's home, this cosy little place has its own entrance & kitchen & is quiet but very close to the city centre. $$

Camping There is informal camping along the Copper River Highway. Camping is allowed anywhere on Forest Service Land as long as it's not visible.

⛺ **Alaska River Expeditions Campground** (18 sites) Mile 12.5 Cordova Hwy; ↘ 424 7238; www.alaskarafters.com. Pleasant sites in a wooded area with toilets but no showers. US$15. Guided hiking & rafting trips can also be booked from their main office on the grounds.

⛺ **Odiak Camper Park** (25 sites) Whitshed Rd; ↘ 424 7282. A standard RV park.

⛺ **Childs Glacier Recreation Area** (11 sites) Located at the end of the Copper River Highway between 2 glaciers (48 miles from town). US$25.

🍴 WHERE TO EAT AND DRINK

🍴 **Powder House Bar & Restaurant** Mile 2.1 Copper River Hwy; ↘ 424 3529; ⊕ 10.00–midnight Mon–Fri, 12.00–01.00 Sat. Follow the Copper River Hwy along Eyak Lake to this funky but good restaurant. Steaks, seafood, sandwiches & soups. Sushi on Fri. $$$

🍴 **Reluctant Fisherman Restaurant** 407 Railroad Av; ↘ 424 3272, 877 770 3272 (TF); www.reluctantfisherman.com; ⊕ 11.30–21.00 daily. Great views from a large deck, OK food. Skip the food & get a drink. $$$

✗ **Baja Taco** I Harbor Loop Rd; ☎ 424 5599; ⊕ 08.00–21.00 daily. Across from the harbour, this funky little place is glued to an old bus & serves good, simple food for US$6–9pp. $$

✗ **Killer Whale Café** 507 First St; ☎ 424 7733; ⊕ 06.30–15.00 Mon–Sat, 06.30–13.00 Sun. A dark little café inexplicably designed so the kitchen has all the windows & the dining area has none. Good diner food served all day for US$6–12. $$

SHOPPING

Orca Books 507 First St; ☎ 424 5305; ⊕ 08.00–17.00 Mon–Sat. A fun space filled with books, toys, gifts & even a small café. The owner, Kelly is extremely knowledgeable about the area &, given the time, will regale you with stories & information. Ask to see the jar of oil he collected after the *Exxon Valdez* oil spill (see box on page 272).

OTHER PRACTICALITIES

Post office 502 Railroad Av; ☎ 424 3564; ⊕ 10.00–17.30 Mon–Fri, 10.00–13.00 Sat.

Public library 622 First St; ☎ 424 6667; www.cordovalibrary.org; ⊕ 10.00–20.00 Tue–Fri, 13.00–17.00 Sat. A cosy library with internet access.

FESTIVALS In May Cordova welcomes millions of migratory birds with the **Copper River Delta Shorebird Festival**. Guest speakers, guided walks and other information is available.

WHAT TO SEE Cordova has extensive hiking trails and other adventure opportunities, but also its fair share of cultural character. The harbour is alive with activity all summer and can be a fun place to walk around and see boats and fishermen. A fishermen's memorial overlooks the south side of the harbour.

Ilanka Cultural Center (*110 Nicholoff Way;* ☎ *424 7903;* ⊕ *10.00–17.00 Tue–Fri*) Near the fishermen's memorial. Features modern and ancient artefacts as well as a rare, complete killer whale skeleton. Call for artist demonstration times.

Prince William Sound Science Center (*300 Breakwater Av;* ☎ *424 5800; www.pwssc.org;* ⊕ *09.00–17.00 Mon–Fri*) On the other (northern) side of the harbour. Scientists research wildlife, climate change and other environmental aspects of Prince William Sound here. While not really a centre for the public, their many summer science adventures are the best guides/educational trips in town. These include beach walks, sea kayaking, and river rafting. Visit their website for a schedule of events.

Cordova Museum (*First St;* ☎ *424 6665; www.cordovamuseum.org;* ⊕ *10.00–18.00 Mon–Sat, 14.00–16.00 Sun*) The museum is small but full of native and more modern artefacts as well as a gift shop. Visitors make a suggested donation of US$1. The town library is right next door.

The rest of the city centre is an odd mix of rustic, gaudy and generally attractive historic buildings.

Copper River Highway and hikes The 48-mile Copper River Highway is undoubtedly one of the best reasons to come to Cordova. The road was built in 1945 following the abandoned railroad tracks. The original plan was to push all the way through to the town of Chitna, allowing access to Cordova from the rest of the Alaska road system. When the 1964 earthquake destroyed much of the road and part of the Million Dollar Bridge, the project was stopped. After years of rebuilding, the road was reopened in 2005. From town, follow the highway along Eyak Lake. At mile 5.1 is the trailhead for one of Cordova's best half-day hikes, the **Heney Ridge**

Trail There are a number of trailheads along the next five miles of road and some informal camping. Look up the river valleys to see glaciers and some of the state's most wild country visible from a car. After passing the **airport**, the **Alaska River Expeditions Campground** (see page 276) is on the left just after mile 12. Shortly after the pavement ends (just before mile 13), a gravel road heads north to the short **Sheridan Glacier Trail**. Hike the hillside to get the best view. Locals ice skate on the lake in the winter. Back on the Copper River Highway, watch for the south turnoff to **Alaganik Slough** near mile 17. This is a popular place to fish or watch migratory birds in the spring. High tide is the best time to view birds, since they are forced up the beach and are closer to the spotter. Alaganik was also the site of a Native village. Near mile 25, a road heads north to the **Saddlebag Glacier Trailhead**. This three-mile trail is an easy walk or mountain bike and ends at an amazing turquoise lake surrounded by steep mountains. The dainty Saddlebag Glacier touches the water at the opposite end of the lake. Near mile 27, the road breaks out of the trees and heads out across the braided Copper River. At the end of the road is an organised campground with top-notch facilities and an unbelievable location with 11 sites for US$25. Just before the Million Dollar Bridge (built in 1910 for US$1.4 million) is a picnic area with the face of the Childs Glacier right across the river. Watch for pieces of ice breaking off. If they are large, climb a tree. Large waves caused by falling ice have crossed the river to inundate the shore opposite. Some radical guys have even surfed them! Check out the videos on YouTube here: www.youtube.com/watch?v=mKRR9RMmcIQ. From the Childs Glacier viewpoint, walk or drive to the Million Dollar Bridge and look across the water to the Miles Glacier. From the end of the road just beyond the bridge, plenty of off-trail hiking taking days or even weeks can be found. You won't see anyone else, but you will see glaciers, mountains, high mountain lakes, rivers and probably lots of wildlife.

Cordova Area Parks
Kayak Island, Canoe Passage and Boswell Bay State Marine Parks are all accessible from Cordova and each offers something unique. Guided and unguided kayak trips can be arranged at **Alaska Coastal Outfitters** (see page 276), **Orca Adventure Lodge** (see page 276) and **Points North Heli-Adventures** (↘ 877 787 6784; *www.alaskaheliski.com*).

Kayak Island State Marine Park
South of Cordova and the Copper River, the little-visited Kayak Island is a long, skinny spit of land known as a landing point for the 1741 Russian Bering Expedition. The island is rugged and exposed to the weather. The island's southern tip has a historic lighthouse and a spectacular knife of rock reaching from the water. Sea lions can often be found here. The lighthouse can be rented from the **Cape St Elias Lightkeepers Association** (see page 276).

6

Interior Alaska

Nestled between three major mountain ranges and with the cosmopolitan town of Fairbanks at its heart, interior Alaska strikes an intriguing balance between civilisation and wilderness. Good roads provide access to much of the region, yet total wilderness is never far away. For those arriving in Alaska by vehicle, interior Alaska will be your first glimpse of the state. Here you will find two of Alaska's most impressive parks: the Denali National Park – home to Mt McKinley, the continent's highest mountain – and the Wrangell-St Elias National Park at the far southern end of the region, bordering Canada and touching the Pacific Ocean. These parks are remote, but accessible, and filled to the brim with massive peaks (many well over 15,000ft) encrusted in glaciers. North of the Alaska Range the landscape leads off in every direction with rolling hills, lakes, rivers – including an impressive 1,000-mile stretch of the state's longest river, the Yukon – and small yet dense forests stunted by the extreme winters. In contrast to all this, is the modern metropolis of Fairbanks, which sits at the region's centre and is full of good museums, fine food and art. Fairbanks is also the jumping-off point for exploring the Brooks Range and for road trippers seeking adventure on the Dalton Highway into the Arctic (see page 414).

HISTORY The interior of Alaska was some of the first land in North America to be settled when the first people crossed the Bering Land Bridge between Siberia and Alaska 10–12,000 years ago and possibly as far back as 25,000 years ago. Known as Athabascans, these native people colonised the whole of interior Alaska as it was some of the only land not covered in glaciers. Without a coastline, interior native groups derived virtually all their subsistence from the major rivers, the largest of which being the Yukon. These rivers also provided transportation during summer and winter, allowing the Athabascan people to trade over a wide area and significantly expand their sphere of influence. As the climate warmed and the ice receded, their populations expanded south to southeast Alaska and the American West.

At the turn of the 19th century, Russian fur traders, having driven sea otters nearly to extinction, began to push up along many of western Alaska's rivers in search of new resources. Finding mostly peaceful natives people, the Russian explorers traded local furs for metal goods throughout western Alaska and into the interior under the umbrella of the Russian-American Company. By the mid-century, interior Alaska was being explored and exploited from both the west by the Russians and from the east by the US Hudson Bay Company. Both parties used the Yukon and other rivers as their means of transport.

The Alaska Commercial Company took over the Alaskan fur trade after the purchase of Alaska in 1867 and, by the 1880s, had a monopoly on trade in the interior. Meanwhile, gold prospecting was taking place all over the region with the first significant find in 1886 on the Fortymile River. Prospectors flooded into the area but major finds were few and far between.

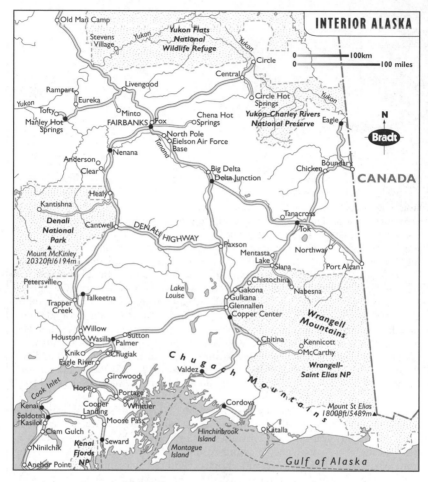

INTERIOR ALASKA

In the 1890s, the Richardson Highway, Alaska's first road was opened to serve the Yukon gold fields and greatly increased the scope of the miners and their cumbersome equipment. Fairbanks was founded around gold on the banks of the Tanana River and immediately attracted prospectors. Unlike other mining towns, though, and thanks to some visionary early residents and Judge J Wickersham, the town was born with the rule of law and a vision of prosperity in mind. The town attracted all manner of people from agronomists and scientists to frontiersmen and gold prospectors. The boom town was even called by some the 'Chicago of Alaska'. Relatively easy access by steamboat helped the town grow even more and, in the 1920s, a railroad connected southcentral Alaska with the interior region. Agriculture and fur also helped the town grow. As air travel gained popularity, much of interior Alaska was opened up to settlers aiding travel and goods transport. Fairbanks further separated itself when a mining technology and agriculture college opened and later became the University of Alaska.

The 1940s and 1950s brought the modern world to the doorstep of interior Alaska. In 1942, the Alaskan Canadian Highway provided a direct link to the outside world while during the 1950s, military airstrips and seaplane bases arrived in nearly every interior town. In the early stages of World War II, the Alaska-Siberia

Aircraft Ferrying Project was responsible for flying planes from the continental US through Fairbanks and onto Russia for use against the Nazis. Between 1942 and 1945, more than 8,000 planes made their way across Alaska to Russia.

In the 1960s and 1970s, gold prospecting and fur hunting were eclipsed by the search for oil. In 1973, the Alaska Pipeline was started to transport North Slope oil to Valdez on Prince William Sound. The project included the construction of hundreds of miles of haul roads and the first bridge to span the Yukon River. This massive project once again brought legions of people to Fairbanks seeking lucrative work.

The history of Interior Alaska is one of boom and bust. Today, the economy has been stabilised somewhat with the University of Alaska as well as a healthy tourism industry.

GETTING THERE AND AWAY Interior Alaska enjoys an extensive network of roads, allowing access to and from Anchorage, Canada and even Deadhorse above the Arctic Circle at the end of the long Dalton Highway. Fairbanks is also served by regular flights from around Alaska as well as international and nation destinations. Many major US airlines now serve Fairbanks directly or via Anchorage. The Alaska Railroad is yet another way to reach the interior. From Seward, visitors can travel all the way to Fairbanks via Anchorage, Talkeetna and the Denali National Park.

THE GEORGE PARKS HIGHWAY

TALKEETNA (*Population: 857*) The charming and old-fashioned town of Talkeetna (✿ 62°18'41"N, 15°5'14"W) is located 11 miles down the Talkeetna Spur Road, which branches off the George Parks Highway at mile 99. The town exudes a funky, arty, frontiersman vibe not commonly found in other much-visited Alaskan towns. Sunburnt and wild-eyed mountaineers, just returned from Denali Mountain, mingle in the streets with tourists, hippies and others. Fine accommodation options, galleries and tasty food can be found here as well as information about the area's gold mining history and the more recent mountaineering history of Denali. The landscape is dominated by Denali and the Alaska Range just 60 miles northwest. The surrounding forests are split by the impressive Susitna and Chuluota Rivers, which converge with Clear Creek right next to town. During the summer, salmon push up the Susitna River and, on clear days, the ever-spectacular Denali seems like it is sitting right on top of the town. Hiking and boating are popular activities here, but most visitors come to charter a plane and take in the spectacular views of Denali.

Getting there and away Talkeetna is located about 100 miles north of Anchorage, 14 miles off the George Parks Highway at the end of Talkeetna Spur Road. Visitors can easily make the journey in their own car, ride the train or bus, or take a shuttle. Daily flights via small planes are also available. See page 282 for flight services.

By bus

🚌 **Alaska Park Connection** ✆ 245 0200, 800 266 8625 (TF); www.alaskacoach.com. Daily bus service between Seward, Anchorage, Talkeetna & Denali National Park. The 1-way fare between Anchorage & Talkeetna costs US$65.

🚌 **Alaska Bus Guy** ✆ 677 9612, 888 340 9612 (TF); www.alaskabusguy.com. An alternative to the larger commercial buses, this one runs on pure, recycled, waste vegetable oil. The fare is US$65 from Anchorage.

🚌 **Alaska Shuttle** ✆ 694 8888; www.alaskashuttle.com. Shuttle service from Anchorage to Fairbanks (US$99) & Denali (US$75). Also from Fairbanks to Denali (US$55) & from Talkeetna to Denali (US$59) & Fairbanks (US$92). Plus service to Whitehorse & Dawson in the Yukon Territory, Canada.

Parks Highway Express 888 600 6001 (TF); www.alaskaone.com/phe. Connects much of Interior Alaska with regular bus service. Extra gear is allowed but bikes cost US$10.

By train
The Alaska Railroad 1745 Johansen Expressway; 265 2494, 800 544 0552 (TF); www.akrr.com.

Tourist information
Talkeetna Denali Visitor Center 733 2688, 800 660 2688 (TF); www.talkeetnadenali.com; 10.00–18.00 daily. Sits at mile 99 of the George Parks Highway at the cut-off to the Talkeetna Spur Rd & has information about Talkeetna & the area.
Talkeetna Visitor Center In Talkeetna (next to Nagley's Store) on Main Street; 733 2689) Has more information on local businesses.

Denali Overland Transportation www.denalioverland.com. Service between Anchorage, Talkeetna & the Denali National Park.

The 1-way fare costs adult/child US$89/45 from Anchorage to Talkeetna.

Talkeetna Ranger Station B St; 733 2231; 08.00–18.00 daily. This new ranger station has a plethora of information about mountaineering & Denali.
Chamber of Commerce www.talkeetnachamber.org. They don't have an office, but their website is a good source of information.

Local tours and activities
Besides walking around town, there is a lot to do in Talkeetna. Rafting, fishing and especially flightseeing are all popular.

Flightseeing
Flights to the Denali area generally cost around US$185–220 and just under US$300 for a glacier landing.

Fly Denali 733 7768, 866 733 d7768 (TF); www.flydenali.com. A variety of flightseeing flights around Denali starting at US$250pp. Add about US$100 for a glacier landing.
Hudson Air 733 2321, 800 478 2321 (TF); www.hudsonair.com. An area family business for more than 60 years.

K2 Aviation 733 2291, 800 764 2291 (TF); www.flyk2.com. Flightseeing & custom charters.
Talkeetna Aero 733 2899, 888-733-2899 (TF); www.talkeetnaaero.com. 6 daily flights from Talkeetna to Denali starting at US$300.
Talkeetna Air 733 2218, 800 533 2219; www.talkeetnaair.com. Flightseeing, support for climbers & a pleasant, small gallery in their office.

Fishing charters
The rivers and streams around Talkeetna are alive with trout, salmon and other species of fish during the summer. In addition to fishing trips, river guides take guests on leisurely floats downriver to look for wildlife and take in the scenery.

Fishbone Charters 841 3963; www.akfishbonecharters.com. Salmon & trout trips for US$155–205.

Just Fly Fish 733 5332; www.justflyfish.net. Walking fly-fishing trips to some of the smaller & lesser-known creeks in the Susitna drainage.

Guided tours
Alaska Nature Guides 733 1237; www.alaskanatureguides.com. Guided day hikes.
Denali View Raft Adventures 733 2778, 877 533 2778 (TF); www.denaliviewraft.com. A variety of river raft trips on the Talkeetna (US$69) & Susitna (US$105) Rivers. They also offer a 'Flag Stop Rail n' Raft Tour' for US$169, which involves the unique Hurricane train.

Denali Trekking Company 733 2566; www.alaskahiking.com. Offer a variety of multi-day hiking adventures for hikers of any experience. Prices start at US$1,250pp.
Mahay's Riverboat Service 733 2223; 800 736 2210 (TF); www.mahaysriverboat.com. Sightseeing river tours & guided fishing. Jet boat tours on the Talkeetna, Chulitna & Susitna. Devil's Gorge tour is for those looking for more of a thrill.

Talkeetna River Guides ✎ 733 2677; www.talkeetnariverguides.com. Find them in the yurt in the city centre.
Tri River Charters ✎ 733 2400; www.tririvercharters.com. A full-service fishing guide, offering full day trips for US$225, half-day trips for US$175. They will also drop you off with your own gear for US$55, or with their gear for US$85.

Where to stay
⌂ **Talkeetna Lodge** (200 rooms) Mile 12.5 Talkeetna Spur Rd; ✎ www.talkeetnalodge.com. A little out of place in the funky town of Talkeetna, this high-end lodge has great views of Denali & 2 good & expensive restaurants. $$$–$$$$$
⌂ **Traleika B&B** (3 rooms) 22216 S Freedom Dr; ✎ 733 2711; www.traleika.com. 3 lovely cabins located 5 miles outside Talkeetna all with stunning views of Denali. $$$–$$$$
⌂ **Susitna River Lodging** (8 rooms) Mile 13.5 Talkeetna Spur Rd; ✎ 733 0505, 866 733 1505 (TF); www.susitna-river-lodging.com. Cabins & lodge rooms in a lovely setting just outside town. Wi-Fi. $$$
⌂ **Swiss Alaska Inn** (20 rooms) 22056 South F St; ✎ 733 2424; www.swissalaska.com. Decent rooms a short walk from town. On F St. near 2nd St. $$$
⌂ **Talkeetna Cabins** (5 rooms) 22137 C St; ✎ 733 2227; www.talkeetnacabins.org. Generic but nice 3-bedroom log cabins sleep 4 people a very short walk from town on C St. $$$
⌂ **Chinook Wind Cabins** (10 rooms) 13770 E 2nd St; ✎ 733 1899, 800 643 1899 (TF); www.talkeetna-alaska.net. Located near town. Wi-Fi. $$–$$$
⌂ **Northern Guest House** (4 rooms) 2nd St; ✎ 733 1314; www.northernguesthouse.com. This pleasant guest house has 3 rooms in the main house & an apartment that sleeps up to 5. $$
⌂ **The House of Seven Trees** (4 rooms) Main St; ✎ 733 7733 Conveniently located right in town offering simple but comfortable rooms, plus a bunk house with 6 bunks. Rumour has it, they have the best shower in town. $–$$
⌂ **Talkeetna Hostel** (6 rooms) 1 St; ✎ 733 4678; www.talkeetnahostel.com. A funky but comfy hostel located a few mins' walk from the city centre with bunks, private rooms, camping & a VW bus converted to a bedroom. Full kitchen. Free Wi-Fi & tea. $–$$
⌂ **Talkeetna Roadhouse** (10 rooms) 13550 E Main St; ✎ 733 1351; www.talkeetnaroadhouse.com. Historic roadhouse offering bunks & rooms. A good café is on the premises (see page 284). $–$$

Camping Camping can be found at the following pay campgrounds or for free with no services at the large gravel pull-out, one mile before Talkeetna on the Talkeetna Spur Road.

⚑ **Montana Creek Campground** Mile 96.5 Parks Hwy; ✎ 733 5267, 877 475 2267 (TF); www.montanacreekcampground.com. Located on Montana Creek just before the Talkeetna Spur Road cut-off. Camping is US$20–33. $
⚑ **Talkeetna Camper Park** (35 sites) ✎ 733 2693; www.talkeetnacamper.com. Located just before Talkeetna off the Talkeetna Spur Road on the north side. Sites are US$30. Coin-operated showers & laundry. $
⚑ **Talkeetna River Campground** (12 sites) Located at the end of Main Street, along the river. Tents only. Pitches US$10. $

Where to eat
✕ **Café Michele** Mile 13.7 Talkeetna Spur Rd; ✎ 733 5300; www.cafemichele.com; ⊙ 11.00–16.00 & 17.30–22.00 daily. Located just before town on the drive in, this high-end eatery has wonderful food & exorbitant prices. Even in Alaska US$17 is a lot for a salad! $$$$
✕ **Wildflower Café** 13572 E Main St; ✎ 733 1782; ⊙ 08.00–21.00 Sun–Thu, 08.00–21.30 Fri & Sat. One of Talkeetna's high-end eateries serving 3 homemade-from-scratch meals a day. B/fasts are yummy & include dishes like wild blueberry pancakes & crab eggs Benedict. Lunch will cost around US$15 & dinners are about US$30 for exquisitely prepared seafood & meat dishes. $$$$
✕ **Twister Creek** 13605 E Main St; ✎ 733 2537; ⊙ 08.00–22.00 daily. Talkeetna's newest eatery, this place is doing it right with 8 beers on tap (5 of them brewed in-house) & a menu full of seafood &

other meat dishes. A wonderful deck for those sunny evenings. 3 meals served a day. **$$$**

✕ **Mile High Pizza Pie** Main St; ☎ 733 1234; www.mhpp.biz; ⏱ 11.30–22.00 daily. This popular pizza joint also has beer & live music. **$$$**

✕ **The Latitude 62°** 22687 S Talkeetna Spur Rd; ☎ 733 2262; ⏱ 08.00–22.00 daily. Located inside the lodge of the same name, this restaurant/bar serves 3 all-American meals a day. Not the best food in town, but they do serve up a hardy b/fast. **$$$**

✕ **Swiss Alaska Inn** (see page 283) Hearty Swiss fare with some local seafood thrown in. **$$$**

✕ **West Rib Pub** 13650 E Main St; ☎ 733 3354; ⏱ 11.00–midnight daily. One of the older businesses in town & popular with climbers. Decent burgers & beer & a perfect patio deck **$$$**

✕ **Talkeetna Roadhouse** (see page 283) Right in town, this bakery offers great baked goods & lunches from 07.00–21.00. The dining area is cosy but crowded. **$$**

Festivals and events Talkeetna is known throughout Alaska as *the* place to party. Virtually all the events are fun, but often get rowdy and are usually noisy all night. If you plan to do any sleeping, find a place to stay miles away from the festivities.

Talkeetna Bluegrass Festival (☎ 488 1494; *www.talkeetnabluegrass.com*) One of Talkeetna's better-known events. The festival is not limited to bluegrass (folk

DENALI STATE PARK

The 325,240-acre Denali State Park is not to be confused with the much larger Denali National Park to the north. Even though the park does not contain Denali, the continent's highest mountain, it is one of the best places to see the famous peak, and is a worthy destination by itself. On a clear day, the information placard at mile 135.2 provides some of the best roadside views of the mountain. The placard lists the names and height of all the mountains in view. Other worthwhile places to stop are at miles 147.1, 158.1 and 162.3. The park is dominated by two parallel ridges, the Curry and Kesugi Ridges, which traverse about 35 miles of the park.

With the Talkeetna Mountains to the east and the Alaska Range to the west, the park is quite literally walled in by mountains. Long, warm summer days, great views of Denali, fantastic hiking on a network of well-maintained trails and a distinct lack of people make this park a must-see for hikers or those looking for great scenery and views of the North America's highest mountain.

GETTING THERE Denali State Park is right off the Parks Highway, 147 miles north of Anchorage and 216 miles south of Fairbanks. The best way to get here is by car, though some of the shuttle companies (see page 282) running to Denali from Anchorage may be willing to drop you off.

TOURIST INFORMATION A small, staffed visitor centre can be found at the Veterans' Memorial and bulletin boards throughout the park give updates and information. A new visitor centre called the South Denali Visitor Complex is proposed for the Curry Ridge area, but a completion date has not been set. Other information can be obtained by calling the Mat-Su area State Parks office (☎ 745 3975; *www.dnr.alaska.gov/parks/units/denali1.htm*).

WHERE TO STAY The park has five campsites along the Parks Highway and three public-use cabins around Byers Lake. Camping is US$10 and cabins are US$45–60 per night.

Public-use cabins The park's three handmade public-use log cabins are found around Byers Lake. PUC #1 has a sod roof and can be driven right up to during the summer. PUC #2 and PUC #3 are near one another and have good views of Mt Denali, but are

music), and a wide variety of musical genres are explored as participants dance, drink and generally have a good time.

Talkeetna Moose Dropping Festival Has an odd theme and namesake but is always fun. The event started in the 1970s as a joke and caught on! Usually taking place the second week in July, the festival is known for various activities revolving around moose poo, a parade through town, music and the famous Mountain Mother Contest.

Winterfest (✆ *733 4709; www.bachelorsoftalkeetna.org*) Takes place during December and is famous for the Wilderness Woman contest, put on by the Talkeetna Bachelor Society.

Other practicalities

Nangle's Store 13650 E Main St; ✆ 733 3663; www.nagleysstore.com; ⊕ 07.00–22.00 Sun–Thu, 07.00–23.00 Fri & Sat. The historic building from the early part of the 20th century was originally a supply store for gold prospectors. It has a general selection of food & goods.

only accessible via a short canoe paddle or a half-a-mile walk. Cabin reservations can be made at www.dnr.alaska.gov/parks/cabins/matsu.htm or by calling the Mat-Su Area Headquarters in Wasilla (✆ 745 3975) or the Public Information Center in Anchorage (✆ 269 8400).

Campsites
🏕 **Byers Lake Campground** (73 sites) Located at mile 147 near the Veterans Memorial, the campground has toilets, drinking water & a boat launch.
🏕 **Byers Lake Lakeshore Campground** (6 sites) This campground has no road access & requires a short walk to reach Park at mile 147. Toilets & boat launch.
🏕 **Denali Viewpoint North Campground** (20 sites) Located at mile 162.7, the campground has toilets & drinking water.
🏕 **Denali Viewpoint South Campground** (9 sites) Located at mile 135.2 at the north end of the park, the campground has toilets & drinking water.
🏕 **Lower Troublesome Creek Trailhead** (20 sites) At mile 137.2, the campground has toilets & drinking water.

ACTIVITIES The park has great hiking on easy, well-maintained trails as well as difficult, multi-day backcountry routes. Along the Parks Highway there are four main areas to start or end a hike. From north to south they are: the Troublesome Creek Trailhead with toilets at mile 137.6; the Alaska Veterans' Memorial and the Byers Lake Campground at mile 147; the Ermine Hill Trailhead, which has a gas station and little else, at mile 156.5; and the Little Coal Creek Trailhead at mile 163 near the Denali Viewpoint North Campground. The trails leaving from these trailheads all interconnect, allowing hikes of more than 36 miles from the Troublesome Creek Trailhead to Little Coal Creek Trailhead or the easy and scenic 4.8-mile Byers Lake Loop Trail. Hikers can start and end at any one of the four main trailheads to create a trip of suitable length. The Kesugi Ridge Trail is particularly scenic, but also reasonably difficult.

Though seldom visited, the east side of the park is remote and wild and well worth exploration for those so inclined. Access is provided by the Alaska Railroad Hurricane Loop flag-stop run where passengers can get off almost anywhere. A good place to get off the train is right after the train crosses the Susitna River.

Market Each Sat, Sun & Mon from 10.00–18.00 the Denali Arts Council (↘ 733 7929) hosts an open-air art market, offering local arts & crafts, behind the post office near the Sheldon Community Arts Hanger.

Internet Wi-Fi can be found at the Library (↘ 733 2359; ◷ 11.00–18.00 Mon–Sat), the Talkeetna Roadhouse (see page 283) & at the West Rib (see page 284).

What to see Unlike many towns in Alaska, or America for that matter, Talkeetna is small and compact and ideal for walking. A good walking tour brochure is available from the information centre right next to Nagley's Store in the city centre.

Museum of Northern Adventure (↘ 733 3999; ◷ 10.00–18.00 daily; adult/child US$2/1) An interesting collection of artefacts and dioramas about the natural and human history of the area including gold mining, dog mushing and bush planes.

Talkeetna Historical Society Museum (↘ 733 2487; www.talkeetnahistoricalsociety.org; ◷ 10.00–18.00 daily; US$3/free adult/child) Mountaineering, aviation and other local history.

NORTH FROM TALKEETNA ON THE GEORGE PARKS HIGHWAY A variety of accommodation options, gas stations and other services are spread out between the Talkeetna turn-off and the Denali National Park and Preserve.

The small town of Trapper Creek is at mile 115 as is the junction for the tiny town of Petersville at the end of the 19-mile Petersville Road. A few accommodation possibilities are available along the road including the **Denali View Chalet** (↘ 733 1333; $$) at mile 2, the **North Country B&B** (↘ 733 3981; www.alaska.com/northcountrybnb; $$) at mile 2.7, and **Gate Creek Cabins** (↘ 733 1393; www.gatecreekcabins.com; $$–$$$) at mile 10.5. The road forks at the historic **Forks Roadhouse** (↘ 733 1851; $$–$$$) at mile 18 where food and lodging can be found. The right hand road is the continuation of the historic Petersville Road and requires a vehicle with some clearance. **Cache Creek Cabins** (↘ 733 5200; www.cachecreekcabins.com; $–$$$) are at mile 39. Proceeding left from the Forks Roadhouse, the road ends at Peters Creek where camping with no facilities is allowed. The fishing can be good here and the Dollar Creek Trail starts at the bridge.

Back in Trapper Creek the **Trapper Creek Inn & General Store** (↘ 733 2302; www.trappercrkinn.com; $$) offers an RV site for US$24 and tent sites for US$10. For 10 minutes in the shower, expect to pay US$4. The four rooms go for US$99–139. Basic food is available in the general store and petrol is out at the front. Nearby is **Trapper Creek Pizza** (↘ 733 3344) with good pizzas and other simple fare. At mile 132 is the southern edge of Denali State Park. At mile 134, **Mary's McKinley View Lodge** (↘ 733 1555; www.mckinleyviewlodge.com; $$) offers dining and lodging. At mile 185, a half a mile paved loop road provides basic camping and access to the Chulitna River.

CANTWELL (Population: 192) Located at the junction of the Denali Highway (see page 333) and the George Parks Highway, the small town of Cantwell (⊕ 63°23'17"N, 148°54'1"W) provides little more than the basics for those heading to Denali National Park and Preserve just 27 miles to the north. The town used to thrive on the railroad and was named after the Cantwell River, now called the Nenana River. The few businesses in town huddle around the convergence of the two highways and include two petrol stations, a post office and the following:

Tours
Atkins Flying & Guiding Service Mile 210 Parks Hwy; ↘ 768 2143. Just north of the Denali Hwy junction, this guide service offers flightseeing, plane charter, guiding & basic accommodation.

Where to stay

🏠 **Backwoods Lodge** Mile 210 Park Hwy; ☎ 768 2232; www.backwoodslodge.com. Decent rooms & free coffee, tea, hot chocolate & popcorn! $$$

🏠 **Cantwell Lodge** Mile 210 Parks Hwy; ☎ 768 2300; www.cantwellodgeak.com. The word 'lodge' could be a little misleading in this case. Extremely bare bones accommodation costs US$35–85, RVs are US$30. Simple fare provided in the café. $$

🏠 **Denali Manor B&B** Mile 210 Parks Hwy; ☎ 768 2223; www.denalimanor.com. Simple but clean rooms. $$

🏠 **Cantwell RV Park** Mile 210 Parks Hwy; ☎ 768 2210. RVs are US$23. $

Heading north from Cantwell, Denali National Park and Preserve is the goal for many visitors. At about mile 224, the Carlo Creek (see page 293) area has a number of accommodation options and restaurants that are often preferable to those found in the Nenana River Canyon (see page 294).

DENALI NATIONAL PARK AND PRESERVE

Stretching out over six million acres, the Denali National Park protects not only the state's most recognised landmark and the continent's highest mountain, Mt McKinley (20,320ft), but also a vast and largely pristine and diverse ecosystem. Wildlife is plentiful in the park as are glaciers, quiet valleys, swift glacial rivers and endless expanses of tundra and stunted spruce forests known by the Russian word, 'taiga'. Despite the fact that as many as half a million people flood into the park each summer, the park's superb management has kept animal-human conflict to a minimum. Park buses provide the only transportation into the park and all visitor activities are tagged, authorised by permit and strictly monitored. This does not mean those who want to see the real park cannot get away and have the wilderness experience of a lifetime. With a single 92-mile gravel road providing access to the park's interior, getting out there is easy. Caribou, bears, wolves, lynx, moose and other wildlife are in abundance and often more easy to spot than the mountain most people come to see. Due to its enormous size, Mt McKinley actually creates its own weather, which affects much of the park. Thick clouds often swirl around the mountain dropping masses of snow onto the upper portions of the peak all summer. Visitors who come to see the mountain and actually do, are considered lucky.

HISTORY For thousands of years, the Athabascan people lived throughout interior Alaska and the area surrounding Mt McKinley. Existing on the abundant wildlife,

---

THE HIGH ONE

Athabascans lived in Alaska's interior – including the present-day Denali National Park – for 12,000 or more years before today. In the Tanana Athabascan language 'Denali' means quite simply 'the high one'. Around the turn of the 20th century, gold was found in the area and prospectors flooded in. One such prospector was a man from Ohio named William A Dickey. Dickey, impressed by the massive mountain, petitioned Congress to name it after his home state governor William McKinley, who had recently been nominated for president. When McKinley was assassinated in 1901, the name gained acceptance. Even today the mountain bears the name of a man who had no connection with Alaska or the mountain. Today, many Alaskans choose to call the mountain by its Athabascan name. I follow this tradition.

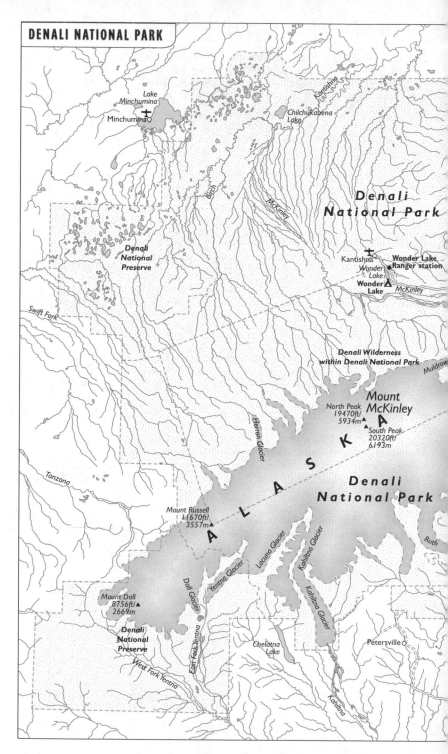

DENALI NATIONAL PARK

Lake
Minchumina
Minchumina

Chilchukabena
Lake

Kantishna

Birch

McKinley

**Denali
National Park**

Denali
National
Preserve

Kantishna
Wonder Lake
Ranger station
Wonder
Lake
Wonder
Lake
McKinley

Swift Fork

**Denali Wilderness
within Denali National Park**

Muldrow

Mount
McKinley
North Peak
19470ft/
5934m
South Peak
20320ft/
6193m

Herron Glacier

**Denali
National Park**

Tonzona

Mount Russell
11670ft/
3557m

Ruth

Lacuna Glacier
Kahiltna Glacier

Dall Glacier
Yentna Glacier

Mount Dall
8756ft/
2669m

Kahiltna Glacier

Denali
National
Preserve

Chelatna
Lake

Petersville

West Fork Yentna

East Fork Yentna

Kahiltna

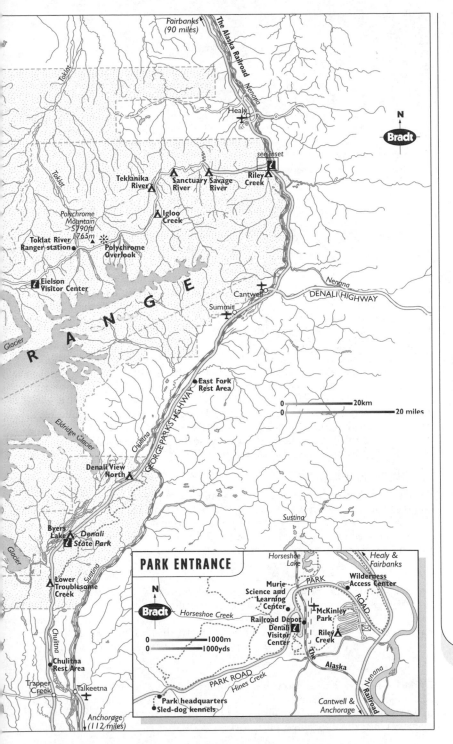

Fairbanks
(90 miles)

The Alaska Railroad

Nenana

Healy

N

Bradt

see inset

Teklanika
River

Sanctuary
River

Savage
River

Riley
Creek

Igloo
Creek

Polychrome
Mountain
5790ft
1765m

Toklat River
Ranger station

Polychrome
Overlook

Toklat

Eielson
Visitor Center

R A N G E

Glacier

Cantwell

Nenana

DENALI HIGHWAY

Summit

Glacier

East Fork
Rest Area

0   20km
0   20 miles

GEORGE PARKS HIGHWAY

Chulitna

Eldridge Glacier

Denali View
North

Sustina

Byers
Lake

Denali
State Park

Glacier

Lower
Troublesome
Creek

Sustina

Chulitna
Rest Area

Chulitna

Trapper
Creek

Talkeetna

Anchorage
(112 miles)

PARK ENTRANCE

Horseshoe
Lake

Healy &
Fairbanks

N

Bradt

Horseshoe Creek

Murie
Science and
Learning
Center

PARK

Wilderness
Access Center

ROAD

Railroad Depot
Denali
Visitor
Center

McKinley
Park

Riley
Creek

0   1000m
0   1000yds

The

Alaska

PARK ROAD

Hines Creek

Cantwell &
Anchorage

Park headquarters
Sled-dog kennels

Railroad

Nenana

berries and wild plants, these semi-nomadic people first encountered westerners in the 1800s. By 1906, the area was swarming with prospectors looking for gold in the hills around the Kantishna Hills. About this same time, the naturalist Charles Sheldon arrived to study Dall sheep, which he feared would be negatively impacted by the sudden influx of people. Harry Karstens, a Fairbanks resident who had explored the area thoroughly, guided Sheldon in search of his sheep. Karstens went on to be the first person to climb Mt McKinley in 1913. When the park was created in 1917, thanks to Sheldon's efforts in Washington, Karstens was named park superintendent. Originally called Mt McKinley National Park, the park was expanded and renamed Denali National Park and Preserve in 1980. Initially the park was only accessible by train, then in the 1950s the Denali Highway (see page 333) provided rough access from the east. In the1960s, the George Parks Highway connected Fairbanks and Anchorage via the park.

GETTING THERE AND AWAY

By car By private vehicle, the park is 237 miles from Anchorage and 125 miles south of Fairbanks. During the summer, this road has a steady stream of cars and RVs, but for the most part congestion is minimal except where there is construction. Moose are common along the way so motorists should drive with their lights on and never speed. Petrol is available at various points along the Park Highway as well as in Cantwell (27 miles south of the park), Denali Village and Healy (11 miles north of the park). Approaching the park from the south, you will first see signs leading to the park headquarters on the left. This is where you will find the Park road, campgrounds, visitor centres and other facilities, as well as the small train station. With the exception of the 15-mile stretch of road to the Savage River, the park is entirely closed to private vehicles. Instead, park buses transport visitors into the park via the 92-mile park road. This is to the wildlife and the landscape.

By bus The park is also accessible by commercial bus or shuttle service from Anchorage or Fairbanks. The trip generally takes about six hours and can cost upwards of US$90 from Fairbanks and US$70 from Anchorage one-way. Many operators offer discounts for groups. (See page 281).

By train Travelling to Denali National Park by train is not the fastest or most affordable way to reach the park, but it is fun. The *Denali Star* (*The Alaska Railroad, 1745 Johansen Expressway;* ↘ *265 2494, 800 544 0552 (TF); www.akrr.com*) links Anchorage with the park travelling at 30mph and giving passengers the chance to see wildlife and some amazing scenery. Summer service is between mid-May and mid-September. Fares from Anchorage to the park are US$146/73 adult/child and from Fairbanks to Denali US$64/32 adult/child. For first-class service add about 50%.

GETTING AROUND To protect the landscape and its wildlife, as well as people, the Denali National Park and Preserve does not allow private vehicles within most of the park. For the most part, Denali exemplifies the way parks should be run, that is, with the natural world given priority over the comforts of humans. The park does a wonderful job of balancing the need to show visitors the wonder of the natural world with keeping the park pristine.

By car Private vehicles are not allowed inside the park except between the park entrance and Savage River (an area with picnic tables, bathrooms, a campground and a pleasant two-mile circular trail) on a 15-mile paved road. A US$20 park entrance fee has to be paid for each vehicle to drive to Savage River. Parking is limited and, on sunny days, boarding the free hourly shuttle is a better idea.

By bus The park's bus system is exemplary because it allows people to see the park without congesting it. The buses ply the 95-mile park road all summer between the park entrance and the end of the road at Kantishna.

There are two types: park-run tour buses and privately run buses. All bus fees quoted are in addition to the US$10 per person park entrance fee. Bus timetables are available at the various park entrance buildings.

Park-run buses
Tour buses The beige tour buses have the added bonus of a guide who narrates history and facts as you explore the park, but they *do not* allow day hikers to get off. See page 281 for a list of operators.

Tourist shuttle bus These green shuttle buses depart every hour all summer 09.00–21.00 and are for general transportation to any point in the park and *do* allow day hikers to get off and on anywhere. However, buses get full quickly, so be prepared to wait an hour or more. The shuttle buses are free to Savage River, but a paid ticket is required to proceed beyond that point. Fares vary from US$22.50/11.25/free adult/youth/child to Polychrome Overlook at mile 47, to US$43.25/21.75/free adult/youth/child to Kantishna at mile 90. Round-trip times vary from two hours to Savage Creek to more than 13 hours to Kantishna.

Camper bus In addition to the standard shuttle buses, there are camper buses (also green) that are for backcountry hikers who require extra space for gear. Tickets cost US$28.75/14.50/free adult/youth/child for a single fare. Because the road climbs in elevation, snow stops the furthest reaches of the road from opening until the first week in June.

Park-run free shuttles
The Riley Creek Loop bus This bus makes a loop around the entrance area every 30 minutes, stopping at the Riley Creek Campground, Wilderness Access Center, Denali Visitor Centre bus stop, Murie Science and Learning Center, Riley Creek Mercantile, and the Horseshoe Lake/Mt Healy Trailhead.

Sled-dog demonstration bus This bus departs from the visitor centre 40 minutes before each sled-dog demonstration. Since demonstration times are not fixed, neither are the shuttle times.

Savage River Shuttle This bus regularly departs from the visitor center and makes the 13 mile trip into the park to the Savage River Campground in about one hour. Take this bus to reach the campground or to hike the Savage River Loop Trail or for a picnic.

Making a booking Some buses fill up quickly so reservations are recommended and can be made as early as 1 December at www.reservedenali.com. Phone reservations can be made starting 15 February by calling ☎ 800 622 7275 (national), ☎ 272 7275 (international and local). Reservations can also be made by mail by writing to Doyon/Aramark (*241 West Ship Creek Av, Anchorage, AK 99501*) or by fax at ☏ 2644684.

Privately run buses Several hotels and operators – including **VANtastic** (☎ *683 7433*), **Denali Taxi** (☎ *683 2504*) and **Caribou Cab** (☎ *683 5000*) – offer transportation to and from the Canyon and the park entrance. But for travel inside the park there are various options, depending on what you want to do.

TOURIST INFORMATION

ℹ **Wilderness Access Center (WAC)** ☎ 683 9274; ⏲ 15 May–20 September 05.00–20.00 daily. WAC can be found by taking the first right after turning off the Parks Highway. The reservation desk opens at 07.00, bus tickets can be obtained at that time. On sunny days the WAC can be very busy.

ℹ **Denali Visitor Center** Mile 1.5 of the park road; www.nps.gov/dena; ⏲ 15 May–18 Sep 08.00–18.00 daily. This facility is generally very crowded & useful only for its fine staff & spectacular map of the park. There is also a bookstore & grill attached.

ℹ **Murie Science & Learning Center** ☎ 683 1269, 888 688 1269 (TF); www.muriesⅼc.org. Across the street from the visitor centre is this excellent & little-visited science centre. Informative displays & staff have information about the park, its history & management. The centre offers educational programmes throughout the summer. The centre hosts a science lecture series on Sat & Sun at 10.00. They also offer field seminars with groups out in the field, staying in wall tents & learning from researchers.

LOCAL TOURS AND ACTIVITIES
In the Canyon there are many guide services that offer everything from flightseeing and river rafting to horseback riding.

Fishing

Denali Fly Fishing Guides PO Box 156, Cantwell; ☎ 768 1127; www.denalifishing.com. Custom fishing trips in the Denali area & throughout the Alaska Range.

Rafting

Denali Outdoor Center Mile 238.9 Parks Hwy; ☎ 683 1925; www.denalioutdoorcenter.com. These friendly folks offer raft trips, a kayak school, mountain bike tours & rentals as well as cabins & campsites on their Otto Lake property (see page 294). Bikes cost US$7/hr, US$25 for a half-day, US$40 for a full-day trip & US$35 per day for 2 days or more. River trips range from US$70–90.

Denali Raft Adventures Mile 238.6 Parks Hwy; ☎ 683 2234, 888 683 2234 (TF); www.denaliraft.com. 2- & 4-hr river trips from US$80–170pp.

Denali Saddle Safaris 3.9 Mile Stampede Rd; ☎ 683 1200; www.denalisaddlesafaris.com. Single day & overnight horseback adventures into the wilderness near the park.

Nenana Raft Adventures Mile 238 Parks Hwy; ☎ 6837238, 800 789 7238 (TF); www.alaskaraft.com. Raft trips in the Denali area for US$80–110 as well as overnight trips.

Too-loo-uk River Guides Mile 239 Parks Hwy; ☎ 683 1542; www.akrivers.com. Short & extended trips in the Denali area & throughout Alaska.

Flightseeing

There are few sights as spectacular as Denali seen from the air. Scenic flights are available from Talkeetna and the Canyon.

Denali Air ✎ 683 2261; www.denaliair.com. Daily flights over Denali in their 6–8 passenger planes cost US$350pp. Their private airstrip is located at Mile 229.5 off the Parks Highway.

Era Helicopters Mile 238 Parks Hwy; ✎ 683 2574, 800 843 1947 (TF); www.flightseeingtours.com. Glacier helicopter landings are US$435pp while a 3.5hr helicopter & hiking tour is US$465pp. Their cheapest option is a general 25mins (1hr total tour time) Denali flight for US$235pp. A general Denali flight is US$349pp.

Fly Denali ✎ 683 2899, 866 733 7768 (TF); www.flydenali.com. Denali flights with glacier landings for US$449pp.

Kantishna Air (see page 294)

Talkeetna Aero Services ✎ 683 2899, 800 660 2688 (TF); www.talkeetnaaero.com. Flights in an out of the Canyon & around the mountain. An all-day flight from Talkeetna into Denali Park, then around the park by bus with a fly by of the mountain on the way in & out, costs US$425pp.

WHERE TO STAY

You have three options when deciding where to stay when visiting Denali: the first is, of course, to stay in the park itself (for these listings see page 294); the second, is to stay in the Canyon – a town of sorts spread along the highway close to the park entrance (see page 294 for these listings); or the third option is to opt for Healy just north of the park (see page 299) or Carlo Creek (see below). These areas are more peaceful and pleasant.

Carlo Creek

Located 14 miles south of the Canyon, Carlo Creek offers some pleasant places to stay. Here are the best:

⌂ **Denali River Cabins** (98 rooms) Mile 231.1 Parks Hwy; ✎ 800 230 7275; www.denalirivercabins.com. Located 6 miles south of the park entrance at mile 231.1 of the Parks Highway. More commercial & less concerned with character than its neighbours, they offer simple cabins for US$160–210 dbl, as well as rooms in the lodge for US$194 dbl. Continental b/fast incl. Wi-Fi. 💲💲💲–💲💲💲💲

⌂ **Denali Grizzly Bear Resort** (105 rooms) Mile 231.1 Parks Hwy; ✎ 683 2696 (summer), 374 8796 (winter), 866 583 2696 (TF); www.denaligrizzlybear.com. Newly expanded, this resort now feels more like Glitter Gulch than its riverside collection of cabins it used to be. The new 72-roomed Cedar Hotel has simple wood-finished rooms, all with a small deck & view of the Nenana River. Rooms are US$192 dbl. Cabins are available with or w/out a bathroom for US$65–105. Wall tents cost US$30–35. Campsites for tents & RVs rent out for US$24. A small store is on the property & Wi-Fi is available just about everywhere. Coin laundry & showers. Shuttle service to the park entrance for US$10 return. 💲💲💲

⌂ **Denali Perch Resort** (24 rooms) Mile 224 Parks Hwy; ✎ 683 2523, 888 322 2523 (TF); www.denaliperchresort.com. South of town at mile 224 of the Parks Highway, this place offers simple cabins with or w/out private baths for

US$85–125. Shuttle service to & from the park. Wi-Fi. 💲💲💲

⌂ **McKinley Creekside Cabins** (21 rooms) (see page 296) Located at mile 224, this collection of rooms & cabins is conveniently located immediately behind Denali's best café. Rooms in the Terrace building are US$189 (4 people) while family cabins are US$199 (6 people). All rooms have a small refrigerator, microwave, coffee maker & free Wi-Fi. 💲💲💲

⌂ **Carlo Creek Lodge** (10 rooms) Mile 224 Parks Hwy; ✎ 683 2576; www.ccldenaliparkalaska.com. At mile 224, this historic homestead site has a little more charm than the average place. Simple log cabins with or w/out bathrooms are available for US$85–145 dbl, as well as a campsite for tents (US$15) or RVs (US$17). 💲💲–💲💲💲

⌂ **Denali Mountain Morning Hostel** (28 rooms) Mile 224.1 Parks hwy; ✎ 683 7503; www.hostelalaska.com. A pleasant collection of buildings located 13 miles south of the park entrance, at mile 224.1. Group bunkrooms are available for US$32, while private cabins can be rented for US$80–160. Free Wi-Fi, a full kitchen, a small store & a free shuttle 4 times a day to the park & town. Some of the area's best restaurants are within walking distance. 💲–💲💲💲

The Canyon In general, accommodation in the Canyon is expensive and not very exciting. There are some exceptions, however, most notably the Denali Salmon Bake with its pleasant staff, simple cabins and reasonable prices.

The Nenana River Canyon – sometimes called Glitter Gulch – is the small but jam-packed collection of businesses near the park entrance. In contrast to the park's remote feel, this 'town' of sorts can feel somewhat like an Alaskan theme park but it does provide some much-needed amenities, including lodging, restaurants, gift shops and tour companies. As a result, this is where most visitors choose to stay, but be warned: accommodation in the Canyon is expensive, not very exciting, and usually booked up solid throughout the middle of the summer. Booking ahead is essential – even for camping.

The Canyon is probably the best option for those travelling on a budget and/or without a car, as many places offer a free local shuttle service to the park, and there are many campgrounds around the park's entrance.

⌂ **Denali Bluffs Hotel** (112 rooms) ☏ 683 8500; www.denalialaska.com/bluffs_index.html. Standard rooms with tolerable décor. $$$$
⌂ **Denali Princess Lodge** (440 rooms) ☏ 800 426 0500; www.princesslodges.com. Sprawls along the west side of the road & caters almost exclusively to tour groups. Free WI-Fi is available for everybody in their comfortable lobby. $$$$
⌂ **Grande Denali Lodge** (166 rooms) ☏ 683.8500; www.denalialaska.com. Perched high on the hill, overlooking the valley & mountains, this hotel is spectacularly situated if not appointed. $$$$

⌂ **Denali Crow's Nest** (39 rooms) Mile 238.5 Parks Hwy; ☏ 683 2723, 888 917 8130 (TF); www.denalicrowsnest.com. High on the hill, these simple cabins have a decent view & a hot tub. Free shuttle. $$$
⌂ **Denali Salmon Bake** (12 rooms) (see page 296) In addition to being one of the better spots to eat, it's also the most affordable place to stay. The cabins are located up the hill behind the restaurant & come in 2 varieties: nice wall tents, & cabins. Wall tents 10, 11 & especially 12 are nice. Cabin 4 is the best. $$–$$$

Campsites Outside the park's boundaries there are a number of campsites within ten miles of the park entrance including:

⋏ **Otto Lake Campground** (30 sites) Otto Lake Rd; ☏ 683 1925. Owned by the Denali Outdoor Center, this has showers & pitches for US$8pp.
⋏ **Denali Riverside RV Park** (85 sites) Mile 240 Parks Hwy; ☏ 866 583 2696 (TF)

⋏ **Denali Riverside Campground** (98 sites) ☏ 888 778 7700
⋏ **Denali Grizzly Bear Cabins & Campground** (58 sites) Mile 231 Parks Hwy; ☏ 866 583 2696 (TF)

In the park

Lodges Five remote lodges exist within the park, allowing guests the unique opportunity to sleep inside the park without sleeping in a tent. At mile 90 of the Denali Park road is the former mining town of Kantishna with four remote lodges. The journey along rough road takes the better part of a day so many guests choose to fly in with **Kantishna Air Taxi** (☏ 683 1223; www.katair.com). The 35-minute flight costs US$215 per person if there are four passengers (US$170pp for just two), or for a 55-minute scenic flight expect to pay US$275 per person for two and US$355 via the scenic route also for two. Flights directly into Kantishna are available from Anchorage, Talkeetna and Fairbanks for US$1,595/US$1,135/US$995 for up to four passengers. Park buses travel the 90+ miles into Kantishna in about seven rough, dusty hours and slightly less on the way out (see page 291 for booking details). Some travellers choose to bus one way and fly the other. Most of the lodges in this area are open only from June to September. Mosquitoes are a big problem during summer so be prepared.

Camp Denali (17 rooms) & **North Face Lodge** (15 rooms) ✆ 907 683 2290; www.campdenali.com. These two lodges are run by the same people & offer top-notch, fully catered experiences. Both lodges charge a premium, but are all-inclusive & offer a well-organised trip for those looking for comfort & their every need taken care of. 3-, 4- & 7-night stays cost US$1,365, US$1,820 & US$3,185pp dbl for both lodges. Rates include bus transportation to & from Kantishna, as well as all meals & activities. $$$$$

Denali Backcountry Lodge (30 rooms) ✆ 376 1992, 877 233 6254 (TF); www.denalilodge.com. Denali Backcountry Lodge caters to the mid-budget traveller with its simple rooms, decent food & minimal-frills service. A dbl cabin costs US$430pp with a price drop during the shoulder season & includes transportation in & out as well as meals & guide services. $$$$$

Hawk's Nest (1 room) A small rustic cabin owned by & located near the North Face Lodge & Camp Denali. The sgl-room homestead cabin is ideal for independent, self-sufficient travellers looking for a semi-rugged backcountry experience. No electricity or running water guarantee the authenticity of the experience. Guests are given a permit, which allows them to drive through the park to the cabin, a privilege in itself. The cabin costs US$375 per night for up to 4 people. Canoes & the first night's meal are included in the price. Make reservations very early. $$$$$

Kantishna Roadhouse ✆ 800 942 7420 (TF); www.kantishnaroadhouse.com. $$$$$

Skyline Lodge (4 rooms) ✆ 683 1223; www.katair.com. This lovely lodge caters to the independent traveller with simple, comfortable cabins, a great chef, but no guide services beyond scenic flights. Cabins are US$225–US$325/night depending on the number of people. $$$$

Campsites The park is full of campsites, but finding a space in one is not as easy as you might think. To ensure a space, reservations are advisable. Campground spaces can be reserved online as early as 1 December at www.reservedenali.com. Phone reservations can be made starting 15 February by calling ✆ 800 622 7275 (national), ✆ 272 7275 (international and local). For backcountry camping information see page 296.

Riley Creek Campground (146 sites) (146 sites) ✆ 800 622 7275 (international), ✆ 272 7275 (domestic); www.reservedenali.com. Located right inside the entrance to the park, Riley has RV & tent spaces available, as well as water & flush toilets. Sites are US$12 for walk-ins & US$20 for those with a car. This campsite is very convenient for those without a car as it's near the post office, grocery store, the visitor centre & the Wilderness Access Center. Free Wi–Fi can be intercepted at the Riley Creek Merchantile (0.5 Park Rd; ✆ 683 9246; ⊕ 06.00–23.00 daily) where basic groceries can be bought. The store also has laundry & showers. Evening educational programs are led by rangers.

Savage River Campground (33 sites) At mile 13 of the park road. Open to RVs for US$22–28 & tents for US$22. Water & toilets are available.

Sanctuary River Campground (7 sites) At mile 23 of the park road. Has toilets, but no water. Since this is past mile 15, there are no private vehicles allowed here, only tents. Pitches are US$9.

Teklanika River Campground (53 sites) At mile 29 of the park road. Has water & toilets for US$16. This campsite is unique because travellers

driving a hard-sided RV-style camper can drive in themselves with a special permit, as long as they stay 3 nights or more. There is nowhere to pump waste or take water, but toilets & drinking water are on site. Once parked in the campground, vehicles are not allowed to move except to leave, making buses the only way to get further into the park from here. Tickets are not available on site, so a Teklanika Shuttle Pass (US$30.75/15.50/free adult/youth/child) should be purchased ahead of time, allowing passengers to travel west of the campground but not east.

Igloo Campground (7 sites) Accessible only by camper bus & located at mile 35 of the park road, this tiny, primitive campground has no potable water or electricity, but is beautifully situated between Cathedral Mountain & Igloo Mountain. Sites are US$9 but reservations can only be made at the Wilderness Access Center (see page 292) no more than 2 days before your first night.

Wonder Lake Campground (28 sites) At mile 85 of the park road. Tent camping is the only option since private vehicles are not allowed here. Toilets & water are available & the fee is US$16.

✖ **WHERE TO EAT AND DRINK** While there are lots of restaurants around the park entrance, these gems, spread between the Canyon and Carlo Creek, are where I eat.

✖ **229 Parks Restaurant & Tavern** Mile 229.7 Parks Hwy; ☏ 683 2567; www.229parks.com; ⊕ 15 May–25 Sep 07.00–11.00 & 17.00 22.00 Tue–Sun & 1 Jan–15 April 08.00–22.00 Fri & Sat, 09.00–13.00 Sun. This exquisite restaurant is the best in the area with handmade local food. Expect to spend US$30 for a meal & make a reservation. $$$$

✖ **Denali Salmon Bake** Mile 238.5 Parks Hwy; ☏ 683 2733; www.denaliparksalmonbake.com; ⊕ 07.00–midnight daily. Located in a fabulously funky & crooked building right off the Parks Highway, this restaurant has a small, simple menu & serves 3 meals a day. They also have free Wi-Fi, poker on Mon night with prizes donated by local businesses, a DJ night on Tue & live music on Wed–Sun. Meals costs US$12–15. Tacos are available at the bar or outside counter usually until 04.00. They also have simple cabins for rent. $$$

✖ **McKinley Creekside Café** 224 Parks Hwy; ☏ 683 2277, 888 533 6254 (TF); www.mckinleycabins.com; ⊕ 06.00–22.00 daily. Wisely keeping its distance

from Glitter Gulch, this lovely little eatery serves 3 great meals a day, has an espresso bar & a small gift shop & is right on Carlo Creek. They also offer pleasant cabins out back. Entrées run US$15–25. Located 13 miles south of the Park entrance. $$$

✖ **Overlook Bar & Grill** Mile 238.5 Parks Hwy; ☏ 683 2723; ⊕ 11.00–23.00 daily. Bad food, OK service, but still a good place to sit & sip a beer & look at the view. Located up a steep hill behind the Denali Salmon Bake. This place is also called the Crow's Nest. $$$

✖ **Panorama Pizza** Mile 224 Parks Hwy; ☏ 683 2523; ⊕ 12.00–23.00 & sometimes until 02.00. Great gourmet pizzas & sandwiches. Wash it down with Alaskan & Northwest beers. Located in Carlo Creek, south of the park. $$$

✖ **Black Bear Coffee Co.** Mile 238.5 Parks Hwy; ☏ 683 1656; www.denaliblackbear.com; closed during winter. The only hip coffee house in the town, this is a great place to start your day. Hot drinks, muffins & some other breakfast items. $$

OTHER PRACTICALITIES

Keys to Denali Mile 248.8 Parks Hwy ☏ 683 1239, 800 683 1239 (TF); www.denalidomehome.com. Run by the friendly owners of Denali Dome Home in Healy. Cars are US$110–130/day.

The Canyon Market 238.4 Parks Hwy; ☏ 683 2259; ⊕ 24hrs. The Canyon Market is Denali's brand-new fresh foods store with basic groceries, a deli, soups, salads, smoothies & coffee.

There are laundry facilities at the Riley Creek Merchantile (see page 295) and a post office nearby too (☏ *683.2291;* ⊕ *09.00–17:30 Mon–Fri, 10.00–12.30 Sat*). Healy also has a post office (⊕ *09.00–17.30 Mon–Fri, 10.00–12.30 Sat*).

WHAT TO SEE AND DO The Denali National Park and Preserve is the promised land for those seeking outdoor activities. The park has a number of tour operators offering everything from flightseeing to river rafting and hiking. However, to appreciate the park's true splendour, one must strap on some hiking boots, don a rucksack and head out, even if only on a day's hike. Few visitors leave the roads and even fewer leave the groomed trail system around the park entrance; they're missing out on the vast and untouched tundra.

Hiking For those wishing to explore the park on foot, the best place to start is at the **Wilderness Access Center (WAC)** (see page 292). The WAC is a cavernous building with a massive chalkboard advertising bus times. Park employees are available to answer questions, but listen to the information carefully as some guides are more knowledgeable than others. Backcountry permits are required for all backcountry camping in the park. Permits can be obtained from the WAC office and are free. Reservations are not accepted and permits cannot be secured more than one day in advance. The park is divided into 43 backcountry units, each is allowed only a certain number of visitors per day. If your heart is set on one area in

Blazed by miners in the 1930s, the Stampede Trail (now more of a road) winds west from the town of Healy just north of the park entrance. The road was made famous by Jon Krakauer's book *Into the Wild*, (see page 432) released in 1996. The true story follows troubled young Christopher McCandless to the Alaskan wilderness where he hiked more than 20 miles down the Stampede Trail to an abandoned Fairbanks school bus. Unprepared for the reality of living in the wild, he couldn't find his way out and eventually died. His body was later found by moose hunters. A cinematic version, directed by Sean Penn and released in 2007, helped fuel a growing contingent of young people, particularly men, travelling to Alaska as part of a larger pilgrimage, who want to see the bus and landscape where Christopher McCandless lived his last days during the summer of 1992. The trail has also brought businesses eager to make money from curious travellers. All summer long, ATV and Jeep tours travel up and down the road.

For those looking for a lovely multi-day hike in the Alaskan wilderness *do not do* the Stampede Road. The road, which is not actually in the park, frequently crosses private land and is largely low, boggy, muddy and wet. The scenery in general is so uninspiring that when making the movie, the film crew often chose to shoot in other, more scenic parts of the Alaska Range. The bus is more than 20 miles from the town of Healy and though much of it is well travelled by vehicles, there are a number of dangerous river crossings including the Savage and Teklanika Rivers. These are icy, glacial rivers that should not be attempted. If you'd like to see the bus, talk to as many park staff as possible, so you're aware of the dangers (or even better hire a guide), bring extra food and clothes, and only attempt to cross the rivers when the water is at its lowest. Bears and mosquitoes are very common so go prepared. Denali rangers almost unanimously resent the story since it costs thousands of dollars annually to rescue hapless parties looking for the bus. While the majority of the general public is sympathetic to Chris, virtually all Alaskans consider his actions little more than suicidal and completely lacking in common sense. Facing the wilds sounds glamorous until you find yourself dying in the woods with no one to come to your rescue. For a map and more information visit their website (*www.denalichamber.com/news.php?item.8.2*).

TOUR OPERATORS Denali ATV Adventures (℡ 978 2094; e *mike@denaliatv.com*) and **Denali Jeep and Backcountry Safaris** (℡ 683 4404) both offer motorised tours of the first part of the Stampede Trail. **Earth Song Lodge** (see page 299) offer winter-time dogsled tours of the Stampede Trail and the bus.

particular, you may have to wait a few days for a permit to become available. Bear-proof food containers are available for hire and a plethora of resources, including maps, videos and knowledgeable staff, will help you enjoy your trip safely. After securing your permit, a US$25 camper bus ticket is required to access the park. Backcountry visitors are allowed to camp anywhere in their unit as long as they are not visible from the road.

Practicalities Looking at maps of the park trying to decide where to go can be overwhelming. While there is no part of the park that is not fascinating in its own right, most visitors wishing to hike and camp will do well to stay above the treeline to avoid the thick brush. Remember that rivers can be extremely cold (especially when flowing from a glacier) and fording even small streams can be dangerous or at least unpleasant. The tundra is sometimes a pleasant hiking surface but it can also be very rough. Following low ridgelines will keep you out of the bogs and rough stuff and will also give you the best views. Mosquitoes can be maddening mid-summer so be sure to bring lots of insect repellent and/or a head net. Choosing campsites with some – but not too much – wind will help keep the bugs down. Some interesting areas off the park road include the Cathedral Mountains near Igloo Creek, the Wyoming Hills and Glacier Creek near the Eielson Visitor Center.

Hiking trails A number of pleasant and less strenuous hikes can be found near the park entrance. From the visitor centre, the **Rock Creek Trail** follows low terrain through the woods, looping back via the Roadside Trail for a four-mile round-trip. For spectacular views, head straight up the mountain on the **Mount Healy Overlook Trail**. This steep and sustained five-mile round-trip is worth it with great views, low bush blueberries in the autumn and Dall sheep sometimes visible in the rocks.

Ranger-led walks Ranger-led walks are another option. The **Discovery Hike** takes place within the park and requires a US$28.75 bus ticket to participate. This hike is generally about six hours with a few hours in the bus. Ranger-led hikes are also available on the trails around the park entrance. Reserve space on any of these hikes a few days ahead at the visitor centre.

Sled-dog kennels The park sled-dog kennel is a fun place to visit rain or shine. The kennels are near the park headquarters a few miles west from the visitor centre. There is no public parking at the kennels, but you can walk to the kennels via the Rock Creek Trail anytime to see the small sled-dog museum and visit with the dogs. Ranger demonstrations are also held three times a day at 10.00, 14.00 and 16.00 and free shuttle buses depart from the visitor centre for the dog kennels 40 minutes before the demonstrations.

Cycling Bicycling in the park is somewhat limited due to the lack of trails. The park road is often dusty and well travelled by park buses, which makes biking unpleasant, even unsafe. Due to the dust problem, the park road is best when the weather is slightly wet, but not too wet or mud can be a problem. Other times to bike along the lovely park road is between the hours of 23.00 and 06.00 when there are virtually no vehicles and more than enough light through most of the summer.

The 15-mile stretch of paved road from the park entrance to Savage River is a pleasant bike ride, especially if you catch a ride in on the Savage River Shuttle (see page 292), then ride back along the long downhill stretch. Technically, only two bikes are allowed on the bus, but drivers often allow many more on the spacious and seldom-crowded, 52-seat buses. An increasingly popular way to experience the park is by obtaining a back country permit and riding the length of the park road, camping along the way. The only condition to this trip is that all your equipment, including your bike and tents must be out of sight from any part of the road. For those venturing beyond Savage River, the camper buses (see page 292) can be taken back to the park entrance for free. Jumping on a bus to go further into the park is another matter, however, since bus drivers cannot sell tickets, the only place to buy tickets and board a bus is at the Eielson Visitor Center at mile 66 of the park road. The section of road between Wonder Lake and Kantishna at the end of the park road is gravel and prone to the same dusty or muddy conditions as the rest of the park road, but receives less traffic and can be a good choice for a short ride.

Located 11 miles north of the Park, Healy (⊕ 63°58'15"N, 149°7'37"W) is a quiet community with basic services including groceries and petrol, but also some good accommodation options that provide a much quieter and cheaper alternative to the Canyon.

TOURIST INFORMATION

⛰ The Healy/Denali Visitor Center Mile 0.5 Healy Spur Rd; ☏ 683 4636; www.denalichamber.com; ⏰ 10.00–18.00 daily. Situated at the corner of Coal Street and Healy Spur Road, this centre has limited information but knowledgeable staff who are eager to help. They can help you find accommodation or book a guided trip.

WHERE TO STAY
Town centre

🏠 **Earth Song Lodge** (12 rooms) Stampede Rd; ☏ 683 2863; www.earthsonglodge.com. Cosy cabins with Wi-Fi & meals available upon request. Located 4 miles down the Stampede Rd. A small café serves basic but delicious food & drinks. They run wintertime dog sled tours to the bus made infamous by Chris McCandless & the *Into the Wild* story (see page 297). $$$

🏠 **Motel Nord Haven** (28 Rooms) Mile 249.5 Parks Hwy; ☏ 683 4500; 800 683 4501 (TF); www.motelnordhaven.com. Basic hotel rooms, some with kitchens. B/fast incl. $$$

🏠 **Denali Dome Home** (7 rooms) Mile 248.8 Parks Hwy; ☏ 683 1239, 800 683 1239; www.denalidomehome.com. Friendly folk & a lovely home make this one of the best accommodation options in Healy. 2 rental cars are available. B/fast incl. $$$

🏠 **Healy Heights Cabins** (6 rooms) Mile 247 Parks Hwy; ☏ 683 2639; www.alaskaone.com/healycabins. Located 0.9 miles down Otto Lake Road, off Hill Top Lane. $$–$$$

🏠 **Touch of Wilderness B&B** (9 rooms) Stampede Rd; ☏ 683 2459, 800 683 2459 (TF); www.touchofwildernessbb.com. Well-decorated rooms with a jacuzzi & gift shop on location. $$

⛺ **McKinley RV Chevron** (75 sites) Mile 248.5 Parks Hwy; ☏ 683 2379. Newly renovated by the folks that run the Denali Salmon Bake, this little gas station & RV park has a nice new delicatessen serving fresh sandwiches. Located at the south end of town. RV spaces are US$29, tents are US$18. Showers are US$2.50. $

Outskirts of town On the road leaving Healy from the south, you'll find the following:

🏠 **Denali Lakeview Inn** (20 rooms) Otto Lake Rd; ☏ 683 4035; www.denalilakeviewinn.com. A large place right on the lake with pleasant rooms. $$$

🏠 **Denali Park Hotel** At mile 247; ☏ 683 1800, 866 683 1800 (TF); www.denaliparkhotel.net. On the left just after the turnoff to Otto Lake Rd, this hotel offers typical rooms & renovated train cars. $$

🏠 **Denali RV Park & Motel** (90 sites & 15 rooms) At mile 245 on the left; ☏ 683 1500, 800 478 1501; www.denalirvpark.com. RV sites cost US$26–30, simple rooms are US$90. Also has Wi-Fi. $$

🏠 **Denali Outdoor Center** (see page 292) (3 cabins) Just under a mile down Otto Lake Road, this store also offers cabins, camping & rental equipment. $$

🏠 **White Moose Lodge** At mile 248 of the George Parks Highway, on the left; ☏ 683 1231; www.whitemooselodge.com. Has a number of decent rooms. $$

WHERE TO EAT

✗ **Black Diamond Grill** Mile 247 Parks Hwy; ☏ 683 4653; www.blackdiamondgolf.com; ⏰ 11.00–23.00 daily. Attached to a golf course, the grill serves decent food all day. $$$

✗ **Totem Inn** Mile 248.7 Parks Hwy; ☏ 683 6500; www.thetoteminn.com. A fair restaurant (⏰ 07.00–22.00 daily) & a lounge (⏰ until late). $$$

Interior Alaska **HEALY**

6

OTHER PRACTICALITIES

Car Quest Mile 248.3 Parks Hwy, ✎ 683 2374, ☉ 08.00–18.00 Mon–Fri, 09.00–17.00 Sat. Sells auto parts.

Keith's Healy Service Mile 249.5 Parks Hwy; ✎ 683 2404; ☉ 24hrs. Petrol, delicatessen & a small gift shop.

Post office 9990 Coal St; ✎ 603 2263; www.usps.com; ☉ 08.00–12.30 & 13.30–17.30 Mon–Fri, 08.30–12.00 Sat.

WHAT TO SEE AND DO

Usibelli Coal Mine (*Healy Spur Rd;* ✎ *683 2226; www.usibelli.com*) is the only one of its kind in the state and provides 'clean' burning, but low BTU (British Thermal Unit) coal to three military bases (Wainwright, Eielson Air Force Base and Clear Air Station) as well as to the city of Fairbanks. Until recently, they also sold almost a million tons of coal annually to South Korea. Free tours are available at 10.00 and 14.00 daily and start from the front gate. Reservations are required. The mine and the Healy airstrip are found down the Healy Spur Road, past the train tracks.

BETWEEN HEALY AND NENANA

Between Healy and Nenana, at mile 298 of the George Parks Highway, a few services can be found.

⚑ Tatlanika Trading Co & RV Park Mile 276 Parks Hwy; ✎ 582 2341; www.tatlanika.com; ☉ 09.00–18.00 daily. Native & other crafts plus RV & tent sites. The giant polar bear marks their location.

✗ Clear Sky Lodge Mile 280 Parks Hwy; ✎ 582 2251. Burgers, steaks & booze. Located at mile 280.

Just off the highway is the small town of Anderson, founded in the 1950s. The town is where the **Anderson Bluegrass Festival** takes place each year during the last week in July. Call the city (✎ *582 2500*) for more information. Also in Anderson is Riverside Park Campground with 40 sites each costing US$12–15. The town also has a post office and medical clinic.

NENANA *Population: 479*

The small but charming town of Nenana (⊕ 64°33'29"N, 149°5'26"W) sits on the banks of the Tanana and Nenana Rivers. The town of just under 400 souls played an integral role in the development of interior Alaska because of its ideal location at the meeting point of the Tanana River and the Alaska Railroad. The town is home to the second-longest steel span bridge in the US and is where the 237ft SS Nenana was built in 1932. Until 1967, motorists wishing to travel from Anchorage to Fairbanks had to use a ferry to cross the Tanana River or drive across the ice in the winter. Grab a bite to eat, walk around town and visit the wonderful museums.

TOURIST INFORMATION

Nenana Visitor Center (*A St & Parks Hwy;* ✎ *832 5435;* ☉ *08.00–18.00 daily*) Engulfed in flowers, the lovely log cabin visitor centre is one of the town's first buildings. Behind the building are some local artefacts including the historic tugboat, the Taku Chief. Across the street is the cheesy Tripod Gift Shop. If you're looking for anything other than postcards, skip it.

FESTIVALS AND EVENTS The town is famous for its **Ice Classic** (✎ *832 5446; www.nenanaakiceclassic.com*) event, which has taken place without a break since

1917. A tripod-like contraption is placed in the ice in February with a cable running to the shore attached to a clock. When the ice starts to break up in the spring the tripod is moved. When the tripod has moved 100ft, the cable stops the clock. Throughout the winter tickets are sold for US$2.50 to people attempting to guess the exact time when the clock stops. Originally intended to mark the arrival of spring, the event has become more of a gambling event. Over US$300,000 in prize money has been up for grabs recently.

WHERE TO STAY AND EAT

🏠 **Kristi's Cuisine** A St; ☏ 832 5656; ⊕ 11.00–20.00 Mon–Fri. Pizzas, submarine sandwiches, salads & ice cream as well as a simple room for rent for US$95. **$$$**

✕ **Monderosa Bar & Grill** Mile 309 Parks Hwy; ☏ 832 5243; ⊕ 10.00–22.00 daily. The best food in Nenana is not, in fact, in Nenana. The Monderosa is located 4 miles north of Nenana on the west side of the road. A sign out at the front proudly proclaims 'still the best burgers in Alaska' which would indicate their claim was at some point in question. Great burgers? The best? Quite possibly. The

pseudo biker bar has lovely flowers out at the front & a dark interior with pool tables. **$$$**

✕ **Rough Woods Inn Café** 623 A St (corner of 2nd & A St); ☏ 832 5299; www.roughwoodsinn.biz; ⊕ 8.00–20.00 daily. A very funky kind of place, popular with locals & displaying pictures of the white moose on the wall. Standard diner food & b/fast served all day. **$$**

🏠 **Coghill's General Store** A St; ☏ 832 5422; ⊕ 09.00–18.00 Mon–Sat. This funky store sells a bit of everything.

WHAT TO SEE AND DO

Alfred Starr Cultural Center *(Front St;* ☏ *832 5520)* Sat between Front Street and the river is one of Nenana's main attractions. The local history, from the region's native cultures to the railroad, is fascinating and presented in detail.

Alaska State Railroad Museum *(Front St;* ☏ *832 5500;* ⊕ *09.30–18.00 daily)* Another must see, this museum – near the river at the corner of A and Front Street – is housed in the original rail depot built in 1922. The items on display are fascinating even for those not obsessed with rail travel. Information about the Ice Classic and even the legendary white moose can be found here. Outside is the tower to which the Ice Classic clock and cable are attached. Inside is a log of each year's winning time and all the losing times.

Public library *(At the corner of Market & 2nd St;* ☏ *832 5812; www.nenanalibrary.com;* ⊕ *11.00–19.00 Wed–Sat)* Offers internet access as well as books, maps and videos about Nenana and Alaska in general.

FAIRBANKS *Population: 31,423*

Fairbanks (⊕ 64°50'16"N, 147°42'59"W) often confounds people's expectations; despite the wild surroundings and wildly fluctuating temperatures, you arrive to find neighbourhoods of modern houses and manicured lawns – with nothing to hint the city's proximity to the Arctic Circle – just 150 miles to the north – and its history of rugged frontiersmen. With a little more than 31,000 residents, Fairbanks is Alaska's second largest city after Anchorage. It sits in the middle of the state, 358 miles north of Anchorage, and is subject to the interior's harsh winters and glorious summers. Without the moderating effects of an ocean, Fairbanks temperatures can rise to 96°F (35.56°C) during the summer months with more than 21 hours of daylight, while winter temperatures can plummet to –62°F (–52.22°C) with as little as three hours of daylight. Despite the harsh environment, Fairbanks is fully modernised with every convenience someone would expect from a large city in the Lower 48. The world's

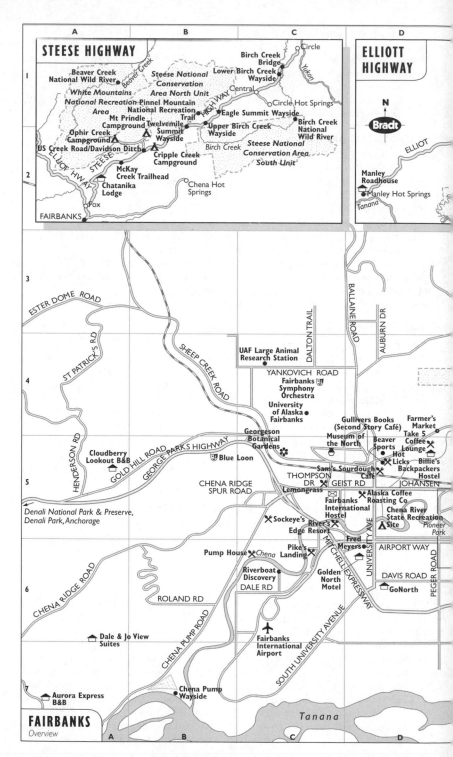

STEESE HIGHWAY

A

1

Beaver Creek
National Wild River
White Mountains
National Recreation
Area
Mt Prindle
Campground
Ophir Creek
Campground
US Creek Road/Davidson Ditch

2

McKay
Creek Trailhead
Chatanika
Lodge

Fox

FAIRBANKS

B

Steese National
Conservation
Area North Unit
Pinnel Mountain
Trail
National Recreation
Trail
Twelvemile
Summit
Wayside

Cripple Creek
Campground

Chena Hot
Springs

Beaver Creek

ELLIOT HWY

STEESE

C

Birch Creek
Bridge
Lower Birch Creek
Wayside

Central

Circle Hot Springs

Eagle Summit Wayside

Upper Birch Creek
Wayside

Birch Creek

Steese National
Conservation Area
South Unit

Birch Creek
National
Wild River

Circle

Yukon

HIGHWAY

ELLIOTT HIGHWAY

D

N

Bradt

Manley
Roadhouse
Manley Hot Springs

Tanana

ELLIOT

3

ESTER DOME ROAD

ST PATRICK'S RD

SHEEP CREEK ROAD

DALTON TRAIL

BALLAINE ROAD

AUBURN DR

4

UAF Large Animal
Research Station

YANKOVICH ROAD

Fairbanks
Symphony
Orchestra

University
of Alaska
Fairbanks

Georgeson
Botanical
Gardens

Gullivers Books
(Second Story Café)

Museum of
the North

Farmer's
Market
Take 5
Coffee
Lounge

HENDERSON RD

GOLD HILL ROAD

GEORGE PARKS HIGHWAY

Cloudberry
Lookout B&B

Blue Loon

Hot
Licks

Beaver
Sports

Billie's
Backpackers
Hostel

Sam's Sourdough
Café

THOMPSON
DR

GEIST RD

JOHANSEN

5

CHENA RIDGE
SPUR ROAD

Lemongrass

Fairbanks
International
Hostel

Alaska Coffee
Roasting Co

Chena River
State Recreation
Site

Pioneer
Park

Denali National Park & Preserve,
Denali Park, Anchorage

CHENA RIDGE ROAD

Sockeye's

River's
Edge Resort

Fred
Meyers

Golden
North
Motel

AIRPORT WAY

DAVIS ROAD

GoNorth

PEGER ROAD

Pump House

Chena

Pike's
Landing

UNIVERSITY AVE

MITCHELL EXPRESSWAY

6

Riverboat
Discovery

DALE RD

ROLAND RD

CHENA PUMP ROAD

Dale & Jo View
Suites

Fairbanks
International
Airport

SOUTH UNIVERSITY AVENUE

7

Aurora Express
B&B

Chena Pump
Wayside

Tanana

FAIRBANKS
Overview

A   B   C   D

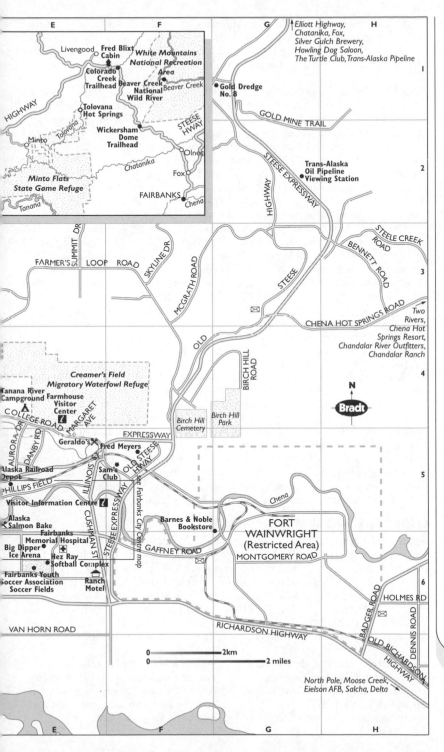

E   F   G   H

Elliott Highway,
Chatanika, Fox,
Silver Gulch Brewery,
Howling Dog Saloon,
The Turtle Club, Trans-Alaska Pipeline

Livengood   **Fred Blixt**
Cabin

White Mountains
National Recreation
Area

Colorado
Creek   Beaver Creek
Trailhead   **Beaver Creek**
National
Wild River

Gold Dredge
No. 8

HIGHWAY

Tolovana
Hot Springs

GOLD MINE TRAIL

Minto   **Wickersham**
Dome
Trailhead

Olnes

STEESE
HWAY

Trans-Alaska
Oil Pipeline
Viewing Station

Chatanika   Fox

Minto Flats
State Game Refuge

FAIRBANKS   Chena

Tanana

STEELE CREEK
ROAD

FARMER'S   SUMMIT DR   LOOP   ROAD   SKYLINE DR   MCGRATH ROAD

BENNETT   ROAD

STEESE

CHENA HOT SPRINGS ROAD

Two
Rivers,
Chena Hot
Springs Resort,
Chandalar River Outfitters,
Chandalar Ranch

OLD

BIRCH HILL   ROAD

Creamer's Field
Migratory Waterfowl Refuge

Tanana River
Campground   **Farmhouse**
Visitor
Center

COLLEGE ROAD

MARGARET
AVE

Birch Hill
Cemetery

Birch Hill
Park

N

Bradt

AURORA DR   DANBY RD

EXPRESSWAY

Geraldo's   Fred Meyers

OLD STEESE HWY

Alaska Railroad
Depot

ILLINOIS   Sam's
Club

PHILLIPS FIELD

Visitor Information Centre

STEESE EXPRESSWAY

see Fairbanks City Centre map

Chena

Alaska
Salmon Bake

Barnes & Noble
Bookstore

Fairbanks
Memorial Hospital

FORT
WAINWRIGHT
(Restricted Area)

Big Dipper
Ice Arena

CUSHMAN ST

Hez Ray
Softball Complex

GAFFNEY ROAD

MONTGOMERY ROAD

Fairbanks Youth
Soccer Association
Soccer Fields

Ranch
Motel

HOLMES RD

BADGER ROAD

DENNIS ROAD

VAN HORN ROAD

RICHARDSON HIGHWAY

OLD RICHARDSON
HIGHWAY

0   2km
0   2 miles

North Pole, Moose Creek,
Eielson AFB, Salcha, Delta

northernmost institute of higher education, the University of Alaska, is found here and has become a draw for visitors with its new and very modern Museum of the North. The frontier spirit responsible for the city's existence is alive and well in this vibrant community which boasts friendly people, good art and great food.

HISTORY In 1901, gold prospector ET Barnette had the noble and, in hindsight, far-fetched dream of establishing a trading post at the site of Tanacross, where the Tanana River crossed the Valdez-Eagle trail. Barnette hired Captain Charles Adams and his steamship, the *Lavelle Young,* to take him, his wife and their mountain of supplies up the Tanana River. They were turned back by shallow water so instead they steamed up the Chena River. After a few short miles, the Chena also became too shallow and Barnette and his wife were promptly deposited on the shore at present-day First Avenue and Cushman, with all their gear. Alone in the middle of the wilderness, the turn of events seemed like a death sentence.

Before long, Felix Pedro, an Italian immigrant searching the region for gold, strode up and greeted Barnette and his wife. Having found enough gold to peak his interest, Felix bought a winter's worth of supplies from Barnette. Within the year Felix would strike it rich, sparking a gold rush and luring prospectors from around the state and beyond. Barnette's first sale of goods to Felix developed into a full-time business supplying prospectors. The tiny outpost thrived with the influx of people and soon needed a name. Mrs Barnette lobbied for Fairbanks, after Charles Fairbanks who later served as Vice President under Theodore Roosevelt. Clearly, the name stuck.

Though the population swelled to nearly 20,000 in just a few short years, the gold in Fairbanks was not easy to get. Buried in frozen mud, miners deforested the entire area, making fires to thaw out the ground. Discouraged, many prospectors left and, by 1920, the town's population had dwindled to just over 1,000. In 1923, the Alaska Railroad made it to town, connecting Fairbanks with Seward and Anchorage. Commercial mining and the Alaska Highway pushed through in 1942, invigorating the economy as the town's population once again began to grow. During World War II, the Fairbanks area received communications systems, bases and airfields, creating jobs and bringing new people to the area. Fairbanks airfields were refuelling stations for American-built warplanes flown to Russia to be used against Nazi Germany. When oil was discovered in Prudhoe Bay in the late 1960s, Fairbanks boomed overnight. During the 1970s, the construction of the Trans-Alaska Pipeline brought a new breed of fortune hunters but the boom was short-lived. Today, Fairbanks thrives on tourism, military dollars and the University.

GETTING THERE AND AWAY

By air Six miles south of the city centre is Fairbanks International Airport. The small airport has an information kiosk as well as a gift shop, snack bar and historic bush plane. Fairbanks is served by a number of major US airlines, as well as the German airline Condor, which flies directly from Frankfurt to Fairbanks all summer. Shuttles, taxis and rental cars are all located at the airport and the public buses (*departs: 07.38, 09.13, 9.59, 11.38, 15.53, 17.38 & 19.05 Mon–Fri, 11.48, 14.07 & 15.37 Sat*) stop in front of the building. There are no buses on Sunday. The airport is currently being remodelled and should be finished by the time this book goes to press.

✈ **Alaska Airlines** ☎ 452 1661, 800 426 0333 (TF); www.alaskaair.com. Flights to other destinations within the state as well as to the Lower 48 states.
✈ **Arctic Circle Air** ☎ 474 0112; www.arcticcircleair.com. Serves much of interior & western Alaska.

✈ **Condor Airlines** ☎ 800 524 6975; www.condor.com. Regular non-stop service between Fairbanks & Frankfurt, Germany. The service is not world class but if you're coming from Europe, there is no quicker way to reach Alaska.

✈ **Era/Frontier** ☎ 266 8394, 800 866 8394 (TF); www.flyera.com. Service to/from Anchorage, as well as to many towns in interior Alaska.
✈ **Warbelow's Air Ventures** ☎ 474 0518, 800 478 0812 (TF); www.warbellos.com.

✈ **Wright Air Service** ☎ 474 0502; www.wrightair.net. Northwest, JAL (Japan) & Delta also serve the Fairbanks International Airport.

By rail The **Alaska Railroad** (*1745 Johansen Expressway;* ☎ *265 2494, 800 544 0552 (TF); www.akrr.com*) *Denali Star* service runs daily between Anchorage and Fairbanks with stops in Wasilla, Talkeetna and Denali. During 1 Jun–31 Aug fares are US$210/105 adult/child for the standard service and US$320/160 for the Gold Star service from Anchorage to Fairbanks. The new railway station is out of town but quite nice.

By bus and shuttle Rarely the most comfortable or efficient way to travel, buses are generally cheaper than the alternatives.

🚌 **Alaska/Yukon Trails** ☎ 800 770 7275; www.alaskashuttle.com. Travels daily between Anchorage & Fairbanks for US$99 1-way.

GETTING AROUND
By bus
MACS (Metropolitan Area Commuter Service) (☎ *459 1002; www.co.fairbanks.ak.us/transportation*) The city's public transport system does a pretty good job of connecting most of Fairbanks and is reasonably convenient. Bus schedules are available at information centres around town. Buses do not run on Sundays. A regular fair costs US$1.50 or US$3 for a day pass but tokens are also available with five for US$5 and a month pass for US$36.

By taxi Taxis are fairly common in the city and always present at the airport.

🚕 **Alaska Cab** ☎ 456 3355

🚕 **Minnie Moose Pedicab** ☎ 347 9719. Eco-friendly tours & transportation downtown in yellow rickshaws.

By shuttle
🚌 **GoNorth** [302–3 D6] 3500 Davis Rd; ☎ 479 7272; www.paratours.net. Shuttle service for those with equipment wanting to get a ride to & from almost any outdoor area in the Fairbanks area. Rents outdoor equipment as well.

By rental car For most of Alaska, a rental car is a necessity and Fairbanks, with its sprawling nature and outlying attractions, is no exception. With the exception of Arctic Outfitters, rental car companies won't allow their cars on gravel roads, especially the Dalton Highway. Parking in the city centre can sometimes be a nightmare. The 380-space city centre parking garage costs US$1 per hour.

Car hire at the airport At the airport you will find the usual suspects:

🚗 **Avis** ☎ 474 0900, 800 331 1212 (TF); www.avis.com

🚗 **Budget** ☎ 474 0855, 800 474 0855 (TF); www.budget.com
🚗 **Dollar** ☎ 451 4360; www.dollar.com

Most of the others around town will pick you up at the airport.

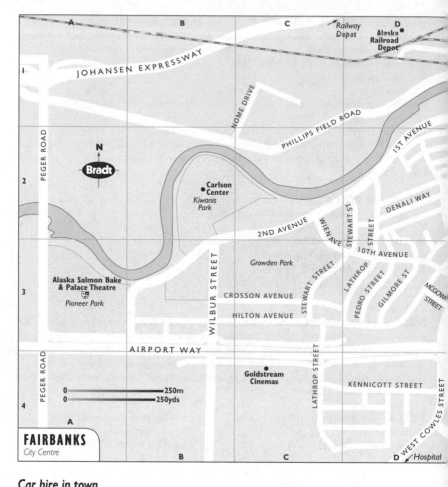

FAIRBANKS
City Centre

Car hire in town

🚗 **Arctic Rent-A-Car** 4500 Dale Road; ✆ 479 8044; www.arcticrentacar.com. Arctic Outfitters ✆ 474 3530 rents cars for the Dalton Highway.

🚗 **Go North** [302–3 D6] 3500 Davis Rd; ✆ 479 7272; www.gonorthalaska.com. Rents trucks, SUVs & campers.

🚗 **Rent-A-Wreck** 615 12th Av; ✆ 452 1606, 800 478 1606 (TF); www.rentawreck.com

By bike

🚲 **Alaska Outdoor Rentals & Guides** [302–3 D5] (see page 308) Bike rentals from the north end of Pioneer Park right on the Chena River. Bikes cost US$27/day & US$99/week.

🚲 **Outdoor Adventure** 505 Yukon Dr; ✆ 474 6027; www.alaska.edu/woodcentre/outdoor; ◷ 10.00–17.00 Mon–Fri. Mountain bikes are available for US$15/day or US$60/week. Located in the William Ransom Wood Campus Center in the University of Alaska Fairbanks.

TOURIST INFORMATION

ℹ️ **Morris Thompson Cultural & Visitors Center** [306–7 G2] 101 Dunkel St; ✆ 456 5774, 800 327 5774 (TF); www.explorefairbanks.com; ◷ 08.00–21.00 daily. This handsome new facility houses the visitor

centre & the Public Lands Information Center. This facility offers 9,000ft² of natural history & cultural displays, knowledgeable staff, free nightly films about culture & wildlife (✆ 459 3730 for film info), &

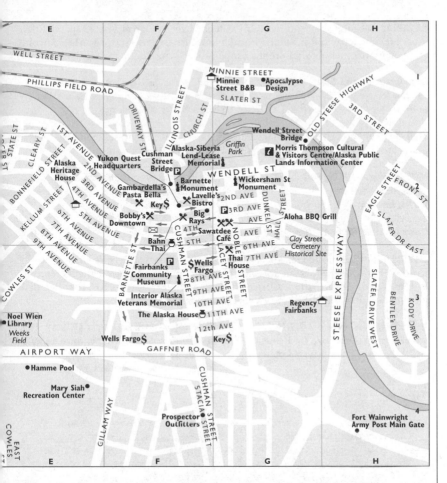

extensive resources in the Public Lands Information Office for planning your next adventure in the Interior or the Arctic. Additionally, information centers can be found at Pioneer Park (2300 Airport Way) at the west Entrance (⏰ *12.00–20.00 daily*) & in the Airport & Alaska Railroad Depot.

LOCAL TOURS AND ACTIVITIES

Boat tours Two riverboat cruises are available in town. Both are narrated over loudspeaker, which can be informative but also annoying.

Riverboat Discovery [302–3 C6] 1975 Discovery Dr; 🝰 479 6673, 866 479 6673 (TF); riverboatdiscovery.com; tours run 12 May–19 Sep 08.45 & 14.00; US$54.95/37.95 adult/child. Discovery is more commercial than its counterpart & is owned by a long-time Fairbanks family. The merging of the Tanana & Chena rivers is something to behold..
Greatland River Tours 1020 Hoselton Rd; 🝰 452 8687; www.greatlandrivertours.com. The *Tanana Chief* offers sightseeing cruises for US$25, which boards at 18.30, as well as dinner cruises for US$50 also

boarding at 18.30. These cruises cater a little more to the independent traveller than Riverboat Discovery. **Gold Dredge No 8** [302–3 G1] 1755 Old Steese Hwy; 🝰 457 6058. The 1928 dredge has been lovingly restored by the cruise ship line Holland of America & has 7 tours/day starting at 09.30 & ending at 15.50 for US$25/12.50 adult/child. Visitors can tour the museum, gift shop & try their hand at panning for gold. Head north on the Steese Highway to the town of Fox, turn left on Goldstream Road & left again on the Old Steese Highway.

Kayaking Messing about on the calm Chena River is a great way to spend a day, especially if that day finishes at the Pump House Restaurant (see page 314). Anyone competent in a small boat can rent a canoe or kayak and enjoy the Class I river.

Alaska Outdoor Rentals & Guides ↘ 457 2453; www.2paddle1.com; ⊕ 11.00–19.00 daily. Located on the northwest corner of Pioneer Park off Peger Road right on the Chena River. Guided kayak & canoe trips as well as rentals are available. They also offer drop off & pick up.

Sled-dog tours The ever-popular sled-dog tours are well represented in Fairbanks. Tours are generally US$50–60 for ½ hour and US$80–90 for an hour.

PAWS for Adventure Sled Dog Tours ↘ 378 3630; www.pawsforadventure.com
Sled Dog Adventures ↘ 479 5090; www.sleddogadventures.com
Alaskan Tails of the Trails ↘ 455 6469; www.maryshields.com; adult/child US$28/12. Mary Shields, the first woman to finish the Iditarod, shares 40 years of dog mushing experience with visitors.
Alaskan Dog Sled & Horse Adventures ↘ 457 3601; www.heavyhorsefarm.com

Fishing The fishing in interior Alaska's many clear streams and lakes is world famous. For those who want to skip the guide and head out on their own, the Public Lands Information Office (see page 306) downtown has detailed information on which lakes and rivers have which fish.

Arctic Grayling Guide Service ↘ 479 0479; www.wildernessfishing.com. Single day & overnight trips to clear water streams south of Fairbanks.

Fly-In Fishing 1195 Shypoke Dr; ↘ 479 5684; www.akpikefishing.com. Operated by Marina Air, these trips are based around the popular species. Fly in & fish your heart out in a secluded setting.

WINTER IN FAIRBANKS

Perhaps more so than anywhere else in Alaska, Fairbanks is expanding its winter tourism to include skiing, dog mushing, snow machining and, most notably, the northern lights (*aurora borealis*). For the best balance of northern lights and winter activities, visit in late February or March. Japanese make up almost 90% of the wintertime guests at both the Aurora Borealis Lodge and the Chena Hot Springs Resort. For many Japanese, seeing the northern lights is a once-in-a-lifetime opportunity and of an almost spiritual importance. The Japanese airline JAL now flies non-stop to Fairbanks through the winter, bringing thousands of Japanese tourists every month.

Most of the hot springs in Fairbanks are accessible in the winter and are much more appreciated when it's –40°F (–4°C) than when it's 96°F (35.56°C).

Ice fishing is also possible for lake trout and a variety of other species. Guides are available but you can also rent an ice hut with a stove for the day. See the Public Lands Office for more information. Like many Alaskan towns, the winter is for locals and Fairbanks has lots of festivals and events during the long winter that are a lot of fun; dog mushing, foot races and ice art (see page 316) to name just a few.

TOUR OPERATORS SPECIALISING IN WINTER ACTIVITIES
Aurora Borealis Lodge ↘ 389 2812; www.auroracabin.com. The lodge invites guests out for evening sessions from 22.00–02.30 for US$175 dbl with hot drinks & transportation from Fairbanks.
Iron Dog Tours ↘ 378 3228; www.irondogadventures.com. Snowmobile tours with all the gear provided.
Moose Mountain Ski Area ↘ 479 4732; www.shredthemoose.com
Mt Aurora Skiland 2315 Skiland Rd; ↘ 389 2314; www.shredthemoose.com
Nordic Ski Club of Fairbanks ↘ 474 4244

Miscellaneous

Midnight Sun Balloon Tours ✎ 456 3028; www.alaskaballoontours.com; adult/child US$175/125. Thrilling balloon flights with amazing views.

Alaskan Arctic Turtle Tours ✎ 457 1798; e wildalaska@Alaska.net. Single & multi-day van tours above the Arctic Circle & around Fairbanks.

HIKING AND RECREATION The Fairbanks area is an outdoor playground during both summer and winter. The city has numerous parks with hiking trails and the outer-lying parks and recreation areas offer everything from hiking to fishing and even swimming. The Chena River is flanked by a lovely trail through much of the town, ideal for getting some exercise and seeing some of the city's historic buildings and sites. Unlike some parts of Alaska, Fairbanks offers outdoor enthusiasts the logistical support that can make their dreams of adventure a reality. Gear can be rented easily, guides hired, planes chartered, just about anything you want to do can be arranged in Fairbanks and the wilderness is always just a bush flight away.

A number of hiking opportunities exist right in Fairbanks including the Birch Hill Trail System at the Birch Hill Ski Area off the Steese Highway, Creamer's Field trails and the extensive trail system at the University. A complete map of the UAF trails can generally be found at the visitor centre and a posted map is located on campus at the ski hut on the West Ridge. A fantastic hiking book can be found in town called *Outside in the Interior* by Kyle Joly.

WHERE TO STAY Fairbanks has numerous accommodation options, from in-city camping to luxury hotels. Most notably though, the city has many wonderful B&Bs that should not be missed.

Hotels

Luxury

⌂ **Pikes Waterfront Lodge** [302–3 C6] (180 rooms) 1850 Hoselton Rd; ✎ 456 4500, 877 774 2400; www.pikeslodge.com. A variety of nice rooms & cabins on the Chena River. Free shuttle to the airport & US$5 elsewhere. **Pikes Landing Restaurant** (see page 313) is right next door & quite good. Rooms & cabins are US$235 & upwards. Good continental b/fast. Dog friendly. Wi-Fi. $$$$

⌂ **River's Edge Resort** [302–3 C5] (90 rooms) 4200 Boat St; ✎ 474 0286, 800 770 3343 (TF); www.riversedge.net. Pleasant cottages crammed together along the Chena River. Decent food in the adjacent **River's Edge Resort Restaurant** (see page 313) & Wi-Fi. If reserving a riverfront cottage (US$244 dbl), be sure it actually faces the river. Garden cottages are US$219 dbl. $$$$

Mid-range

⌂ **Alpine Lodge** (115 rooms) 4920 Dale Rd; ✎ 328 6300, 800 455 8851 (TF); www.akalpinelodge.com. A standard hotel with clean rooms. $$$

⌂ **Fountainhead Hotels** www.fountainheadhotels.com. Fairbanks has 3 of these hotels scattered around town. **Bridgewater Hotel** (94 rooms) 723 First Av; ✎ 452 6661. Located near the downtown visitor centre on the Chena River. **Sophie Station** (150 rooms) 1717 University Av; ✎ 479 3650. Has free Wi-Fi throughout the hotel & pleasant suites with full kitchens for US$189–205 dbl. A restaurant & lounge are also on the premises. **Wedgewood Resort** (295 rooms) 212 Wedgwood Dr; ✎ 452 1442) has

apartment-style rooms with a living room, kitchen & 1 or 2 bedrooms for US$165–255 for 2–6 people. $$$

⌂ **Extended Stay Deluxe** (100 rooms) 4580 Old Airport Rd; ✎ 457 2288; www.extendedstaydeluxe.com. Pay Wi-Fi, pool & small in-room kitchens. $$$

⌂ **Regency Hotel** [306–7 G3] (128 rooms) 95 10th Av; ✎ 452 3200, 800 348 1340 (TF); www.regencyfairbankshotel.com. Downtown hotel near the Chena River with nice large rooms & kitchens. Pleasant restaurant with passable food. Free shuttle. Wi-Fi. $$$

These historic roadways and many of the towns along them were originally created as gold prospectors branched out from Fairbanks at the turn of the century in search of the next strike. Today, they serve small communities and allow visitors access to some remote country.

THE STEESE HIGHWAY The Steese Highway starts at the town of Fox (*population: 300*), situated 11 miles north of Fairbanks. Fox was established in the early 1900s as a gold mining settlement, but is now known mainly as a place where Fairbanks locals drive to get a good meal at one of the restaurants, or a beer at the brewery (see page 315 for listings).

From Fox, the Steese Highway cuts northeast to the town of Central at mile 127, and finally ends in Circle at mile 162. Along the way there are numerous trails and campsites.

At mile 16.5, the monument to Felix Pedro (see page 304) commemorates the first person to find gold in the area. The rough road continues to Cleary Summit at 2,233ft and onto the Chatanika Gold Camp at mile 27.9. The **Chatanika Lodge** (✆ 389 2164; $$) has simple rooms with shared bathrooms. This is where locals gather in March for Chatanika Days, a fun event filled with drinking and bizarre sports such as human bowling and outhouse races. Stop by the delightfully funky bar to see the John Wayne shrine.

At mile 39 is the **Upper Chatanika State Recreation Site** (25 sites) with toilets, water and a lovely location right on the river. Boaters can launch here for an all day, 20-mile trip to the Lower Chatanika State Recreational Area on the Elliott Highway. The pavement ends at mile 44.

Davidson Ditch at mile 57.3 represents a marvel of Arctic engineering on a par with the Trans-Alaska Pipeline. The system of pipes and 'ditches' transported water from the Chatanika River to the gold mining operation in Fairbanks. The piped sections worked as siphons. Also at mile 57.3 is the Nome Creek Road, heading north to the White Mountains Nation Recreation Area with two campsites and numerous trails. **Ophir Creek Campground** (19 sites; US$6) has good hiking and fishing. After turning onto Nome Creek Road, take a left at the T-junction and continue another 12 miles to the campground. **Mount Prindle Campground** (13 sites; US$6) is situated in a spectacular alpine setting with Mount Prindle (5,286 feet) looming nearby. It is a great spot to start a high country hike. After taking the Nome Creek Road, go right at the T-junction and the campground is four miles further on.

At mile 60, the **Cripple Creek Campground** (12 sites; US$6) offers camping, fishing and river access. At mile 85.5 is your first chance to start the Pinnell Mountain Trail. The multi-day trail borders the Steese National Conservation Area North Unit, an alpine environment important to the local caribou population. Caribou can sometimes be seen on the road in the autumn.

At mile 94, an access road on the right leads to the **Birch Creek National Wild River** where boaters start a seven–ten day float on the class I–III river to Lower Birch Creek Wayside at mile 140.

Eagle Summit, at mile 107, is the second and preferred place to start the Pinnell Mountain Trail.

The small town of **Central** unceremoniously appears in the trees at mile 127.8. **Circle Air** (✆ 520 5223, 866 520 5223 (TF); www.circleair.com) offers charter flights in the area and rents rafting equipment. The **Steese Roadhouse** (✆ 520 5800; ⊕ 08.00–21.00, 07.00–23.00 Sat, 07.00–19.00 Sun), formerly Crabb's Corner, serves good food, has a small grocery store and friendly staff although the rooms are a little dingy.

Lower Birch Creek at mile 140.4 is a good place to start the 16-mile float of calm water to the Birch Creek Bridge at mile 147. The end-of-the-road town of **Circle** was once a booming mining town but lost most of its population as other, more lucrative, claims were discovered. The founding miners named the town 'Circle', incorrectly believing it was on the Arctic Circle. The town is actually 50 miles to the south of the Arctic. In its heyday, the town had its own newspaper, the *Yukon Press*, as many as ten dance halls, an opera house and more than 700 residents. Located on the mighty Yukon River, the town served as a goods distribution point for regional mining camps. Today, the town has a large native Athabascan community and many active miners. Pioneer Cemetery is the town's best record keeper with stones dating back to the 1800s. To find the cemetery, head upriver on the gravel road. After a barricade and some brush, the cemetery is off to the left. The **Circle Museum** (✆ 520 1893; ⊕ 12.00–17.00 daily; US$1 adult) has historic items representing the area's gold mining history. The town is still has an active mining community. The town is also known for its **Circle Hot Springs**, which unfortunately are now closed. The springs were used by the native Athabascans and later by gold miners. The hotel is said to be haunted. **HC Company Store** (✆ 773 1222) offers tyre repair, petrol and basic groceries. There is no lodging in Circle beyond the free campsite on the river. **Warbelow's Air** (✆ 474 0518; www.warbelows.com) flies the mail into town and offers charter flights in the area as well as a scheduled service Monday to Friday between Circle and Central. They also offer a flight to the town of Fort Yukon and a short tour once you're on the ground. **Elbert Carol Jr** (✆ 773 1233) is the town's unofficial guide and can take you out in his boat for fishing or sightseeing.

The large building on the river is the ill-fated Circle Lodge that was started and not completed, presumably due to financial shortfalls. Princess Cruises is rumoured to have bought it, but construction plans are a little fuzzy.

THE ELLIOTT HIGHWAY The Elliott Highway strikes out west from Fox, 11 miles north of Fairbanks and ends at Manley Hot Springs, 151 miles later. The highway was named after Malcom Elliott, the Alaska Railroad commissioner and completed in 1959. Between Fox and the Dalton Highway junction there are a few landmarks worth mentioning. The White Mountains National Recreation Area is accessible from the highway via a number of trails (see page 322). At mile 11, the **Lower Chatanika State Recreation Area** is a 570-acre recreation area with two paying campsites and access to the Chatanika River. Wickersham Dome Trail is at mile 27.7, Colorado Creek Trail is at mile 57.1 and a public-use cabin is available by reservation at mile 62.5. Contact the BLM office in Fairbanks. At mile 49, the **Arctic Circle Trading Post** (✆ 474 4565) has basic supplies, but no gas or lodging.

At mile 70.8, a road leads to what's left of the town of **Livengood**. Prospector Jay Livengood, who discovered gold there in 1914, founded the town. The infamous Dalton Highway (see box on page 414) heads north at mile 73.1, providing the only arctic road access in Alaska.

At mile 93, a primitive 11-mile trails leads to the private **Tolovana Hot Springs** (✆ 455 6706; www.tolovanahotsprings.com). Three cabins are available here for US$50–150, depending on the season. The best way to get in, winter or summer, is by plane.

At mile 103 is the **Hutlinana Hot Springs.** A poorly-marked trail starts at the Hutlinana Creek bridge. Do not attempt this trip without a healthy sense of adventure and the topographical maps 'Livengood A-6' and 'Tanana A-1'. The trail follows Hutlinana Creek for five to six miles. The pool is right on the river and is a steady 105°F. Because of the variable quality of the trail, locals generally ski in during the winter or spring.

At mile 110, the tiny Athabascan town of **Minto** is 11 miles down the road to the south. Finally, the road ends at mile 151 in the town of **Manley** and the Tanana River

continued overleaf

6

just beyond. During the gold rush days at the turn of the century, Manley was much larger, supplying mining camps in the area. In 1902, a prospector named John Karshner claimed the springs and started a vegetable farm on 278 acres. Five years later, Frank Manley built the 45-room Hot Springs Resort Hotel, helping the town to thrive until it burned to the ground in 1913. In 1957, the town's name was changed from Hot Springs to Manley Hot Springs. When the Elliott Highway was completed in 1959, the town began its regeneration. Today, the quiet, friendly town of 72 people has a school, post office, a store, a roadhouse and a new resort built around the hot springs. The **Manley Roadhouse** (672 3161) serves decent food, has a bar and simple rooms with private or shared bathrooms for US$120 double and US$65, cabins cost US$100. A large grassy area across the street is available for campers (US$5) and showers can be had in the lodge for US$3. **Manley Hot Springs** (672 3171) has a few cement hot tubs for soaking in a greenhouse filled with plants. Using the heat from the springs on their property, they are able to grow plants in their greenhouses all winter.

Budget

Golden North Hotel [302–3 D6] (62 rooms) 4888 Old Airport Rd; 479 6201, 800 447 1910 (TF); www.extendedstaydeluxe.com. Small, simple rooms are US$96 dbl with free Wi-Fi, private bathroom & shuttle service. $$

Ranch Motel [302–3 E6] (30 rooms) 2223 Cushman St; 452 4783. This small family-run hotel doesn't look very good from the outside but some of the rooms can be quite nice for the price. Some rooms are better than others (watch for sagging beds), so ask to choose your own room. US$95 dbl. $$

B&Bs Fairbanks has numerous B&Bs, some better than others. The visitor centre maintains a list of available accommodation as well as fliers for most of them. The Fairbanks Association of Bed and Breakfasts has a reasonably wide membership of local B&Bs. Find more information at www.ptialaska.net/~fabb.

Aurora Express B&B [302–3 A7] (8 rooms) 1540 Chena Ridge Rd; 800 221 0073; www.fairbanksalaskabedandbreakfast.com. A unique B&B with elaborately decorated historic railcar rooms. US$145–160 dbl. $$$

Cloudberry Lookout B&B [302–3 A5] (4 rooms) 351 Cloudberry Ln; 479 7334; www.mosquitonet.com/ ~cloudberry. An amazing 5-storey custom home with antique furniture throughout. Dbl rooms are US$85–125. $$$

Dale & Jo View Suites [302–3 A6] (6 rooms) 3260 Craft Rd; 378 0186; www.daleandjo.com. Not run by a gay couple, as many people think, this lovely & tastefully decorated B&B is run by the fabulous cook & painter Jo & her husband Dale. Every detail of each well-appointed room has been attended to. Dbl rooms are US$150–200, while a downstairs 2-room suite is US$285. Wi-Fi. $$$

Alaska Heritage House B&B [306–7 E2] (6 rooms) 410 Cowles St; 388 9595. Jackie & Frank renovated this historic 1916 house over 2 years & recently opened as a B&B. Historic photos & gorgeous details everywhere. 3 rooms have kitchenettes & the darker downstairs rooms are ideal for those having trouble adjusting to the midnight sun. Full b/fast & coin laundry. The beautiful Georgia Lee Boudoir is dedicated to the ladies of the night (prostitutes), who worked Fairbanks infamous 4th Street red-light district which was active from 1902 until the 1950s. Rooms are US$89–US$200 dbl. $$$

Minnie Street B&B [306–7 F1] (12 rooms) 345 Minnie St; 456 1802; 888 456 1849 (TF); www.minniestreetbandb.com. Simple rooms with & without shared bathrooms as well as very nice large luxury suites. Rooms are US$139–239. Wi-Fi. $$$

Hostels

🛏 **Billie's Backpackers Hostel** [302–3 D5] (20 rooms) 2895 Mack Blvd; ☎ 479 2034; www.alaskahostel.com. Dorm beds are US$25 & rooms are US$50. Tents are US$15. Kitchen, showers & Wi-Fi. $

🛏 **Chandalar Ranch** (20 rooms) 5804 Chena Hot Springs Rd; ☎ 488 8402; www.chandalarranchalaska.com. Bunks are US$30, rooms are US$40 sgl & US$60 dbl & cabins are US$40 sgl & US$70 dbl. Transportation to the ranch costs US$50 return. $

🛏 **Fairbanks International Hostel** [302–3 C5] (30 rooms) 4316 Birch Ln; ☎ 479 0751; www.fairbankshostel.com. Nice and affordable. US$25 sgl, US$75 dbl, US$10 tent. $

🛏 **GoNorth** [302–3 D6] (20 rooms) 3500 Davis Rd; ☎ 479 7272; www.gonorthalaska.com. Beds in wall tents are US$24 & tent sites are US$12. 4 cabins are built around a central fire & BBQ area. Showers, kitchen & toilets are in an adjacent building. Canoes, bikes & camping gear for rent. Free Wi-Fi. $

Camping In addition to these in-city campsites, many others can be found on the roads heading out of town including the Steese Highway (see box on page 310), the Elliott Highway (see box on page 310) and Chena Hot Springs Road (see page 321).

⛺ **Chena River State Recreation Site** [302–3 D5] (see page 322) Located right in town where University Av crosses the Chena River.

⛺ **Tanana River Campground** [302–3 E4] (50 Sites) 1800 College Rd; ☎ 456 7956 (summer), 451 5557 (winter); www.tananavalleyfair.com. Just off College

Road near Creamer's Field, UAF & the fairground, this cramped campground has simple sites but all the facilities including hot showers, Wi-Fi, coin laundry, table & fire pits. The 30 RV spaces go for US$18–20 with or without electricity & the 20 tent sites cost US$16.

Public-use cabins For more information on the area's cabins, see the sections on the Steese Highway, the Elliott Highway and Chena Hot Springs Road. Visit the Public Lands Office in Fairbanks (see page 306) for more information on cabins and how to book them.

✗ WHERE TO EAT

Fairbanks has some great dining options, particularly for Thaiophiles like me. Besides the many restaurants, don't forget about grabbing lunch at the farmers' market where cheap American, Chinese, Thai and Middle Eastern fare can be enjoyed. The Pita Place is popular so show up for an early lunch or you will stand in line for 15 minutes. For those eating lunch downtown, a 15% tip is sometimes added automatically so don't be shocked. This is not so common at dinner. Other than the many restaurants in town, the dinner cruise on the sternwheeler *Tanana Chief* (see page 307) can be a good time. Dinner cruises leave at 18.45 and cost US$49.95. Sunday brunch is US$36.95 and the boat leaves at 12.00. The **Fairbanks Arts Association** (☎ 456 6485; www.fairbanksarts.org) organises 'Dinners in Homes', when local families host visitors in their homes for an evening of food and good conversation for US$35. Call the FAA and talk to Melissa Hougland about the programme. Finally, many residents often drive to the nearby town of Fox for a bite to eat. Listings for this town have also been included below.

City centre

✗ **Alaska Salmon Bake** [306–7 A3] 2300 Airport Way; ☎ 452 7274, 800 354 7274 (TF); www.akvisit.com; ⏰ 17.00–21.00 daily. Widely considered the best salmon bake in Alaska. All you can eat salmon, halibut, prime rib, cod, salad & dessert for US$31. Shuttles are US$5. Located in Pioneer Park (see page 319). $$$$

✗ **River's Edge Resort Restaurant** [302–3 C5] 4200 Boat St; ☎ 474 3644; www.riversedge.net; ⏰ 11.00–14.00 & 17.00–22.00 daily. Seafood, steak & pasta served inside or on a lovely riverside deck. $$$$

✗ **Pike's Landing** [302–3 C6] 1850 Hoselton Rd; ☎ 456 4500; ⏰ 10.00–22.00 Mon–Fri,

10.00–23.00 Sat & Sun. An extensive menu of decent but overpriced food served on a huge deck right on the river. A great place to have an appetiser, or dessert & a drink on a sunny day. Next to Pike's Waterfront Lodge. Make a reservation. $$$$

✗ **Bahn Thai** [306–7 F2] 541 3rd Av; ☏ 452 8424; ⏲ 11.00–16.00 daily. Good, mild food in a clean, lovely space. $$$

✗ **Bobby's Downtown** [306–7 F2] 609 2nd Av; ☏ 456 3222; ⏲ 16.00–22.00 Mon–Thu, 16.00–23.00 Fri, 17.00–23.00 Sat. Don't be fooled by the drab exterior, this new restaurant's owner is passionate about fine food & the meals are fantastic. Many dishes are Greek-themed but other cuisines are also represented. Locals flock here for dinner so be sure to get a reservation. $$$

✗ **Gambardella's Pasta Bella** [306–7 F2] 706 2nd Av; ☏ 479 4657; www.gambardellas.com; ⏲ 11.00–21.00 daily. Good food, service & reasonable prices. The upstairs dining area is light & pleasant. $$$

✗ **Geraldo's Restaurant** [302–3 E5] 701 College Rd; ☏ 452 2299; ⏲ 11.30–22.00 Mon–Fri, 12.00–22.00 Sat & 17.00–22.00 Sun. With the

official motto 'Say Yes to Garlic', it must be good. Pizza, sandwiches & more. $$$

✗ **Lavelle's Bistro** [306–7 F2] 575 First Avenue; ☏ 450 0555; ⏲ 16.30–22.00 Tue–Sat, 16.30–21.00 Sun & Mon. A modern place with nice outdoor seating right on the street. Lunch is US$12–15 & dinner is usually about US$22. Huge wine list. $$$

✗ **Lemongrass** [302–3 C5] 388 Old Chena Pump Rd; ☏ 456 2200; ⏲ 11.00–16.00 & 17.00–22.00 Mon–Fri. Located in a dismal strip mall off Chena Pump Road, this little gem serves up great food made with organic & local ingredients. $$

✗ **Sawatdee Café** [306–7 G2] 404 Lacey St; ☏ 452 1339; ⏲ 07.00–21.00 Mon–Sat. Decent Thai & American food. $$

✗ **Thai House** [306–7 G3] 412 5th Av; ☏ 452 6123; ⏲ 17.00–20.30 Mon–Sat. A simple but hip interior & great affordable food. Top-notch, but hot, curries. No meal is complete without the fried bananas & ice cream for dessert. $$

✗ **Hot Licks** [302–3 D5] 3453 College Rd; ☏ 479 7813; http://hotlicks.net; ⏲ 12.00–23.00 Mon–Sat, 12.00–22.00 Sun. The homemade ice cream is out of this world. Locals spend a lot of time here. $

Around town

✗ **Pump House Restaurant** [302–3 C6] 796 Chena Pump Rd; ☏ 479 8452; www.pumphouse.com; ⏲ 11.30–23.00 daily. Located 1.3 miles outside town on Chena Pump Rd, the historic Pump House Restaurant is right on the river & serves good food in a rustic turn-of-the-century building. Seafood, elk, reindeer, beef & many other options are available. The Sun brunch is popular, but expensive. Has a decent wine list & Alaskan beers. $$$$

✗ **Aloha BBQ Grill** [306–7 G2] 402 5th Av, ☏ 479 7770; ⏲ 10.30–21.30 daily. Off the tourist track, this little gem serves up the diverse flavours of Hawaiian cuisine. If you can't decide what to order get the mixed plate for US$13 or if you are a meat fan, the kalua pork for US$10 cannot be beaten. $$$

✗ **Sockeye's** [302–3 C5] 446 Chena Pump Rd; ☏ 456 7427; ⏲ 11.00–14.00 & 17.00–20.00 Tue–Fri, 11.00–20.00 Sat. Decent Mexican food, large burgers & delicious ribs. $$$

In Fox

✗ **The Turtle Club** Mile 10 Old Steese Hwy; ☏ 457 3883; www.alaskanturtle.com; ⏲ 18.00–22.00 Mon–Sat, 17.00–21.00 Sun. Good meat-centric dishes served in large quantities but lacking in ambience. The average entrée costs US$20–30. $$$$

✗ **Silver Gulch Brewery** 2195 Old Steese Hwy; ☏ 452 2739; ⏲ 16.00–closing Mon–Fri, 11.00–closing Sat & Sun. They claim the distinction

of being America's northernmost brewery with beers made in-house & countless others on tap. Also decent burgers, fries, fish & chips & pizza. No reservations. 8 miles north of Fairbanks on the Old Steese Highway. $$$

✗ **Howling Dog Saloon** A rowdy place to drink & see live music.

CAFÉS

✗ **Alaska Coffee Roasting Co** [302–3 D5] 4001 Geist Rd; ☏ 457 5282; www.alaskacoffeeroasting.com; ⏲ 07.00–22.00 Mon–Fri, 08.00–22.00 Sat, 09.00–22.00 Sun. A hip hangout with great food.

Baked goods & pizzas made in a wood-fired oven. Free Wi-Fi with food purchase. $$

✗ **College Coffee House** 3677 College Rd; ☏ 374 0468; ⏲ 07.00–midnight Mon–Fri, 08.00–midnight

Sun. Located in a strip mall behind a petrol station off College Road, this coffee house is a popular late-night spot for locals. Computer terminals with internet access & live music on occasion. Wi-Fi is US$5 for a day pass. **$$**

✕ Cookie Jar 1006 Cadillac Ct; ✆ 479 8319; www.cookiejarfairbanks.com; ⏰ 06.30–20.00 Mon–Thu, 06.30–21.00 Fri–Sat, 08.00–16.00 Sun. A bakery full of tasty treats. **$$**

✕ Second Story Café [302–3 D5] Located in the second storey of Gulliver's Books (see page 317). Sit among the books & sip while you use the free Wi-Fi. Soups, sandwiches, salads & baked goods. **$$**

✕ Sam's Sourdough Café [302–3 D5] 3702 Cameron St; ✆ 479 0523. Presently rebuilding after a fire, call to check opening times.

✕ Take 5 Coffee Lounge [302–3 D5] 1755 Westwood Way, #2; ✆ 456 1610; ⏰ 08.00–21.00 Mon–Sat. Located in the hip new Artisans Courtyard building, the coffee shop is a pleasant & quiet place to sip a drink & read or use the free Wi-Fi. Also offers baked goods, soups, sandwiches & salads. **$$**

WHERE TO DRINK

♀ Silver Gulch Brewery [302–3 G1] ✆ 452 BREW; www.silvergulch.com. America's northernmost brewery, they make their own beers & have many others on tap. Located north of Fairbanks in Fox.

♀ The Pumphouse, Pikes Landing (see page 313) & **River's Edge Resort** (see page 313) are all pleasant places to grab a pint with an appetiser or meal. All have lovely outdoor seating for those sunny days & mid-summer nights!

♀ Howling Dog Saloon [302–3 G1] Mile 10 Steese Hwy; ✆ 456 4695; www.howlingdogsaloon.com; ⏰ 16.00–midnight Mon–Thu, 16.00–03.30 Fri, 12.00–03.30 Sat, 12.00–midnight Sun. Rowdy, grungy biker-style bar with good music occasionally. Located 11 miles north of Fairbanks in the town of Fox. Locals drink & dance here on the w/ends.

ENTERTAINMENT AND NIGHTLIFE A free and largely local event is Gazebo Nights put on by the Fairbanks Arts Association (see page 313). Musicians, storytellers and dancers perform every night June to August at 19.00 in Pioneer Park.

Ester Gold Camp and the **Malemut Saloon** (✆ *479 2500, 800 676 6925 TF*) are located ten miles south of Fairbanks in a complex on National Register of Historic Places. Nightly performances about the early gold rush days and Robert Service (famed gold rush poet) poetry readings happen at 21.00. Entrance costs US$18/9 adult/child. Food and drink is available.

Palace Theatre [306–7 A3] (*2300 Airport Way;* ✆ *452 7274, 800 354 7274 (TF); www.akvisit.com*). A well-done comedy show about the history of Fairbanks. Located in Pioneer Park near the Salmon Bake. Nightly shows are at 20.15 and sometimes at 18.45. Tickets cost US$18/9 adult/child and can be bought at 3175 College Rd or at the Salmon Bake.

Fairbanks Symphony Orchestra [302–3 C4] (*234 Fine Arts Complex, 312 Tanana Dr;* ✆ *474 5733; www.fairbankssymphony.org;* ⏰ *10.00–17.00 Mon–Fri*). Those interested in classical music should visit the Fairbanks Symphony Orchestra. Tickets can be bought online, by phone or at the box office one hour before the performance. Tickets for concerts cost US$30/10 adult/child, recitals US$25/5 adult/child.

Live music Fairbanks nightlife is at its best during winter, but everything from a concert to all-night dancing can still be found during the summer.

Blue Loon [302–3 B5] 2999 Parks Hwy; ✆ 457 5666; www.theblueloon.com; ⏰ 17.00–22.00 Tue–Thu, 17.00–23.00 Fri & Sat. Movies, concerts & free karaoke every Wed at 21.30. Good bar food & a number of beers on tap.

The Marlin 3412 College Rd; ✆ 479 4646; www.themarlin.alaskansavvy.com; ⏰ 16.00–02.00 Mon–Thu, 16.00–03.30 Fri & Sat. The Marlin is a great little bar in the basement of a hostel where tons of people come to drink cheap beer & catch cool shows.

Cinema

Blue Loon (see page 315) Movies shown in an alternative theatre with food & beer. Closed Sun & Mon.

Goldstream Cinemas [306–7 C4] 1855 Airport Way; ↘ 456 1882; www.regalcinemas.com. A large, modern theatre with many movies playing every night of the week.

FESTIVALS AND EVENTS

February

Yukon Quest A 1,000-mile sled dog race from Fairbanks and Whitehorse in the Yukon Territory, Canada. Starts 8 February.

Iron Dog (↘ 563 4414) Held between 10 and 16 February, Iron Dog is considered the most brutal snowmobile race on earth. The race ends in Fairbanks.

Winterfest (↘ 457 6874) Winter sports demonstrations in Denali National Park between 22 and 24 February.

World Ice Art Championship (↘ 451 8250; www.icealaska.com) Almost 200 ice sculptors gather from around the world to show off their amazing talents, sculpting this unlikely material. On show from 26 February until 23 March.

March

Chatanika Days Quirky competitions and fun, including outhouse races at the Chatanika Lodge on 8 March.

April

Arctic Man (↘ 456 2626; www.acticman.com) A fun ski and snowmobile race held 9–13 April.

May

Design Alaska Wild Arts Walk Artists & musicians perform and show their work in Creamer's Park in the afternoon on 7 May.

June

Folk Festival (www.alaskafolkmusic.org) A day of free music in Pioneer Park held on 14 June.

Summer solstice Usually on 21 June, the longest day of the year, is a big deal in Alaska, but particularly in Fairbanks with its abnormally long days. The solstice is a great time to be in Fairbanks, but deciding which events and parties to attend is the problem. All of the following take place:

Midnight Sun Festival (↘ 452 8671) A summer solstice event downtown with food, music, art, shows, hay rides and more.

Midnight Sun Baseball Game (↘ 451 0095) The local team, the Gold Panners, play from 22.00 past midnight in this fun, annual ritual game.

Midnight Sun Run (↘ 452 7211; www.midnightsunrun.com) A 10k run from UAF to Pioneer Park. Serious runners as well as those wearing costumes are welcome!

Yukon 800 (↘ 452 5377; www.yukon800.com) An 800-mile boat race on the Chena, Tanana and Yukon Rivers.

July

4 July celebrations (✆ *459 1087; www.co.Fairbanks.ak.us/parks&rec/pioneerpark for more information*) Head to Pioneer Park where food, entertainment, even an Air Force fly-over can be seen. The small town of North Pole just outside Fairbanks also hosts events. Call 488 2242 for more information.

Arts Festival (✆ *474 8869; www.fsaf.com*) An art and music extravaganza held 13–27 July.

Golden Days (✆ *452 1105; www.explorealaska.com*) Historic re-enactments, shows, fun competitions including costume wagon races in Pioneer Park and a 'build your own boat' competition in the Chena River. Free hamburgers and hot dogs. Held on 15–20 July.

World Eskimo Olympics (✆ *452 6646; www.weio.org*) Held on 16–19 July. An amazing event of traditional dances, songs and competitions demonstrated by native groups from around the state. Don't miss the seal- and fish-skinning competitions as well as the high jump, ear pull and blanket toss.

August

Tanana Valley State Fair (✆ *452 3750; www.tananavalleyfair.org*) Music, shows, food and large produce. Held on 1–9 August.

Tanana Valley Sandhill Crane Festival (✆ *452 5162*) Held on 22–24 August, this is a celebration of the sandhill cranes that migrate to the area each year. Head out to Creamer's Field for talks, demonstrations and hopefully some cranes.

SHOPPING Fairbanks has numerous gift shops downtown, mostly with gaudy tourist trinkets. A number of galleries and shops do stand out and don't forget to swing by the Farmers' Market (see page 319) on Wednesday and Saturday where vendors sell art and crafts.

Bookshops

Gulliver's Books [302–3 D5] 3525 College Rd; ✆ 474 9574; www.gullivers-books.com; ⏲ 09.00–20.00 Mon–Fri, 09.00–19.00 Sat, 11.00–17.00 Sun. A fantastic, locally owned bookstore near Hot Licks. A café upstairs & every new or used book you could desire. A great selection of Alaska books. Free Wi-Fi.

Barnes & Noble [302–3 G5] 421 Mehar Av; ✆ 452 6400; www.barnesandnoble.com; ⏲ 09.00–23.00 daily.
A large commercial, but quite complete bookstore. Pay Wi-Fi.

Food shopping The Farmers' Market (see page 319) on Wednesday and Saturday is a great place to get lunch and stock up on local veggies and other goodies. Fairbanks also has the usual line-up of large grocery stores with a wide variety of foods and other items.

Fred Meyers [302–3 F5 & D6] 930 Old Steese Hwy; ✆ 459 4200; ⏲ 07.00–midnight daily. One of the better grocery stores in Alaska with clothes, books, a delicatessen, a full assortment of foods, as well as an organic section.
Safeway 30 College Rd; ✆ 374 4100; ⏲ 24hrs. Another quality grocery store with a full selection of foods & a delicatessen. Other locations include: 3620

Airport Way (✆ 374 4000; ⏲ 24hrs); & North Pole at 301 N Santa Claus Lane (✆ 490 2700; ⏲ 24hrs).
Sam's Club [302–3 F5] 48 College Rd; ✆ 451 4800; www.samsclub.com; ⏲ 10.00–20.30 Mon–Sat, 10.00–18.00 Sun. Huge quantities of food sold in bulk. It's some of the cheapest food around, but you're not likely to find anything organic here.

Galleries and gifts

Fairbanks Arts Association (see page 313) Puts together art shows & performances in the Alaska Centennial Center for the Arts in Pioneer Park. Their gift shop is open 11.00—21.00 daily.

The Alaska House [306—7 F3] 1003 Cushman St; ✆ 456 6449; www.thealaskahouse.com; ⏰ 11.00—19.00 Mon—Sat. A wonderful gallery in a lovely building. Native & local art as well as 'First Friday' shows & other events.

The Alaskan Bowl Company 4630 Old Airport Rd; ✆ 474 9663, 800 770 4222; www.woodbowl.com. This company uses locally obtained woods to create lovely wooden bowls.

UAF Museum Store [302—3 C5] (see page 320) ⏰ 09.00—19.00 daily. Located inside the UAF Museum of the North, this fine little gallery has a good selection of Alaska-themed books & local art.

Outdoor

Apocalypse Design [306—7 G1] 201 Minnie St; ✆ 451 7555, 866 451 7555 (TF); www.akgear.com; ⏰ 09.00—18.00 Mon—Fri, 10.00—16.00 Sat. Hand-sewn outdoor gear made for the extremes of Alaska.

Beaver Sports [302—3 D5] 3480 College Rd; ✆ 479 2494; www.beaversports.com; ⏰ 10.00—19.00 Mon—Sat, 11.00—17.00 Sun. The most complete outdoor store in Fairbanks with bikes, boats, camping equipment, climbing gear & much more.

Big Rays [306—7 F2] 507 2nd St; ✆ 452 3457; www.bigrays.com; ⏰ 09.00—20.00 Mon—Fri, 09.00—18.00 Sat, 11.00—18.00 Sun. Camping equipment & clothing.

Prospector Outfitters 1512 South Cushman St; ✆ 457 7372, 800 495 7372 (TF); www.prospectoroutfitters.com; ⏰ 09.00—20.00 Mon—Sat, 11.00—20.00 Sun. A large selection of outdoor gear & non-technical clothing.

Outdoor equipment rental

Alaska Outdoor Rentals & Guides 1101 Peger Rd; ✆ 457 2453; www.akbike.com; ⏰ 11.00—19.00 daily. Boat & bike rentals from the northwest corner of Pioneer Park. Canoes rent for US$71—52/day while rafts rent for US$45/day.

Chandalar River Outfitters 5804 Cheena Hot Springs Rd; ✆ 488 8402. Located 25 miles out of town, these guys rent canoes from their home. Call before you stop by.

PARA Tours/Go North [302—3 D6] 3500 Davis Rd; ✆ 479 7272; call ahead. Everything for the outdoors.

OTHER PRACTICALITIES

Banks

$ **Key Banks** [306—7 F2 & G3] ATMs are located at: 100 Cushman St (✆ *459 3300*; ⏰ *09.00—17.00 Mon—Fri*); 612 Gaffney Rd (✆ *459 3306*; ⏰ *Mon—Thu 10.00—17.00, Fri 10.00—18.00, 11.00—15.00 Sat*); 33 College Rd (✆ *459 3245*; ⏰ *10.00—17.00 Mon—Thu, 10.00—18.00 Fri, 10.00—14.00 Sat*); 401 N Santa Claus Ln (North Pole) (✆ *459 3266*; ⏰ *10.00—17.00 Mon—Thu, 10.00—18.00 Fri, 11.00—15.00 Sat*). The ATM at 100 Cushman St is open 24hrs.

$ **Wells Fargo Banks** [306—7 F3] ATMs are located at: 613 Cushman St (✆ *459 4300; 10.00—17.00 Mon—Thu, 10.00—18.00 Fri, 10.00—16.00 Sat*); 620 Gaffney Rd (✆ *459 4370*; ⏰ *09.00—18.00 Mon—Fri*); 40 College Rd (✆ *459 4361*; ⏰ *10.00—18.00 Mon—Fri, 10.00—16.00 Sat*). ATMs open 24hrs can be found at: 205 E 3rd St, 48 College Rd.

Healthcare

Pharmacies

✚ **Safeway** www.safeway.com. Has 3 branches: 30 College Rd (✆ *456 8501*; ⏰ *09.00—19.00 Mon—Sat, 10.00—18.00 Sun*); 3620 Airport Way (✆ *374 4000*); & North Pole at 301 N Santa Claus Lane (✆ *490 2700*).

✚ **Fred Meyers** [302—3 F5 & D6] www.fredmeyer.com. Has 2 locations: 930 Old Steese

Hwy (✆ *459 4200*; ⏰ *09.00—21.00 Mon—Fri, 09.00—19.00 Sat, 10.00—18.00 Sun (pharmacy), 07.00—23.00 daily (store)*); 3755 Airport Way (✆ *474 1400*; ⏰ *09.00—21.00 Mon—Fri, 09.00—18.00 Sat, 11.00—17.00 Sun (pharmacy), 07.00—23.00 daily (store)*).

Hospitals

✚ **Fairbanks Memorial Hospital** [302–3 E6] 1650 Cowles St; ☎ 452 8181

Dentists

Barrera Dental Clinic 1001 Noble St # 420; ☎ 479 6400; www.barreradental.com

Internet Fairbanks has plenty free Wi-Fi hot spots, so you should be able to get away with not paying.

🄴 **College Coffeehouse** (see page 314) Free Wi-Fi.

🄴 **Blue Loon** [302–3 B5] (see page 315) Free Wi-Fi.

🄴 **Fairbanks Princess Riverside Lodge** 4477 Pikes Landing Rd; ☎ 455 4477; www.princesslodges.com. Free Wi-Fi in lobby.

🄴 **Noel Wien Public Library** [306–7 E3] 1215 Cowles St; ☎ 459 102; www. library.fnsb.lib.ak.us; ⊕ 10.00–21.00 Mon–Thu, 10.00–18.00 Fri, 10.00–17.00 Sat.

🄴 **Pump House Restaurant** (see page 314) Free Wi-Fi.

🄴 **Sophie Station Hotel** (see page 309) Free Wi-Fi in lobby.

Post offices

✉ **Downtown** [306–7 F2] 315 Barnette St; ☎ 452 3223; ⊕ 09.30–17.30 Mon–Fri.

✉ **Walnwright** [302–3 H6] 3726 Neely Rd; ☎ 356 7602; ⊕ 09.30–17.30 Mon–Fri.

✉ **College** [302–3 C5] 4025 Geist Rd; ☎ 479 6021; ⊕ 10.00–18.00 Mon–Fri, 11.00–15.00 Sat.

✉ **Steese** 646 Rohloff St; ☎ 456 4258; ⊕ 10.30–18.00 Mon–Fri, 10.30–16.00 Sat.

✉ **Badger** 771 Badger Rd; ☎ 488 2/88; ⊕ 13.00–19.00 Mon–Fri, 09.00–15.00. Located in North Pole.

WHAT TO SEE AND DO

Farmers' Market [302–3 D4] Fairbanks has a wonderful farmers' market where local vendors sell everything from sausages to vegetables as well as arts and crafts. The market is held each Wednesday from 11.00–16.00 and Saturday from 09.00–16.00 about a half a mile west of the Tanana Fairgrounds on College Road. Pita Place is locally famous and always has a long line. Get there early for lunch when Thai, Chinese and good ol' American food is served. Picnic tables litter a small adjacent birch forest, it's the perfect place to enjoy lunch on a sunny day.

Large Animal Research Station [302–3 C4] (☎ 474 7207; *www.usaf.edu/lars; tours every hour between 10.00–16.00; US$10*) Run by UAF as a research and education facility for large Alaskan animals such as musk ox and caribou.

Pioneer Park [306–7 A3] (*Between Airport Way & Chena River, near Peger Rd;* ⊕ *11.00–21.00 daily; free admission*) An Alaskan-frontier theme park. Though gaudy and meant for mass tourism, the park offers some sights worth checking out. Many of the city's historic treasures have been moved to the park, including some turn-of-the-century log cabins, President Warren Harding's railroad car and the second-largest wooden boat on earth, the sternwheeler SS *Nenana*. The Salmon Bake Restaurant (see page 313) is a fun and filling, though very expensive, place to eat. At the far end of the park, kayaks and canoes can be rented for cruising the river. Near the Salmon Bake is a garden of rusting and antiquated heavy machinery used to build the Panama Canal.

Also contains several museums. **Georgeson Botanical Gardens** [302–3 C5] (☎ 474 1944; ⊕ 09.00–17.30 Mon–Sat. 12.00–17.00 Sun; US$2 adult) Across from the University at 117 W Tanana Drive, the lovely manicured gardens explode with flowers during the summer. Free tours are available on Friday at 14.00 or you are welcome to stroll through the Eden on your own.

The **Bear Gallery** (⊕ *12.00–22.00 daily; free*), run by the Fairbanks Arts Association (see page 313), features a new art show every month, kicking off with a soirée at 17.00 on the first Friday. The gallery also has a gift shop.

Interior Alaska **FAIRBANKS**

6

Creamer's Field National Wildlife Refuge [302–3 E4] Originally a dairy farm started in 1903 by an intrepid dairy farmer named Charles Hinckley. After 1927, Charles Creamer ran the farm with his wife until the state bought the land and established the wildlife refuge in 1969. The rolling hills, wetlands and forests of the refuge are now home to countless migratory birds and other wildlife. A network of trails wind through the refuge and free naturalist-led walks happen Monday to Friday at 10.00.

Farmhouse Visitor Center [302–3 E4] (*1300 College Rd;* ❧ *459 7307; www.creamersfield.org;* ☉ *10.00–17.00 daily*) Has information on the land's history and is where all group hikes start .

Birch Hill Park [302–3 G4] Miles of well-maintained trails through the woods where bikers and hikers can roam free. Drive out of town on the Steese Expressway to mile 2.8. Call ❧ 457 7638 for more information.

Trans-Alaska Pipeline [302–3 G2] An eyesore for some, but for others, it's a beautiful marvel of modern engineering – a glittering monument to capitalism. A good place to see it is from a pull-out off the Steese Highway, north of Fairbanks at mile 8.4. Interpretive placards detail the pipeline's construction and function.

University of Alaska Fairbanks [302–3 C4] (❧ *474 7505; www.uaf.edu*) A driving force in Fairbanks, bringing students from around the world to study everything from maths to arctic biology. At the west end of the campus, the new **Museum of the North** (see below) is a testament to the city's commitment to modernity with its gleaming, swooping lines. Inside, the state's natural and cultural history is on display in wonderful and informative displays. The **International Arctic Research Center** (❧ *474 7558*) hosts tours 4 June–27 August on Wednesdays at 16.00. The centre is a leader in global climate studies. The **Geophysical Institute** (❧ *474 7558*) is where the state's seismology lab is located. Tours run 4 June–27 August on Wednesdays at 14.30. The virtual reality displays at the **Arctic Region Supercomputing Center** (❧ *450 8600*) are impressive and worth a look. Tours run 4 June–27 August on Wednesdays at 13.00. The **Cold Climate Housing Research Center** (❧ *474 2402*) addresses the unique challenges of building in cold climates. New materials and techniques are developed and put through the ringer here. Tours are offered all year round on Thursdays at 14.00, or by appointment.

Yukon Quest Headquarters (*550 1st Av;* ❧ *452 7954; www.yukonquest.com*) This quaint little cabin serves as the headquarters for one of the most gruelling sled-dog races on earth. Stop by to learn about the race and dog-mushing.

Museums

Museum of the North [302–3 C5] (❧ *474 7505; www.auf.edu/museum;* ☉ *09.00–19.00 daily; US$10/5 adult/child*) Housed in possibly the state's most modern building, the University of Alaska's new museum has fantastic human and natural history displays. An amazing visual feast called 'the Place Where You Go to Listen' features light and sound, driven by the sun, moon, the *aurora borealis* and seismic activity. A café and gallery are also on the premises.

Fairbanks Community Museum [306–7 F3] (*410 Cushman St;* ❧ *457 3669; www.fairbankscommunitymuseum.com;* ☉ *10.00–18.00 Tue–Sat*) This free museum, located in the historic 1933 old City Hall building is full of information and simple displays about the history of Fairbanks and interior Alaska. Located in the same building is the Dog Mushing Museum.

Pioneer Park [306–7 A3] (*2300 Airport Way; http://co.fairbanks.ak.us/PioneerPark/ default.htm*; ⊕ *24hrs*) Has a handful of museums that are worth a visit: the **Pioneer Museum** (✆ *456 8579; www.akpub.com/akttt/pione.html*; ⊕ *11.00–19.00 daily; US$2/0.50 adult/child*) has Interior Alaska history with artefacts and photos; the **Pioneer Air Museum** (✆ *451 0037; www.akpub.com/akttt/aviat.html*; ⊕ *12.00–20.00 daily; US$2 adult/child*) has a collection of historic planes and photos from the first half of the 20th century; the **Wickersham House Museum** (✆ *455 8947; www.fairbankshistory.org*; ⊕ *12.00–20.00 daily*) is a small house museum that details the fascinating life of Judge James Wickersham and his exploits around the state; the free **Native Museum** (⊕ *12.00–20.00 daily*); and **Railroad Museum** (⊕ *12.00–20.00 daily*) are also worth a visit.

Hot springs The Fairbanks area is not only the land of snow and ice, but also of hot springs.

Chena Hot Springs Resort (*Mile 56.6 Chena Hot Spring Rd*; ✆ *451 8104, 800 478 4681 (TF); www.chenahotsprings.com*) The resort can be found at mile 58 of the Chena Hot Springs Road. Hotel style rooms cost US$179–249, yurts are US$65 and RV or tent camping is US$20. Hot water passes are US$10. The restaurant is open 07.00–22.00. The odd but strangely alluring ice museum is kept cold all summer and features ice sculptures as well as a bar where drinks are served in ice glasses.

Other area hot springs Manley Hot Springs (see page 311), Tolovana Hot Springs (see page 312) and Kanuti Hot Springs (see page 416).

Fairbanks Area State Parks Fairbanks is blessed with an ideal summer climate and a host of parks and recreation sites in which to enjoy it. All the parks and recreations sites described here are accessible from the road.

Contact the **Fairbanks Department of Natural Resources** (*Mile 267 Richardson Hwy*; ✆ *451 2695*) for more information.

Harding Lake State Recreation Area The recreation area is located 45 miles south of Fairbanks off the Richardson Highway and has 90 campsites with toilets, tables and water for US$10 per night. The lake is open to motorised boats which can be annoying. Fishing can be good for lake trout, arctic char and burbot.

Salcha River State Recreation Site At mile 323.3 of the Richardson Highway, half-way between Fairbanks and Delta Junction is the Salcha River State Recreation Site. The area has campsites with tables, water and toilets for US$10 as well as a boat launch. A public-use cabin is also available. Reserve by visiting dnr.alaska.gov/parks/cabins/north.htm or by calling either the Fairbanks or Delta Junction parks offices. The Salcha River is home to king salmon, grayling and pike.

Chena River State Recreation Area This 397-square-mile recreation area is located about 30 miles east of Fairbanks off the Chena Hot Springs Road. The park follows the clear Chena River with three campsites, hiking trails as well as fishing and boating opportunities.

The hiking in this area is fantastic with well-groomed, clearly-marked trails and spectacular scenery. The Angel Rocks Trail starts at mile 48.9 of the Chena Hot Springs Road and takes a few hours. The Chena Dome Trail is one of the longest in the area at 29 miles and quickly gains elevation to a sublime alpine environment. The trail starts at mile 50.5 of the Chena Hot Springs Road. The 15-mile Granite Tors Trail starts at mile 39. After winding through bogs and forests, the trail ascends to high rolling hills where amazing granite formations known as 'tors' protrude from the landscape.

⌂ Where to stay

Campsites Three campgrounds are found along the road. At mile 27 of Chena Hot Springs Road is **Rosehip Campground** with 37 sites for US$10. At mile 39, the **Tors Trail Campground** has 24 sites for US$10. **Red Squirrel Campground** at mile 43 has 12 sites also for US$10. All have basic facilities.

Public-use cabins A network of public-use cabins are also available to those willing to hike to them. The popular **North Fork Cabin** is accessible by car at mile 47.7 of Chena Hot Springs Road. The cabin is a short walk from the road and though not the wilderness setting some might want, the cabin is ideal for families with young children or for those who simply want a place to stay rather than an adventure. The cabin sleeps six and costs US$50 per night. The **Chena River Cabin** is also accessible by car and is surrounded by birch and spruce trees. The cabin sleeps nine people and is also US$50 per night.

For those seeking a more unique adventure, the following cabins all require a hike to reach them. Cabins can be reserved at www.dnr.alaska.gov/parks/cabins/north.htm or by contacting the Fairbanks public land information office (see page 306).

⌂ **Colorado Creek Cabin** An older log cabin, situated 5.8 miles from the Chena Hot Springs Road. Park at mile 31.6 & hike in. The cabin sleeps 4 & costs US$25/night.

⌂ **Stiles Creek Cabin** In the high country & has a great view. The cabin is located half way down the 15-mile Stiles Creek Trail about 7–8 miles from either end. Park at mile 31.6 or 36.4 to start the hike in. The cabin sleeps 6 & costs US$25/night.

⌂ **Nugget Creek Cabin** Reached by hiking in about 6 miles from either mile 31.6 or mile 36.4. The trail at mile 36.4 is not well marked or maintained. The cabin sleeps 3 & costs US$25/night.

⌂ **Upper & Lower Angel Creek Cabins** Located at miles 3.1 & 6.7 of the Angel Creek Trail. Park at mile 50.5 of the Chena Hot Springs Road. Lower Angel Creek Cabin sleeps 6 & Upper Angel Creek Cabin sleeps 5. Both cost US$25/night.

The Chena River State Recreation Site [302–3 D5] This pleasant recreation site is located in Fairbanks where the Chena River is crossed by University Av. The site has 60 campsites as well as lots of room to picnic or lounge in the sun. The campsite has water, tables and toilets and even Wi-Fi. The park is run by a private company, Northern Parks Management (✆ 452 7275; *www.chenawayside.com*). Tent sites are US$10 while RVs are US$25 with water and electricity and US$17 without. Call ahead to reserve riverside spots.

Birch Lake State Recreation Site Birch Lake is south of Fairbanks at mile 305.2 of the Richardson Highway. The site has 17 RV spaces and eight tent campsites for US$10 per night. A public-use cabin is also in the area for US$35 per night. The cabin sleeps six people. Make reservations at dnr.alaska.gov/parks/cabins/north.htm or by calling the Fairbanks parks office (see page 306).

White Mountains National Recreation Area This one-million-acre recreation area is a favourite playground for Fairbanks residents due to its network of summer and winter trails, 12 public-use cabins and its proximity to the city. For a complete list of trails and cabins, visit or call the **BLM Office** (*1150 University Av;* ✆ *474 2251*). The area has two campgrounds accessible via the Nome Creek Road.

NORTH POLE (*Population: 2,099*) In the 1940s, a couple of enterprising homesteaders subdivided their 160-acre plots and called the area the North Pole. The idea was to lure toy manufactures to the area so they might gain a competitive advantage over their competitors by printing 'made at the North Pole' on their toys. Sadly, not a single toy manufacturer took the bait, but countless Christmas fans eventually made their home there. Just 14 miles southeast of Fairbanks on the Richardson Highway, the town of 1,750 people also serves as a suburb of Fairbanks.

Christmas pervades every inch of the town from business names to street signs. The town seems to run on gifts and trinkets bearing the town's name. The post office receives thousands of letters every year from children around the world. During summer thousands more drop by to send a letter with a 'North pole' cancellation stamp on it. The town is still so taken with the idea of a town 'where the spirit of Christmas lives year round', that they are planning a Christmas land theme park.

Tourist information

Visitor Center 2550 Mistletoe Dr; 488 2242; www.northpolechamber.us; 10.00–18.00 daily. Situated in a log cabin at Mission Road.

Where to stay

Beaver Lake Motel (18 rooms) 2555 Mission Rd; 488 9600; www.beaverlakeresort.com. Simple rooms with Wi-Fi, TV etc right on Beaver Lake. Rooms are US$140–180 dbl. $$$

North Pole Cabins (2 rooms) 2502 Outside Blvd; 490 6400; www.northpolecabins.com. Cabins in the woods are US$129–189 for up to 5 people. Located a short walk from the Santa Clause House. $$$

Jolly Acres Motel (8 rooms) 3068 Badger Rd; 488 9339; www.jollyacres.com. Funky but adequate rooms with kitchens for US$96 dbl. $$

Riverview RV Park (160 sites) 1316 Badger Rd; 488 6392; www.riverviewrvpark.net. Located in North Pole, this has every amenity & river frontage.

Santaland RV Park (85 sites) 125 St Nicholas Dr; 488 9123; 888 488 9123; www.santalandrv.com. Right next to Santa Claus House & the massive Santa statue, this RV park has a store, a few reindeer & sites for US$25–35/night. Free Wi-Fi.

Shopping

Santa Claus House 101 St. Nicholas Dr; 488 2200, 800 588 4078 (TF); www.santaclaushouse.com. For those who just can't get enough of Christmas, the gift shop stocks all kinds of North Pole gifts & has a Santa on staff for photo opportunities & wishes.

ESTER (*Population: 1,982*) Long ago, Ester experienced its heyday and today the town is little more than a collection of dirt streets and homes. The mining town was the centre for extensive dredging from the turn of the century until the 1950s.

Where to stay and eat Today, most people make the six-mile drive from Fairbanks down the George Parks Highway to the **Ester Gold Camp** (479 2500, 800 676 6925 TF) and the famous **Malamute Saloon** (479 2500, 800 676 6925 TF). The gold camp has rooms for US$50–90 double and the restaurant serves a delicious family-style buffet daily from 17.00–21.00 for US$28. Tents and RVs cost US$10/15. Transportation is available from Fairbanks, call to make a reservation.

The **Golden Eagle Saloon** is technically the centre of town where characters and beer are readily available. The **Gold Hill Liquor and Grocery** (*3040 George Parks Hwy;* 479 2333) is a general store with a little of everything.

What to do Just down the street is the gallery of Alaskan photographer LeRoy Zimmerman (*www.photosymphony.com*). A slide show with musical accompaniment of LeRoy's northern lights photos can be seen in the Firehouse Theatre (*showings: Wed–Sat at 18.45 & 19.45; tickets US$8/4 adult/child*).

ALASKA HIGHWAY

TOK Arranged around the intersection of the Tok Cut-off and the Alaska Highway, Tok (⊕ 63°19'27"N, 143°1'5"W) is more of a stopover than a destination. The town brags paradoxically that they are 'the coldest inhabited place in North America' but also that they have 'warm summers and friendly people'. For many, the town of Tok (rhymes with 'spoke') is their introduction to the state, being just 90 miles from the border and the first town of any size after entering the state on the Alaska Highway. Besides using Tok as a base for exploration of Tetlin National Wildlife Refuge (see box opposite) or simply to grab a bite or rest your head, the town offers little in the way of useful visitor services. Still, a number of fine B&Bs have sprung up in the surrounding suburbs and the town now has a small health food store and a good visitor centre. Fishing is possible in some of the surrounding lakes and limited hiking can be found in the hills south of town. A trade centre for a number of Athabascan native villages, Tok has a good selection of native arts and crafts in its many gift stores.

History Tok began as a road construction camp when the Alaska Highway was being constructed in the 1940s. In the autumn of 1942, US government engineers, forging the path that would become the Tok Cut-off, named the camp in honour of their favourite husky pup, Tok.

Getting there Tok is 206 miles from Fairbanks, 328 miles from Anchorage and 254 miles from Valdez.

Festivals and events Tok is famous for its winter activities. Dog mushers from around Alaska travel here to run their dogs on local trails and compete. In March, the **Alaska Trailblazers Snow Machine Club** (✆ 883 7669; *www.alaskatrailblazers.com*) hosts an annual snowmobile trip from Tok to Dawson City in Canada via Chicken on the snowed-in Taylor Highway. The club encourages visitors to participate by helping arrange accommodation in Dawson City and even renting snowmobiles locally or in Anchorage. Those interested should register by the end of January.

Tourist information

🛈 **Tok Visitor Center** Mile 1314 Alaska Hwy; ✆ 883 5775; www.tokalaskainfo.com; ⏰ 08.00–19.00 daily. Located right at the junction of the Tok Cut-off & Alaska Hwy, this large log building has some simple displays & lots of information.

🛈 **Alaska Public Lands Information Center** Mile 1314 Alaska Hwy; ✆ 883 5667; www.nps.gov/aplic/about_us/taplic.html. Next door to the Visitor Center, this has a good bookstore.

🏠 Where to stay

🏠 **A Mooseberry Inn** (5 rooms) #3 Maes Way; ✆ 883 5496, 877 880 5496 (TF); www.amooseberryinn.com. A new & very tasteful B&B a few miles outside town. Owners Maggie & Damon are charming & have attended to every detail. Mooseberry & Snowberry rooms are best. Free Wi-Fi. US$99–149. $$$

🏠 **Cleft of the Rock B&B** (9 rooms) 0.5 Sundog Trail; ✆ 800 478 5646; www.cleftoftherock.net. Private rooms & cabins for US$95–145 dbl. East of town on Sundog Trail in a lovely secluded setting. $$$
🏠 **Burnt Paw** (7 rooms) Mile 1314.3 Alaska Hwy; ✆ 883 4121; www.burntpawcabins.com. Cabins for rent & a gift shop in a great sod-roofed building. Next to the post office. $$

The Tetlin National Wildlife Refuge follows the Alaska Highway from the border of Canada almost to the small town of Tok. At 730,000 acres, the refuge is many visitors' first glimpse of the state as they drive north. The landscape is dominated by the monumental Wrangell-St Elias Mountains to the south and low black spruce and muskeg (marsh) elsewhere. The incredible number of lakes, rivers and other waterways, including the massive Chisana and Nabesna Rivers, make the refuge an ideal environment for thousands of migratory birds, fish and other wildlife. Frequent storms ignite wildfires, which play an important role in the area's ecosystems, actually creating habitats and food for wildlife.

GETTING THERE The refuge skirts the Alaska Highway for 65 miles, giving visitors unparalleled access. Small boats can be launched and used to explore the refuge from a variety of places, including Desper Creek at mile 1225.4 (on a dirt pull-out across from the **Border City** campground (✆ 774 2205), the Chisana River bridge in Northway at mile 1264, the Riverside airstrip at mile 1281, and at the Tanana River bridge at mile 1303.6.

TOURIST INFORMATION At mile 1229 of the Alaska Highway, the Tetlin National Wildlife Refuge Visitor Center has interpretive programs, displays, information and a pleasant viewing deck. The refuge headquarters are in Tok at 1.3 mile off Borealis Avenue (✆ 883 5312; www.tetlin.fws.gov).

WHERE TO STAY
Camping The refuge has two free campsites, both of which are right off the highway.

⊼ **Deadman Lake Campground** (16 sites) At mile 1249.3 & just over a mile off the highway down a dirt road. The campground has all the facilities & is free for up to 14 days.
⊼ **Lakeview Campground** (8 sites) At mile 1256.7, 0.2 miles from the highway down a gravel road right on Yarger Lake. Toilets & other facilities, but no drinking water.

Public-use cabins The refuge also has three public-use cabins available by reservation. Wellesley Lake and Jatahmund Lake cabins are accessible by seaplane while the Nabesna River cabin can be reached by boat. Reservations can be made by phone or in person at the refuge headquarters no more than 120 days before you want to stay.

ACTIVITIES The refuge is known to fishermen and birders alike. Pike, whitefish, burbot and grayling are common throughout the refuge and rainbow trout can be found in Hidden Lake at mile 1240 of the Alaska Highway. Other options include boating through the lake systems, but once you leave the road, the park is wild and you will be on your own. The soggy nature of much of the land can make it difficult to find a dry place to sleep.

🏠 **Golden Bear Motel** (60 rooms) Mile 124.3 Tok Cut-off; ✆ 883 2562; www.alaskagoldenbear.com. Very basic motel rooms. $$

🏠 **Off the Roadhouse** (4 rooms) Mile 1318.5 Alaska Hwy; ✆ 883 5600; www.offtheroadhouse.com. Simple but pleasant rooms with 1 cabin. $$

Camping Other camping options are available outside town.

⊼ **Tok RV Village** (160 sites) 1313.4 Alaska Hwy; ✆ 883 5878; www.tokrv.net. Clean & organised campground populated mainly with the older RV crowd. Showers, laundry & Wi–Fi. $

Interior Alaska **ALASKA HIGHWAY**

6

Just over 100 miles east of the city of Fairbanks, the Yukon-Charley Rivers National Preserve protects 128 miles of the 2,300-mile Yukon River and the entire Charley River basin. This sub-arctic environment of rolling hills and cold glacial water is home to a significant percentage of the nation's peregrine falcons as well as other wildlife and many cabins and homestead sites dating back to the historic Klondike Gold Rush. This roadless preserve is best seen from a raft as you float down one of the preserve's many rivers.

GETTING THERE The preserve can only be accessed by boat or small plane. Charter flights are available from Fairbanks into any part of the preserve including the rough upper portion of the Charley River. Visitors can access the preserve by boat from the town of Circle at the end of the 162-mile Steese Highway or from Eagle at the end of the 161-mile Taylor Highway. The river is generally ice-free from mid-April to mid-October.

GETTING AROUND Boats can be rented from **Eagle Canoe Rentals** (⟍ *547 2203; www.eaglecanoerentals.com*) for travel between Dawson City, Eagle and Circle on the Yukon River. Rates are US$120 between Dawson City and Eagle, US$195 between Eagle and Circle and US$295 between Dawson City and Circle. For four days on the 40 Mile River a canoe is US$170 and a raft is US$350.

TOURIST INFORMATION
ℹ The **National Park Service** 4175 Geist Rd ⟍ 457 5752; ⊕ 08.00–16.30 Mon–Fri in Fairbanks is a great source of information.
ℹ **Yukon–Charley Rivers National Preserve Visitor Center** First & Fort Egbert Av; ⟍ 547 2233; www.nps.gov/yuch; ⊕ 08.00 –17.00 Mon–Fri. Information about Eagle & the preserve.

WHERE TO STAY Camping is generally good on the river's many gravel banks, but six public-use cabins are also available along the river on a first-come-first-serve basis. For details see www.nps.gov/yuch/planyourvisit/publicusecabins.htm.

ACTIVITIES The Preserve is ideal for boaters with its extensive network of wild and scenic rivers. Floating the clear 108-mile Charley River is one of the best trips in the preserve. Rapids are a frequent reality of this river, so novice boaters would do well to choose the calm Yukon River instead. Boaters generally fly in to one of three landing strips at the Charley River's headwaters. Gelvin's airstrip is the most popular but Three Fingers and Joseph are also available. Boaters generally fly in from Tok, Fairbanks or Circle and float down the Charley to the Yukon, then on to the town of Circle where they take out. This trip is about 75 miles and takes around six days. Although permits are not required to float the Charley River, boaters are asked to file a float plan with the Eagle Preserve office (⟍ *547 2233*).

Floating the historic and mighty Yukon River from Eagle to Circle is another fantastic trip. The silted, glacial river flows 128 miles through the preserve across a vast wooded floodplain between steep bluffs. This large, slow river is ideal for novice boaters. Boaters can fly or drive to Eagle then float the 158 miles through the preserve and end in the town of Circle. The average trip length is five days but weather can change the trip length considerably. For more prolonged exposure to the elements start in Dawson City and experience the customs in Eagle.

Ⓧ Sourdough Campground (74 sites) 1.75 miles down the Tok Cut-off from town; ✆ 883 5543, 800 789 5543; www.sourdoughcampground.com. Tents are US$20 & RVs are US$30–40. Free Wi–Fi. Restaurant, gift shop & events include the pancake toss. $

Ⓧ Tundra Lodge & RV Park (78 sites) 1315 Alaska Hwy; ✆ 883 7875. RV & tent sites with all the amenities.

Where to eat

✗ Fast Eddy's 1313.3 Alaska Hwy; ✆ 883 4411; ⊕ 06.00–23.00 daily. A large diner with decent steaks & burgers & a large salad bar. Young's Motel ($$–$$$) is attached with standard rooms. $$$

✗ Gateway Salmon Bake 1313.3 Alaska Hwy; ✆ 883 5555; ⊕ 11.00–21.00 daily. During research for this guidebook, this iconic restaurant was closed, but it plans to reopen. Call ahead to check. It costs US$18 for an all-you-can-eat extravaganza. $$$

✗ Grumpy Grizzly Café Tok Cut-off & Alaska Hwy intersection; ✆ 883 2233; ⊕ 06.00–21.00 daily. A trucker's stop with fine dinners & local characters. $$

Other practicalities

Tok General Store Mile 1313.5 Alaska Hwy; ✆ 883 8343; www.tokgeneralstore.com; ⊕ 09.00–17.30 Mon–Fri, 13.00–17.00 Sun. Health foods, bulk snacks & mobile phones available.

Three Bears Foods 1314 Alaska Hwy; ✆ 883 5195; ⊕ 07.00–22.00 daily. A large selection of groceries & a little of everything else. ATM inside.

FROM TOK TO GLENNALLEN (TOK CUT-OFF)

Those entering Alaska from Canada and heading to Valdez, Anchorage or the Wrangell St Elias National Park (see page 335) will find themselves on the lovely Tok Cut-off Highway. The road travels through low black spruce and wide river valleys with the spectacular Wrangell-St Elias Mountains to the east and the Chugach Mountains dead ahead. Listed below are a few of the sites you'll encounter along the way.

The **Eagle Trail State Recreation Site** is 16 miles outside Tok and is worth a stop, if not a hike or night's rest. Situated 50 miles from Tok, the **Mentasta Lodge** (Mile 78 Tok Cut-off; ✆ 291 2324; www.mentastalodge.com), located 61 miles outside Tok, has gas and basic food. **Porcupine Creek Recreation Site** (12 sites; US$15), just off the highway has pleasant sites with basic facilities. Twelve miles further on, the private **Grizzly Lake Campground** (24 sites; Mile 53 Tok Cut-off; ✆ 822 5214) has cabins, camping spaces and boat rentals. At mile 59, the 42-mile **Nabesna Road** (see page 328) provides one of only two vehicle access points into Wrangell-St Elias National Park. The **Red Eagle Lodge** (✆ 822 5299; www.redeaglelodge.net; $$) is just beyond and offers cabins for US$95–110 and camping for US$13 for tents and US$25 for RVs. The **Gakona RV Park** (✆ 822 3550) near the Gakona Junction has 42 camping spaces, showers, laundry and Wi-Fi and is situated shortly after the tiny town of Gakona at the confluence of the Copper and Gakona Rivers. The **Gakona Lodge** (9 rooms, 3 cabins; ✆ 822 3482; www.gakonalodge.com; $$–$$$); ask them about renting equipment and guides for fishing and rafting. Heading north from **Gakona Junction,** the Richardson Highway leads to Fairbanks via Paxson (the start of the Denali Highway, see page 333) and Delta Junction. Between Gakona Junction and Glennallen there are a number of good places to fish in season. Just before the junction with the Glenn Highway, is the **Dry Creek State Recreation Site** (50 sites; ✆ 822 5608; US$12). The junction of the Richardson and Glenn Highways is marked most notably by a massive petrol station complex called **The Hub** (✆ 822 3555) with typical gas station fare and a gift shop.

Finished in 1933, the Nabesna Road was built to facilitate the removal of precious metals from the town of Nabesna at the end of the road. The road starts at mile 63 of the Glenn Highway and continues for 43 miles into the park. The Nabesna Road gets a lot less traffic than the McCarthy Road, helping it stay generally in good condition. Three streams cross the road at miles 29, 30.8 and 34.3. While they are generally little more than a trickle, during the spring they can be quite intimidating. At the road's start, the Slana Ranger Station offers maps, exhibits and good information about the park and road. Just beyond is the **Slana Post Office** (⏰ *10.00–14.00 Mon, Wed & Fri*). Over the next 40 plus miles, more than eight primitive campsites can be found along the road with varying levels of facilities. Rufus Creek at mile 7 is good for fishing and camping. Fishing is also possible at Copper Lake at mile 12.2, Long Lake at mile 22.9, Tanada Lake at mile 24 and at the Twin Lakes area at mile 27.8 where there is also camping. Primitive camping can be found between miles 16 and 18 and again at Rock Lake Rest Area at mile 22. At mile 22.5 is the Viking Lodge public-use cabin. This simple cabin is located at the end of a ¼-mile trail north of the road and can be reserved for nightly rental (US$25) by calling or stopping by the Slana Ranger Station (✆ *822 7401*). More camping and fishing can be found at Jack Creek at mile 35. A number of pleasant day hikes can be found along the route including Skookum Volcano Trail at mile 36.2 where strange volcanic formations can be seen. At mile 42, the state-maintained portion of the road ends and private land dominates. Flights into the park can be arranged through **Devil's Mountain Lodge**.

A few accommodation options do exist along the Nabesna Road including the **Hart D Ranch** (✆ *822 3973, www.hartd.com*) at mile 0.5, **Huck Hobbit's** (✆ *822 3196*) at mile 4, and the **End of the Road B&B** (✆ *822 5312; e nabesna@cvinernet.net*).

What to see and do

Tok Area State Parks Tok is generally considered little more than a place to buy petrol and spend the night if you have to. However, the area is warm and dry during the summer and offers a number of pleasant parks and recreation sites, many of which have trails, river or lake access and fishing. For more information contact **Fairbanks Department of Natural Recourses** (*Mile 267 Richardson Hwy;* ✆ *451 2695; dnr.alaska.gov/parks/units/tok.htm*).

Eagle Trail State Recreation At mile 109.5 of the Tok Cut-Off Highway (16 miles south of Tok), this 35-site campsite has toilets, water and tables as well as a few decent hiking trails.

Moon Lake State Recreation Site Located 15 miles south of Tok at mile 1332 of the Alaska Highway, Moon Lake has 15 campsites, a boat launch, toilets and water. Swimming options for the brave.

Tok River State Recreation Site At mile 1309 of the Alaska Highway (4.5 miles east of Tok) is the Tok River State Recreation area. The campground has 43 sites for tents and RVs with toilets, water and tables. The campground is on the Tok River.

GLENNALLEN (*Population: 454*) An ordinary town in an extraordinary setting is perhaps the best way to describe this town of just under 1,000 people. Located at the intersection of the Glenn and Richardson Highways along the Copper River, Glennallen (⊕ 62°6'35"N, 145°33'26"W) enjoys unrivalled views of the Wrangell-

St Elias Mountains. From left to right, the biggest of these peaks are Mount Sanford (16,237ft), Drum (12,010ft), Wrangell (14,163ft) and Blackburn (16,390ft). The conservative town hugs the Glenn Highway for a few miles and is home to large Christian and native Alaskan contingents. Glennallen is the only place in Alaska where you can attend a four-year bible college. Glennallen is also a base for many guiding and flightseeing outfits taking visitors into the Wrangell-St Elias National Park or the Copper River.

Where to stay and eat The accommodation options in town are a little dismal. It is better to stay north of town at **Gakona Lodge** (see page 327), at **Dry Creek Campground** (see page 327) or in Copper Center. Also try the **Northern Nights RV Park and Campground** (*188.7 Glenn Hwy;* ☎ *822 3199; www.northernnightscampground.com*) right in town. Tent places costs US$15 and RVs are US$30, while showers are two for US$5. **Omni Parks Place** (☎ *822 3334;* ⊕ *07.00–00 daily*) offers groceries, a deli and a bakery. It is located two miles west of the junction in the big metal building.

The Freeze (*Mile 187 Glenn Hwy;* ☎ *822 3923;* ⊕ *10.30–20.00 daily; $$*) provides good old-fashioned American cooking.

DELTA JUNCTION Delta Junction (✪ 64°2'52"N, 145°43'7"W) is known mainly as the end of the Alaska Highway: Mile 1,422. The town of just under 1,000 people is also at the junction of the Alaskan and Richardson Highways. Lastly, the town is known for its two historic roadhouses, which served turn-of-the-century prospectors on the Valdez-Fairbanks trail. Bison brought in during the 1920s have populated the area with some success and can sometimes be seen along the road. In the 1970s, the state promoted agriculture in the interior and the farmers at Delta Junction began to grow barley, wheat, peas and potatoes on farms ranging from 20 to 3,000 acres. The pipeline and the military base, Fort Greely, as well as limited farming keep the town going today. The small visitor centre in town has basic displays and decent information but is usually awash with tourists bussed in to have their picture taken with the Alaska Highway's end marker.

Tourist information
Visitor Centre ☎ 895 5068; ⊕ 08.00–20.00 daily. Located at the junction of the Alaska & Richardson Highways.

Where to stay
⌂ **Black Rapids Lodge** (10 rooms) Mile 227.4 Richardson Hwy; ☎ 877 825 9413; www.blackrapids.org. Built on the site of a historic roadhouse, this new & entirely custom lodge was built by the owners Annie & Mike Hooper. The lodge has an amazing natural setting, great food & undoubtedly the most comfortable beds outside of heaven. Located between Delta Junction & Paxson. B/fast/lunch/dinner are US$10/15/25. $$$–$$$$
⌂ **Bald Eagle Ranch B&B** (3 rooms) Mile 272 Richardson Hwy; ☎ 895 5270, 877 895 5270 (TF); www.baldeagleranchbb.com. Accommodation ranges from camping to garishly decorated rooms for up to

US$225. Situated at mile 272 of the Richardson Hwy. $$$
⌂ **Alaska 7 Motel** (16 rooms) Mile 270.3 Richardson Hwy; ☎ 895 4848; www.alaska7motel.com. Dingy standard rooms with Wi–Fi. $$
⌂ **Clearwater B&B** (6 rooms) 3170 Clearwater Rd; ☎ 895 4842; www.wildak.net/~dean. This B&B has 2 suites & 4 rooms for US$89–105. Laundry. TV. $$
⌂ **Diamond Willow Inn** (11 rooms) 1456 Decker Ln; ☎ 895 4373; www.diamond-willowinn.org. Cabins & rooms for US$115–125. $$
⌂ **Garden B&B** (4 rooms) 3103 Tanana Loop Extension; ☎ 895 4633; www.alaskagardenbandb.com. Pleasant room with a lovely garden. Wi–Fi. $$

🏠 **Kelly's Alaska Country Inn** (21 rooms) 1616 Richardson Hwy; ☎ 895 4667; www.kellysalaskacountryinn.com. Located right in town, within walking distance to various shops & the visitor centre. Simple, but pleasant, rooms go for US$110 dbl. $$

Camping
🏕 **Smith's Green Acres** Mile 268 Richardson Hwy; ☎ 895 4369, 800 895 4369 (TF); www.smithsgreenacres.com. About 2 miles north of the visitor centre. Tents cost US$16, RVs go for US$17–30.

Also see **Delta State Campground** (see page 332), **Quartz Lake Recreation Area** (see page 330), **Clearwater State Campground** (see page 332).

✕ Where to eat
✕ **Alaskan Steak House & Motel** 1271 Richardson Hwy; ☎ 895 5175; ⏰ 05.00–21.00 daily. A meaty menu. $$$

✕ **Pizza Bella** 265 Richardson Hwy; ☎ 895 4841; www.pizzabellarestaurant.com; ⏰ 16.00–21.00 daily. A large menu including pizza, sandwiches & pasta. $$$

✕ **Buffalo Center Drive-In** Mile 265.5 Richardson Hwy; ☎ 895 4055; ⏰ 11.00–22.00 Wed–Mon. Tasty burgers made from local beef, & milkshakes made from local dairy. $$

✕ **Poor Boys** 1755 Richardson Hwy; ☎ 895 1805; ⏰ 05.00–15.00 daily. Known for their omelettes & burgers. $$

✕ **IGA Food Cache** 266 Richardon Hwy; ☎ 895 4653; www.iga.com; ⏰ 06.00–21.00 Mon–Sat, 07.00–20.00 Sun. Located at mile 266 of the Richardson Hwy. Groceries, a delicatessen & a bakery.

RICHARDSON HIGHWAY (GLENNALLEN TO VALDEZ)

The 115-mile drive from Glennallen to Valdez – particularly the stretch just outside Valdez – on the Richardson Highway is one of the most beautiful in the state. Ten miles south of Glennallen is the **Wrangell-St Elias National Park Visitor Center** (☎ 822 5234; www.nps.gov/wrst/home.htm; ⏰ 08.00–18.00 daily) with amazing views, great information and helpful staff. Tourists are bussed in regularly, so the place can get very crowded.

At mile 106, the Old Richardson Highway branches off to the east and passes through the small town of Copper Center.

COPPER CENTER (*Population: 294*) The town was established in the late 19th century by prospectors travelling north to Alaska's Interior gold fields through the mountains from Valdez

Tourist information
ℹ **Copper River Valley Visitor Center** Glenn & Richardson Hwys; ☎ 822 5555; www.coppervalleychamber.com; ⏰ 09.00–19.00 daily.

Where to stay
🏠 **Copper Center Lodge** (14 rooms) ☎ 822 3245, 866 330 3245 TF; www.coppercentrelodge.com. Has standard hotel rooms & a decent restaurant on location. The lodge stands where the historic 1896 Blix Roadhouse used to be. $$$

🏠 **Pippin Lake B&B** (1 room) Mile 82.2 Richardson Hwy; ☎ 822 3046; www.pippinlakebnb.com. Half an hour outside town, Pippin has a charming spot on the lake with a full kitchen & canoes to use. $$$

🏠 **Sawing Logzz** ☎ 822 3242; www.sawinglogzz.com. Right in the centre of town. $$$

🏠 **Willow Lake B&B** (1 room) ☎ 822 3961; www.willowlakebb.com. Near the Copper Center. Offers just 1 cosy cabin for US$150. $$$

Shopping

Farmers' Market Held 10.00–16.00 Wed & Sat at the visitor centre.

Delta Meat & Sausage 1413 Alaska Hwy; ☏ 895 4006, 800 794 4206 (TF); www.deltameat.com; ⏰ 08.00–17.00 Mon–Fri; 10.00–16.00 Sat. Local smoked & fresh meat, much of which is organic. The building is all alone at mile 1413 of the Alaska Highway.

Other practicalities

Public library 2288 Deborah St; ☏ 895 4656; ⏰ 10.00–18.00 Mon–Fri, 10.00–17.00 Sat, 12.00–17.00 Sun. Wi-Fi & internet terminals.

What to see and do

Rika's Roadhouse (see page 332)

Sullivan Roadhouse (*1422 Alaska Hwy;* ☏ *895 4656;* ⏰ *09.00–17.30 Mon–Sat; free admission*) The oldest roadhouse in Interior Alaska, the structure was built in 1905 and still retains many original artefacts. Helpful volunteers dressed in period outfits can help with questions. The roadhouse is located next to the visitor centre.

Delta Junction Area State Parks A number of pleasant parks and recreation sites can be found around the town of Delta Junction. While not an adventure destination, the well-maintained parks and trails are worth a stop. Expect good hiking trails, fishing, boat trips, wildlife and informative historical monuments. In 1928, 23

⌂ **Copper River Princess Lodge** (85 rooms) ☏ 822 4000; www.princesslodges.com. Has pleasant rooms & a killer view. $$–$$$

✕ **The Fishing Widow** Mile 101 Old Richardson Hwy; ☏ 822 5608; www.thefishingwidowak.com. Serves soups, smoothies, coffee & ice cream.

What to see and do Built in 1942, **Chapel on the Hill** on Loop Road was the first church in the area. Today visitors are free to tour the chapel and a slide show is available. The chapel and the **George Ashby Museum** (*Mile 101 Old Richardson Hwy;* ☏ *822 3922;* ⏰ *11.00–17.00 daily; free admission*) both have information about the local history and are worth a visit.

Heading south from Copper Center toward Valdez, the Edgerton Highway branches off east to Chitina, McCarthy, and Kennicott (see page 343) about 18 miles south of Copper Center. Just beyond is the **Squirrel Creek State Recreation Area** (25 sites; US$10). Other accommodation possibilities along the way include: **Tiekel River Lodge** (*Mile 56 Richardson Hwy;* ☏ *822 3259; www.tiekelriverlodge.com*), **Alaska Rendevous Lodge and Tavern** (*Mile 45 Richardson Hwy;* ☏ *822 3330*), **Thompson Pass Mountain Chalet** (*Mile 19 Richardson Hwy;* ☏ *835 4817; www.alaska.net/~chalet*) and the **Blueberry Lake State Recreation Site** (25 sites; US$14) about 24 miles from Valdez.

Just before Thompson Pass, the menacing but beautiful Worthington Glacier splits the peaks and descends to road level. A small State Recreation Site provides a viewing area and is where the rugged Ridge Trail starts. Though not very high in elevation, **Thompson Pass** (2,678ft) gets record amounts of snow in the winter. In the mid 1950s, almost 1,000ins was recorded. From there, the road descends into **Keystone Canyon**, an amazing bit of road flanked by the Lowe River and countless waterfalls tumbling down the 30ft cliffs. The town of **Valdez** (see page 267) is just beyond.

bison were transplanted to the area from Montana. Today, the herd numbers 375 and can often be seen in the grass along the road.

For more information on these recreation areas swing by the **Delta Junction Department of Natural Resources** (*Mile 267.5 Richardson Hwy;* ✆ *895 4599; www.dnr.alaska.gov/parks/units/deltajct;* ☉ *08.00–17.00 Mon–Fri*). They don't have much printed information, but the staff are knowledgeable. Alternatively, try the **Public Lands Information Center** (*250 Cushman St;* ✆ *456 0527;* ☉ *09.00–18.00 daily*) in Fairbanks. For locals maps and outdoor gear check out **Granite View Sports** (*Mile 267 Richardson Hwy;* ✆ *895 4990;* ☉ *09.00–19.00 Mon–Sat; 10.00–18.00 Sun*).

Activities Most of the areas listed below have marked hiking trails and some have boat launches for river and lake access. The Delta Clearwater River is an excellent single-day float trip. The 20-mile river is crystal clear and is the only such tributary of the Tanana River. Boaters can put in at Clearwater State Recreation Site and end at either the Richardson Highway Bridge, a 28-mile trip or at Clearwater Lake, a 12-mile trip. There is great fishing and floating either way. Visit www.dnr.alaska.gov/parks/units/deltajct for more information.

Donnelly Dome is located 18 miles south of Delta Junction on the Richardson Highway and offers good hiking and views.

Big Delta State Historical Park The park is centred around historic Rika's Roadhouse, which dates back to the turn of the 20th century. Roadhouses such as Rika's served gold miners, hunters, trappers, the army and others seeking fame and fortune as they travelled between Valdez and Fairbanks between 1909 and 1947. Lovely manicured lawns and gardens are interspersed with historic buildings and other artefacts from the roadhouse heyday. The park has a store and restaurant, but a picnic lunch under a sunny sky in the grass along the Tanana River is the best way to go. The park also allows up to 23 RVs to camp in the carpark for US$5 a place. Toilets, water and waste-disposal points are nearby. Tiny wild strawberries can be found on the north side of the carpark. Tours are available, ask at the store. Be sure to go and visit the friendly sheep and garish peacock.

The park is located eight miles north of Delta Junction at mile 274.5 of the Richardson Highway.

Clearwater State Recreation Site On the banks of the crystal clear Delta Clearwater River, this well-kept campsite offers a boardwalk through the forest, great fishing for grayling and salmon and a boat launch for those starting a float trip. The Delta Clearwater River allows access to the Tanana and Goodpaster Rivers. The campground has 17 sites with toilets, tables and water for US$10 a place. Take the Clearwater Road at mile 1415 of the Alaska Highway and proceed for 8.5 miles. Jack Warren Road at mile 268 of the Richardson Highway can also be used.

Delta State Recreation Site Right in town, this 25-site campground is a good option for those who want to walk around town. Facilities include toilets, water and shelters with showers and laundry nearby. Places cost US$10 per night. Located in Delta Junction at mile 267 of the Richardson Highway.

Donnelly Creek State Recreation Site South of town on the Richardson Highway, the Donnelly Creek State Recreation Site is on the banks of the Delta River and has good views of the Alaska Range on a clear day. The campground has 12 sites for US$10 and is rarely full. Look for bison across the river. Located 32 miles south of Delta Junction at mile 238 of the Richardson Highway.

Fielding Lake State Recreation Area Located above treeline, this lovely 17-site campground sits on Fielding Lake and offers great hiking, boating and fishing for wild grayling, lake trout and burbot. Camping costs US$10 per night. A public-use cabin on the lake can sleep up to six and can be reserved in advance for US$35. Reserve the cabin here (*www.dnr.alaska.gov/parks/cabins/north.htm*) or by calling the Fairbanks or Delta Junction Park offices (see opposite). Located two miles west of the Richardson Highway at mile 200.5.

Quartz Lake State Recreation Area The Quartz Lake State Recreation Area sits on 600 acres and borders two lakes. The area is popular with locals boating, swimming, fishing and just hanging out. Five short hiking trails have good views in clear weather. Quartz Lake has rainbow trout up to 18 inches in length, and silver salmon up to 13 inches long. The lake is also stocked with dolly varden and king salmon. Lost Lake has rainbow trout.

The Quartz Lake area has 103 campsites for US$10 per night. Lost Lake is quieter and has 12 sites for the same price. Both areas have water, picnic tables and toilets. Two public-use cabins can also be reserved by visiting (*www.dnr.alaska.gov/parks/cabins/north.htm*) or by calling the Fairbanks or Delta Junction Park offices (see opposite). The Quartz Lake cabin is on Quartz Lake and sleeps three people. The Glatfelder Cabin is on Lost Lake at the end of a half-mile trail. Both cabins are US$25.

DENALI HIGHWAY

The 135-mile Denali Highway is one of the states most scenic roadways giving visitors a glimpse of what driving through Alaska must have been like half a century ago. The rough, mostly gravel road connects the town of Cantwell (just south of Denali National Park) in the west with Paxson in the east. Those with an extra tyre and ample patience (driving can be slow) will never forget their experience on Denali Highway. Mountain vistas, great fishing, hiking, boating, biking and wildlife viewing are all excellent and in abundance here. With the Alaska Range, the Wrangell-St Elias Range and the Chugach Mountains all around, the skyline is filled with peaks like Mt Hess (11,940ft) to Mt Sanford rising (16,000ft). Autumn is an excellent time to visit as caribou are easily seen, often in large numbers, the mosquitoes are less abundant and the tundra is ablaze with reds, oranges and yellows.

HISTORY In the early 1900s a small gold rush took place at Veldez Creek and supplies were shuttled in from Cantwell and Paxson on rough trails. When Denali became a park in 1917, the first easy access for visitors was via the Denali Highway when it was built in 1957. Since 1971 the Parks Highway connecting Anchorage with Fairbanks shifted traffic away from the Denali Highway and today it is rarely used.

GETTING THERE AND AWAY The Denali Highway can be accessed from either Paxson on the Richardson Highway, or from Cantwell on the Park Highway. Travelling from Anchorage on a loop via the Denali Highway is 600 miles, while a loop trip from Fairbanks is 436 miles. The Denali Highway, though relatively short, is a slow road and many side trips via bike, foot or boat make the trip much more enjoyable. The highway is generally free of snow from mid-May through to 1 October, but visitors would do well to call the **Gennallen BLM office** (↘ *822 3217*) to be sure. During the winter some residents follow the route by dog sled, snowmobile, or ski to ice-fish and hunt. The highway is all gravel except 21 miles

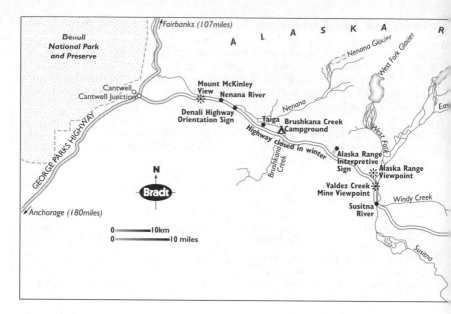

of pavement on the Paxson end, and a handful of paved miles on the Cantwell end. Camping is possible anywhere on Borough of Land Management (BLM) land and a number of campgrounds exist as well.

ON THE ROAD The small town of Paxson on the east end of the highway has little, but offers a few basic services and lodges. **Paxson Lodge** (↖ *822 3330; www.paxson-lodge.com; $$*) has basic rooms and a simple restaurant (⊕ *08.00–21.00 daily*). North of town is the **Black Rapids Lodge** (see page 329). Other businesses in Paxson include: **Paxson Alpine Tours/Denali Highway Cabins** (↖ *822 5972; www.denalihwy.com; $$–$$$*) offers guiding services and cabins.

Travelling from Paxson on the Denali Highway, the Tangle Lakes area, at mile 15, provides excellent boating and fishing in a network of interconnected lakes. This is also an archeological site where human habitations thought to be over 10,000 years old can be found. Right about the time the pavement ends at mile 21, the Tangle Lakes Campground presents itself and is a great starting point for boaters wanting to explore Round and Long Lakes and others. This area also has many dirt tracks off the highway suitable for hikers as well as bikers. The **Tangle River Inn** (↖ *822 3970; www.tangleriverinn.com; $–$$$*) is found here and has bunks and cabins and a restaurant, as well as gas. Boating down the Delta River from here will eventually lead back to the Richardson Highway after three days and 29 miles of whitewater rapids that reach Class IIII (see box on page 78). Another longer boat trip from here follows the Upper Tangle Lakes with a portage to Dickey Lake, then down the rough and wild middle fork of the Gulkana River. The Richardson Highway, with some stretches of Class IV rapids, will present itself after six days and 76 miles.

Some wonderful hiking can be found in the Amphitheater Mountains just past the Tangle Lakes are. A day hike to Landmark Gap (a five-mile round trip) is well worth the effort. The highest point on the highway is Mclaren Summit (4,086ft), 37 miles west of Paxson. This is a great viewpoint as well as starting point for day and overnight hikes. Because of the elevation, the landscape is tree and brush free and the hiking is generally good. The first part of the trail is a two track and can be good for bikers as well.

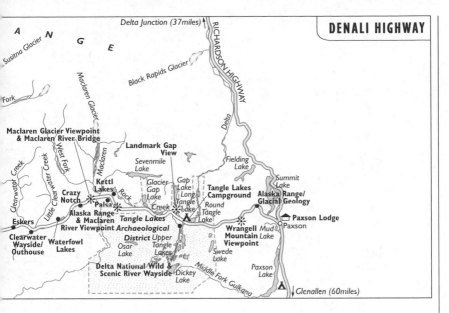

Delta Junction (37miles)
RICHARDSON HIGHWAY
Susitna Glacier
A N G E
Black Rapids Glacier
Maclaren Glacier
Fork
Delta
Maclaren Glacier Viewpoint
& Maclaren River Bridge
West Fork
Landmark Gap View
Sevenmile Lake
Fielding Lake
Summit Lake
Maclaren
Clearwater Creek
Little Clearwater Creek
Kettl Lakes
Glacier Gap Lake
Gap Lake
Tangle Lakes Campground
Alaska Range/ Glacial Geology
Crazy Notch
Palsa
Rock
Creek
Long Tangle Lake
Round Tangle Lake
Eskers
Alaska Range & Maclaren River Viewpoint
Tangle Lakes Archaeological District
Paxson Lodge
Wrangell Mud Lake
Mountain Lake Viewpoint
Paxson
Clearwater Wayside/ Outhouse
Waterfowl Lakes
Upper Tangle Lakes
Osar Lake
Lower Tangle Lakes
Swede Lake
Delta National Wild & Scenic River Wayside
Dickey Lake
Middle Fork Gulkana
Paxson Lake
Glenallen (60miles)

At mile 42, the **Maclaren River Lodge** (✆ 822 5444; *www.maclarenlodge.com;* $$) offers rooms, cabins and duplex rooms, as well as a restaurant with full bar and gas in on sale. More affordable communal cabins can be had for US$25. They also offer canoe rentals and guided and unguided fishing, canoeing and glacier viewing trips for US$45–US$75. Ten miles later the **Gracious House** (✆ 333 3148 *(winter), 259 1111 (summer); www.alaskaone.com/gracious*) offers cabins, camping, a restaurant as well as tours and charter-flight service and gas.

At mile 85, the Valdez Creek Mine site was extracting gold from the creek until is closed in 1995. At mile 104, the 22-site Brushkana River Campground offers toilets, campsites and fire rings. As you approach the end of the highway – and it's a clear day – you'll be rewarded with fantastic views of Mt Denali.

WRANGELL-ST ELIAS NATIONAL PARK AND PRESERVE

In terms of the number of massive peaks and cascading glaciers, Wrangell-St Elias National Park beats Denali hands down. Exploring this park is much more of a challenge but well worth the effort.

At 13.2 million acres, the Wrangell-St Elias National Park and Preserve is not only the nation's largest park, but also one of its most rugged. The Chugach, Wrangell and St Elias mountain ranges converge to form the backbone of the park and one of the most impressive collections of mountains and glaciers on Earth. The park is home to more peaks above 16,000ft than anywhere else in the country, as well as Mount St Elias (18,008ft), the nation's second highest peak after Denali. The park is home to an incredible variety of fish and wildlife and offers amazing opportunities to get away in a secluded mountain environment. Only two roads – McCarthy and Nabesna (see box on pages 340 and 328) – cross the park's boundaries and both offer stunning views and an exciting road trip into the heart of the wilderness.

GETTING THERE AND AWAY The park is normally accessed from the only two roads that penetrate the park, the Nabesna and McCarthy Roads as well as from the town of Copper Center where park headquarters is located. Glennallen is the largest

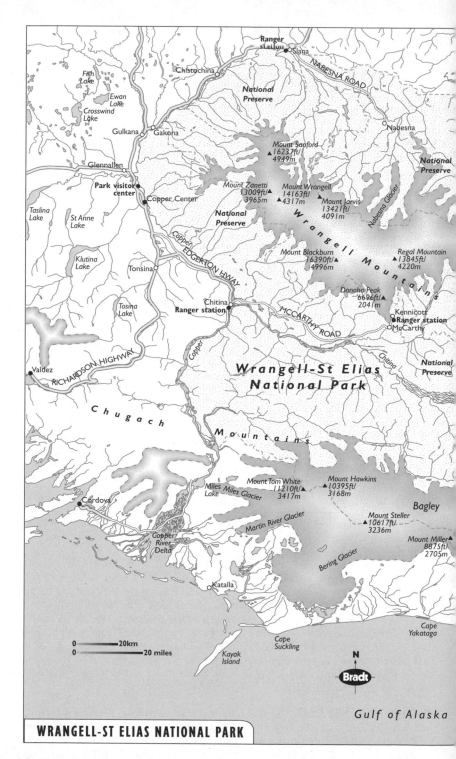

WRANGELL-ST ELIAS NATIONAL PARK

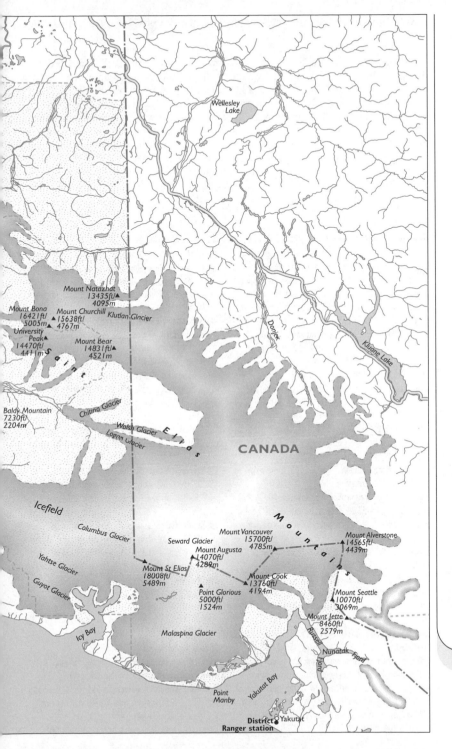

Wellesley
Lake

Mount Natazhat
13435ft/▲
4095m

Mount Bona
16421ft/
5005m

Mount Churchill
15638ft/▲
4767m

Klutlan Glacier

University
Peak▲
14470ft/
4411m

Mount Bear
14831ft/▲
4521m

Donjek

Kluane Lake

Saint

Baldy Mountain
7230ft/
2204m

Chitina Glacier

Walsh Glacier

Logan Glacier

Elias

CANADA

Icefield

Columbus Glacier

Seward Glacier

Mount Vancouver
15700ft/
4785m

Mountains

Mount Alverstone
14565ft/
4439m

Yahtse Glacier

Mount Augusta
14070ft/
4289m

Mount St Elias
18008ft/
5489m

Mount Cook
13760ft/
4194m

Guyot Glacier

Point Glorious
5000ft/
1524m

Mount Seattle
10070ft/
3069m

Icy Bay

Malaspina Glacier

Mount Jette
8460ft/
2579m

Nunatak Fjord

Russell Fjord

Point
Manby

Yakutat Bay

District ⊙ Yakutat
Ranger station

town near the park and can be reached by bus, plane or private car from Anchorage or Fairbanks.

By air Small planes can also be chartered to anywhere in the park. For those who do not wish to drive the McCarthy Road, Ellis Air and Wrangell Mountain Air, fly between Chitina and McCarthy and between Anchorage and Glennallen. Visitors choose to fly into McCarthy for many reasons. The McCarthy Road, though not as bad as it once was, is 60 miles of gravel and can destroy tyres. A flight also affords the opportunity to see the mountains from the air, which is an unforgettable experience. Once in McCarthy, those who fly in can easily walk around town or ride the local shuttle. Yet another option for reaching McCarthy is to fly from Anchorage to Valdez where you can rent a car, then drive into the park. **Levi Car Rental** (*1135 E Dowling Rd; ☏ 563 2279; www.levicarrental.net*) allows their cars to be driven on this road.

By bus

🚌 **Alaska Direct Bus** ☏ 770 6652, 800 770 6652 (TF). Buses travel on Wed, Fri & Sun & reservations are required. Buses leave Anchorage at 06.00 & arrive at Tok at 13.45 (tickets: US$105), with stops along the way inc Palmer (US$10) and Glennallen (US$75). Buses leave Fairbanks at 09.00 and arrive in Tok at 13.30 (tickets: US$80) with stops in between. Buses from Tok to Whitehorse, Canada leave at 14.30 and arrive at 24.00 with stops in between (tickets: US$135).
🚌 **Alaska Yukon Travel** ☏ 822 5978; www.alaskayukontravel.com. Buses leave Anchorage at 08.00 (will pick you up) on Tues & Sat & arrives in McCarthy at 18.00 (tickets: US$165) with stops at the Wrangell-St Elias National Park Visitor Center and Chitina. The trip back to Anchorage leaves on Mon & Fri at 08.00. Buses also run from Kenny Lake & Chitina every day at 08.00 (arriving at 10.00) for US$65.
🚌 **Backcountry Connection** ☏ 822 5292; www.kennicottshuttle.com. Buses leave Glennallen daily at 07.00 & arrive at McCarthy at 11.00, with stops along the way. Tickets cost US$79, or US$99 for a roundtrip if done in the same day. The return trip leaves at 16.30 from McCarthy & arrives in Glennallen at 20.00.

TOURIST INFORMATION The park headquarters and a new visitor centre are located in the small town of Copper Center (see page 330), ten miles south of Glennallen.

ℹ️ **Chitina Ranger Station** ☏ 823 2205 (summer); 🕐 14.00–17.00 Fri–Mon.
ℹ️ **Slana Ranger Station** Mile 0.5 Nabesna Rd; ☏ 822 7401; 🕐 08.00–17.00 daily. This station has books, maps, restrooms, & limited interpretive information about the park.
ℹ️ **Wrangell-St Elias National Park & Preserve Visitor Center** Mile 106.8 of the Richardson Highway; ☏ 822 5234; 🕐 08.00–18.00 daily. Located between Copper Center & Glennallen. This centre is state of the art & full of information & knowledgeable staff.

ℹ️ **Kennecott Ranger Station** ☏ 554 1105; 🕐 09.30–17.00 daily. A simple information centre with limited printed info but friendly & helpful rangers.
ℹ️ **Yakutat Ranger Station** ☏ 784 3295; 🕐 08.30–16.30 daily. Covering the far end of the park, this ranger station has exhibits & printed information on both the Wrangell-St Elias & Glacier Bay National Parks.

LOCAL TOURS AND GUIDES

Trek Alaska ☏ 554 4554 (summer), 350 3710 (winter); www.trekalaska.com. Top-notch guided backcountry hiking & camping trips in the park. Greg has an office in McCarthy & is the author of a fantastic hiking & trekking guide to the park called *Hiking Alaska's Wrangell-St Elias National Park and Preserve* (see page 335)

St Elias Alpine Guides ☏ 345 9048; www.steliasguides.com. Rafting, hiking, camping & other outdoor adventures within the park.
Kennecott Wilderness Guides ☏ 554 4444 (summer), 888 933 5427 (winter); www.kennicottguides.com. A locally owned business with an office in Kennecott, these seasoned outdoorsmen offer

mountaineering, hiking, camping, rafting & a host of other activities.
Copper Oar ☎ 554 4453, 800 523 4453 (TF); www.copperoar.com. Multi-day raft trips in the park.

Nova ☎ 800 746 5753; www.novalaska.com. Raft trips in the park & around Alaska.

ACTIVITIES Wrangell-St Elias National Park and Preserve is one of Alaska's best places to explore the back country. Access is reasonably straightforward and the park is vast and little visited. Once away from the roads and towns, the park has no trails or facilities. Days or even weeks can be spent drifting down rivers or hiking through the mountains. Part of what makes the park so appealing to adventurers is also what makes it dangerous. Fast-moving glacial rivers, wild animals, dangerous terrain and a host of other obstacles combined with no real search-and-rescue options make this a place where self-sufficiency can mean the difference between life and death. Always file a trip report with the nearest ranger station and try to stick to it. The southern portion of the park meets the ocean in a spectacular melding of mountains, ice and sea. Icy Bay formed after 1900 when a number of glaciers retreated to form a lovely protected bay full of ice and rich in wildlife. The best way to explore this region is by sea kayak. Access is provided by small plane from Yakutat to Kageet Point or Pt Riou. Pt Riou is located on Chugach Alaska Native Corporation land and permission is required before using the land. Write to the Chugach Alaska Corporation (*560 E 34th Avenue, Suite 200, Anchorage, Alaska 99503*). Alsek Air and Yakutat Coastal Airlines are the only two air taxis approved to operate in this area. **Icy Bay Lodge** (☎ *800 950 5133; www.icybayalaska.com*) offers guided kayak trips as well as meals and accommodation. **Alaska Discovery** (see page 45) out of Juneau occasionally leads trips here. Contact the Yakutat Ranger station for advice (see opposite). A wonderful resource for hiking trails and trip planning in the park is www.wrangellsteliaspark.com, run by Greg Fensterman, owner of Trek Alaska in McCarthy.

Flightseeing If you haven't been willing to shell out the cash to go flightseeing anywhere else in Alaska, treat yourself and do it here. Flights can be chartered from Glennallen, McCarthy or Chitina.

Glennallen operators
Alaskan Airventures ☎ 822 3905
Copper Air Service ☎ 822 4200; www.coppervalleyair.com
Copper Valley Air Service ☎ 822 4200; www.coppervalleyair.com

Ellis Air Taxi ☎ 822 3368, 800 478 3368 (TF); www.ellisair.com
Wrangell Mountain Air ☎ 554 4411, 800 478 1160 (TF); www.wrangellmountainair.com
Lee's Air Service ☎ 822 3574

McCarthy operators
Alsek Air Service ☎ 784 3231; www.alsekair.com. Flies to Yakutat.
K-Air Service ☎ 822 5312. Flies to Gakona.
McCarthy Air ☎ 554 4440; www.mccarthyair.com

Ultima Thule Outfitters ☎ 688 1200; www.ultimathulelodge.com. Flies to Chitina.
Yakutat Coastal Airlines ☎ 784 3831; www.flyyca.com. Flies to Yakutat.

WHERE TO STAY The park has 13 public-use cabins, all of which can be used on a first-come-first-serve basis except the Esker Stream Cabin near Yakutat, and Viking Lodge Cabin along the Nabesna Road. The Esker Stream cabin can only be reached via small plane and can be reserved through the Yakutat Ranger Station (☎ *784 3295*) up to six months ahead for US$25/night. The Viking Lodge cabin, located at mile 22.5 of the Nabesna Road a quarter of a mile to the north, is a rustic cabin built by hand in the 1970s. To reserve this cabin call the Slana Ranger Station (☎ *822 7401*).

Most of the cabins are simple former hunting or homestead cabins with bunks, an oil stove and little else. With the exception of the Viking Lodge Cabin off the Nabesna Road and the Nugget Creek Cabin off the McCarthy Road, all the cabins require a small plane to reach. The Nugget Creek Cabin can be reached by foot, horse or mountain bike via a 14-mile trail. The cabin is a simple handmade wood structure with moose antlers on the outside and spectacular mountain views all around.

Other cabins include: the Chelle Lake, Orange Hill, Too Much Johnson, Glacier Creek, Peavine, May Creek, Jake's Bar, and Huberts Landing cabins. For more information please visit www.nps.gov/wrst/planyourvisit/backcountry-cabins.htm

CHITINA, MCCARTHY AND KENNICOTT

One of Alaska's best adventure road trips is the McCarthy Road, leading out of Chitina at the end of the 33-mile Edgerton Highway. While the 60-mile gravel road beyond Chitina is stunningly gorgeous and an adventure in itself, the towns of McCarthy and Kennicott at the end are the real prize. If you have always felt like you were born in the wrong century and would have felt more at home in 1900, this is the place for you. The two towns' quaint and historic charms are no match, however, for the overwhelming beauty and grandeur of Wrangell-St Elias National Park all around. Nestling in the heart of the park, the towns of McCarthy and Kennicott provide the best access to the park, allowing hikers to literally step into the park's remote core. For more information about the drive, see below.

The Kenny Lake area off the Edgerton Highway on the way into Chitina has some basic services including a few accommodation options. The **Kenny Lake Mercantile** (*Mile 7.2 Edgerton Hwy;* ✆ *822 3313; www.kennylake.com*) has petrol, food and campsites. The diner serves three meals a day, rooms are US$80 dbl, laundry is US$2.50, RV sites cost US$20, tent sites are US$12. The **Copper Moose B&B** (*4 rooms; Mile 5.85 Edgerton Hwy;* ✆ *822 4244, 866 922 4244 (TF); www.coppermoosebb.com*) has rooms with private entrances and Wi-Fi for US$125 dbl with b/fast.

CHITINA (*Population: 125*) The town of Chitina roughly marks the start of the McCarthy Road. Chitina may not look like much, but take some time to walk

> ### THE ROAD TO MCCARTHY
>
> The drive to McCarthy is one of the classic adventure road trips in the state. Almost nowhere else can you drive through such utterly unspoilt and grand terrain. In recent years, the road has been improved and may eventually be 'chipped' (tarred) which will make it practically modern (much to the dismay of many McCarthy residents). For now the road is in fine condition (except for the first few miles) and has been much improved in recent years. However, calling ahead to the Kennicott visitor centre for an update would be wise. The road starts in the small town of Chitina with its own summer-time-only ranger station (see opposite). Shortly after passing through a narrow passage that used to be a tunnel, the road crosses the mighty Copper River where locals are often seen fishing for salmon. At mile 17, the road crosses the 1910 Kuskulana Bridge, 238ft over the Kuskulana River. At mile 60, the road ends at a small footbridge crossing the Kennicott River. An extortionate fee of US$5 per day is levied to visitors and locals alike to park their cars in the carpark by the bridge. Camping is US$20. McCarthy is one mile past the bridge and Kennicott is another five miles. The McCarthy Road has few campsites or services except right at the end and beyond in McCarthy and Kennicott.

around this historic town. Run-down remnants of a bygone era litter the area. The town thrived in the first decade of the 20th century when tons of copper were transported out of the Kennicott mine to the Lower 48 states. When the railroad arrived in 1910, the town boomed until 1938, when the train stopped running.

Tourist information

🛈 **Chitina Ranger Station** Fairbanks St; ☎ 823 2205; ⏰ 14.00–18.00 Mon–Fri. Information about Chitina's history & park recreation opportunities. They have a good ¹/₂hr video about the park.

🛈 **Chitina Chamber of Commerce** ☎ 259 2239; www.chitinachamber.org. No physical location but a decent source of info.

Where to stay and eat

🏠 **Chitina Hotel** (11 rooms) Fairbanks & Main St; ☎ 823 2244; www.hotelchitina.com. One of only a few newer-looking buildings in town & was in fact restored from one of town's original buildings. A fine restaurant & lounge are on the premises. $$$

🏠 **Chitina Red House B&B** (2 rooms) ☎ 823 2298. A historic structure in a lovely location. $$–$$$
✕ **Chitina Trading Post** ☎ 823 2211. Sells a little of everything from food to hardware.
🍷 **Uncle Tom's Tavern** ☎ 823 2253. A local watering hole.

Other practicalities

Spirit Mountain Art Works ☎ 823 2222. Arts & crafts located in one of town's only *other* renovated building.

Chitina I Stop Pumps petrol from a giant tank & sells basic supplies from a blue trailer.

MCCARTHY (*Population: 53*) Downhill from Kennicott is the town of McCarthy (⊕ 61°25'58"N, 142°54'39"W), which shares much of the same history. Today, McCarthy is the vision of a frontier town in the middle of the Alaskan wilderness. Fantastic summer weather, friendly people and monolithic mountains and glaciers in every direction make this town one of my favourite places in the state. The unparalleled access to pristine wilderness and a limited number of tourists don't hurt either. The town is tucked in the woods a little less than a mile east of the bridge. Be sure to pay the US$5 fee per day for parking your car in the gravel lot known as Base Camp. Don't bother getting too mad about this, even the locals have to pay. Camping here is US$20 night. A bathroom is provided and washing can be done in the ridiculously cold river. Shuttles are available from the other side of the bridge into McCarthy or Kennicott for US$10. You can call the **Wrangell Mountain Bus** (☎ 554 4411) from the payphone. If you are staying at a hotel in McCarthy or Kennicott, they will pick you up. While a shuttle is required to get to Kennicott, McCarthy can easily be walked to. To find town cross the bridge then turn right at the small **McCarthy–Kennicott Museum** (⏰ *daily*) or take a right at the 'drinking water' sign before the museum for a short cut. In town you will find a small collection of businesses in historic buildings.

Getting there and away While most visitors choose to drive in, shuttle buses are also available from Anchorage and Glennallen.

By car The state recently poured some money into the McCarthy Road, and now almost any car can make the trip, and if you go slow, you may not even get a flat tyre! Check current road conditions here: http://wsen.net. Unlike a few years ago, most rental car companies now allow their cars on this road, but be sure to ask anyway. Some that do include: **High Country** (☎ 562 8078), **Enterprise** (☎ 563 5050) and **A-1 Car Rental** (☎ 929 1222), all have office in Anchorage, as well as **Go North** (☎ 479 7272), which has offices in Fairbanks as well. Flying into McCarthy is also possible, and with the amazing views, is worth the US$100–150.

By bus

Wrangell-St Elias Tours 822 5978; www.alaskayukontravel.com. Van service from Anchorage to McCarthy for US$365 return trip.

Alaska/Yukon Trails (see page 344) Bus service from Fairbanks & Glennallen to McCarthy.

By air

Wrangell Mountain Air 554 4411, 800 478 1160 (TF); www.wrangellmountainair.com. Flights to McCarthy with the added bonus of a free flightseeing trip!

McCarthy Air 554 4440; www.mccarthyair2.com With just one pilot, they are a small & personal air service able to take you just about anywhere.

Tourist information

McCarthy Park Service Office Located at mile 58 of the McCarthy Road about ¹/₄ mile before the road's end. ⏲ 09.30–17.30 daily.

Where to stay and eat

In town The Golden Saloon offers a limited menu of good food, an annual 'liars' contest' and open mic on Thursday. Next door the **McCarthy Bistro** serves breakfast from 08.00. **Ma Johnson's Hotel** (554 4402; *www.mccarthylodge.com;* $$$) across the street offers very small rooms with shared bathrooms. The hotel is worth a stay for the authentic old-time experience. Get room No 3, if you can, or any room not sharing a wall with a bathroom. **Lancaster's Backpacker Hotel** is owned by Ma Johnson's Hotel and caters to backpackers exclusively with simple rooms for US$48 single, US$68 double. All these businesses share ownership and can be contacted through Ma Johnson's Hotel.

Nearby is the **McCarthy Mercantile** with a selection of baked goods, limited groceries and a wonderful deck for those sunny days. In July and August, the spoils of locals gardens can be bought here. **The Potato** (⏲ *08.00–20.00 daily*) is located on the edge of town in an old bus. Their creative menu features wraps, pork sandwiches, burritos, fries, houmous etc.

Trek Alaska (*City centre;* 350 3710; *www.trekalaska.com*) is run out of a funky little office by Greg Fensterman who authored one of the best books on hiking in the Wrangell-St Elias Range called *Hiking Alaska's Wrangell-St Elias National Park and Preserve* He offers a range of guiding services in the park. **Backcountry Connection** (822 5292; *www.kennicottshuttle.com*) has a shuttle service from Glennallen, Copper Center, and Chitina to McCarthy for US$79 one-way. Service is also provided from the Kennicott Bridge to McCarthy or Kennicott for US$5 one-way.

Out of town

Currant Ridge Cabins (6 rooms) 554 4424, 877 647 2442 (TF); www.currantridgecabins.com. If you don't mind being a little out of town, this is the best accommodation. Beautifully constructed individual cabins with kitchens & private bathrooms. Run by a lovely family with 2 children. Wi-Fi. $$$

Kennicott River Lodge & Hostel 554 4441; www.kennicottriverlodge.com. Just before the end of the road on the north side. Great views with a variety of accommodation possibilities from bunks for US$25 to cabins for US$100. Kitchen, sauna, fire pit & a game of horseshoes. Non-guests are allowed to take showers for US$7. Trails right out the back door. $$

McCarthy B&B (5 rooms) 554 4433; www.mccarthy-kennicott.com/mccarthybb. Simple funky cabins with private bathrooms. John also does the local tyre repair. $$

Wrangell-St Elias News B&B (3 rooms) 554 4454; www.mccarthy-kennicott.com/WSENBB. 3 funky cabins with remote bathrooms & kitchen, 2 miles from the end of the road. Owners print bi-monthly local newspaper. $$

Glacierview Campground (26 sites) 554 4490 (summer), 243 6677 (winter);

www.glacierviewcampground.com. Off the McCarthy Road on the south side just before the end. Simple campsites are US$20 & cabins are US$85. A tiny hot food booth serves meals from 10.00–22.00 daily. Bikes are available for US$25.

What to see and do Great hiking and bike riding can be found around McCarthy. The Nizina Creek Road starts at the south end of town at a small privately-owned bridge. The seven-mile road can be bug-infested in the summer but the views are grand and an old mining bridge and ghost town are at the end. Another pleasant hike starts from the Kennicott Mine and leads north along the Root Glacier. One route leads to the ice and the other follows the glacier but glacial erosion has destroyed much of the trail. This is the access point for the Erie Mine high on the hill. Hiking to the Erie Mine is more of a climb than a hike and should only be tried by extremely competent and fit individuals. The crumbling mine clings to the cliff and is a marvel of engineering. Yet another hike worth doing follows the west side of the Kennicott Glacier on flat ground from the parking lot at the end of the McCarthy Road. Be sure to talk to the rangers in McCarthy or Kennicott about any hike before setting out. **Copper Oar** (↖ *554 4453; www.copperoar.com*) is a good operator to contact for hiking, rafting and a variety of other guided activities in the McCarthy area.

KENNICOTT About five miles beyond McCarthy is the town of Kennicott (⊕ 61°30'36"N, 142°52'5"W), perched on the side of the mountain and built around the closed Kennicott copper mine. Situated more dramatically than McCarthy but much more polished and a little more touristy, Kennicott makes a great day's destination from McCarthy. The five miles from McCarthy to Kennicott can be walked or biked but dust is a problem and it's all uphill. Conversely a van runs frequently for US$5 one-way from the centre of McCarthy.

History In 1906, the Kennicott Mine was built on the side of Bonanza Ridge with the Kennicott Glacier just a few feet below. The rich copper resources helped the mining town flourish with a school, theatre and hospital to accommodate the many miners and their families. Until the 1930s, the mines produced hundreds of millions in copper, gold, and silver. The mine employed more than 500 miners on average and the town of McCarthy, five miles away, was developed to accommodate them. When the mine shut down in 1939, due to a drop in copper prices and rising operating costs, the town went from prosperous boomtown to ghost town overnight. Today, the Park Service owns the land and has spent millions restoring the site. Kennicott's main drag is lined with former mining buildings in various states of repair. Some are homes, some are businesses and some are just falling down.

Tourist information
🛈 **Kennicott Park Service Office** ↖ 554 4417; ⊙ 09.00–17.30 daily. Daily ranger-led hikes & general information.

🛈 **Kennicott Wilderness Guides** ↖ 800 664 4537; www.kennicottguides.com. A one-stop adventure shop right on the main drag in Kennicott. Guided rafting, hiking, mountaineering, ice climbing & anything else you might want to do outdoors.

Where to stay
🏠 **Kennicott Glacier Lodge** (35 rooms) ↖ 800 582 5128; www.kennicottlodge.com. The lodge is responsible for most of the people in town. The original building brims with character while the newer south wing is nice but generic. The lodge serves 3 meals in their dining room & is a great place to eat a nice meal with views of the glacier. B/fast is from 07.00 to 10.00, lunch from 12.00 to

15.00 & dinner is from 19.00 on. If you're not a guest, be sure to make reservations. Free slide shows are given every night at 20.30. Movies are screened in the hall across from the lodge on Wed & Sat. $$$–$$$$

⌂ **Kennicott B&B** (1 room) ☏ 554 4500 (summer), 554 4420 (winter); www.kennecottbb.com. A strangely modern apartment a stone's throw from the glacier. Located under the **Fireweed Mt Art & Crafts**. The owners sometimes choose to close it for the summer, so call ahead. $$$

TAYLOR HIGHWAY

The scenic Taylor Highway branches off the Alaska Highway at Tetlin Junction (mile 1302, 12 miles east of Tok) and winds its way northeast for 160 miles before ending in the town of Eagle on the Yukon River. For those heading to Dawson Creek in Canada's Yukon Territory, this is the fastest path, at about 170 miles. The border crossing is open from mid-May to mid–September from 08.00–20.00 Alaska time (09.00–21.00 Pacific time). The Taylor Highway traverses some lovely country and is well worth the drive if you're patient and subscribe to the motto, 'the journey is the destination'. Leaving the Alaska Range and Wrangell-St Elias Mountains behind, the landscape unfolds with rolling hills, rivers, lakes and wildflowers.

The first 64 miles of the highway are paved, after that the gravel road is good except in early spring and after rains. The Taylor Highway is not ploughed, meaning it's usually closed from mid-October to April. Petrol is available in Chicken, Eagle and, once in Canada, can be found in Dawson City. Though the distances are not so great that extra gas cans are required, be sure to get petrol whenever available. Fuel is very expensive and many stations will only accept cash. As with any remote gravel road, an extra full-sized spare tyre is advisable.

Driving north from Tetlin Junction on the Alaska Highway, frost heaving has distorted the road and can slow progress. The occasional burned areas of forests attests to the abundance of wildfires in Interior Alaska. Started mostly by lighting, these fires play a crucial role in the eco-system, rejuvenating soils, dispersing seeds and keeping the landscape's flora dynamic. The **Tanana Valley State Forest** starts at mile 6 and encompasses 1.8 million acres. At mile 50, the **West Fork Campground** (*25 sites; US$8*) offers pleasant campsites with water, toilets, tables and fire pits.

CHICKEN (*Population: 21; www.chickenalaska.com*) The town of Chicken at mile 66 has barely 20 residents during the summer and less than half that in winter. Turn-of-the-century gold prospectors wanted to name their town 'Ptarmigan' after the common chicken-like bird found throughout Alaska but were unable to spell it. They settled on the name 'Chicken' instead. The town has changed little except that the road now brings visitors who put a strain on the local infrastructure, or rather the lack of it. Chicken has no public water, sewer or electricity and just a few businesses. To see the real town be sure to turn off the highway onto Airport Road and have a walk around old town.

Getting there and away
Alaska/Yukon Trails (☏ 479 2277, 888 770 7275; www.alaskashuttle.com) Shuttle bus service between Fairbanks and Dawson City via Chicken for US$169 per person.

⌂ Where to stay and eat
⌂ **Chicken Gold Camp** Airport Rd; ☏ 235 6396 (winter), 413 1480 (summer); www.chickengold.com. Camping for US$10–18 with free wood & Wi-Fi as well as cabins for US$90–105 & a small café with

sandwiches, waffles, whole roasted chickens, ice cream & beer. Tours of the nearby Pedro Dredge are also offered.

♣ The Goldpanner Free camping & Wi-Fi with gas fill-up as well as pay RV sites & cabins. Tours of the local Tisha's Schoolhouse & a gift shop.

✕ Chicken Mercantile Emporium Good food, free Wi-Fi & a decent gift shop located on the north side of the Taylor Hwy.

CONTINUING ON THE TAYLOR HIGHWAY... Heading north out of Chicken, the **Cowden Gold Dredge** can be hiked to via a three-mile trail starting at mile 68 of the Taylor Highway. The scenery is lovely and the 1936 dredge is fun for history buffs. **Walker Fork Campground** (20 sites) can be found at mile 82 on the west side of the road. Water, wood & outhouses for US$8. At mile 95 the **Jack Wade Junction** leads north 65 miles to the town of Eagle or 13 miles east to the US/Canadian border and 71 miles to Dawson City in Canada.

From Jack Wade Junction head north on the Taylor Highway toward Eagle. This section of road is fun for some and a nightmare for others. Expect lots of steep grades, tight turns and precipitous drop-offs. Allow a few hours for this little-travelled and relatively short section of road. Primitive camping can be found at mile 135 and just before Eagle.

EAGLE (*Population: 129*) Right at the end of the road on the banks of the Yukon River is the small historic town of Eagle. Eagle is a wonderfully friendly and historically important town in the middle of the Alaskan wilderness. The town's history has been well preserved and besides a few modern trucks, you could be looking at a turn-of-the-century Alaskan village. The town provides access to the **Yukon-Charley Rivers National Preserve** (see page 326) and was once a booming supply town, serving much of Interior Alaska. Right on the upper Yukon River, the town was ideally positioned to receive supplies and distribute them to the legions of gold prospectors swarming the area at the end of the 19th century. Fort Egbert was built near the current town site by the army in 1899 and in 1900

CROSSING THE BORDER ON THE ALASKA HIGHWAY

Driving to Alaska through Canada on the Alaska Highway (also known as the Alcan or Alaskan–Canadian Highway) is one of the continent's last great road trips. Thankfully the border crossing at mile 1,187 of the Alaska Highway is beautifully located and generally quite easy to cross.

The location of the border was originally agreed upon by England and Russia in 1825 and later delineated Alaska prior to its statehood when the US bought the land from Russia in 1867. The border is now marked by a cleared swathe of forest from the Arctic Ocean to the Gulf of Alaska. The border crossing itself and **US Customs** (☎ 774 2252) are open 24 hours a day all year and has toilets and a telephone. When crossing the border, make sure you have your vehicle's registration, a driver's licence and also proof of insurance handy. Everyone in the car will also need a passport. Do not take pictures anywhere near the border. Foreign visitors entering the US for the first time must pay a US$6 per person 'paper processing' fee. The fee can only be paid with US dollars or travellers cheques. Visitors are allowed to enter the US with up to one litre of alcohol, up to 200 cigarettes, 50 cigars (not Cuban) or 4.4lbs of tobacco. If you use medicinal drugs be sure to keep the quantities low (enough for personal use) and have a written prescription. Pets should be up to date on all their shots and proof is required. Canada has cracked down on those with DUI (Driving Under the Influence [of alcohol]) violations and very often will not let you into the country if you have a count on your record. Lastly, Alaska has its own time zone so set your clocks back an hour.

Visit www.travel.state.gov for more information.

Judge Wickersham established the interior's first federal court in Eagle. In 1901 Eagle was incorporated and had 1,700 people. However, as gold was found in Nome and elsewhere and the court was eventually moved to Fairbanks, the town's population shrank practically overnight to just under 200. Eagle continued to shrink until the Taylor Highway was finished in the 1950s and the town's population rebounded, if only slightly.

The **Eagle Historical Society** (\ *547 2325; www.eagleak.org*) does a wonderful job of preserving the town history and showing it to the public. The society offers a two-hour walking tour for US$5 that should not be missed. Meet at the 1901 Wickersham House at 09.00 and bring your camera and questions. The nearby city well, dug by hand in 1903, has crisp, clear water and is where the majority of the town still gets its water. The tour includes the Wickersham House, the Customs House, Fort Egbert and other sights. Follow Village Road upstream three miles to Eagle Village, an Athabascan native village where many of the 30 or so residents still live a subsistence lifestyle.

Practicalities

MV Yukon Queen II A high-speed ferry run by **Grey Line of Alaska** (\ *800 544 2206; www.greylineofalaska.com*). The ferry takes passengers between Dawson City & Eagle via the Yukon River for US$90 each way but caters mainly to those on organised tours.

Everts Air \ 800 434 3488. Connects Eagle with much of Interior Alaska.
Warbelow Air \ 800 478 0812 (TF); www.warbelows.com. Connects Circle with Fairbanks. For simple rooms check out **Falcon Inn B&B** (\ *547 2254*) & **Eagle Trading Motel** (\ *547 2326*).

7

Southwest Alaska

The southwest Alaska (*www.southwestalaska.com*) region encompasses the remote Lake Clark National Park, the Katmai National Park, Kodiak Island, Bristol Bay, the Alaska Peninsula and the Aleutian Islands – and is one of my favourite places on earth. This is one of Alaska's most remote and scenic regions with pockets of civilisation few and far between. With fewer than 50 communities (about 20,000 residents) in 60,906 square miles of land, southwest Alaska is wild and remote to say the least. Visitors come for adventure and to get a sense of how the state might have looked 100 or even 1,000 years ago. Those who venture into this wilderness pay a small fortune for transportation but have the privilege of witnessing a part of Alaska barely touched by the hand of man.

Largely volcanic, the Alaska Peninsula boasts more than 57 volcanoes, many of which are still active. The unexpected sight of white sand beaches can be found along Shelikof Straight – a reminder of the 1912 Novarupta eruption near Katmai. From sights of the world's largest brown bears on Kodiak Island to visits to the largest red salmon fishery on Earth in Bristol Bay, southwest Alaska is a place where visitors will find themselves in awe of nature.

HISTORY After the initial waves of emigrants walked across the Bering Land Bridge 12,000–25,000 years ago, another wave of people came about 5,000 years ago, this time by boat. These mariners expanded through western Alaska and those who colonised the Aleutians became the Unangan (Aleut). The Unangan were masters of the kayak, which they used for hunting, fishing and travel. By all accounts, the Unangan prospered in one of Earth's harshest environments. In the 1740s, Russian fur traders seeking sea otter pelts discovered the Aleutian Islands and island hopped to mainland

EARTHQUAKES AND TSUNAMIS

The Alaska Peninsula is geologically very active with regular eruptions and earthquakes. Earthquakes are frequent in Alaska and it's estimated that one in ten worldwide occur somewhere within the state. One in particular caught the world's attention: on 1 April 1946, a magnitude 7.2 quake shook the Aleutian Islands destroying the Scotch Cap Lighthouse on Unimak Island. Its five keepers were killed and a massive underwater landslide released. For a short time, the damage was thought to be limited to the lighthouse until a tsunami generated by the underwater landslide hit Hawaii, killing 159 people, less than five hours after the initial quake. Nine 25ft waves pounded the town of Hilo on the Big Island of Hawaii at 20-minute intervals.

The tsunami had been preceded by only feeble warnings and so in 1949, the Seismic Sea Wave Warning System was established. Tragically, because the tsunami struck on April Fools' Day, the limited warnings were thought to be a prank.

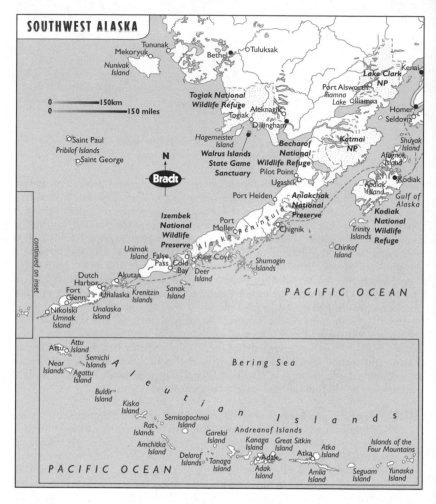

SOUTHWEST ALASKA

Alaska and beyond. Vitus Bering, a Dane in the service of Russia and a Russian, Alexei Chirikov, were sent in 1741 to explore the unknown waters east of Russia. Bering was shipwrecked and died on Bering Island with half his crew. The other half made it back to Russia in rafts, telling tales of waters teeming with sea otters. Shortly thereafter fur traders, or *promyshleniki,* found their way to the Aleutians, killing and enslaving Unangan as they went. They enslaved and killed the native people, decimated the sea otter population and hunted the Steller's sea cow into extinction along the way. Unangan hunters were so efficient at hunting marine animals, even with their comparatively primitive weapons, that they were often enslaved as captive hunters and their families held also. The ransom was sea otter pelts. Hunters and their families were often killed anyway. Russian fur traders, in their brutal and relentless search for sea otter pelts, pushed past the Alaska Peninsula, through southeast Alaska all the way to California, building forts and churches all the way. It is estimated that as many as 25,000 Unangan lived on the Alaska Peninsula before the Russian occupation began in the 1740s. Within 150 years there were just a few thousand.

At the turn of the 19th century, the Shelikhov Company controlled much of the fur trade in Alaska. As trading expanded to the Pribilof Islands and their immense seal populations, international pressure and the work of some Russian Orthodox leaders, helped to improve the treatment of Native peoples. Until Russia sold Alaska to the United States in 1867, Native labour was the backbone of the Russian Fur trade. To this day, the Russian Orthodox religion is the dominant faith in southwest Alaska.

World War II brought further hardship to the land and its people. Before the US entered World War II in 1942, the Aleutian Islands of Attu and Kiska were occupied by Japanese forces, the only part of American soil ever controlled by a foreign power. Native Alaskans from these islands were sent to forced labour camps in Japan and only a few lived to return after the war. As US troops flooded into the Aleutians to confront the Japanese, many of the remaining Unangan people were interned in southeast Alaska. Many died, and of those who returned home, many found their homes bulldozed and their islands littered with military rubbish. To this day, remnants of the US occupation remain throughout the Aleutians. Wrecked warplanes, immense runways, trenches, buildings, communications towers and bunkers are common sights in the landscape and the tundra is only now

ALASKA MARITIME NATIONAL WILDLIFE REFUGE

The 4.9-million-acre Alaska Maritime National Wildlife Refuge includes much of Alaska's 44,000 miles of coastline from the southeast to Attu at the far end of Aleutian Islands and north to the Arctic Ocean. This is the largest and richest refuge in the US, supporting an estimated 40 million sea birds and countless other species. For more information contact **Homer Islands and Oceans Center** (*95 Sterling Hwy;* ℘ *235 6546; www.islandsandocean.org, or www.alaska.fws.gov/nwr/akmar/index.htm*)

GETTING THERE Access to this refuge is virtually always with a boat. The Alaska ferry serves many communities in southwest, southeast and southcentral Alaska from which visitors can launch their trip into the refuge.

ACTIVITIES The park is so large and varied, there is little you cannot do here. Kayaking, boating, hiking, camping and wildlife viewing are the main attractions. The Islands and Oceans Center in Homer has a great deal of information on the refuge and the Homer area is also rich in wildlife and adventure. Homer is also where the annual Shorebird Festival is held each May (see page 70). Birders and other wildlife enthusiasts gather to watch huge flocks of migrating shorebirds arriving from South America, Asia and Hawaii. The following are some of the more popular attractions within the refuge for seeing seabirds, sea otter, seals, sea lions, whales and other wildlife and native and western history.

- **Chiswell Islands** Rich in seabirds and Steller sea lions and accessible from Seward.
- **Pribilof Islands** Often called the 'Galapagos of the North', they are home to three million seabirds and one million marine mammals such as fur seals. Unalaska Here you can kayak, fish, hike, learn about Alaska's World War II history and see wildlife aplenty.
- **Safety Sound** Near Nome. You can see rare migratory species in abundance through the early spring.
- **St Lazaria Island** Near Sitka. Half a million seabirds nest amongst old growth forests here.
- **Kachemak Bay** The staging point for trips to other parts of the refuge such as Kodiak and the Barren Islands, and a spring stopover for millions of migratory birds.

LAKE CLARK NATIONAL PARK AND PRESERVE

This 2.6 million-acre park occupies a rugged and wild bit of land on the east side of Cook Inlet an hour or two away from Anchorage by plane. Fishermen, backpackers and river runners are drawn to this wild yet easily accessible landscape of mountains, glaciers and lakes. For more information contact the **Port Alsworth Visitor Center** (✆ 781 2218; www.nps.gov/lacl; ⊕ May–Oct 08.00–17.00 daily).

GETTING THERE AND AWAY Port Alsworth on Lake Clark is where many adventures start ,but with such a short flight time to Anchorage, Homer, Kenai and Soldotna, visitors can land exactly where they want to, without stopping in Port Alsworth.

ACTIVITIES The park is undeveloped except for a small network of trails around Port Alsworth on Lake Clark providing access to the dramatic Tanalian Falls and Kontrashibuna Lake. The park is home to many excellent raftable rivers including the Mulchatna River, Chilikadrotna River and the Tlikakila River, all of which are swift but generally mellow.

Telaquana Trail The original inhabitants of the area, the Dena'ina, maintained a network of trails throughout the upper Alaskan Peninsula. The trails allowed quick travel between the hunting and fishing grounds and were later used by miners and trappers in the 1800s and 1900s. The Telaquana Trail, used today by backpackers, is a part of that network. The trail connects Lake Clark and Telaquana Lake with many river crossings and amazing scenery between. Generally backpackers are flown to Telaquana Lake or another lake along the route and return to Lake Clark on foot. Call the ranger station at Port Alsworth for more information on the trail.

DICK PROENNEKE

Richard Louis Proenneke, known as Dick, first visited Lake Clark in 1962 and later built a cabin from local materials and largely with tools he fashioned himself. He lived alone in the wilderness for more than 30 years and held the belief that his presence should have little or no impact on the environment. His sustainable wilderness ethic inspired people around the world.

Proenneke was born in Iowa in 1916. He worked on the family farm before enlisting in the Navy shortly after Pearl Harbor was bombed. After he was discharged from service, and after briefly working in ranching, he visited a friend in Alaska in 1949. He worked in the state on and off until 1962 when he first visited the Twin Lakes near Lake Clark. He set about building a cabin by hand in 1967 and finished it a year later. Dick filmed the construction of his cabin and meticulously noted in journals about his life and experiences. In the 1970s Proenneke's journals were published under the name *One Man's Wilderness* and a short film called *Alone in the Wilderness* was created from his original footage. The film is available on You Tube (www.youtube.com).

Proenneke's cabin was entrusted to the park when he left in 1998, aged 82. He had decided that the –50°F –46°C) winters were too cold for his old bones. Proenneke's cabin is now open to the public and will hopefully inspire a new generation of wilderness activists.

beginning to reclaim them. For more information about the World War II in the Aleutians see page 393.

Today, southwest Alaska is driven by commercial fishing with Unalaska bringing in 613 million pounds of seafood in 2008 (it is the top US port for the 20th straight year) while Bristol Bay landed more than 30 million red salmon in 2009. Tourism is also expanding, but relatively slowly due to the region's remoteness.

GETTING THERE AND AWAY Southwest Alaska is one of the most challenging places in Alaska to visit, which is how some travellers prefer it. Unpredictable weather plus limited and expensive transportation are among the reasons. Crowds are unknown in all areas of the southwest; even tourists as we know them don't exist here for the simple reason that they cease to be tourists the moment they board the plane or ferry and instead become explorers. The ferry heads out to the Aleutians once per month and is the trip of a lifetime; the ferry serves Kodiak far more often (see page 375 for more information on ferries). Other than the ferry, expensive flights are the best way to get around, and the only way to get to the Bristol Bay area.

For flight and ferry options see individual towns.

GETTING AROUND Getting around southwest Alaska is done by boat and plane, except in Kodiak where a small road system allows limited travel by car. In many of southwest Alaska's small towns, boats can be chartered as water taxis, some of them are licensed to do so and others are not. Likewise, small planes can be chartered from almost anywhere for 'flightseeing' or for passengers to be dropped off in the backcountry.

KODIAK Population: 14,000

The town of Kodiak (✪ 57°28'0"N, 153°26'0"W), on Kodiak Island feels like civilisation's last outpost. Despite its relative modernity the town feels dwarfed by the rugged enormity of southwest Alaska and wildness of the island – most of whichlies within the remote and beautiful Kodiak National Wildlife Refuge. The town of Kodiak, even with its large road system, occupies a very small portion of the island's northeast corner. Leaving Kodiak on the ferry bound for Unalaska, passengers inevitably feel that with every passing mile, they are closer to Siberia and further from the US.

Known as the Emerald Isle, Kodiak's hills spring to life each summer with a rich green carpet of flower-studded tundra and valleys filled with lush, spruce rainforests. Kodiak is home to Alaska's largest bears; the Kodiak Island grizzly and other wildlife, including fox, elk, deer, mountain goats, river otters, whales, sea otters, sea lions and many birds. The accessibility and yet the remoteness of Kodiak make it an ideal location for those seeking a wilderness experience of any kind. Lodges of varying qualities offer seclusion, fishing, and wildlife viewing; while charter planes and water taxis can drop travellers in the middle of nowhere. The tundra provides easy hiking terrain, while hundreds of miles of convoluted and protected coastline offer kayakers safe passage almost anywhere. For those not comfortable spending weeks in a tent, the 100-mile network of roads on the island offers great road tripping. The Chiniak Highway leading south along the coastline is mostly paved and allows access to some beautiful scenery, crystal clear rivers often teeming with fish and even sandy beaches.

Kodiak Island is the largest island in Alaska and the second largest in the US, covering some 3,465 square miles. The island is 100 miles long and has many deep fjords and bays, and ranges 10–60 miles wide. Kodiak Island is part of a larger archipelago, including the islands of Afognak and Shuyak to the north and the

7

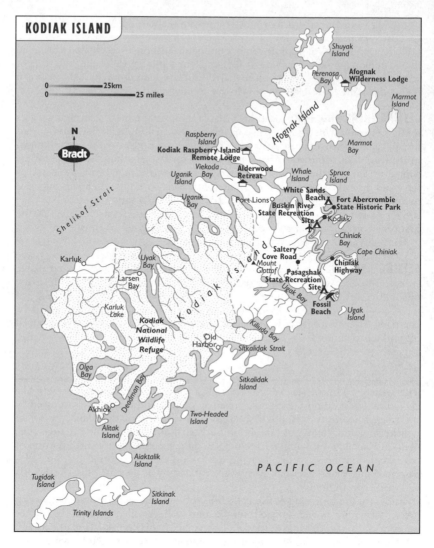

KODIAK ISLAND

0 ————— 25km
0 ————— 25 miles

N

Bradt

Shuyak
Island

Perenosa
Bay

**Afognak
Wilderness Lodge**

Marmot
Island

Afognak Island

Raspberry
Island

**Kodiak Raspberry Island
Remote Lodge**

Viekoda
Bay

Uganik
Island

**Alderwood
Retreat**

Whale
Island

Marmot
Bay

Spruce
Island

Uganik
Bay

Port Lions

**White Sands
Beach**

**Buskin River
State Recreation
Site**

**Fort Abercrombie
State Historic Park**

Kodiak

Chiniak
Bay

Shelikof Strait

Karluk

Uyak
Bay

Larsen
Bay

Karluk
Lake

**Kodiak
National
Wildlife
Refuge**

Kodiak Island

**Saltery
Cove Road**

Mount
Glottof

**Pasagshak
State Recreation
Site**

Ugak Bay

Cape Chiniak

**Chiniak
Highway**

**Fossil
Beach**

Ugak
Island

Old
Harbor

Sitkalidak Strait

Killuda Bay

Sitkalidak
Island

Olga
Bay

Deadman Bay

Akhiok

Alitak
Island

Two-Headed
Island

Aiaktalik
Island

PACIFIC OCEAN

Tugidak
Island

Sitkinak
Island

Trinity Islands

Trinity Islands to the south. The climate is wet and relatively mild with fog common in the summer and rain showers the norm throughout the year.

Kodiak is one of Alaska's top fish-producing ports; the harbours are full of fishing boats and you can hear the canneries at work from some distance away. The island is also home to the largest US Coast Guard base in the Pacific. Beside these two major groups, Kodiak's personality has been built by a small native population and a decent arts community.

HISTORY The Russian fur trader, Stephan Glotov, was the first westerner to explore Kodiak in 1763. More than 20 years later, fellow fur trader, Gregorii Shelikhov, established the first permanent settlement, after defeating the Alutiiq at their town site in Three Saints Bay in Kodiak. This later became the Russian-American Company in 1799. On 25 December 1793, Russian Empress Catherine sent eight monks and two novices to establish the Church of the Holy Resurrection in Kodiak. They arrived on

24 September 1794 after travelling for 293 days and 7,327 miles from St Petersburg – the longest missionary journey in the history of the Orthodox Church.

In 1791, Alexander Baranov replaced Shelikov as manager of the Russian–American Company, choosing to relocate the settlement to present day Kodiak after an earthquake destroyed much of Three Saints Bay. Kodiak quickly grew to become the centre of Russia's presence in Alaska. A sea-otter-pelt warehouse built by Baranov still exists today as the Baranov Museum (see page 366) on Marine Way.

Before Alaska was sold to the United States in 1867, Russian fur traders moved most of their operation to Sitka in 1808 leaving Kodiak to recover from nearly half a century of heavy resource exploitation. The Russian Orthodox religion proved the most memorable aspect of the Russian occupation. The faith is widespread in Kodiak and the lovely blue onion domes of the Holy Resurrection Church are visible from almost everywhere in town.

The 20th century marked yet another time plagued with misfortune for Kodiak. Just as commercial fishing began to take hold as a viable means for locals to make a living, the Novarupta volcano on the mainland near Katmai erupted on 6 June 1912. The explosion was one of the largest of the 20th century, ten times more powerful than the infamous 1980 eruption of Mt St Helens in Washington. Ash as deep as 700ft was deposited within a 40-square-mile radius of the volcano. Kodiak was blanketed in two feet of grey ash and the skies were dark for three days. The Valley of Ten Thousand Smokes was created by the eruption and is now protected in the 4.7-million-acre Katmai National Park.

KODIAK GRIZZLY BEARS

It's a popular myth that brown bears and grizzly bears are different species, but they are in fact one; *Ursus arctos*. However, the brown bears found on the Kodiak Island archipelago are a distinct subspecies called *Ursus arctos middendorffi*, having been separated from the mainland for 12,000 years. In general, the term 'brown bear' can be used for bears living in coastal environments feeding to a large extent on salmon. 'Grizzly bears' are bears of the same species living inland away from salmon streams, feeding primarily on plants, berries, carrion and small mammals.

The density of Kodiak bears rivals those of the famous Admiralty Island in southeast Alaska with as many as 0.7 bears per square mile with an estimated 3,500 bears in total. When salmon begin to congregate to spawn mid to late summer around the mouths of streams, the bear populations can explode in certain areas with ten or more bears per square mile. In the past this did pose a problem, especially for the Russians (whose cattle grazed the same tundra as the bears) and ranchers (who lost their cows to the bears). Ranchers used everything from big, mean dogs and 'bear proof' fences, to mass slaughtering of bears from airplanes to keep their livestock safe. Happily, though, most efforts to reduce the number of bears, or keep them off of grazing land, ceased in the 1960s.

Ironically, modern bear hunters are some of the biggest advocates for bears and the preservation of their habitat, having played a large part in creating the Kodiak National Wildlife Refuge during the first half of the 20th century.

Traditionally, the Alutiiq – the native people of the Kodiak archipelago – hunted the bears using only spears, arrows and copious amounts of courage. Today, the hunt continues but it is one of the most well-managed large game hunts in North America. About 500 permits are issued (received from more than 5,000 applicants) per year with only about 180 bears actually killed. Non-Alaskan US residents pay US$585 for a hunting permit and a bear tag (US$685 for non-US residents) and usually another US$20,000–30,000 in guide fees, transportation, taxidermy, equipment and logistics.

The 4.7-million-acre Katmai National Park is one of Alaska's premier destinations for viewing brown bears, receiving more than 60,000 visitors annually. During the summer, the Naknek River becomes a highway for millions of spawning salmon. These salmon attract large numbers of brown bears and other wildlife. Also within the park is the Valley of Ten Thousand Smokes, an otherworldly landscape created in 1912 by the Novarupta volcanic eruption.

Though the park is remote and vast, most of the park's annual visitors squeeze into a small area called Brooks Camp. The action centres around the short Brooks River, which connects Naknek Lake and Brooks Lake. The private enterprise of **Katmailand** (800 544 0551; www.katmailand.com) operates most of the facilities including a small lodge, guest cabins and a store. They also operate a bus from Brooks Camp to Ukak Falls and the Valley of Ten Thousand Smokes. Lodge rates start at US$1500/pp dbl including a flight from Anchorage. Katmailand also runs two other remote lodges (**Grosvenor Lodge** and **Kulik Lodge**) catering primarily to fishermen. Other lodges in the area include the **Royal Wolf** (248 3256; www.royalwolf.com; $$$$$) and the **Enchanted Lake Lodge** (694 6447; www.enchantedlakelodge.com; $$$$$).

The National Parks Service operates a campground (18 sites; US$8) right on the lake with a picnic table, bathrooms, food storage, water and cooking shelters all inside an electric 'bear fence.' Make reservations well ahead by calling the office in King Salmon (see page 371) or by visiting www.recreation.gov. A total of 60 campers can be accommodated. **Brooks Lodge** (800 544 0551 (TF); www.katmailand.com; $$$$$) offers three meals per day – campers, tired of cooking for themselves are welcome – for US$20–30. The lodge store sells white gas for camp stoves. If the campground is full, backcountry camping is allowed 1.5 miles or more from the Brooks River Falls and bear-proof food containers can be borrowed at no charge from the visitor centre. Campsites 2, 3, 4, 5, 17 and 18 are the closest to the lake.

From the lodge, trails and boardwalks lead to the best bear-viewing areas along the Brooks River, the most famous of which is Brooks Falls where bears sometimes catch salmon mid-jump as they fight to get up river. Fishing is still very popular here, creating a strange dynamic between bears, bear viewers and fishermen. Fishermen are instructed to cut their line if they have a fish on and a bear approaches. This is to stop bears from associating people with food. During peak season (July and August) the camp can feel very crowded and it can seem like the bears have shown up to watch the people rather than the other way around.

Responding to the crowded conditions, visitors have started to seek bears and other wildlife elsewhere in the park. Recently the east side of the park, along Shelikof Strait has become popular. Guests generally visit this area by staying at one of the lodges, chartering a boat for an extended cruise from Homer or Kodiak or by flying in for the day from Homer, Kodiak, Anchorage or King Salmon. Hallo Bay, Geographic Harbor, Moraine Creek and Funnel Creek and Swikshak Lagoon are also far less crowded and can host bears during the summer. Brooks River is best for seeing bears in July and September, Hallo Bay in June, Moraine Creek, Funnel Creek and Geographic Harbor in August and Swikshak Lagoon in June.

GETTING THERE Katmailand operates Katmai Air (800 544 0551; www.katmailand.com) and offers a number of guided and unguided trips in the park. For US$615 they will fly

During the 1930s and 1940s Kodiak was heavily fortified against the possibility of a Japanese invasion and to supply the Aleutian campaign. An air base, a submarine base and an army outpost were built in the tiny town of Kodiak,

visitors from Anchorage to King Salmon (the park's headquarters), then transport them to Brooks Camp in a small plane. From King Salmon to Brooks Camp the fare is US$176. Guided bear viewing trips start at $US600 for a one-day trip.

For a full list of air carriers, visit the park's website or call the King Salmon Ranger office (see page 371).

TOURIST INFORMATION

Refuge Visitor Center Bldg 4, Fish & Wildlife Service Rd; 246 4250 or 246 3339; e akpeninsula@fws.gov. Located near the airport.

Brooks Camp Visitor Center 481 1781; www.nps.gov/katm; 1 Jun–7 Sep.

ACTIVITIES The park offers endless hiking, rafting, fishing, hunting, sightseeing and exploring opportunities. The 86-mile **Savoniski Loop** canoe route is a fantastic trip for intermediate paddlers. The route starts at Brooks Camp and heads northeast along Naknek Lake through the Bay of Islands to Fures Cabin (make reservations at the park office in King Salmon). A one-mile, muddy, unmarked portage leads to Lake Grosvenor. A further 14 miles leads to Grosvenor River where a few easy miles upstream lead to the Savoniski River which empties into the Iliuk arm of Naknek Lake. From the mouth of the river, a 20-mile paddle completes the loop at Brooks Camp for a ten-day trip. Canoes (US$40/day) and double kayaks (US$16/day) are available for rent at the lodge.

Around the Brooks Camp area, visitors can easily keep busy with hikes and ranger-led tours and programmes. Every evening during the summer a ranger leads a free, one-hour cultural walk detailing the prehistoric inhabitants of the area. Archaeologists have found more than 900 home sites in the area, more than anywhere else in North America. Also, bus tours leave daily for the Valley of Ten Thousand Smokes and Ukak Falls. Campers and lodge guests gather just about every evening at the auditorium for a presentation.

Follow the Dumpling Mountain Trail uphill from the campground for a pleasant hike. The trail is 1.5 miles one-way and gains over 800 feet of elevation. This portion of the trail is led by a ranger each day. Independent hikers can continue up the mountain unguided a further 2.5 miles and an additional 1,600 feet of elevation to the summit of Dumpling Mountain for great views.

TOUR OPERATORS

Bald Mountain Air Service Homer Spit Rd; 235 7969; www.baldmountainair.com. Located in Homer.

Hallo Bay Lodge 235 2237, 888-535-2237 (TF); www.hallobay.com. A remote lodge along Shelikof Strait with simple accommodation in tent-like structures.

Homer Air 2190 Kachemak Dr; 235 8591, 800 478 8591 (TF); www.homerair.com.

Katmai Coastal Bear Tours 235 8337, 800 532 8338 (TF); www.katmaibears.com. Lodging is provided by The Waters, a 73ft converted tug boat out of Homer. Guests are able to see a great deal of coastline from their floating lodge.

Katmai Wilderness Lodge 486 8767, 800 488 8767 (TF); www.katmai-wilderness.com. A reasonably well-appointed lodge in a very remote area. Kayaks are available.

Mythos Expeditions (see page 357) Multi-day trips out of Kodiak on the converted fishing boat, the F/V Mythos.

ballooning the population to more than 25,000 people. The best evidence of this period can be seen at Fort Abercrombie north of town and at Chiniak and on Long Island just a few miles east of town.

Two decades later, on 27 March 1964, the Good Friday earthquake struck southcentral Alaska, rocking Kodiak for more than five minutes, causing massive damage, flooding and ultimately a series of devastating 30ft waves.

One of Alaska's richest commercial fishing ports, Kodiak was hit hard in 1989 by the infamous *Exxon Valdez* oil spill. Commercial fishing was halted when oil showed up in Kodiak and fishermen and other residents went to work cleaning beaches and trying to save the wildlife. While monetary settlements could never reverse the harm done, they did help to pay for the Alutiiq Museum (see page 366) and added land to a number of state parks and wildlife refuges around the island.

Today, Kodiak's economy is driven by commercial fishing, tourism, and the US Coast Guard base. An odd addition to the small town of Kodiak came in 1998 when the Kodiak Launch Complex at Narrow Cape near Pasagshak was built. The sterile white missile silo stands many storeys high in stark contrast to the green tundra all around. Located around the building are surveillance cameras, fences and signs indicating the national security threat level.

GETTING THERE AND AWAY
By air
✈ **Alaska Airlines** ✆ 800 252 7522, 487 4363 (local); www.alaskaair.com. Daily flights to Kodiak from Anchorage for US$375 return.

✈ **ERA/Frontier** ✆ 266 8394, 800 866 8394 (TF); www.frontierak.com. ERA flies to Kodiak from Anchorage on a regular basis.

By ferry
Alaska Marine Highway (✆ *800 526 6731, 786 3800 (local); www.dot.state.ak.us/amhs*) Kodiak is served by the Alaska Ferry from Homer. The trip takes about 13 hours and is always overnight. A cabin is a good idea since the trip can be rough, with the worst part often coming just before arrival in Kodiak. The ferry travels to Kodiak from Homer three to four times per week for US$76, or US$129 for a cabin.

GETTING AROUND
By rental car
🚗 **Avis** 1647 Airport Way, Kodiak Airport; ✆ 487 2264, 800 331 1212 (TF); www.avis.com

🚗 **Rent-a-Heap** Kodiak Airport; ✆ 487 2220; www.budget.com. A second location can be found at 508 Marine Way; ✆ 486 8550.

By taxi or shuttle
🚗 **A & B Taxi** ✆ 486 2461
🚗 **Ace Mecca Taxi** 1816 Mill Bay Rd; ✆ 486 3211
🚗 **Anderson Taxi** ✆ 486 2461

🚗 **Garrett's Taxi Service** 1212 Purtov St; ✆ 654 3535
🚗 **Robbie's #1 Limousine Service** 3851 Woodland Dr; ✆ 486 3604

By bike
58 Degrees North [358–9 C3] 1231 Mill Bay Rd; ✆ 486 6249. Bike rentals.

Flights Kodiak has a number of flight services, most of them offering essentially the same service in similar planes. Always ask about the pilot's experience of flying in Alaska.

Andrew Airways ✆ 487 2566; www.andrewairways.com. Flight service, gear rental & remote cabin rental.
Harvey Flying Service Kodiak State Airport; ✆ 487

2621; www.harveyflyingservice.com. With just 1 plane, a spectacular 1943 Grumman Widgeon, Steve & Mary Ann Harvey offer bear viewing, flightseeing & charter flights to about everywhere.

Island Air 1420 Airport Way; ℡ 487 4596, 800 478 6196 (TF); www.kodiakislandair.com. Scheduled & charter flights almost anywhere in Kodiak.

Kingfisher Air 1829 Mill Bay Rd; ℡ 486 5155; www.kingfisheraviation.com
Paklook Air/Servant Air ℡ 487 4400; www.servantair.com

TOURIST INFORMATION
ℹ️ Kodiak Chamber of Commerce [358–9 B4] 100 E Marine Way # 300; ℡ 486 5557; www.kodiak.org. Located near the ferry dock & Kodiak Wildlife

Refuge Visitor Center (see page 366). For more information visit www.southwestalaska.com/kodiak.html

LOCAL TOURS AND ACTIVITIES
Memory Makers ℡ 486 7000; www.memorymakersink.com. Walking tours of various local museums as well as the harbour & tide pooling.
Burton's Ranch Narrow Cape; ℡ 486 3705. Occasionally offer horse rides on their stunning property, where you can see bear, deer, elk &

bison. Rides are US$50–60pp/hr, but be sure to call ahead to check availability. This ranch also offers hunts for many of the game species on their land.
Northland Resort Mile 30.3 Chiniak Pasagshak Hwy; ℡ 486 5578. Also offer horse rides.

Wildlife Brown bears are the big draw on Kodiak Island, and there are a number of ways to see them. Fly out to a remote lodge for a week or more, or fly out for the day to any number of locations on Kodiak Island or nearby Katmai National Park.

Kodiak Treks 11754 S Russian Cr Rd; ℡ 487 2122; www.kodiaktreks.com. Wildlife guiding from their location in the remote Uyak Bay.
True North Adventures ℡ 486 5188; www.truenorthfishing.com. Bear-viewing trips to

Katmai in the autumn & to a remote lodge on an island in Karluk Lake during the rest of the summer. An expensive but top-notch experience.

Hiking/Adventure
Kodiak Treks (see above) Guided single- or multi-day hikes led by biologist Harry Dodge with all gear provided. Remote camp stays are also available.

Orion's 1247 Mill Bay Rd; ℡ 486 8380. A full-service outdoor shop offering a local hiking guide.

Cruise/Kayak/Canoe
Alaska Wilderness Adventures 12372 S Russian Creek Rd; ℡ 487 2397; www.akwildadventures.com. A small & very personal kayak adventure company offering some of the more affordable paddles in Kodiak. US$160pp for 1–3 people & US$145pp for 4 or more people.
Galley Gourmet ℡ 486 5079, 800 253 6331 (TF); www.galleygourmet.biz. A lovely evening dinner cruise aboard the 42ft Sea Breeze. Sea otters & other wildlife are often spotted. The owners also have a pleasant B&B.
Mythos Expeditions Kodiak ℡ 486 5536; www.thewildcoast.com. Kayak, fishing & sightseeing trips throughout the Kodiak archipelago. The M/V

Mythos, originally a fishing boat, provides accommodation & transportation to remote areas.
Orcas Unlimited Charters ℡ 654 1979; 📧 aschroeder@gci.net; www.orcasunlimited.com. This very green business offsets their footprint on the Earth at every step. They offer day kayak trips & multi-day adventures with accommodation provided on their former fishing boat; the MV Celeste. Custom trip ideas can usually be accommodated.
Single Star ℡ 486 4093; www.mvsinglestar.com. This 58ft yacht provides accommodation & transportation to Kodiak's most remote areas. They specialise in wildlife viewing (especially bears) & fly fishing.

Fishing Kodiak's rivers are all crystal clear and teeming with fish. While remote locations are best for fishing, roadside rivers can be productive as well.

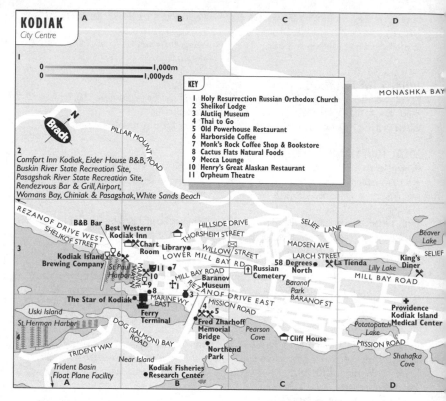

KODIAK
City Centre

0 ——————— 1,000m
0 ——————— 1,000yds

MONASHKA BAY

KEY

1 Holy Resurrection Russian Orthodox Church
2 Shelikof Lodge
3 Alutiiq Museum
4 Thai to Go
5 Old Powerhouse Restaurant
6 Harborside Coffee
7 Monk's Rock Coffee Shop & Bookstore
8 Cactus Flats Natural Foods
9 Mecca Lounge
10 Henry's Great Alaskan Restaurant
11 Orpheum Theatre

PILLAR MOUNTAIN ROAD

Comfort Inn Kodiak, Eider House B&B,
Buskin River State Recreation Site,
Pasagshak River State Recreation Site,
Rendezvous Bar & Grill, Airport,
Womans Bay, Chiniak & Pasagshak, White Sands Beach

REZANOF DRIVE WEST
SHELIKOF STREET

B&B Bar
Best Western
Kodiak Inn
Chart
Room
Library
HILLSIDE DRIVE
THORSHEIM STREET
WILLOW STREET
LOWER MILL BAY RD
MADSEN AVE
LARCH STREET
SELIEF LANE
Beaver Lake
SELIEF
King's Diner
Lilly Lake
MILL BAY ROAD
58 Degrees
North
La Tienda

Kodiak Island
Brewing Company
St Paul
Harbour
MILL BAY ROAD
Russian
Cemetery
Baranof
Museum
Baranof
Park
Baranof ST
BARANOF ST

The Star of Kodiak
MARINE WAY EAST
REZANOF DRIVE EAST
MISSION ROAD

Uski Island
St Herman Harbor
Ferry
Terminal
DOG (SALMON) BAY ROAD
Fred Zharhoff
Memorial
Bridge
Pearson
Cove
Cliff House
Providence
Kodiak Island
Medical Center
Potatopatch
Lake
MISSION ROAD

TRIDENT WAY
Near Island
Northend
Park
Shahafka
Cove

Trident Basin
Float Plane Facility
Kodiak Fisheries
Research Center

Can't Get Enough ATV Fishing ✆ 487 2162; www.cantgetenoughfishing.com. All-terrain-vehicle fishing trips may not be a quiet, low-impact way of seeing the Alaskan wilderness, but visitors can be sure of reaching remote areas quickly.

Memory Makers (see page 357) Fishing trips from the Kodiak Road system.

True North Adventures (see page 357) High-end fly-out fishing trips for halibut, salmon & trout.

HIKING AND RECREATION Kodiak is a hikers' paradise. Though an extensive trail system exists around the road system, much of Kodiak is tundra, which is very hiker-friendly. The Kodiak National Wildlife Refuge offers eight public use cabins that can be booked at the refuge office (see page 366). Be sure to check out *Hiking on Kodiak – A Trail Guide* by Hans Tschersich and *Kodiak Mountain Bike Guide – The Joys of Riding on 'The Rock'* by Phillip Tschersich. Semi-wild bison herds are common near Pasagshak. Hikers should keep a safe distance, especially when they have calves. Before venturing any distance from the road, hikers should be well-versed in bear safety (see page 53).

The **Kodiak Audobon Society** (✆ 486 8148 (Margie), 539 1264 (Katie)) offers free hikes most Saturdays throughout the summer. The society also produces a fantastic hiking and birding map for the northeast part of Kodiak Island called *Hiking and Birding Guide* written by Hans Tschersich and Stacy Studebaker. The map can be ordered from the society or purchased around town.

Some great trails in the area are **Termination Point Loop Trail** (see page 367), **Pyramid Peak** (trailhead off Anton Larson Bay Rd), the **Pasagshak** area and the **Chiniak Loop** (see page 366).

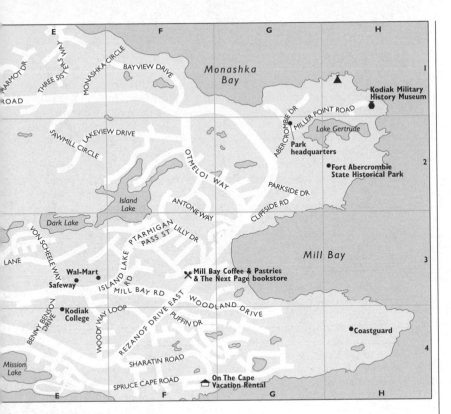

WHERE TO STAY
Hotels

🏠 **Best Western Kodiak Inn** [358–9 B3] (81 rooms) 236 Rezanof Drive W; ☎ 486 5712, 888 563 4254 (TF); www.kodiakinn.com. Located near the small boat harbour, the hotel has clean but pricey standard rooms with a good central location. Free airport pickup, fridge, microwave, Wi-Fi, b/fast incl. $$$

🏠 **Comfort Inn Kodiak** [358–9 A2] (50 rooms) 1395 Airport Way; ☎ 487-2700, 800 544 2202 (TF); www.comfortinn.com/hotel/ak025. Right across the street from the airport & 5 miles from town. Taxi rides to town can be as much as US$25 each way. Free airport pickup. Fridge, microwave, Wi-Fi. $$$

B&Bs

🏠 **Cliff House** [358–9 C4] (4 rooms) (see page 357) The owners of the dinner cruise Galley Gourmet run this lovely B&B near town. Clean, modern rooms with art & murals. 3 rooms (US$124–150) share a separate building with a shared full kitchen & common area. The suite (US$190) has the best views & shares a bath with hosts. BBQ, freezer space, Wi-Fi. $$$

🏠 **On the Cape** [358–9 F4] (3 rooms) 3476 Spruce Cape Rd; ☎ 486 4185; www.onthecape.net. A modern house outside town dedicated to the guests. The Cape Suite has great views & luxury amenitites (US$160). The other 2 rooms are simple but nice. Full kitchen & stocked fridge, freezer space, laundry, Wi-Fi. $$$

🏠 **Eider House** [358–9 A2] (3 rooms) 782 Sargent Creek Rd; ☎ 487 4315; www.eiderhouse.com. Located in a rural area south of the airport. Simple, affordable rooms. Wi-Fi. $$

Camping

⛺ **Buskin River State Recreation Site** [358–9 A2] (15 sites) (see page 366) A popular fishing area, this park has tent & RV spaces, pit toilets, shelters & tables. Tent/RV US$15.

Located on the northern edge of Katmai National Park, McNeil is perhaps the most famous and tightly controlled place on Earth for seeing wild brown bears. The 200-square-mile sanctuary is 100 miles from Homer and 250 miles from Anchorage. During a few short summer months each year, McNeil River hosts the greatest concentration of brown bears on Earth. Brown bears normally need hundreds of miles of separation between one another, but here briefly tolerate each other's company to feed on the abundant dog (chum) salmon. As many as 72 bears have been observed at one time!

To protect both bears and people, the sanctuary is run, carefully controlled and monitored by the Alaska Department of Fish and Game (AFG&G). A permit drawn by lottery is required to enter and it's not uncommon for bear enthusiasts to wait years to get the chance to visit. Two types of permits exist, a Guided Viewing Permit and a Camp-Standby Viewing Permit. After the application is submitted (1 March) and the US$25 application fee paid, 250 or so permits are issued after a payment of US$350 (non-Alaskan residents) or US$150 (Alaskan residents) is made by 15 April. Camp-Standby permits are US$175 for non-residents and US$75 for residents. A Guided Viewing Permit allows guests to stay for three days and the visitors are guided by an ADF&G guide each day. Camp-Standby permits allow visitors to enter the camping area and portions of the coast but not enter the main viewing areas at McNeil Falls or Mikfik Creek unless a Guided Viewing Permit holder decides to not go with the group that day and his/her place is freed up. Most people who apply for a guided permit also apply for a Camp-Standby permit to improve their chances. No more than ten people a day are allowed at the main viewing area between June 7 and August 25.

Flights into the sanctuary are available from Homer, Anchorage, King Salmon and Kodiak. The sanctuary is primitive with a camping area, pit toilets and a cabin for cooking. Permits are easier to get for June before the dog salmon start to show up in McNeil Creek and bears are still often seen on the tidal flats and at Mikfik Creek where an earlier run of red salmon spawn. July and August are the best months for seeing bears gorge on dog salmon at McNeil Falls but permits are also much harder to get for this. Visitors spend six to eight hour a day sitting on a 10'x10' gravel pad overlooking the falls. Having been safely accustomed to the presence of people, the bears will sometimes walk within 30ft of the visitors, but more commonly they remain a few hundred feet away. Due to the efforts of long-time sanctuary steward Larry Aumiller and others, bears and people have existed in harmony since the permit process began.

For more information contact McNeil River staff (↳ 267 2253; e dfg.dwc.mcneil-info@alaska.gov; www.wildlifenews.alaska.gov/index.cfm?adfg=mcneil_river.main).

Ӽ **Fort Abercrombie State Historical Park** [358–9 H1] (13 sites) (see page 366) Most campsites have great views over the ocean & are nestled in amongst World War II bunkers. Tent/RV US$15.

Ӽ **Pasagshak River State Recreation Site** [358–9 A2] (12 sites) (see page 366) Located about 1hr from Kodiak with undeveloped camping, good fishing & no charge.

Ӽ **White Sands Beach** [358–9 A2] (see page 367) Free camping is allowed on the beach but be careful of the tide. Loud at w/ends. The tyre swing is amazing.

Cabins The Kodiak National Wildlife Refuge maintains seven public-use cabins around the island costing US$30 each. These cabins are simple structures with platforms for sleeping, pit toilets and a gas heater (bring your own kerosene).

Cabin reservations are scheduled by lottery. For the months of April, May and June, campers should make applications by post before January. For the months of July, August and September, mail your application before April. Obtain an application from the Kodiak National Wildlife Refuge website (*www.kodiak.fws.gov/pdf/Cabin_Application.pdf*).

Wilderness lodges Kodiak has a host of wilderness lodges and while most offer the same activities and promise the same experience, some are far better than others.

⌂ **Afognak Wilderness Lodge** ➘ 486 6442; www.afognaklodge.com. Located on the remote Afognak Island north of Kodiak Island, this rustic lodge offers bear viewing, fishing & hunter-lodge-style accommodation.

⌂ **Alderwood Retreat** ➘ 486 4773; www.alderwoodretreat.com. A pleasant lodge a short flight west of Kodiak right on the water at the base of Mt Kupreanoff. One of the few lodges offering spa getaways as well as the usual hunting & fishing packages. Ask about their cooking classes with the famous local French chef Joël Chanet.

⋏ **Kodiak Treks** ➘ 487 2122; www.kodiaktreks.com. One of the more affordable remote camps on Kodiak

Island. Simple accommodation in Uyak Bay near the small town of Larson Bay in southwest Kodiak. A stay at the camp can be combined with single- or multi-day hikes further afield led by biologist Harry Dodge.

⋏ **Kodiak Raspberry Island Remote Lodge** ➘ 701 526 1677; www.raspberryisland.com. A secluded camp on Raspberry Island, located a short flight or boat ride heading north from Kodiak. Birch, Tiffany, & their kids are wonderful hosts & Tiffany is an excellent cook. A very friendly environment with great kayaking, fishing & bear viewing a short plane ride away.

✖ WHERE TO EAT

✖ **Henry's Great Alaskan Restaurant** [358–9 B3] 512 Marine Way, ➘ 486 8844; ⊕ 11.25–22.00

Mon–Thu, 11.25–22.30 Fri & Sat, 12.00–21.30 Sun. Facing the harbour in a small mall, this sports

---

SHUYAK ISLAND STATE PARK

Located 54 air miles north of Kodiak past Afognak Island, Shuyak Island is a small but remote and wild island. The rugged coastline is ideal for extended kayak trips and, with the island's small size of just 11 x 12 miles (47,000 acres), it is possible to circumnavigate the island. Most of the island is cloaked in Sitka spruce forests and virtually the entire island is protected by the park. Due to the extensive coastal environment, sea birds are plentiful as are otters, whales, seals, sea lions and porpoise. Inland, visitors will find bear and deer. A few trails exist on the western side of the island but thick brush makes boat travel preferable to overland travel.

Four cabins for public use can be found on the western side of the island but reservations are required and all supplies must be brought in and waste hauled out. Cabins have non-potable water, propane and stoves, wood stoves, gravity-fed showers, basic pots and pans and foam pads resting on wooden bunks. A ranger station in Big Bay on the west coast is manned during the summer months.

Afognak Island, to the north of Shuyak, is the second largest island in the Kodiak archipelago just north of Kodiak. Unlike on Shuyak Island, only a small portion of Afognak Island is protected within the park and some logging has taken place. Still, the park is very large, encompassing 75,000 acres in the island's northwest corner. The island has lots of salmon and brown bears as well as deer and elk. Two cabins for public use can be found at Laura and Pillar Lakes. These are accessible by seaplane only.

For more information contact Alaska State Parks (*1400 Abercrombie Dr;* ➘ *486 6339; www.alaskastateparks.org*).

This 1.9-million-acre, roadless wilderness covers most of Kodiak Island and some of the outerlying islands. The park was originally established in 1941 at the behest of brown bear hunters to protect the creatures from overhunting. Today, the park is home to all five species of salmon, an estimated 600 nesting pairs of bald eagles, millions of seabirds, more than 3,000 brown bears, elk, deer, otters and many other animals. The park has hundreds of rivers and creeks, 4,000ft peaks, lush spruce forests, tundra and hundreds of miles of rugged coastline with sandy beaches.

GETTING THERE Kodiak Island is accessible by commercial airlines from Anchorage or a ferry through the Alaska Marine Highway System. The refuge is accessible only by seaplane or boat. Air charters are available in the city of Kodiak.

TOURIST INFORMATION

Kodiak National Wildlife Refuge Visitor Center 402 Center St; ☎ 487 2626; 888 592 6940 (TF); www.kodiakwildliferefuge.org, www.kodiak.fws.gov/index.htm; ⊕ 09.00–17.00 daily.

ACTIVITIES Like most of Alaska's protected wild lands, the Kodiak National Wildlife Refuge has unlimited adventure possibilities from kayaking the coastline to hiking overland for days on end. The climate is generally cool and wet with rain and fog common in many areas throughout the summer.

bar/restaurant serves a little of everything, doing it all well, but not brilliantly. A full bar with a number of beers on tap, TVs & smoking permitted. $$$$

✗ **Old Powerhouse Restaurant** [358–9 B4] 516 E. Marine Way; ☎ 481 1088; ⊕ 11.30–14.00 & 17.00–21.00 Tue–Thu, 11.30–14.00 & 17.00–22.00 Fri & Sat, 17.00–21.00 Sun. Located close to the Near Island bridge in an old electric power building. One of Kodiak's most classy establishments with fair yet affordable sushi & unpredictable steaks & seafood. Either good food *or* good service but rarely both simultaneously. There's a pleasant surprise for women in the ladies bathroom: heated toilet seats! $$$$

✗ **Chart Room** [358–9 B3] 236 W Rezanof Dr; ☎ 486 5712; ⊕ 07.00–14.00 & 16.00–22.00 daily. Good Sun brunch with nice views. Music on Fri. Located inside the Best Western Kodiak Inn. $$$

Cafés

✗ **Mill Bay Coffee & Pastries** [358–9 F3] 3833 E. Rezanof Dr; ☎ 486 4411; www.millbaycoffee.com; ⊕ 06.30–19.00 Mon–Sat, 08.00–17.00 Sun. Located in an unassuming, grey strip mall north of town next to the Gas-N-Go, this little gem is almost a reason in & of itself to go to Kodiak. French couple, Joël & Martine Chanet own the place & are delightful to talk to. Joël is a relatively famous

✗ **Rendezvous Bar & Grill** 11652 Chiniak Hwy; ☎ 487 2233; ⊕ 11.30–15.00 & 17.00–19.30 Tue–Sun. Located south of town, the 'Rondi' is a wonderfully funky spot to eat a great meal prepared by chef Tony. Get a drink & some interesting conversation. Burgers only on Mon. $$$

✗ **King's Diner** [358–9 D3] 1941 Mill Bay Rd; ☎ 486 4100; ⊕ 05.30–15.00 Mon–Sat, 06.30–15.00 Sun. Cheap, large portions of generic American food — good for what it is. $$

✗ **Shelikof Lodge Restaurant** 211 Thorsheim Av; ☎ 486 4141; ⊕ 06.30–21.00 daily. Serves b/fast all day. $$

✗ **Thai To Go** [358–9 B4] 420 Marine Way; ☎ 486 0600; ⊕ 11.00–20.00 daily. This odd new Thai restaurant can be found in a blue Connex shipping container covered in plastic flowers next to the Near Island Bridge. Unfortunately the food is not as exciting as the landscaping. No credit cards. $$

French pastry chef who has cooked all over the world before settling in Kodiak. Kodiak's best b/fast & lunch spot. Free Wi-Fi. $$$

✗ **Harborside Coffee** [358–9 A3] 216 Shelikof; ☎ 486 5862; ⊕ 06.30–19.00 Mon–Sat, 07.00–19.00 Sun. A locals' coffee house right on the harbour. Hot drinks, baked goods & art. $$

✕ **Monk's Rock Coffee Shop & Bookstore** [358–9 B3] 202 E Rezanof Dr, Ste I; ☎ 486 0905; ⏱ 7.00–16.00 Mon–Fri. An interesting café full of Russian Orthodox icons, books & art. Good smoothies & OK sandwiches. **$$**

WHERE TO DRINK, ENTERTAINMENT AND NIGHTLIFE

♀ **B&B Bar** [358–9 A3] 326 Shelikof St; ☎ 486 3575. Fishermens' bar
♀ **Henry's Great Alaskan Restaurant** [358–9 B3] (see page 361) A family bar — If there is such a thing.
♀ **Kodiak Island Brewing Company** [358–9 A3] 338 Shelikof Av; ☎ 486 2537; www.kodiakbrewery.com. Free samples or by the jug.

♀ **Mecca Lounge** [358–9 B3] 302 W Marine Way; ☎ 486 3364: ⏱ 09.00–closing. Suit & cologne or raingear & fish, whatever you're wearing you will feel right at home. Get 'Mecca-nised' Sat night on the dance floor.
♀ **Tony's Bar** 518 W Marine Way; ☎ 486 9489. Fishermen's bars.

Cinema

Orpheum Theatre [358–9 B3] 102 Center Av; ☎ 486 5449. Movies shown every night all year.

FESTIVALS AND EVENTS

April

Whalefest (*www.whalefestkodiak.com*) This mid-April event celebrates the return of the whales to Kodiak waters with whale watching, arts and festivities.

Earth Day Triathlon (☎ *486 8665*) Features a 1km swim, 5km run and a 20km bike event.

May

Kodiak Crab Festival (*www.kodiak.org/crabfest.html*) Always held the Thursday before Memorial Day, this festival is a lot of fun. Events include a tennis tournament, food, booths, local art, music, a US Coast Guard Search and Rescue Demonstration, an arm-wrestling competition, a parade, a rubber duck race, survival suit races and more. Be sure to sample the locally famous 'Bruin Burger' from the Bruin's Snow Mobile Club stand. A hunk of hamburger and Velveta cheese deep-fried – a Kodiak right-of-passage meal!

Kodiak's Annual Salmon Run (☎ *486 2455*) A 5km run or walk to celebrate the returning of salmon to the Buskin River. Smoked salmon prizes.

Kodiak Salmon Celebration (☎ *267 2265, 486 9000*). Children can help release salmon fry into the ocean and learn about the resource.

June

All American Soap Box Derby (☎ *486 8665*) A qualifying race for the world championships in Akron, Ohio.

July

4 July (☎ *486 3258*) Fireworks at midnight on 3 July and on the following day, a parade, music, a free BBQ, a chili cook-off and a kids' pie-eating contest.

Bear Country Music Festival (☎ *486 8766*) As many as 50 bands play everything from bluegrass to rock.

Barefoot in the Park Quintathlon (☎ *486 0809*; e *dunbarfamily@gci.net*) Swim, bike, shoot, kayak and run with a picnic at Fort Abercrombie afterwards.

August

Warm August Nights Music Fest (↘ *539 2010*) An annual music event at the State Fair Grounds with bonfires and BBQ.

Annual Garden Tours (↘ *486 3074*) The second week in August, join a group of local garden enthusiasts and visit the best gardens around town.

Silver Salmon Derby (*117 Lower Mill Bay Rd;* ↘ *486 3900*) Starts at the end of August and runs until the end of September.

Kodiak State Fair and Rodeo Held on Labour Day (the last few days of August) this event features bull riding, pie eating, nail pounding, halibut cleaning, watermelon seed spitting, music, food and other events.

Pilgrimage to St Herman's Monks Lagoon (↘ *486 3854*) An annual pilgrimage held on 7– 9 August to the home site of father Herman on Spruce Island to celebrate his canonisation in 1970.

October

Oktoberfest Held 7 October. The town hosts music and drinking with sponsorship by Kodiak's own brewery, the Kodiak Island Brewing Company.

SHOPPING
Bookshops

The Next Page [358–9 F3] 3833 E Rezanof Dr; ↘ 481 7243; ☺ 11.00–18.00 Mon–Sat, 11.00–17.00 Sun. Next door to Mill Bay Coffee. Books & local art.

Food shopping

Cactus Flats Natural Foods [358–9 B3] 338 Mission Rd; ↘ 486 4677; ☺ 10.00–18.00 daily. A small selection of natural foods. By the harbour.
La Tienda [358–9 C3] 1315 Mill Bay Rd; ↘ 486 1415; www.latienda-kodiak.tripod.com; ☺ 11.00–19.00 Mon–Sat. A locally owned Latin-American food store.

Safeway [358–9 E3] 2685 Mill Bay Rd; ↘ 486 6811; www.safeway.com; ☺ 06.00–midnight daily. A large selection of foods & a pharmacy. Another smaller location can be found at 502 Marine Way; ↘ 486 6227; ☺ 09.00–midnight daily.

Native arts The best place in town to get authentic native arts and crafts is the **Alutiiq Museum** (see page 366).

Outdoor

58 Degrees North [358–9 C3] 1231 Mill Bay Rd; ↘ 373 2453. Outdoor gear incl bikes sales & rentals, kayaks etc.

Kodiak Kamps ↘ 486 5333; www.kodiakkamps.com. Outdoor equipment rental from tents & cots to fishing poles & boats (US$85/day).
Orion's (see page 357) A good supply of outdoor gear. Guides available.

OTHER PRACTICALITIES
Banks

$ First National Bank Alaska 218 Center Av; ↘ 800 856 4362 (TF); www.fnbalaska.com; ☺ 10.00–17.00 Mon–Fri, 10.00–14.00 Sat.
$ Key Bank 422 E Marine Way; ↘ 486 6104; www.key.com; ☺ 10.00–17.00 Mon–Fri.

$ Wells Fargo Bank 202 Marine Way; ↘ 869 3557; www.wellsfargo.com; ☺ 09.00–18.00 Mon–Fri, 10.00–14.00 Sat.

Healthcare

Pharmacies

Safeway [358–9 E3] (see opposite) ☎ 481 1560; ⏰ 09.00–19.00 daily.

Wal-Mart [358–9 E3] 2911 Mill Bay Rd; ☎ 481 1675; www.walmart.com; ⏰ 09.00–19.00 Mon–Fri, 09.00–18.00 Sat.

Hospitals

✚ **Providence Health and Services** [358–9 D4] 1915 E Rezanof Dr; ☎ 486 3281.

Dentists

Nathan Faber 413 E Rezanof Dr; ☎ 486-3257; www.kodiakdentistry.com; ⏰ 08.00–17.00 Mon–Fri.

Internet

🄴 **Best Western Kodiak Inn** [358–9 B3] (see page 359) Free Wi-Fi.
🄴 **Mill Bay Coffee & Pastries** [358–9 F3] (see page 362) Free Wi-Fi.

🄴 **Public library** [358–9 B3] 319 Lower Mill Bay Rd; ☎ 486 8680; www.city.Kodiak.ak.us; ⏰ 10.00–21.00 Mon–Fri, 10.00–17.00 Sat, 13.00–17.00 Sun. No Wi-Fi but free internet access on terminals.

Post offices

✉ **City Center Locations** [358–9 C3] 419 Lower Mill Bay Rd; ☎ 486 4721; ⏰ 09.00–17.00 Mon–Fri.

Another location can be found at 111 W Rezanof Dr; ⏰ 10.00–18.00 Mon–Sat.

WHAT TO SEE Unlike most Alaskan islands, Kodiak has a well-maintained road system allowing access to a number of lovely areas. Without a car, a visitor's experience of Kodiak will be limited.

City centre A very complete visitors guide is available at the Visitor Information Office featuring a walking-tour itinerary and map with descriptions of most of the town's attractions.

Kodiak Fisheries Research Center [358–9 B4] (*301 Research Ct;* ☎ *481 1700; www.afsc.noaa.gov/Kodiak;* ⏰ *09.00–17.00 Mon–Fri, closed 13.00–14.00*) A research station with two tanks and lots of information on marine biology. Cross the Near Island Bridge and stay left. Take the second right.

The Star of Kodiak [358–9 B4] Protruding from the collection of buildings off Marine Way E is a massive ship called the Star of Kodiak. The ship was the last World War II *Liberty Ship* built and found its way to Kodiak after the 1964 tsunami to become a part of the Trident Seafoods complex.

Holy Resurrection Russian Orthodox Church [358–9 B3] (*410 Mission Rd;* ☎ *486 5532*) With traditional blue onion domes, this building cannot be missed. Tours are available at 13.00 Monday–Friday, and services are held on Thursday at 18.30 and Sunday at 20.30.

Saint Herman's Chapel (*414 Mission Rd;* ☎ *486 3524*) Just down the street from the Russian Orthodox Church, this building is almost as impressive and is usually open.

Near Island Until 1986, fishermen and visitors took a small ferry to Near Island from Kodiak. The new bridge allows access to St Herman's Harbor (called Dog Bay by locals), a seaplane dock, the Fisheries Research Center and Northend Park with a short trail. To access the trailhead, park on the left immediately after the bridge.

Kodiak Island Brewing Company [358–9 A3] (*338 Shelikof Av;* ☎ *486 2537; www.kodiakbrewery.com;* ⊕ *12.00–19.00 Mon–Sat, 12.00–17.00 Sun*) Free samples of their many locally made brews. All beers are available by the jug.

Museums

Kodiak Wildlife Refuge Visitor Center [358–9 B4] (*402 Center St;* ☎ *487 2626; 888 592 6940 (TF); www.kodiakwildliferefuge.org;* ⊕ *09.00–17.00 daily; free admission*) This fantastic centre is the best way to get acquainted with the flora, fauna and cultures of Kodiak.

Alutiiq Museum [358–9 B3] (*215 Mission Road, Ste 101;* ☎ *486 7004; www.alutiiqmuseum.org;* ⊕ *09.00–17.00 Mon–Fri, 10.00–17.00 Sat; US$5/free adult/child*) Various permanent and travelling displays, artefacts and photographs depict the history of the Alutiiq people.

Baranov Museum [358–9 B3] (*101 Marine Way;* ☎ *486 5920; www.baranovmuseum.org;* ⊕ *10.00–16.00 Mon–Sat, 12.00–16.00 Sun; US$3/free adult/child*) Located in Alaska's oldest building, the museum celebrated the building's 200th anniversary in 2008. The museum provides the most complete story of Kodiak's history with information on the Alutiiq people, the Russian period and World War II.

Kodiak Military History Museum [358–9 H1] (*1623 Mill Bay Rd;* ☎ *486 7015; www.kadiak.org;* ⊕ *13.00–16.00 Sat & Sun (incl Memorial Day, May 26); US$3/free adult/child*) Located inside a World War II ammunition bunker at Miller Point in Fort Abercrombie State Park. Inside this unconventional little museum you will find various artefacts from World War II. Two eight-inch gun mounts overlook the sea and, just beyond, a bald eagle frequents the rock spire.

Around town

Fort Abercrombie State Historical Park [358–9 H2] A few miles north of town, this lovely forested park has trails, camping, picnic areas and World War II attractions. To reach the park, follow Rezanof Drive north for about three miles. Turn right onto Abercrombie Drive.

Buskin River State Recreation Area Located off the Chiniak Hwy on the way to the airport, this park has a number of hiking trails and camp sites but is primarily known as a sport fishing destination. Riverside trail to the sea.

Cape Chiniak A 40-mile drive south along the Chiniak Highway leads to the small community of Chiniak. Past the Road's End Restaurant at mile 42.8, drivers cross Chiniak Creek; a great place to watch masses of pink salmon squirm through the culvert mid-summer. At mile 42.8, a dirt road accessible only by 4x4 leads to the left. Follow this road and travellers will eventually find a World War II bunker with a commanding view.

Fossil Beach At mile 30.3 of the Chiniak Highway, head south at the T-junction to Pasagshak. Within a mile the road turns to gravel, but is generally very good. At mile 9, Pasagshak State Recreation Area offers great fishing and camping. As you pass through the Kodiak Rocket Launch Complex, look for a tall radar tower on the right and take a right just before it. A steep, dirt road descends to Fossil Beach where fossils can be found at low tide. Follow the shoreline in a northeasterly direction to get to Narrow Cape. Here you will find World War II bunkers and, on a calm day in April, the grey-whale watching can be amazing.

White Sands Beach At mile 11.5 of Rezanof Drive north of town, the road ends at a lovely beach with good fishing and camping. Thrill seekers can hike the short and very steep hill behind the parking area and ride the 'extreme' buoy swing. One of Kodiak's best hikes, the **Termination Point Loop Trail** (5 miles) starts here.

Port Lions (*Population: 190*) Port Lions (✣ 57°52'5"N, 152°52'48"W) is 19 miles north of the city of Kodiak in Settlers Cove. About half of the Alaska ferry trips to Kodiak make a quick stop in Port Lions. Three quarters of the 250 or so inhabitants are at least part Alutiiq native and the majority of people derive their income from commercial fishing or processing.

Tourist information
ℹ **City of Port Lions** ↘ 454 2332

Where to stay
🏠 **Port Lions Lodge** 620 Main St; ↘ 454 2264; www.portlionslodge.com
🏠 **Whale Pass Lodge** ↘ 454 2500; www.whalepasslodge.com. A pleasant lodge in a remote location near Port Lions.

🏠 **Wilderness Beach Lodge** 431 Main St; ↘ 454 2301; www.wildernessbeachlodge.com. Next to the Port Lions Lodge, offering fishing & simple accommodation.

BRISTOL BAY

The Bristol Bay (*www.visitbristolbay.org*) region, located north of the Alaska Peninsula is home to the largest red salmon fishery on Earth as well as some of Alaska's most remote land. Fishing villages are few and far between and wildlife is abundant with more bears in the region than people – as many as 10,000. Migratory birds pass through by the millions and places like Round Island are home to huge numbers of walrus. Some of the best sport fishing in the world can be enjoyed here. The area is relatively accessible with short flights available from Anchorage to King Salmon, Dillingham or Iliamna. From these transportation hubs, small bush planes and water taxis carry visitors to their final destination.

GETTING THERE AND AWAY These three airlines will get you almost anywhere in the Bristol Bay.

✈ **Alaska Airlines** ↘ 800 252 7522; www.alaskaair.com
✈ **Era/Frontier Air** ↘ 450 7200, 800 478 6779 (TF); www.frontierflying.com

✈ **Peninsula Air** ↘ 771 2640, 800 448 4226 (TF); www.penair.com

DILLINGHAM (*Population: 2,400*) Dillingham (✣ 59°2'48"N, 158°30'31"W) is the largest town in Bristol Bay and the region's economic hub. Located 325 air miles southwest from Anchorage, the town is at the head of Nushagak Bay at the confluence of the Wood and Nushagak Rivers. In addition to a large commercial fishing fleet of almost 600 boats, the Dillingham area is known as one of the best sport fishing destinations in the world. Dillingham is also a staging point for the 4.7-million-acre Togiak National Wildlife Refuge (see page 373) bordering the 25-mile road to the small town of Aleknagik. The Wood-Tikchik State Park (see box on page 369) and the Walrus Islands State Game Sanctuary (see page 374) 60 miles west, are also accessed through Dillingham. The drive north to Aleknagik

The controversial Pebble Mine has brought international media attention to a remote and beautiful part of Alaska, 200 miles southwest of Anchorage, between Lake Clark and Lake Iliamna. The proposed (as of 2008) gold, copper and molybdenum mine has divided the state with environmental advocates and commercial fishermen on one side and those looking for jobs and tax revenue on the other. Possibly the greatest amount of gold ever found has been pitted against the greatest red salmon run on earth. Fishermen and environmentalists worry that the mine, directly upstream from their fishery, will harm fish and could possibly destroy the fishery. They cite the poor environmental track record of mines throughout history and around the world as a reason not to proceed. Proponents of the mine quote the 2,000 temporary jobs created and the 1,000+ permanent jobs during the 30–60-year life of the mine. The mine will also be a significant source of tax revenue for the state.

Located within the circum-Pacific ring of fire, the mine site is less than 70 miles from two large and active volcanoes, Iliamna and Augustine, which can often be seen smoking. The little-understood seismic nature of the area could mean that even a slight earthquake would break the dams and release huge amounts of waste into rivers. As little as two parts per billion of copper can effect a salmon's sense of smell, preventing them identifying mates or even finding their way upstream. Records show that, worldwide, at least two mining waste lake dams fail per year. Alaska has a history of sympathy and leniency toward mining, most likely because it creates more income than any other resource besides oil. Many parts of the state are littered with abandoned commercial and private mining operations and their waste. Having made their money, the owners and workers simply leave and the state and its residents are left with a permanently degraded natural environment and the clean-up bill. These costs are rarely taken into account when determining the value of mining in Alaska.

Owned jointly by Canadian company Northern Dynasty and the US mining company Anglo American, the Pebble Mine is divided into two sections, east and west, with the mine's total value estimated at US$300 billion. The mine is slated to open in 2015 and with the recent (August 2008) defeat of the Clean Water Act, the mine is closer to being approved by the Alaska Department of Natural Resources. Pebble West will likely be a pit-mine two miles wide and several thousand feet deep. With 99% of the materials extracted being valueless, an estimated 2.5 billion tons of earth will need to be removed from the pit using millions of gallons of local water in the process. Dammed lakes are the traditional way to store chemical and other waste from such mines. A proposed dammed lake would be 4.3 miles long and 740ft deep. To date, Northern Dynasty has invested US$225 million into the project with about US$85 million of that going to environmental studies.

Unfortunately, non-renewable resource extraction from Alaska's state lands (let's not forget these lands are owned by residents) virtually always wins out over renewable resources like commercial fishing, timber and tourism. In the case of the Pebble Mine, which has the potential to significantly harm the Bristol Bay salmon fishery, renewable versus non-renewable resources extraction has never been more black and white. For the first time many commercial fishermen are finding themselves in the same camp as the environmentalists. The New York Times perhaps said it best when they asked the simple yet profound question in an article published in August 2008: 'Gold or Fish? It increasingly seems clear we can not have both.'

The 1.6 million-acre Wood-Tikchik State Park is a boater's paradise with rivers, lakes and mountains in equal measure. The landscape is dramatic with the Nushagak lowlands on the east and the Wood River Mountains rising from water edge to the west. A series of 12 very large lakes are connected by short rivers and portages, allowing boaters access to virtually the entire park without having to leave their boat. At the northern end of the lake system, Chikuminuk Lake is closed to the use of motorised watercraft but is accessible by airplane. All other lakes in the park are open to motorised boats.

Camping is allowed anywhere in the park but special permits are required for the Nishlik, Slate, Upnuk and Chikumink Lakes at the north end of the park. The Tikchik River also requires a permit to float or camp. Camping and floating permits are US$100.

GETTING THERE Most visitors fly to the northern end of the park from Dillingham, then paddle the lakes connected by shallow, swift rivers. Paddlers can finish at the small town of Aleknagik and from there, drive south to Dillingham.

TOURIST INFORMATION
Dillingham Ranger Station 842 2641; www.dnr.state.ak.us/parks/units/woodtik.htm or www.southwestalaska.com/bristol/index.html

ACTIVITIES The park is ideal for self-sufficient boaters. Nowhere else in Alaska is there such an extensive interconnected waterway with such amazing and varied scenery. The lakes are also known for their excellent fishing. The treeline is at 900ft, above that the hiking is limitless. Camping is easy on countless sand and gravel beaches distributed throughout the lakes.

(*population: 200*) is pleasant but flat until the mountains begin to rise near Lake Aleknagik. Other than by plane, this is the main access point to the Wood-Tikchik State Park, which starts around Lake Nerka.

Getting around
By air taxi Alaska Airlines, Pen Air, and Frontier Flying Services offer regularly scheduled flights to Dillingham and to many smaller communities in the area. The smaller flying services can be chartered to get everywhere else.

+ **Bay Air** 842 2570; www.bayair-alaska.com
+ **Frontier Flying Services** 800 478 6779
+ **Grant Aviation** 842 2955
+ **Mulchatna Air Service** 842 4500
+ **Nushagak Air** 842 1656
+ **Shannons Air Taxi** 842 5609

+ **Sky Trekking Alaska** 357 3153; www.alaskaonthefly.com
+ **Tikchik Airventures** 842 5841; www.tikchikairventures.com. Charter flights for fishermen, hikers, rafters & adventurers of all kinds.
+ **Tucker Aviation** 842 1023
+ **Yute Air Alaska** 842 5333; www.yuteairtaxi.com

Tourist information
Chamber of Commerce 842 5115; www.dillinghamak.com. Next to the Sam Fox Museum.

Togiak National Wildlife Refuge Office 842 1063; www.togiak.fws.gov; 08.00–17.00 Mon–Fri

Local tours and activities

Alaska Rafting Adventures ☎ 842 5454, www.alaskaraftingadventures.com. Outdoor gear rentals & logistical support.
Dan's Rentals ☎ 877 423 3400; www.dansrentals.com. Inflatable boat rentals & camping gear.
Eskimo Fishing Adventures ☎ 842 5678. Fully equipped tent camp with guided sport fishing services.

Nushagak Outfitters ☎ 842 2710, 842 2711 (summer); www.nushagakoutfitters.com/index.html. With a locally owned remote fishing camp.
Reel Wilderness Adventures ☎ 726 8323; www.reelwild.com. Guided river trips for fishermen or sightseers.
Wild Streams Alaska ☎ 842 3440, 888 684 0177 (TF). Offers comfortable float fishing trips.
Wood River Expeditions ☎ 456 6696. Hunting, fishing & photo trips in the Wood River area.

Where to stay

⌂ **Aleknagik Schoolhouse Inn** (3 rooms) Lake Aleknagik; ☎ 842 1629. Stay in this 1938 former schoolhouse on the lake with all the amenities. plus a BBQ, freezer space for your fish & boats for your use. $$$$
⌂ **Beaver Creek Bed & Breakfast** (5 rooms) ☎ 842 7335; www.dillinghamalaska.com. A number of nice, clean cottages around the property all with kitchens, internet & TV. Free airport shuttle, b/fast incl. US$95pp dbl, US$150 sgl. Car rental for US$70/day. $$$

⌂ **Bunk House** ☎ 842 2715, 888 848 2715 (TF); www.dillinghamservices.com. A few miles outside town on Squaw Creek. Sleeps 8. BBQ, TV, phone, Wi-Fi. US$135 sgl, US$90pp dbl/trpl, US$80pp 4, US$65pp 5–8. $$$
⌂ **The Overlook Bed & Breakfast** (4 rooms) ☎ 842 4524. Overlooking Nushagak Bay & near town, this pleasant B&B offers airport pick-up, a full b/fast, & Wi-Fi. $$–$$$
⌂ **Thai Inn** (4 rooms) ☎ 842 7378; www.thai-inn.com. A lovely Thai-themed house. US$120 dbl. Wi-Fi. b/fast incl. $$

Where to eat

✗ **Windmill Grille** 1544 Kanakanak Rd; ☎ 842 1205; ⏰ 16.00–21.00 Mon–Sat & 11.00–14.00 Wed–Fri. A sustainably run restaurant with recycled energy used just about everywhere. Great pizzas, plus steaks, seafood & some Mexican fare. $$$

✗ **Twin Dragon** 732 Airport Rd, ☎ 842 2172; ⏰ 11.00–15.00, 16.00–20.00 Mon–Sat. Chinese food in the airport. $$

Other practicalities

Post office 9998 D St; ☎ 842 5633; ⏰ 09.00–17.00 Mon–Fri, 09.00–12.00 Sat.
Public library 361 D St; ☎ 842 5610; ⏰ 08.00–18.00 Mon–Fri, 10.00–14.00 Sat. Free Wi-Fi & books for US$0.25.
Kanakanak Hospital 6000 Kanakanak Rd; ☎ 842 5201
D & J Rentals 537 Woodriver Rd; ☎ 842 2222. Van & car rentals.

Ernies Cab ☎ 842 2606
Nushagak Cab ☎ 842 4403
Alaska Commercial 1st & Main St; ☎ 842 5444; ⏰ 07–22.00 Mon–Sat & 09.00–21.00 Sun. The large grocery store in town.
N&N Market 219 Main St; ☎ 842 5283; ⏰ 08.00–21.00 Mon–Sat, 09.00–20.00 Sun. A smaller & more expensive grocery store.

Festivals and events

March
Beaver Round–Up (*www.dillinghamak.com/roundup/roundup.html*) From the 4–8 March, the town comes alive with games, competitions, food, music and a parade.

June
A Century of Salmon Tours of old canneries still in operation. Late June through late July.

July
Salmon Bake Hosted by the Chamber of Commerce on 4 July.

August
No-See-Um Festival A fun celebration with food and games centred around the pesky, hard to see, biting insect, the infamous No-See-Um.

What to see and do
Sam Fox Museum (✆ *842 5610; www.ci.dillingham.ak.us/museum1.html;* ⊕ *10.00–17.00 Mon–Fri; free admission*) A collection of Dillingham area Native and Russian history. The museum was named after Yupik artist and teacher Sam Fox (1935–83) who moved to Dillingham in 1973. He worked with ivory, stone and wood. Some of his work can be seen in the museum.

KING SALMON AND NAKNEK
King Salmon (⊕ 58°41'24"N, 156°39'38"W) and Naknek are connected by a 15-mile road along the Naknek River and are accessible by air and boat only.

Getting there and away Most visitors fly into King Salmon with Alaska Air (see page 367) or Pen Air (see page 367) where the park's headquarters are located, then catch an air taxi out to the river. See *Getting there and around* under King Salmon for air-taxi services, or contact **Branch River Air Service** (✆ *248 3539; www.branchriverair.com*). They offer bear-viewing trips for US$200 (three person minimum) as well as rafting packages for US$1,400 for two people, which includes

---

ANIAKCHAK NATIONAL MONUMENT AND PRESERVE

The little-visited Aniakchak National Monument on the Alaska Peninsula is 150 miles southwest of King Salmon and 10 miles east of Port Heiden. The 600,000-acre monument contains southwest Alaska's most dramatic volcanic activity with a six-mile-wide, 2,000ft-deep collapsed 'caldera' or crater. The caldera was formed when a 7,000ft tall volcano collapsed 3,500 years ago. Recent volcanic activity has built a 2,200ft cinder cone called Vent Mountain inside the caldera. The Aniakchak River flows from Surprise Lake inside the caldera through its rim to the sea. In 1931, an eruption from the monument was heard as far as 200 miles away. Chignik Bay, 45 miles away was covered in ash and, in Bristol Bay, a massive raft of floating pumice five miles in diameter was reported. One year before the eruption, explorer and geologist from Santa Clara University, Bernard Hubbard, flew into the caldera and reported 'a world within a mountain' and called it 'paradise found.' He returned after the 1931 eruption to find his paradise smothered under ash and rock. Today only the faintest signs of life exist within the caldera itself.

GETTING THERE Aniakchak National Monument is accessible by air from King Salmon, a 1.5hr flight, and from Port Heiden, a ½hr flight. The weather is notoriously bad and flights may be delayed for days. Floatplanes can land at Surprise Lake but flights from King Salmon – the monument's main jumping-off point – are expensive.

TOURIST INFORMATION
🏛 **Refuge Visitor Centre** Bldg 4, Fish & Wildlife Service Rd, in King Salmon; ✆ 246 4250 or 246 3339; e akpeninsula@fws.gov; www.nps.gov/ania. Located near the airport.

ACTIVITIES Experienced river rafters can float the Aniakchak River from the put-in at Surprise Lake inside the volcanic caldera to the ocean – generally three to four days. Potential boaters should be very experienced before attempting this trip. Only a few parties attempt this river each year.

7

the flight from King Salmon and a raft for five–seven days. Charter rates are US$400–600/hr.

King Salmon *(Population: 409)* King Salmon is a local hub for flights bringing visitors in and taking commercially harvested red salmon out. Many local residents are descended from Alutiiq natives who relocated from the Katmai area in 1912 when the Novarupta volcanic eruption covered the area in ash.

Tourist information
🄴 **King Salmon Visitor Center** ☎ 246 4250;
🕐 08.00–17.00 daily. Located at the airport.

Getting around
King Salmon Air ☎ 246 6318
Branch River Air ☎ 246 3437;
www.branchriverair.com. Air taxi & raft trips
Aleutian Aviation ☎ 246 3030

C-Air ☎ 246 6318
Egli Air Hauling ☎ 246 3554;
www.heliadventuresak.com. Helicopter & small-plane flightseeing, fishing, & charter service.

Where to stay and eat
🏠 **Rainbow Bend Lodge** (4 rooms) ☎ 888 575 4249; www.bristolbayfishing.com. This unique lodge allows you to customise your trip to suit your interests, whether they be bear viewing, fishing, etc. Boats are available for rent, as are fishing rods & anything else you might need to explore & play. Head out guided or on your own. All-inclusive packages are also available starting at US$1,130pp for 2 days. $$$$–$$$$$
🏠 **King Ko Inn** (16 rooms) King Salmon Airport Rd; ☎ 246 337; www.kingko.com. Located in town with decent duplex cabins. A restaurant ($$$) & bar

are on the premises. Open only in the summer. $$$–$$$$
🏠 **King Salmon Inn** (32 rooms) Mile 13, AK Pen Hwy; ☎ 246 3444; www.kingsalmoninn.com. Accommodation & guided fishing as well as car (US$75) & boat rental. Meals are also served here for US$12–24. $$$.
🏠 **Eddie's Fireplace Inn** 1 Alaska Peninsula Hwy; ☎ 246 3435; 🕐 07.00–23.00 daily. Restaurant & bar (🕐 19.00–02.00 daily) serve three meals & rent videos. Burgers (US$11) & steaks (US$17) are popular. $$$

Other practicalities
Health clinic ☎ 246 3322

Post office 13 Alaska Hwy; ☎ 246 3396; 🕐 08.30–16.30 Mon–Fri, 09.00–13.00 Sat.

Naknek *(Population: 552)* Naknek is a native fishing community with over 6,000 years of Yup'ik and Athabascan history. Today, the town is crowded with lodges and other businesses focused around the visitor. Naknek is also the seat of the Bristol Bay government. Across the river lies South Naknek, a more traditional native village accessible by boat.

Getting around The only flying outfits in Naknek are **King Flying Service** (🕐 *246 4414*) and **Naknek Aviation** (🕐 *246 3385*)

Where to stay
🏠 **Bear Trail Lodge** (5 rooms) ☎ 246 2327; www.fishasl.com. A fancy new lodge right on the water offering all-inclusive packages starting at US$3,900. $$$$$
🏠 **Al-Lous B&B** (1 room) 1717 Aspelund Dr; 246 4270. A private room with kitchen. $$$

🏠 **Naknek Hotel** (D&D Hotel) (5 rooms) 1 Alaska Peninsula Hwy; ☎ 246 4430. Decent rooms with a restaurant (🕐 08.00–midnight daily; $$) in the building. $$$
🏠 **A little house B&B** (1 room) Michael St; ☎ 246 4486. Self-contained, private cabin with everything you need. $$

ALAGNAK WILD RIVER

Flowing from the rugged Aleutian Range near Katmai National Park, the Alagnak River is one of Alaska's most beautiful and pristine rivers. A boat trip down this calm river gives visitors an amazing experience of the area's scenery, wildlife and native cultures. The river is known for its excellent sport fishing. During peak fishing times, the number of fly-in trips from King Salmon and Naknek lodges can be a little annoying because of the noise. During the early spring, you will have the river to yourself and the mosquitoes will be at a minimum.

GETTING THERE Flights can be chartered from King Salmon, Iliamna and Anchorage to the Nonvianuk or Kukaklek Lakes at the headwaters of the river.

TOURIST INFORMATION
Z **Refuge Visitor Center** Bldg 4, Fish & Wildlife Service Rd; ℄ 246 4250, 246 3339; e akpeninsula@fws.gov; www.nps.gov/alag. Located near the airport.

ACTIVITIES Rafting or kayaking the river to sightsee or fish is the most popular way to explore. Rapids up to class III can be encountered. The river 'braids' as it travels toward the sea, making decent route-finding skills a must. Indeed, the word 'Alagnak' means 'making mistakes' or 'going the wrong way'. Native Alaskans from a number of groups own the land along the river and they fish and hunt there during the summer.

✕ Where to eat and drink

✕ **D&D Restaurant** 1 Alaska Peninsula Hwy; ℄ 246 4430; ⊕ 08.00–midnight daily. Located in the Naknek Hotel. Italian & America food with decent pizza. $$
✕ **Nacho Mama's** Mile 3 Alaska Peninsula Hwy; ℄ 246 4688. Good Mexican food & burgers from a drive-through place. $$

♀ **Fisherman's Bar** 73 Alaska Peninsula Hwy; ℄ 246 4252; ⊕ 10.00–closing
♀ **Hadfield's Bar** 101 Main St; ℄ 246 4440; ⊕ 10.00–closing
♀ **Red Dog Inn** 87 Monsen St; ℄ 246 4213; ⊕ 10.00–closing

Other practicalities

Public library 101 Main St; ℄ 246 4465; ⊕ 10.00–18.00 Tue & Thu, 09.00–17.00 Fri & Sat. Wi-Fi.

Camai Clinic 2 School Rd; ℄ 246 6155. Naknek

TOGIAK (*Population: 802*) Togiak (⊕ 59°3'33"N, 160°22'59"W) is located at the head of Togiak Bay, 67 miles west of Dillingham. The town is entirely within the 4.7-million-acre Togiak National Wildlife Refuge and is a staging point for visiting the Walrus Island Game Sanctuary 25 miles offshore. Togiak's residents subsist in this traditional Yup'ik village primarily on commercial herring and salmon fishing as well as subsistence food gathering. Togiak is accessible by small plane from Dillingham. Try **Alaska Island Air** (℄ *493 5120*) or **Coupchiak Aviation** (℄ *842 1705*).

Other practicalities

Post office 9998 Airport Way; ℄ 493 5228; ⊕ 08.15–12.00 & 13.00–16.45 Mon–Fri, 09.15–12.45 Sat.

What to see and do
Togiak National Wildlife Refuge The 4.7-million-acre Togiak National Wildlife Refuge encompasses a beautiful 600-mile stretch of coastline on the northern side of Bristol

Bay. The land has changed little in the past few thousand years with Yu'pik natives leading predominantly subsistence lives and all five species of salmon providing the land's lifeblood. All the major Alaskan terrestrial mammals live here with more than 150,000 caribou, moose, brown and black bear, wolverine, wolves, red fox, marmots, beavers and others. At least 200 species of birds can be found in the refuge as well, particularly at Cape Peirce where millions of seabirds nest on high sea cliffs.

Walrus Island State Game Sanctuary Located 25 miles from Togiak, the Walrus Island State Game Sanctuary is famous for hosting large numbers of walrus during the summer. A number of rocky islands form the Walrus Islands. Round Island is the best known with 14,000 walrus once counted in a single day. Camping is allowed on the northeast side of the island and a US$50/pp permit is required. Visitor numbers are tightly controlled so permits need to be obtained as far in advance as possible (1 September the year before). Only 15 visitors are allowed per day with only 12 staying overnight. Permits are available for trips between 1 May and 31 August with July being the best but also the most 'crowded'. Obtain permits on the website (*www.wildlifenews.alaska.gov/index.cfm?adfg=refuge.rnd_is*).

Getting there Togiak lies in the heart of the refuge and is the best jumping-off point for almost anywhere in the refuge, including the Walrus Islands. Flights are available daily from Anchorage to Dillingham and from Dillingham to Togiak. A number of very expensive transportation and guided options exist from Togiak to the Walrus Islands.

Don Winkelmen's Round Island Boat Charters ℡ 493 5127
Togiak Outfitters ℡ 493 5000 or 522 6259; www.visitbristolbay.org/togiakoutfitters. Paul Markoff offers trips to the Walrus Islands for US$650 in a 12hr round trip, as well as cultural tours of Togiak for US$20/pp. Paul is a very friendly guy & can find a place for you to stay or camp in town if bad weather alters your schedule.
Walrus Islands Expeditions ℡ 235 9349; www.alaskawalrusisland.com. 2- & 3-day trips to the Walrus Islands & along the coast of the Togiak National Wildlife Refuge. Custom trip & drop-offs are available.

Tourist information
🛈 **Togiak National Wildlife Refuge Office** 6 Main St; ℡ 842 1063; e togiak@fws.gov; www.togiak.fws.gov

Activities There are no roads, trails, campgrounds or any other facilities in the refuge. The refuge's many rivers are a natural place to look for transportation and

---

BECHAROF NATIONAL WILDLIFE REFUGE

Located at the base of the Alaska Peninsula, the 477,000-acre refuge is a paradise of rivers, fjords, glaciers, mountains and, most notably, Becharof Lake. The lake covers an astounding 300,000 acres and is the second largest in Alaska. Millions of salmon spawn in the lake each summer, attracting large numbers of brown bears and other animals.

GETTING THERE Regular flights serve King Salmon from Anchorage and charter flights can deposit visitors inside the park.

TOURIST INFORMATION
🛈 **Refuge Visitor Center** Bldg 4, Fish & Wildlife Service Rd; ℡ 246 4250 or 246 3339; e akpeninsula@fws.gov; http://becharof.fws.gov. Located near the airport.

a great many raft trips are available for the self-sufficient adventurer. The Kanektok, Goodnews, and Togiak Rivers are the longest and calmest in the refuge.

THE ALEUTIAN RUN

For many, riding the Alaska ferry, the MV *Tustumena,* from Homer to Unalaska is the adventure of a lifetime. The journey takes four days with stops in a number of very remote native villages along Alaska Peninsula. With clear weather, the scenery is unrivalled. Jagged peaks, volcanoes, shipwrecks and wildlife are all in abundance. A naturalist on board answers questions, points out wildlife and gives a number of informative slide talks throughout the trip.

WHEN TO SAIL The best time of year to make this voyage all depends on the kind of experience you want to have. The weather can be good or bad at any time of year, but in general May is more stormy and therefore the boat less crowded and snow will be present. June is much greener and as a result the boat more crowded. July has the best weather, but the ferry is generally filled to capacity.

BOOKING ONBOARD ACCOMMODATION Accommodation on the 'Trusty Tusty' come in many forms, but only one of them involves a bed. The rest are a variation of the floor or a bench.

Cabins Cabins will add significantly to the cost but are a good idea for all but the most penniless adventurer. However, getting a cabin is not as easy as simply having the desire and the cash. Since the ferry travels this route so infrequently, the cabins for the mid-summer months sell out in a matter of days and sometimes hours. Schedules are generally posted mid-winter but sometimes they appear as late as February. It's best to be in constant contact with the ferry office. When the tickets go on sale, buy what you need if it's available because it may not be there in a few hours. Most of the cabins have two bunks and a small bathroom. The two cabins at the back of the ship are best for smokers as they provide easy access to the deck. In addition to the standard rooms, there are two cabins with four beds, but without a bathroom. Cabin 202 has four beds and can sleep two more on the floor. Cabin 220 also has four beds, but is smaller.

Advice for sleeping on deck For those travelling on the cheap, and not booking a cabin, here are a few tips that will dramatically improve your experience on board. Bring most of your own food supplies, as the food on the ferry is expensive and barely edible. A microwave and hot water are available but no stove, kitchen or fridge. A comfortable place to sleep is of the utmost importance on a ferry ride of this length. Bring a pillow and sleeping bag or blanket as well as a pad. Ferry officials recommend passengers get to the ferry two hours before departure. Normally, this is more than enough time, but for the trip to Unalaska, get there four or more hours ahead. Check in at the counter in Homer and form a queue at the fence at the base of the dock so you are sure to be the first one to board.

Once on board head upstairs to the cabin deck and race for the front of the ship where there are a number of benches with tables and some reclining chairs, all with great views. Assuming you're here first you have your choice of the best spots. The padded benches with the tables are generally the best since they afford some privacy while sleeping and give you an area to spread out and prepare food or read. Be sure to get a table with the six-foot benches. The port booth is best. The reclining seats and floor are also an option.

Yet another option is the Solarium, a must for first time Aleutian run passengers who want to cut their teeth properly. The Solarium is the ship's top deck and is partially covered where tents are allowed. The views are unrivalled here and the open air is never more than a few steps away. Heaters hang from the ceiling and I've seen people use them for heating food, though I'm sure ferry authorities would discourage this. The drawbacks to the Solarium are that the smoke stacks are very near and very loud but can be used to warm your hands when it's cold. The upper decks move more in heavy seas, so this spot may not be ideal for those prone to sea-sickness.

EXCURSIONS To make the most of your time 'off board' and to help you explore the small towns along the way, bring a bicycle on the ferry. The cost is just US$54 all the way to Unalaska from Homer. Many of the small Aleutian towns have miles of road that are only possible to explore by bike in the short time the ferry is in port.

If you're off exploring, remember to leave plenty of time to get back to the ferry. If you are left behind, a very expensive charter flight to the ferry's next stop awaits. When you disembark the ferry, be sure to ask the purser (the officer responsible for administration on the ship) exactly what time to arrive back. Generally the horn sounds 15–30 minutes before departure, but they often forget.

CHIGNIK (*Population: 59*) Chignik (⊕ 56°17'54"N, 158°24'16"W) is the ferry's first stop after the 250-mile ride from Kodiak. The Chignik area is an outdoor man's paradise with great fishing, hunting, bear viewing and hiking. The town is simple with 80 buildings and about 120 people, 60% of whom are native Alaskan. Lovely hills carpeted in lush green tundra rise on both sides of the bay and on a clear day Mt Veniaminof (8,225ft) can be seen. A large fish-processing plant sits at the base of the dock and a boardwalk and adjacent road lead through town. The town has a small gift shop right on the main drag and a grocery store run by Trident Seafoods. The city building at the northwest end of town rents comfortable rooms for US$80 (✆ 749 2280) and can answer questions.

Unlike some small Alaska Peninsula towns, Chignik has much to offer the visitor. For those just getting off the ferry while it's in port, the **Donut Hole** (walk down the dock and turn right. Follow the boardwalk until it ends, the shop is on the right) is the spot to visit. Get there before everyone else or they may run out! Beside the Donut Hole there are a number of short hikes to occupy your time in port. A road follows the river at the far end of town by the city building to a small reservoir. The beach is also pleasant to stroll down. It's amusing to watch passengers flood off the ferry seeking donuts while locals wait to board the ferry to have burgers at the ferry restaurant.

Getting there
🚢 **Alaska Ferry** ✆ 800 526 6731, 786 3800 (local); www.dot.state.ak.us/amhs.
✈ **Peninsula Air** ✆ 771 2640, 800 448 4226 (TF); www.penair.com

✈ **Alaska Airlines** ✆ 800 252 7522; www.alaskaair.com

Where to stay
🏠 **Lindholm's Lodge** (4 rooms) ✆ 696 4037; www.fishchignik.com. A pleasant but simple fishing lodge at Chignik Lake outside the town of Chignik. Week-long trip starts at US$3,500pp for an all-inclusive package with fishing & wildlife viewing. $$$$$
🏠 **Eagles Roost B&B** (2 rooms) ✆ 840 2273. Located in Chignik Lagoon, 5mins by plane from Chignik, this affordable accommodation offers 3 meals & friendly company. Your host can also help you find local guides for fishing & sightseeing. $$
🏠 **Chignik Bay Alaska Adventures** ✆ 360 671 1423 (winter), 749 2448 (summer); e johnr@ chignikbayadventures.com; www.chignikbayadventures.com. A nice lodge/home in Chignik town centre. Comfortable accommodation possibilities with lake & ocean views. Fishing, hunting & sightseeing trips. Wi-Fi.

A dramatic spine of glaciated volcanoes splits the Refuge with rolling hills and wetland on the north side and abrupt wind battered sea-cliffs and beaches on the south side. Many of the area's volcanoes are still active and frequently smoke. Virtually all of Alaska major wildlife species can be found here with the exception of black bears. As with most places in coastal Alaska, salmon provide the backbone of the ecosystem with all five species spawning in the Refuge's many streams.

GETTING THERE Chignik is the closest town to the refuge but the headquarters is located in King Salmon. Access is by plane and boat.

TOURIST INFORMATION
Refuge Visitor Center Bldg 4, Fish & Wildlife Service Rd; ☎ 246 4250 or 246 3339; e akpeninsula@fws.gov; www.alaskapeninsula.fws.gov Located near the airport.

🏠 **Chignik Lake** A small native Alutiiq village just a few miles away. Simple accommodation opportunities are available, as well as a number of guides including Ronald Lind (see below).

Local guide
Ronald Lind ☎ 845 2255 or 569 5463; www.visitbristolbay.org/bearskincreek. A local guide of Alutiiq-Swedish descent who is extremely knowledgeable & friendly. Fly fishing & photography trips can be arranged for US$350pp.

SAND POINT (*Population: 958*) Nine hours after leaving Chignik, the 'Tusty' docks in the small fishing village of Sand Point (⊕ 55°20'12"N, 160°29'36"W) on Popof Island. Many of the town's residents are of native Unangan and Scandinavian descent. The town has a small health clinic and a dentist flies in when needed. Many residents live on a combination of store-bought food and subsistence fare such as kelp, berries, ptarmigan, fish, gull eggs, clams, and bison. Each year the Shumagin Corporation sells permits to hunt bison from the island's herd of 120, established in 1955. The area has a mild maritime climate and is sometimes called the 'Banana Belt of the Aleutians', with 21°C/70°F summertime temperatures fairly common.

Getting there and away
🚢 **Alaska Ferry** ☎ 800 526 6731, 786 3800 (local); www.dot.state.ak.us/amhs

✈ **Peninsula Air** ☎ 771 2640, 800 448 4226 (TF); www.penair.com

Tourist information Sand Point doesn't have a visitor centre but most questions can be answered by the **City of Sand Point** (☎ *383 2696*).

Hiking and recreation Unga Island next door is a popular place to visit with a petrified sequoia forest as well as a ghost town – the remnants of an old gold mine. On the east side of Sand Point there are some nice hikes past the school. This is also a good place to see bison.

Where to stay
🏠 **Anchor Inn Motel** (17 rooms) 189 Maine St; ☎ 383 3272 ext. 120; e motel@shumagin.com; ⏰ 09.00–16.00 Mon, 10.00–15.00 Tue–Sat. Simple rooms in a variety of sizes with refrigerators & microwaves. Guests get 50% off pizza at the Sand Point Tavern. Rental cars for US$104.95/day. TV. $$
🏠 **Marine View B&B** (9 rooms) 247 Chichagof St; ☎ 383 5607. Located just uphill from the Anchor Inn Motel. Kitchen. Wi–Fi. $$

Southwest Alaska **THE ALEUTIAN RUN**

7

✕ Where to eat and drink

✕ **Aleutian China** 100 Main St; ✎ 383 5676;
⏲ 10.30–midnight. Located at the AC store, they
serve Chinese & American food & alcohol. $$
✕ **Bozo Burgers** ✎ 383 4777; ⏲ with ferry. A
local favourite serving burgers, sandwiches & ice
cream. Always open when the ferry is in town. $$
✕ **Harbor Café** ✎ 383 3677; ⏲ with ferry.
Overlooking the harbour this pleasant little place
serves burgers, sandwiches & has a salad bar. Clam
chowder on Fri. $$
✕ **Trident Seafoods Galley** ✎ 383 4848. Visitors are
welcome to eat at the Trident Galley in the Trident

processing plant. Get a meal ticket at the main
office. $$
♀ **Sand Point Tavern** 189 Main St; ✎ 383 5050;
⏲ 15.00–02.00 Sun–Thu, 15.00–03.00 Fri–Sat.
This dismal watering hole is usually brimming with
Sand Point characters. Mixed drinks & beer as well
as a variety of frozen foods they reheat & serve
'fresh'. Pool tables, football & a big screen TV. $$
✕ **Cut 'R Loose Coffee** ✎ 383 2633; ⏲ with ferry.
Located just uphill from St Nicholas Chapel, this cute
little café serves ice cream & hot drinks, & has a
small selection of native artwork. Wi-Fi. $

Other practicalities

Alaska Commercial ✎ 383 3111; ⏲ 08.00–20.00
Mon–Fri, 10.00–18.00 Sat, 11.00–15.00 Sun.
The local grocery store with a little bit of everything.
Post office 9998 Main St; ✎ 383 2955;
⏲ 09.00–17.00 Mon–Fri, 10.00–12.00 Sat. On the
east side of town by Toy's Plus & Napa Auto.
Shumagin Island Gifts ✎ 383 2161; ⏲ with ferry.
Toy's Plus ✎ 383 5614. Toys, food & video rentals.

Shumigan Corporation ✎ 383 3525; www.shumagin.com
Unga Corporation ✎ 383 5215
Health Clinic ✎ 383 3151
City Taxi ✎ 383 2000
Sand Point School ✎ 383 2393. Located on the far
eastern side of town off Red Cove Rd, the school
has a nice public gym & a swimming pool with
showers available.

What to see and do The ferry generally remains in port for a little over two hours.
From the ferry dock follow South Harbor Access Road toward town – just under
one mile. After you pass the harbour you will cross a bridge over the lagoon. On
the right you will see the Russian Orthodox Church, **St Nicholas Chapel**, built
in 1933, which is on the register of National Historical Places. Follow the road
uphill passing Trident Seafoods on the left and the Anchor Inn Motel on the right.
Take a right at Sand Point Avenue to explore the 'town centre'. Behind the AC
store a small cemetery is worth a look. Ingrid at **Cut 'R Loose Coffee** is very
friendly and can answer just about any question you may have about Sand Point.

KING COVE (*Population: 750*) Seven or so hours after leaving Sand Point, the
Tustumena arrives in the small fishing town of King Cove (✦ 55°4'20"N,
162°19'5"W). The Agdaagux tribe is based here and about 50% of the residents are
native. Peter Pan Seafoods has an enormous fish processing plant here, employing
some 500 seasonal workers. With the cannery at its core, the town thrives on
commercial fishing all year round. A total of 62 residents hold commercial fishing
permits and the annual catch is generally worth in excess of US$6 million.

Getting there and away

🚢 **Alaska Ferry** ✎ 800 526 6731, 786 3800
(local); www.dot.state.ak.us/amhs

✈ **Peninsula Air** ✎ 771 2640, 800 448 4226 (TF);
www.penair.com

The **AEB Hovercraft** (✎ 497 2070) provides a service from Lenard Harbor near
King Cove to Cold Bay every Tuesday, Thursday and Sunday for US$76pp one-
way. Vehicles are US$0.06/lb and an ATV is US$100.

Tourist information

☑ **City of King Cove** ✎ 497 2340;
www.cityofkingcove.com

Where to stay

⌂ **Salmonberry B&B** (1 room) ☏ 497 2856. A room in the host's home with b/fast & dinner served. $$

Where to eat and drink

✕ **King Cove China** Windy Walkway; ☏ 497 5676; ⏰ 12.30–01.00 daily. Decent Chinese food. $$

✕ **Uptown Pizza** ☏ 497 3161. Tasty pizzas delivered or for pick-up. $$$

Other practicalities

Village Corporation ☏ 497 2312
My Cab ☏ 497 2226
Alaska Commercial 1 Bayview Dr; ☏ 497 263; ⏰ 07–22.00 Mon–Sat & 09.00–21.00 Sun

Post office 38 Windy Walkway; ☏ 497 2363; ⏰ 09.00–17.00 Mon–Fri, 12.00–14.00 Sat

What to see and do With just an hour or two to explore town, it's hard to see very much. Monolithic piles of king crab pots line the streets, behind them almost sheer walls of green tundra rise up. The town is sandwiched between the ocean and King Cove Lagoon with a small cemetery and church at the east end of town. A road follows the lagoon north 4.5 miles to the airport. Take a left just after the airport and you will come to Lenard Harbor or you can hike west past the runway to Belkofski Bay. Flights are often cancelled because of high winds. A 27-mile road is proposed through the Izembek National Wildlife Refuge to access the runway at Cold Bay.

COLD BAY (*Population: 90*) Two hours after leaving King Cove, the ferry arrives in the very small, mostly non-native town of Cold Bay (⊕ 55°12'33"N, 162°42'51"W). On a clear day the scenery is stunning with the Shishaldin Volcano (9,372ft), 50 miles to the west on Unimak Island, Frosty Peak (5,803ft) just behind town and Pavlov Volcano (8,200ft) to the east.

IZEMBEK NATIONAL WILDLIFE REFUGE

Izembek National Wildlife Refuge is the nation's smallest at just 315,000 acres in area, but it is also one of North America's most important. Izembek Lagoon, on the north side of the Alaskan Peninsula and accessible by car and plane from Cold Bay, is the heart of the refuge. The lagoon has the largest expanse of eel grass on Earth and is home to hundreds of thousands of migratory birds and, most notably, a significant portion of the worldwide populations of Pacific black brant (population 150,000), Taverner's Canada geese (population 55,000), emperor geese (population 6,000) and 23,000 threatened Steller's eiders. The refuge is also home to all five species of salmon and most of Alaska's marine and terrestrial mammals.

GETTING THERE The small town of Cold Bay is within the refuge and around 40 miles of gravel roads provide access to a very small portion of the park from town. Further access is provided by plane and boat from Cold Bay. The Alaska ferry serves Cold Bay as does Peninsula Air (see opposite).

TOURIST INFORMATION
🏛 **Izembek Visitor Center** 1 Izembek St; ☏ 532 2445; e izembek@fws.gov; www.izembek.fws.gov. Located in Cold Bay.

Getting there and away While Cold Bay and King Cove are currently only connected by the Alaska Ferry and the hovercraft, a law was passed in March 2009 allowing for a road to connect the two towns. This will be a boon for King Cove where flights are grounded more than 50% of the time due to gale-force winds. A completion date for the road has not been announced.

🚢 **Alaska Ferry** ☎ 800 526 6731, 786 3800 (local); www.dot.state.ak.us/amhs

✈ **Peninsula Air** ☎ 771 2640, 800 448 4226 (TF); www.penair.com

For information on the **AEB Hovercraft** to King Cove see page 378.

Tourist information and guide services

🏛 **City of Cold Bay** ☎ 532 2401; www.coldbayak.com; ⏱ 08.00–12.00 Mon–Fri

K Pursue Guide Service ☎ 532 2612. Sightseeing, hunting, fishing & accommodation.
R&R Guide Service ☎ 532 2767

Where to stay

⌂ **Cold Bay Lodge** (21 rooms) ☎ 532 2767; www.coldbaylodge.com. Simple accommodations in town. The friendly host can help arrange guided trips. 3 meals/day are US$60 in addition to the cost of the room. Travellers can also pop in for a meal at US$16 for b/fast & lunch or US$30 for dinner. Wi-Fi. $$$

⌂ **Bearfoot Inn Alaska** (8 rooms) ☎ 532 2437. Groceries & standard (no bathroom) as well as deluxe (with bathroom) rooms for rent. Located right in town. $$

Other practicalities

Allen & Letty Truck Rental ☎ 532 2478
Health clinic ☎ 532 2000
Post office | Letty Av; ☎ 532 2464:
⏱ 09.00–17.00 Mon–Fri, 12.00–14.00 Sat

Public library ☎ 532 2878; ⏱ 19.00–21.00 Mon–Fri

What to see and do On a good day, Cold Bay is a wonderful place to explore with wild country in all directions including the 307,982-acre Izembek National Wildlife Refuge (see box on page 379). For those just hopping off the ferry while it's in port, there are a few options to see the country and maybe even some wildlife. The onboard naturalist usually organises an excursion in a van to the refuge. A fiercely competitive lottery is held before the ferry arrives in port to select the few who get to go on the excursion. For those not selected, a bike is handy. Occasionally passengers can hitch a ride with the Tustumena crew who sometimes take a vehicle inland for fishing or sightseeing. Making friends with various members of the crew is therefore advisable and useful. A truck or bike can be taken just a few miles southeast to a lovely clear river flowing through the tundra. Great silver salmon fishing is found here in the late summer and autumn and steelhead in the spring. Birds and World War II debris can be seen in the tundra.

North of town, a gravel road winds through the tundra for 15 miles to Grant Point, where a viewing platform overlooks the Izembek Lagoon. This is a wonderful place to observe everything from shore birds to sea otters and even whales. A number of interpretive panels explain the environment and animals. Along the road, bears, fox and caribou are common. Local guides can sometimes be arranged last minute for a quick guided tour of the refuge.

Those staying in town can walk to the Izembek Refuge headquarters at the northeast end of town. This tiny centre has some good wildlife displays and large maps showing the surrounding countryside and the refuge. The knowledgeable staff can answer questions.

During World War II, the area served as a strategic airbase called Fort Randall and was home to nearly 20,000 personnel. The 10,000-foot runway still exists and is used daily by small aircraft.

FALSE PASS (*Population: 39*) About five hours after leaving Cold Bay, the ferry veers north and heads through the narrow and dramatic Isanotski Strait to the small town of False Pass (⊕ 54°49'40"N, 163°23'57"W) on Unimak Island – the first Aleutian Island. The town's name is derived from the shallow channel, which is inaccessible to larger vessels. When a cannery was built in the early 1900s, native Unangan migrated to the area for work. The cannery burned down in 1984 but the vast majority of the 60 or so residents still make their living from the sea. Incomes are supplemented by subsistence hunting, fishing and gathering. Sanak Island to the south provides home for geese, seals and semi-wild cattle.

Getting there and away
🚢 **Alaska Ferry** ✆ 800 526 6731, 786 3800 (local); www.dot.state.ak.us/amhs

✈ **Peninsula Air** ✆ 771 2640, 800 448 4226 (TF); www.penair.com

Tourist information
ℹ **City of False Pass** ✆ 548 2319

ℹ **Isanotski Corporation** ✆ 548 2217

✕ Where to eat
Isanotski Store, at the base of the ferry dock, sells food and a little bit of everything, including False Pass T-shirts. Fishermen frequent this store, stocking up for the trip to Bristol Bay. Local children sometimes sell glass balls (old Japanese fishing net floats). Locals occasionally host a salmon bake for ferry guests at the base of the dock.

Other practicalities
Post office 170 Umiak Dr; ⏱ 13.00–16.00 Mon–Sat

Health clinic ✆ 548 2742

What to see
Fog is common during the summer but, on a clear day, Isanotski Volcano (8,104ft) is an impressive sight right behind town. Behind Isanotski, the massive Shishaldin Volcano (9,372ft) has the quintessential volcano look. Unimak Island is the only Aleutian Island where brown bears are found.

AKUTAN (*Population: 796*) Ten hours after leaving False Pass, the ferry arrives in Akutan (⊕ 54°8'42"N, 165°48'5"W). A small sign on the dock welcomes visitors. Residents – about 20% of whom are native Unangan – work in the fisheries. The large Trident Seafoods cannery west of town processes crab, cod and pollock.

History
The town is on the traditional site of an Unangan village. In 1878, the Russian Western Fur and Trading Company built a fur storage warehouse, fish plant and a church. In 1912, the Pacific Whaling Company built a whale processing facility across from Akutan, operating until 1939. Akutan residents were evacuated from their homes when the Japanese attacked Unalaska in 1942. Natives were interned in southeast Alaska near Ketchikan until 1944 when villagers were allowed to return, however many chose not to.

Getting there and away
🚢 **Alaska Ferry** ✆ 800 526 6731, 786 3800 (local); www.dot.state.ak.us/amhs

✈ **Peninsula Air** ✆ 771 2640, 800 448 4226 (TF); www.penair.com

Tourist information
City of Akutan ☎ 698 2228

Akutan Corporation ☎ 698 2206

Other practicalities
Health clinic ☎ 698 2208

Post office 101 Salmon Berry Rd; ☎ 698 2200;
⏰ 09.00–12.00 & 13.00–17.00 Mon–Fri,
13.00–17.00 Sat

What to see and do Visitors generally have less than one hour in port. Boardwalks lead through some of town but for extended hikes, walk along the beach west at low tide. The Alexander Nevsky Chapel, built in 1912, is just a few minutes' walk from the ferry dock and is surrounded by a scenic cemetery. Mount Akutan (4,275ft) is at the far end of the island.

UNALASKA (*Population: 4,300*) The small, but very busy, fishing community of Unalaska (⊕ 53°53'22"N, 166°31'38"W) is located at the end of the Alaska ferry Aleutian run or it can be reached by a three-hour flight from Anchorage. Unalaska occupies a bit of land where Amaknak Island nearly touches the island of Unalaska. About half of the town's residents live on Amaknak Island, the focus of commercial fishing, the airport, Dutch Harbor and where most new development is taking place. The city centre of Unalaska is on Unalaska Island on a lovely beach between Unalaska Lake and Iliuliuk Bay. Here you will find the visitor centre, the iconic Holy Ascension Russian Orthodox Cathedral, the Ounalashka Corporation building and some local neighbourhoods.

For 20 years, Unalaska has been the top seafood-producing port in the country; the Discovery Channel show *The Deadliest Catch* – about Bering Sea commercial king crab fishing – has turned their job (and the town) into a household name. A staggering 600 million pounds of seafood pass through Unalaska every year. Often eclipsed by the hustle and bustle of the fishing industry, the natural beauty of Unalaska Island is not to be missed. Furthermore, the history of the area from the Native Unangan people to the Russians and World War II has been well preserved and is visible everywhere.

History The Unangan (preferable to the name Aleut) people inhabited the Aleutians and Unalaska Island for many thousands of years before the first Russian fur traders began arriving in the 1740s. Despite the harsh environment, the Unangan thrived. At least 25 villages sites have been identified within two miles of Unalaska.

World War II affected Unalaska and there is evidence everywhere of gun bunkers, Quonset huts (military shelters made of corrugated steel sheets, the equivalent of a Nissen hut) and barracks in what is sometimes called the 'Forgotten War'. In June 1942, Japanese soldiers invaded the Aleutian Islands of Kiska and Attu, making it the first time since 1812 that American soil was occupied by a foreign force. Earlier that month, the Japanese had bombed Unalaska for two days, leaving more than 100 soldiers and civilians dead. Native residents of Unalaska Island were immediately sent to camps in southeast Alaska where many died from disease. When they returned in 1945, many found their homes and villages bulldozed and military junk littering their island. In 2002, the World War II National Historic Area on Amaknak Island was created to preserve the unique World War II history of the island.

Commercial king crab fishing dominated the economy in Unalaska through the 1970s until a crab population crash in the 1980s slowed the fishing industry considerably. Other rich fish sources emerged including pollock, halibut, black cod and snow crab. During the concentrated fishing seasons of the 1980s and 1990s, the population of Unalaska would sometimes swell to 15,000 or more. Today,

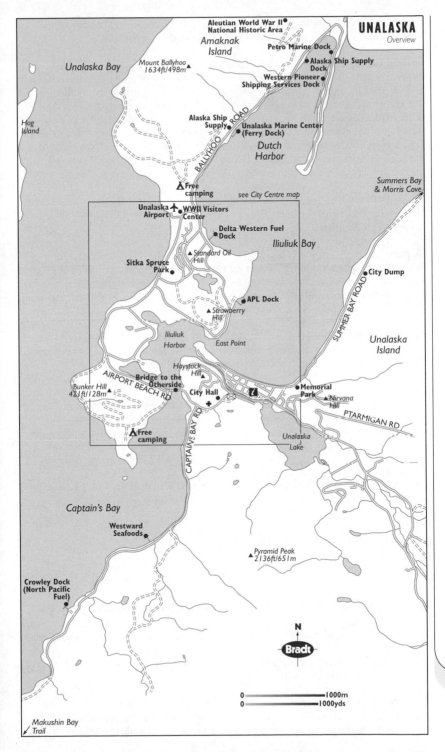

UNALASKA
Overview

Aleutian World War II
National Historic Area

Amaknak
Island

Unalaska Bay

Mount Ballyhoo
1634ft/498m ▲

Petro Marine Dock

Alaska Ship Supply
Dock

Western Pioneer
Shipping Services Dock

Hog
Island

Alaska Ship
Supply

Unalaska Marine Center
(Ferry Dock)

*Dutch
Harbor*

BALLYHOO ROAD

⛺ Free
camping

*Summers Bay
& Morris Cove*

see City Centre map

Unalaska ✈
Airport

WWII Visitors
Center

Delta Western Fuel
Dock

Iliuliuk Bay

▲ Standard Oil
Hill

Sitka Spruce
Park

City Dump

APL Dock

SUMMER BAY ROAD

▲ Strawberry
Hill

*Unalaska
Island*

*Iliuliuk
Harbor*

East Point

Haystack
Hill ▲

AIRPORT BEACH RD

Bunker Hill
421ft/128m ▲

Bridge to the
Otherside

City Hall ✚

Memorial
Park

▲ Nirvana
Hill

CAPTAINS BAY RD

PTARMIGAN RD

⛺ Free
camping

*Unalaska
Lake*

Captain's Bay

Westward
Seafoods

Pyramid Peak
2136ft/651m ▲

Crowley Dock
(North Pacific
Fuel)

N
Bradt

0 ———— 1000m
0 ———— 1000yds

*Makushin Bay
Trail*

fishing is still the economy's cornerstone. The fishing seasons are now spread out over the year with only slight population influxes during the winter.

Getting there and away Though tourism has increased somewhat in recent years, largely because of the popular TV show, *The Deadliest Catch*, Unalaska has remained one of Alaska's hidden gems. The expense and difficulty of the trip is the greatest deterrent with ferries making the trip just once a month (a trip costs US$700–800), with Alaska Air charging about the same for a round-trip ticket. An ideal way to travel to Unalaska – and a monumental adventure in its own right – is to ride the Alaska ferry to Unalaska. After a week or so in Unalaska, fly one-way with Alaska Air back to Anchorage.

By air
Alaska Airlines (↘ *800 252 7522; www.alaskaair.com*) Three flights a day (except Wednesday and Sunday when there are only two flights) for US$700–1000. Alaska Air uses Pen Air planes.

By ferry
Alaska Marine Highway (↘ *465 3941; www.dot.state.ak.us/amhs*) The MV *Tustumena* travels to Unalaska once a month from Homer. The 1,700 nautical-mile trip takes four days with short stops in a number of small towns along the Alaska Peninsula, including Kodiak. For more information on taking the ferry to Unalaska, see page 375.

Getting around Though Unalaska is a small island, a car is extremely handy. Where 4x4 trucks are available, they are recommended for those who want to explore the small but rough and extremely beautiful road system.

By car
🚗 **BC Vehicle Rental** 300 Airport Beach Way; ↘ 581 6777; www.bcvehiclerental.com. Located in the airport with cars out back.

🚗 **North Port Rentals** 429 Airport Cargo Bldg; ↘ 581 3880; www.northportrentals.net; ⊕ 06.00–21.00 daily. Located in a building adjacent to the airport, these guys are friendly & rent out mobile phones in addition to trucks.

By taxi and shuttle
🚗 **Mr Kab** ↘ 581 2000, 359 2000 (mobile); e taranto_sheila@yahoo.com.

Miss Sheila offers World War II tours & transportation.
🚗 **Alaskan Taxi** ↘ 581 2129.

By bike
🚲 **Unalaska City Community Center** ↘ 581 1251. Occasionally bikes & other sporting equipment can be rented here.

Tourist information
ℹ **Ounalashka Corporation** 400 Salmon Way; ↘ 581 1276; www.ounalashka.com. The corporation was formed in 1973 & manages native affairs on the Island of Unalaska. They own much of the land on the island & ask that everyone purchase a land use permit before venturing onto the island.

ℹ **Unalaska Convention and Visitors Bureau** ↘ 581 2612, 877 581 2612 (TF); www.unalaska.info. Located on 5th St, the tiny office is a great place to gather maps & information.

Local tours and activities
The Extra Mile Tours ↘ 581 6171; www.unalaskadutchharbortour.com. Longtime local

Bobbie Lekanoff leads natural history & World War II focused tours with prices starting from US$50.

Activities

Wildlife Hundreds of bird species can be found in the Unalaska area including a huge population of bald eagles and the extremely rare Whiskered Auklet. Besides birds, the Bering Sea is home to a profusion of marine mammals including sea lions, whales, sea otters, porpoises and seals. Shore-side visitors will find foxes, ground squirrels, meadow voles, lemmings and a herd of horses at Morris Cove. Sadly, Unalaska does not have bears.

Aleutian Island Outfitters ↘ 581 4557. Water taxi service as well as sightseeing & wildlife tours around Unalaska Island.

Mac Enterprises ↘ 581 1386; www.missalyssa.com. Jimmer offers charters, tours & adventures of any kind aboard the MV *Miss Alyssa*.

FV *Lucille* ↘ 581 5949; www.unalaskahalibutfishing.com; e lucille@arctic.net. Fishing & wildlife viewing aboard Dave's 32ft boat.

Fishing Unalaska is famous for its great fishing and world-record halibut. These 'barn doors' can reach 450lbs or more. Many types of fishing can be arranged through the following guides. Fishermen can also book a trip through the Grand Aleutian Hotel.

Mac Enterprises (see above)
FV *Lucille* (see above) Half & full day charters for cod, halibut & salmon. US$165/pp.

Volcano Bay Adventures ↘ 581 3414; www.volcano-bay.com. Greg Hawthorne has run this unique fly-in fishing camp for almost 10 years.

Hiking and recreation Adventures in Unalaska can be as tame as a driving tour of the 38-mile scenic road system, or as wild as kayaking the Island of the Four Mountains, 150 miles away. Since there are no bears, trees or obstacles of any kind, Unalaska is an amazing place to hike and explore. The town is easily left behind and any number of remote peaks, valleys and bays are within a day's hike.

Since most of the land on Unalaska Island is owned by the Ounalashka Corporation (OC), hikers and campers need to get a US$6 land-use permit from their office behind the Grand Aleutian Hotel (see page 387). Permits can also be issued from the Aleutian World War II Visitor Centre, see page 391. Daily permits expire 24 hours after the time of purchase. Respectful camping is allowed anywhere in OC land. OC agents patrol the roads. A good hiking trail map can be procured from the Ounalashka Corporation office (see opposite).

Grand Aleutian Hotel administrator Dan Young (↘ 581 7150) leads free hikes on Sundays all year.

Priest Rock This is the dramatic rock pinnacle off Cape Kalekta. A fantastic hike leads from Morris Cove to Constantine Bay and finally to the rear side of Priest Rock. This

---

WHAT'S IN A NAME?

The town seems to go by two names, Dutch Harbor and Unalaska. The name Dutch Harbor was originally assigned to a small deep-water bay in Unalaska Bay by Russian fur traders at the turn of the 20th century, referring to a Dutch ship that was supposedly the first to enter the bay. After World War II, the name gained wider use and usurped the original name of 'Angunalaksha' given to the area by the native Unangan people (sometimes incorrectly called Aleut). The name was later modified to the more pronounceable Unalaska. Though many people call the town Dutch Harbor or simply 'Dutch', Dutch Harbor is technically only the harbor area on Amaknak Island and Unalaska forms the rest.

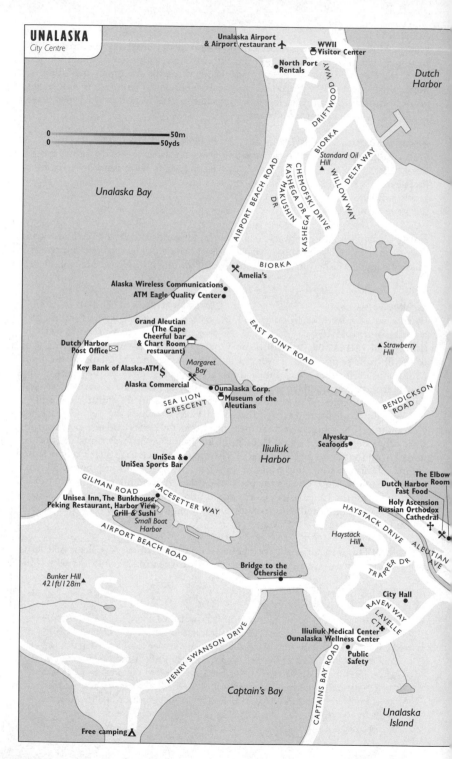

UNALASKA
City Centre

Unalaska Airport
& Airport restaurant ✈

WWII
Visitor Center

North Port
Rentals

Dutch
Harbor

DRIFTWOOD WAY

BIORKA

Standard Oil
Hill

KASHEGA DR

CHEMOFSKI DRIVE

KASHEGA DR

MAKUSHIN DR

WILLOW WAY

DELTA WAY

AIRPORT BEACH ROAD

Unalaska Bay

0 ————————— 50m
0 ————————— 50yds

BIORKA

Amelia's ✗

Alaska Wireless Communications
ATM Eagle Quality Center

EAST POINT ROAD

Strawberry
Hill

Grand Aleutian
(The Cape
Cheerful bar
& Chart Room
restaurant)

Dutch Harbor
Post Office ✉

Key Bank of Alaska-ATM $

Margaret
Bay

Alaska Commercial ✗

Ounalaska Corp.
Museum of the
Aleutians

BENDICKSON
ROAD

SEA LION
CRESCENT

Iliuliuk
Harbor

Alyeska
Seafoods

UniSea &
UniSea Sports Bar

The Elbow
Dutch Harbor Room
Fast Food

GILMAN ROAD

PACESETTER WAY

Holy Ascension
Russian Orthodox
Cathedral ✝

HAYSTACK DRIVE

ALEUTIAN AVE

Unisea Inn, The Bunkhouse,
Peking Restaurant, Harbor View
Grill & Sushi

Small Boat
Harbor

AIRPORT BEACH ROAD

Haystack
Hill

TRAPPER DR

Bunker Hill
421 ft/128m

Bridge to the
Otherside

City Hall

RAVEN WAY

LAVELLE
CT

HENRY SWANSON DRIVE

Iliuliuk Medical Center
Ounalaska Wellness Center

CAPTAINS BAY ROAD

Public
Safety

Captain's Bay

Unalaska
Island

Free camping ⛺

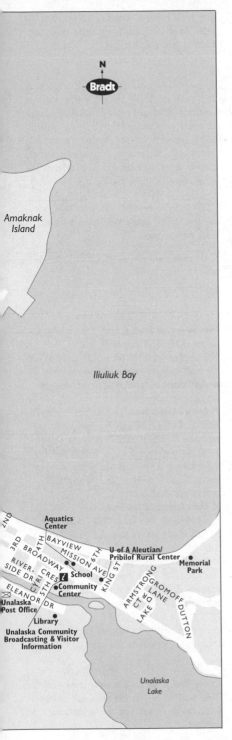

trip can be done in one very long day by those in shape or in three days by others.

Pyramid Peak This is the large peak sometimes visible behind town. The hike is easy except for the peak. Drive toward the head of Captain's Bay and take the gravel road uphill at the cannery complex.

Ugadaga Bay This trail descends from an official trailhead off Overland Drive. The trail follows a small creek and winds through a beautiful prehistoric valley to the ocean. A longer option is to descend the Peace of Mind Trail, then follow the cliffs – staying up high – to Ugadaga Bay and return via the Ugadaga Bay Trail.

Makushin Bay This remote and beautiful bay is accessible by boat, plane or on foot from the head of Captain's Bay. The Makushin Bay Portage Trail starts at the end of the Captain's Bay Road and leads uphill for four miles to a small lake before it descends for six miles to Makushin Bay. These are rough miles that may take two days with any significant load. Makushin Bay is protected from most weather conditions and for anyone willing to carry a folding kayak over the pass, the bay offers amazing paddling, fishing, hiking and hot springs. Contact Dave Magone from the charter fishing boat *Lucille* for details. See page 385.

Where to stay Unalaska has just three hotels and no B&Bs. Homestays can sometimes be arranged through the visitor centre.

Hotels
🏠 **Grand Aleutian Hotel** (112 rooms) 498 Salmon Way; ☎ 581 3844, 800 891 1194 (TF); www.grandaleutian.com. This large hotel seems out of place in tiny, remote Unalaska. Visitors & well-to-do fishermen stay here. The best rooms have even numbers & are on the upper floors. While the rooms are standard issue, the Sunday brunch in the Chart Room is to die for. 2 restaurants, 2 bars. Wi-Fi. $$$–$$$$

🛏 **Unisea Inn** (42 rooms) 📞 886 581 3844. A mid-range option located on Gilman Drive opposite the massive, grey Unisea housing complex. $$$
🏠 **The Bunkhouse** 📞 581 4900. Located on Gilman Road in the middle of Unalaska's fish processing sector. Shared bathrooms & very simple rooms used mostly by fishery workers. $$

Camping Unalaska has no organised campgrounds but camping is allowed anywhere on Ounalashka Corporation (OC) land with a permit. They ask only that visitors respect the land and do not have campfires on the tundra. From Amaknak Island, head towards the bridge but just before it take Henry Swanson Drive south around Bunker Hill. There are stunning views and even some privacy. Another reasonably secluded camping area is on Amaknak Island just north of the airport. A few hundred feet north of the airport runway, a gravel road exits west up a small hill to a large flat area with some World War II debris. Noise from planes can be annoying.

🏕 **Broad Bay Adventures** 📞 581 4377, 359 3645 (mobile); www.broadbayadventures.com. A rustic camp located in Broad Bay, a 20min boat ride from Unalaska. Simple tents with bedding can be rented for US$25–60/day or for US$20 visitors can bring their own gear. Facilities include water, toilets & showers. US$25 more for meals. $

Remote lodges
🏠 **Ugludax Lodge** (see page 392)

✗ Where to eat
✗ **Chart Room** (see page 387) Located inside the Grand Aleutian, the Chart Room hosts 3 dining events per week that should not be missed. For big eaters, they could even be called a good deal. Fishermen in work clothes mingle with visiting investors in pressed suits. The Sunday brunch is served 10.00–14.00 featuring all-you-can-eat fresh shrimp, king crab, desserts, & other goodies for US$25pp. Seafood buffet night Wed 18.00–22.00 & BBQ night Fri 18.00–21.00. $$$$
✗ **Airport Restaurant** 📞 581 6777 or 581 5966; ⏰ 09.00–22.30 daily. Located inside the airport, this is where fishermen get drunk before jumping on a plane to fly out. It's also a good place to get Asian food, pizza & burgers. $$$
✗ **Harbor View Grill & Sushi** Salmon Way; 📞 581 7246; ⏰ 11.30–01.00 Mon–Sat, 11.30–21.00 Sun. Next to the Unisea Inn, this is the spot where locals go for sushi. $$$
✗ **Margaret's Bay Café** (see page 387) Located inside the Grand Aleutian Hotel, this café offers decent American fare for b/fast & lunch. A lunch buffet is set out 11.30–13.30 daily. Wi-Fi. $$$
✗ **Peking Restaurant** 100 Gilman Rd; 📞 581 5555; ⏰ 11.00–midnight daily. This Chinese/American/Japanese restaurant is surprisingly tasty, with good but expensive sushi. $$$
✗ **Amelia's** Airport Beach Rd & E Point Dr; 📞 581 2800; ⏰ 06.00–22.00 daily. This smoky little diner could have the largest menu in all Alaska. Burgers, hot & cold sandwiches & lots of Mexican food. Milk shakes come in a variety of odd flavours including avocado. B/fast is served all day. The sourdough pancakes are great! $$
✗ **Alaska Commercial** 100 Salmon Way; 📞 581 1245; ⏰ 07.00–22.00 Mon–Sat & 09.00–21.00 Sun. In the back of this grocery store is a decent Chinese place. $$
✗ **Dutch Harbor Fast Food** 11 N Second St; 📞 581 5966; ⏰ 11.00–22.00. A brand-new Chinese, Vietnamese & Thai restaurant next to the Russian Orthodox Church in old town. $$

Where to drink Unfortunately the world-famous Elbow Room bar (see box opposite) has closed. However, take heart, drunken fishermen are just as common at the following bars:

♀ **Airport Restaurant** (see above) Nervous about the flight? Take the edge off here.
♀ **The Cape Cheerful** 📞 581 3844; ⏰ 14.00–22.00 Mon–Sat, 12.00–22.00 Sun. Located inside the Grand Aleutian Hotel. A full bar & a rowdy crowd when fishing boats are in port. Live music isn't uncommon & food can be ordered from the Margaret's Bay Café next door.

The Elbow Room bar put Unalaska on the map decades before the Discovery Channel TV show *The Deadliest Catch* (see page 382) aired. During the king-crab fishing heyday of the 1970s and 1980s, the bar was known throughout the world as one of the roughest around. Gnarly fishermen, sporting fistfuls of cash, made the Elbow Room into the legend it would become – a place where hard drugs, alcohol and as many as eight fights a night were the norm.

Larry Shaishnikoff and Carol Moller bought the Blue Fox Cocktail Lounge in 1966 for US$800 and converted it into the Elbow Room. Their timing could not have been better. Within a few years, king crab were fished for months on end and most nights the queues at the Elbow Room stretched out of the door. Lines of cocaine on the bar were a common sight and, for a number of years, the few police officers working in Unalaska refused to go anywhere near the place. The dingy interior said little about the amount of money spent and made there – as much as US$1 million a year. The building was small, cramped and dark with a dubious aroma. Still, the bar's appeal was undeniable. To the right of the front door, a tiny stage hosted such greats as Jimmy Buffet while a stout railing kept the rowdy patrons at bay.

During the 1980s, a number of factors combined to lead eventually to the closure of the Elbow Room in April 2005. Almost overnight, the king crab fishery went bust and Unalaska began the slow process of gentrification. Federal and state money brought new schools and a health clinic to town. This created job positions that needed to be filled, often by people from out of town who increasingly objected to the riotous scene created every night at the bar. In the 1990s, another bar opened called Carl's, which took business from the Elbow Room. As Unalaska's population swelled, fewer and fewer residents made their living from fishing and they didn't want to spend their nights puking and fighting at the Elbow Room.

Getting on in years, Shaishnikoff eventually sold the bar in April 2005 to a couple who renamed it Latitudes. To the horror of hard drinkers the world over, two years later the bar's doors closed for good.

♀ **Unisea Sports Bar** ☎ 581 7246; ⏰ 15.00–close. A classic sports bar with TV & billiards located inside the UniSea plant. Good views of the harbour & appetisers served late.

Festivals and events

May
Cinco de Mayo Held annually 5 May.

June
Archaeological Dig Program (☎ *581 5150*) Held mid-June through to the end of the summer, the Museum of the Aleutians takes guests along on archaeological digs.

All American Soap Box Derby (☎ *581 1864*) A qualifying race for the world championships in Akron, Ohio.

July
Fourth of July Fireworks, parade and a softball tournament.

Mount Ballyhoo Run A race up and down the largest mountain on Amaknak Island.

August
Summer Bay Bike and Run Classic A 13.5-mile bike and running competition from Unalaska to Summer Bay.

Heart of the Aleutians Festival Live music and food.

Camp Qungaayax (Unanga Culture Camp) (✆ *581 2920*) A week-long celebration of the Unangan culture at Morris Cove. Learn to skin marine mammals, fish, make baskets, make bent wood hats and more.

Tundra Golf Classic (✆ *581 4242*) A nine-hole golf tournament at Pyramid Peak with prizes and food.

September
Blueberry Bash (✆ *581 2612*) Normally held on the last weekend of the month, locals make various blueberry concoctions and are awarded prizes.

December
New Year's Eve Fireworks The festivities kick off on the last day of the year.

Shopping
Alaska Ship Supply 1352 Ballyhoo Rd; ✆ 581 1284 www.alaskashipsupply.com; ⏰ 06.00–22.00 daily. Located across from the Alaska ferry dock, this warehouse sells bait, food, commercial fishing supplies & *Deadliest Catch* paraphernalia.
Carolyn Reed ✆ 581 4679; ⏰ 12.00–18.00 Wed–Sat. Local artwork & gifts in the 2nd floor of the Intersea Mall across the street from the UniSea.
Grand Aleutian Gift Shop ✆ 581 3844; ⏰ 10.00–20.00 Mon–Sat, 12.00–18.00 Sun. Get

your postcards here, but don't expect anything too unique.
Gert Svarny ✆ 581 1597. Native Unalaskan, Gert doesn't have a shop but can be met by appointment. She has stories & wonderful artwork, such as Unangan bent wood hats, baskets & ivory carving to share.
Museum of the Aleutians Gift Shop (see opposite) Cool museum shirts & the best selection of Unalaska books in town with some native artwork.

Food shopping
Eagle Quality Center 2029 Airport Beach Rd; ✆ 581 4040; ⏰ 07.00–23.00 daily. A great selection of food with the highest prices on Earth. Groceries, delicatessen & souvenirs.
Alaska Ship Supply 487 Salmon Way, ✆ 581 1284; ⏰ 06.00–22.00 daily. Located in the old Alaska Commercial building, this new store sells everything

including groceries, lumber, hardware, fishing gear, liquor, even coffee.
Alaska Seafood 2315 Airport Beach Rd; ✆ 581 1864, 877 581 1864 (TF); www.aleutianfreshseafood.com; ⏰ 08.00–18.00 daily. Buy anything that comes out of the sea from these guys, or have them ship it to your home.

Other practicalities
Banks
$ **Eagle Quality Center** (see above) ⏰ 07.00–23.00 daily. ATM inside.

$ **Key Bank** 487 Salmon Way; ✆ 581 1300; ⏰ 09.00–18.00 Mon–Fri, 11.00–15.00 Sat

Hospital
✚ **Health Clinic** ✆ 581 1202

Internet
🖥 **Unalaska Public Library** 64 Eleanor St; ✆ 581 5060; ⏰ 10.00–21.00 Mon–Fri, 12.00–18.00 Sun. Free internet with a 30min limit.

🖥 **Grand Aleutian Hotel** (see page 384) Surf the internet free on Wi-Fi from comfortable chairs in the lobby. Best in the morning.

Laundry/showers
Aquatics Center 37 S 5th St; ✆ 581 1649; ⏰ 06.00–22.00 Mon–Fri, 08.00–22.00 Sat,

12.00–19.00 Sun. Visitors can take showers incl in the price of admission to the pool, sauna & weight room.

Phone service
Alaska Wireless Communications 2029 Airport Beach Rd; ✆ 581 5071, www.alaska-wireless.com. To use your home mobile phone in Unalaska stop by this office to buy credits & get a temporary Unalaska number.

Post offices
✉ **Amaknak Island Post Office** 82 Airport Beach Rd; ✆ 839 2214; ⏰ 09.00–11.30 & 12.30–17.00 Mon–Fri, 09.00–13.00 Sat

✉ **Unalaska Island Post Office** 1745 Airport Beach Rd; ⏰ 09.00–12.30 & 13.20–17.00 Mon–Fri, 13.00–17.00 Sat

What to see
The Aleutian World War II National Historic Area Located on Amaknak Island, this is one of the most accessible remnants of World War II's 'forgotten' Aleutian war. Drive north past the airport and ferry dock on Ballyhoo Road. Follow the narrow, steep road leading up the mountain on the left. The road braids at the top with the dilapidated remains of the US Army base Fort Schwatka everywhere. To the right is an 867ft cliff. The free brochure called *Aleutian World War II Historic Area* is the best guide to the area. Find it at the tourist information office and the Aleutian World War II Visitor Centre at the airport. Be sure to get a land use permit from the OC (see page 384).

Church of the Holy Ascension Russian Orthodox Cathedral This is Unalaska's most impressive building and the state's oldest church, built between 1894 and 1896. The fact that eagles frequent the Russian cross on the highest dome only increases the building's photogenic nature. Attend services at 06.30 on Saturday and at 10.00 on Sunday or arrange a tour by calling the church (✆ *581 6404*) or the visitor centre.

Memorial Park A short walk west of the visitor centre on Bayview Road, the park is less interesting than the cemetery just behind. Few places are more pleasant than on a sunny day than amidst the flowers, rolling hills and old grave stones.

City Dump From the city centre follow Summer Bay Road heading north. After 1.2 miles you will see a massive pile of rubbish on the right and unless the fish processors are pumping fish waste into the water at the other end of town, there will be legions of bald eagles.

Summer Bay Road Drive north on Summer Bay Road from the city centre past the city dump. Large sea otter rafts are common along this stretch of coast as are eagle nests tucked into the cliffs. Summer Bay has a nice beach and a lake with a small stream. Overland Drive splits off the main road right after the lake and leads back to town through the mountains. This is a steep and rocky road that may be snowed in, even during mid-summer. The views are worth any hardship and a number of amazing trails are accessible from this road. From Summer Bay, the road continues east to Morris Cove. The road follows the bluff and at the edge, large gun mounts are overgrown but worth a look. Below, a small pinnacle of rock usually has an active eagle's nest. Morris Cove is where the 'wild' horses hang out – bring a bag of carrots to make a herd of new friends.

Museums
Museum of the Aleutians (*314 Salmon Way;* ✆ *581 5150; www.aleutians.org;* ⏰ *09.00–17.00 Mon–Sat, 11.00–17.00 Sun; US$5 adult/child*) A wonderful collection of Russian icons and old and new Unangan artwork and artifacts. Some of the highlights include a seal-gut rain jacket, an extensive collection of arrowheads, fish hooks, etc, and a grass basket exhibit – an art form the Unangan were well known for.

Aleutian World War II Visitor Center (☎ *581 9944;* ⊕ *11.00–20.00 daily; US$4 adult/child*) Located in a historic World War II building next to the airport. Information on the World War II Aleutian campaign and its impact on the native people. World War II era films play in the theatre and the radio room has been reconstructed from old photos. Mt Ballyhoo and the museum are owned by the Ounalashka Corporation but the National Park Service helps with management.

OTHER ALEUTIAN ISLANDS

Despite the feeling in Unalaska of being on the edge of the Earth, the Aleutian chain actually continues east for 500 miles with more than 50 more major islands before running into the Kamchatka Peninsula in Russia. These windswept islands are home to abundant marine life, sea birds, a few people and little else. Scientists, fanatical birders, and a few hardy residents have so far been the only parties willing to pay the enormous cost of transportation to these far-flung places.

UMNAK ISLAND Immediately east of Unalaska Island is Umnak Island, the third largest island in the Aleutians. The island is dominated by three volcanoes; Mount Okmok (3,519ft) in the west, and Mount Recheshnoi (6,510ft) and Mount Vsevidof (7,051ft) in the east near the island's only town, Nikolski. The town has only 39 residents and, beside the seasonal lodge at Fort Glenn, are the island's only inhabitants. Mount Okmok once had a large caldera lake at the summit. The caldera, or crater, was more than 500ft deep but was drained when a crack formed in the rim. Today, a lovely but much smaller lake fills part of the caldera. On 12 July 2008, Okmok exploded with no warning, sending ash 50,000ft into the air. Commercial jets travelling between the US and Asia were diverted to avoid the plume. The former World War II site of Fort Glenn at the base of the mountain, where the Nikolski Lodge now sits, was hit by ash and falling rocks and the coast guard evacuated everyone.

 Where to stay

⌂ **Nikolski Adventures at Ugludax Lodge** ☎ 929 5273, 888 430 8329 (TF); www.nikolskiadventures.com. The Nikolski Lodge is also the westernmost fishing lodge in the country. The lodge accommodates up to 8 people during the summer & offers fishing, hiking, wildlife viewing & 4-wheeler tours on a deteriorating World War II road system. A week's stay will cost US$2,900pp but the lodge is nice & well appointed, unlike many remote Alaskan lodges. Guests fly in from Unalaska.

ISLANDS OF THE FOUR MOUNTAINS Amukta, Chagulak, Yunaska, Herbert, Carlisle, Chuginadak, Uliaga, Kagamil – the Islands of the Four Mountains – are unique in their perfect shape and classic volcanic symmetry. Grouped together and perpetually smoking, the islands – in particular Kagamil – are considered by some to be the ancestral home of the Unangan people. Mummified bodies, dating back thousands of years, have been found high on the mountains in caves.

On Chuginadak Island a three-mile sandy beach is one of the only such beaches in the islands, and is perfect for landing kayaks. Rising above the beach is Mount Cleveland (5,675ft), a spectacular and perfectly symmetrical volcano. A mirror of Mount Cleveland, Carlisle Volcano (5,315ft) is two miles away on Carlisle Island. An eruption of this volcano in 1944 killed a US serviceman – the only death ever reported in the Aleutians from a volcano.

ATKA ISLAND (*Population: 73*) Atka has a small village and a large volcano; Korovin Volcano (5,030ft). The small native village of Atka in Nazan Bay has a population of about 100 people. The village has a harbour and landing strip with occasional supplies coming from Unalaska. A military road provides access to a traditional summer fishing camp at Korovin Bay. The Unangan language is still spoken in most homes and local waters support a small commercial fishing fleet.

Where to stay and eat The Atka tribal council operates a store with limited hours and an even more limited supply of food as well as a three-bedroomed house with a kitchen available for rent. There is also the Nazana Inn and the city has some small apartments for rent. The Community Hall has a snack bar and hosts bingo once a week. In the public school is a small library and a tiny museum with artefacts displayed. Reindeer were introduced to the island in 1912 and now number more than 2,000. They are hunted by locals throughout the year and are an important source of food.

Other practicalities

Atka Village Clinic ⟍ 839 2232.
City of Atka ⟍ 839 2233 or 522 0384;
e Administrator goldcreekwater@yahoo.com or
Mayor atkacity@gci.net

Village Corporation (Atxam Corporation) ⟍ 839 2237.
Village Council ⟍ 839 2229.
Peninsula Air ⟍ 771 2640, 800 448 4226 (TF); www.penair.com. Flies to Atka twice per week from Unalaska.

ADAK ISLAND (*Population: 178*) Adak Island, just east of Atka and 450 miles from Unalaska has a small population of just 136 people in the town of Adak on Kuluk Bay. Mount Moffett (3924ft) rises directly from behind the town and has been skied in the spring by worldly ski bums. The lower portion of the mountain actually had a ski lift at one time. In 2000, a navy base of more than 6,000 servicemen closed leaving the massive infrastructure including an airport, runway and lots of buildings. An abandoned McDonalds restaurant is an amusing sight in this distant settlement. The land is now owned by the Native Corporation. The Alaska Department of Fish and Game introduced caribou to Adak at the behest of the navy for hunting and to safeguard against famine. Today, some 3,000 caribou roam the island and provide an important source of meat for locals. Hunters from Alaska and outside the state have started to hunt here because of the large herds and few restrictions.

KANAGA ISLAND Eight miles to the east of Adak Island is Kanaga Island. The northern tip of the island is dominated by Kanaga Volcano (4,287ft) and is reported to have springs. The volcano is active with eruptions as recently as the 1990s. Lava flows can be seen on its slopes.

THE RAT ISLANDS

Kiska Island Japanese forces invaded the island of Kiska on 7 June 1942 and captured a team of US Aerological servicemen stationed there. The group fled inland but were all eventually captured except for William House who survived on plants and worms for 50 days before surrendering to the Japanese. He weighed just 80lbs.

Seven millions pounds of bombs were dropped on Kiska in the following year while the Allied Forces simultaneously cut off supply lines to Kiska and Attu. On 29 July 1943, 5,000 Japanese soldiers escaped the island on ships by luring US ships to the opposite side of the island with phony radar bleeps. The entire escape took only 55 minutes. When 35,000 Allied troops landed on the island on 15 August, they were greeted not by the massive Japanese force they expected, but by booby traps, destructed facilities and supplies and a few dogs originally owned by the US Aerological servicemen, then cared for by Japanese soldiers.

Kiska Volcano (4,004ft) At the northern part of the island is the westernmost active volcano in the Aleutian Islands. Because of its historical significance the island has been declared a National Historic Landmark. The harbour and island are littered with artefacts from both the Japanese and US occupation.

Rat Island The island was populated with Norway rats in the late 1700s by a Japanese shipwreck. Their impact on the ground-nesting seabirds has been devastating but in recent years the US Fish and Wildlife Service has sponsored an eradication program that may have recently proven successful.

Amchitka Island The island was used during World War II as an air base and later as a radar and radio relay station between Attu and Unalaska. During the 1960s and 1970s, the United States Atomic Energy Commission conducted underground nuclear testing on the island. Some environmental groups reported that the commission studied the effects of the blasts on sea otters and other marine life. The island is no longer used for nuclear testing but is monitored for leakage and contamination. The US Fish and Wildlife Service reintroduced the endangered Aleutian goose in the 1970s to bolster southwest Alaska's dwindling populations.

Attu Island Attu Island is located at the westernmost part of the Aleutian Islands and the US. The island was also the site of the only land battle on US soil during World War II and has been declared a National Historic Landmark for that reason. Currently, the island has a US Coast Guard LORAN (Long Range Navigation) station and 20 residents who man the station. Attu is not only the westernmost piece of land in the US, it is also the easternmost, lying nearly seven degrees east of longitude 180°. The island is situated more than 1,500 miles from Anchorage, 450 miles from the Russian mainland and almost 5,000 miles from Washington DC.

From the original Unangan inhabitants to the Japanese and US occupations during World War II, the island's history is fascinating. On 7 June 1942, Japanese forces invaded Attu as well as Kiska. The native Unangan were taken prisoner and sent back to Japan. Of the 40 taken, only 16 survived their imprisonment to return to US soil in 1945. After their long imprisonment, they returned home through the Philippines and San Francisco, but were told they could not return to Attu because the cost of cleaning and rebuilding their island was too great. The displacement of the Unangan during World War II is without a doubt one of the most underreported and embarrassing parts of US history.

On 2 May 1943, US soldiers landed on Attu to confront Japanese soldiers already entrenched there. Poorly prepared for the extreme weather, US soldiers starved, froze and suffered trench foot at a far greater rate than they were killed or wounded by the enemy. Soldiers often kept moving to stay warm even though it usually meant their deaths from Japanese sniper fire. Soldiers also took and wore the outer clothing of dead Japanese soldiers even though they were often mistakenly shot by fellow soldiers. Supply planes were often delayed for days or weeks with thick fog and 120mph winds. Battles were initiated simply to procure food from the enemy and some soldiers threw grenades into the water to kill fish. The grizzly nature of war was in some ways overshadowed by the fight for survival against the elements.

The island was won by the US on 29 May, when the much-depleted Japanese force opted for an honourable death. While some charged at the US force on a suicide mission, others killed themselves. The Bushido Code was followed by virtually all Japanese soldiers and dictated that they kill themselves rather than suffer the dishonour of being captured. The code was taken seriously not only by soldiers but also by their families. The wives of some Japanese POWs killed themselves when they learned of their husbands' capture.

In terms of the percentage of combatants killed, the battle of Attu ranks second to Iwo Jima for the Pacific portion of the war. The battle was one of the most bloody of the war and also one of the least well known. Today, a monument to peace stands on the island, erected by the Japanese government in 1987.

The US Fish and Wildlife Service manages the island and is occasionally visited by birders with deep pockets. Flights are by special charter only and can cost as much as US$5,000. Rare Asian bird species such as the spoon-billed sandpiper, the Siberian blue robin and others can be seen here.

PRIBILOF ISLANDS

The Pribilof Islands of St Paul, St George and three smaller islands are some of the most isolated in Alaska. More than 200 miles north of the Aleutian Islands, the Pribilofs are an oasis of life in the middle of the frigid Bering Sea.

During the short summer months the beaches teem with more than one million fur seals and the volcanic cliffs are covered by millions of nesting seabirds. Visitors venture out to the Pribilofs for one reason; wildlife. Many animals are surprisingly approachable and few places on Earth have such an abundance. The islands are also home to the largest native Unangan community in the world.

HISTORY Russian explorers originally stumbled across the Pribilof Islands in 1786, landing on St George and naming the islands to the north St Peter and St Paul Islands. Until the sale of Alaska to the US, the Russian American Company enslaved the natives and harvested fur from seals. After the sale of Alaska, the American Commercial Company continued harvesting fur seals until the turn of the century when populations plummeted. The right to hunt seals was eventually handed over to the Pribilof native groups in 1985. Today, fur seals are only harvested by natives for subsistence purposes.

For more information visit www.southwestalaska.com/pribilof/index.html.

GETTING THERE AND AWAY

Peninsula Air (↘ 771 2640, 800 448 4226 (TF); www.penair.com) Flights from Anchorage to St George are offered three times a week and to St Paul seven times a week. Weather frequently grounds the flights in and out.

PRACTICALITIES The islands are cool, wet, and windy all summer. Low clouds often blanket the islands with the temperatures hovering between 4°C/40°F and 10°/50°F and the winds often blow at 10–20mph. Warm, layered clothes are essential. Virtually all of the land on both islands is owned by the Tanadgusix and Tanaq Corporations and camping is not allowed.

ST PAUL (*Population: 450*) St Paul is the larger and more populated of the two islands with 760 people, about 65% of whom are of native descent. The island's beaches are where a great many fur seals haul themselves out of the water to give birth and sun themselves. Males arrive in the early spring and females join them in June. Russian history is readily visible in the amazing St Peter and Paul Russian Orthodox Church on St Paul Island. St Paul also has a large herd of caribou, introduced in 1911.

Tours

St Paul Island Tours ↘ 278 2311; www.alaskabirding.com. Wildlife & cultural guiding service. Tours start at US$1,650pp for 2 nights & 3 days & are all inclusive. A week long tour will cost US$2,670pp.

7

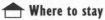 Where to stay

King Eider Hotel & Restaurant (25 rooms) ✆ 546 2477. The only accommodation in St. Paul, the hotel is owned by the Tanadgusix Corporation & although it looks run-down, it is actually not bad. Communal bathrooms. During the w/ends the bar next door can get loud. B/fast inc. $$$$$

Other practicalities

Tanaq Corporation ✆ 272 9886. The local Native Corporation.

Health clinic ✆ 859 2245
City of St George ✆ 859 2263

ST GEORGE South of St Paul is the smaller island of St George (*www.stgeorgealaska.com*) with just 150 people, who are vastly outnumbered by fur seals. With its higher sea cliffs, St George is known for its large numbers of seabirds and is an international hotspot for birders. Even if birds are not your obsession, many consider St George more scenic.

Where to stay and eat

St George Hotel (10 rooms) ✆ 272 9886. The hotel was converted from federal government housing by the local Native Corporation & is now reasonably comfortable & quiet though expensive. US$170/pp. TV, phone. $$$$$
✕ St George Canteen & Variety Store ✆ 859 2241

Other practicalities

Health Clinic ✆ 546 2310
City of St Paul ✆ 546 2331
Northstar Truck Rental ✆ 546 2645
Tanadgusix Corporation ✆ 546 2312. The local Native Corporation.

Zees Cab ✆ 546 2352
Alaska Commercial ✆ 546 2209; ⏰ 10.00–19.00 Mon–Sat. A decent selection of expensive groceries.

8

Western Alaska

From the Yukon Delta to the Arctic Circle, western Alaska is a rarely visited and remote land thriving on gold and salmon. Not a single road penetrates this pure, unadulterated wilderness. Instead, the many rivers and waterways are used like highways by salmon, wildlife and people alike. In the winter, 'ice roads' are used by trucks and snowmobiles, while boats are the preferred means of transportation during the rest of the year. The region is walled in by the Alaska Range to the east, the Brooks Range to the north, and the Bering Sea in all other directions. In the south, the 19-million-acre Yukon Delta National Wildlife Refuge is a flat, emerald green landscape dotted with millions of lakes and ponds and criss-crossed by rivers. Elsewhere, older, non-glaciated mountains form impressive low–lying ranges as far as the eye can see. Yup'ik and Inupiat native Alaskans have long called the area home and, to this day, many exist much as they have done for centuries, living off the land and communicating in their native languages.

Without ferry service or roads, getting to western Alaska is expensive and almost always by air. Despite the expense and trouble, visitors who choose to visit the villages and many remote refuges and parks are rewarded with an experience like no other. Wildflowers carpet the treeless landscape during mid-summer and musk ox, bear, wolves and caribou sightings are more common here than almost anywhere else in the state. Visitors often visit the southern part of the region to view the millions of migratory birds that visit the Yukon Delta while Nome in the north offers a small but lovely road system and history galore. Wherever you go in western Alaska, don't forget to enjoy the journey as well as the destination since the former can sometimes take longer than the latter.

HISTORY

Yup'ik and Cup'ik native Alaskans inhabit the southern part of the region while the Seward Peninsula in the north is generally populated by the Inupiat (or Inupiaq). Due to its isolation, and lack of easily procured natural resources, western Alaska was not confronted by the west until the 1800s, when Russians first explored the coast. During the late 1800s, Russian missionaries began to convert the Yup'ik to Christianity and a number of churches were built that still stand today. The Yup'ik, while not expressly resistant to the new religion, only accepted the parts of the new religion that blended well with their personal religious beliefs. The late discovery of the Yup'ik is perhaps the reason their culture remains so intact today with the language commonly heard on the street and even on local TV and radio. While much of the Yup'ik culture persists, there have been changes. Native corporations provide modern housing to many of their members and supplies are flown in from the outside world. Rather by choice or because of the tremendous cost of imported goods, native and non-native residents alike derive much of their food from subsistence gathering, hunting and fishing.

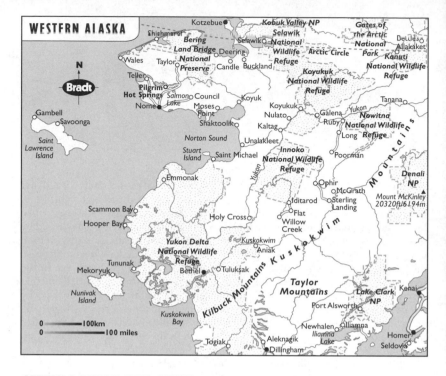

WESTERN ALASKA

GETTING THERE AND AWAY

Getting to western Alaska is expensive and almost always by air. While the remoteness of the landscape necessitates small plane travel within the region, Alaska Airlines planes do serve Bethel, Nome, King Salmon and Dillingham. See individual towns for further details.

BY AIR

✈ **Alaska Airlines** ☎ 800 252 7522;
www.alaskaair.com. See individual towns.
✈ **Bering Air** ☎ 443 5464, 800 478 5422 (TF);
www.beringair.com. Serving Little Diomede Island, St.
Laurence Island & virtually every community on
Norton Sound & the Seward Peninsula.

✈ **Era/Frontier Aviation** ☎ 266 8394, 800 866
8394 (TF); www.frontierak.com. See individual towns.
✈ **Grant Air** ☎ 543 2000; www.flygrant.com.
Regular summer service from Anchorage to Bethel
& other small communities in the area.

BETHEL *Population: 5,449*

The remote yet sizeable town of Bethel (✆ 60°47'32"N, 161°45'21"W) is 400 miles from Anchorage and lies at the heart of the 19-million-acre Yukon Delta National Wildlife Refuge (see page 401). Most of Bethel's residents are native Yup'ik and it is not uncommon to hear the language around town. On the banks of the Kuskokwin River, Bethel serves as a supply and transportation hub for more than 50 outer lying villages. With just 25 miles of road in and around town, the river serves as the local highway. After the river freezes mid-winter cars and snowmobiles use the ice like a highway.

Bethel is where most visitors begin their trip to the Yukon Delta National Wildlife Refuge. The refuge visitor centre has lots of information about wildlife viewing, adventure, fishing, hunting, and boating opportunities there. In town, taxis aid getting around and there are a number of decent restaurants and accommodations as well as a few guide services. With the exception of a handful of fishermen and bird watchers, Bethel is mostly off the average visitor's radar and they are not well set-up for tourism.

HISTORY Bethel was originally established by Yup'ik Eskimos and called Mumtreklogamute, or 'Smokehouse People'. In 1885, Moravian missionaries built a church and founded a mission near the original village, which they called Bethel. Still standing today, the church is Bethel's most interesting building and well worth a visit. The settlement gradually grew as villagers migrated to the area for work and education.

GETTING THERE AND AROUND Bethel is accessible from Anchorage by two airlines: Alaska Air, Era/Frontier Aviation who run three or more flights per day. Once there, taxis are common, rental cars are available, and charter plane outfits provide transportation to the surrounding area.

By air
✈ **Alaska Airlines** ☎ 800 252 7522; www.alaskaair.com. Up to 3 flights per day from Anchorage for US$400 return.
✈ **Era/Frontier Aviation** ☎ 266 8394, 800 866 8394 (TF). Up to 5 flights a day for US$400 return.
✈ **Grant Aviation** ☎ 800 764 7607 (TF); www.flygrant.com. Daily flights to many western Alaskan communities from Bethel.

✈ **Yukon Helicopters** ☎ 543 3280; www.yukonhelicopters.net. Helicopter & small plane charter service around Bethel.
✈ **Yute Air** ☎ 543 5089; www.yuteairtaxi.com. Charter flights to remote locations around Bethel.

By car
🚗 **Payless Car Rental** 3340 Airport Rd; ☎ 543 3058. For about US$100/day you can have a car. They also offer free airport pick-up & drop-off.

TOURIST INFORMATION
🛈 **Chamber of Commerce** ☎ 543 2911; e bethelchamber1@alaska.com; www.bethelak.com.

WHERE TO STAY
🏠 **Bentley's Porter House** (35 rooms) ☎ 543 5923. A large main building with many outbuildings right on the river. More motel than B&B. TV, VCR, kitchen, freezer, b/fast incl. $$$
🏠 **Brown Slough B&B** (8 rooms) ☎ 543 4334; www.bethelhotel.com. 2 houses, incl a lovely log house, accommodate guests in nice, clean rooms. All rooms share bathrooms except 1 suite. B/fast incl, Wi-Fi. $$$
🏠 **Lakeside Lodge B&B** (3 rooms) ☎ 543 5275; www.lakesidelodge.com. On the outskirts of town by a lake with simple clean rooms. $$$

🏠 **Longhouse Bethel Inn** (39 rooms) 751 3rd Av; ☎ 543 4612; www.longhousebethel.com. A large, standard issue hotel. Wi-Fi. $$$
🏠 **The White House B&B** (4 rooms) ☎ 543 2388. A nice 2-storey log home within walking distance of town. All rooms have shared bathrooms. $$$
🏠 **Allanivik Hotel** (30 rooms) 1220 Chief Eddie Hoffman Hwy; ☎ 543 4305, www.allanivik.com. The native-owned blue complex with the VIP restaurant inside. Laundry, ATM. $$–$$$

WHERE TO EAT AND DRINK
✖ **Alaska Commercial Deli** 135 Ridgecrest Dr; ☎ 543 2662; ⏱ 07.00–23.00 Mon–Fri & 09.00–21.00

Sun. Offers basic deli food for a reasonable price. $$

✕ Arctic Sun Café 3551 State Hwy; ☎ 543 3566; closed during winter. In the airport terminal, this place does a decent b/fast & lunch. **$$**

✕ Dimitrie's Restaurant 281 4th Av; ☎ 543 3434; ⏰ 11.30–13.00 & 16.30–21.00 Mon–Sat. Italian, Greek & even some Middle Eastern fare. Most locals will tell you it's the best place in town. **$$**

✕ VIP Restaurant 1220 Chief Eddie Hoffman Hwy; ☎ 543 4777; ⏰ 07.00–22.00 daily & closed the 2nd & 4th Sun of every month. Inside the Allanivik Hotel, the VIP serves Asian & American food. **$$**

OTHER PRACTICALITIES

Alaska Commercial Co 135 Ridgecrest Dr; ☎ 543 2661; ⏰ 07.00–22.00 Mon–Sat & 09.00–21.00 Sun. A large grey warehouse with a decent selection of groceries & a delicatessen.

Art Guild ☎ 543 5876; ⏰ 15.00–18.00 Wed, 16.00–19.00 Fri, 12.00–18.00 Sat. Local artists display their work here, call ahead to make sure work is available to see.

Bethel Car Rental ☎ 543 3058. It costs US$93 for a mid-sized car; one day free with a week rental.

Kuskokwim Wilderness Adventures ☎ 543 3900; www.kuskofish.com. Guided fishing & wildlife watching trips & transportation. A 1-day

birdwatching trip with a US Fish & Wildlife specialist is US$125pp. Boat charters are US$125/hr.

Public library 420 State Hwy; ☎ 543 4516; ⏰ 12.00–19.00 Mon–Thu & 12.00–17.00 Fri & Sat. Free Wi-Fi & computer terminals with internet access.

Recreation center 208 East 6th Av; ☎ 443 5431; ⏰ 05.30–22.00 Mon–Fri, 14.00–22.00 Sat–Sun. A nice pool, gym & bowling alley. US$5.

Yukon-Kuskokwim Hospital PO Box 528; ☎ 543 6300. The large yellow building.

FESTIVALS AND EVENTS
Camai Festival (see page 70)

Kuskokwin-300 Sled Dog Race (*www.k300.org*) Before planes and snowmobiles existed, mail and supplies were transported via dog sled. The Kuskokwin-300 is a celebration of that tradition, and has taken place every January since 1979. Fireworks, concerts and other festivities are usually held before and after the race.

WHAT TO SEE
Yup'ik Cultural Center (*420 Eddie Hoffman Hwy;* ☎ *543 1819;* ⏰ *12.00–16.00 Tue–Sat; free admission*) A large grey building housing the library and the University of Alaska's Kuskokwim campus. Dance performances, lessons, concerts and a Sunday market are held here. A wonderful collection of Yup'ik artwork, artefacts and historic photographs can also be found there.

NOME (*Population: 3,600*)

Nome (✪ 64°30'14"N, 165°23'58"W) is western Alaska's most refined, historically rich and tourist-centric city. The town itself is a rustic, but historically rich, place

---

CAMAI – A CELEBRATION OF CULTURE

Dance and language constitute some of the Yup'ik's strongest ties to their past. The Camai celebration – a three-day event held annually in Bethel in April – brings together native American musicians and dancers from around the state and continent. It's common for 500 participants to perform, each showing the unique traditions and attire of their ancestry. John Active of Bethel summed up the event and tradition best when he said: 'I dance for it lifts my spirits. I reach out and touch the hands of my ancestors and know that I've come home'.

In the southern portion of Western Alaska the 19-million-acre Yukon Delta National Wildlife Refuge occupies a vast and unique piece of land. The Yukon and Kuskokwim rivers provide the main arteries for the area acting like boat highways for the nearly 35,000 Yup'ik living in 35 villages within the refuge. The park is typically low and flat with thousands of rivers, small streams, lakes and ponds dotting the landscape, 70% of which are 100ft or less above sea level. Trees cover less than 5% of the refuge. The Kilbuck Mountains rise to 4,000ft in the east, creating an elevated area supporting wildlife less dependent on the lower lying wetlands.

The expanses of tundra and coastal tidal flats are home to a multitude of wild animals, particularly birds. Each spring, millions of migratory birds pass through the park and many stay to feed and raise their young. Other wildlife includes musk ox, both species of bears, wolves, moose and some caribou. Some 44 species of fish, including all five species of Pacific salmon, live and spawn in the rivers and lakes.

The refuge also covers the southern half of Nunivak Island (see page 407) and the resident population are reindeer and musk ox. The island has a small native village with a rich history.

GETTING THERE There are no roads leading into the park making small planes and boats the best way to get around. The park's headquarters is in Bethel. Regular flights to Bethel depart from Anchorage.

TOURIST INFORMATION
Yukon Delta National Wildlife Refuge Visitor Center State Hwy (Bethel); ☏ 543 3151; www.yukondelta.fws.gov. Simple displays and knowledgeable staff.

ACTIVITIES The many rivers and lakes in the refuge make overland travel difficult by any means other than by boat. The Andreafsky River is a wonderful floating trip with grizzly bear sightings just about guaranteed.

Eruk's Wilderness Float Tours 12720 Lupine Rd (Anchorage); ☏ 345 7678; www.alaska.net/~erukwild. Wildlife & fishing float trips in the refuge.

where gold mines still line the beaches just as they did more than a century ago. Nome has been accommodating legions of visitors for more than 100 years from the invasion of 10,000 gold miners at the turn of the 20th century to more than 20,000 'Visa gold'-wielding tourists per year today. What makes Nome special is its fascinating native and mining history and its position as the starting point for one of Alaska's most remote road trips on more than 230 miles of road. The Iditarod Sled Dog Race also ends here.

The town wears its history on its sleeve, with much of the mining history on display where it was left 100 years ago or in the Memorial Museum. The local road system offers unparalleled views of musk ox and other wildlife, and the fishing is great. Nome is an excellent location for visitors seeking a remote Alaskan frontier town with a few refinements such as shopping, restaurants, accommodations and tours. Nome is also one of Alaska's best places to buy native arts and crafts; what costs US$2,000 in Anchorage could easily cost half that in Nome.

HISTORY Though Inupiat native Alaskans inhabited the northern part of western Alaska for thousands of years before Nome became a town, the specific town site of Nome never supported any prehistoric settlements. The area became more than just a beach when Swedes Erik Lindblom, Jafet Lindberg, John Brynteson known collectively as the 'Three Lucky Swedes' found gold in Anvil Creek in 1898. By the following summer, the town's population had gone from three to 10,000 as prospectors from the Klondike gold fields flooded in. Famous southwest gunman and entrepreneur Wyatt Earp even spent a few years in Nome, supposedly turning a handsome profit managing various saloons. As the wealth of gold in the rivers and streams and in the beach sand became evident, news began to reach the outside world, bringing steamships full of hopeful gold seekers from across the US.

At that time the town was called Nome, but in 1899 a group of miners petitioned to change the name to Anvil City because 'Nome' was being confused with nearby Cape Nome and the Nome River. As it turned out, the name Nome had been chosen quite by accident. When the area was mapped it the 1850s by an English explorer, they noted a point had not been named. The cartographer scrawled '? Name' on the map. Later, when the map was copied the messy handwriting was thought to mean Cape Nome, with the '?' mistaken for a 'C' and the word 'Name' mistaken for 'Nome'. Apparently the Nome Post Office refused to accept the new name of Anvil City because they thought it would be confused with the nearby town of Anvik. The name, based on a spelling error, would stay.

Nome quickly became Alaska's largest city with 12,488 people living in tents in 1900. A full one third of all white Alaskans resided in Nome. In 1934, a series of storms and a devastating fire destroyed much of the town. The few original buildings still standing are not spectacular examples of the architecture of the town but give a hint of the town's original charms. During World War II, Nome was used to supply the USSR with warplanes.

Today Nome is a 'modern' bush community, served daily by jet from Anchorage. While little of Nome's income comes from gold these days, prospectors still migrate to Nome each summer to sift through beach sand. Despite other less elusive sources of wealth (such as tourism and goods distribution), Nome clings to its gold mining past. Whether this is due to nostalgia or because they are actually finding gold, few of us can say, and the gold miners are a notoriously tight-lipped bunch.

GETTING THERE AND AWAY The Nome airport is about two miles outside town. A taxi costs US$5 per person. The runway has buckled from extreme weather and is like a roller coaster to land and take off on. Many of the Alaska Airlines planes serving Nome and Kotzebue are primarily transporting cargo. Don't be alarmed if you enter a full-size plane only to find five rows of seats and a makeshift bulkhead separating cargo from passengers. Bering Air also serves Russian towns across the Bering Strait by special charter.

By air
Alaska Airlines (✆ 800 252 7522; *www.alaskaair.com*) Many visitors come as part of an organised tour, often through Alaska Airlines. Unless you want to really get off the beaten path and stay there, these packages – which include airfare, hotel and tours – are always cheaper than doing it on your own. Up to three flights a day connect Anchorage with Nome for US$450 return.

TOURIST INFORMATION
ⓘ Bering Land Bridge Interpretive Centre 214 West Front St; ✆ 443 2522; ⏱ 08.00–18.30 daily; www.nps.gov/bela. Located on Front St, the small office has simple displays, a film & knowledgeable staff. Regular ranger talks & hikes.

ⓘ Bureau of Land Management (BLM) ✆ 443 2177; ⏱ 08.00–17.00 Mon–Fri. Stop here for information before embarking on any adventure.

i **Nome Visitor Centre** 310 Front St; ☏ 443 6624
www.nomealaska.org; ⏰ 09.00–21.00 daily.
Knowledgeable staff & a variety of free brochures &
maps.

WHERE TO STAY
Free camping can be found two miles east of town on the beach without facilities. The Salmon Lake Campground, 38 miles out on Kougarok Road, is a lovely and secluded place to pitch a tent. Showers, laundry and water are located at the Senior Centre.

Aurora Inn (68 rooms) 302 E Front St ☏ 443 3838, 800 354 4606 (TF); www.aurorainnome.com. Decent rooms from US$138–220 dbl & rental cars for US$90. Laundry. $$$

Nugget Inn (47 rooms) 315 Front St ☏ 443 4189, 877 443 2323 (TF). An old building with simple, funky rooms & a historic lobby. The Dust Saloon & Fat Freddies Restaurant ($$) are located off the lobby. Wi-Fi. $$$

Bering Sea B&B (2 rooms) 1103 E 5th Av; ☏ 304 1208; www.beringseabb.com. 2 comfortable rooms for US$120 dbl. TV. $$

Chateau de Cape Nome (4 rooms) ☏ 443 2083. Located on the edge of town with hunting lodge décor & run by a long time Nome resident. $$

Extra Dry Creek B&B (2 rooms) ☏ 443 7615. Nice but basic rooms with a private entrance & access to a kitchen. $$

Sweet Dreams B&B (3 rooms) ☏ 443 2919; www.leaknomeak.com/aboutnome.htm. Pleasant rooms in a private home for US$125. The owners are very knowledgeable about Nome. $$

WHERE TO EAT AND DRINK
Nome has lots of bars. If you head out for a late night drink, go to the historic Board of Trade Saloon, built in 1900. Drunk people can be common in town after dark (or what passes for dark during Nome's long summer days). Keep to the busier streets to avoid confrontations.

Nome has a plethora of easy-to-find restaurants serving defrosted and deep-fried foods. Here are some of the exceptions.

✕ Airport Pizza 406 Bering St; ☏ 443 7992; www.airportpizza.com; ⏰ 07.00–22.00 Mon–Fri, 09.00–22.00 Sat & Sun. Perhaps the best food in town. Great pizza plus sandwiches, salads & beer on tap. Tasty & affordable lunch special & some of the best coffee in town. Wi-Fi. $$$

✕ Milano's Pizzeria 503 Front St; ☏ 443 2924; ⏰ 11.00–23.00 daily. One of the larger restaurants in town with decent Italian & Japanese food & relatively expensive. $$$

✕ Husky Restaurant 235 Front St; ☏ 443 1300; ⏰ 11.00–23.00 Mon–Sat & 13.00–23.00 Sun. A greasy spoon with a decent all American b/fast. $$

✕ Subway 135 Front St; ☏ 443 8100; ⏰ 10.00–23.00 daily. A chain restaurant, but good value. $$

✕ Taste of the West 1 Airport Rd; ☏ 443 6012; ⏰ 07.45–16.00 daily. Hot drinks & smoothies. $$

OTHER PRACTICALITIES
Alaska Commercial Company 185 E Front St; ☏ 443 2243; ⏰ 07.00–23.00 Mon–Fri & 09.00–21.00 Sun. Hunting, fishing, & groceries.

Arctic Trading Post 302 West Front St; ☏ 443 2686; ⏰ 08.00–20.00 Mon–Sat; e arctictrading@gci.net. Good selection of books about Nome.

Checker Cab ☏ 443 5211

Chukotka-Alaska 309 Bering St; ☏ 443 4128. An importer of art & other goods from Russia.

Hansons 415 Bering St; ☏ 443 5454. Hunting, fishing, & groceries.

Movie theatre 135 E Front St; ☏ 443 8200. A very comfortable, modern theatre showing films every night all summer.

Nome Discovery Tours ☏ 443 2814. Richard, the owner, is very knowledgeable about Nome & offers tours.

Public library 223 Front St; ☏ 443 6628; ⏰ 12.00–20.00 Mon–Thu, 12.00–18.00 Fri & Sat. Free Wi-Fi & computer terminals with internet access.

The 2.7-million-acre Bering Land Bridge Preserve on the Seward Peninsula protects the site where the first humans set foot in the Americas. This was the true discovery of the New World. The Bering Land Bridge Preserve in Alaska and its counterpart in Russia, the Beringia Nature-Ethnic Park, protect most of the land that was the location of one of the most important human migrations of all time. Despite being separated by 50 miles of water and 10,000 years of history, native people in Russia and Alaska to this day share a similar language, culture and history.

GETTING THERE This remote preserve is accessed only by boat and plane, usually from Nome. Contact Bering Air (*1470 Sepalla Dr;* 443 5464; *www.beringair.com*).

TOURIST INFORMATION
Bering Land Bridge Information Center 179 Front St, Nome; 443 2522. Trip planning resources & information on the Beringia Nature-Ethnic Park in Russia.

ACTIVITIES A popular trip is to fly to Serpentine Hot Springs for an overnight stay and soak. Beautiful scenery surrounds the springs and odd granite shapes protrude from the tundra. A few buildings house the hot pools and there are some first-come-first-serve bunks for overnighters. A lovely creek flows through the hilly landscape, mixing with the hot water to make the pools just the right temperature. Tough hikers can also trek from Taylor. The park is home to most of Alaska's major wildlife including whales and millions of migratory birds.

Stampede Car Rentals Located inside the Aurora Inn; 443 3838; www.aurorainnome.com/Stampede.htm. Rental cars available for US$90.

Wells Fargo Bank 109A Front St; 443 7688; 10.00–17.00 Mon–Thu, 10.00–18.00 Fri

FESTIVALS AND EVENTS Nome keeps its summer calendar full. Community trips to Pilgrim Hot Springs happen a few times a month and regular ranger talks about local history and wildlife are also held. Summer solstice events (20 or 21 June) are guaranteed fun.

The **Nome River Raft Race** takes place toward the end of June at mile 13 of the Nome–Taylor Highway. The **4 July** is a hoot with the Anvil Mountain Run, the Mother Goose Parade, free ice cream and, of course, fireworks.

WHAT TO SEE The **city hall building**, near the visitor centre, has a wooden burl arch out front that's hauled into the street each winter when the Iditarod race ends in Nome. Also, in front of the city hall, is a bronze bust of Roald Amundsen who piloted the dirigible *Norge* from Europe to Teller, (near Nome) Alaska in 1926. A historical marker in front of the building describes Wyatt Earp's profitable exploits at the turn of the century. **Anvil City Square,** at the corner of Division Street and Third in town, has a statue of the famous Three Lucky Swedes, a very large gold pan and St Joseph's Church, Nome's oldest building. Established in 1901, the high tower served as a beacon for dog-sled teams. **The Little Creek Rail Depot** is behind the Little Creek Mining Station. Both are worth seeing for a taste of Nome's gold-mining history. The **Carrie M McLain Memorial Museum** (*223 E. Front St;* 443 6630; *www.nomealaska.org/museum;* 09.30–1.30 daily; free admission) has Nome history on display from the Three Lucky Swedes and the gold rush, to sled dog racing and Inupiat culture. Some 14,000 historic photographs are on display and available as reprints.

Around town Outside town there is just as much to do, if not more than in town. For those interested in hiking, Anvil Mountain behind the town is an all day hike and well worth it on a clear day. Other hikes of interest include the beaches in front of town where gold miners sift the sand for 'pay dirt' (gold). The **Swanberge Dredge** on the east end of town operated until the 1990s, excavating dirt from the ground and sorting out the gold. The dredge is just one of 38 on the peninsula, most of which were decommissioned in the 1950s. The **historic cemetery** is also worth visiting.

Nome road trips Unlike other isolated Alaskan towns, Nome has an extensive road system (230 miles) allowing access to the communities of Teller, Council and Taylor as well as some of western Alaska's most beautiful landscapes. The cost of renting a car is usually about US$100 per day, making a road trip here a costly but worthy prospect. The roads are gravel with little traffic and the scenery is unparalleled. Wildlife sightings, including musk ox and bear, are common and the fishing is superb. Get the *Nome Roadside* fishing guide from the visitor centre. Camping is allowed almost everywhere and the lack of traffic makes this one of the best remote places to bike tour in the state. Whether on bike or in a rental car, be sure to have an extra tyre/tube and all the normal accoutrements for self-sufficiency. There are no services between Nome and the villages. The Alaska Department of Transportation (✆ 443 3444) can give up-to-date information on the roads and the BLM should be consulted for land status and camping. These trips are more about the journey than the destination since there is little to see or do in any of the three villages.

Nome to Teller (73 miles) This stretch of road generally takes about two hours one-way without stops. The gravel road winds through lovely country with some good fishing creeks and a good chance of seeing reindeer herded by Teller locals. The town of Teller clings to a precarious bit of land right on the sea. The town of less than 300 is predominantly Inupiat. A small store sells basic food and supplies and a gift shop has local crafts. Sometimes locally made art can be purchased directly from locals.

Nome to Taylor (85 miles) Sometimes called the Kougarok Road, this 85-mile gravel road takes about two hours one-way without stopping by car. This scenic route follows the Nome River and passes many abandoned mining claims. Some houses can be seen just off the road. After ten miles, the Dexter Road House – allegedly once owned by Wyatt Earp – is a good place to get a drink. As the Kigluaik Mountains close in, the **Salmon Lake Campground** is at mile 38 on the right. The free campground has toilets, tables and grills. Off the road near mile 65, Pilgrim Hot Springs has both artificial and natural pools that are rustic but pleasant. The area even has trees; a real novelty in western Alaska. The chapel of Our Lady of Lourdes can be found nearby. The building housed orphaned children after many of their parents were killed in the 1918 influenza epidemic in Nome. The Catholic church owns the land and are allegedly planning a campground. Currently, the hot springs are open to anyone but travellers should ask at the visitor centre first. The road to Taylor ends when it crosses the Kougarok River for the second time. Continue on foot, ATV or bike if desired but there is no town beyond a semi-abandoned mining claim. Intrepid travellers can hike overland from here to Serpentine Hot Springs in the Bering Land Bridge Preserve. The trip is hard and long but it can be done. Talk to Mitch at the visitor centre.

Nome to Council (72 miles) This stretch of road is famous for the Last Train to Nowhere, a failed railway designed for transporting gold, but abandoned in 1907. The rusting hulk sits all alone in the tundra and in the right light makes a wonderful photo. The engines were shipped from New York to Alaska in 1903. The train was used to transport gold until 1907, when it was abandoned mainly because of the challenging terrain and the mighty Bering Sea storms that ultimately destroyed much of the tracks. Safety Sound is a fantastic place to see migratory birds.

The **Safety Roadhouse** sits by itself on a lonely stretch of sand about 20 miles from Nome. The roadhouse is open only during the summer and, during the Iditarod Race, serves as the last official stop for racers. The ceiling is plastered with dollar bills bearing witty messages and also some Iditarod memorabilia. This is one of the more remote and interesting places in Alaska to have a cup of coffee. After the roadhouse, the road crosses a number of rivers, all good for fishing. Native fish camps along the way dry fish on wooden racks. The road runs right through a river before entering the mostly Caucasian village of Council. Locals drive through or boat across, and sometimes rides can be negotiated. A few old log cabins can be seen around town from the days when Council supported 15,000 gold seekers. Nowadays, the town is primarily a summer destination for Nome residents.

ST LAWRENCE ISLAND

Located 120 miles from mainland Alaska, less than 45 miles from Russia and inhabited by Siberian Yup'ik's, the remote St Laurence Island (✪ 63°24'54"N, 170°23'57"W) is far more Russian than Alaskan. Russia is easily visible on a clear day with the mountains appearing almost close enough to touch. Ice is common in the sea and on the beach all summer. Local people speak English as well as Siberian Yup'ik – the same language spoken by 900 contemporary Yup'ik living on the Chukchi Peninsula in Russia. The island is about 100 miles long with two small native villages – Gambell and Savoonga – of about 650 people each. (Savoonga is the self-proclaimed 'Walrus Capital of the World'.) The treeless island is littered with whale and other marine mammal bones from millennia of hunting. Subsistence is the way of life here, so drying skins and various marine-mammal body parts are often found lying about. Besides bird watching, the culture and their ancient lifestyle are the main attractions of the island. Few people left on Earth live in such direct contact with nature and are so susceptible to its whims. Whale blubber (fat) and other native foods are generally available including 'eskimo ice cream' (whale or other wild animal fat mixed with berries). You'll also find some wonderful and affordable ivory carvings are available, especially in Gambell. Ivory can be sold by native Alaskans only after it has been carved, so don't buy uncarved ivory.

HISTORY The island was occupied by Siberian Yup'ik native Alaskans on and off for about 2,000 years. The Yup'ik name for the island is Sivuqaq. Then as now, residents live a mostly subsistence diet of whales, walrus and other marine mammals. Because the populations of these animals naturally fluctuate dramatically, food was not always readily available and periods of starvation were common. As a result, the island was used only occasionally as a permanent settlement and more often as a seasonal hunting area. However, during the 18th and 19th centuries, the island supported some 4,000 people in 35 villages. They travelled and hunted from 'umiaq', large open boats covered in animal skin, sometimes 25 or more feet long. Even today, some residents use skin boats. Vitus Bering – the famous Danish explorer sailing under the Russian flag – briefly visited the island in 1728. In 1900,

President Roosevelt created a reindeer reservation on the island to combat starvation. Artefacts from the island can be seen at the University of Alaska Fairbanks museum and include rain jackets made from intestines and amazing bowls made of fish skins, still bearing the fins and scales.

GETTING THERE AND AWAY Bering Air (see page 409) flies semi-regularly to St. Lawrence Island.

TOURIST INFORMATION
🄸 **City of Gambell** ☎ 985 5112;
e cityofgambell@yahoo.com
🄸 **City of Savoonga** ☎ 984 6614
🄸 **Gambell IRA Council** ☎ 985 5346;
www.kawerak.org/tribalHomePages/gambell

🄸 **Native Village of Savoonga IRA Council** ☎ 984 6414; www.kawerak.org/tribalHomePages/savoonga
🄸 **Sivuqaq Native Corporation (Gambell)** ☎ 985 5826; e sivuqaq@gci.net

WHERE TO STAY AND EAT The island is not set up for tourism, which suits some travellers perfectly. If you are in need of accommodation, it can be arranged through the native corporations. A small store and cafeteria with hamburgers in Gambell can meet basic food needs.

OTHER PRACTICALITIES
Gambell Health Clinic ☎ 985 5346   Savoonga Health Clinic ☎ 984 6513

WHAT TO SEE AND DO There are no vehicles on the island except ATVs (All Terrain Vehicles). Virtually the entire island is controlled by the two native groups and permission is required for any activity outside the villages. Birders in organised groups are the most common visitors to the island. Sea birds are abundant and many rare Asian species can be seen as they migrate through. A whale festival, including music and dancing in the school, is held in July. This event – conducted almost entirely in the Yup'ik language – is not for tourists, though they are generally invited to attend.

NUNIVAK ISLAND

Nunivak Island (⊕ 60°04'54"N, 166°22'51"W) is a large flat volcanic island resting just 30 miles offshore in the southern part of western Alaska. The island has just one village, Mekoryuk, with 200 Cup'ik native residents. Locals speak a variation of the more common Yup'ik language found elsewhere in the region. The southern half of the island is managed under the Yukon Delta National Wildlife Refuge while the rest is native-owned. Much of the island is lined with low sea cliffs, populated with thousands of seabirds. The island is also a stopping point for many migratory species of birds. The island's interior has some cinder cones and other evidence of relatively recent volcanic activity as well as many craters, some of which contain lakes. Reindeer were introduced in 1920 and today there is a large herd of some 4,000 hunted for meat by locals. In 1936, a few musk ox were transplanted to the island from Greenland by the state authorities. This was part of a larger effort to repopulate the state with musk ox after their extinction (in Alaska) in the late 1800s. Today, more than 500 roam the island providing *quivuit* – the under hairs of the musk ox, considered to be one of the softest natural materials on Earth – and meat to local people.

Tourism on Nunivak Island is in its infancy and there is essentially no tourist infrastructure. Visitors need to be self-sufficient, flexible and should not require many of the luxuries used when travelling elsewhere in Alaska. Everything must be done by special arrangement. Visitors will be rewarded with an experience of nature and culture like no other. Instead of learning about history from a museum, visitors can seek that information out amongst local elders. The University of Alaska Fairbanks Kuskokwim campus is working with the Nunivak Island Mekoryuk Native Corporation and has recently formed the Nunivak Island Cultural Education and Adventures (NICEA). NICEA offers guided outdoor activities such as kayaking, hiking and backpacking as well as cultural education for regional students and visitors alike. In addition, Cruise West recently started visiting the island a few times a year. These small luxury ships are the only way to visit the island in luxury while still having some exposure to the culture and environment.

HISTORY Cup'ik native Alaskans have inhabited Nunivak Island for more than 2,000 years, developing a rich tradition S of art and dance. Russian explorer Mikail S Vasilev was the island's first contact with the outside world in 1821. At that time, 400 people lived in 16 villages around the island, including a summer camp where Mekoryuk is today. In 1900, a flu epidemic decimated the population, leaving only a few families alive. In the 1930s the Eskimo missionary Jacob Kenick built the Evangelical Covenant Church and banned the native language as well as all traditional cultural activity. A school was built a few years later and most of the island's villages consolidated to be situated nearby. Throughout the 1940s, traditional life was mostly restored but, in 1957, a runway brought considerable change to the island. Before the island built its own high school in 1978, many families moved to Bethel to educate their children. Many of the island residents

THE BERING STRAIT BRIDGE

The concept of a bridge or tunnel from Alaska to Russia began at the turn of the 20th century with Colorado governor William Gilpin, who envisioned a railway that would circumnavigate the globe. Later, Joseph Strauss, the designer of hundreds of US bridges – most famously the Golden Gate Bridge in San Francisco – planned a bridge to connect the two continents, but it was rejected by the Russians. Until the Alaska Highway was completed in the 1940s, the bridge was just a pipe dream. Suddenly though, Alaska was opened to the rest of North America and the idea of a bridge enjoyed another moment in the sun. The first serious plan was put forward by Chinese-born cement engineer TY Lin in 1968. He took into account the immense difficulty and expense of crossing not only Alaska, but one of the most turbulent and ice-choked stretches of water on Earth. He estimated a cost of more than US$4 billion, which was probably very modest. The bridge was meant to signify the unity of the two countries. Sadly though, the Cold War broke out and Lin's plans were resigned to history.

The project's prohibitive costs are in some ways the lesser obstacle. The environmental impacts of such a project could be devastating. Hundreds, if not thousands, of rivers and streams would have to be crossed in both Russia and Alaska just to reach the Bering Strait. The ramifications of bringing road access to many native villages has not been studied and could be devastating to some communities. Furthermore, the Bering Strait is a whale and king crab migration path. The massive support pillars required to withstand the pack ice would have a large footprint on the seabed and the possible changes in currents, ice pack and movement cannot be predicted. If the bridge were to ever find funding, it would not likely come from free trade and tourism, but from oil mega-corporations looking to transport their product. This in itself carries a huge risk; an oil spill into the fast moving and ecologically rich Bering Sea could make the *Exxon Valdez* spill (see box on pages 272–3) look trivial.

have made a concerted effort to regain their language and cultural traditions and, in 2002, US federal government awarded them a significant grant to help them in their mission. The Cup'ik language is now taught in island schools.

TOURIST INFORMATION

Era/Frontier Air (✆ *450 7200, 800 478 6779 (TF); www.frontierflying.com*) Provides limited service to Mekoryuk, but travellers should be flexible as fog is common and flights are often grounded. Contact NICEA or the Native Corporation to arrange a visit and activities.

✉ Nunivak Island Cultural Education and Adventures
e wdon@nimacorporation.com;
www.nimacorporation.com/NICEALLC.htm

✉ Nunivak Island Mekoryuk Alaska ✆ 827 8636;
www.nimacorporation.com
✉ City of Mekoryuk ✆ 827 8828;
e cityofmekoryuk@yahoo.com

DIOMEDE ISLANDS

The Diomede Islands (✜ 65°45'35"N, 168°55'39"W), Little and Big Diomede, occupy a unique location in space and even time. With both the international dateline and the US/Russian border running between them, Little Diomede is always on the edge of tomorrow and both are on the front doorstep of the two countries. Located exactly in the middle of the 50-mile gap between the US and Russian mainland in the Bering Strait, only 2.5 miles of water separate Little Diomede (US) from Big Diomede (Russia). The town of US Diomede on Little Diomede Island consists of a collection of about 30 houses on stilts clinging precariously to the island's steep and rocky western slopes. The island's 146 residents are almost exclusively Ingalikmiut. Russian-owned Big Diomede is visible just off the coast. Flat space is almost non-existent on both islands, preventing the construction of a runway or even a graveyard. Instead the dead are entombed in stones on the hillside. Supplies, mail and passengers arrive by helicopter, boat, or by seaplane during the winter when pack-ice connects the two islands and blurs the line between land and sea. Though locals can easily travel on the ice between the islands, visitors need to show a passport.

Tourism is non-existent here with just a few outsiders visiting each year. The Native Village of Diomede levies a fee for visiting the island and can sometimes arrange for accommodation for visitors. A visit of a few hours is a more realistic choice, flying with the mail helicopter 45-minutes from Nome. Evergreen Helicopters (✆ *443 5334*) provide this service. **Bering Air** (✆ *443 5464; www.beringair.com*) also operates flights to the village, but only during the winter. A visit to the island can feel like a step back in time, as the island is dotted with the skins of various marine mammals stretched tight to dry in the sun and skin boats pulled up along the shore. Meat and fish hang to dry on wooden racks for months, before being stored for the winter. In addition to seals and walrus, residents hunt beluga whales and even polar bears. Elegant ivory carvings can sometimes be bought from local carvers. The island supports a huge number of seabirds, while walrus are common on both the Diomede Islands. Diomede school children have assembled an interactive panoramic image of the island. Visit: www.bssd.org/download/dio_standing_place.mov

HISTORY Ingalikmiut native Alaskans have inhabited the islands for centuries, fearlessly travelling the sea and ice to trade with both continents. When the American naturalist John Muir (see page 18) visited the island in 1881, there were just 40 people in a village known as Inalet. He said about the village:

No margin is left for a village along the shore, so, like the seabirds that breed here and fly about in countless multitudes darkening the water, the rocks and the air, the natives had to perch their huts on the cliffs, dragging boats and everything up and down steep trails, The huts are mostly of stone with skin roofs. They look like mere stone heaps, black dots on the snow at a distance, with whalebone posts set up and framed at the top to lay their canoes beyond the dogs that would otherwise eat them.

The islands were first visited by western travellers when Danish explorer Vitus Bering, sailing under the Russian flag, happened across them in 1728.

During World War II, Russia built a military base on Big Diomede and moved its residents to the mainland. Though the border between the islands had been drawn decades earlier, islanders were not affected by the invisible line until then. Being so close to one another, the two islands had formed one community, with free travel and intermarriage between them. Following World War II politics kept families apart and fostered opposing ideals and different languages. The 'Iron Curtain' was felt here perhaps more than anywhere else.

TOURIST INFORMATION
City of Diomede ✆ 686 3071;
e dio.city@yahoo.com

Diomede Native Corporation ✆ 686 3221

KING ISLAND

King Island (⊕ 64°58'00"N, 168°05'00"W) clings to a cliff 35 miles from the mainland southwest of Nome. Just a few hardy souls live in this nearly deserted town during the summer in order to hunt marine mammals.

HISTORY Traditionally, the island was inhabited all year round by about 200 Uguivangmuit. Captain James Cook named the island after a member of his crew, James King, in 1778 when natives lived in walrus-skin houses along the 700ft rocky faces that lined the one square mile island. The island experienced a boom in the 1930s and 1940s, when villagers travelled to Nome to sell their intricate ivory carvings. With this wealth, the village built a church, a school and more than 40 houses, all with electricity. During the 1950s, the island's population dwindled as villagers began to spend their winters in Nome, using the island as a summer camp for subsistence hunting. By the end of the 1970s, the island had no winter-time residents. Today, villagers still use the island for subsistence purposes during the summer and have their own native corporation. King Islanders are a distinct population within the larger Nome community and they own a number of Nome businesses in which they continue to sell their ivory carvings.

GETTING THERE AND AWAY The island is accessible via boat, helicopter and occasionally by seaplane.

TOURIST INFORMATION
King Island Native Corporation ✆ 443 5494;
e king@nome.net. Contact the corporation to make arrangements to visit.

For more information visit www.kawerak.org/tribalHomePages/kingIsland.

WHAT TO SEE The spectacular town clings to the steep hillside and looks as if it will slide into the sea at any moment. Indeed, most of the town and its original buildings

– including a grand schoolhouse – are falling apart. Marine life, sea birds and the island's unique history are the main reasons to go, but visitors will have to be entirely self-sufficient as there are no services at all. Bad weather is common so be prepared to get wet, buffeted by the wind and possibly stuck for a few days or more.

WESTERN ALASKA'S REMOTE REFUGES

Detailed topographic maps of the following areas are available through the US Geological Survey (USGS) (*4230 University Dr, Anchorage;* ↘ *786 7011*).

INNOKO NATIONAL WILDLIFE REFUGE The 3,850,000-acre Innoko National Wildlife Refuge straddles the Kaiyuh Mountains and is flanked on the western edge by the Yukon River. The refuge is marked by two distinct habitats: low, flat, wet ground studded with black spruce and low lying mountains. Around 130 species of birds – numbering 300,000 – make their home in or near the refuge's many bodies of water each year. River otter, beaver, both species of bears, lynx, fox and wolverine are all found here.

Getting there and away The Innoko Refuge is extremely remote and gets very few visitors each year. Some parts of the refuge are accessible via boat, but seaplanes are the best way to get in. The town of McGrath is the refuge's main access point. McGrath is accessible from Anchorage and other regional villages.

Tourist information
☑ Innoko National Wildlife Refuge 40 Tonzona Av (McGrath); ↘ 524 3251; www.innoko.fws.gov;

⏱ 08.00–16.30 Mon–Fri. This office has limited information, but knowledgeable staff.

Activities Like its neighbour the Yukon Delta National Wildlife Refuge, Innoko is best seen on a floating trip on one of its rivers. The Innoko River and others can provide great fishing and wildlife viewing.

NOWITNA NATIONAL WILDLIFE REFUGE Just northwest of Denali National Park and Preserve and south of the Yukon River, the two-million-acre Nowitna National Wildlife Refuge is yet another remote and little-visited refuge in western Alaska. Most of Alaska's major wildlife is found in abundance here with beautiful and varied landscapes to boot. The Nowitna River forms the heart of the refuge with wetlands and large spruce forests in lower areas transitioning to tundra in the hills.

Getting there and away Galena, just down the Yukon River from the refuge, is the main point of entry for visitors. Ruby and Tanana are closer to the park but are less commonly served by aircraft, though charters flights are always possible. McGrath is another entry point by charter plane. Yet another way to visit the park is by boat from the bridge where the Dalton Highway crosses the Yukon River 240 miles downriver or 280 miles from Nenana on the Tanana River. This trip is commonly made by village residents in the summer by boat and in the winter by snowmobile.

Tourist information
☑ National Wildlife Refuge 101 Front St (Galena); ↘ 656 1708; www.nowitna.fws.gov; ⏱ 08.00–16.30 Mon–Fri. The Nowitna Refuge

Visitor Centre in Galena has a lot of great information on the park & the many opportunities for adventure there.

Activities The 283-mile Nowitna is a mellow river ideally suited for river trips. Wildlife and fish are abundant as are mosquitoes. The extremely remote nature of

8

this park necessitates total self-sufficiency. Some fish species not found in other parts of western Alaska can be found here including sheefish, burbot, whitefish, pike and grayling as well as dog and king salmon.

KANUTI NATIONAL WILDLIFE REFUGE The 1.6-million-acre Kanuti National Wildlife Refuge straddles the Arctic Circle at the headwaters of the Koyukuk River just west of the Dalton Highway. The refuge is hit by lightning strikes all summer, sparking many wildfires that create a cycle of burn and regeneration, which is key to this particular boreal ecosystem. The many rivers in the refuge are home to a number of salmon species that travel more than 1,000 miles from the sea to spawn. Bear, wolves, moose and caribou and migratory birds are all found here.

Getting there and away The refuge is usually accessed from Bettles, which is served by small plane from Fairbanks. The park is also reasonably close to the Dalton Highway making it possible to hike into the park, although skiing in during the winter would be more practical.

Tourist information
⚠ Kanuti National Wildlife Refuge 101 12th Av (Fairbanks); ✆ 456 0329; www.kanuti.fws.gov.

Information on the refuge is available at both the Fairbanks & Coldfoot (Dalton Hwy) refuge offices.

Activities The refuge is one of the least visited in the state. Wildlife is abundant and, in most cases, the animals have not seen people before. Fishing and wildlife viewing from a boat are the best options for leisure pursuits here, as much of the ground is unsuitable for hiking.

KOYUKUK NATIONAL WILDLIFE REFUGE The 3.5-million-acre Koyukuk National Wildlife Refuge is a rich breeding ground for migratory birds, moose and world record fish. This remote wilderness is near the base of the Seward Peninsula and surrounds the flood plain of the Koyukuk River. The Three-Day Slough in the refuge's 400,000-acre Koyukuk Wilderness has been known to support ten or more moose per square mile, some of the highest densities in Alaska. As many as half a million caribou head south each winter through the Brooks Range to feed in the northern part of the refuge. Both species of bear, wolverine, lynx and other wildlife can also be found here.

Getting there and away The village of Galena is near the southern border of the refuge on the Yukon River and is served regularly by flights from Anchorage and Fairbanks. Charter flights are available from Galena to access the park. Conversely, visitors can use a motorboat to travel 312 miles down the Yukon from the Dalton Highway or down the Tanana River from Nenana, then motor up the Koyukuk River into the refuge.

Tourist information
⚠ Koyukuk National Wildlife Refuge Visitor Center
101 Front St, Galena; ✆ 656 1708;
www.nowitna.fws.gov; ⏰ 08.00–16.30 Mon–Fri

Activities To get an understanding of the extent of this modestly-sized refuge, two days are required to traverse the refuge by motorboat on the Koyukuk River. Again, a floating trip is generally the best way to see the refuge, especially since the fishing is spectacular. The Koyukuk River gets motorboat traffic making the many side rivers quieter places to paddle.

9

Northern Alaska: Arctic Circle

The Arctic region is defined in this book as everything north of the Arctic Circle at 66° latitude north. The region is dominated by the ancient and well-worn Brooks Range running roughly east to west, just north of the Arctic Circle. The range extends more than 1,100 miles from the Lisburne Peninsula across the top of Alaska to Canada. The mountains are some of the oldest in the state rising to a maximum of approximately 9,000ft and with less glaciation than other major ranges. North of the range, there are virtually no trees and the mountains give way to a seemingly endless flat expanse of tundra dotted with thousands of lakes, ponds, creeks and rivers. This area is known as the 'north slope' and it is where most of Alaska's oil comes from.

Arctic Alaska gives a new significance to the words 'vast' and 'wilderness'. Only a handful of towns dot the landscape and though oil exploration is considered by some people to be detrimental to local cultures and the environment, the actual footprint is relatively small. Arctic Alaska is penetrated by only one road; the 414-mile, all-gravel Dalton Highway, which follows the Trans-Alaska Pipeline from Fairbanks to the Arctic Ocean. The almost constant mid-summer sunlight in Arctic Alaska, combined with the amazing array of parks and refuges, makes this region popular with hardy adventurers eager to see one of the world's most remote and beautiful places.

GETTING THERE AND AWAY Arctic Alaska has only one road leading into the region; the Dalton Highway (see box on page 414). This highway should be considered as an adventure rather than an efficient way of getting anywhere. Daily flights to Kotzebue and Barrow from Anchorage and Fairbanks are fairly expensive. Small planes connect the remaining small villages.

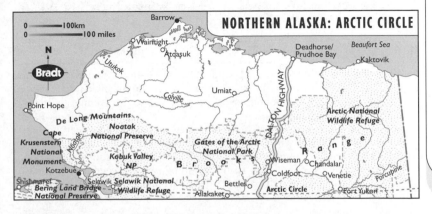

WHAT ARE THE NORTHERN LIGHTS?

The fantastic light displays that occur over Arctic and Antarctic regions of the earth are called *Aurora borealis* in the northern hemisphere (and *Aurora australis* in the southern hemisphere). In Alaska they are generally referred to as the northern lights. The phenomenon was first documented in the 16th century by the famed Italian scientist Galileo. Before him, countless ancient cultures from northern and southern regions described the lights in stories and folklore and incorporated them into their religions. Scandinavians believed the northern lights were the reflection of millions of herring in the ocean while some native people of Alaska believed them to be their ancestors dancing across the sky.

The northern lights can be seen regularly in most regions of Alaska, particularly in the north and during the winter. The lights are created when particles from the sun strike the earth's magnetosphere and, due to its shape, are directed to the north and south poles. Gases in the earth's atmosphere stop these solar particles *en route* to the earth's surface and the resulting collision emits photons visible as the northern lights. Each gas in the earth's atmosphere emits a unique colour when struck by solar particles. Greens and blues occur at about 100 miles up, while red is created much higher. During periods of intense solar activity, the northern lights are at their brightest and are visible at their furthest distance from the poles.

More than 5,000 Japanese visitors come to Alaska each winter to see the northern lights. While some come to simply watch and maybe take a few photos, others believe a new marriage consummated under the northern lights will be a happy one. Eitherway, those involved in Alaskan tourism are excited to see winter tourism increasing. Fairbanks and some of the surrounding villages have become a Mecca for winter tourists seeking this spectacular natural light show. Any time between October and April is a good time to see the lights, but braving the sub-polar conditions of mid-winter can ensure a sighting on almost every night. For many it's the sight and highlight of a lifetime. Remember to wrap up warm though: a cup of hot coffee thrown into the air will freeze instantly at temperatures of −60°C.

By air

✈ **Alaska Airlines** ☎ 800 252 7522; www.alaskaair.com

✈ **Arctic Air Guides** ☎ 442 3030. Charter flights from Kotzebue.

✈ **Bering Air** ☎ 442 3943 or 442 3187, 800 478 3943 (TF); www.beringair.com. Serves Kotzebue & other regional communities including Kobuk & Ambler.

✈ **Frontier Air** ☎ 450 7200, 800 478 6779 (TF); www.frontierflying.com. Serves most Arctic villages of any size from Fairbanks.

✈ **Mavrik Air** ☎ 442 3949. A small charter outfit operating in Kotzebue.

✈ **Arctic Northwestern Aviation** ☎ 442 3525

DALTON HIGHWAY

Cutting the Arctic in half, the 414-mile Dalton Highway provides a unique opportunity to drive through Alaska's vast and largely uninhabited Arctic region. The word 'highway' is slightly misleading, however, since it's technically a gravel road built for, and used by, large, fast-moving trucks servicing the Trans-Alaska Pipeline and bringing supplies to the Prudhoe Bay oil fields. The scenery from the road is possibly the best on Earth, not to mention the views after a hike up a roadside peak. Wildlife commonly seen along the road includes musk ox, caribou, bears and sometimes wolves. The roadside fishing is also excellent. The gates of the Arctic National Park and the Arctic National Wildlife Refuge are within hiking distance of the road, making the road a great access point for those wanting to explore these parks without paying for a charter flight.

Driving the all-gravel Dalton Highway is not the same as cruising down your home highway or even the semi-rugged Denali Highway for that matter. The road winds its way through some of the world's most remote terrain, climbs through the Brooks Range and traverses the massive North Slope before ending unceremoniously in the depressing oil town of Deadhorse. At least one flat tyre is almost inevitable, so bring at least two spare tyres. The road is still used by commercial traffic shuttling supplies north. Give these enormous 18-wheel lorries a wide berth: they drive extremely fast and spew rocks that break windshields. Gas, towing and repair services are few and far between so plan to be almost totally self-sufficient. For a vehicle with an average-sized fuel tank, the trip does not require extra fuel in cans, but it doesn't hurt to take one just in case. If you think fuel is expensive in Fairbanks, wait till you fill up in Coldfoot!

Early August is perhaps the best time to drive the Dalton Highway with bug numbers reduced and autumn colours sweeping across the tundra in waves of red, yellow and orange. However, cool nights, rain and even snow are common.

Most motorists camp along the way but simple lodging is available in Yukon Crossing, Coldfoot, Wiseman and Deadhorse. Camping is allowed almost anywhere along the road except near the Toolik Lake Area (at miles 278–293). Three free, primitive campsites are at Five Mile (mile 60), Arctic Circle (mile 115) and Galbraith Lake (mile 275). Marion Creek at mile 180 is the only organised campground on the highway with the usual facilities, a fee of US$8 and a host. Only Marion Creek and Five Mile have potable water. Treat all stream water before drinking it.

The Dalton Highway was originally called the Haul Road since all the food

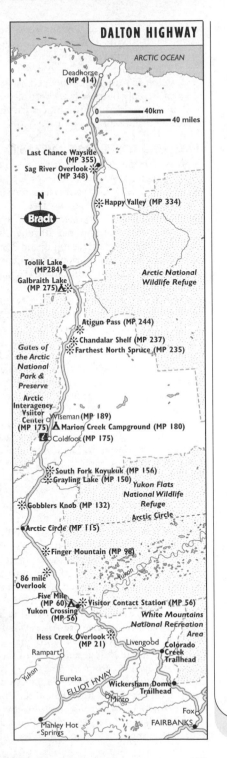

and equipment the oil workers used on the north-slope oil fields was 'hauled' north. In 1981, the road was named in honour of Alaska-born Arctic engineer James Dalton, known for his work on the Distance Early Warning Line (DEW), a Cold War era enemy detection system. The road was closed to the public until 1981, when 211 miles were opened. In 1994, the road was opened to Deadhorse, a small oil-supply outpost just short of the Arctic Ocean. Unfortunately, the short road to the Arctic Ocean is not open to the public, but tours to the sea can be organised in Deadhorse (see page 426).

TRAVELLING NORTH FROM FAIRBANKS At mile 56 is the Yukon River and an impressive bridge. On the north side is the **Yukon River Camp** (↘ 474 3557) with gas, tyre repair, food and rooms for US$150–200. A little further north is the **Hot Spot Café** (↘ 451 7543) with the same services. At mile 105.3, the road crosses the Kanuti River. At 14 miles downriver is the remote and seldom-visited **Kanuti Hot Springs**. Winter is the preferred time to visit as skis or snowmobiles can be used, but more than one intrepid traveller has ventured to the springs during the summer. One possibility is to raft the Kanuti River to the springs, then hike the 12 or so miles back via Caribou Mountain. The water is very hot and the pools generally need some modification. Arctic Circle is at mile 115 (latitude 66°) and is marked by a large sign.

Driving all the way to Deadhorse is generally just for those who have a burning desire to see (or even swim in) the Arctic Ocean. The best trip for hiking, camping and general scenery is from Fairbanks to somewhere around the **Toolik Lake** area. The most scenic part of the trip is travelling through the Brooks Range and once the land starts to flatten on the north side many motorists turn back. Be sure to make it at least to the amusing sign at mile 235, pointing out Alaska's northernmost spruce tree and warning you not to cut it. **Atigun Pass** at mile 244 is the highway's highest point and a great place to hike from. As the landscape flattens, the scenery become more repetitive, but your chances of seeing musk ox improve.

Coldfoot, at mile 175 of the Dalton Highway, is little more than a truck stop in the Arctic – the most northerly truck stop in the world, in fact. The town of 35 people (12 in the winter) has struggled along since it was founded in 1898 as a gold mining camp. The name changed from Slate Creek when prospectors got 'cold feet' at the onset of winter. The town's heyday was during the first few years of the 20th century and, by 1912, the town was practically deserted. The discovery of oil in Prudhoe Bay in 1969 and the subsequent construction of the Dalton Highway and the pipeline reinvigorated the area. The town – even though it is 60 miles north of the Arctic Circle – has all the essentials, but only just. Rooms are converted trucker quarters and funky to say the least. The Truck Stop serves diner food (burgers and sandwiches) during the day but put on a 'fancier' spread when Princess Tours rolls in. Also offering rooms is **Coldfoot Camp** (↘ 474 3500; www.coldfootcamp.com) located next to the post office. It has petrol, a café, RV spaces and rooms for rent. Rooms are US$219 dbl and RV spaces are US$35 or US$15 for tents. The café is open 05.00–midnight daily. Remember to get petrol here. In town you'll also find **Coyote Air** (*Office on the Coldfoot airstrip;* ↘ 678 5995, 800 252 0603 (TF); www.flycoyote.com) who charter flights in the area and fly to the Arctic National Wildlife Refuge and Gates of the Arctic; and the **Alaska State Troopers** (*near the Coldfoot airstrip;* ↘ 678 5201). If you would like to sly straight in to Coldfoot, try **Air Arctic** (↘ 474 3550; www.airarctic.com) with regular small-plane flights from Fairbanks for US$430 return.

The town of **Wiseman** at mile 189 was formed around 1919 when a few Coldfoot residents decided to do their own thing a little further north. There are a few accommodation options here too, including: **Arctic Getaway** (*3 rooms; Igloo*

Straddling the Arctic Circle, less than 20 miles east of Kotzebue, the Selawik National Wildlife Refuge is a vast, remote and largely untouched wilderness about the size of the state of Connecticut. The park has more than 24,000 lakes, which – along with its abundance of wildlife – aren't so much 'managed' as left in nature's hands. The park gets its name from the Inupiat word *siilvik*, the large fish found throughout the Arctic and more commonly known as the *sheefish*. This fish grows to more than 50lbs and is known to sporting fishermen as the 'tarpon of the north'. Nine other species of fish make their home in the refuge, as do 30 mammal species and more than 160 migratory bird species. The western Arctic caribou herd – the largest herd in Alaska – migrate through the refuge numbering in their hundreds of thousands. On the north side of the Waring Mountains, the massive Kobuk River Delta is a landscape perforated with bodies of water, forming ideal habitats for fish and birds and is a much-used thoroughfare for locals in small boats as well as adventurers. On the south side of these mountains, the Selawik River provides further habitat and transportation for the small Inupiat town of Selawik. The refuge is also of significant historical importance as it was an integral part of the Bering Land bridge migration path used by the first people to set foot in North America some 12,000 years ago.

GETTING THERE Kotzebue, served by daily jet service from Anchorage, is where most visitors start their journey. From Kotzebue, the refuge can be reached by boat or small plane in the summer and by snowmobile in the winter.

TOURIST INFORMATION
🖥 **Selawik National Wildlife Refuge** 160 2nd Av; ☎ 442 3799; e selawik@fws.gov; www.selawik.fws.gov; ⏰ 08.00–17.00 Mon–Fri. The refuge office is in Kotzebue within walking distance of the airport.

ACTIVITIES The Selawik National Wildlife Refuge is ideally explored by boat on the scenic, meandering Selawik River. The river and its tributaries have great fishing for the refuges' namesake, the mighty *sheefish* as well as Northern pike, burbot, Arctic grayling, dolly varden and others. As the Selawik River cleaves the park neatly in two, a trip down this river affords visitors the best and most prolonged experience of the park.

8; ☎ 678 4456; *www.arcticgetaway.com*), which has three cabins for US$95–195 per night with kitchens and breakfast; and **Boreal Lodging** (*5 rooms; 1 Timberwolf Trail;* ☎ 678 4566; *www.boreallodge.com*). Located on the western edge of town, they have a small lodge and cabin for US$90 double and US$140 double, plus satellite TV and a phone!

To reach the tiny town of Wiseman, head three miles down a spur road at mile 185 of the Dalton Highway. The town consists of a collection of rustic cabins with some impressive mountains looming in the background. The old post office and the outdoor Koyukuk Mining Museum are worth seeing. The trading company is occasionally open but doesn't keep much on sale anyway.

FURTHER INFORMATION For information on the Dalton Highway and some handy brochures, visit the **Public Lands Information Center** (*250 Cushman St;* ☎ 456 0527; ⏰ 09.00–18.00 daily) in Fairbanks. The impressive new **Arctic Interagency Visitor Center** (*Mile 175 Dalton Hwy;* ☎ 678 5209; ⏰ 10.00–22.00 daily) in Coldfoot is by far the best place to get up-to-date information on the area and road. Ask the rangers about hikes, camping, fishing and wildlife activity. For driving conditions call the **Arctic Interagency Visitor Center** in Coldfoot or the **Fairbanks Department of Transportation** (↘ 456 7623). Finally, the **Dalton Highway Express** (↘ 474 3555; www.daltonhighwayexpress.com) run a shuttle service on the Dalton Highway. Tickets cost US$106 to Coldfoot and US$221 to Deadhorse one-way.

KOTZEBUE Population: 3,200

Located 190 miles north of Nome and just 30 miles north of the Arctic Circle, Kotzebue (⊕ 66°53'50"N, 162°35'28"W) is the second-largest town in the region (after Barrow). The town sits at the end of the Baldwin Peninsula, a long gravel spit on Kotzebue Sound at the mouth of the Kobuk and Noatak Rivers. The town is predominantly Inupiat and the economy is based around the transportation of goods to distant villages and also the nearby Red Dog Zinc Mine – the largest zinc mine in the world.

Visitors seldom visit Kotzebue except when jumping immediately onto another plane to travel to a more remote part of the bush. Many charter services shuttle hunters into the surrounding countryside to chase bear, moose and caribou. During the late autumn, the tiny airport looks like a camouflage convention. Many groups, who go rafting along the Noatak or Kobuk rivers, start and end in Kotzebue. The town of Kotzebue does have some sights and it is fun to walk around for a day.

GETTING THERE AND AWAY
By air
Alaska Airlines ↘ 800 252 7522; www.alaskaair.com. Daily flights from Anchorage.

Frontier Air ↘ 450 7200, 800 478 6779 (TF); www.frontierflying.com

GETTING AROUND
By air
✈ **Arctic Air Guides Flying Service** ↘ 442 3030. Canoe & raft rental & also a charter flight service.
✈ **Bering Air** ↘ 442 3943 or 442 3187, 800 478 3943 (TF); www.beringair.com
✈ **Mavrik Air** ↘ 442 3949. A small charter outfit in Kotzebue.

✈ **Northwestern Aviation** ↘ 442 3525. Charter flight service with staff who are knowledgeable about regional boating, hiking & wildlife viewing opportunities.

By road
🚗 **B&D Cab Company** ↘ 442 2244
🚗 **Kikiktagruk Inupiat Corporation** (see below). Rents vehicles including 3 SUVs & 1 truck.

🚗 **Kobuk Cab Company** ↘ 442 3651

TOURIST INFORMATION
ℹ **City of Kotzebue** 258A Third Av; ↘ 442 3401; www.kotzpdweb.tripod.com/city
ℹ **Kotzebue IRA Council** ↘ 442 3467; www.kotzebueira.org
ℹ **Kikiktagruk Inupiat Corporation** 373A Second Av; ↘ 442 6118; www.kikiktagruk.com

ℹ **Innaigvik Education and Information Center** ↘ 442 3890. Natural & cultural history presentations are often held at the centre during the summer. Call for a schedule of events.
ℹ **National Park Visitor Center** Second St; ↘ 442 3760

LOCAL TOURS AND ACTIVITIES
Arctic Tours ↘ 800 468 2248. Offer tours of town & the museum, including cultural & natural history information. Arctic Tours works with Alaska Airlines

to offer 1-day tours of Kotzebue including airfare from Anchorage, starting at US$375.

The Cape Krusenstern National Park occupies a unique piece of coastal tundra just north of Kotzebue and west of the Noatak River. The monument is of particular natural, as well historic, importance since ancient peoples may have lived there as early as 9,000 years ago. Many former village sites are visible today, resembling low coastal ridges. Because of deposits of sand along the coastline, the oldest town sites are the furthest from the shore. While the sites are not as impressive as the Egyptian pyramids at Giza, the people who inhabited this area predated the pinnacle of Egyptian civilisation.

The landscape is typified by low rolling hills and wet tundra permeated by streams and lakes. Much of the monument's coastline is protected by sand spits, shielding the coastal environment from harsh weather and winter ice. These lagoons provide ideal habitat for birds, fish and marine mammals. A single road crosses the northern portion of the monument, leading to the Red Dog Mine. The lead and zinc pit mine is 50 miles from the coast and the largest of its kind in the world. A tide-water port allows supplies to come in and raw metals to leave. The mine hires workers from regional native villages almost exclusively and the pay is very good. Still, some residents and environmentalists are concerned about the mine's effects on the environment and traditional ways of life.

GETTING THERE Most visitors to the park start their journey in Kotzebue after flying in from Anchorage or Fairbanks. The southern end of the monument can be reached by small boat in good weather from Kotzebue. From there, the intrepid and totally self-sufficient adventurer could continue along the beach by foot as far as he/she dared go. About 100 miles of beach walking will take you to the small Inupiat Eskimo village of Kivalina where you can fly back to Kotzebue via small plane. The town has 6 cars and no visitor facilities of any kind.

TOURIST INFORMATION
Z Cape Krusenstern National Monument ✆ 442 3890; www.nps.gov/kova; ⏱ 08.00–17.00 Mon–Fri.

ACTIVITIES Cape Krusenstern National Park is completely undeveloped – a boon for some, a drawback for others. The monument has many miles of beach hiking and a number of large protected lagoons for sea kayaking. Hiking inland is scenic but wet so visitors should wear rubber boots. Musk ox, caribou and nesting birds are reasonably common sights. High winds can make life tough, transportation impossible and the temperatures can be below freezing even during mid-summer.

Arctic Circle Educational Adventures ✆ 442 3509; www.fishcamp.org. This interesting non-profit tour company, run by LaVonne Hendricks, is designed to empower local native youth by presenting aspects of their culture to visitors. Visitors who stay overnight at the camp also receive meals & are welcome to help by catching & preparing salmon, picking berries etc. The camp is 5 miles outside Kotzebue on the beach.

WHERE TO STAY
Nullagvik Hotel (79 rooms) ✆ 442 3331; www.nullagvik.com. A new building was recently constructed to replace the old one & although more expensive, it is quite nice for a hotel in the Arctic. Simple & clean, generic rooms often have good views of the sound. The hotel restaurant isn't bad & a small gift shop has some locally made crafts. Expect to pay US$200 or more for a dbl. TV. $$$$
Sue's Bed & Breakfast (4 rooms) 587 Bison St; ✆ 442 3770. Simple rooms with no b/fast. $$

⚔ WHERE TO EAT AND DRINK

✗ **Bayside Restaurant** 303 Shore Av; ☎ 442 3600; ⏲ 07.00–23.00 Mon–Sat & 07.00–22.00 Sun. Near the Nullagvik Hotel (see page 419), this Chinese/American place offers some of the better fare in town. $$$

✗ **Empress Restaurant** 301 Shore Av; ☎ 442 4304; ⏲ 11.00–22.45 Mon–Sat & 13.00–23.00 Sun.

Chinese/American cuisine. Not very pretty from the outside but one of the better meals in town. Good views. Lunch & dinner only, with large portions. $$$

✗ **Arctic Sun Coffee** 308 Shore Av; ☎ 442 2828; ⏲ 12.30–18.00 Mon–Fri. $$

OTHER PRACTICALITIES

Alaska Commercial 395 Bison St; ☎ 442 3285; ⏲ 07.00–22.00 Mon–Sat & 09.00–21.00 Sun. A grocery store in town with a little of everything.
Bison Street Store ☎ 442 2758
EZ Market 24hr Store 606 Bison St; ☎ 442 4544
Maniilaq Medical Health Center ☎ 442 3321
Public Library ☎ 442 2410; ⏲ 12.00–20.00 Mon–Fri, 12.00–18.00 Sat. Internet access, photocopies etc.

Recreation Center Third Av & Wanda St; ☎ 442 3045; ⏲ 06.00–21.00 Mon, 12.00–21.00 Tue–Sat. This large grey building has some surprisingly modern facilities incl a gym, racket ball court, sauna & showers for US$5/day.
Uutuku Store 571 Friends Way; ☎ 442 3337

WHAT TO SEE AND DO About 25 miles of road surround the town, providing some moderately scenic hiking. An interesting cemetery can be found in the middle of town at Lagoon Street and Third Avenue. Walking toward the sea from the airport, visitors can see a collection of massive jade boulders near some old industrial junk. Just beyond the boulders is a well-preserved native dwelling. The new Northwest Arctic Heritage Center is probably the best place in town to learn about the area and its history or prepare for an adventure into one of the surrounding parks and refuges. Shore Avenue can also be an enjoyable stroll with houses perched right on the turbid sea and locals going about their business.

Northwest Arctic Heritage Center (☎ 442 3890; ⏲ 08.00–17.00 Mon–Fri; free admission) This brand new museum is currently being built and should be open for the summer of 2010. The facility will feature a museum with native artwork and information on nearby parks and refuges.

Kobuk Valley National Park Kobuk Valley National Park lies about 60 miles east of Kotzebue, between the Baird and Waring Mountain ranges. In addition to the 500,000 plus caribou that pass through the park each spring and autumn, the park is home to the Arctic oddity of sand dunes. The park encompasses a central portion of the Kobuk valley and around 61 miles of the Kobuk River. The river and the wildlife it supports have been central to the lives of local native people for almost 9,000 years. Onion Portage, a National Historic Landmark, is a site on the Kobuk River where native people have gathered for thousands of years to hunt caribou as they cross the river each year. Even today, locals hunt caribou as they cross the river. Every part of the animal is used and is an important winter food source.

Arctic Sand Dunes Drifting down the placid, but distinctly Arctic Kobuk River, a surprising sight reveals itself – a vast expanse of white sand dunes. Stranger yet is the sight of thousands of caribou crossing the dunes as they have done so for thousands of years on their way north and south each year. The dunes stretch over an area of more than 200,000 acres near the small native town of Ambler, but much of that area is covered in tundra. Still, more than 20,000 acres of active dunes poke above the surrounding landscape and can be seen along the Kobuk River. They are the Great Kobuk, Little Kobuk, and the Hunt River Dunes.

In 2007, I embarked on a trip to the Noatak River in Arctic Alaska with a plan to float the river, and also to hike and thrash my way through hundreds of miles of terrain in a desperate attempt to do something unique and 'fun'. Forbidden by my parents to go it alone, I invited a friend from Massachusetts, purposefully withholding the trip's gruesome details until he was safely in Alaska and couldn't bail out. We flew from Anchorage to Kotzebue, then boarded a small plane to the native Alaskan bush community of Ambler. As we assembled our folding canoe on the banks of the Kobuk River, the town's people came down, no doubt thinking we were yet another party going downriver. When they discovered we were in fact going *upriver*, they were shocked. Though we had never paddled up *any* river before and didn't even know if it was possible, we talked tough and almost convinced ourselves.

A few days of sun, warm weather and upriver paddling brought us deep into the Brooks Range where we eventually left the river, broke down our folding canoe and began hiking into the mountains with more than 275lbs of food, gear and the boat. Suddenly, the sunny weather was replaced by a dark overcast sky threatening rain. It didn't rain, it snowed! From that day on the temperature dropped between −15°C/5°F and −12°C/10°F each day. After 12 days of breaking ice with our paddles, pitching our tent every night on the snow, and progressively getting lower on food supplies, we finally reached the town of Noatak. Despite the hunger and fear, we will never forget the massive herd of caribou that passed right by our hiding place, hoofing the snow from the frozen ground to nibble at the icy lichens and grasses; the brown bear that peacefully watched us from the bank as we silently floated by, our eyes tracking his magnificent bulk and his nose trying to solve the mystery of our identity; and the profound and unexpected effect of so many days in a pure wilderness filled to the brim with beauty and terror. The following snippet from one of our conversations sums it up perfectly, I think:

'Are you ok?' asks Peter.

Any question asked with enough frequency eventually becomes rhetorical. This particular question, however, had become not only rhetorical, but a symbol of our entire trip.

'Are you ok?' he asks again.

I try to form an answer in my mind before I speak so I don't insight panic.

'Peter', I want to say, 'We are above the Arctic Circle. We are on a 400-mile canoe trip. Need I remind you, neither of us have ever canoed before? Things have been OK until now, but for Christ's sake, I just sprained my ankle on a frozen puddle in the corner of the tent! There's snow falling from the rainfly and last night, the Gore-Tex on my down sleeping bag froze so solid I couldn't move, remember that? We've done the 45-mile upriver paddle. We even made it through the Brooks Range with 275 pounds of gear. But who could have known winter could hit in one single night? I've never heard of that! We have more than 300 miles to go and nothing but freezing temperatures, frozen rivers and snow ahead. I'll be honest with you Pete, I'm just not sure we're going to make it. While I'm spilling my guts, those missing Brazil nuts and cheese? A marmot didn't eat it man, I did. Also, it's time you know that the EPIRB (Emergency Position Indicating Radio Beacon) was brought more as a symbol of safety rather than an actual device *for* safety. The batteries I brought don't even fit. And no, we don't have enough food to get us out. I'm sorry man, if one of has to eat the other, you can have me'.

But instead, I wriggle deeper into my sleeping bag, pull my hat over my eyes and dumbly answer:

'Yeah man, I'm ok'.

The dunes are a reminder of the park's heavily glaciated history, though no glaciers exist in the park today. The grinding action of glaciers on stone over the past 10,000–20,000 years created masses of sediment that was washed down river, then blown west along the valley by high winds. The dunes are the largest of their kind in Arctic Alaska.

Getting there The Kobuk Valley National Park is remote with no roads. Access is provided by charter flight from Kotzebue, either directly into the park or to one of the outlying villages, then into the park via small boat.

Tourist information
Kobuk Valley Nation Park ❧ 442 3890;
www.nps.gov/kova; ⊕ 08.00–17.00 Mon–Fri

Activities With the prevailing sunny, but cool weather, hiking, camping, fishing and boating are all very popular in the park. A great way to see the park is by rafting along the Kobuk River from Ambler (or further upstream). The upper portion of the river is the best but also the most technically challenging stretch with class IV and V rapids just below Watson Lake. The 30 miles above Watson Lake are rarely floated. Though this is a popular trip and you may see other groups, it is well worth sharing the experience with the 'crowds'. Having personally done long trips in this area, I can attest to the rugged beauty of the landscape. Always plan more days than you will need since the weather can make paddling hard or ground your pick-up flight for days on end. Even if the weather is not a variable, you will want extra days to take advantage of the amazing hiking throughout the park.

The Noatak National Preserve
The 6.7-million-acre Noatak National Preserve protects one of North America's most pristine river systems. Because almost 90% of the park is designated wilderness, the preserve forms an amazingly complete ecosystem with virtually no development. Like the neighbouring parks and refuges, the Noatak National Preserve is home to hundreds of thousands of caribou as well as other wildlife including bear, wolves and thousands of migratory birds. The most common way to see the preserve is to float along the Noatak River. The scenery is normally low rolling hills with mountains rising in the distance. As there are no trees, the opportunities for wildlife viewing are excellent.

Getting there The preserve is remote and wild with no roads or facilities. Access is by boat or small plane, usually from Kotzebue but sometimes by plane from the Dalton Highway communities.

Tourist information
Noatak National Preserve ❧ 442 3890;
www.nps.gov/noat; ⊕ 08.00–17.00 Mon–Fri

Activities Though the most popular way to see the preserve is by boat on the Noatak River, hiking and camping are also possible. The terrain is generally fairly friendly with the best hiking above the brush line along the sides or tops of ridges and hills. The Noatak River is a popular raft trip because of its mellow nature and amazing, unspoiled scenery. The fishing and hiking are excellent and for the most part the river is very calm with only light turbulence (class II) at the headwaters and near Noatak Canyon a few days' journey upstream from the town of Noatak. Boaters can start at the river's headwater at the Gates of the Arctic National Park and float for nearly 400 miles to Kotzebue or get picked up by small plane anywhere in between.

Allow 18 days or more to travel from the headwaters to Kotzebue Sound. The autumn is a less crowded, less bug-infested and a more colourful time to visit the preserve, although winter can hit literally overnight so be prepared for the worst. Even during the summer, temperatures can drop suddenly and the weather can change quickly, so always 'over-prepare' in Arctic Alaska.

Those looking for a trip like ours (see box *A Noatak River Epic* on page 421), try hiking though the Brooks Range and floating along the Noatak River in September. For everyone else, early August is much more civilised.

BARROW *Population: 4,541*

Barrow (⊕ 71°18'21"N, 156°44'29"W) has the distinction of being the most northerly community of any size in the US. Another claim that the locals are less boastful of is that Barrow consistently records the lowest average temperatures in the state. While the state's interior achieves the coldest days, Barrow's average July temperature is 4°C/40°F and the average for February is –26°C/–15°F making the yearly average temperature little more than –12°C/–10°F. Yet another Barrow distinction is that it is one of the cloudiest places in Alaska: fog and wind are very common all summer and ice is often pressed up to the beach, in front of town, until July. Most visitors fly in for a day just to say they have been there, but a few days or more would better suit the intrepid, culturally curious traveller. Cultural events and rituals are wonderful to witness here, and include the centuries-old bowhead whale ceremonies. Another phenomenon many visitors travel north to see is the midnight sun, more dramatic in Barrow than anywhere else in the US. In early May, the sun rises and does not set again for more than 80 days, finally dropping below the horizon around 1 August. Conversely, during the winter, the sun does not rise for more than 60 days – a spectacle that less visitors are keen to see!

Barrow is north of just about everything except the North Pole. The town is more than 700 miles north of Anchorage, some 2,000 miles north of Seattle and 320 miles north of the Arctic Circle. The population, the vast majority of whom are native Inupiat, hovers around 4,000 people. The town is a regional goods distribution centre for the northwest coast of Alaska. Sitting on more than 1,300ft of permafrost, locals need to do little more than dig a hole to get year-round refrigeration. 'Perma-fridges' – reinforced holes in the ground caked with ice – can be seen around town and are often used for storing whale meat.

Barrow is colourful in character, if not in landscape. One house has palm trees ingeniously made from upright driftwood logs topped with whale baleen fronds. The local high school football team plays on a new astroturf field right on the ocean, across from the very odd DEW (Distant Early Warning) station, built to warn the US of enemy aircraft. The muddy road system has only one stop light and there is some discussion amongst locals as to whether it has ever turned red. While some areas are tundra and make for easy hiking, others are choked with shrubs. Stick to the waterways or the hillsides where the walking is easiest.

HISTORY Barrow has been inhabited by native peoples since around 500AD, partly because of the many whales that migrated past the point each year. Today, remnants of their culture such as whalebones and artefacts wash from the eroding bluffs along the sea. Whales and other marine life were the mainstays of the Inupiat people's subsistence lifestyle, much of which continues to this day. When Captain Beechey of the English Royal Navy charted the coastline, he named Point Barrow after Sir John Barrow of the British Admiralty. The town, just to the south, later borrowed the name. In the 19th and 20th centuries, American whaling parties plied the waters often employing some native Alaskans

Barrow area Inupiat have been hunting bowhead whales for more than 2,000 years. Bowhead whales are often called 'Ice Whales' because they spend their entire lives in the world's Arctic regions and do not migrate to warmer climates like many other species. So closely linked are the bowhead and the native peoples of the area, the Inupiat are often called 'people of the ice whale'. Inupiat have traditionally taken less than 50 whales each year, but in the 1840s commercial whaling started in earnest around Alaska, depleting the population of these slow-moving creatures by more than 60%, from 50,000 to less than 20,000. Like their relative, the right whale, bowhead whales were favoured because they were slow moving (and therefore easier to catch), float when killed and are extremely rich in oil. When the US became a member of the International Whaling Commission (IWC) in 1946, commercial whaling was banned in Alaska and around the US. The IWC now allows Inupiat Eskimos to take as many as 56 whales per year, a harvest not expected to hurt the bowhead's recovery, which has been significant since commercial whaling was stopped. Under the stewardship of the Inupiat and the IWC, the Alaskan population of bowhead whales has exploded from less than 1,000 when commercial whaling was banned in Alaska, to more than 12,000 today.

The Inupiat hunt the bowhead each spring and autumn as they have done so for centuries. During April and May, hunters travel out onto the pack-ice in white parkas to watch for whales travelling along 'leads' (ice-free passages). Even today, seal-skin kayaks called *umiaq* are used insteadof rigid-hull boats because they can be dragged silently across the ice. These *umiaq* can be launched and paddled through the ice without a sound, unlike metal boats, which scare the whales away with their metallic clanking.

The autumn hunt takes place during September and October. Hunters use modern metal boats with outboard motors, as the seas are generally rougher. It takes about ten hours to drag a 50ft whale less than 25 miles. When the whales are hauled onshore, the entire town turns out to participate in the butchering process.

After a successful hunt, the town of Barrow erupts in the Nalukataq celebration held at the end of June. The day-long festival and feast includes a blanket toss using coarse whale meat. Afterward a dance is held and the community shares 20–40 tons of meat and other products from each whale.

The bowhead lives farther north than any other whale species and uses its arched head to break through the ice to create breathing holes. Using their baleen (fine fibres on 'fronds' in the whale's mouth) they filter huge amounts of plankton from the sea. Scientists speculate the bowhead may live to be 200 or more years old. Stone spearheads have been found lodged in the flesh of living whales, suggesting that individual hunting may have pre-dated commercial whaling.

as crew members. Many came from New Bedford, Massachusetts on a journey of more than 20,000 miles circling South America (there was no Panama Canal until 1914!). The Inupiat Heritage Center in Barrow is the best place to learn about this fascinating history.

GETTING THERE AND AWAY Barrow has no roads in or out and is most commonly accessed by plane from Anchorage or Fairbanks. **Alaska Airlines** (✆ 800 252 7522 *(TF); www.alaskaair.com*) makes the trip from Anchorage (US$575 return) and from Fairbanks (US$515 return) every day during mid-summer. Alaska Airlines also offers day and overnight trips to Barrow that include airfare and a simple tour that touches on wildlife and culture for US$575pp. The overnight version is US$689pp for a couple and US$804 if your alone. **Frontier/Era** (✆ *266 8394, 800 8668394 (TF); www.flyera.com*) also makes the trip to Barrow from Fairbanks (daily except Sat; US$505 return) and from Anchorage (daily; US$575 return).

TOURIST INFORMATION

☑ **City of Barrow** ✆ 852 5211; www.cityofbarrow.org. A tiny, grey visitor information office is located next to a pole with signs indicating how incredibly far away the rest of the world is.

☑ **Inupiat Heritage Center** ✆ 852 0422; ⏱ 08.30–17.00 Mon–Fri; US$10/5/3 adult/student/senior. The Heritage Center was dedicated in February 1999 & houses exhibits, artefact collections, library, gift shop & a room showing traditional craft demonstrations. Free cultural programs are held each Sat 12.00–13.30. Free science & culture meetings are held on the 3rd Wed of each month 18.00–21.00.

☑ **Ukpeagvik Inupiat Corporation** ✆ 852 4460; www.ukpik.com

LOCAL TOURS AND ACTIVITIES

Tundra Tours ✆ 852 3900. These tours can be booked through the Top of the World Hotel & can incl as little or as much as you would like to see. Flights to Barrow, accommodation, trips to see native traditions & sightseeing can all be arranged.

NorthernMost Tours ✆ 852 5893; www.northernmosttoursbarrow.com. Owned by a local native family, the company offers 2 tours per day plus a midnight tour in nice vans. Tours include city excursions & trips to Point Barrow for birdwatching & the chance to see walrus & even polar bears. Tours cost US$70–100pp.

Northern Alaska Tour Company ✆ 474 8600, 800 474 1986 (TF); www.northernalaska.com. Offers trips to Barrow that include a stop in the minuscule town of Coldfoot along the Dalton highway, followed by a short tour of Barrow. Small planes run by Air Arctic (✆ *474 3550; www.airarctic.com*) provide the transportation and keep the groups small and make the flight more exciting than the Alaska Air jets. The trip from Fairbanks costs US$749pp.

WHERE TO STAY

🏠 **King Eider Inn** (19 rooms) 1752 Ahkovak St; ✆ 852 4700; www.kingeider.net. Quite good rooms with the added benefit of a guest sauna. $$$

🏠 **Airport Inn** (16 rooms) 1815 Momeganna St; ✆ 852 2525; e Airportinn@barrow.com. Clean & pleasant rooms with a friendly staff & decent prices. Fresh bread & continental b/fast served every morning. Fridge, microwave, TV, Wi-Fi. $$$

🏠 **Top of the World Hotel** (50 rooms) 1200 Agvik St; ✆ 852 3900; www.tundratoursinc.com. Simple but clean rooms. Mexican restaurant & gift shop are attached. TV, telephone, fridge. $$$

WHERE TO EAT AND DRINK

✗ **Arctic Pizza** 125 Apayuik St; ✆ 852 4222; ⏱ 11.00–23.00 daily. Mexican Italian, seafood & of course, pizza. A large with one topping is US$18. $$$

✗ **Pepe's North of The Border** 1204 Agvik St; ✆ 852 8200; ⏱ 06.00–22.00 daily. This colourful Mexican restaurant has good food & décor reminiscent of an exploded piñata. The owner is Fran Tate who hosts the local radio show Jazz Below Zero on KBRW. She is also the one that visitors should contact about joining the Polar Bear Club. $$$

✗ **Shogun Teriyaki House** 1906 Pakpuk St; ✆ 852 2276; ⏱ 11.00–11.30 daily. The lunch buffet is US$15 & is a good value for big eaters. $$$

OTHER PRACTICALTIES The public is welcome to use the high school's pool and gym in the evenings and at the weekends. Taxis are common and can take you almost anywhere around town for less than US$10.

Taxis

🚕 **Alaska Taxi** ✆ 852 3000

🚕 **Barrow Taxi** ✆ 852 2222

🚕 **City Cab** ✆ 852 5050

Hospitals

✚ Samuel Simmonds Memorial Hospital ↘ 852 9248 ✚ North Slope Borough Health Clinic ↘ 852 0260

Miscellaneous

Alaska Commercial ↘ 442 2704; ⏲ 07.00–22.00 Mon–Sat & 09.00–21.00 Sun. On Ahkovak Street, this is the large grocery store in town.
Piuraagvik Recreation Center 2026 Ahkovak St; ↘ 852 2514. Gym, racketball courts, weight room & sauna.

Public library 5421 N Star St; ↘ 852 1720; www.tuzzy.org. Located in the same building as the Inupiat Heritage Center. Internet access & a cosy place to hang out.
UIC Rental 1764 Ahkovgak St; ↘ 852 2700. Car rentals.

FESTIVALS AND EVENTS The best way to visit Barrow is to time your trip to coincide with a summer event. Every July, the Top of the World Baby Contest – where native babies are judged on general cuteness – is held in addition to other celebrations and various Eskimo games, such as the traditional high-kick and ear-pull competitions. The high-kick involves the participant kicking a ball hanging from ceiling; the higher the better. The ear-pull, on the other hand, is a pain and strength test where two opponents face one another with a loop of string hooked over one ear of each competitor. The goal is to pull the head back until the pain is too great and someone gives up. **Nalukataq** is held on the third week of June only if the whale hunt has been successful. Festivities include dancing, celebration and the blanket toss. The autumn whale hunt happens in October.

WHAT TO SEE Walking the shoreline in front of Barrow is a good way to see the town and a number of sights are located there. A welcome sign, written partially in Inupiat, is right on the sea and is surrounded by bowhead whale skulls. Another sign along the sea has a picture of a snowy owl and explains the traditions of the original people to inhabit the area. Along Stevenson Street, a pair of whale bones form an arch that is always popular with tourists looking for a unique photo. Near the small visitor centre, a sign indicates the direction and distance of many international and US cities including Lake Placid in Florida (4,774 miles). The **Will Rogers and Wiley Post Memorial** is an odd, stone structure commemorating the death of the famous comedian Will Rogers and his friend Wiley Post who crashed in a small plane just south of Barrow. A few blocks from the airport is the **cemetery**, an interesting place to take a stroll.

Perhaps the most coveted sight, and the one most people come to Barrow to see, is the northernmost point in the US: Point Barrow. The views are stark in their beauty and polar bears have been seen. Buses can be arranged from the Top of the World Hotel (see page 425). Hiking to Emaiksoun Lake can be lovely in good weather with many birds nesting in the area. Starting from the west end of the runway, follow the gravel road south for about three miles past a number of satellite dishes to the lake. Joe 'the Waterman' Shults, who also works at Pepe's (see page 425), has a personal museum across the street with a collection of fascinating Native Alaskan artefacts and some stuffed local wildlife. Call ahead to Pepe's to let him know you are coming, then meet at the restaurant at 22.00 for a free tour of Joe's Museum.

PRUDHOE BAY/DEADHORSE

The oil town of Deadhorse (✥ 70°12'20"N, 138°40'32"W) and the surrounding area of Prudhoe Bay, the largest oil field in America, is located 200 miles southeast of Barrow at the end of the Dalton Highway. Deadhorse is the beginning of the Trans-Alaska Pipeline, which crosses Alaska and ends at Valdez. A city of oil workers, Deadhorse is an otherworldly place where caribou and other Arctic wildlife, including fox and even the occasional polar bear, wander between buildings and oil machinery. Tough men drive large trucks little concerned with the crisis in the fuel economy, they are – after all – practically driving on oil. The day the oil workers start driving hybrid cars is the day we know our national oil reserves are running out.

Deadhorse got its name as a result of a young man from New York with a large trust fund. As the story goes, the young man's father told his son he was to receive a US$6 million dollar trust fund, but not until he turned 35 years old. The young man travelled to Fairbanks Alaska to work and came across a gravel business which was going bankrupt. With his father's help he bought the business. The business is believed to have been named Deadhorse Haulers for one of two reasons: the first, was that the business had the contract to haul dead horses out of Fairbanks; the second, and more likely story is that the young man's father referred to his continued support of the failing business in terms of paying to feed a dead horse. Deadhorse Haulers was hired to build the new Prudhoe Bay airstrip that soon became known as the Deadhorse runway and later the area became known as Deadhorse, eventually even receiving its own US postal zip code.

Visitors to the area can fly or drive along the Dalton Highway. Because of the oil leases held in the area, access to the Arctic Ocean is restricted and allowed only by tour bus. These tours can be arranged by any of the hotels in Deadhorse. For most people there is little reason to go to Deadhorse. Most visitors arrive as part of a larger trip along the Dalton Highway and only visit to complete their trip north. Though the wildlife viewing can be excellent with thousands of caribou regularly passing through, the oil field backdrop is not as quintessentially Alaska as it could be. Bring all your own alcohol and cash since Deadhorse is a dry town and there is no ATM.

GETTING THERE AND AROUND In addition to driving in via the Dalton Highway, daily flights are also available from Fairbanks and Anchorage.

By air
✈ **Alaska Airlines** ☎ 800 426 0333; www.alaskaair.com. Regular service to Prudhoe Bay from both Anchorage & Fairbanks.

✈ **Alaska Air Taxi** ☎ 659 2743. Charter flight service.
✈ **Frontier Aviation** ☎ 800 478 6779; www.frontierflying.com. Daily service to Prudhoe Bay from Fairbanks.

WHERE TO STAY AND EAT Existing primarily for oil workers, Deadhorse offers just a few services with not many facilities that visitors expect. Still, a decent but expensive meal can be had and the rooms have walls and a roof – but little more.

🏠 **Arctic Caribou Inn** (196 rooms) ☎ 659 2368; www.arcticcaribouinn.com. Yet another low, depressing building on the Prudhoe Bay landscape. This hotel is also right across from the airport & offers rooms with private baths & 2 twin beds for US$190. The hotel operates Tatqaani Tours, which is the only way to get to the Arctic Ocean. Tours last about 2hrs &

leave 4 times per day 25 May–1 Sep for US$40pp (visitors must present the hotel with an ID or passport 24hrs in advance of the tour). $$$
🏠 **Prudhoe Bay Hotel** (170 rooms) 100 Airport Rd; ☎ 659 2449. Right across from the airport, this dismal hotel offers meals, rooms, & bunks for US$110 sgl, US$250 dbl. $$$

OTHER PRACTICALTIES
Brooks Range Supply ☎ 659 2550. Auto parts & hardware.
Conam ☎ 659 9282. Auto & tyre repair.
Prudhoe Bay General Store 1 Oldspine Rd; ☎ 659 2412: ⏰ 07.00–21.00 daily. This little shop has

everything from warm clothes to food to native arts & crafts. The post office is next door.
Nana Oilfield Services ☎ 659 2840. A 24hr petrol station & RV services.

Detailed topographic maps of the following areas are available through the US Geological Survey (USGS) (*4230 University Dr, Anchorage;* \ *786 7011*).

GATES OF THE ARCTIC NATIONAL PARK AND PRESERVE Straddling a particularly rugged part of the Brooks Range, the Gates of the Arctic National Park and Preserve is covered with light forest in the south and a vision of stark Arctic beauty in the north. The Arrigetch Peaks form rocky needles in the heart of the park and the gravel Dalton Highway skirts the park's eastern flank, providing unusually convenient access to such a remote park. Six recognised wild and scenic rivers are found here: the Alatna River, the John River, the Kobuk River, the upper Noatak River, the North Fork of the Koyukuk River and the Tinayguk River. A traditional home for a number of native groups, the park includes ten villages, with populations numbering around 1,500 people, all with subsistence hunting and fishing rights. Upright stones can sometimes be found in the tundra. These were used by ancient hunters to scare caribou into better hunting configurations.

Getting there and away Because the Dalton Highway borders the park's eastern edge, access is a little less restricted here than in the neighbouring parks and preserves. Still, most visitors choose to fly into the park for flightseeing or to be dropped off for an adventure. Visitors can drive from Fairbanks north along the Dalton Highway to any number of jumping-off points including Bettles (accessible only by plane or snowmobile in winter) and Coldfoot. Both of these locations have informative ranger stations. From these towns, visitors can either hike or fly into the park. Anaktuvuk Pass (fly in only), along the park's northern border also has a ranger station and is a popular jumping-off point. A wilderness orientation session to acquaint visitors with wilderness travel and bear safety is required to enter the park and is offered in Bettles, Coldfoot and Anaktuvuk Pass.

Tourist information

🛈 Alaska Public Lands 250 Cushman St; \ 456 0527; ◷ 09.00–18.00 daily 25 May–1 Sep. Located in Fairbanks under the historic post office.
🛈 Arctic Interagency Visitor Center \ 678 5209; ◷ 10.00–22.00 daily late May–Early Sep. Located in Coldfoot.

🛈 Anaktuvuk Pass Ranger Station \ 661 3520. Summer only.
🛈 Bettles Ranger Station/Visitor Center \ 692 5494; www.nps.gov/gaar; ◷ 08.00–17.00 daily. Located in Bettles.

Activities With the variety of terrain found in the park, there is little one can't do here. Hiking, camping, river running, fishing, mountain climbing and wildlife viewing are just some of the possibilities. Visitors need to be totally self-sufficient in the park as the weather can be extreme and help is never very close.

ARCTIC NATIONAL WILDLIFE REFUGE The 19.2-million-acre Arctic National Wildlife Refuge occupies the entire northeast corner of state, forming the largest piece of protected land on Earth. The refuge is home to all three species of bear (black, brown and polar), musk ox, wolf, wolverine, Dall sheep, moose and tens of thousands of caribou. A total of 45 species of mammals, 36 species of fish and more than 180 species of bird make their home in the refuge. The towering peaks of the Brooks Range form the park's spine with endless tundra leading to the Beaufort Sea in the north and vast boreal forests in the south. Three designated wild and scenic rivers are found here; the Sheenjek, Wind, and Ivishak Rivers. These provide not only great fishing, but also remote and scenic raft trips. What makes

The Arctic National Wildlife Refuge (ANWR, pronounced *Anwar*) in remote northeast Alaska has been the source of a heated land-use debate since its inception in 1960. The crux of the matter is the need for increased domestic oil production, which is perpetually at odds with the need to protect the designated wilderness. The 19-million-acre refuge was created at the behest of visionary members of the Sierra Club, the National Parks Service and scientific and conservation communities, '…to preserve the unique landscape, flora and fauna in its original state for the people of the US and the world in perpetuity.' Today, ANWR is the largest and most pristine tract of protected land on earth.

In 1980, the Alaska National Interest Lands Conservation Act designated eight million acres as wilderness and called for portions of the coastal plain to be considered for oil exploration, only with the prior approval of Congress. Area 1002, as this area is now called, covers approximately 1.5 million acres along the refuge's northern shoreline. Of the projected 11 billion barrels of oil located in ANWR, more than seven billion are within Area 1002. The area is prime habitat for the porcupine and central caribou herds and conservationists worry that the herd's migration patterns will be disrupted if oil development is allowed. Developers argue that the caribou and other wildlife found in the nearby Prudhoe Bay oil fields have experienced minimal impact since the 23-million-acre National Petroleum Reserve (NPR) was established.

In 1989, a bill allowing drilling in Area 1002 was days from being approved by the Senate when the *Exxon Valdez* oil spill (see box on page 272) shocked the world and temporarily turned public opinion against the oil industry. During the first decade of the 21st century, the US government went back and forth on bills allowing drilling in ANWR with former president George W Bush leading the charge to drill. With a few exceptions, the Conservative Alaskan government is in favour of drilling. The majority of the Alaskan public also approve of drilling in ANWR, while just over half of the US public approve. Entrenched in the Iraq war and with defence on everyone's mind, Alaska Senator Ted Stevens tried to add wording to a defence-spending bill to allow drilling in ANWR. Democrats successfully filibustered the bill and the wording was changed. While some native Alaskan groups are excited about the job potential from development of ANWR, the village of Kaktovik – located within the refuge – called the Shell Oil company 'a hostile and dangerous force' and are adamantly opposed to any drilling.

Though an estimated 750,000 barrels of oil per day could be produced from ANWR between 2018 and 2028, the US currently uses more than 20 million barrels per day. The Organisation of the Petroleum Exporting Countries (OPEC), of which the US is a member, estimates that by 2030 ANWR oil would account for less than 1% of the world's total oil consumption and would not affect oil prices. With the US currently only producing five million barrels per day domestically and importing the remaining 15 million barrels, ANWR oil would not likely reduce the US's need for foreign oil. Furthermore, ANWR oil reserves, if drilled, would peak in 2028 with significant declines in daily production thereafter. In short, importing foreign oil needs to be slowed and eventually stopped, but drilling in ANWR will not significantly advance this goal. What many Americans don't realise, is that with current (or even lower) energy usage, the dream of oil independence is only possible if the country shifts to a 'green' economy.

Today, the Arctic National Wildlife Refuge remains what it was intended to be – an area 'where the earth and its community of life are untrammeled by man'.

this refuge unique, though, is the long unbroken series of untouched Arctic environments. There are few other places on Earth where one can travel so far within a completely intact and thriving ecosystem.

Getting there and away The majesty of the refuge is in part due to the fact that access is difficult and few visitors venture very far into the refuge each year. On the refuge's western edge, the Dalton Highway passes within hiking distance of the refuge just after the Atigun Pass. To get the best experience out of the park, however, visitors should charter a plane from Fairbanks deep into the park.

Tourist information
Alaska Public Lands 250 Cushman St; ☎ 456 0527; ⏰ 25 May–1 Sep 09.00–18.00 daily. Located in Fairbanks under the historic post office.

Activities The refuge is ideal for those self-sufficient adventurers eager to explore one of the last great wildernesses on Earth. Very few visit the refuge each year so getting away from the crowds is easy, practically guaranteed, once inside the refuge. One of the best ways to see the refuge is on a floating trip. On some of the more popular rivers you may encounter another party but, venture a little farther and you will be alone for hundred of miles in any direction. With this isolation comes some danger though, so be prepared for any weather including high winds, rain and even snow. Endless hiking is also possible in the lower elevations of the Brooks Range.

YUKON FLATS NATIONAL WILDLIFE REFUGE Just north of Fairbanks and bisected by the Arctic Circle, the nine-million-acre Yukon Flats National Wildlife Refuge forms a forested basin along the Yukon River, and is very important for fish and wildlife. Without the moderating effects of a maritime climate, the area is typified by extreme temperatures, soaring to over 37°C/100°F in the summer and plummeting to –59°C/–75°F in the winter. Despite these extremes, the refuge is home to the greatest number of ducks in Alaska as well as lynx, beaver and other fur bearers. Moose also do very well in the refuge and form the primary source of food for native peoples here. The abundance of birch makes the autumn a colourful time to visit.

Getting there and away Situated less than 100 miles north of Fairbanks, the refuge is easier to reach than most other Arctic parks. Access is provided by small planes, boats and by hiking in. Scheduled flights are available from Fairbanks to any one of the seven small towns in or near the refuge. Alternatively, visitors can follow the Steese Highway from Fairbanks to the town of Circle (see page 310) on the Yukon River where they can proceed by boat into the refuge. Visitors can also access the refuge from the Dalton Highway at the Yukon River Bridge.

Tourist information
Alaska Public Lands 250 Cushman St; ☎ 456 0527; ⏰ 25 May–1 Sep 09.00–18.00 daily. Located in Fairbanks under the historic post office.

Activities Because of the lack of developed trails in the refuge, the best way to explore is by boat on any number of rivers, including the massive Yukon. The fishing is good and the boating opportunities are practically limitless. Tundra hiking and camping are possible mostly in the White Mountains in the refuge's southern region.

Appendix I

GLOSSARY

Bushwack	To make one's way through thick undergrowth.
Bycatch	Fish caught during commercial fishing that are discarded because they are not the right size or species.
Calving	The act of ice breaking off a glacier and falling into the water.
Combat fishing	Extremely crowded fishing conditions, often when the salmon are running, and fishermen are jockeying (or even fighting) for a spot to cast. The flying hooks and tense mood can put fishermen in a 'combative' mood.
Eskimo ice cream	A traditional native Alaskan food made by blending whale or game fat with berries.
Fly-out fishing	Flying into a remote area to fish. Also called fly-in fishing.
Lower 48	A term used by Alaskans to describe the contiguous 48 states of the US.
Midden	A term used by archeologists to describe a site where waste is deposited. In Alaska these are the 'trash piles' of ancient peoples and usually contain animal bones, shells and sometimes tools. Nettles (a stinging plant) often grow in the rich soil of these sites and are a tell-tale sign. Never dig in these sites or take artifacts.
Muskeg	A swamp or bog
Old Believers	Rebelling against church reforms, the Old Believers separated from the Russian Orthodox Church in the 17th century. Some stayed in Russia while others moved their communities to places like Brazil, Romania, Turkey, China and some now live in the US states of Oregon and Alaska. Many Old Believers dress traditionally, speak Russian and live in communities separated from surrounding populations.
Shoulder season	Alaska's shoulder seasons are May and August and the first half of September. During these seasons you'll encounter fewer tourists and fewer bugs.
Socked in	A term used to describe bad weather that has moved in and grounded planes.
Switchback	When a steep trail zig-zags up a hill to make the climb more manageable.
Turn	When a salmon enters a river in preparation for spawning, it undergoes a transformation including colour (changing from silver to red, green, or stripped), and physical features such as a hooking of the nose and longer teeth. The moment a salmon enters a river and shows any of these signs, it has started to 'turn'.
Williwaw	A sudden, and often violent, gust of wind descending from the mountains near the sea.

Appendix 2

FURTHER INFORMATION

BOOKS
Literature

Beach, Rex *The Spoilers* BiblioBazaar, 2009 (originally pubed in 1906) A true story about swindlers and gold prospectors during the Nome gold strike.

Bowermaster, Jon *Birthplace of the Winds* National Geographic, 2002. A well-told story about a 25-day kayak and mountaineering trip in the Islands of the Four Mountains in the Aleutian chain.

Brown, Emily Ivanoff *The Roots of Ticasuk* Alaska Northwest Publishing, 1982. The unique tale of a native Alaskan woman from Unalakleet. The author recounts her own story and that of her elders.

Carter, Bill *Red Summer: The Danger, Madness, and Exaltation of Salmon Fishing in a Remote Alaskan Village* Scribner, 2008. An accurate and entertaining story about glory and pitfalls of commercial fishing in Bristol Bay.

Chadwick, Jerah *Story Hunger* Salmon Poetry, 1999. A collection of poems by a long-time Unalaksa poet.

Davidson, Art *Minus 148 Degrees: The First Winter Ascent of Mount McKinley* Mountaineers Books, 1999. An epic story of survival on Mt Denali in the winter.

Haines, John *The Owl in the Mask of the Dreamer: Collected Poems* Graywolf Press, 1993. A collection of powerful poems, many of which are about the 30 years the author spent in Alaska.

Heacox, Kim *The Only Kayak: A Journey into the Heart of Alaska* The Lyons Press, 2006. The author has been exploring Glacier Bay since 1979. This book chronicles those adventures with an ever vigilant eye on the past and future.

Keith, Sam & Proenneke, Richard *One Man's Wilderness: An Alaskan Odyssey* Alaska Northwest Books, 2003. The amazing story of a normal guy who dropped out to live alone in the Alaskan wilderness.

Kent, Rockwell (ed) *Wilderness: A Journey of Quiet Adventure in Alaska* Wesleyan, 1996. An account of Alaska's wild lands with illustrations.

Krakauer, Jon *Into the Wild* Anchor, 1997. The fascinating story of Chris McCandless as he struggles to cope with life before dying in the wilderness near Denali National Park. Everyone should read this book before travelling to Alaska and keep in mind that Alaskans almost unanimously lack any sympathy for the protagonist, while many Lower48-ers consider him a cult hero.

London, Jack *The Call of the Wild* Puffin Classics, 1903. The classic story of a pampered dog that becomes a sled dog in Alaska and gets back in touch with his instincts.

London, Jack *White Fang* Prestwick House, Inc, 2007 (Originally published in 1906). The story of a wolf pup reared during Alaska's gold rush days.

Lord, Nancy *Fishcamp Life on an Alaskan Shore* Counterpoint, 2000. A story about the author commercial fishing and observing nature woven together with native Alaskan stories and folklore.

Lopez, Berry *Of Wolves and Men* Scribner, 2004. A thorough discussion of wolves and the hunting of them.

McPhee, John *Coming into the Country* Farrar, Straus and Giroux, 1991. A well-rounded look at nearly every facet of the state, from business to bush and travel to history and politics.

Muir, John *Travels in Alaska* CreateSpace, 2009. A contemplative account of turn-of-the-century Alaska.

Orth, Joy *Island: Our Alaskan Dream and Reality* Alaska Northwest Publishing, 1987. The story of a couple who dreamed of Alaska, then faced the reality of living there, usually with good humour.

Ott, Riki *Not One Drop: Betrayal and Courage in the Wake of the Exxon Valdez Oil Spill* Chelsea Green Publishing, 2008. A touching account of the economic and emotion toll the Exxon Valdez oil spill had on the community of Cordova.

Proenneke, Richard and Sam Keith *One Man's Wilderness: An Alaskan Odyssey* Alaska Northwest Books, 2003. One of the best homesteading stories of all time. Proenneke built a cabin near Lake Clark and lived alone off the land for much of his later life.

Rich, Kim *Johnny's Girl: A Daughter's Memoir of Growing Up in Alaska's Underworld* William Morrow & Co, 1993. Not your average Alaskan tale: the author researched the lives of her murdered mobster father and ex-stripper mother while they lived in Alaska.

Ricks, Byron *Homelands: Kayaking the Inside Passage* Harper Perennial, 1999. A modern adventure tale of a couple who kayak through the southeast, observing many natural and cultural wonders along the way.

Rustad, Dorothy Scott *I Married a Fisherman*. Alaska Northwest Publishing, 1986. The tale of a fisherman's wife living, fishing and raising a family in southeast Alaska.

Service, Robert *The Best of Robert* Service Running Press, 2003. Immensely entertaining poems about drinking, starving and lusting after gold in Canada's gold fields.

Sexton, Tom *For the Sake of the Light: New and Selected Poems* University of Alaska Press, 2009. A collection of poems from the former Poet Laureate of Alaska.

Sherwonit, Bill *To the Top of Denali: Climbing Adventures on North America's Highest Peak* Graphic Arts Center Publishing Company, 2000. A thorough discussion of Denali politics and adventures.

Staender, Vivian and Gil *Our Arctic Year* Alaska Northwest Publishing, 1984. A couple tough out a season in the Brooks Range working for the US Fish and Wildlife Service.

Thomas, Mickey *You Can't Ride a Bike to Alaska. It's an Island!* iUniverse, Inc, 2005. A story about all the trials and tribulation one would expect on a 3,400-mile bike trip from Montana to Alaska.

Tremblay, Ray *Trails of an Alaskan Game Warden* Alaska Northwest Books, 1985. Working as a rural game warden, Tremblay recounts his many adventures around the state. The author also wrote *Trails of an Alaskan Trapper* about his experiences trapping in sub-zero temperatures in the 1940s.

Walker, Spike *Working on the Edge: Surviving In the World's Most Dangerous Profession: King Crab Fishing on Alaska's HighSeas* St Martin's Griffin, 1993. An account of the glory days of king crab fishing in the Bering Sea – considered some of the most dangerous commercial fishing on earth and in all likelihood, the inspiration for the TV show, *The Deadliest Catch*.

Walker, Spike *Nights of Ice: True Stories of Disaster and Survival on Alaska's High Seas* St. Martin's Griffin, 1999. The writing can be overly-dramatic at times, but commercial fishing-philes will love the hair-raising stories of near-death experiences off Alaska's coast.

Wallis, Velma *Two Old Women: An Alaska Legend of Betrayal, Courage and Survival* Harper Perennial, 2004. Two native Alaskan women fight the elements after being abandoned by their tribe.

Waterman, Jonathan *In the Shadow of Denali: Life and Death on Alaska's Mt. McKinley* The Lyons Press, 2009. A gripping collection of stories about climbing on Denali.

Weiss, Miranda *Tide, Feather, Snow: A Life in Alaska* Harper, 2009. A wonderfully honest account of a woman who moves to Alaska and reinvents herself according to the land.

Wright, Sam *Edge of Tomorrow: An Arctic Year* Washington State University, 1998. The author, a philosopher and ecologist, recounts the year he spent with his wife in the isolated Brooks Range of Alaska.

History

Allen, Arthur James *A Whaler and Trader in the Arctic* Alaska Northwest Publishing, 1978. An interesting account of the life of a whaler around the turn of the century.

Bancroft-Hunt, Norman *People of the Totem: The Indians of the Pacific Northwest* University of Oklahoma Press, 1988. A comprehensive look at the native peoples of southeast Alaska, the northwest and coastal Canada.

Beaglehole, John (editor) *The Journals of Captain Cook* Penguin Classics, 2000. A condensed version of Cook's journals as he explored much of the Pacific, including Alaska.

Green, Lewis *The Gold Hustlers* Alaska Northwest Publishing, 1977. This atypical gold rush story following the business side of the Klondike gold strike.

Rennick, Penny (ed) *Russian America, Volume 26, Number 4 of Alaska Geographic* Alaska Geographic, 1999. A wonderful resource for anyone looking for more information on Alaska's Russian history.

Ritter, Harry *Alaska's History: The People, Land, and Events of Alaska* Alaska Northwest Books, 1993. A short, but very readable, account of Alaska's history.

Art

Black, Lydia *Aleut Art: Unangam Aguqaadangin* Aleutian Pribilof Islands Association, 2003. Images of Aleut (Unangan) art from museums around the world.

Brown, Steven C & Carro, Paz Cabello (eds) *Spirits of the Water: Native Art Collected on Expeditions to Alaska and British Columbia 1774-1910* University of Washington Press, 2000. Masks and other art from the native peoples around southeast Alaska and British Columbia, Canada.

Hessell, Ingo *Arctic Spirit: The Albrecht Collection of Inuit Art at the Heard Museum* Douglas & McIntyre, 2006. A lovely glossy book filled with large colour plates of Inuit art.

Troll, Ray *Rapture of the Deep: The Art of Ray Troll* University of California Press, 2004. Ketchikan's own Ray Troll has a playful style all its own.

Woodward, Kesler E *Sydney Laurence, Painter of the North* University of Washington Press, 1990. A wonderful collection of colour images by one of Alaska's most famous painters.

Reference

Alaska Atlas and Gazetteer DeLorme Publishing, 2004. A detailed collection of topographic, trail and road maps of the state.

The Alaska Wilderness Guide Morris Communications, 2005. This guide is as useful to the adventurer as the *Milepost* is to the road tripper. Detailed information about camping, trails, river-running and other adventures.

Austin, Rosemary *Mountain Bike Anchorage: A Comprehensive Guide to Dirt, Gravel and Paved Bicycle Trails from Eklutna Lake to Girdwood* Alaska Publication Consultants, 2005. One of the best resources to biking (or even hiking) around Anchorage.

Coombs, Colby *Denali's West Buttress: A Climber's Guide to Mount McKinley's Classic Route* Mountaineers Books, 1997. A complete guide focusing only on Denali's most popular route.

Duffus, Joshua *A Recreational Guide to Kachemak Bay State Park and Wilderness Park* self-published, 2005. The best (and only) guide to hiking across the bay from Homer. To order, write to the author at: PO Box 84, Girdwood, AK 99587.

Evans, Polly *Yukon: The Bradt Travel Guide* Bradt Travel Guides, 2009

Field, Carmen & Conrad *Alaska's Seashore Creatures: A Guide to Selected Marine Invertebrates* Alaska Northwest Books, 1999. The only book you will need for tide pooling Alaska's waters.

Gates, Nancy (ed) *The Alaska Almanac: Facts about Alaska* Alaska Northwest Books, 2009. Fun facts and interesting details about Alaska.

Fensterman, Greg *Hiking Alaska's Wrangell-St Elias National Park and Preserve: From Day Hikes to Backcountry Treks* Falcon, 2008. The only complete guide to this range.

Gunnar, Pedersen *The Highway Angler: Fishing Alaska's Road System* Fishing Alaska Publications, 2007. Fishing visitors traveling the state's roads will want a copy of this on hand.

Hodges, Montana *Best Easy Day Hikes Fairbanks* Falcon, 2009. 20 of the best easy hikes around Fairbanks.

Hulten, Eric *Flora of Alaska and Neighboring Territories* Stanford University Press, 1968. This large and heavy book is a must for anyone serious about Alaska's diverse flora.

Jettmar, Karen *The Alaska River Guide: Canoeing, Kayaking, and Rafting in the Last Frontier* Menasha Ridge Press, 2008. With so few roads in the Alaska, using a boat to navigate one of the state's many waterways is a great way to go.

Joly, Kyle *Outside in the Interior: An Adventure Guide for Central Alaska* University of Alaska Press, 2007. The best hiking book for the interior with maps and detailed information about a plethora of hikes.

Jubenville, Alan *South Central Alaska: A Comprehensive Guide to the Hiking & Conoeing Trails & Public-Use Cabins* Hunter Publishing, 1997. A worthwhile resource for planning trips to southcentral Alaska.

King, ML *Ninety Short Walks around Juneau* Published locally, 1987. This is an older but still quite useful guide to Juneau's best trails.

Larson, Richard *Mountain Bike Alaska: 49 Trails in the 49th State* Glacier House Publishing, 1991. One of the few books out there on the subject, but getting quite outdated.

Littlepage, Dean *Hiking Alaska: A Guide to Alaska's Greatest Hiking Adventures* Falcon, 2006. A good book for getting an overview of Alaska's hiking opportunities, but not a substitute for local hiking guides.

Maclean, Dan *Paddling Alaska: A Guide to the State's Classic Paddling Trips* Falcon, 2009. An intermediate paddling guide to the state's best paddling routes.

Nienhueser, Helen D. and John Wolfe *55 Ways to the Wilderness in Southcentral Alaska* Mountaineers Books, 1994. This good book covers many of the best hikes in southcentral Alaska.

Praetorius, Pete and Alys Culhane *Alaska Bicycle Touring Guide: Including Parts of the Yukon Territory and Northwest Territories* Denali Press, 1992. A good resource (but getting outdated) for those dreaming of cycling through Alaska.

Puryear, Joseph *Alaska Climbing* SuperTopo, 2006. A complete guide to the alpine ascents of the Alaska Range.

Scoggins, Dow *Discovering Denali: A Complete Reference Guide to Denali National Park and Mount McKinley* Alaska iUniverse, 2004. A decent guide to Denali National Park.

Secor, R. J. Denali *Climbing Guide* Stackpole Books, 1998. Maps, photos and details about most climbing routes on Denali.

Sheperd, Shane and Wozniak, Owen *50 Hikes in Alaska's Chugach State Park* Mountaineers Books, 2001. A good hiking guide to the mountains outside Anchorage.

Schofield, Janice J *Discovering Wild Plants* Alaska Northwest Books, 2003. The best book out there on Alaska's edible and medicinal plants.

Tally, Taz *50 Hikes In Alaska's Kenai Peninsula* Countryman, 2008. One of the best hiking guides to the Kenai Peninsula.

Valencia, Kris (ed) *The Milepost 2009: Alaska Travel Planner.* Morris Communications Company, 2009. There is no guide more complete than this in describing every sight, hazard and detail of Alaska's road system.

Tyson, John *Best Hikes Near Anchorage* Falcon, 2009. A must-have guide for hiking near Anchorage.

Waits, Ike *Denali National Park Guide to Hiking, Photography & Camping* Wild Rose Guidebooks, 2010

Wood, Michael & Coombs, Colby *Alaska: A Climbing Guide* Mountaineers Books, 2002. A collection of Alaska's best alpine climbing.

Health

Wilson-Howarth, Dr Jane, and Ellis, Dr Matthew *Your Child Abroad: A Travel Health Guide* Bradt Travel Guides, 2005

Wilson-Howarth, Dr Jane, *Bugs, Bites & Bowels* Cadogan, 2006

WEBSITES

http://alaska.fws.gov Alaska Fish and Wildlife Service. Information on wildlife, habitat and protected land in Alaska.

http://vilda.alaska.edu The Alaska Digital Archive is a wonderful resource for etchings, photographs and other historical art depicting Alaska's past. Digital files can be purchased for US$25.

www.adfg.state.ak.us Extensive information about Alaskan sport and commercial fisheries and hunting as well as natural history information on Alaska's plants and animals.

www.ak.blm.gov Information about Alaska's Bureau of Land Management.

www.alaskachamber.com A list of every chamber of commerce in the state.

www.alaska.com An invaluable website for general information created by the Anchorage Daily News.

www.arh.noaa.gov Alaska weather.

www.awrta.org The Alaska Wilderness Recreation and Tourism Association is a great place to find environmentally minded businesses and organisations in Alaska.

www.commerce.state.ak.us/dca – The Division of Community and Regional Affairs is the place to get detailed information on any Alaskan town or city. Click 'Alaska Community Database', then 'Detailed Community Information'.

www.dnr.alaska.gov The Alaska Department of Natural Resources (DNR) has detailed information on all of Alaska's state parks.

www.fs.fed.us/r10 The Alaska US Forest Service is the best place to find information on Alaska's two national forests, Chugach and Tongass.

www.nps.gov/state/AK/index.htm Information on all of Alaska's National Parks.

www.recreation.gov Reserve campsites and public use cabins around the state.

www.state.ak.us Many details about state government and business.

www.travelalaska.com Great website for general information run by the state.

www.travelerphotography.com The author's website featuring his photography and writing.

Index